A SPIRITUALITY OF EVERYDAY FAITH

Louvain Theological and Pastoral Monographs is a publishing venture whose purpose is to provide those involved in pastoral ministry throughout the world with studies inspired by Louvain's long tradition of theological excellence within the Roman Catholic tradition. The volumes selected for publication in the series are expected to express some of today's finest reflection on current theology and pastoral practice.

LOUVAIN THEOLOGICAL & PASTORAL MONOGRAPHS
——————————— 23 ———————————

A SPIRITUALITY OF EVERYDAY FAITH

A THEOLOGICAL INVESTIGATION OF THE NOTION OF SPIRITUALITY IN KARL RAHNER

Declan Marmion

PEETERS PRESS
LOUVAIN

ISBN 90-6831-988-4
D. 1998/0602/7

FOREWORD

It is said that "the doctoral student ploughs a lonely furrow." I think that this is only partly true, however. While one has to take personal responsibility, ultimately, for what one has written, this is an opportunity to thank a number of people and institutions, without whose help, this book — originally a dissertation — would not have been possible.

Firstly, I would like to thank Professor Terrence Merrigan of the Faculty of Theology, Catholic University of Leuven, whose consistent encouragement, perceptive reading of my text, and constructive criticisms have helped me greatly. It is an honour to be included in the Louvain Theological and Pastoral Monographs Series.

I also owe a debt of gratitude to the former Provincial of the Irish Province of the Marist Fathers, Fr John Hannan sm. He it was who suggested I come to Leuven, and he has supported not only me, but also our International House of Studies since its inception in 1992.

A number of Rahner "experts" gave me of their time and wisdom. A number of visits to the Karl Rahner Archives in Innsbruck enabled me to clarify some issues with Professor Karl-Heinz Neufeld, its Director. In particular, Dr. Roman Siebenrock, the assistant in the Archives and in the Department of Fundamental Theology, guided me through the literature available on my topic and was always available for discussion. In Heythrop College, (University of London), I raised some of the issues dealt with in this study with Dr. Philip Endean SJ, former editor of *The Way*, and lecturer in theology at the college. His insights on the Ignatian aspect of Rahner's spirituality confirmed some of my own ideas while discounting others. He also kindly sent me on a copy of his soon to be published doctoral thesis. Finally, Professor emeritus Herbert Vorgrimler, of the University of Mnster, despite a hectic schedule of lecturing and writing, graciously answered a number of questions my topic and endorsed its basic thrust and conclusions.

Back to Leuven, and I was consistently fortunate to find most of the primary and secondary literature I needed in our own library. Some members of the Faculty kindly agreed to reading portions of the text and gave me valuable feedback. To these and the many others who have helped me in countless ways, I dedicate this book as a token of my gratitude and appreciation.

8th August 1997   Declan MARMION

TABLE OF CONTENTS

Bibliography   XI
Introduction XXXIX

Chapter One:
The Notion of Spirituality

Introduction   1
   a. Spirituality Today   1
   b. Spirituality — An Ambiguous Term   3
1. The Changing Meaning of the Term   4
   a. Meaning in Paul   4
   b. Subsequent Development of the Term after Paul   9
   c. Twelfth and Thirteenth Centuries 12
   d. Further Developments in the Use of the Term 15
2. Towards a Definition of Spirituality 18
   a. Spirituality and Spiritual Theology 19
   b. Spirituality and Spiritualities 24
   c. Components of a Definition 26
3. Theology and Spirituality 29
   a. The Divorce between Spirituality and Theology 29
   b. Spirituality and Experience 33
   c. Spirituality — An Immature Discipline 37
   d. Summary 39

Chapter Two:
The Notion of Spirituality in Karl Rahner

Introduction 41
1. The Spiritual Basis of Rahner's Theology 42
   a. Experiences of God 42
   b. Ignatian Influences 46
   c. Rahner's Early Spiritual Theology 48
2. Key Themes in Rahner's Notion of Spirituality 55

   a. God as Mystery   55
   b. Christian Life: A Mysticism of Everyday Faith   61
   c. Prayer as Surrender of the Heart   69
   d. Love of Neighbour as Love of God   79
3. Towards a Definition of Spirituality in Rahner.   88
   a. The Link between Theology and Spirituality   88
   b. Components of a Definition 100

Chapter Three:
The Experiential Dimension of Rahner's Notion of Spirituality

Introduction
1. The Rahnerian Notion of Religious Experience 109
   a. Rahner's Concept of Experience — Terminological
      Clarification 111
      i) Experiential and Conceptual Knowledge. 111
      ii) Human Experiences and the Experience of God. . . . 115
   b. Experience of God as Experience of Transcendence . . . 124
   c. Rahner's Transcendental-Anthropological Method 130
   d. Implications for Spirituality 140
2. Experience of the Spirit and Enthusiasm 145
   a. Experience of the Spirit — Terminological Clarification . 145
   b. Experience of the Spirit and Existential Decision. . . . 150
   c. Experience of Enthusiasm 152
   d. Comments and Questions 157
3. Experience of Grace. 163
   a. A Reinterpretation Of Grace. 163
   b. Rahner's "Supernatural Existential" 170
   c. Consequences 178
      i) From an Anonymous to an Explicit Spirituality 178
      ii) Rahner's "Three Appeals" 186
   d. Conclusion: "I believe in Jesus Christ". 194

Chapter Four:
The Ignatian Dimension of Rahner's Spirituality

Introduction
1. The Ignatian Background 301

a. Rahner and the *Exercises*: Introduction and Context . . . 202
b. Rahner's Appropriation of Ignatian Mysticism 206
   i) A Tension of Opposites. 206
   ii) Ignatian "Indifference". 211
2. Rahner's Ignatius Interpretation 216
a. The Problem of the "Election" in the *Exercises* 216
b. Discernment of Spirits 219
c. An Interim Appraisal 228
   i) "Consolation without previous cause". 228
   ii) The Preferred Time of Election 235
d. The Christological Dimension of the Ignatian Election. . 240
3. Rahner and Ignatian Mystagogy 252
a. Rahner's Spiritual Testament 252
b. Mystagogy and the Application of the Senses 261
c. Conclusion: Towards a Mystagogical Spirituality 274

Chapter Five:
An Evaluation of Rahner's Notion of Spirituality

Introduction 281
1. A Synthesis of Various Criticisms 282
a. Criticism from the Right. 282
b. Criticism from the Left 296
c. Gathering the Threads 305
2. The "Specifically Christian" Nature of Rahner's Spirituality . 312
a. The Christocentric Character of Rahner's Spirituality . . 312
b. The Ecclesial Aspect of Rahner's Spirituality. 319
c. The Sacramental Aspect of Rahner's Spirituality 327
3. Rahner and Beyond: Towards a New Vision of Spirituality. 336
a. Liberation Spirituality: Jon Sobrino. 336
b. Feminist Spirituality: Anne Carr 346
4. Retrospect and Prospect. 357

Index of Names and Subjects. 370

SELECT BIBLIOGRAPHY

Introductory Note

This bibliography is divided into two main sections. The first section concentrates on the primary sources, i.e., on Karl Rahner's works in article and in book form. Both the German original and, where possible, the English translation are given. A number of bibliographies on Karl Rahner have already appeared in both English and in German. We will, firstly, refer to the principal bibliographies of Rahner. There is little point, here, in repeating work already covered, especially when one considers that, even by 1974, Rahner's prodigious literary output had reached almost 3000 publications (including reviews, translations, new editions and reprints). Hence our bibliography of Rahner's works is not exhaustive, but rather represents a selected, working bibliography listing the principal Rahnerian sources consulted in the course of writing this thesis. The lists of Rahner's articles and books are given in chronological order, i.e., according to date of publication. Rahner also collaborated with other authors in editing a number of important reference works, handbooks and dictionaries. We refer to the most significant of these at the end of Section One.

As most of Rahner's theological writings were originally composed as separate articles, we always refer initially to the article concerned, and then to its location in a particular collection, (e.g., in *Theological Investigations*). Further, in order to distinguish between the German original and the corresponding English translation of multi-volume works, the English translations are referred to by Arabic numerals, and the volumes of the German original by Roman numerals.

Section Two, is comprised of the secondary literature by authors other than Rahner both on him and on our topic itself. Once again, this section is divided between bibliographies of the secondary literature on Rahner, books, articles in journals, articles in encyclopaedias and dictionaries, and Church documents consulted. All lists are arranged alphabetically according to author.

Section One
(Primary Literature)

1. Bibliographies on Karl Rahner

Bleistein, Roman, and Elmar Klinger. *Bibliographie Karl Rahner 1924-1969.* Freiburg: Herder, 1969.
Bleistein, Roman, ed. *Bibliographie Karl Rahner 1969-1974.* Freiburg: Herder, 1969.
Imhof, Paul, and Heinrich Treziak. "Bibliographie Karl Rahner 1974-1979," *Wagnis Theologie: Erfahrungen mit der Theologie Karl Rahners.* Edited by Herbert Vorgrimler. Freiburg: Herder, 1979, 579-97.
Imhof, Paul, and Elisabeth Meuser. "Bibliographie Karl Rahner 1979-1984," *Glaube im Prozess.* Edited by Elmar Klinger and Klaus Wittstadt. Freiburg: Herder, 1984, 854-88.
Pedley, C. J., "An English Bibliographical Aid to Karl Rahner," *The Heythrop Journal* 25 (1984): 319-65.

2. Works of Karl Rahner — Articles In Periodicals

"Warum uns das Beten not tut," *Leuchtturm* 18 (1924-25): 10-11.
"Le début d'une doctrine des cinq sens spirituels chez Origène," *Revue d'Ascétique et de Mystique* 13 (1932): 113-145.
"Die geistliche Lehre des Evagrius Ponticus. In ihren Grundzügen dargestellt." *Zeitschrift für Aszese und Mystik* 8 (1933): 21-38.
"La doctrine des 'sens spirituels' au Moyen-Âge. En particulier chez St-Bon-aventure." *Revue d'Ascétique et de Mystique* 14 (1933): 263-99.
"Die ignatianische Mystik der Weltfreudigkeit," *Zeitschrift für Aszese und Mystik* 12 (1937): 121-37.
"Hans Urs von Balthasar — 60. Geburtstag," *Civitas* 20 (1965): 601-605.
"Frömmigkeit heute und morgen," *Geist und Leben* 39 (1966): 326-42.
"Dimensions of Martyrdom: A Plea for the Broadening of a Classical Concept," *Concilium* 163 (1983): 9-11.
"Im Anspruch Gottes. Bemerkungen zur Logik der existentiellen Erkenntnis," *Geist und Leben* 59 (1986): 241-47.

3. Articles in the *Schriften zur Theologie (Theological Investigations)*

Schriften zur Theologie Bd. I, *Gott, Christus, Maria, Gnade.* Einsiedeln: Benziger, 1954, 3rd ed. 1958.
[ET: *Theological Investigations* Vol. 1, *God, Christ, Mary and Grace.* Translated with an Introduction by Cornelius Ernst. London: Darton, Longman & Todd (DLT), 1961, 1965].
"The Development of Dogma," 39-77.

"Theos in the New Testament," 79-148.
"Current Problems in Christology," 149-97.
"On the Question of a Formal Existential Ethics," 217-34.
"Concerning the Relationship between Nature and Grace," 297-317.
"Some Implications of the Scholastic Concept of Uncreated Grace," 319-46.
"The Theological Concept of Concupiscentia," 347-382.

Schriften zur Theologie Bd. II, *Kirche und Mensch.* Einsiedeln: Benziger, 1955, 3rd ed. 1958.
[ET: *Theological Investigations* Vol. 2, *Man in the Church.* Translated by Karl-H. Kruger. London: DLT, 1963].
"Membership of the Church According to the Teaching of Pius XII's Encyclical 'Mystici Corporis Christi'," 1-88.
"Personal and Sacramental Piety," 109-133.
"Forgotten Truths Concerning the Sacrament of Penance," 135-74.
"On the Question of a Formal Existential Ethics," 217-34.

Schriften zur Theologie Bd. III, *Zur Theologie des geistlichen Lebens.* Einsiedeln: Benziger, 1956.
[ET: *Theological Investigations* Vol. 3, *The Theology of the Spiritual Life.*
Translated by Karl-H. and Boniface Kruger. London: DLT, 1967].
"Reflections on the Problem of the Gradual Ascent to Christian Perfection," 3-23.
"Thoughts on the Theology of Christmas," 24-34.
"The Eternal Significance of the Humanity of Jesus for Our Relationship with God," 35-46.
"Reflections on the Theology of Renunciation," 47-57.
"The Passion and Asceticism," 58-85.
"Reflections on the Experience of Grace," 86-90.
"Some Thoughts on 'A Good Intention'," 105-28.
"The Apostolate of Prayer," 209-219.
"A Spiritual Dialogue at Evening: On Sleep, Prayer, and Other Subjects," 220-238.
"Priestly Existence," 239-263.
"The Ignatian Mysticism of Joy in the World," 277-98.
"Priest and Poet," 294-317.
"'Behold this Heart!': Preliminaries to a Theology of Devotion to the Sacred Heart," 321-330.
"Some Theses for a Theology of Devotion to the Sacred Heart," 331-354.
"The Christian Among Unbelieving Relations," 355-72.
"Science as a 'Confession'?" 385-400.

Schriften zur Theologie Bd. IV, *Neuere Schriften.* Einsiedeln: Benziger, 1960.
[ET: *Theological Investigations* Vol. 4, *More Recent Writings.* Translated by
    Kevin Smyth. London: DLT, 1966].
    "The Concept of Mystery in Catholic Theology," 36-73.
    "On the Theology of the Incarnation," 105-120.
    "Dogmatic Questions on Easter," 121-33.
    "Nature and Grace," 165-188.
    "Questions of Controversial Theology on Justification," 189-218.
    "The Theology of The Symbol," 221-52.
    "The Theology of Power," 391-409.

Schriften zur Theologie Bd. V, *Neuere Schriften.* Einsiedeln: Benziger,
    1962, 3rd ed., 1968.
[ET: *Theological Investigations* Vol. 5, *Later Writings.* Translated by Karl-
    H. Kruger. London: DLT, 1966].
    "What is a Dogmatic Statement?" 42-66.
    "Christianity and the Non-Christian Religions," 115-34.
    "Dogmatic Notes on 'Ecclesiological Piety'," 336-65.
    "Some Theses on Prayer 'In the Name of the Church," 419-38.
    "The 'Commandment' of Love in Relation to the Other Command-
        ments," 439-59.

Schriften zur Theologie Bd. VI, *Neuere Schriften.* Einsiedeln: Benziger, 1965.
[ET: *Theological Investigations* Vol. 6, *Concerning Vatican Council II.*
    Translated by Karl-H. and Boniface Kruger. London: DLT, 1969].
    "The Man of Today and Religion," 3-20.
    "Reflections on the Contemporary Intellectual Formation of Future
        Priests," 113-40.
    "Theology of Freedom," 178-96.
    "Reflections on the Unity of the Love of Neighbour and the Love of
        God," 231-49.
    "The Church of Sinners," 253-69.
    "The Sinful Church in the Decrees of Vatican II," 270-94.
    "Anonymous Christians," 390-99.

Schriften zur Theologie Bd. VII, *Zur Theologie des Geistlichen Lebens.* Ein-
    siedeln: Benziger, 1966.
[ET: *Theological Investigations* Vol. 7, *Further Theology of the Spiritual
    Life 1.* Translated by David Bourke. London: DLT, 1971].
    "Christian Living Formerly and Today," 3-24.
    "Being Open to God as Ever Greater," 25-45.
    "Intellectual Honesty and Christian Faith," 47-71.
    "'I Believe in the Church'," 100-118.
    "Mysteries of the life of Jesus," 121-201.
    "Proving Oneself in Time of Sickness," 275-84.

Schriften zur Theologie Bd. VII, *Zur Theologie des Geistlichen Lebens*. Ein-
siedeln: Benziger, 1966.
[ET: *Theological Investigations* Vol. 8, *Further Theology of the Spiritual
Life 2*. Translated by David Bourke. London: DLT, 1971].
  "Why and How Can We Venerate the Saints?," 3-23.
  "The Position of Woman in the New Situation in which the Church
  Finds Herself," 75-93.
  "The Theological Meaning of the Veneration of the Sacred Heart,"
  217-28.
  "Unity — Love — Mystery," 229-47.

Schriften zur Theologie Bd. VIII, *Theologische Vorträge und Abhandlungen*.
Einsiedeln: Benziger, 1967.
[ET: *Theological Investigations* Vol. 9, *Writings of 1965-67, 1*. Translated
by Graham Harrison. London: DLT, 1972].
  "Theology and Anthropology," 28-45.
  "Observations on the Doctrine of God in Catholic Dogmatics," 127-44.
  "Atheism and Implicit Christianity," 145-64.
  "'I Believe in Jesus Christ': Interpreting an Article of Faith," 165-68.
  "One Mediator and Many Mediations," 169-86.
  "Christian Humanism," 187-204.
  "Self-realisation and Taking Up One's Cross," 253-57.

Schriften zur Theologie Bd. VIII, *Theologische Vorträge und Abhandlungen*.
Einsiedeln: Benziger, 1967.
[ET: *Theological Investigations* Vol. 10, *Writings of 1965-67, 2*. Translated
by David Bourke. London: DLT, 1972].
  "On the Theology of Hope," 242-59.

Schriften zur Theologie Bd. IX, *Konfrontationen*. Einsiedeln: Benziger, 1970.
[ET: *Theological Investigations* Vol. 11, *Confrontations 1*. Translated by
David Bourke. London: DLT, 1974].
  "Pluralism in Theology and the Unity of the Creed," 3-23.
  "Reflections on Methodology in Theology," 68-114.
  "The Experience of God Today," 149-65.
  "The Position of Christology in the Church Between Exegesis and Dog-
  matics," 185-214.

Schriften zur Theologie Bd. IX, *Konfrontationen*. Einsiedeln: Benziger, 1970.
[ET (A Translation of the second part of *Schriften IX*): *Theological Investigations* Vol. 12, *Confrontations 2*. Translated by David Bourke. London: DLT, 1974].
  "Concerning our Assent to the Church as She Exists in the Concrete,"
  142-60.

"Anonymous Christianity and the Missionary Task of the Church,"
    161-78.
"The Question of the Future," 181-201.
"The Function of the Church as a Critic of Society," 229-49.

Schriften zur Theologie Bd. X, *Im Gespräch mit der Zukunft.* Einsiedeln:
    Benziger, 1972.
[ET: *Theological Investigations* Vol. 13, *Theology, Anthropology, Christol-
    ogy.* Translated by David Bourke. London: DLT, 1975].
"On Recognizing the Importance of Thomas Aquinas," 3-12.
"Possible Courses for the Theology of the Future," 32-60.
"On the Relationship between Theology and the Contemporary Scien-
    ces," 94-104.
"Institution and Freedom," 105-21.
"Experience of Self and Experience of God," 122-32.
"The Quest for Approaches Leading to an Understanding of the
    Mystery of the God-Man Jesus," 195-200.
"Remarks on the Importance of the History of Jesus for Catholic Dog-
    matics," 201-212.
"The Two Basic Types of Christology," 213-23.

Schriften zur Theologie Bd. X, *Im Gespräch mit der Zukunft.* Einsiedeln:
    Benziger, 1972.
[ET: *Theological Investigations* Vol. 14, *Ecclesiology, Questions in the
    Church, the Church in the World.* Translated by David Bourke. Lon-
    don: DLT, 1976].
"What is a Sacrament?," 135-48.
"Considerations on the Active Role of the Person in the Sacramental
    Event," 161-84.
"The Relationship between Personal and Communal Spirituality and
    Work in the Orders," 220-44.
"Observations on the Problem of the 'Anonymous Christian'," 280-94.

Schriften zur Theologie Bd. XI, *Frühe Bussgeschichte in Einzeluntersuchun-
    gen.* Bearbeitet von Karl-Heinz Neufeld. Einsiedeln: Benziger, 1973.
[ET: *Theological Investigations* Vol. 15, *Penance in the Early Church.*
    Translated by Lionel Swain. London: DLT, 1983].
"The History of Penance," 1-22.
"Sin as Loss of Grace in Early Church Literature," 23-54.

Schriften zur Theologie Bd. XII, *Theologie aus der Erfahrung des Geistes.*
    Bearbeitet von Karl-H Neufeld. Einsiedeln: Benziger, 1975.
[ET: *Theological Investigations* Vol. 16, *Experience of the Spirit: Source of
    Theology.* Translated by D. Morland O.S.B. London: DLT, 1979].

"Experience of the Spirit and Existential Commitment," 24-34.
"Religious Enthusiasm and the Experience of Grace," 35-51.
"Anonymous and Explicit Faith," 52-59.
"Faith between Rationality and Emotion," 60-78.
"The 'Spiritual Senses' according to Origen," 81-103.
"The Doctrine of the 'Spiritual Senses' in the Middle Ages," 104-134.
"Modern Piety and the Experience of Retreats," 135-55.
"Reflections on a New Task for Fundamental Theology," 156-66.
"The One Christ and the Universality of Salvation," 199-224.
"The Hiddenness of God," 227-43.

Schriften zur Theologie Bd. XII, *Theologie aus der Erfahrung des Geistes.*
    Bearbeitet von Karl-Heinz Neufeld. Einsiedeln: Benziger, 1975.
[ET (A Translation of the second part of *Schriften* XII): *Theological Investi-*
    gations Vol. 17, *Jesus, Man, and the Church.* Translated by Margaret
    Kohl. London: DLT, 1981].
    "Christmas in the Light of the Ignatian *Exercises*," 3-7.
    "On the Spirituality of the Easter Faith," 8-15.
    "Mystical Experience and Mystical Theology," 90-99.
    "Transformation in the Church and Secular Society," 167-180.
    "Religious Feeling Inside and Outside the Church," 228-42.
    "Some Clarifying Remarks About My Own Work," 243-48.

Schriften zur Theologie Bd. XIII, *Gott und Offenbarung.* Bearbeitet von Paul
    Imhof. Einsiedeln: Benziger, 1978.
[ET: *Theological Investigations* Vol. 18, *God and Revelation.* Translated by
    Edward Quinn. London: DLT, 1983].
    "The Human Question of Meaning in Face of the Absolute Mystery of
        God," 89-104.
    "What Does It Mean Today to Believe in Jesus Christ?," 143-56.
    "Following the Crucified," 157-70.
    "Experience of Transcendence from the Standpoint of Catholic Dog-
        matics," 173-88.
    "Experience of the Holy Spirit," 189-210.
    "Faith as Courage," 211-25.
    "Christian Dying," 226-56.

Portions of *Schriften* XIII and XIV have been translated in *Theological
    Investigations* Vol. 19, *Faith and Ministry.* Translated by Edward
    Quinn. London: DLT, 1983.
    "Foundations of Christian Faith," 3-15.
    "Theology and Spirituality of Pastoral Work in the Parish," 87-102.
    "The Spirituality of the Secular Priest," 103-116.
    "The Spirituality of the Priest in the Light of His Office," 117-38.

"On the Theology of Worship," 141-49.
"Why Does God Allow Us to Suffer?," 194-208.
"Mary and the Christian Image of Woman," 211-17.

Schriften zur Theologie Bd. XIV, *In Sorge um die Kirche.* Bearbeitet von Paul Imhof. Einsiedeln: Benziger, 1980.
[ET: *Theological Investigations* Vol. 20, *Concern for the Church.* Translated by Edward Quinn. London: DLT, 1981].
"Courage for an Ecclesial Christianity," 3-12.
"Women and the Priesthood," 35-47.
"The Church's Responsibility for the Freedom of the Individual," 51-64.
"The Spirituality of the Church of the Future," 143-53.
"The Inexhaustible Transcendence of God and Our Concern for the Future," 173-86.

Schriften zur Theologie Bd. XV, *Wissenschaft und christlicher Glaube.* Bearbeitet von Paul Imhof. Einsiedeln: Benziger, 1983.
[ET: *Theological Investigations* Vol. 21, *Science and Christian Faith.* Translated by Hugh M. Riley. London: DLT, 1988. [A Translation of the first three sections of *Schriften zur Theologie* XV].
"A Theology That We Can Live With," 99-112.
"The Mature Christian," 115-29.
"Christianity's Absolute Claim," 171-84.
"Jesus Christ — The Meaning of Life," 208-219.
"Christology Today," 220-27.
"Brief Observations on Systematic Christology Today," 233-34.

Schriften zur Theologie Bd. XV, *Wissenschaft und christlicher Glaube.* Bearbeitet von Paul Imhof. Einsiedeln: Benziger, 1983.
[ET: *Theological Investigations* Vol. 23, *Final Writings.* Translated by Hugh M. Riley. London: DLT, 1983, Chapters 1 to 7].
"Nuclear Weapons and the Christian," 16-32.
"Plea for a Nameless Virtue," 33-37.
"Intellectual Patience with Ourselves," 38-49.

Schriften zur Theologie Bd. XVI, *Humane Gesellschaft und Kirche von morgen.* Bearbeitet von Paul Imhof. Einsiedeln: Benziger, 1984, (First three sections).
[ET: *Theological Investigations* Vol. 22, Humane Society and the Church of Tomorrow. Translated by Joseph Donceel. London: DLT, 1991].
"Christian Pessimism," 155-62.
Schriften zur Theologie Bd. XVI, *Humane Gesellschaft und Kirche von morgen.* Bearbeitet von Paul Imhof. Einsiedeln: Benziger, 1984, (Last two sections).
[ET: *Theological Investigations* Vol. 23, *Final Writings.* Translated by Joseph Donceel. London: DLT, 1984, Chapters 8 to 19].

"Intellectual Patience with Ourselves," 38-49.
"Devotion to the Sacred Heart Today," 117-28.
"Courage for Devotion to Mary," 129-39.
"Art against the Horizon of Theology and Piety," 162-68.
"Faith and Sacrament," 181-94.

4. Works of Karl Rahner — Books

E Latere Christi: Der Ursprung der Kirche als zweiter Eva aus der Seite Chris-ti des zweiten Adam. Eine Untersuchung über den typologischen Sinn von Jo 19, 34. Unpublished Thesis. Innsbruck, 1936.

Worte ins Schweigen. Innsbruck: Rauch Verlag, 1938.
  [ET: *Encounters with Silence.* Translated by J. Demske. Westminster: Newman, 1960; London: Burns and Oates, 1975].

With Marcel Viller, *Aszese und Mystik in der Väterzeit. Ein Abriß.* Freiburg: Herder, 1939; 2nd ed. With an Introduction by Karl-Heinz Neufeld, 1989.

Geist in Welt. Zur Metaphysik der endlichen Erkenntnis bei Thomas von Aquin. Innsbruck: Rauch Verlag, 1939; 2nd ed. Edited by J. B. Metz. Munich: Kösel, 1957.
  [ET: *Spirit in the World.* Translated by William Dych. New York: Herder and Herder, 1968].

Von der Not und dem Segen des Gebetes. Innsbruck: Rauch Verlag, 1949; 10th ed. Freiburg: Herder, 1980.
  [ET: *Happiness Through Prayer.* London: Burns and Oates, 1958, 1978].

Zur Theologie des Todes. Quaestiones Disputatae 2. Freiburg: Herder, 1958.
  [ET: *On the Theology of Death.* Quaestiones Disputatae. New York: Herder and Herder, 1961].

Visionen und Prophezeiungen. Quaestiones Disputatae 4. Freiburg: Herder, 1958.
  [ET: *Visions and Prophecies.* Quaestiones Disputatae 10. London: Burns and Oates, 1963].

Hörer des Wortes: Zur Grundlegung einer Religionsphilosophie. Munich: Kösel-Pustet, 1941; 2nd rev. ed. Edited by J. B. Metz, 1963.
  [ET: *Hearer of the Word: Laying the Foundation for a Philosophy of Religion.* Translation of the First Edition by Joseph Donceel. Edited and with an Introduction by Andrew Tallon. New York: Continuum, 1994; *Hearers of the Word,* 2nd rev. ed. Edited by J. B. Metz. Translated by Ronald Walls. London: Sheed and Ward, 1969].

Das Dynamische in der Kirche. Quaestiones Disputatae 5. Freiburg: Herder, 1958.
  [ET: *The Dynamic Element in the Church.* Translated by William J. O'Hara. Quaestiones Disputatae 12. London: Burns and Oates, 1964].

Sendung und Gnade. Beiträge zur Pastoraltheologie. Innsbruck: Tyrolia Verlag, 1959, 3rd ed. 1961. [ET: *Mission and Grace: Essays in Pastoral Theology.* 3 Vols. Translated by Cecily Hastings. London and New York: Sheed and Ward, 1963].

Kirche und Sakramente. Quaestiones Disputatae 10. Freiburg: Herder, 1963. [ET: *The Church and the Sacraments.* New York: Herder and Herder, 1963].

Alltägliche Dinge. Einsiedeln, Benziger Verlag, 1964. [ET: *Everyday Things.* Theological Meditations 5. Edited by Hans Küng. London and Melbourne: Sheed and Ward, 1965].

Biblische Predigten. Freiburg: Herder, 1965. [ET: *Biblical Homilies.* Translated by Desmond Forristal and Richard Strachan. Dublin: Herder and Herder, 1966].

Betrachtungen zum ignatianischen Exerzitienbuch. Munich: Kösel, 1965. [ET: *Spiritual Exercises.* London: Sheed and Ward, 1976, reprint, 1986].

Das Konzil — ein neuer Beginn. Freiburg: Herder, 1966.

With Angelus Häussling, *Die vielen Messen und das eine Opfer: Eine Untersuchung über die rechte Norm der Messhäufigkeit.* Quaestiones Disputatae 31. Freiburg: Herder, 1966.

Glaube, der die Erde liebt: Christliche Besinnung im Alltag der Welt. Freiburg: Herder, 1966. [ET: *Everyday Faith.* London: Burns and Oates, 1967].

Knechte Christi. Meditationen zum Priestertum. Freiburg: Herder, 1967. [ET: *Servants of the Lord.* Translated by Richard Strachan. London and New York: Burns & Oates, Herder and Herder, 1968].

Ich glaube an Jesus Christus. Theologische Meditationen 21. Einsiedeln: Benziger Verlag, 1968.

Gnade als Freiheit: Kleine theologische Beiträge. Freiburg: Herder, 1968. [ET: *Grace and Freedom.* Translated by Hilda Graef. New York: Herder and Herder, 1969].

Zur Reform des Theologiestudiums. Quaestiones Disputatae 41. Freiburg; Herder, 1969.

Einübung priesterlicher Existenz. Freiburg: Herder, 1970. [ET: *Meditations on Priestly Life.* Translated by Edward Quinn. London: Sheed and Ward, 1970].

Chancen des Glaubens: Fragmente einer modernen Spiritualität. Freiburg: Herder, 1971. [ET: *Opportunities for Faith: Elements of a Modern Spirituality.* Translated by Edward Quinn. London: SPCK, 1970].

With Eberhard Jüngel, *Was ist ein Sakrament? Vorstöße zur Verständigung.* Kleine ökumenische Schriften 6. Freiburg: Herder, 1971.

With Wilhelm Thüsing, *Christologie — systematisch und exegetisch: Arbeitsgrundlagen für eine interdisziplinäre Vorlesung.* Quaestiones Disputatae 55. Freiburg: Herder, 1972. [ET: *A New Christology.* New York: Seabury Press, 1980].

With Hugo Rahner, *Worte ins Schweigen; Gebete der Einkehr.* Freiburg: Herder, 1973.

Strukturwandel der Kirche als Aufgabe und Chance. Herderbücherei 446. 3rd ed. Freiburg: Herder, 1973. [ET: *The Shape of the Church to Come.* Translated and Introduced by Edward Quinn. London: SPCK, 1974].

Die siebenfältige Gabe. Munich: Verlag Ars Sacra, 1974. [ET: *Meditations on the Sacraments.* New York: Seabury Press, 1977].

Wagnis des Christen. Geistliche Texte. Freiburg: Herder, 1974. [ET: *Christians at the Crossroads.* London: Burns and Oates, 1975].

Herausforderung des Christen. Meditationen — Reflexionen — Interviews. Freiburg: Herder, 1975.

Grundkurs des Glaubens: Einführung in den Begriff des Christentums. Freiburg: Herder, 1976. [ET: *Foundations of Christian Faith: An Introduction to the Idea of Christianity.* Translated by William V. Dych. London: Darton, Longman & Todd, 1978].

Erfahrung des Geistes: Meditation auf Pfingsten. Freiburg: Herder, 1977. [ET: *The Spirit in the Church.* London: Burns and Oates, 1977].

With J. B. Metz, *Ermutigung zum Gebet.* Freiburg: Herder, 1977. [ET: *The Courage to Pray.* Translated by Sarah O'Brien Twohig. London: Search Press, 1980].

With Helmuth Nils Loose, and Paul Imhof, *Ignatius von Loyola.* Freiburg: Herder, 1978. [ET: *Ignatius of Loyola.* With an Historical Introduction by Paul Imhof. Translated by Rosaleen Ockenden. London: Collins, 1979].

With Karl-Heinz Weger, *Was sollen wir noch glauben?* Freiburg: Herder, 1979. [ET: *Our Christian Faith: Answers for the Future.* Translated by Francis McDonagh. London: Burns and Oates, 1981].

[*Wer ist dein Bruder?* Freiburg: Herder, 1981].

[*Was heißt Jesus lieben?* Freiburg: Herder, 1982]. [ET: *The Love of Jesus and the Love of Neighbour.* Translated by Robert Barr. New York: Crossroad / London: St. Paul Publications, 1983].

Praxis des Glaubens: Geistliches Lesebuch. Edited by Karl Lehmann and Albert Raffelt. Freiburg: Herder, 1982. [ET: *The Practice of Faith: A Handbook of Contemporary Spirituality.* London: SCM Press, 1985].

Karl Rahner. Bilder eines Lebens. Edited by Paul Imhof and Hubert Biallowons. Freiburg: Herder/Benziger: Zurich: 1985.

Karl Rahner im Gespräch. Edited by Paul Imhof and Hubert Biallowons. 2 Vols. Munich: Kösel, 1982, 1983. [ET: *Karl Rahner in Dialogue: Conversations and Interviews 1965-1982.* Translated by Harvey Egan. New York: Crossroad, 1986].

Glaube in winterlicher Zeit: Gespräche mit Karl Rahner aus den letzten Lebensjahren. Edited by Paul Imhof and Hubert Biallowons. Düsseldorf: Patmos, 1986.
[ET: *Faith in a Wintry Season: Conversations and Interviews with Karl Rahner in the Last Years of his Life.* Translation Edited by Harvey Egan. New York: Crossroad, 1990].
Politische Dimensionen des Christentums. Ausgewählte Texte zu Fragen der Zeit. Edited by Herbert Vorgrimler. Munich: Kösel, 1986.
Das große Kirchenjahr. Geistliche Texte. Edited by Albert Raffelt. Freiburg: Herder, 1987.
[ET: *The Great Church Year. The Best of Karl Rahner's Homilies, Sermons and Meditations.* Edited by Albert Raffelt. Translated by Harvey D. Egan. New York: Crossroad, 1993].
Sehnsucht nach dem geheimnisvollen Gott: Profil, Bilder, Texte. Edited by Herbert Vorgrimler. Freiburg: Herder, 1990.

5. Works of Karl Rahner — Dictionaries, Encyclopaedias, and Handbooks

Kleines Theologisches Wörterbuch. Edited by Karl Rahner and Herbert Vorgrimler. Freiburg: Herder, 1961, 13th ed. 1981.
[ET: *Theological Dictionary.* Edited by Cornelius Ernst. Translated by R. Strachan. New York: Herder and Herder, 1965].
Lexikon für Theologie und Kirche. Edited by Karl Rahner and Josef Höfer. 10 Vols. Freiburg: Herder, 2nd ed. 1957-65.
LThK I (1957):
"Anima naturaliter christiana," 564-565.
"Anthropologie, theologische," 618-27.
"Atheismus," 983-89.
LThK IV (1960):
"Formale und fundamentale Theologie," 205-206.
"Gebet," 542-45.
"Gnadenerfahrung," 1001-1002.
LThK V (1960):
"Heilswille Gottes, allgemeiner, 165-68.
LThK VI (1961):
"Liebe. V. Heutige Problematik," 1038-1039,
LThK VII (1962):
"Martyrium," 136-38.
"Mysterien des Lebens Jesu," 721-22.
"Mystik," 743-45.
LThK IX (1964):
"Sakramententheologie," 240-43.
LThK X (1965):
"Theologia crucis," 61.

Sacramentum Mundi: Theologisches Lexikon für die Praxis. Edited by Karl Rahner, Adolf Darlap, et al. 4 Vols. Freiburg: Herder, 1967-69. [ET: *Sacramentum Mundi. An Encyclopedia of Theology.* 6 Vols. New York: Herder and Herder, 1968-70].
Sacramentum Mundi 2 (1968):
"Conversion," 4-8.
"Existence," 306-307.
"Freedom, Theological," 361-62.
"Grace, Systematic," 415-22.
Sacramentum Mundi III (1969):
"Liebe," 234-52 (ET: Not Translated).
Sacramentum Mundi 4 (1969):
"Mystery," 133-36.
"Missions II," 79-81.
"Order, Supernatural," 297-300.
Sacramentum Mundi 5 (1970):
"Potentia Oboedientalis," 65-67.
Sacramentum Mundi 6 (1970):
"Transcendental Theology," 287-89.
Handbuch der Pastoraltheologie: Praktische Theologie der Kirche in ihrer Gegenwart. Edited by Franz Xaver Arnold, Karl Rahner, Viktor Schurr, and Leonhard M. Weber. 5 Vols. Freiburg: Herder, 1962—1972.
HPTh I/2 (1964):
"Grundlegung der Pastoraltheologie als praktischer Theologie," 117-215.
HPTh II/1 (1966):
"Die Rücksicht auf die verschiedenen Aspekte der Frömmigkeit," 61-79.
"Die grundlegenden Imperative für den Selbstvollzug der Kirche in der gegenwärtigen Situation," 256-76.
HPTh II/2 (1966):
"Menschliches Scheitern und Weltverhältnis des Christen," 34-38.
"Die Notwendigkeit einer neuen Mystagogie," 269-71.
Encyclopedia of Theology. A Concise Sacramentum Mundi. New York: Seabury, 1975.

Section Two
(Secondary Literature)

1. Bibliographies of Secondary Literature on Rahner

Raffelt, Albert. "Karl Rahner — Bibliographie der Sekundärliteratur 1948-1978," *Wagnis Theologie: Erfahrungen mit der Theologie Karl Rahners.* Edited by Herbert Vorgrimler. Freiburg: Herder, 1979, 598-622.

Raffelt, Albert. "Karl Rahner — Bibliographie der Sekundärliteratur 1979-1983 und Nachträge," *Glaube im Prozeß*. Edited by Elmar Klinger and Klaus Wittstadt. Freiburg: Herder, 1984, 872-85.

Raffelt, Albert, and Roman Siebenrock. "Karl Rahner — Sekundärliteratur 1984-1993," *Karl Rahner in Erinnerung*. Freiburger Akademieschriften, Band 8. Edited by Albert Raffelt. Düsseldorf: Patmos, 1994, 165-205.

Tallon, Andrew. "Rahner Studies, 1939-89: Part 1, 1939-73," *Theology Digest* 36: 4 (1989): 321-46.

Tallon, Andrew. "Rahner Studies, 1939-89: Part 2, 1974-89," *Theology Digest* 37: 1 (1990): 17-41.

Tallon, Andrew. "Rahner Bibliography Supplement," *Theology Digest* 38: 2 (1991): 131-140.

2. Books

Albrecht, Carl. *Das mystische Wort: Erleben und Sprechen in Versunkenheit*. Edited by H. A. Fischer-Barnicol. Mainz, 1974.

Au, Wilkie. *By Way of the Heart: Towards a Holistic Christian Spirituality*. New York/Mahwah: Paulist Press, 1989.

Bacik, James J. *Apologetics and the Eclipse of Mystery: Mystagogy According to Karl Rahner*. Notre Dame: University of Notre Dame Press, 1980.

Bakker, Leo. *Freiheit und Erfahrung. Redaktionsgeschichtliche Untersuchungen über die Unterscheidung der Geister bei Ignatius von Loyola*. Würzburg: Echter Verlag, 1970.

Barry, William A. *Allowing the Creator to Deal Directly with the Creature: An Approach to the Spiritual Exercises of Ignatius of Loyola*. New York/Mahwah, N.J.: Paulist Press, 1994.

Barthes, Roland. *Sade, Fourier, Loyola*. Translated by Richard Miller. Berkeley and Los Angeles: University of California Press, 1976.

Bernard, Charles-André. *Traité de théologie spirituelle*. Paris: Les Éditions du Cerf, 1986.

Beker, J. Christian. *Paul the Apostle: The Triumph of God in Life and Thought*. Philadelphia: Fortress Press, 1980.

Böhme, Wolfgang, and Josef Sudbrack, eds. *Der Christ von morgen — ein Mystiker?* Würzburg: Echter, 1989.

Bonaventure, *The Soul's Journey Into God, The Tree of Life, The Life of St Francis*. Translated and Edited by Ewert Cousins. Classics of Western Spirituality Series. New York: Paulist Press, 1978.

Bornkamm, Günther. *Paulus*. 3rd ed. Stuttgart: Kohlhammer, 1977. [ET: *Paul*. Translated by D. Stalker. London: Hodder and Stoughton, 1971].

Bouyer, Louis. *Introduction à la vie spirituelle. Précis de théologie ascétique et mystique*. Paris-Tournai: Desclée, 1960.

Bouyer, Louis. *La Spiritualité du Nouveau Testament et des Pères*. Histoire de la spiritualité chrétienne Vol. 1. Paris: Aubier, 1960.

Callahan, Annice. *Karl Rahner's Spirituality of the Pierced Heart: A Reinterpretation of Devotion to the Sacred Heart.* Lanham MD: University Press of America, 1985.

Callahan, Annice, ed. *Spiritualities of the Heart.* New York: Paulist Press, 1990.

Carabine, Deirdre. *The Unknown God. Negative Theology in the Platonic Tradition: Plato to Eriugena.* Louvain Theological & Pastoral Monographs 19. Louvain: Peeters Press/ W. B. Eerdmans, 1995.

Carr, Anne E. *The Theological Method of Karl Rahner.* Missoula, Montana: Scholars Press, 1977.

Carr, Anne E. *Transforming Grace: Christian Tradition and Women's Experience.* San Francisco: Harper and Row, 1988, 1990.

Cerfaux, Lucien. *L'Itinéraire spirituel de saint Paul.* Paris: Cerf, 1966. [ET: *The Spiritual Journey of St Paul.* Translated by John Guinness. New York: Sheed and Ward, 1968].

Congar, Yves. *Je crois en l'Esprit Saint,* Vol 1: *L'expérience de l'Esprit.* Paris: Les Editions du Cerf, 1979. [ET: *I Believe in the Holy Spirit,* Vol. 1. *The Holy Spirit in the 'Economy.'* Translated by David Smith. London: Chapman, 1983].

Conn, Joann Wilski, ed. *Women's Spirituality: Resources for Christian Development.* New York: Paulist Press, 1986.

Conway, Eamonn. *The Anonymous Christian — A Relativized Christianity? An Evaluation of Hans Urs von Balthasar's Criticisms of Karl Rahner's Theory of the Anonymous Christian.* European University Studies 485. Frankfurt am Main: Peter Lang, 1993.

Delgado, Mariano, and Matthias-Lutz Bachmann, eds. *Theologie aus Erfahrung der Gnade: Annäherungen an Karl Rahner.* Berlin: Morus Verlag, 1994.

De Guibert, Joseph. *The Jesuits: Their Spiritual Doctrine and Practice. A Historical Study.* Translated by William J. Young. Edited by George E. Ganss. St. Louis: The Institute of Jesuit Sources, 1972.

De Lubac, Henri. *Surnaturel: Études historiques.* Paris: Aubier, 1946.

De Schrijver, Georges. *Kiezen voor de God van het Leven: Maatschappijkritische Opstellen rond Geloven.* Niké Reeks 7. Leuven/Amersfoort: Acco, 1985.

Dister, John E, ed. *A New Introduction to the Spiritual Exercises of St. Ignatius.* Collegeville, Minnesota: The Liturgical Press, 1993.

Divarkar, Parmananda R. *The Path of Interior Knowledge: Reflections on the Spiritual Exercises of St Ignatius of Loyola.* Study Aids on Jesuit Topics, No. 5. Rome: Centrum Ignatianum Spiritualitatis. 1982.

Drewermann, Eugen. *Glauben in Freiheit oder Tiefenpsychologie und Dogmatik.* Vol. 1. *Dogma, Angst und Symbolismus.* Solothurn und Düsseldorf: Walter-Verlag, 1993.

Duffy, Stephen J. *The Graced Horizon: Nature and Grace in Modern Catholic Thought.* Theology and Life Series 37. Collegeville, Minnesota: The Liturgical Press, 1992.

Dych, William V. *Karl Rahner.* Outstanding Christian Thinkers Series. Edited by Brian Davies. Collegeville, Minnesota: The Liturgical Press, 1992.

Egan, Harvey D. *The Spiritual Exercises and the Ignatian Mystical Horizon.* Foreword by Karl Rahner. St. Louis: The Institute of Jesuit Sources, 1976.

Egan, Harvey D. *What are they saying about Mysticism?* New York: Paulist Press, 1982.

Egan, Harvey D. *An Anthology of Christian Mysticism.* Collegeville, Minnesota: The Liturgical Press, 1991.

Eicher, Peter. *Die anthropologische Wende: Karl Rahners philosophischer Weg vom Wesen des Menschen zur personalen Existenz.* Freiburg: Freiburger Universitätsverlag, 1970.

Evdokimov, Paul. *L'amour fou de Dieu.* Paris, Éditions du Seuil, 1973.

Farmer, Jerry T. *Ministry in Community: Rahner's Vision of Ministry.* Louvain Theological and Pastoral Monographs 13. Louvain: Peeters Press, 1992.

Fiorenza, Elisabeth Schüssler. *In Memory of Her: A Feminist Theological Reconstruction of Christian Origins.* New York: Crossroad, 1983.

Fiorenza, Elisabeth Schüssler. *Discipleship of Equals: A Critical Feminist Ekklesia-logy of Liberation.* New York: Crossroad, 1993.

Fischer, Klaus P. *Der Mensch als Geheimnis: Die Anthropologie Karl Rahners. Mit einem Brief von Karl Rahner.* Freiburg: Herder, 1974.

Fischer, Klaus P. *Gotteserfahrung: Mystagogie in der Theologie Karl Rahners und in der Theologie der Befreiung.* Mainz: Grünewald, 1986.

Fitzmyer, Joseph. *To Advance the Gospel. New Testament Studies.* New York: Crossroad, 1981.

Fox, Matthew. *Original Blessing: A Primer in Creation Spirituality.* Santa Fe: Bear and Co., 1983.

Ganss, George E. et al., eds. *Ignatius of Loyola: The Spiritual Exercises and Selected Works.* Classics of Western Spirituality Series. Mahwah, New Jersey: Paulist Press, 1991.

Gelpi, Donald L. *The Turn To Experience In Contemporary Theology.* New York/Mahwah, N.J.: Paulist Press, 1994.

Grün, Anselm. *Erlösung durch das Kreuz. Karl Rahners Beitrag zu einem heutigen Erlösungsverständnis.* Münsterschwarzacher Studien 26. Münsterschwarzach: Vier-Türme-Verlag, 1975.

Guenther, Titus F. *Rahner and Metz: Transcendental Theology as Political Theology.* Boston: Univ. Press of America, 1994.

Gutierrez, Gustavo. *Beber en su propio pozo: En el itinerario espiritual de un pueblo.* Lima: Centro de Estudios y Publicaciones (CEP), 2nd ed. 1983. [ET: *We Drink from Our Own Wells: The Spiritual Journey of a People.* Translated by Matthew J. O'Connell. London: SCM, 1984].

Haight, Roger. *The Experience and Language of Grace*. Dublin: Gill and Macmillan, 1979.

Haight, Roger. *An Alternative Vision: An Interpretation of Liberation Theology*. New York, Mahwah: Paulist Press, 1985.

Haslinger, Herbert, *Sich selbst entdecken — Gott erfahren. Für eine mystagogische Praxis kirchlicher Jugendarbeit*. Mainz: Grünewald, 1991.

Hilberath, Bernd Jochen. *Karl Rahner: Gottgeheimnis Mensch*. Mainz: Grünewald, 1995.

Hoye, William J. *Gotteserfahrung? Klärung eines Grundbegriffs der heutigen Theologie*. Zurich: Benziger, 1993.

Johnson, Elisabeth. *She Who Is: The Mystery of God in Feminist Theological Discourse*. New York: Crossroad, 1993.

Karrer, Otto. *Der Heilige Franz von Borja*. Freiburg: Herder, 1921.

Kelly, Geffrey B. ed. *Karl Rahner: Theologian of the Graced Search for Meaning*. The Making of Modern Theology Series. Minneapolis: Fortress Press, 1992.

Kelly, William J. ed. *Theology and Discovery: Essays in Honour of Karl Rahner, S.J.* Milwaukee: Marquette University Press, 1980.

Klinger, Elmar. *Das absolute Geheimnis im Alltag entdecken: Zur spirituellen Theologie Karl Rahners*. Würzburg: Echter Verlag, 1994.

Kuss, Otto. *Paulus: Die Rolle des Apostels in der theologischen Entwicklung der Urkirche*. Regensburg: Pustet, 1971.

LaCugna, Catherine Mowry. *God for Us: The Trinity and Christian Life*. San Francisco: HarperCollins, 1991.

Lagrange, Reginald Garrigou. *Les trois ages de la vie interieure, prelude de celle du ciel: traite ascétique et mystique*. 2 Vols. Paris: Cerf, 1938. [ET: *The Three Ages of the Interior Life*. 2 Vols. Translated by T. Doyle. New York: Herder, 1948].

Lash, Nicholas. *Easter in Ordinary: Reflections on Human Experience and the Knowledge of God*. London: SCM, 1988.

Latourelle, René. *Theology, Science of Salvation*. New York: Alba House, 1969.

Leclerq, Jean. *L'amour des lettres et le desir de Dieu: initiation aux auteurs monastiques du Moyen Age*. Paris: Cerf. 1957. [ET: *The Love of Learning and the Desire for God: A Study of Monastic Culture*. Translated by Catherine Mishrahi. New York: Fordham University Press, 1974].

Leijssen, Lambert, Herman Lombaerts, and Bert Roebben, eds. *Geloven als toekomst. Godsdienstpedagogische visies en bijdragen aangeboden aan Professor Jozef Bulckens bij zijn emeritaat*. Leuven/Amersfoort: Acco, 1995.

Lennan, Richard. *The Ecclesiology of Karl Rahner*. Oxford: Clarendon Press, 1995.

Libbrecht, Ulrich, et al., eds. *De geur van de roos. Over zingeving en spiritualiteit*. Leuven: Davidsfonds, 1994.

Lohmeyer, Ernst. *Der Brief an die Philipper.* Kritisch-exegetischer Kommentar über das Neue Testament. Edited by H. A. W. Meyer 9/1; 14th ed. Göttingen: Vandenhoeck and Ruprecht, 1974.

Lonsdale, David. *Eyes To See, Ears To Hear: An Introduction to Ignatian Spirituality.* London: DLT, 1990.

Louth, Andrew. *Discerning the Mystery: An Essay on the Nature of Theology.* Oxford: Clarendon Press, 1983.

Maréchal, Joseph. *Le point de départ de la métaphysique: Leçons sur la développement historique et théorique du probleme de la connaissance.* 5 Vols. Paris: Desclée de Brouwer; and Brussels: L'Edition Universelle, 1922-26.

Metz, J. B. *Christlicher Anthropozentrik. Über die Denkform des Thomas von Aquin.* With an Introduction by Karl Rahner. Munich: Kösel, 1962.

Metz, J. B. *Zur Theologie der Welt.* Mainz: Grünewald, 1968. [ET: *Theology of the World.* New York: Herder and Herder, 1969].

Metz, J. B. *Glaube in Geschichte und Gesellschaft.* Mainz: Grünewald, 1977. [ET: *Faith in History and Society: Toward a Practical Fundamental Theology.* Translated by David Smith. New York: Crossroad, 1980].

Metz, J. B. *Zeit der Orden. Zur Mystik und Politik der Nachfolge.* Freiburg: Herder, 1977. [ET: *Followers of Christ. The Religious Life and the Church.* London: Burns and Oates, 1978].

McBrien, Richard P. *Catholicism.* 2 Vols. London: Geoffrey Chapman, 1980.

Miggelbrink, Ralf. *Ekstatische Gottesliebe im tätigen Weltbezug. Der Beitrag Karl Rahners zur zeitgenössischen Gotteslehre.* Münsteraner Theologische Abhandlungen. Altenberge: Telos Verlag, 1989.

Moltmann, Jürgen. *Gott in der Schöpfung: Ökologische Schöpfungslehre.* Munich: Kaiser Verlag, 1985. [ET: *God in Creation: An Ecological Doctrine of Creation.* Translated by Margaret Kohl. London: SCM, 1985].

Moltmann, Jürgen. *Der Geist des Lebens: Eine ganzheitliche Pneumatologie.* Munich: Kaiser Verlag, 1991. [ET: *The Spirit of Life: A Universal Affirmation.* Translated by Margaret Kohl, London: SCM, 1992].

Mommaers, Paul. *Was ist Mystik?* Frankfurt: Insel Verlag, 1979.

Neufeld, Karl H. *Die Brüder Rahner: Eine Biographie.* Freiburg: Herder, 1994.

Neumann, Karl. *Der Praxisbezug der Theologie bei Karl Rahner.* Freiburger Theologische Studien 118. Freiburg: Herder, 1980.

Peters, William A. M. *The Spiritual Exercises of St Ignatius: Exposition and Interpretation.* Rome: C. I. S., 1968.

Pöhlmann, Horst Georg. *Gottesdenker. Prägende evangelische und katholische Theologen der Gegenwart. 12 Porträts.* With an Introduction by Milan Machovec. Reinbek bei Hamburg: Rowohlt Verlag, 1984.

Pourrat, Pierre. *La spiritualité chrétienne,* 3rd ed. Paris: Gabalda, 1918. [ET: *Christian Spirituality,* 4 Vols. Translated by W. H. Mitchell and S. P. Jacques. Westminster: Newman, 1953-55].

Przywara, Erich. *Deus semper major: Theologie der Exerzitien.* 2 Vols. Freiburg: Herder, 1938-39.

Przywara, Erich. *Ignatianisch. Vier Studien zum vierhundertsten Todestag des Heiligen Ignatius von Loyola.* Frankfurt am Main. Josef Knecht Verlag, 1956.

Puhl, Louis J. *The Spiritual Exercises of St Ignatius. Based on Studies in the Language of the Autograph.* Chicago: Loyola University Press, 1951.

Raffelt, Albert, and Karl Lehmann, eds. *Rechenschaft des Glaubens. Karl Rahner-Lesebuch.* Freiburg: Herder, 1979. [ET: *The Content of Faith. The Best of Karl Rahner's Theological Writings.* Translation Edited by Harvey D. Egan. New York: Crossroad, 1993].

Raffelt, Albert, ed. *Karl Rahner in Erinnerung.* Freiburger Akademieschriften, 8. Düsseldorf: Patmos, 1994.

Rahner, Hugo. *Ignatius von Loyola als Mensch und Theologe.* Freiburg: Herder, 1964. [ET: *Ignatius the Theologian.* Translated by Michael Barry London: Chapman, 1968, 1990].

Regan, David. *Experience the Mystery: Pastoral Possibilities for Christian Mystagogy.* London: Geoffrey Chapman, 1994.

Rinser, Luise. *Gratwanderung. Briefe der Freundschaft an Karl Rahner 1962-1984.* Edited by Bogdan Snela. Munich: Kösel, 1994.

Saudreau, Auguste. *Manuel de spiritualité.* Paris: Amat, 1916; 3rd rev. ed., Paris: Téqui, 1933.

Schilson, Arno, ed. *Gottes Weisheit im Mysterium. Vergessene Wege christlicher Spiritualität.* Mainz: Grünewald, 1989.

Schnackenburg, Rudolph. *Die sittliche Botschaft des Neuen Testaments,* 2nd ed., Munich: Max Hüber Verlag, 1962. [ET: *The Moral Teaching of the New Testament.* New York: Herder, 1969].

Schneider, Michael. *"Unterscheidung der Geister:" Die ignatianischen Exerzitien in der Deutung von E. Przywara, K. Rahner und G. Fessard.* 2nd ed. Innsbrucker theologische Studien 11. Innsbruck: Tyrolia, 1987.

Schneiders, Sandra. *Women and the Word.* New York: Paulist Press, 1986.

Schweitzer, Albert. *Die Mystik des Apostels Paulus.* Tübingen: Mohr, 1930.

Schwerdtfeger, Nikolaus. *Gnade und Welt: Zum Grundgefüge von Karl Rahners Theorie der "anonymen Christen."* Freiburger Theologische Studien 123. Freiburg: Herder, 1982.

Segundo, Juan Luis. *El Cristo de los ejercicios espirituales.* Madrid: Ediciones Cristianidad, 1982. [ET: *The Christ of the Ignatian Exercises. Jesus of Nazareth Yesterday and Today.* Vol. 4. Edited and Translated by John Drury. Maryknoll, NY: 1987].

Sheehan, Thomas. *Karl Rahner: The Philosophical Foundations.* Preface by Karl Rahner, SJ. Ohio: University Press, 1987.

Sheldrake, Philip. *Spirituality and History: Questions of Interpretation and Method*. London: SPCK, 1991.

Sheldrake, Philip, ed. *The Way of Ignatius Loyola: Contemporary Approaches to the Spiritual Exercises*. St Louis, Missouri: The Institute of Jesuit Sources/London: SPCK, 1991.

Sievernich, Michael, and Günter Switek, eds. *Ignatianisch. Eigenart und Methode der Gesellschaft Jesu*. Freiburg: Herder, 1990.

Skelley, Michael. *The Liturgy of the World: Karl Rahner's Theology of Worship*. Collegeville, Minnesota: The Liturgical Press, 1991.

Sobrino, Jon. *Liberacíon con espíritu*. San Salvador and Santander: Editorial Sal Terrae, 1985. [ET: *Spirituality of Liberation: Toward Political Holiness*. Translated by Robert R. Barr. Maryknoll, New York: Orbis, 1988].

Sobrino, Jon. *Christology at the Crossroads. A Latin American View*. Translated by John Drury. Maryknoll, New York: Orbis, 1978.

Sobrino, Jon. *The Principle of Mercy. Taking the Crucified People from the Cross*. Maryknoll, New York: Orbis, 1994.

Sudbrack, Josef. *Mystik: Selbsterfahrung — Kosmische Erfahrung — Gotteserfahrung*. 3rd ed. Stuttgart: Quell Verlag; Mainz: Grünewald Verlag, 1992.

Tafferner, Andrea. *Gottes- und Nächstenliebe in der deutschsprachigen Theologie des 20. Jahrhunderts*. Innsbrucker theologische Studien 37. Innsbruck/Wien: Tyrolia, 1992.

Tanquerey, Adolphe. *Précis théologie ascétique et mystique*. 9th ed. Paris: Desclée, 1928. [ET: *The Spiritual Life: A Treatise on Ascetical and Mystical Theology*. Translated by H. Branderis. 2nd rev. ed. Tournai: Desclée, 1930].

Tinsley, Lucy. *The French Expression for Spirituality and Devotion: A Semantic Study*. Studies in Romance Languages and Literature, 47 Washington, DC: Catholic University of America Press, 1953.

Toner, Jules. *A Commentary on St Ignatius' Rules for the Discernment of Spirits*. St Louis: The Institute of Jesuit Sources, 1982.

Toner, Jules. *Discerning God's Will. Ignatius of Loyola's Teaching on Christian Decision Making*. St Louis: The Institute of Jesuit Sources, 1991.

Van der Heijden, Bert. *Karl Rahner: Darstellung und Kritik seiner Grundpositionen*. Sammlung Horizonte 6. Einsiedeln: Johannes Verlag, 1973.

Vass, George. *The Mystery of Man and the Foundations of a Theological System: Understanding Karl Rahner*. 2 Vols. London: Sheed and Ward, 1985.

Viller, Marcel. *La Spiritualité des premiers siècles chrétiens*. Paris: Bloud and Gay, 1930.

Von Balthasar, Hans Urs. *Verbum Caro: Skizzen zur Theologie I*. Einsiedeln: Johannes Verlag, 1960, 3rd. ed. 1990. [ET: *Word and Redemption: Essays in Theology 2*. Translated by A. V. Littledale and Alexander Dru. New York: Herder and Herder, 1965].

Von Balthasar, Hans Urs. *Cordula oder der Ernstfall*. Einsiedeln: Johannes Verlag, 1966. [ET: *The Moment of Christian Witness*. Translated by Richard Beckley. San Fransisco: Ignatius Press, 1969].

Vorgrimler, Herbert. *Karl Rahner verstehen: Eine Einführung in sein Leben und Denken*. Freiburg: Herder, 1985. [ET: *Understanding Karl Rahner: An Introduction to his Life and Thought*. Translated by John Bowden. London: SCM Press, 1986].

Vorgrimler, Herbert, ed. *Wagnis Theologie. Erfahrungen mit der Theologie Karl Rahners*. Freiburg: Herder, 1979.

Walsh, Michael J. *The Heart of Christ in the Writings of Karl Rahner: An Investigation of its Christological Foundation as an Example of the Relationship between Theology and Spirituality*. Analecta Gregoriana 209. Rome: Università Gregoriana Editrice, 1977.

Weger, Karl-Heinz. *Karl Rahner: Eine Einführung in sein theologisches Denken*. Freiburg: Herder, 1978. [ET: *Karl Rahner: An Introduction to his Theology*. New York: The Seabury Press, 1980].

Wong, Joseph H. P. *Logos-Symbol in the Christology of Karl Rahner*. Biblioteca di Scienze Religiose 61. Rome: Libreria Ateneo Salesiano, 1984.

Wright, John H. *A Theology of Christian Prayer*. 2nd ed. New York: Pueblo, 1988.

Wulf, Friedrich, ed. *Ignatius von Loyola: seine geistliche Gestalt und sein Vermächtnis (1556-1956)*. Würzburg: Echter-Verlag, 1956.

Zulehner, Paul M. *"Denn du kommst unserem Tun mit deiner Gnade zuvor ..." : Zur Theologie der Seelsorge heute. Paul M. Zulehner im Gespräch mit Karl Rahner*. Düsseldorf: Patmos, 1984.

3. Articles in Journals

Arnold, Patrick M. "In Search of the Hero: Masculine Spirituality and Liberal Christianity," *America* 161 (1989): 206-210.

Bechtle, Regina. "Theological Trends: Convergences in Theology and Spirituality," *The Way* 23 (1985): 305-14.

Benjamin, Harry S. "Pneuma in John and Paul: A Comparative Study of the Term with particular reference to the Holy Spirit," *Biblical Theology Bulletin* 6 (1976): 27-48.

Buckley, James. "On Being a Symbol: An Appraisal of Karl Rahner," *Theological Studies* 40 (1979): 453-73.

Callahan, Annice. "Karl Rahner's Theology of the Symbol: Basis for his Theology of the Church and the Sacraments," *The Irish Theological Quarterly* 49 (1982): 195-205.

Callahan, Annice. "Traditions of Spiritual Guidance: Karl Rahner's Insights for Spiritual Direction," *The Way* 29 (1989): 341-47.

Carson, D. A. "When is Spirituality Spiritual? Reflections on Some Problems of Definition," *Journal of the Evangelical Theological Society* 37 (1994): 381-94.

Cousins, Ewert. "Spirituality: A Resource for Theology," *Proceedings of the Catholic Theological Society of America* 35 (1980): 124-37.

Daniélou, Jean. "À propos d'une introduction à la vie spirituelle," *Études* 94 (1961): 270-74.

Deidun, Thomas. "Beyond Dualisms: Paul on Sex, Sarx and Soma," *The Way* (1988): 195-205.

De Schrijver, Georges. "Postmodernity and Theology," *Philippiniana Sacra* 27 (1992): 439-52.

Duquoc, Christian. "Theology and Spirituality," *Concilium* 19 (1966): 88-99.

Dulles, Avery. "Finding God's Will: Rahner's Interpretation of the Ignatian Election," *Woodstock Letters* 114 (1965): 139-52.

Edwards, Denis. "Experience of God and Explicit Faith: A Comparison of John of the Cross and Karl Rahner," *The Thomist* 46 (1982): 33-74.

Egan, Harvey D. "Christian Apophatic and Kataphatic Mysticisms," *Theological Studies* 39 (1978): 399-426.

Egan, Harvey D. "Prayer and Contemplation as Orthopraxis," *Proceedings of the Catholic Theological Society of America* 35 (1980): 102-112.

Egan, Harvey D. "Karl Rahner: Theologian of the *Spiritual Exercises*," *Thought* 67 (1992): 257-70.

Eicher, Peter. "Wovon spricht die transzendentale Theologie? Zur gegenwärtigen Auseinandersetzung um das Denken von Karl Rahner," *Theologische Quartalschrift* 156 (1976): 284-95.

Endean, Philip. "Spirituality and the University," *The Way Supplement* (1995): 87-99.

Fraling, Bernhard. "Überlegungen zum Begriff der Spiritualität," *Zeitschrift für Katholische Theologie* 92 (1970): 183-98.

Fischer, Klaus P. "'Wo der Mensch an das Geheimnis grenzt'. Die mystagogische Struktur der Theologie Karl Rahners," *Zeitschrift für Katholische Theologie* 98 (1976): 159-70.

Fischer, Klaus P. "Gott als das Geheimnis des Menschen. Karl Rahners theologische Anthropologie — Aspekte und Anfragen," *Zeitschrift für Katholische Theologie* 113 (1991): 1-23.

Galvin, John P. "Before the Holy Mystery: Karl Rahner's Thought on God," *Toronto Journal of Theology* 9/2 (1993): 229-37.

Giuliani, Maurice. "Une introduction à la vie spirituelle," *Christus* 8 (1961): 396-411.

Hilberath, Bernd Jochen, and Bernhard Nitsche. "Transzendentale Theologie? Beobachtungen zur Rahner-Diskussion der letzten Jahre," *Theologische Quartalschrift* (1994) 4: 304-15.

Irwin, Kevin W. "Sacramental Theology: A Methodological Proposal," *The Thomist* 54 (1990): 311-42.

Johnson, Elisabeth. "Jesus, the Wisdom of God: A Biblical Basis for a Non-Androcentric Christology," *Ephemerides Theologicae Lovaniensis* 50 (1985): 261-94.

King, Norman J. "The Experience of God in the Theology of Karl Rahner," *Thought* 53 (1978): 174-202.

Knauer, Peter. "Die Wahl in den Exerzitien von Ignatius von Loyola," *Theologie und Philosophie* 66 (1991): 321-37.

Laguë, Micheline. "Spiritualité et théologie: d'une même souche: Note sur l'actualité d'un débat," *Église et Théologie* 20 (1989): 333-51.

Lane, Dermot. "Anthropology and Eschatology," *The Irish Theological Quarterly* 61 (1995): 14-31.

Leclerq, Jean. "Spiritualitas," *Studi Medievali* 3 (1962): 279-96.

Leclerq, Jean. "Jalons dans une histoire de la théologie spirituelle," *Seminarium* 26 (1974): 111-21.

Lee-Pollard, Dorothy A. "Feminism and Spirituality: The Role of the Bible in Women's Spirituality," *The Way* 32 (1992): 23-32.

Lehmann, Karl. "Theologie aus der Leidenschaft des Glauben: Gedanken zum Tod von Karl Rahner," *Stimmen der Zeit* 202 (1984): 291-98.

Leijssen, Lambert. "Grace as God's Self-Communication: The Starting-Point and Development in Rahner's Thought," *Louvain Studies* 20 (1995): 73-78.

Liberatore, Albert. "Symbols in Rahner: A Note on Translation," *Louvain Studies* 18 (1993): 145-58.

Maher, Mary V. "Rahner on the Human Experience of God: Idealist Tautology or Christian Theology?," *Philosophy & Theology* 7 (1992): 127-64.

Marmion, Declan. "The Notion of Spirituality in Karl Rahner," *Louvain Studies* 21 (1996): 61-86.

Megyer, Eugene. "Theological Trends: Spiritual Theology Today," *The Way* 21 (1981): 55-67.

Metz, Johann Baptist. "Karl Rahner — ein theologisches Leben," *Stimmen der Zeit* 192 (1974): 305-14.

Michiels, Robrecht. "De Theologie van Karl Rahner," *Collationes* 8 (1978): 264-92.

Molnar, Paul D. "Can We Know God Directly? Rahner's Solution From Experience," *Theological Studies* 46 (1985): 228-61.

Neufeld, Karl-Heinz. "Umkehr und Buße im Denken Karl Rahners," *Wort und Wahrheit* 30 (1989): 30-33.

Neufeld, Karl-Heinz. "Worte ins Schweigen: Zum erfahrenen Gottesverständnis Karl Rahners," *Zeitschrift für Katholische Theologie* 112 (1990): 427-36.

O'Donovan, Leo. "Living into Mystery: Karl Rahner's Reflections at Seventy-five," *America* 140 (March 10, 1979): 177-80.

O'Donovan, Leo. "Orthopraxis and Theological Method in Karl Rahner," *CTSA Proceedings* 35 (1980): 47-65.

O'Donovan, Leo. "A Journey Into Time: The Legacy of Karl Rahner's Last Years," *Theological Studies* 46 (1985): 621-46.

O'Donnell, John. "The Mystery of Faith in the Theology of Karl Rahner," *The Heythrop Journal* 25 (1984): 301-18.

O'Hanlon, Gerard. "The Jesuits and Modern Theology — Rahner, von Balthasar and Liberation Theology," *The Irish Theological Quarterly* 58 (1992): 25-45.

Principe, Walter H. "Toward Defining Spirituality," *Studies in Religion/ Sciences Religieuses* 12 (1983): 127-41.

Sachs, John R. "Transcendental Method in Theology and the Normativity of Human Experience," *Philosophy & Theology* 7 (1992): 213-25.

Schneiders, Sandra. "Theology and Spirituality: Strangers, Rivals, or Partners?," *Horizons* 13 (1986): 253-74.

Schneiders, Sandra. "Spirituality in the Academy," *Theological Studies* 50 (1989): 676-97.

Sobrino, Jon. "Karl Rahner and Liberation Theology," *Theology Digest* 32 (1985): 257-60.

Splett, Jörg. "Mystisches Christentum? Karl Rahner zur Zukunft des Glaubens," *Theologische Quartalschrift* 174 (1994): 258-71.

Stanley, David M. "Pauline Allusions to the Sayings of Jesus," *Catholic Biblical Quarterly* 23 (1961): 26-39.

Steger, Albert. "Primat der göttlichen Gnadenführung im geistlichen Leben nach dem hl. Ignatius von Loyola," *Geist und Leben* 21 (1948): 94-108.

Sudbrack, Josef. "Vom Geheimnis christlicher Spiritualität: Einheit und Vielfalt," *Geist und Leben* 39 (1966): 24-45.

Sudbrack, Josef. "Literaturbericht: Über Mystik und Spiritualität in modernen Lexika," *Geist und Leben* 2 (1993): 144-51.

Sullivan, Francis. "Baptism in the Holy Spirit," *Gregorianum* 55 (1974): 49-68.

Tetlow, Joseph A. "The Emergence of an American Catholic Spirituality," *Theology Digest* 40 (1993): 27-36.

Thompson, William. "Renewed Interest in the Discernment of Spirits," *The Ecumenist* 13 (1975): 54-59.

Tracy, David. "The Uneasy Alliance Reconceived: Catholic Theological Method, Modernity, and Postmodernity," *Theological Studies* 50 (1989): 548-70.

Vandenbroucke, François. "Le divorce entre théologie et mystique: ses origines," *Nouvelle Revue Théologique* 72 (1950): 372-89.

Vandenbroucke, François. "Spirituality and Spiritualities," *Concilium* 9 (1965): 45-60.

Vinay, Gustavo. "'Spiritualità': Invito a una discussione," *Studi Medievali* 2 (1961): 705-709.

Von Balthasar, Hans Urs. "The Gospel as Norm and Test of all Spirituality in the Church," *Concilium* 9 (1965): 7-23.

Weger, Karl-Heinz. "'Ich glaube, weil ich bete.' Für Karl Rahner zum 80 Geburtstag," *Geist und Leben* 57 (1984): 48-52.

Wiseman, James A. "'I have experienced God': Religious Experience in the Theology of Karl Rahner," *American Benedictine Review* 44 (1993): 22-57.

4. Articles in Encyclopaedias, Dictionaries, Collections, etc.

Bacik, James J. "The Basis for a Dialectical Spirituality," *Being and Truth: Essays in Honour of John Macquarrie.* Edited by Alistair Kee and Eugene T. Long. London: SCM Press, 1986, 168-82.

Brown, Raymond. "Aspects of New Testament Thought: Eschatology and Apocalypticism," *The New Jerome Biblical Commentary.* Edited by Raymond Brown, Joseph Fitzmyer, and Roland Murphy. London: Geoffrey Chapman, 1990: 1359-64.

Clarke, Thomas E. "A New Way: Reflecting on Experience," *Tracing the Spirit.* Edited by James Hug. Woodstock Studies 7. New York: Paulist Press, 1983, 13-37.

Cousins, Ewert. "Preface to the Series," *Christian Spirituality* 1: *Origins to the Twelfth Century.* Edited by Bernard McGinn and John Meyendorff. Vol. 16. [Title Series: *World Spirituality: An Encyclopedic History of the Religious Quest,* ed. Ewert Cousins, 25 Vols.] New York: Crossroad, 1985: xiii.

Crouzel, Henri. "Exegese, Spirituelle Exegese," *Sacramentum Mundi.* Vol. I. Edited by Karl Rahner et al. Freiburg: Herder, 1967: 1278-89. [ET: *Sacramentum Mundi.* Vol. 1. New York: Herder and Herder, 1970: 201-207].

DiNoia, J. A. "Karl Rahner," *The Modern Theologians. An Introduction to Christian Theology in the Twentieth Century.* Edited by David F. Ford. Vol. 1. Oxford: Blackwell, 1989, 183-204.

Dupuy, Michel. "Spiritualité," *Dictionnaire de Spiritualité Ascétique et Mystique.* Vol. 14. Edited by Marcel Viller, Ferdinand Cavallera, and Joseph de Guibert. Paris: Beauchesne, 1990: 1160-73.

Dubois, Elfrieda. "Fénelon and Quietism," *The Study of Spirituality.* Edited by Cheslyn Jones, Geoffrey Wainwright, and Edward Yarnold. London: SPCK, 1986: 408-19.

Egan, Harvey. "Mysticism and Karl Rahner's Theology," *Theology and Discovery: Essays in Honour of Karl Rahner.* Edited by William Kelly. Milwaukee: Marquette Univ. Press, 1980, 139-58.

Egan, Harvey. "Ignatian Spirituality," *The New Dictionary of Catholic Spirituality.* Edited by Michael Downey. Minnesota: The Liturgical Press/Glazier, 1993: 521-29.

Fiorenza, Francis Schüssler. "Systematic Theology: Tasks and Methods," *Systematic Theology: Roman Catholic Perspectives.* Edited by Francis

Schüssler Fiorenza and John P. Galvin. Dublin: Gill and Macmillan, 1992, 1-87.

Fitzmyer, Joseph A. "Pauline Theology," *The New Jerome Biblical Commentary.* Edited by Raymond Brown, Joseph Fitzmyer, and Roland Murphy. London: Geoffrey Chapman, 1990: 1396-97.

Funk, Virgil C. "The Liturgical Movement," *The New Dictionary of Sacramental Worship.* Edited by P. Fink. Minnesota: Liturgical Press/ Gla-zier, 1990: 695-715.

Haight, Roger. "Grace," *The New Dictionary of Catholic Spirituality.* Edited by Michael Downey. Minnesota: The Liturgical Press/Glazier, 1993: 452-64.

Harrington, Daniel J. "Early Christian Spirituality," *The New Dictionary of Catholic Spirituality.* Edited by Michael Downey. Minnesota: The Liturgical Press/Glazier, 1993: 300-309.

LaCugna, Catherine Mowry. "The Trinitarian Mystery of God," *Systematic Theology: Roman Catholic Perspectives.* Edited by Francis Schüssler Fiorenza and John P. Galvin. Dublin: Gill and Macmillan, 1992, 149-92.

Lehmann, Karl. "Erfahrung," *Sacramentum Mundi.* Vol. I. Edited by Karl Rahner et al. Freiburg: Herder, 1967: 1117-123. [ET: *Sacramentum Mundi.* Vol. 2. New York: Herder and Herder, 1968: 307-309].

Lehmann, Karl. "Karl Rahner," *Bilanz der Theologie im 20. Jahrhundert.* Edited by Herbert Vorgrimler and Robert Vander Gucht. Freiburg: Herder, 1970, 143-81.

Leijssen, Lambert. "La contribution de Karl Rahner (1904-1984) au renouvellement de la sacramentaire," *Current Issues in Sacramental Theology.* Edited by Josef Lamberts. Leuven: Abdij Keizersberg/Faculteit Godgeleerdheid, 1994, 84-102.

Metz, J. B. "Politische Theologie," *Sacramentum Mundi.* Vol. III. Edited by Karl Rahner et al. Freiburg: Herder, 1969: 1232-1240. [ET: *Sacramentum Mundi.* Vol. 5. New York: Herder and Herder, 1970: 34-38].

Metz, J. B. "Prophetic Authority," *Religion and Political Society.* Edited by J. B. Metz, Jürgen Moltmann, et al. Translated by David Kelly and Henry Vander Goot. New York: Harper and Row, 1974, 177-209.

Meye, R. P. "Spirituality," *Dictionary of Paul and His Letters.* Edited by Gerald F. Hawthorne and Ralph P. Martin. Illinois: Intervarsity Press, 1993: 906-16.

Mühlen, Heribert. "Der gegenwärtige Aufbruch der Geisterfahrung und die Unterscheidung der Geister," *Gegenwart des Geistes: Aspekte der Pneumatologie.* Edited by Walter Kasper. Quaestiones Disputatae 85. Freiburg: Herder, 1979, 24-53.

Pissarek-Hudelist, Herlinde. "*'Die Frau ist der Frau aufgegeben'.* Die Entwicklung des Frauenbildes bei Karl Rahner," *Wie Theologen Frauen sehen — von der Macht der Bilder.* Edited by Renate Jost and Ursula Kubera. Freiburg: Herder, 1993, 159-92.

Purvis, Sally B. "Christian Feminist Spirituality," *Christian Spirituality: Post-Reformation and Modern*. Edited by Louis Dupré and Don E. Saliers, in collaboration with John Meyendorff. World Spirituality Series. London: SCM, 1989, 500-519.

Rahner, Hugo. "Eucharisticon Fraternitatis," *Gott in Welt*. Vol. 2. Edited by J. B. Metz, W. Kern, A. Darlap, H. Vorgrimler. Freiburg: Herder, 1964, 895-99.

Rondet, Henri. "Nouvelle Théologie," *Sacramentum Mundi*. Vol. III. Edited by Karl Rahner et al. Freiburg: Herder, 1969: 816-20. [ET: *Sacramentum Mundi*. Vol. 4. New York: Herder and Herder, 1969: 234-36].

Schütz, Christian, "Spiritualität," *Praktisches Lexikon der Spiritualität*. Edited by Christian Schütz. Freiburg im Breisgau: Herder, 1992: 1170-1180.

Schneiders, Sandra. "Scripture and Spirituality," *Christian Spirituality* Vol. 1: 1-20. (See under Cousins, Ewert above for complete bibliographical information).

Schneiders, Sandra. "Feminist Spirituality," *The New Dictionary of Catholic Spirituality*. Edited by Michael Downey. Minnesota: The Liturgical Press/Glazier, 1993: 395-406.

Schweizer, Eduard. "Pneuma," *Theologisches Wörterbuch zum Neuen Testament*. Band VI. Edited by Gerhard Friedrich. Stuttgart: Kohlhammer, 1959: 413-53. [ET: *Theological Dictionary of the New Testament*. Vol. 6. Translated and Edited by Geoffrey W. Bromiley. Grand Rapids, Michigan: Eerdmans, 1968: 415-50].

Sobrino, Jon. "Spirituality and the Following of Jesus," *Systematic Theology: Perspectives From Liberation Theology*. Edited by Jon Sobrino and Ignacio Ellacuría. Translated by Robert R. Barr. London: SCM Press, 1996, 233-56.

Sobrino, Jon. "Bearing with One Another in Faith," *Theology of Christian Solidarity*. Edited by Jon Sobrino and Juan Hernández Pico. Translated by Philip Berryman. Maryknoll, New York: Orbis, 1985, 1-41.

Solignac, Aimé. "Spiritualité — Le mot et l'histoire," *Dictionnaire de Spiritualité Ascétique et Mystique*. Vol. 14. Edited by Marcel Viller, Ferdinand Cavallera, and Joseph de Guibert. Paris: Beauchesne, 1990: 1142-60.

Sudbrack, Josef. "Spiritualität," *Sacramentum Mundi*. Vol. IV. Edited by Karl Rahner et al. New York: Herder and Herder, 1970: 674-91. [ET: *Sacramentum Mundi*. Vol. 6. New York: Herder and Herder, 1970: 147-57.

Sudbrack, Josef. "Karl Rahner und die Theologie der Exerzitien," *Gott neu buchstabieren. Zur Person und Theologie Karl Rahners,* ed. Hans-Dieter Mutschler. Würzburg: Echter Verlag, 1994., 41-50.

Tracy, David. "Recent Catholic Spirituality: Unity amid Diversity," *Christian Spirituality: Post-Reformation and Modern*. Edited by Louis Dupré and Don E. Saliers, in collaboration with John Meyendorff. *World Spirituality Series*. London: SCM, 1989, 143-73.

Weismayer, Josef. "Spirituelle Theologie oder Theologie der Spiritualität?" *Spiritualität in Moral: Festschrift für Karl Hörmann zum 60. Geburtstag*. Wiener Beiträge zur Theologie. Wien: Wiener Dom-Verlag, 1975, 59-77.

Wiseman, James A. "Mysticism," *The New Dictionary of Catholic Spirituality*. Edited by Michael Downey. Minnesota: The Liturgical Press/Glazier, 1993: 681-92.

Zizioulas, John D. "The Early Christian Community," *Christian Spirituality* 1: 23-31. (See under Cousins, Ewert, above for complete bibliographical information).

5. Unpublished Papers, Dissertations, etc.

Endean, Philip. "Die ignatianische Prägung der Theologie Karl Rahners: Ein Versuch der Präzisierung," Private Paper, London, 1989.

Endean, Philip. "The Direct Experience of God and the Standard of Christ: A Critical and Constructive Study of Karl Rahner's Writings on the *Spiritual Exercises* of Ignatius of Loyola." Doctoral Dissertation, University of Oxford, 1991.

Pajarillo, Manuel R. "Confrontation With The Real: Jon Sobrino's View of Spirituality. Analysis and Study of Its Presuppositions," STL Dissertation, Katholieke Universiteit Leuven, 1995.

6. Church Documents

Neuner, Joseph, and J. Dupuis, *The Christian Faith in the Doctrinal Documents of the Catholic Church*. Revised Edition. London: Collins, 1982.

Optatam Totius (28 October 1965). *Vatican Council II: The Conciliar and Post Conciliar Documents*. Edited by Austin Flannery, O.P., Vatican Collection Series. Vol. 1. New Revised Edition. Dublin: Dominican Publications, E. J. Dwyer, 1992, 707-24.

Gaudium et Spes (7 December 1965). *Vatican Council II: The Conciliar and Post Conciliar Documents*. Edited by Austin Flannery, O.P., Vatican Collection Series. Vol. 1. New Revised Edition. Dublin: Dominican Publications, E. J. Dwyer, 1992, 903-1001.

Pastores Dabo Vobis: Apostolic Exhortation of John Paul II on the Formation of Priests (25 March 1992). London: Catholic Truth Society, 1992.

Ratio Fundamentalis Institutionis Sacerdotalis (6 January 1970). *Acta Apostolica Sedis* 62 (1970): 368-74.

INTRODUCTION

Spirituality is in vogue today. Religious bookshops have large sections devoted to this theme, even if one is not always sure what sort of literature one can expect to find under the category "spirituality." For example, there has been an explosion of interest in "new age" spiritualities whose characteristics include a concern for holistic health, an emphasis on self-improvement techniques, and on non-conventional therapies and medicines. Moreover, the plethora of available literature on spirituality cannot be assumed to be specifically Christian in tone or in message. However, the focus of the present work is on Christian spirituality and, in particular, on how this notion is operative in the work of one of the giants of twentieth century Catholic theology, Karl Rahner.

Why have we chosen Rahner as the choice of our study? To answer this question we need to refer to a sub-text operating throughout the book, namely, the need to rediscover the connection between spirituality and theology. It is our contention that Rahner has made an invaluable contribution to the ongoing debate on how such a link can be developed. Specifically, we will endeavour: i) to ascertain what lies at the core of Rahner's understanding of spirituality, and ii) to point out the underlying unity of spirituality and theology within Rahner's corpus as a whole.

Although spirituality plays an uncertain role within the theological academy, there is no denying that Christians are searching for an experience of God. Karl Rahner has recognized this. He has recognized how the Christian faith commitment, if it is to survive at all, needs to be grounded in a personal experience of God. His oft-quoted dictum: "the Christian of tomorrow will either be a 'mystic' — someone who has 'experienced' something — or will not exist" already rings true in Europe, where Christian faith is no longer a cultural habit.

This notion of the experience of God emerges in *Chapter One*, where we study the changing meaning of the term spirituality. In a second section, we shall clarify precisely what we mean by the term spirituality, and how this is understood among contemporary theologians. Our preferred definition is that of the German theologian, Josef Sudbrack, who holds that the core of Christian spirituality involves all of the following elements: a "being-grasped" of the whole person, a personal encounter with Christ applied to our contemporary situation, and a "concretization" in the specific historical context of each person. However, we also discuss some theologians in the English-speaking (Schneiders, Principe), and in the French-speaking world (Solignac, Dupuy, Bernard), who have written in this area. It will become apparent that spirituality has to do with an investigation of "spiritual experience," i.e., with an investigation not only of religious experience in the more strict sense, but also of those analogous experiences that are perceived to convey ultimate meaning and value for individuals and groups. Further, we maintain that it is to this concept of spirituality as an examination of Christian religious experience that contemporary authors return in their debate on how spirituality might prove a resource for theology. In other words, having traced the gradual separation or divorce between spirituality and theology into two distinct disciplines, we shall see that theologians are rediscovering a common basis or root between theology and spirituality in an exploration of Christian religious or spiritual experience.

The notion of spirituality is then developed in greater detail in *Chapter Two*, where we concentrate on Rahner's understanding of the term. Our claim is that there is a very definite, if often overlooked, spiritual basis to Rahner's theology. We shall discuss a number of Rahner's early publications, particularly his more spiritual writings, with this thesis in mind. Further, we believe that one of the basic convictions running throughout Rahner's writings is that theology cannot be divorced from experiential knowledge of God. What constitutes the "spiritual" dimension of Rahner's thought, and how this finds expression in Rahnerian categories and language, are two questions that occupy the first part of the second chapter.

In the second half of Chapter Two, we address some of the key-themes operative in Rahner's understanding of spirituality. These themes include: an understanding of God as "holy mystery;" Christian life as a mysticism of everyday faith; prayer as a surrender of the heart; and the linking of the love of neighbour with the love of God. By outlining these themes our intention is to provide an overview of Rahner's view of spirituality. On one level, spirituality for Rahner has to do with the practical aspects of Christianity, that is to say, with the practice of faith in its various expressions. Indeed, Rahner has written on different kinds of spiritualities, e.g., Marian spirituality, Sacred-Heart spirituality, Lay Spirituality, etc. On another level, and underlying all these "forms" or expressions of spirituality is that unavoidable experience of mystery that lies at the heart of human life and which every person undergoes. Rahner offers many examples where someone can "make" such experiences: experiences of solitude, of trust, of hope, etc., whereby a person acts out of that which is most authentic in him or herself, elsewhere described by Rahner as being faithful to the dictates of one's conscience. The depth dimension in such experiences Rahner argues, serves as a pointer to where and how God can be experienced in the midst of everyday life.

It will be apparent that some of the issues that arose in the first chapter, e.g., the place of experience in spirituality, and the relationship between spirituality and theology, resurface in our discussion of Rahner's spiritual theology. The third section of the chapter will concentrate more explicitly on how Rahner understands the term "spirituality," and on how he links this to his understanding of theology. Once more, the notion of the experience of God emerges as the core of Rahner's conception of spirituality.

In fact, the importance of the concept of religious experience for Rahner's notion of spirituality warrants a separate chapter in its own right. This is necessary not only because of the ambiguous nature of religious experience but also because this topic takes us to the heart of Rahner's theology. In his view, all theological reflection, all theological statements, have their root in the holy mystery of God. Indeed Rahner often referred to the perennial *tension* that exists between theological concepts, and the attempt to relate these back to an original experience of God. The acknowledgement of the dimension of mystery in theology and the analogical nature of all theological statements thus forms a basic part of Rahner's theological method. This method has been described by Herbert Vorgrimler as the attempt to focus a multiplicity of theological themes (and Rahner *has* addressed a great number of such themes!) onto a very small number of basic ideas, i.e., key-concepts *(Schlüsselbegriffe)* or, more precisely, key-experiences *(Schlüsselerlebnisse)*. *The* key-concept or key-experience, which, in our view, provides the connecting link between Rahner's spiritual and theological reflections, is that of the experience of God *(Gotteserfahrung)*. Accordingly, a significant part of *Chapter Three* is devoted to teasing out Rahner's understanding of the experience of God under a variety of headings. We shall analyze the meaning of those terms that frequently crop up in Rahner's writing on religious or spiritual experience, namely, the "experience of transcendence," the "experience of God," the "experience of the Holy Spirit," and the "experience of grace." The concluding part of the chapter investigates Rahner's reinterpretation of grace in greater detail, and draws some consequences for a contemporary understanding of spirituality.

Our analysis of Rahner's conception of grace will show how he distanced himself from a reified or entitative understanding, and instead reinterpreted grace as the personal self-communication of God. This gratuitous offer of God's self-communication is present as a permanent "existential" in the life of every person. A question that arises in relation to Rahner's stress on the universality of grace, and with which we shall also have to grapple in our final chapter, concerns the distinctively Christian character of Rahner's understanding of spirituality, and how this finds expression in practice. Prior to that, however, we look in *Chapter Four* at the distinctively Ignatian features of Rahner's spirituality. Our task here is primarily to treat of Rahner's own writings on Ignatian spirituality, and, in particular, his writings on the *Spiritual Exercises* of Ignatius Loyola. Having previously underscored the central role of spiritual experience in Rahner's theology, we now relate this to his interpretation of the *Exercises*, where, in Ignatius' words, God deals directly with the creature. In short, the *Exercises* facilitate an experience of God, and have, what Rahner calls, a "mystagogical" function. There is also the further (Ignatian) claim that in the *Exercises* a person may discover God's specific will for him or herself. In the light of this claim, we shall critically evaluate Rahner's interpretation of the Ignatian notions of "election" and "consolation."

Rahner's Ignatian studies took place alongside his early historical research into the role of the spiritual senses in Origen and Bonaventure. By turning to these studies we shall indicate how they shed light on the concept, central to his interpretation of the *Exercises*, of the immediate experience of God. The issue to be dealt with here is the question of a "felt-knowledge," (a *sentire*, as Ignatius calls it), rather than with a conceptual knowledge of God. The theme of a direct encounter with God is also the subject of what Rahner later described as his spiritual testament. This testament, published in 1978, contains many significant insights into Rahner's appropriation of Ignatian spirituality and on how he conceives the contemporary significance of Ignatius. We conclude the chapter by exploring how these insights might be applied in the direction of what we have designated as Rahner's "mystagogical" spirituality.

In *Chapter Five*, our concluding chapter, we shall try to attain some distance from Rahner's presentation of spirituality by examining some of the typical criticisms of his position. These criticisms came from different ends of the theological spectrum. We shall take the comments of Hans Urs von Balthasar and J. B. Metz as representative examples of these two poles of opinion on the validity or otherwise of Rahner's idea of Christianity and the implications for spirituality. Besides evaluating the merits of these criticisms, we shall see how Rahner integrated many of the criticisms levelled at him into his own theologizing. This appropriation results in a spirituality with both a mystical and a societal component, the roots of which, lie in Rahner's assertion of the unity of love of neighbour and love of God.

Our second part of the final chapter attempts to clarify in more detail the specifically Christian characteristics of Rahner's notion of spirituality. This will entail an elucidation of what we describe as the Christocentric, ecclesial, and sacramental characteristics of Rahner's spirituality, and of how Rahner considers all three aspects integral to an authentic Christian spirituality.

Rahner never claimed his ideas to be the last word or that it was unnecessary to move beyond him. In this light, we shall devote the final part of the chapter to two important developments in spirituality, both of which find some implicit resonance in Rahner. The first can be described as "Liberation Spirituality," and we shall take Jon

Sobrino as a representative example of this development. The second development has been described as "Feminist Spirituality," and our focus here will be on the American theologian Anne Carr. Both Sobrino and Carr have acknowledged their debt — personal and theological — to Rahner. At the same time, they have taken his thought further in an attempt to devise a spirituality that will be more in tune with the needs and concerns of contemporary Christians.

We bring our work to a close with an overview of some of the main points that have emerged in the course of our study. We shall refer here to a helpful retrospective or *Rückblick* over Rahner's theological career which he gave shortly before his death. We conclude with a synthesis of what Rahner considered the essential elements of any future spirituality and indicates why he can be regarded as having made a most significant contribution towards achieving a *rapprochement* between theology and spirituality so needed today.

CHAPTER ONE

THE NOTION OF SPIRITUALITY

Introduction

a. Spirituality Today

One of the most significant developments in Catholicism since Vatican II has been the growing interest in spirituality. This trend is not just confined to Catholicism, but has affected almost every Christian denomination.[1] Yet the use of the term "spirituality" remains extraordinarily fluid and often quite ambiguous. For some, spirituality has primarily to do with prayer, the interior life, and one's personal relationship to God. Others, however, react against this rather private, individualised understanding (which has been operative for a century or more in Catholic theology),[2] and prefer to broaden the term

---

[1] Catholic theologians who have analysed this trend include Sandra Schneiders, "Theology and Spirituality: Strangers, Rivals, or Partners?" *Horizons* 13 (1986): 253-74, and Regina Bechtle, "Theological Trends: Convergences in Theology and Spirituality," *The Way* 23 (1985): 305-14. See also Joseph A. Tetlow, "The Emergence of an American Catholic Spirituality," *Theology Digest* 40:1 (1993): 27-36. Especially relevant for the focus of our study is Karl Rahner, *Praxis des Glaubens: Geistliches Lesebuch,* eds. Karl Lehmann and Albert Raffelt (Freiburg: Herder, 1982). [ET: *The Practice of Faith: A Handbook of Contemporary Spirituality* (London: SCM Press, 1985)].

[2] It will only be possible in the first part of this chapter to give a brief overview of the history of the use of the term. This has meant, inevitably, a selective historical synthesis. More detailed and extensive studies are available in *World Spirituality: An Encyclopedic History of the Religious Quest,* ed. Ewert Cousins, 25 vols. (New York: Crossroad, 1985 -), of which vols. 16, 17, and 18 are devoted to Christianity. Other significant works here include: *Dictionnaire de Spiritualité Ascétique et Mystique,* eds. Marcel Viller, Ferdinand Cavallera, and Joseph de Guibert (Paris: Beauchesne, 1932 -); *The New Dictionary of Catholic Spirituality,* ed. Michael Downey (Minnesota: The Liturgical Press, 1993), (hereafter cited as *NDCS*); *The Study of Spirituality,* eds. Cheslyn Jones, Geoffrey Wainwright, and Edward Yarnold (London: SPCK, 1986). See also Jean Leclercq, "Spiritualitas," *Studi Medievali* 3 (1962): 279-96. This article was a response to the Italian historian Gustavo Vinay, who expressed

to indicate an intensified faith life which embraces the whole of one's
daily experience — especially those elements of experience, at times
denigrated by traditional Catholic theology, i.e., the body and the
emotions. One often hears the use of the term "holistic spirituality"
in this context. There is also a growing desire on the part of many
theologians to highlight the social and political implications of spirituality.[3] Related to the above is the emergence of a feminist spirituality — arising out of women's experience and involving a critical,
interactive dialogue with the Bible and the traditions of the Church.[4]
And, finally, in the threatening circumstances of the world's current
ecological crisis, there is an increased emphasis on the importance of
a spirituality (and theology) of creation in an attempt to more appro-
priately rethink humanity's relationship to nature.[5]

In this chapter we will investigate this rather fluid notion of
spirituality as follows: First, we examine the changing meanings of
the term. We begin with St Paul, and then move on to the development of the term — indicating how the meaning of the term subsequently shifted at various stages in the history of Western Christianity. This approach should provide us with some sense of the rather
fluid understanding of spirituality. In a second step, we will note certain points of convergence on the basis of the results of some recent
studies on the meaning of spirituality. We will also focus here on the

---

his unease at the way the term was used by historians in their research. See Gustavo
Vinay, "'Spiritualità': Invito a una discussione," *Studi Medievali* 2 (1961): 705-9.
Leclercq's study has been summarized and augmented by Walter H. Principe,
"Toward Defining Spirituality," *Studies in Religion/Sciences Religieuses* 12 (1983):
127-41.

[3] See for example Gustavo Gutierrez, *We Drink from Our Own Wells: The Spiri-
tual Journey of a People*, trans. Matthew J. O'Connell (London: SCM, 1984), 33-53.
See also Jon Sobrino, *Spirituality of Liberation: Toward Political Holiness,* trans.
Robert R. Barr (Maryknoll, New York: Orbis, 1988), 46-79.

[4] For a good overview of recent feminist literature on this subject, see Dorothy A.
Lee-Pollard, "Feminism and Spirituality: The Role of the Bible in Women's Spiritu-
ality," *The Way* 32 (1992): 23-32. See also Joann Wilski Conn. ed., *Women's Spiri-
tuality: Resources for Christian Development* (New York: Paulist Press, 1986); Anne
E. Carr, *Transforming Grace: Christian Tradition and Women's Experience* (San
Francisco: Harper and Row, 1988), 201-14.

[5] Matthew Fox, *Original Blessing: A Primer in Creation Spirituality* (Santa Fe:
Bear and Co., 1983). See also Jürgen Moltmann, *God in Creation: An Ecological
Doctrine of Creation*, trans. Margaret Kohl (London: SCM, 1985), 1-39.

distinctions between spirituality and spiritual theology and between spirituality and spiritualities. Is there just one Christian spirituality or can one justifiably speak of various Christian spiritualities? A third section will develop some of these themes — concentrating in particular on the relationship between theology and spirituality. It will be necessary, in this context, to discuss the divorce between theology and spirituality (that had occurred by the beginning of the thirteenth century) and the consequences that ensued from this separation. Particular attention will be given to the concept of "experience," since this concept plays a central role in much current discussion on spirituality. This concept will occupy us in greater detail when we come to discuss the spirituality of Karl Rahner in the second, and subsequent chapters.

b. Spirituality — An Ambiguous Term

One of the reasons for the ambiguity of the term "spirituality" is that the term can refer to: (1) that inner dimension or spiritual core that is the deepest centre of the human person,[6] (2) the lived experience which actualizes that dimension, and (3) the academic discipline which studies that experience.[7] A further distinction made by some writers involves reserving the term "spirituality" for the lived experience, while referring to the discipline as "spiritual theology."[8] Thus, there exists today quite a degree of vagueness, not to mention an amount of confusion, as to the exact meaning of the word.[9] In attempting to come to some understanding of what is

[6] Ewert Cousins, "Preface to the Series," *Christian Spirituality* 1: *Origins to the Twelfth Century,* eds. Bernard McGinn and John Meyendorff, World Spirituality: An Encyclopedic History of the Religious Quest, 16 (New York: Crossroad, 1985), xiii.

[7] We follow here Schneiders' distinction in the use of the term "spirituality," in "Spirituality in the Academy," *Theological Studies* 50 (1989): 676-97, esp. 678. See also Principe, "Toward Defining Spirituality," 135-37, who makes a similar threefold distinction in defining spirituality.

[8] Ewert Cousins, "Spirituality: A Resource for Theology," *Catholic Theological Society of America Proceedings* 35 (1980): 124-37. See also Eugene Megyer, "Theological Trends: Spiritual Theology Today," *The Way* 21 (1981): 55-67.

[9] Philip Sheldrake, *Spirituality and History: Questions of Interpretation and Method* (London: SPCK, 1991), 32-56. See also the "Note on 'Spirituality'" *The Study of Spirituality*, xxiv-xxvi, where this ambiguity is briefly discussed.

meant by the term "spirituality," we will begin, firstly, with the
sense of the term in Paul. Then, we will illustrate how the meaning
of the term subsequently shifted from its original Pauline understanding. It will obviously not be possible, in such a short space, to
trace the entire history of the use of the word in Western Christianity. Our aim is merely to give some evidence for the claim that its
meaning has fluctuated widely in history — with the result that
there is no widespread contemporary consensus regarding a general
definition of spirituality.

1. The Changing Meaning of the Term

a. Meaning in Paul

Behind the English word "spirituality" lies the Latin term
spiritualitas, derived from the noun *spiritus* and the adjective *spiri-
talis* or *spiritualis*. The adjective "spiritual," from which the noun
"spirituality" is derived, has been traced to the Latin translations of
the Pauline terms *pneuma* and *pneumatikos*.[10] In Pauline theology
pneuma or *spiritus* is contrasted with flesh (*sarx* or *caro*), but not in

---

[10] Leclercq, "Spiritualitas," 279-96. He, in turn, is summarizing and augmenting
the detailed work on the history of the term "spirituality" by Lucy Tinsley, *The
French Expression for Spirituality and Devotion: A Semantic Study*, Studies in
Romance Languages and Literatures, 47 (Washington, DC: Catholic University of
America Press, 1953). Aimé Solignac has also traced the history of the word "spiritualité" in Latin and in French in *Dictionnaire de Spiritualité Ascétique et Mystique*
vol. 14 (Paris: Beauchesne, 1990): 1142-60. Because Paul provided the basis for the
later development of the term *pneumatikos*, we have confined our remarks here to
his teaching. It would be beyond the scope of this chapter to consider the complicated question of the role of Scripture in early Christian spirituality or to treat of
specifically Johannine or Lucan spiritualities. On the former, see Henri Crouzel,
"Spiritual Exegesis," *Sacramentum Mundi*, eds. Karl Rahner et al. (New York:
Herder and Herder, 1970) 1: 201-207. [*Sacramentum Mundi. Theologisches Lexikon
für die Praxis* (Freiburg/Basel/Wien: Herder, 1967) I: 1278-1289]. See also Sandra
Schneiders, "Scripture and Spirituality," in *Christian Spirituality* 1: 1-20. On the
latter, see Eduard Schweizer, "Pneuma," *Theological Dictionary of the New Testament*, ed. Gerhard Friedrich, trans. and ed. Geoffrey W. Bromiley, vol. 6 (Grand
Rapids, Michigan: Eerdmans, 1968): 415-50, (hereafter cited as *TDNT*). [*Theologisches Wörterbuch zum Neuen Testament*, vol. 6 (Stuttgart: Kohlhammer, 1959):
413-53].

opposition to *soma* or *corpus*.[11] For Paul, the spirit is that aspect of human nature that makes one open to God's Spirit, whereas the "flesh" represents everything in human beings that opposes this influence of the Spirit of God.[12] The opposition is thus not between the incorporeal and the corporeal, but between two ways of life.[13]

Despite the differing emphases given by various commentators[14] on Paul, there remains an underlying coherence to his spirituality. While Paul did not know the earthly Jesus, he was certainly acquainted with the incarnation (Phil 2:6-11) and with the cruci-

[11] See Harry S. Benjamin, "Pneuma in John and Paul: A Comparative Study of the Term with particular reference to the Holy Spirit," *Biblical Theology Bulletin* 6 (1976): 27-48.

The relevant biblical material is summarized by Josef Sudbrack, "Spirituality," *Sacramentum Mundi*, eds. Karl Rahner, Adolf Darlap, et al. 6 vols. (Freiburg, Herder, 1968-70), 6: 148-49 (*SM* IV: 674-75), and by Thomas Deidun, "Beyond Dualisms: Paul on Sex, Sarx and Soma," *The Way* (1988): 195-205. See also Louis Bouyer, Jean Leclercq, François Vandenbroucke, eds., *A History of Christian Spirituality*, 3 vols. trans. Mary P. Ryan (London: Burns and Oates, 1963; reprint ed., New York: Seabury Press, 1982), vol. 1: *The Spirituality of the New Testament and the Fathers,* by Louis Bouyer, 58-81.

[12] See Gal 3:3, 5:13, 16-25; 1 Cor 3: 1-3; Rom 7-8. Joseph Fitzmyer notes that, for Paul, the Spirit is an "energizer," a Spirit of power (1 Cor 2:4; Rom 15:13), and the source of Christian love, hope and faith. See his "Pauline Theology" [82: 61-67], *The New Jerome Biblical Commentary,* eds. Raymond Brown, Joseph Fitzmyer, Roland Murphy (London: Geoffrey Chapman, 1990): 1396-97, (hereafter cited as *NJBC*). In contrast, human preoccupation with "flesh" (Rom 8: 5-7), according to Paul, is one of the causes of their estrangement from God. Such estrangement and hostility (Col 1:21) is the situation of humanity without the gospel. On this, see Joseph Fitzmyer, *To Advance the Gospel. New Testament Studies,* (New York: Cross-road, 1981), 166-70.

[13] Bouyer, *Spirituality of the New Testament and the Fathers*, 80: "In other words, the flesh is not the body, but it is what man (woman) becomes when his (her) created spirit no longer submits itself to the divine Spirit ..." According to Bouyer, Paul is not so much concerned with the specifically Greek dichotomy between the soul and the body. Instead, he always thinks of man (woman) as a whole. Moreover, what is striking with Paul is how he drew out the consequences of the resurrection in a series of contrasts or oppositions: between the "flesh" and the "Spirit"; "law" and "grace"; "the present age" and "the age to come;" and especially between Adam and Christ. Bouyer sees in this scheme of contrasts: "... the matrix, as it were, of Paulinian spirituality" (p. 63).

[14] Apart from Sudbrack, Fitzmyer, Schweizer, etc., mentioned above, see also Yves Congar, *I Believe in the Holy Spirit*, vol. 1, *The Holy Spirit in the 'Economy,'* trans. David Smith (London: Chapman, 1983), 29-43; R. P. Meye, "Spirituality," *Dictionary of Paul and His Letters,* eds. Gerald F. Hawthorne and Ralph P. Martin (Illinois: Intervarsity Press, 1993): 906-16.

fixion.[15] However, his experience of the Spirit is directly related to the event of Easter and to the resurrection and glorification of Jesus as Christ and Lord. For Paul, the decisive moment of God's plan of salvation was reached in the passion, death, and resurrection of Jesus. In fact, Paul sees the passion and death as a prelude to the resurrection. All three phases make up "the story of the cross" (1 Cor 1:18). Paul thus links the death and resurrection of Christ — the resurrection is seen not simply as making up for the cross, but contributed as much as the passion and death of Christ to the "objective redemption"[16] of humanity. "If Christ has not been raised, then ... you are still in your sins" (1 Cor 15:17).[17]

---

[15] While Paul gives no evidence for knowing Jesus personally in his earthly ministry, his acquaintance with what Jesus did and taught reveals his dependence on early church tradition. The main reason why Paul does not focus on the minutiae of Jesus' manner of life, his ministry or personality is his desire to emphasize the salvific effect of the passion, death, and resurrection of Christ, which, for him, transcend the data of the historical ministry of Jesus. On this, see Fitzmyer, "Pauline Theology," *NJBC* [82: 16-20]: 1386-87; Otto Kuss, Paulus: *Die Rolle des Apostels in der theologischen Entwicklung der Urkirche* (Regensburg: Pustet, 1971), 440-51, and David M. Stanley, "Pauline Allusions to the Sayings of Jesus," *Catholic Biblical Quarterly* 23 (1961): 26-39.

It is an open question whether Paul composed the Christ-Hymn in Phil 2:6-11. The widespread view, since the foundational study of Lohmeyer is that Paul is quoting an independent hymn to summon the Philippians to live out the selfless attitude that should develop in them on the basis of their being "in Christ." See Ernst Lohmeyer, *Der Brief an die Philipper* Kritisch-exegetischer Kommentar über das Neue Testament, ed. H.A.W. Meyer 9/1; 14th ed. (Göttingen: Vandenhoeck and Ruprecht, 1974).

[16] Fitzmyer, "Pauline Theology," *NJBC* [82: 55-60]: 1395-96. The effects of what Christ has accomplished for humanity is referred to by Fitzmyer [82: 67] as the "objective redemption." He explains how the different aspects of this objective redemption are described by Paul under various images, e.g., justification, salvation, transformation, new creation, etc. Correlative to this is our attempt to appropriate or apprehend the Christ-event through faith and baptism, often regarded as the "subjective redemption" [82: 108-137].

[17] Thus, the cross, death and resurrection of Christ form the cornerstones of Paul's spirituality. The implications of this understanding of the Christ-event for the spirituality of early Christianity are discussed by John D. Zizioulas, "The Early Christian Community," in *Christian Spirituality* 1: 23-31: "Christian spirituality was based on accepting as one's own the scandal of the crucified Son of Man, an acceptance that could lead to suffering and death, to *martyrdom*" (p. 24, italics mine). We cannot pursue the question of martyrdom here — merely noting its importance for the spirituality of the early Church. For a discussion of why martyrdom can be considered the supreme example of the imitation of Christ, see Bouyer, *Spirituality of the New Testament and the Fathers*, 190-210.

A crucial event in Paul's life which shaped his spirituality was his "conversion" experience and call near Damascus (Acts 9: 1-19; 1 Cor 15: 8-11; Gal 1:15-16) — an encounter with the risen Lord (*Kyrios*) that he never forgot.[18] Pauline spirituality is the product of a highly personal experience, an experience, however, that also included a new awareness of the presence of the risen Jesus, now reigning as Lord in and among his people. At the same time, this presence of the risen Jesus brings believers into a new relationship with God through faith. Paul calls this new union a "new creation" (Gal 6:15; 2 Cor 5:17), i.e., a life in union with the risen Christ, a share in his own risen life (1 Cor 6:14; 2 Cor 4:14; Rom 6:4-5; 8:11).

Believers share in this risen life also by faith and baptism which incorporate them into Christ and his Church.[19] This "obedience of faith" (Rom 1:5; 16:26) or heartfelt response of the believer encapsulates for Paul the "commitment" or "submission" of the whole person to God in Christ — which lies at the heart of his spirituality. Faith, then, is not a mere intellectual assent to the proposition "Jesus is Lord." Instead,

> "it is a vital, personal commitment, engaging the whole person to Christ in all his or her relations with God, other human beings, and the world ... This awareness underlies the statement of Paul, 'It is no longer I who live, but Christ who lives in me; and even now the physical life I am living (lit., what I now live in the flesh) I live through faith in the Son of God who loved me and gave himself for me' (Gal 2:20)."[20]

---

[18] Paul's conversion experience and apostolic calling are treated by the following authors: Günther Bornkamm, *Paul*, trans. D. Stalker (London: Hodder and Stoughton, 1971), 16-25; Lucien Cerfaux, *The Spiritual Journey of St Paul*, trans. John Guinness (New York: Sheed and Ward, 1968), 19-29, and J. Christian Beker, *Paul the Apostle: The Triumph of God in Life and Thought* (Philadelphia: Fortress Press, 1980), 3-23. Beker notes that Paul is reticent about his conversion experience, and yet extremely outspoken about his apostleship (p.5). He refers to Paul's call as "a primordial experience" (p.10), and rightly portrays him as preoccupied by this call to the apostolate and to the service of the Gospel.

[19] Congar, *I Believe in the Holy Spirit*, 32. The ecclesial dimension of Pauline spirituality is especially stressed by Congar who laments the fact that it is a topic little studied by exegetes. For example, there is nothing about this dimension in Eduard Schweizer's article "Pneuma," in *TDNT*.

[20] Fitzmyer, "Pauline Theology," *NJBC* [82: 109]: 1407.

The experience of being incorporated into Christ needs to be seen in the context of what has been called the "dual polarity" of Christian life.[21] On the one hand, Christians, Paul insists, have become a "new creation" (Gal 6:15) in whom Christ really lives. On the other hand, they still have to be delivered "from the present wicked world" (Gal 1:14; 1 Cor 7:29-31). The Christian who has experienced the effects of the Christ-event still has to work out his or her salvation in fear and trembling (Phil 2:12).

The challenge to Pauline spirituality was therefore to keep a balance between the "already" and the "not yet."[22] At one level, Paul could claim that, with the Christ-event, the messianic age had already begun. A new perspective was introduced into salvation history — the *eschaton*, or "end-time," so long awaited, had started (1 Cor 10:11). Yet, a definitive stage of this stage of salvation history had still to be realized: the Messiah had come, but not yet in glory. Hence Paul (and the early Christian community) found themselves in a double situation: they both looked back upon the death and resurrection of Jesus as the inauguration of the new age, and looked forward to his coming in glory, his Parousia. Living in the *eschaton*, the age of the Messiah, is yet another aspect of the dual polarity of Christian life referred to above.[23] This age initiated a status of union with God

[21] Fitzmyer, "Pauline Theology," *NJBC* [82: 138-139]: 1412-13. See also Rudolph Schnackenburg, *The Moral Teaching of the New Testament* (New York: Herder, 1969), 261-78.

[22] The eschatological dimension of Pauline thought later became a dominant factor in shaping the spirituality of early Christianity. See, for example, John D. Zizioulas, "The Early Christian Community," in *Christian Spirituality* 1: 23-31: "It was this final act of God, the *eschaton*, that became for the first Christians the source of their spirituality ... Christian spirituality was thus centred on the person of Jesus of Nazareth as the *christos* or the 'Son of Man,' the eschatological figure ... This meant that Christian spirituality had to be experienced as a dialectic between history and eschatology, a firm conviction that the kingdom of God had come and at the same time a fervent prayer and expectation that it may come soon" (pp. 24-25). See also Daniel J. Harrington, "Early Christian Spirituality," *NDCS*: 300-309.

[23] It is beyond the scope of this section to provide a detailed account of the various explanations of the tensions in Paul's eschatology. Further discussion can be found, for example, in Raymond Brown, "Aspects of New Testament Thought: Eschatology and Apocalypticism," *NJBC* [81: 47-51]: 1359-64; and Schweizer, "Pneuma," *TDNT* 6: 415-24. For a thoroughgoing eschatological understanding of Pauline mysticism, see Albert Schweizer, *Die Mystik des Apostels Paulus* (Tübingen: Mohr, 1930), 1-26.

which destined believers to a final union with him in glory, and which, in turn, formed the basis of Christian hope and patience (Rom 8:18-25).

Such dual polarity in Christian life provides the reason why Paul insists that the Christian — energized by the Spirit of God — can no longer live a life bound by a merely natural, earthly horizon. The Christian believer is no longer *psychikos*, "material," but *pneumatikos*, "spiritual." Unlike the material person who does not welcome what comes from the Spirit, the spiritual person does not stifle the Spirit or disregard its promptings, but tests all things and holds on to what is good (1 Thess 5:19-22). The spirituality of Paul rests on the foundation of God's gracious work, a grace mediated to believers by and in the power of the Spirit of God — the Spirit which Paul sees as "poured out" (Rom 5:5) in the life of the believer in and through the response of faith (Gal 3:1-6; 4:1-7).[24] Spirituality in Paul can therefore be described as the personal appropriation, on the part of the believer, of the effects of the Christ-event — an appropriation that is expressed in attitude and action. It involves the obedience of faith and takes shape in the believer's grateful response in the Spirit to the call of God.

b. Subsequent Development of the Term after Paul

We began our attempt at clarification of the meaning of the term 'spirituality' with a description of its meaning in Paul. In this, and in the following section, our aim is to show how the Pauline understanding gradually changed — so that the term *pneumatikos* (or its Latin equivalent, *spiritualis*) gradually takes on other nuances and meanings.[25]

Our reference to martyrdom above (n. 17) can also be seen to have an *eschatological* dimension: martyrdom came to crystallize a new form of eschatological hope of Christians (Bouyer). The true and perfect disciple is the one who is ready to go with Christ to the cross. "Hence, indeed, it comes about that the believer accepts very real sufferings unhesitatingly, because he also expects, thanks to Christ, a resurrection which will be equally real." See Bouyer, *Spirituality of the New Testament and the Fathers*, 195.

[24] Bornkamm, *Paul*, 151-56.

[25] Leclercq, "Spiritualitas," *Studi Medievali* 3 (1962): 279-96, divides his study of the history of the term into two major periods: in the first, more ancient, period from around the fifth century, the Latin form *spiritualitas* is the term used. The second,

The first mention of the Latin word *spiritualitas* has been traced to a letter ascribed to Jerome in the early part of the fifth century.[26] The addressee is a recently baptized adult, and the context a paranetic one — the person is urged: "So act as to advance in spirituality" ("Age ut in spiritualitate proficias"). Here, the term *spiritualitas* is used in the sense of the spiritual life, that is, life according to the Spirit resulting from the new grace of baptism. The Christian is to live according to the Spirit to which he or she was initiated by baptism, i.e., a life of detachment from sin and attachment to God.[27]

more recent, period from around the end of the thirteenth century, reveals a more frequent use of derivatives of this word in languages issuing from Latin. In French the term *spiritualité* became the most widespread example of this development. In the following historical survey of the word we are also indebted to the article by Solignac, "Spiritualité," *DSAM*: cols. 1142-60. Both authors acknowledge their dependence on the classic work of Lucy Tinsley, *The French Expressions for Spirituality and Devotion*, (see note 10 above). Also pertinent to our study, which is by no means exhaustive, are the articles by Bernhard Fraling, "Überlegungen zum Begriff der Spiritualität," *Zeitschrift für Katholische Theologie* 92 (1970): 183-98; and by Josef Sudbrack, "Vom Geheimnis christlicher Spiritualität: Einheit und Vielfalt," *Geist und Leben* 39 (1966): 24-45.

[26] Leclercq, "Spiritualitas," 280. The relevant text of Hieronymus' letter is: "Verum, quia tibi, honorabilis et dilectissime parens, per novam gratiam omnis lacrimarum causa detersa est, age, cave, festina. Age, ut in *spiritualitate* proficias. Cave, ne quod accepisti bonum, incautus et negligens custos amittas ..." *De scientia divinae legis*, PL 30, 114 D-115 A. Principe, "Toward Defining Spirituality," 130, n. 19, describes how the above text has been variously ascribed to Pelagius, Faustus of Riez, Tertullian, or some unknown semi-Pelagian writer of the fifth century in Gaul. [In order to highlight the term in this, and in the following references, the term *spiritualitas* and its derivatives will be italicized.]

[27] Solignac, "Spiritualité," *DSAM:* cols. 1143-44. See also Fraling, "Begriff der Spiritualität," 185, who points out that the context of the term *spiritualitas* used above is unclear: is the term used primarily in a theological sense, i.e., referring to the human being under the Spirit of God or does it refers to the rationally-acting spirit of man or woman? Fraling's point is that the theological meaning of the term *spiritualitas* was gradually infiltrated by Greek anthropological thinking in that the 'material' and the 'spiritual' were set over against one another, the 'material' meaning being devalued. ("... immer mehr gewinnt das griechische Denkmodell an Bedeutung, in dem das Materielle dem Geistigen gegenüber abgewertet wird ... das Wort (ist) hier ganz vom griechischen anthropologischen Denken bestimmt.")

Further, both Sudbrack and Fraling align themselves with Leclercq, "Spiritualitas," 281, in claiming to have found another example of the term *spiritualitas* (in a similar context as above) in a Latin translation of Gregory of Nyssa (*De hominis opificio*, PL 67, 357 D) by Dionysius Exiguus in the first half of the sixth century. Referring to the two texts above, Sudbrack detects the "... Unterton von 'Spiritualitas' als Gegensatz zum Körperlichen, Materiellen und Fleischlichen durch." Sudbrack, "Vom

In this period (i.e., between the sixth and the eleventh centuries), while *spiritualitas* is a rather rare term, it nonetheless serves as a neologism for the spiritual life.[28] However, even at this early stage in the history of its development, *spiritualitas* begins to be equated with *incorporalitas* — anticipating a new meaning which would be given to the word in the twelfth century. Spirituality here is opposed to the fact of being corporeal, i.e., to *corporalitas* or *materialitas*.[29]

We also find the term in a Eucharistic context around 1060 (with Bérenger of Tours), where the reference is to the presence of the body and blood of Christ after the consecration, "in that which concerns the spiritual aspect," (quantum ad *spiritualitatem*).[30] For Bérenger, a spiritual attitude, or act of faith is necessary for a perception of the Eucharistic presence.

A further example of the use of *spiritualitas* is found in the *Chronica* of Hugues of Flavigny.[31] He describes a reforming abbot, Jarenton of the monastery of Saint-Bénigne of Dijon, who, wishing to restore the fervour of his monastery, took eight monks from Cluny because of their love of *spiritualitas* — here used in an ascetic or religious sense to designate an intense living of the Christian life based on the Beatitudes.

Thus, even given the varying nuances in the use of the term between the sixth and the eleventh centuries, *spiritualitas* retains a homogenous core of meaning: referring to that reality or those aspects of the human person under the influence, not of nature, but of

Geheimnis christlicher Spiritualität," 34. Solignac, on the other hand, notes that the reading of the second text is unclear, since most of the manuscripts contain *spiritalem* and not *spiritualitatem*. Hence Solignac excludes this latter text from his discussion.

[28] Solignac, "Spiritualité," *DSAM:* col. 1144.

[29] Principe, "Towards Defining Spirituality," 131, comments on this development as follows: "By opposing *spiritualitas* to *corporalitas* or *materialitas*, this new usage of the word changed its Pauline moral sense to an entitative-psychological sense. In this shift one can foresee the confusion of spirituality with disdain for the body or matter that was to mark many later movements dealing with spiritual life."

[30] "... quamvis panis et vinum altaris post consecrationem sint corpus Christi et sanguis, quantum ad *spiritualitatem* vel rem sacramenti." *De sacra cena,* éd. Vischer, (Berlin, 1834), 194, cited by Leclercq, 283, who remarks: "Il s'agit donc ici du mode spirituel selon lequel le pain et le vin eucharistiques, après la consécration, sont plus que ce qu'ils étaient avant."

[31] Solignac, "Spiritualité," *DSAM:* col. 1144.

the Holy Spirit; in short, to that which has traditionally been called the "spiritual" or "supernatural" life.[32]

c. Twelfth and Thirteenth Centuries

In the twelfth century two different groups of texts may be distinguished. The first group retains the connotation of "supernatural" for the term *spiritualitas* — which is placed in opposition to *carnalitas* or *mortalitas*. In these cases, the Pauline nuance of *spiritualitas* as the life of grace under the influence of the Holy Spirit is retained. A first example of such usage is found in the autobiography of Guibert of Nogent, a young monk of Beauvais.[33] He uses the term in the account of his "conversion" whereby he changed from a decadent lifestyle to the study of the Scriptures.[34] A similar idea, based this time on the conflict between the flesh and the spirit (as treated in Gal 5:17), is described in an anonymous treatise on the love of God, possibly the work of a Cistercian in the twelfth century.[35] *Spiritualitas* here refers to the taste (*sapor*) of the heavenly realities and is identified with spiritual love and wisdom.

A second group of texts uses the term to designate the intellectual creature in contrast to non-rational creation. Here, the term is used in what has been called the "philosophical" sense: to designate the individuality and incorporeality of the soul.[36] This use of the term *spiri-*

---

[32] Leclercq, "Spiritualitas," 284.

[33] *De vita sua*, written between 1114 and 1117, cited by Solignac, "Spiritualité," *DSAM:* col. 1144.

[34] "Cum itaque poena peccati intellectum dedisset auditui, tunc demum inutilis studii marcente socordia, cum tamen otii impatiens essem, quasi ex necessitate reiectis imaginationibus, *spiritualitate* recepta, ad exercitia commodiora perveni." I,17, PL 156, 874B. Guibert had been engaged in the writing of imaginative love poems. On the instruction of St Anselm, then abbot of Bec, he renounces the fantasies of poetry having found a taste instead for the sacred Scriptures! In this context, the term refers to a return to the study of Scripture — considered *the* spiritual book. See Solignac, "Spiritualité," *DSAM:* cols. 1144-45.

[35] *Caelestinus de caritate*, cited by Leclercq, "Spiritualitas," 286. The relevant passage is as follows: "Cum anima quod carnale est sapit, carnaliter diligit; cum vero quod spirituale est diligit, *spiritualitatem* sapit. Sapor carnalis est amor carnalis, sapor spiritus amor spiritualis. Unde etiam sapientia dicitur ab eo quod est sapere, id est gustare."

[36] In other words, creatures endowed with *spiritualitas* are said to possess an "intel-lectual matter." See Leclercq, 286, who claims that in the twelfth century:

tualitas becomes more frequent from about the middle of the twelfth century, and is evident in scholastic writings dealing with philosophical problems.[37] In such cases, the meaning of *spiritualitas* is no longer related to its original Pauline conception — where the term was contrasted with the flesh, (i.e., the human being subject to earthly tendencies as opposed to the human being under the influence of God's Spirit).

Likewise, in the thirteenth century, the term is used in two distinct senses. The first, and more frequent use attributes to *spiritualitas* a purely profane meaning (i.e., opposed to *corporalitas*). However, another, more religious or theological meaning is also evident. An example of both uses is evident in the writings of William of Auvergne, (bishop of Paris, 1228-49) who passes easily from the profane to the religious sense. In the second chapter of his *De anima*, he uses the term in the profane sense to designate the incorporeality (and individuality) of the soul.[38] But later, in chapter five, the term *spiritualitas* has a religious meaning referring to that "rebirth" and "recreation" characteristic of the redeemed human person.[39] Set over against *spiritualitas* here, are the terms *brutalitas* or *animalitas* — representing those aspects of humanity which are the consequences of original sin. The sacrament of baptism then removes the dominating hold of the *animalitas* on the person and replaces it with *spiritualitas*.[40]

"*spiritualitas* s'oppose simplement à *corporalitas*, comme ce qui est immatériel à ce qui est matériel."

[37] "Cette utilisation du mot, devient surtout fréquente à partir du milieu du XIIe siècle, dans des écrits, souvent de caractère scolastique, traitant de problèmes philosophiques." See Leclercq, "Spiritualitas," 287, who refers to Gilbert de la Porrée writing at the beginning of the twelfth century: "Necesse est ut illa subsistentia spiritus ... i.e., ipsa, si quis eam ita nominare vult *spiritualitatis* non modo de hominis illa parte sed etiam de toto homine recte praedicetur."

[38] "... declarare nobilitatem substantiae ipsius (animae), cuius pars aliqua *spiritualitas* est ... *spiritualitas* et corporeitas contraria sunt." *De anima*, II, 3, éd. *Opera omnia,* (Orléans, 1674), t. I, p.178, cited by Lerclecq, "Spiritualitas," 288.

[39] "*Spiritualitas* autem est perfectio, per quam avertimus imprimis ab animabus nostris mala spiritualia, quae sunt vitia et peccata ... Per hanc similiter quaeruntur animabus bona spiritualia, quae sunt virtutes omnes et dona gratiarum, sed et praemia futura ...
... Ipsa *spiritualitas*, quam dixi contrariam animalitati seu brutalitati quae animabus nostris est ex antedicta (i.e. peccati originalis) corruptione." *De anima*,V, 130-31.

[40] "... qua scilicet non animaliter sed spiritualiter vivitur." *De anima*,V, 130. Here we are approaching a usage of the term with a meaning familiar today, i.e., *spiritualitas* in the sense of the *vita spiritualis* or spiritual life.

Thomas Aquinas uses *spiritualitas* above all in an ascetic sense, i.e., that through which one has succeeded in triumphing over *carnalitas*.[41] He thus distinguishes three grades of spirituality: those of virgins, widows, and married people. In other cases, he uses the term in a more general Pauline sense to describe the new "spiritual" status of the person renewed by the grace of God.[42]

A final nuance in meaning appears towards the end of the thirteenth century to designate the ecclesiastical jurisdiction of those (clerics) responsible for the government of a church.[43] Thus, there emerged the phrase "spiritual jurisdiction" applied to clerics who were the *spiritualitas* or "lords spiritual."[44] Contrasted with these were the *temporalitas* or "lords temporal" who exercised civil jurisdiction. A further twist in this development gave *spiritualitas* the designation of ecclesiastical property in contrast to the property of the secular ruler whose property or power was referred to as *temporalitas*.

It can be seen from the texts cited above that the meaning of the term *spiritualitas* has, at times, shifted far from the original sense inspired by Paul. However, the original Pauline sense never totally disappeared. In short, where the term is opposed to *carnalitas*, (i.e., to the flesh and to sin), it is used in a *religious* sense — retaining its Pauline meaning of life according to the Holy Spirit (sometimes referred to as the supernatural life). On a second level, where the term is contrasted with *corporalitas*, it is used in a profane or *philosophical* sense to denote the incorporeality and individuality of the soul.[45]

---

[41] See, *In Sent.* IV d.49, q.5, a.2, sol. 3, where the term occurs nine times. Elsewhere, he describes how the sins of the spirit are more serious than those of the flesh on the basis of this distinction between *carnalitas* and *spiritualitas*. See also, *Summa Theologiae*, 1a 2ae, q. 73, a.5.

[42] In the majority of texts, the term *spiritualitas* refers to the Pauline notion of life according to the Holy Spirit, or life according to what is highest in the human person. In Thomas' writings, the term occurs about seventy times. See "Spiritualitas," *Index thomisitcus: Sancti Thomae Aquinatis operum omnium indices et concordantiae*, ed. Robertus Busa, Sectio II: *Concordantiae operum thomisticorum: Concordantia prima*, vol. 21 (Stuttgart: Frommann-Holzboog, 1975): 111, cited by Principe, "Toward Defining Spirituality," 131.

[43] Leclercq, "Spiritualitas," 291-92.

[44] Principe, "Toward Defining Spirituality," 131.

[45] Here, the term was used to signify that quality by which beings could move and breathe, or to describe how such beings were more than inert or purely material mat-

And finally, where the term refers to the administration of church goods or property, it is used in a *juridical* sense, and the opposing term in this case is *temporalitas*.[46]

d. Further Developments in the Use of the Term

Towards the end of the thirteenth century, derivatives of the Latin term *spiritualitas* made their way into the Romance languages, especially in French.[47] According to Tinsley, the term was used between the thirteenth and sixteenth centuries almost exclusively in the juridical sense (i.e., indicating ecclesiastical jurisdiction).[48] However there were some rare uses of the term in its religious sense (i.e., to indicate an affective piety or to describe the "interior life"), but it was not until the seventeenth century that the term experienced a revival. In the first half of the seventeenth century, the use of the adjective "spiritual" in the sense of the "spiritual (or devout) life" becomes more common.[49] But there was also a pejorative use of the term by those who opposed unorthodox developments of an enthusiastic and quietistic nature.[50] Perhaps this is one of the reasons for the infrequent use

ter. Leclercq cites Albert the Great in this context, who speaks of a *"spiritualitas corporis"* possessed by certain bodies and animals. See *Quaestiones super libris de animalibus* (attributed to Albert the Great), I, 55, *Alberti Magni: Opera Omnia.* XII, ed. E. Filthaut (no publisher given, 1955), 108, cited by Leclercq, "Spiritualitas," 289.

[46] Fraling, "Begriff der Spiritualität," 185, notes how this "Verrechtlichung" of the term was at the origin of the German term "Geistlichkeit" — the equivalent of the French *spiritualité*. The term designates a fixed and privileged ecclesiastical position within the Church. Sudbrack, "Vom Geheimnis christlicher Spiritualität," 34-38, sees this development as part of the continual emptying ("ständige Ausleerung") and impoverishing ("Verarmung") of the term, eventually robbing it of its supernatural content.

[47] Solignac, "Spiritualité," *DSAM:* cols. 1146-47. The equivalent terms here include the following: *espirituaulté, esperitalité* and *spiritalité*. These terms made their entrance into French at the end of the thirteenth century, above all in religious and devotional poetry.

[48] Tinsley, *The French Expressions for Spirituality and Devotion*, 152-53.

[49] Here the term refers to *les relations affectives* with God. See Tinsley, *The French Expressions for Spirituality and Devotion*, 227-28. Of interest here, too, is the conclusion of Solignac, "Spiritualité," *DSAM:* col. 1150: "Le sens juridique a pratiquement disparu à la fin du 16e siècle. Par contre, le sens religieux a fini par prédominer."

[50] The dispute between Bossuet and Fénelon at the end of the century over *la nouvelle spiritualité* is an example of this. For Bossuet, the term "spiritualité" took on a

of the term in the latter part of the eighteenth and nineteenth centuries.[51] By the end of the seventeenth century, however, the term came to denote all that pertained to the interior life and the quest for perfection. This pursuit was related to the perceived distinction between the ordinary Christian life and the life of perfection, and understood in a more and more interiorized and individualistic sense. "Spirituality" in this sense involved the practice of specialized spiritual exercises and the pursuit of virtue above and beyond what is required by the commandments.[52] Moreover, the word continued to be used in its more profane or "philosophical" sense (i.e., in contrast to that which is corporeal, or to denote the incorporeality and individuality of the soul) up until the present century.[53]

While the term experienced a certain "eclipse" in the eighteenth century, it makes a gradual reappearance at the beginning of the nine-

pejorative, quietistic meaning, whereas Fénelon claimed to be merely returning to the ancient sources, e.g., the writings of the saints, for a deeper understanding of the term. This controversy, in turn, led to the attempt to distinguish between true and false spiritualities. Solignac, "Spiritualité," *DSAM:* col. 1148. See also Elfrieda Dubois, "Fénelon and Quietism," in *The Study of Spirituality*, 408-19.

[51] Principe, "Toward Defining Spirituality," 132-133. He notes that the use of the term in English has been mainly the result of translation into English of French studies using the word "spiritualité". In other words, the term is used in English at the end of the eighteenth century in a religious or devotional sense. German, on the other hand, was slower in accepting the term "Spiritualität." The *Lexikon für Theologie und Kirche,* vol. 9 (Freiburg: Herder, 1960): 975, lists the word, but refers readers to "Frömmigkeit" — a term which expresses the more "subjective" side of religion — equated with interiority and with a strong individualistic connotation. See also Christian Schütz, ed., "Spiritualität," *Praktisches Lexikon der Spiritualität* (Freiburg im Breisgau: Herder, 1992): 1171. For an excellent, critical overview of the the terms "mysticism" and "spirituality" in contemporary dictionaries, above all in German, see Josef Sudbrack, "Literaturbericht: Über Mystik und Spiritualität in modernen Lexika," *Geist und Leben* 2 (1993): 144-51.

[52] The emphasis was thus on the experiential and practical aspects of the spiritual life. In 1918, Pierre Pourrat published the first volume of his comprehensive history of spirituality, *La spiritualité chrétienne,* 3rd ed., (Paris: Gabalda, 1918). [ET: *Christian Spirituality,* 4 vols., trans. W. H. Mitchell and S. P. Jacques (Westminster: Newman, 1953-55)].

[53] See Leclercq, "Spiritualitas," 294-96, who, in his "provisional" conclusion, believes that the former Pauline meaning of the term has been rediscovered in the present century. He attributes this to the writings, among others, of Pierre Pourrat, Henri Bremond and Étienne Gilson. In Leclercq's view (p. 294), the word *"spiritualité"* designates today: "la vie spirituelle en tant qu'expérience vécue — celle-ci impliquant l'ascèse, la mystique et leurs ramifications —, soit la science de la vie spirituelle."

teenth century, with the various manuals and historical studies of spirituality.[54] This era also saw the appearance in France of new Dictionaries in the literary and linguistic sciences,[55] some of which contain entries on the term "spirituality." Towards the end of the nineteenth and in the early part of the twentieth century, spirituality also begins to be conceived as an academic discipline — the science of the spiritual life; it belongs to that part of theology which deals with Christian perfection.[56]

How did the use and understanding of the word develop in the twentieth century? This question will be the concern of the next section where some perceptive contemporary studies of the use of the term will be considered. Our brief historical survey up to the nineteenth century does, however, permit us to draw some "provisional" conclusions. Firstly, "spirituality" is originally a Christian term; until the late nineteenth century, it was an exclusively Roman Catholic term, more prevalent in France than elsewhere. Secondly, while retaining for the most part its original reference to life according to the Holy Spirit, the word also takes on other nuances: philosophical, juridical, etc. And, thirdly, at the end of the nineteenth century, the

[54] Apart from Pourrat's, *La spiritualité chrétienne,* Auguste Saudreau's *Manuel de spiritualité* (Paris: Amat, 1916; 3rd rev. ed., Paris: Téqui, 1933) also helped give the term *droit de cité* among French authors. In this work, which had a large circulation, Saudreau describes spirituality as: "the science that teaches (one) how to progress in virtue and particularly in the love of God" (p. 7). See also Reginald Garrigou-Lagrange, *The Three Ages of the Interior Life,* 2 vols., trans. T. Doyle (New York: Herder, 1948).

[55] See, for example, É. Littré, "spiritualité," *Dictionnaire de la langue française,* vol. 4 (Paris: Hachette, 1883): 2035. Alongside the philosophical meaning of the term (as "le qualité de ce qui est esprit"), it was also perceived as a term of devotion, applied to the "exercices intérieurs d'une âme dégagée des sens, qui ne cherche qu'à se perfectionner aux yeux de Dieu."

[56] See Adolphe Tanquerey, *The Spiritual Life: A Treatise on Ascetical and Mystical Theology,* trans. H. Branderis, 2nd rev. ed. (Tournai: Desclee, 1930), 1.

In 1928, the publisher Gabriel Beauchesne began an ambitious project of a Dictionary of Spirituality. The title chosen was *Dictionnaire de Spiritualité ascétique et mystique,* and edited by the Jesuits: Marcel Viller, Joseph de Guibert and Ferdinand Cavallera. Its subtitle *Doctrine et Histoire* indicated the double orientation of the enterprise: 1) a study of the main doctrinal themes in relation to the spiritual life; and 2) an historical study of spiritual authors, schools of spirituality and spiritual currents in various countries. The first volume appeared in French in 1932.

word designated either: a) the practice of the spiritual life (often understood in a very individualized and interiorized sense), or b) the science (in the sense of *Wissenschaft* or academic discipline) of the spiritual life.

2. Towards a Definition of Spirituality

In attempting to formulate a definition of spirituality, it is possible to distinguish three different but related levels of meaning.[57] The first and most basic level is that of a person's lived experience, which has been called the *real* or *existential* level, i.e., the way a person understands and lives a chosen religious ideal within his or her historical context. In Christian terms, this approach corresponds to the Pauline teaching of a life influenced by the indwelling of the Holy Spirit or Spirit of God. However, the question could be asked whether a more universal definition of spirituality is possible — one which could be applied to the spiritual life and experience of non-Christians.[58] In this sense, spirituality would refer to "that basic practical or existential attitude (*Grundhaltung*) of a person which is the consequence and expression of the way in which they understand and live their religious — or more generally, their ethically committed — existence."[59]

---

[57] This helpful division into "levels" of spirituality has been devised by Principe, "Toward Defining Spirituality," 135-37. See also his article, "Christian Spirituality," *NDCS*: 931-38. It is important, however, to see these levels as intimately connected to one another. Otherwise a distorted understanding of the term could result. For example, while the first level highlights that aspect of Christian spirituality as a lived personal experience, this experience is neither received nor lived in isolation. Christian life in the Spirit takes place in an ecclesial context; hence, the second level of Christian spirituality is that of a group, whether the family, the parish, or specialized groups giving rise to various schools or traditions of spirituality.

[58] This question has been discussed by Leclercq, "Spiritualitas," 295-96, and also by Hans Urs von Balthasar, "The Gospel as Norm and Test of all Spirituality in the Church," *Concilium* 9 (1965): 7-23.

[59] Von Balthasar, "The Gospel as Norm and Test of all Spirituality in the Church," 7. His definition of spirituality in the German original [*Concilium* 1 (1965): 715] is as follows: "... je praktische oder existentielle Grundhaltung eines Menschen, die Folge und Ausdruck seines religiösen — oder allgemeiner: ethisch-engagierten Daseinsverständnisses ist: eine akthafte und zuständliche (habituelle) Durchstimmtheit seines Lebens von seinen objektiven Letzteinsichten und Letztentscheidungen her."

Such a definition of spirituality, according to Von Balthasar, has to do with "the way in which one acts and reacts habitually throughout life according to one's objective and ultimate insights and decisions."[60]

A second level of spirituality is the *formulation of a teaching about the lived reality*, often influenced by the life and example of some outstanding person (e.g., Francis of Assisi, or Ignatius of Loyola). This has been sometimes called the "theology of the spiritual life,"[61] and, here, history has seen the emergence of many schools or traditions of spirituality (e.g., Benedictine, Jesuit, Franciscan, etc.), each with its own particular emphasis or teaching.

The third level or dimension of spirituality refers to the *study* of the first and especially the second levels. Here the focus is on the study and analysis of various spiritual doctrines, traditions and practices, etc. While there exists a variety of opinions on what should be included in such study and analysis, contemporary studies on spirituality consistently return to two main problems: 1) what is the meaning of "spirituality," and hence of "spiritual theology"? and 2) what is the status of such a "spiritual theology" among the other theological disciplines (e.g., dogmatic or moral theology)?[62] It is to these questions that we now turn.

a. Spirituality and Spiritual Theology

We have already referred to the Pauline term *pneumatikos* as the *terminus technicus* for Christian existence. The "spiritual" person is the one who has received the Spirit of Christ and who thus has

---

[60] Von Balthasar, "The Gospel as Norm and Test of all Spirituality in the Church," *Concilium* 9 (1965): 7.

[61] Principe, "Toward Defining Spirituality," 136, n. 47. Following Jacques Maritain, *Distinguer pour unir, ou Les degrés du savoir,* 4th ed. (Paris: Desclée de Brouwer, 1946), 615-97, Principe distinguishes between "savoir spéculativement pratique" and "savoir pratiquement pratique." An example of the former is the doctrine of a speculative theologian like Thomas Aquinas concerning life in the Spirit and union with God, whereas the latter refers to the practical teaching of a spiritual guide such as John of the Cross.

[62] These two central questions recur in all the major studies we have referred to thus far: Solignac, Leclercq, Bouyer, Sudbrack, von Balthasar, Fraling, Principe, Schneiders, etc.

become a new person (1 Cor 2: 12-16). If we reflect on the results of some of the recent studies on the meaning of the term "spirituality," a number of points of convergence emerge. On one level, spirituality tends to be considered as an interior, personal attitude, influenced by the action of the Holy Spirit, and oriented towards the following of Christ. But this "inner" side of spirituality is only one of its aspects. The majority of authors we have considered also place equal emphasis on an "outer" side. By this we mean that spirituality involves a certain "concretisation" or *Verleiblichung*[63] in the specific historical context of each person. It would be a misunderstanding and a limiting of the action of the Spirit, were one not to acknowledge that the Spirit renews the human person in all their dimensions.[64] This emphasis is necessary, because the notion of spirituality or spiritual life has too often confined itself to the transformation of the interior life.[65]

Spiritual theology, for its part, has been described as a theological discipline, founded on revelation, which studies the Christian (spiritual) experience in all its aspects, and, in the light of this study, describes the structures of the spiritual life and its processes of growth.[66] The term "spiritual theology," originated in the seven-

---

[63] Fraling, "Begriff der Spiritualität," 188, speaks of a "Verobjektivierung" of the term spirituality. What he is arguing for, is not so much a private, interiorized, understanding of the term, as a lived spirituality, a "gelebte Spiritualität." Both inner *and* outer aspects are important, but he warns: "Nicht die Häufung von Übungen, sondern ihre Wirksamkeit in der gelebten christlichen Existenz ist das Entscheidende ... Geistigkeit ohne gesellschaftliche Auswirkung hat keinen rechten Sinn" (p. 191). Sudbrack, "Vom Geheimnis christlicher Spiritualität," 38, speaks in similar terms: "Sie (Spiritualität) existiert nicht in Vorschriften, Mahnungen, Anweisungen und Systemen, sondern in Personen, im gelebten Christentum." Aimé Solignac, "Spiritualité," *DSAM:* col. 1153, who discusses both the studies of Fraling and von Balthasar, also notes this emphasis which both authors place on the importance of the *réalisation* of spirituality in society and in the Church.

[64] One of these dimensions is the body, which Paul sees as also influenced by the Spirit (Gal 5: 16-26). Michel Dupuy, "Spiritualité," *Dictionnaire de Spiritualité Ascétique et Mystique* vol. 14 (Paris: Beauchesne, 1990): cols. 1161-62, thinks that one of the reasons for the confusion of the "spiritual" with the "interior" life is that commentators frequently situated the Spirit in the "soul" of the person, without clarifying precisely what they meant by the word "soul."

[65] Dupuy, "Spiritualité," *DSAM:* col. 1161.

[66] See Charles André Bernard, *Traité de théologie spirituelle*, (Paris: Les Éditions du Cerf, 1986), 66. In commenting on the development of this "spiritual theology," Solignac, "Spiritualité," *DSAM:* col. 1154, notes two tendencies that characterize this

teenth century.[67] This theological discipline then developed as a branch of moral theology dealing with the science of the spiritual life. It had two branches or subdivisions: "ascetical theology," which studied the life of perfection up to the beginning of passive mystical experience, and "mystical theology," which studied the life of perfection subsequent to the onset of passive mystical experience.[68] The primary aim of such spiritual theology was (through the systematic study of the spiritual life in its various aspects) the promotion of virtue in the life of the Christian. Thus, this spiritual theology consisted in a speculative part exploring the doctrinal principles of the Christian life, and in a practical part which described the means of applying these principles to the individual.[69]

According to Bernard[70], spirituality (or spiritual theology) can therefore be related to moral theology, in that both have as their focus the growth of the human person in charity, and the following of Christ in individual and social life. While moral theology could be understood as the scientific presentation of the following of Christ, it does not study, *primarily,* the ways of realizing this ideal of perfection.[71]

spiritual theology as an academic discipline (and which characterize most intellectual disciplines): the first is the increasing *specialization* which can lead to a kind of "schizophrenia," with the expert trapped inside the circle of his or her particular speciality; the second is a corrective to the previous tendency, best described as *interdisciplinarity*, whereby the expert is aware of the results of research in other disciplines, especially as these (disciplines) relate to one's own. Authentic spiritual theology can only develop in a dialogue with the other theological disciplines. In this sense, one can legitimately speak of a biblical spirituality, a liturgical spirituality, a pastoral spirituality, etc.

[67] Solignac, "Spiritualité," *DSAM:* col. 1156.

[68] "Spirituality is that part of theology which deals with Christian perfection and the ways that lead to it. *Dogmatic Theology* teaches what we should believe, *Moral Theology* what we should do or not do … and above them both, though based upon them both, comes *Spirituality* or *Spiritual Theology*. This, again, is divided into *Ascetic Theology* and *Mystical Theology*." Pourrat, *Christian Spirituality* 1: v, cited by Schneiders, "Theology and Spirituality," 263.

[69] Tanquerey, *The Spiritual Life*, 5-26.

[70] We are presenting Bernard's view here. See, for example, "Spiritualité et théologie," *Traité de théologie spirituelle,* 51-64, where the terms spiritual theology and spirituality are used interchangeably. To avoid such terminological confusion, however, we prefer to follow Sandra Schneiders' more nuanced position: "Spirituality in the Academy," 687-91. See also n. 80 below.

[71] Bernard, *Traité de théologie spirituelle,* 60-63. According to Bouyer, *The Spirituality of the New Testament and the Fathers*, ix, it is not by its concern with perfection that spirituality is to be distinguished from morality, but by the fact that spiri-

The study of styles of Christian life, i.e., particular ways of living the Gospel in its personal, historical, and experiential dimensions, belongs to spiritual theology. And in this study, the place of religious experience plays a crucial role: traditionally the experience of the saints through the centuries, but also, increasingly, the everyday experience of all who are living the Christian life.[72] Spirituality and moral theology can thus be seen as two complementary ways of looking at the Christian journey.[73]

In relation to dogmatic theology, the traditional view has been that, whereas dogma studies the objects of belief, as it were, in the abstract, spirituality studies the reactions which these objects arouse in the religious consciousness.[74] Moreover, the difference between spiritual theology and dogmatic theology proper lies not in *what* is apprehended (the divine Mystery), but in *how* it is apprehended.[75]

The early part of the twentieth century saw the publication of standard textbooks in spiritual theology.[76] There was general agreement among scholars on this basic outline and division of spiritual theology

tuality concentrates on those dimensions of human life (the life of prayer, contemplation, mystical experience, etc.) where the reference to God is not only explicit but immediate. His view is reiterated by François Vandenbroucke, "Spirituality and Spiritualities," *Concilium* 9 (1965): 45-60.

[72] René Latourelle, *Theology, Science of Salvation* (New York: Alba House, 1969), 146-51. The significance of the notion of religious experience in contemporary discussions of spirituality will be explored in the third section of the chapter.

[73] See Cousins, "Spirituality: A Resource for Theology," 126, who notes how the term "journey" has become one of the primary symbols in spiritual literature dealing with the stages of growth in the life of faith.

[74] Bouyer, *The Spirituality of the New Testament and the Fathers*, viii. According to Principe, "Towards Defining Spirituality," 137-41, this view is limited, in that it does not directly avert to the need to refer to the belief-systems or theologies implied in any spirituality; it simply presupposes them.

[75] Schneiders, "Spirituality in the Academy," 689: "Systematic theology remains discursive and categorical even when it reflects on mystical experience, including the experience of the theologian himself or herself." In this context, she cites Thomas Merton, *New Seeds of Contemplation* (New York: New Directions, 1962), 149: "And yet when the contemplative returns from the depths of his simple experience of God and attempts to communicate it to humanity, he necessarily comes once again under the control of the theologian and his language is bound to strive after the clarity and distinctness and accuracy that canalize Catholic tradition."

[76] E.g., Tanquerey, *The Spiritual Life;* Reginald Garrigou-Lagrange, *The Three Ages of the Interior Life*, 2 vols., trans. T. Doyle (New York: Herder, 1948).

for most of this century, until Vatican II.[77] Until the conciliar era, the only real controversy had to do with the place of mysticism in the life of the Christian. The problem was whether mysticism was a normal development of the life of faith, or whether it was an extraordinary state (accompanied by visions, ecstasies, locutions, etc.) to which only some were invited.[78] However, since Vatican II's stress on the universal call to holiness, the distinction between an "ordinary" and a "mystical" (i.e., extraordinary) way of Christian life has receded, and it is the former position that has been increasingly favoured.[79] And, today,

[77] On the place of spiritual theology among the other theological disciplines, Vatican II is somewhat unclear. The decree *Optatam Totius* (28 October 1965), on the training of priests, insists that all such formation is to be connected to the nourishment of the spiritual life (n. 16), but it does not mention "spiritual theology" in its list of theological subjects. Rather, the document speaks of "spiritual formation" (n. 8), meaning, by this, a life in union with God according to the standard of the Gospel, and the practice of the virtues of faith, hope and charity. *Vatican Council II: The Conciliar and Post Conciliar Documents,* ed. Austin Flannery, O.P., Vatican Collection Series, vol. 1, new rev. ed., (Dublin: Dominican Publications, E. J. Dwyer, 1992), 707-24. (Unless otherwise stated, all subsequent references to Vatican II documents are taken from the Flannery edition).

The most recent apostolic exhortation on priestly formation, *Pastores Dabo Vobis* (25 March 1992) reiterates this view (n. 45), by citing the above conciliar decree on the subject of spiritual formation. See *Pastores Dabo Vobis: Apostolic Exhortation of John Paul II on the Formation of Priests* (London: Catholic Truth Society, 1992), n. 45, 122-24.

On the other hand, the term "spiritual theology" does appear in the list of theological disciplines in the *Ratio Fundamentalis Institutionis Sacerdotalis* (6 January 1970). Chapter twelve of the document places spiritual theology alongside moral: "Haec doctrina moralis completur in theologia spirituali ..." However, the term *completur* is ambiguous; it does not mean that spiritual theology is merely a complement to moral theology, but that it is a specific discipline treating questions that are not covered by moral theology (e.g., priestly spirituality, the nature of religious life, spiritual theology, etc.). See *AAS* 62 (1970): 368-74, cited by Aimé Solignac, "Spiritualité," *DSAM:* col. 1153.

[78] Tanquerey is a representative of the discontinuity position, i.e., the mystical life is discontinuous with the life of Christian holiness to which all are called. Examples of the continuity position include Garrigou-Lagrange, *The Three Ages of the Interior Life,* and Thomas Merton who, towards the end of his life, emphasized not so much the differences between various stages of spiritual growth as the basic continuity underlying them all. See his *Contemplation in a World of Action* (New York: Doubleday, 1973). This question has been discussed by Karl Rahner whose position will be examined in detail later. See his "Everyday Mysticism," *The Practice of Faith: A Handbook of Contemporary Spirituality,* 69-70.

[79] *Lumen Gentium,* nn. 39-42, 43-47, *Vatican Council II,* ed. Flannery, vol. 1, 396-402. See also the helpful article by James A. Wiseman, "Mysticism," *NCDS:* 681-92.

the term "spirituality" (as a designation for the field which studies Christian religious experience) is used far more frequently[80] than the term "spiritual theology" with its division into ascetical and mystical theology.

b. Spirituality and Spiritualities

In 1960, the French Oratorian, Louis Bouyer published his *Introduction à la vie spirituelle*,[81] where he reacted to what he considered to be the rather artificial way in which so many various "spiritualities" have sprung up today. He traced the origin of this development to the restoration of the religious orders in the nineteenth century.[82] For Bouyer, however, there is just one spirituality — that of the Gospel, or, as he also calls it, the spirituality of the Church.[83] This assertion brought a number of critical responses, above all, from Jean

[80] We follow Schneiders here, "Spirituality in the Academy," 687-91, who prefers to use the term "spirituality" instead of "spiritual theology." The latter term, according to her, still has nineteenth-century connotations of the study of "the life of Christian perfection." Hence, it is important that the contemporary academic discipline of "Christian spirituality" acquires new terminology to underscore the development that has taken place in spirituality studies, especially since Vatican II. However, Dupuy, "Spiritualité," *DSAM:* col. 1169, retains the former distinction. The term "spiritualité," in his view, is better reserved "… au niveau de l'expérience et de l'expression spontanée, en appelant théologie spirituelle l'élaboration réflexive." But this distinction has not always been rigorously observed. As we have seen, the term "spirituality" can also refer to an organized body of knowledge concerning the spiritual life.

[81] Louis Bouyer, *Introduction à la vie spirituelle. Précis de théologie ascétique et mystique* (Paris-Tournai: Desclée, 1960). The work was intended both as an overview of the many facets of the spiritual life (prayer, sacramental life, the development of the spiritual life, mysticism and union with God, etc.), and also as a practical manual of spiritual growth. For a summary of Bouyer's position, see the preface of *Spirituality of the New Testament and the Fathers,* vii-xi.

[82] Bouyer, *Spirituality of the New Testament and the Fathers,* x. For example, Benedictine, Carmelite, Jesuit and Franciscan spiritualities, according to Bouyer, were defined in reciprocal opposition to one another. In addition, one spoke of a spirituality for diocesan priests, another spirituality for the laity, and other spiritualities for different apostolic groups active in the Church. For Bouyer, these are all attempts to build a kind of *Ersatz* spirituality, rather than focusing on the one spirituality — that of the Gospel.

[83] Bouyer, *Spirituality of the New Testament and the Fathers,* xi. He distances himself from the discussions on the different "schools of spirituality," seeing instead the central problem of Christian spirituality as "the problem of how to apply as integrally as possible … the Gospel of Jesus Christ, 'the same yesterday, today and for ever'."

Daniélou and Maurice Giuliani,[84] who claimed that Bouyer failed to acknowledge that these various "spiritualities" (e.g., those of the various religious orders) were an expression of the one Spirit at work in the Christian community. More than a superficial controversy about words, this discussion highlighted the evangelical foundation of spirituality, i.e., the fact that the Gospel is the basis, norm and test of all spirituality in the Church.[85] Yet, the four Gospels (in addition to the Pauline teaching we have already discussed) represent four different approaches to the life and teaching of Jesus. Herein lies the basis for the multiple expressions of spirituality or "spiritualities" which have arisen in history. In turn, the many spiritual traditions, while attempting to model themselves on the teachings of Jesus and the apostles, emphasize and express different aspects of this message. Hence, while there is only *one* Christian spirituality, based on the Gospel, it is, nevertheless, acceptable to speak of various Christian spiritualities, since it is possible to live the *one* Christian vocation in a variety of ways.[86] At the same time, this one spirituality finds concrete expression in the specific circumstances of each person in the Christian community.[87] As there is a variety of gifts (1 Cor 12: 4-14), so, too, is there a variety of spiritualities — all guided by the *one* Spirit.[88]

---

[84] Jean Daniélou, "À propos d'une introduction à la vie spirituelle," *Études* 94 (1961): 270-74; Maurice Giuliani, "Une introduction à la vie spirituelle," *Christus* 8 (1961): 396-411.

[85] Probably, the most significant article here is the (highly condensed) study of Hans Urs von Balthasar, "The Gospel as Norm and Test of all Spirituality in the Church," *Concilium* 9 (1965): 7-23.

[86] François Vandenbroucke, "Spirituality and Spiritualities," *Concilium* 9 (1965): 45-60. See also, Principe, "Christian Spirituality," in *NDCS*: 933. Bouyer, *Spirituality of the New Testament and the Fathers*, xi, seems to view these various "Christian spiritualities" in too negative a light. He associates such expressions of spirituality with "deviations" and "distortions" — hence his reservations about using the term "spirituality" in the plural. However, our discussion above supports a more positive assessment of such "spiritualities."

[87] Josef Weismayer, "Spirituelle Theologie oder Theologie der Spiritualität?" in *Spiritualität in Moral: Festschrift für Karl Hörmann zum 60. Geburtstag,* Wiener Beiträge zur Theologie (Wien: Wiener Dom-Verlag, 1975), 59-77, 67. See also n. 63 above.

[88] See Sudbrack, "Vom Geheimnis christlicher Spiritualität," 40, where he refers to "die *Vieleinheit* (or pluriform unity of) christlicher Spiritualität" (italics mine). So, while there are as many "spiritualities" as there are active Christians, these are all based on the one, single, Christian spirituality — the teaching of Christ, his life and

c. Components of a Definition

Thus far in this study, we have pursued an adequate working definition of the term spirituality. Despite the controversy reported above, and the different nuances given by the various authors we have discussed, there exists, nonetheless, a certain degree of agreement about the meaning of the term spirituality.

Firstly, there is agreement on two essential points: on the one hand, Christian spirituality has to have a direct reference to Christ, the Spirit, and the community of the Church; and, on the other, it implies an activity, an *engagement* (as an expression of this spirituality), adapted to the concrete situations in which Christians find themselves.[89] Secondly, spirituality can be understood on two levels: the first, on a more intellectual or academic level, concentrating primarily on the study of the history of spiritualities, teachings, etc., and the second, on a more practical level, dealing not simply with "theories" of spirituality, but with their concrete manifestation, i.e., focusing on spirituality as lived Christianity. In this context (i.e., on the second, more practical level), it has been claimed that "spirituality, as the term is used today, did not begin its career in the classroom but among practising Christians, mostly Catholics, whose religious experience intensified in the wake of Vatican II."[90]

presence through the Spirit in the Church. Furthermore, this "one and only" spirituality is not simply an idea vaguely connected with Christian discipleship, but has been exemplified in the concrete person of Mary, as model of the Church: "In dieser Frau ist tatsächlich die eine Spiritualität, die eine und einzige Begegnung mit Christus in ihrer ganzen runden Fülle personal-menschliche Wirklichkeit geworden" (p. 40). Sudbrack acknowledges his debt here to Von Balthasar, who likewise speaks of the Marian characteristic of all Christian spirituality. See the latter's article, "Spiritualität," in *Verbum Caro: Skizzen zur Theologie I* (Einsiedeln: Johannes Verlag, 1960), 226 - 44.

[89] See Solignac, "Spiritualité," *DSAM:* col. 1155, "... la référence au Christ, à l'Esprit, à l'Église qu'il s'agit de suivre, d'un côté, l'engagement adapté aux situations concrètes, de l'autre."

On the notion of *service* in the Church as that common element which manifests the essentially ecclesial form of all Christian spirituality, see Sudbrack, "Spirituality," *Sacramentum Mundi* 6: 152.

[90] Schneiders, "Theology and Spirituality," 254. However, even here, the use of the term is ambiguous. For some, the term spirituality had to do primarily with prayer (e.g., those involved in the Charismatic Renewal, or in retreat work). Others viewed spirituality in a less restricted way as related not only with prayer, but with an intensified faith life (e.g., the Cursillo movement or Marriage Encounter groups) embrac-

It is probably fair to say that our considerations, thus far, have provided us more with a description of spirituality (and spiritual theology), than with a precise definition, in the strict sense of the term. The most helpful definition of the term is given, in our view, by the German theologian Josef Sudbrack, and developed by the moral theologian Bernhard Fraling. For Sudbrack, Christian spirituality refers to that by which one becomes, to use Pauline terms, *spiritualis* or *pneumatikos*, as a result of God's Spirit at work in the person. Of course, one can develop theories and definitions and types of spiritualities, but, in such a process, according to Sudbrack, the essential core of what "spirituality" is, gets lost.[91] This core, as we have noted in the previous sections, involves all of the following elements: a "being-grasped" of the whole person (*ein Ergriffenwerden des Subjekts*), a personal encounter with Christ relevant to our contemporary situation (*Begegnung mit Christus; auf unsere heutige Situation hin verdeutlicht*), and a "concretisation" (*Verleiblichung*) in the specific historical context of each person (*Situationsbezogenheit*).[92]

ing the whole of one's daily experience. A third group widened the scope of the term even further: spirituality is rightly concerned with prayer, the intensification of the faith dimension of daily life, but it is also concerned "with the whole of personal experience, especially those elements of experience which Catholic theology and morality had tended to denigrate, i.e., the body and the emotions." (p. 254). A fourth group focused on the implications of a Christian spirituality for social and political life, i.e., the struggle for justice and the building of a better world. In all of these approaches to spirituality, we notice a gradual widening of its scope to include all the dimensions of a person's life, even if, at times, the term spirituality is used in one or more of the senses outlined above.

[91] Sudbrack, "Vom Geheimnis christlicher Spiritualität," 39, warns that all legitimate definitions can indeed be valuable ways of understanding the meaning of the term, but cannot form the ground for such an understanding: "... nicht aber dies Verständnis selbst begründen können; die alle erst im Überschreiten ihrer selbst zur Erfüllung ihrer Aussage kommen."

[92] Drawing together these individual components, Fraling, "Begriff der Spiritualität," 189, gives the following definition of Christian spirituality as: "... die geistgewirkte Weise ganzheitlich gläubiger Existenz, in der sich das Leben des Geistes Christi in uns in geschichtlich bedingter Konkretion ausprägt." In an effort at clarification, Fraling compares his description of spirituality to what is called a "style." A Gothic style, for example, does not solely consist of particular types of arches, vaults, and stain-glassed windows. It also reflects an (not easily grasped) inner dimension, a "spirit" *(Geistigkeit),* of which the architectural forms are an external expression. Such a style determines the whole of a cathedral or church, but is also connected to a particular historical epoch, without which it would not have arisen.

But is it possible to offer a definition of spirituality without the use of explicitly theological language? Sandra Schneiders has made a valuable contribution in this regard with her analysis of the subject matter of spirituality.[93] Surveying a number of definitions of spirituality offered by modern authors, Catholic and Protestant, she notes that the notion of *self-transcendence* (to which we shall return later in the context of Rahner's understanding of spirituality) is the unifying concept in such definitions — one "which gives integration and meaning to the whole of life ... by orienting the person within the horizon of ultimacy in some ongoing and transforming way."[94] Summarizing, she concludes "that spirituality refers to the experience of consciously striving to integrate one's life in terms not of isolation and self-absorption but of self-transcendence toward the ultimate value one perceives."[95] The value of Schneiders' approach is that by avoiding (initially at least) the use of specifically theological language, and by focusing on the "common experience of *integrating self-transcendence within the horizon of ultimacy*, one keeps open the possibility of dialogue among people of very different world views."[96] It is important to note here, however, that this approach is not a plea for a "generic" definition of spirituality which would be so fluid and vague as to be devoid of meaning. Although Schneiders is aware of this danger, it does serve as a reminder: i) of the necessity of circumscribing the parameters of the term, and ii) that every spirituality involves a "concretisation" in the specific historical context of each person, as we noted in our description above. We shall return to Schneiders' contribution in the context of the relationship between spirituality and religious experience.

Having developed a framework for a more precise understanding of this rather ambiguous term "spirituality," it remains, now, in a third section, to examine how our developing understanding of the term relates to, or can be connected with, our understanding of theology.

---

[93] Schneiders, "Theology and Spirituality," 264-69.
[94] Schneiders, "Theology and Spirituality," 266.
[95] Schneiders, "Theology and Spirituality," 266.
[96] Schneiders, "Theology and Spirituality," 267.

3. Theology and Spirituality

a. The Divorce between Spirituality and Theology

We have already discussed the Pauline term *pneumatikos* as a designation for "the spiritual," and, from Paul's time on, the word has been used "to denote the harmonious unity that should exist between Christian doctrine and life, theology and piety."[97] In the second and third centuries, for example, the more speculative, dogmatic works of some Christian theologians[98] (which were mainly concerned with the interpretation of dogma and the refutation of heresies), were accompanied by more practical writings, whose principal aim was the promotion of the moral and spiritual life of the Christian.

Thus, the understanding of theology that existed in the patristic era was that this was not a purely intellectual, but also a "spiritual"[99] activity, an "affaire d'amour," inseparable from prayer. Philosophy and theology were here often used as synonyms for *theoria* or contemplation.[100] In the West, Augustine and Gregory the Great serve as

[97] Megyer, "Theological Trends," 55. See also, Christian Duquoc, "Theology and Spirituality," *Concilium* 19 (1966): 88-99.

[98] One such example, cited by Solignac, "Spiritualité," *DSAM:* col. 1156, is Tertullian who, alongside his doctrinal works (e.g., *Adversus Praxean, De Anima*), also wrote works concentrating on particular aspects of the Christian life (e.g., *De Oratione, De Patientia, De Paenitentia* ...). Similar examples can be found in the works of Origen, Ambrose, and Augustine.

[99] According to Jean Leclercq, "Jalons dans une histoire de la théologie spirituelle," *Seminarium* 26 (1974): 112, such theological activity was synonymous with "doxology." Theology was, first of all, contemplation of the word of God, which was then proclaimed in poetry, chant, and praise. It was a type of spiritual explication of the faith. In the following, we are indebted to Leclercq, while, at the same time, reiterating his caveat that it is impossible, in a few paragraphs, to retrace the whole history of spiritual theology spanning twenty centuries. Instead, he outlines the principal stages of the gradual separation of theology from spirituality, beginning from their original unity in the patristic era up to (and including) the era of the great scholastic theologians.

[100] Leclercq, "Jalons dans une histoire," 112. See also, Megyer, "Theological Trends," 56, where he describes the meaning of "wisdom" in St Augustine's teaching, or the "loving contemplation" of St Gregory the Great as representative of the kind of theology which is never separated from love.

Associated with this approach is the idea of the *numinosity* of nature. Such nature-related religiosity can be traced back to the Greek philosophers and Fathers of the Church. This appreciation of the numinosity of nature is again evident in many quar-

powerful symbols of this current, which, according to Leclercq, never distinguished between knowledge and love, between the understanding and the experience of the spiritual life.[101] And, in the East, two of the names that stand out, in this context, are Origen and Gregory of Nyssa, whose commentaries on the Song of Songs, for example, represent the beginnings of a (not yet systematic) spiritual theology.[102]

Such unity continued into the high Middle Ages, finding expression in the spiritual treatises of monastic theology.[103] This harmony lasted into the thirteenth century: Bonaventure, Aquinas and the other great scholastics knew that theology could not be divorced from experiential knowledge of God.[104] But, little by little, after the period of the great scholastic theologians, the gradual dissociation of theol-

---

ters today. The Greek philosophers comprehended things "with their eyes." They "theorized" in the literal sense of the word (*theorein* = to look at). The underlying assumption here is that we arrive at understanding only through participation, through becoming part of the object. Such a way of perceiving transforms the perceiver, not what is perceived. Perception thus confers communion: we know in order to participate, not in order to dominate. Knowledge, as the Hebrew word *(yada)* tells us, is an act of love: we can only know to the extent to which we are capable of loving what we see, and, in love, are able to let it be wholly itself. See Jürgen Moltmann, *The Spirit of Life: A Universal Affirmation*, trans. Margaret Kohl (London: SCM, 1992), 198-213.

[101] Leclercq, "Jalons dans une histoire," 114.

[102] Bernard, *Traité de théologie spirituelle*, 52. See also Paul Evdokimov, *L'amour fou de Dieu* (Paris, Éditions du Seuil, 1973), 43, who claims: "La tradition orientale n'a jamais distingué nettement entre mystique et théologie, entre l'expérience personnelle des mystères divins et le dogme confessé par l'Église. Elle n'a jamais connu divorce entre la théologie et la spiritualité, ni *devotio moderna*."

[103] Bernard, *Traité de théologie spirituelle*, 53, notes that such treatises emphasized "progression" ("la gradualité") in the spiritual life (e.g., Richard of Saint-Victor speaks of the degrees of charity, Saint Bernard of the degrees of humility).

Leclercq, likewise, views monastic theology as a prolongation of patristic theology. One of the fundamental characteristics of such monastic theology is that it was based on experience, specifically the experience of spirituality practised in the monastic environment. See his *The Love of Learning and the Desire for God: A Study of Monastic Culture,* trans. Catherine Misrahi (New York: Fordham University Press, 1974), 233-66. The relationship between spirituality and experience will be the focus of the next section.

[104] François Vandenbroucke, "Le divorce entre théologie et mystique: ses origines," *Nouvelle Revue Théologique* 72 (1950): 373-76. An excellent example of Bonaventure's approach can be seen in his *The Journey of the Mind to God*, in *The Works of Bonaventure: Cardinal, Seraphic Doctor, and Saint, I: Mystical Opuscula,* trans. José de Vinck (Patterson, New Jersey: St Anthony Guild Press, 1960), 1-58.

ogy from spirituality began.[105] Beginning with Abelard, the term "theology," in the West, towards the end of the thirteenth century, began to develop in a more exclusively systematic, speculative and abstract direction.[106] There emerged, in effect, two parallel "theologies:" one, a more scientific and theoretical speculation; the other, a more pious, affective theology which was rarely nourished by theological doctrine.[107] Some commentators evaluate the seriousness of this divorce (between a speculative and a spiritual theology) within the framework of an inevitable specialization in knowledge, which undercuts any understanding of theology as a unitary science.[108] In any case, by the end of the thirteenth century, this more "scientific" theology, in the West, had lost interest in the questions and problems of the spiritual life.

One reaction to this was the gradual emergence of a *devotio moderna* (an example of the pious and affective theology mentioned above), which eschewed concern for speculative theology, preferring

---

[105] Leclercq, "Jalons dans une histoire," 118: "Mais, peu à peu, ... la théologie scolastique se dissocia de plus en plus de la recherche contemplative, l'activité spéculative de la vie de prière." The emergence of these two parallel "theologies" persisted until the second half of the nineteenth century.

[106] This point is emphasized by Dupuy, "Spiritualité," *DSAM:* col. 1165, by Leclercq, "Jalons dans une histoire," 118, and by Bernard, *Traité de théologie spirituelle*, 53. Leclercq, for example, claims that, with Abelard, theology acquires a "scientific" meaning, i.e., it develops into a theology of thought ("théologie-pensée"), a theology that could be discussed, disputed, and which came to be practised in "schools." This theology can be distinguished from a "theology of prayer" ("théologie-prière"), examples of which can be found in Abelard's sermons and religious poems. See Jean Leclercq, "'Ad ipsam sophiam Christum'." Le témoinage monastique d'Abelard," *Revue d'ascétique et de mystique* 46 (1970): 161-82, for a more detailed discussion, as well as a citation of the relevant texts. Our point here is that what began as a distinction developed towards the end of the thirteenth century into a complete separation.

[107] Leclercq, "Jalons dans une histoire," 119. See also Megyer, "Theological Trends," 56, citing Evdokimov, *L'amour fou de Dieu*, 4, who claims that: "The theologian became a specialist in an autonomous field of knowledge, which he could enter by the use of a technique independent of the witness of his own life, of its personal holiness or sinfulness. The spiritual man, on the other hand, became a *dévot* who cared nothing for theology; one for whom his own experience ultimately became an end in itself, without reference to the dogmatic content to be sought in it."

[108] See Solignac, "Spiritualité," *DSAM:* col. 1156, who distinguishes here between *l'intelligence de la foi* ("fides *quae* creditur") and *la vie de foi* ("fides *qua* creditur"), each requiring different theological approaches.

instead to stress the practice of simple piety and asceticism.[109] The true spiritual life, in this case, consisted in the imitation of Christ — through meditating on and contemplating his humanity — enabling the Christian to attain union with God. A certain individualism crept into such writings, which resulted in a further narrowing of the scope of this "spiritual" theology. In other words, this theology gradually developed into a study of the mystical experiences of the saints. However, there was also a certain disaffection with this approach, because it seemed that such mystical experience was the preserve of an élite few.[110]

We have mentioned how the development of these two parallel "theologies" persisted until the end of the nineteenth century. Subsequently, some attempts were made to restore the unity between theology and spirituality. A number of theologians (e.g., Pourrat, Garrigou-Lagrange) begin to consider mystical experience:

> "not as something extraordinary and strange to Christian life, but as the normal manifestation of a way to perfection; such as is found, for example, in the simplicity of a Thérèse of Lisieux or Charles de Foucauld. For them, the universal call to holiness implies also the universal call to mystical life."[111]

However, a fuller expression of the restoration of the unity between theology and spirituality had to wait until the decades after the second World War with the development of the liturgical renewal and the intensification of biblical and patristic studies.[112] We then see the

---

[109] Geert Groote (1340-1384) is regarded as the founder of the spiritual movement later labelled *devotio moderna*, which spread from the Low Countries as far as Switzerland and northern Germany. The classic example of such spirituality is the *Imitation of Christ*, generally attributed to Thomas à Kempis (1380-1471). Its focus is principally on the study of the interior life and the Eucharist. Thomas also advocated a strict separation from the world and placed a consistent emphasis on repentance and conversion. Originally written separately, the four books of the *Imitation* have had an immense impact on spirituality in subsequent centuries.

[110] Leclercq, "Jalons dans une histoire," 119. See also Bernard, *Traité de théologie spirituelle*, 55, who acknowledges, at the same time, the spiritual classics which appeared in the fifteenth and subsequent centuries, e.g., the *Spiritual Exercises* of Ignatius of Loyola, and the spiritual writings of Teresa of Avila and John of the Cross.

[111] Megyer, "Theological Trends," 57. We will later explore this issue in relation to Karl Rahner's understanding of mysticism in the next and in subsequent chapters.

[112] It is beyond the scope of this section to trace the contribution of the liturgical renewal begun by Dom Guéranger (1805-1875) of Solesmes to contemporary Christian spirituality. See, for example, Virgil C. Funk, "The Liturgical Movement," *The*

emergence of a growing interest on the part of spiritual theology in the *experiential* aspect of the Christian life, and it is to this relationship between spirituality and experience that we now turn.

b. *Spirituality and Experience*

Increasingly today, theology has become an aggregate of multiple, highly specialized, auxiliary disciplines.[113] The question then arises, for our study, whether, and in what sense, spirituality can be a resource for theological reflection. We have seen how the theologians of the patristic and early medieval period were convinced of the "extreme value of their inner experience,"[114] and how such experience formed the basis for their theology. And it is to this concept of spirituality as *experience*[115] that contemporary authors return, in their attempts to illustrate how spirituality may prove a resource for theology. In this section (and also in the second and third chapters), therefore, we will explore the role of experience in the contemporary understanding of spirituality, and the implications of such an understanding for theological reflection.[116]

Having traced the Christian etymology of the term, and described the various levels of meaning in the use of the word

---

New Dictionary of Sacramental Worship, ed. Peter E. Fink SJ, (Collegeville, Minnesota: Liturgical Press/Glazier, 1990): 95-715.

[113] This fact has been acknowledged by (among others) Karl Rahner. See his *Grundkurs des Glaubens: Einführung in den Begriff des Christentums* (Freiburg: Herder, 1976), 18-20. [ET: *Foundations of Christian Faith: An Introduction to the Idea of Christianity,* trans. William V. Dych (London: DLT, 1978), 7-8]. This work will be henceforward abbreviated *FCF*.

[114] Vandenbroucke, "Le divorce entre théologie et mystique: ses origines," 372.

[115] For an account of how spirituality can help theology to examine its presuppositions, and thus open itself to spiritual experience, see Ewert H. Cousins, "Spirituality: A Resource for Theology," *Proceedings of the Catholic Theological Society of America* 35 (1980): 124-37. In his discussion, Cousins understands spirituality in the context of the *experience* of faith and of growth in the life of faith. Another attempt at relating the notion of "spirituality" to experience, is Schneiders, "Spirituality in the Academy," 680-97.

[116] Following Dupuy, "Spiritualité," *DSAM:* col. 1166, we do not emphasize the importance of experience to the detriment of doctrinal precision: "L'accent ne doit pas non plus être mis sur l'expérience au détriment de l'exactitude doctrinale. Il est possible de les unir."

"spirituality," we moved to a discussion of the gradual dissociation
of theology from spirituality and the consequences of this separation. It will be our contention that spirituality (understood in terms
of experience) *can* be an important resource for theology. In subsequent chapters, we will discuss the work of Karl Rahner with this
thesis in mind. Before we develop this claim however, we will
examine how spirituality is understood, today, primarily in an *experiential* sense.[117] Specifically, this understanding of spirituality has
to do with an investigation of "spiritual experience," i.e., an investigation not only of religious experience in the technical sense, but
also of those analogous experiences that are perceived to convey
ultimate meaning and value for individuals and groups.[118] In
Schneiders' view,

> "What this means is that spirituality, for Christians, is *Christian* and
> therefore theological considerations are relevant at every point; it is
> also *religious*, which means that it is affective as well as cognitive,
> social as well as personal, God-centred and other-directed all at the
> same time; and it is *experience*, which means that whatever enters into
> the actual living of this ongoing integrating self-transcendence is rele-
> vant, whether it be mystical, theological, ethical, psychological, politi-
> cal, or physical. The Transcendent who is the horizon, the focus, and
> the energizing source of Christian spirituality is an Other who is per-
> sonal, living, and loving and is fully revealed in a human being, Jesus
> of Nazareth."[119]

What are the characteristics of this emerging discipline which pur-
ports to study "Christian religious experience"? First, this discipline
of spirituality is *descriptive* and *analytic* rather than prescriptive and
evaluative, that is, it "is not the 'practical application' of theoretical

---

[117] The recognition of the importance of *Christian experience,* personal and social,
as the most appropriate starting point and referent for spirituality studies is evident,
for example, in the writings of Schneiders, Conn, Dupuy, and Principe.

[118] Schneiders, "Spirituality in the Academy," 692.

[119] Schneiders, "Theology and Spirituality," 267. As a primordial notion, the term
experience is not easy to define, but a certain circumscribing of its sense is helpful in
the present context. Thomas E. Clarke, "A New Way: Reflecting on Experience,"
Tracing the Spirit, ed. James Hug, Woodstock Studies 7 (New York: Paulist Press,
1983), 13-37, has provided a good initial description of experience as: "designating
those aspects of human behavior which have to do with the *perception* of reality, with
receptiveness toward the real in all its dimensions. Experience is our encounter with
life — or at least the initial phase of encounter ..." (p. 20).

principles, theological or other, to concrete life experience. It is the critical study of such experience."[120] Second, spirituality is an *interdisciplinary* discipline, that is, it uses whatever approaches are relevant to the reality being studied; for Christian spirituality, these include biblical studies, history, theology, psychology, and comparative religion. Third, spirituality is *ecumenical, interreligious,* and *cross-cultural.* Even the study of Christian spirituality cannot assume "that Christianity exhausts or includes the whole of religious reality or that only Christian data is relevant for an understanding of Christian spiritual experience."[121] Fourth, spirituality is an *inclusive* or *holistic* discipline. In its investigation of spiritual experience, spirituality does not confine itself to an exploration of the explicitly religious, i.e., to the "interior life," but examines all the elements integral to this experience, e.g., "the psychological, bodily, historical, social, political, aesthetic, intellectual, and other dimensions of the human subject of spiritual experience."[122] Fifth, the methodological style of spirituality is a *participative* one. The student or researcher, in most cases, comes to the discipline because of a personal involvement with the subject matter. Without some type of personal participation in a spiritual life, it is difficult to imagine how one could develop an adequate grasp of such topics as discernment, prayer, spiritual direction, mysticism, etc.[123] Thus, research in spirituality is not an abstract, speculative, self-distancing exercise, but there is the

[120] Schneiders, "Spirituality in the Academy," 693. See also Dupuy, "Spiritualité," *DSAM:* col. 1169, who writes in a similar vein: "La théologie spirituelle ... déploie l'expérience spirituelle pour elle-même: non seulement elle suppose cette expérience comme la condition d'intelligibilité de son discours, mais encore elle la prend comme objet d'étude ..." For his distinction between spirituality and spiritual theology, see n. 80 above.

[121] Schneiders, "Spirituality in the Academy," 693.

[122] Schneiders, "Spirituality in the Academy," 693. See also her "Theology and Spirituality," 268. For a reaction to Schneiders' valuable contribution to the discussion, see Principe, "Christian Spirituality," *NDCS:* 936-38.

[123] Principe, "Christian Spirituality," *NDCS:* 934, distinguishes two distinct approaches to spirituality in academic circles today: "One operates within a community of faith perspective responding to a revelation accepted as normative, ... The other is the approach of secular religious studies, which examines spirituality without such a faith commitment. Such an approach ... seeks to produce a description of different spiritualities, a presentation derived from the sources, ... but these are not judged in terms of a theology elaborated within a faith community."

explicit intention (in such study) to foster one's own spiritual life as well as that of others.[124]

It can be seen from the foregoing that spirituality is developing into a specialized field of study. Is it then impossible, or at least utopian, to insist on the maintenance of a fundamental unity in theological study given that the demands of specialization (in e.g., biblical, historical, liturgical, pastoral studies, etc.) require that each of these areas of study has its own methodology, vocabulary, etc.? Even if we admit the impossibility of rewriting history, we can still find a point of intersection between theology and spirituality namely, in the notion of Christian experience. Theology itself, particularly in this century, has rediscovered the notion of Christian experience. Such theology, informed by and built on religious experience points out how such experience can lead to fuller religious knowledge. And, increasingly, theologians are discovering a common basis, in Christian experience, between theology and spirituality. Experience serves as a common foundation or root (*souche*)[125] and renders each discipline mutually interdependent "with theology examining the various components of this experience and spirituality investigating the way this experience becomes particular or personal according to different emphases in living the gospel."[126] It is not our intention here to examine in detail the development of the concept of religious experience in modern theology, though we will focus, in the second and third chapters, on the place of experience in Karl Rahner's understanding of spirituality.

---

[124] An excellent basis for such a value-committed intellectualism can be found in Michael Polanyi, *Personal Knowledge* (New York: Harper and Row, 1964).

[125] Micheline Laguë, "Spiritualité et théologie: d'une même souche: Note sur l'actualité d'un débat," *Église et Théologie* 20 (1989): 333-51. She cites Marie-Dominique Chenu (from the preface of the French translation of Gustavo Gutiérrez', *La libération par la foi. Boire à son propre puits ou l'itinéraire spirituel d'un peuple*. (Paris: Les Éditions du Cerf, 1985), 9: "car une théologie qui marginalise la spiritualité comme subjective, tout comme une spiritualité qui ne s'articulerait pas sur l'architecture d'une théologie seraient un échec à l'unité psychologique et théologale de notre être chrétien." Laguë also refers to the work of Sudbrack, who, as we have seen, also stresses the mutual interrelationship between spirituality and theology; she summarizes the *leitmotiv* of Sudbrack's approach in the pithy phrase: "*Non pas l'une sans l'autre.*" (p. 337).

[126] Principe, "Christian Spirituality," in *NDCS*: 935, citing Laguë, "Spiritualité et théologie: d'une même souche," 350-51.

c. Spirituality — An Immature Discipline

The status of spirituality as a relatively immature discipline (in comparison with theology) with regard to its concepts, its distinct methodology and a commonly accepted vocabulary has been acknowledged by contemporary writers.[127] However, no clear consensus exists, at present, on the subject of the precise relationship between spirituality and theology. Some scholars have argued for a direct subordination of spirituality to theology, i.e., theology should provide doctrinal principles that can be applied to the life of the individual.[128] For others, (e.g., Schneiders or Principe):

> Theology, itself must use the resources not only of philosophy but of all the human sciences. Hence theology, when focused on Christian life in the Spirit, must take account of these aspects in a multidisciplinary dialogue; further, it must have as part of its data not only the revealed word of God as developed in authentic tradition but also the range of human experience, historical and especially contemporary.[129]

In the case of spirituality, its dialogue partner is not solely theology, but a whole range of other disciplines including history, anthropology, psychology, and sociology. Were spirituality not to develop an interdisciplinary approach, and instead develop in isolation, the danger of a divorce from other academic disciplines (as one consequence of increased specialization) which has threatened theology, would also threaten spirituality. We have also mentioned how academic studies in Christian spirituality attempt to be ecumenical and to dialogue with non-Christian religions. But there must, above all, exist an intimate link between Christian spirituality and *theology* — especially where the question of the *criteria for the critical judgement* of

---

[127] Cousins, "Preface to the Series," *Christian Spirituality 1: Origins to the Twelfth Century* , xii. See also Schneiders, "Spirituality in the Academy," 696.

In "Spirituality: A Resource for Theology," *Catholic Theological Society of America Proceedings* 35 (1980): 124-37, Cousins describes one of the most important tasks facing contemporary spirituality as that of acquiring depth and maturity, by grounding itself in its spiritual roots, and by appropriating the wisdom of its classical heritage.

[128] For the dependence of spirituality on dogmatic theology, see Bernard, *Traité de théologie spirituelle,* 60-63.

[129] Principe, "Christian Spirituality," *NDCS*: 935. For a helpful overview of recent attempts to overcome the separation between religious experience and theological reflection, see Philip Endean, "Spirituality and the University," *The Way Supplement* (1995): 87-99.

Christian spiritualities is concerned. This point is significant given
the wide diversity of expressions of spirituality among Christians
today, each representing distinctive ways of striving to live the
Gospel. Such increased multiplication of spiritualities inevitably
brings with it serious distortions or exaggerated emphases — hence,
the need to have adequate *theological* criteria by which to make a
critical judgement of whether any Christian spirituality is both
authentically human and Christian.[130] Concretely, this means asking
such questions as: what view of God, and what view of the human
person's relationship with God is implied or expressed?; what role is
given to Christ and the Spirit, the liturgy and the sacraments?; what
understanding of grace and evil is operative?; What underlying
anthropology is at work? Such questions can help clarify the particular theological foundations operative in any Christian spirituality. We
have noted how other influences e.g., psychological, historical, sociological etc., also need to be considered as these, too, are significant
contributions in the shaping of a person's spirituality.[131]

In this context, the *specificity* of Christian spirituality is a related
problem that remains to be clarified. It raises the question whether the
subject matter of spirituality can be independent of theology. This
problem surfaces when one attempts to provide too wide a description of the term "spirituality." While we are indebted to Schneiders'
contribution to this debate, it seems that her very wide (and general)
description of spirituality, could *also* be applied to theology.[132] Many

---

[130] Two related topics that arise in this context include: i) the relation of Christian
spirituality to that of other religions, and ii) the recognition that not all spiritualities
are truly Christian. The first topic is, however, beyond the scope of this study. For the
need for both a "discernment of spirits" and sound theological criteria to evaluate
various spiritualities, see Richard P. McBrien, *Catholicism*, 2 vols. (London: Geoffrey Chapman, 1980), 2: 1088-93. The possibilities of quite varied types of mystical
experiences, not all of which are equally helpful, are discussed by Harvey D. Egan,
"Prayer and Contemplation as Orthopraxis," *Catholic Theological Society of America
Proceedings* 35 (1980): 107-11. On the need for a critical evaluation of such mystical
experiences, which includes a chapter on Karl Rahner's theological approach to mysticism, see Harvey D. Egan, *What are they saying about Mysticism?* (New York:
Paulist Press, 1982), 98-108.

[131] Principe, "Towards Defining Spirituality," 138.

[132] This forms part of Principe's criticism, "Christian Spirituality," *NDCS*: 936-
37, of Schneiders' position. Schneiders, "Spirituality in the Academy," 683, is aware
that "the disadvantage of giving the term 'spirituality' such a wide application (is)

of the characteristics of the emerging discipline of spirituality previously described could also be applied to theological method today. The specificity of spirituality is perhaps better clarified by Schneiders' description of its practice: spirituality is characteristically involved in the study of the individual as opposed to the general,[133] i.e., in the study of texts, persons, particular spiritual traditions, elements of spiritual experience such as spiritual direction, discernment, etc.; it involves a participative methodological style; it proceeds by way of description, critical analysis, and constructive appropriation where the theological, human and social sciences play a part;[134] it seems to have an irreducibly triple finality, i.e., the accumulation of knowledge, the assistance of students in their spiritual lives, and a concern to help foster the spiritual lives of others.

d. Summary

Throughout this discussion, we have kept in mind the two main senses in which the term spirituality has been used. Spirituality has been considered as referring to both (Christian) religious experience and to the academic discipline which critically studies such experience. We are moving away here from the phrase "spiritual theology" and the way this term came to be used in the eighteenth and nineteenth centuries. The main reason for this is that the term spirituality has developed in meaning. It is no longer considered simply as a branch of moral theology consisting of doctrinal principles derived from revelation and their subsequent application in the life of the individual.[135] (In considering the relation of spirituality to theology, we have attempted

that it is very difficult to achieve the clarity and distinction requisite for a useful definition." For the purposes of this study, spirituality refers to *Christian* spirituality; hence, our insistence on an intrinsic link to theology.

[133] Schneiders, "Spirituality in the Academy," 693-94.

[134] See Schneiders, "Spirituality in the Academy," 695, n. 68, where by "appropria-tion" Schneiders means the "transformational actualization of meaning." Here she follows Paul Ricoeur, *Interpretation Theory: Discourse and the Surplus of Meaning* (Fort Worth: Texas Christian University, 1976), 91-95.

[135] Bernard, *Traité de théologie spirituelle*, 84-88, calls such an approach the "deductive" method of spiritual theology, as it seeks to "deduce" from *a priori* theological principles specific consequences for growth in the spiritual life. His preferred method, which cannot be elaborated in detail here, is a synthesis of a descriptive

to keep these two senses in mind). As more than a mere addendum to theology, whether dogmatic or moral, spirituality is a *theological* discipline based on revelation (understood as God's *self*-revelation, the gift of God's own being, — leading to the unfolding of a relationship which mediates to us the mystery of God's love). In the light of this, the discipline of spirituality studies Christian spiritual experience, the structures of the spiritual life, its processes of growth, and the underlying theological principles at work.[136]

We saw how, for Paul, his experience of the risen Jesus is intimately linked to his theological reflection on Christian life in the Spirit. Subsequently, we described how the term *pneumatikos* developed in meaning, although a Pauline core of meaning never totally disappeared. We also noted how, throughout the Patristic era, indeed until the end of the twelfth century, theological reflection was never sharply separated from experiential knowledge of God. This "synthesis" between knowledge and experience lasted until the beginning of the thirteenth century, when, with the movement toward specialization in theology and the growth of scientific knowledge and rationality, theology no longer had a monopoly on questions of knowledge and truth. Theology itself did not remain immune from the effects of such division, and, in this context, we traced the emergence of a divorce between theology and spirituality, which, from the thirteenth century, provoked their separate development, and the effects of which are still visible today.[137]

---

method (see below) with the deductive method. Such a synthesis of the two methods he calls the "phenomenological" method, i.e., spiritual theology must be solidly grounded on the "givens" of revelation while, at the same time, a systematic elaboration and ordering of the various stages in the spiritual life is called for (the descriptive method). For the reasons why I prefer not to use the term "spiritual theology" in the way Bernard does to describe the academic discipline of spirituality, see n. 80 above.

[136] For our preferred definition of spirituality and the two levels on which the term can be understood, see the section: "Components of a Definition" earlier in this chapter.

[137] For an analysis of how this sense of division has penetrated into modern culture and society, resulting in what T. S. Eliot has called a "dissociation of sensibility" — a dissociation between thought and feeling, between the mind and the heart, see Andrew Louth, *Discerning the Mystery: An Essay on the Nature of Theology* (Oxford: Clarendon Press, 1983), 1-16.

CHAPTER TWO

THE NOTION OF SPIRITUALITY IN KARL RAHNER

Introduction

In this second chapter, we approach the notion of spirituality from another perspective, that is, by examining the understanding of this term in the writings of one of the giants of twentieth-century Catholic theology — Karl Rahner. The question of how Rahner understands spirituality (including its relationship to theology) is, however, the main theme of our work. Thus, we will attempt here to indicate the *foundational* role of Rahner's spirituality for his theology. Firstly, we examine some of the more significant influences on his spirituality, and then, in a second step, a number of the main characteristics and themes underlying this spirituality are introduced. We shall see that some themes mentioned in the first chapter, e.g., the place of experience in spirituality, and the relationship between theology and spirituality, resurface again in Rahner's work. Our third section will then explore some points of intersection between Rahner's theology and spirituality. We conclude by focusing more particularly on Rahner's use of the term "spirituality," the contexts in which this term arises, and the meaning he attributes to it. In short, we are asking what lies at the *core* of Rahner's conception of spirituality.

Our aim, moreover, in this chapter, is to plot the course we intend to follow in exploring the central themes of Rahnerian spirituality. Subsequent chapters will take up and develop these themes in greater detail, and with more precision. Hence, we cannot claim to offer, at this stage, an exhaustive treatment of any one of the themes that arise here, opting rather to develop the discussion in the remainder of our work.

1. The Spiritual Basis of Rahner's Theology

a. *Experiences of God*

Probably the main reason for the enduring success of Karl Rahner's spiritual and theological writings lies in his conviction that theology cannot be divorced from experiential knowledge of God. Not
content with providing renewal programmes for theology and the
Church, Rahner writes about himself and the history of *his* life with
God.[1] In theologizing, therefore, from an experiential starting point,
Rahner does not simply deal with human experience in general, or in
the abstract, or even with the experience of others, but explores the
depths of his *own* human and Christian experience.[2] This is why he
kept insisting, in his later years, that his life and work could not be
separated.[3] Thus, Rahner's more "spiritual" writings are not merely
the "overflow" or practical application of his more scientific, theological or philosophical investigations. In this sense, what Rahner
once said of Aquinas can also be said of him:

---

[1] See Karl Rahner, "Why Am I a Christian Today?," *The Practice of Faith*, 17
(*Praxis des Glaubens*, 38), where he gives an example of such personal reflection:
"Both in my life and in my thinking I keep finding myself in situations of confusion
which cannot be 'cleared up.' At first even I feel that one just has to carry on, even if
one doesn't know where it's all leading ... But then I find I cannot avoid or keep
silent about the question of what underlies this carrying on. What I find when I ask
that question is the hope which accepts no limits as final."

[2] Herbert Vorgrimler, *Karl Rahner verstehen: Eine Einführung in sein Leben
und Denken* (Freiburg: Herder, 1985), 11-13. [ET: *Understanding Karl Rahner: An
Introduction to his Life and Thought,* trans. John Bowden (London: SCM Press,
1986), 2-3].

[3] Johann Baptist Metz, "Karl Rahner — ein theologisches Leben," *Stimmen der
Zeit* 192 (1974): 305-14. He refers to "die hier begegnende Einheit von Lehre und
Leben, von Dogmatik und Lebensgeschichte" (p. 309) evident in Rahner's work. See
also, Robrecht Michiels, "De Theologie van Karl Rahner," *Collationes* 8 (1978):
264-92. We will forego here a biographical exposition of Rahner's life. Apart from
the works cited above (Vorgrimler, Metz, and Michiels), see Karl Lehmann: "Karl
Rahner, Ein Porträt," in *Rechenschaft des Glaubens,* eds. Karl Lehmann and Albert
Raffelt (Freiburg: Herder, 1979), 13*- 53,* and Lehmann's "Theologie aus der Leidenschaft des Glauben: Gedanken zum Tod von Karl Rahner," *Stimmen der Zeit* 202
(1984): 291-98. However, the most significant recent biographical work on both Rahner brothers is Karl H. Neufeld, *Die Brüder Rahner: Eine Biographie* (Freiburg:
Herder, 1994).

"Thomas' *theology is his spiritual life and his spiritual life is his theology*. With him we do not yet find the horrible difference which is often to be observed in later theology, between theology and spiritual life. He thinks theology because he needs it in his spiritual life as its most essential condition, and he thinks theology in such a way that it can become really important for life in the concrete."[4]

Rahner's experiences of God are best captured in his prayers and meditations which reveal the "mystical" dimension of his religious thought.[5] The point about Rahner's prayers is not so much that they form a teaching about prayer, but rather, that they are an encouragement for "readers" to express themselves in a similar way, i.e., to

---

[4] Karl Rahner, "Thomas von Aquin," in *Glaube, der die Erde liebt: Christliche Besinnung im Alltag der Welt* (Freiburg: Herder, 1966), 152. [ET: "Thomas Aquinas," *Everyday Faith* (London: Burns and Oates, 1967), 188]. Referring to the "theological life" of Rahner, Metz comments: "In Karl Rahners Lebenswerk ist der Versuch gemacht und in wichtigen Ansätzen der Versuch gelungen, lange Gezweites, ja Entzweites zusammenzuführen, das Schisma zwischen Dogmatik und Lebensgeschichte zu beenden, und dies in einer schöpferischen Vermittlungskraft, mit einem Einbewältigungsvermögen, das mich an die großen Vermittlungen in der abendländischen Theologiegeschichte, an Augustinus und an Thomas von Aquin, denken läßt. Man mag dieses Werk immer noch 'transzendentale Theologie' nennen. Ich nenne es hier, versuchsweise und um die Absicht zu kennzeichnen, lebensgeschichtliche Dogmatik, eine Art Existentialbiographie, eine Art mystische Biographie in dogmatischer Absicht inmitten unserer Zeit." Metz, "Karl Rahner — ein theologisches Leben," *Stimmen der Zeit* 192 (1974): 308.
[5] The term "mysticism" is almost as ambiguous and elusive as the term "spirituality." Rahner's reflections on mysticism are discussed in section 2, b, of this chapter. For Rahner, the term "mysticism" can refer to "(a) an experience, the interior meeting and union of a person with the divine infinity that sustains him or her and all other being," and (b) "the attempt to give a systematic exposition of this experience or reflection upon it (hence a scientific discipline)." Karl Rahner and Herbert Vorgrimler, *Theological Dictionary*, ed. Cornelius Ernst, trans. R. Strachan (New York: Herder and Herder, 1965), 301. [*Kleines Theologisches Wörterbuch* (Freiburg: Herder, 1961; 13th ed., 1981), 289-90]. See also Rahner's, *Worte ins Schweigen* (Innsbruck: Rauch, 1938). While we do not wish to overlook the intellectual influence of Thomas Aquinas, Maréchal, Kant, Hegel, and Heidegger upon Rahner, we are emphasizing in this and in the next chapter that Rahner's theology is also a *mystical* theology. Rahner, especially in his early writings, returns to the spiritual teachings of the Fathers whom he considered to be genuine *Lehrmeister* for contemporary theology. For a development of this theme in Rahner, see Harvey Egan, "'The Devout Christian of the Future Will ... Be a Mystic': Mysticism and Karl Rahner's Theology," *Theology and Discovery: Essays in Honour of Karl Rahner, S.J.* ed. William J. Kelly (Milwaukee: Marquette University Press, 1980), 139-58.

speak from the heart to God.[6] Similarly, his early writings on the mystical doctrine of Origen and Bonaventure for example, led him to take seriously such teaching as valid *theological* sources.[7] For Rahner, no crude frontiers exist between doing theology in the context of Church, on the one hand, and the life of prayer, meditation, and commitment to people, on the other.[8] All form part of faith's seeking to understand the meaning of God's love.[9] Furthermore, this mystical dimension of Rahner's theology has a quite personal and deeply rooted basis in his experience of God:

> "I have experienced God directly. I have experienced God, the name-less and unfathomable one, the one who is silent and yet near, in the trinity of his approach to me. I have really encountered God, the true and living one, the one for whom this name that quenches all names is fitting. God himself. I have experienced God himself, not human words about him. This experience is not barred to anyone. I want to communicate it to others as well as I can."[10]

[6] Karl Rahner, "Gebet im Alltag," *Von der Not und dem Segen des Gebetes,* 10th ed. (Freiburg: Herder, 1980), 60-79. [ET: *Happiness through Prayer* (London: Burns and Oates, 1958, 1978)].

[7] Significant writings of Rahner here include: Karl Rahner and Marcel Viller, *Aszese und Mystik in der Väterzeit: Ein Abriß,* (Freiburg: Herder, 1939, 2nd ed., with an Introduction by Karl Heinz Neufeld, 1989); Karl Rahner, "Die 'geistlichen Sinne' nach Origenes," and "Die Lehre von den 'geistlichen Sinnen' im Mittelalter," *Schriften zur Theologie* XII (Zürich-Einsiedeln-Köln: Benziger, 1975), 111-72. [References to this series will henceforward be abbreviated to *ST* followed by volume and page number(s), thus, *ST* XII: 111-72].

[8] Our interest in exploring Rahner's understanding of spirituality and its relation-ship to his more scientific theological writings emerges as a result of our conclusions in the first chapter, where we traced the increasing divorce between spirituality and theology. By concentrating in this work on the *theologian,* Rahner, we hope to show the inner unity between his theology and spirituality, a point which has been fre-quently overlooked by many commentators. This point has been made by Karl Lehmann who, referring to Rahner's prayers, maintains that these "… kann aber auch die innere Nähe von Frömmigkeit und Theologie in diesem Denken entdecken lassen. Die fast uferlose Literatur über Karl Rahner hat, mit wenigen Ausnahmen, davon kaum Notiz genommen. Aber ohne diese Dimension würde man die theologische Gestalt Karl Rahners radikal verkennen." Karl Rahner, *Gebete des Lebens,* ed. Albert Raffelt, with an Introduction by Karl Lehmann (Freiburg: Herder, 1984), 10.

[9] See Geffrey B. Kelly, ed., *Karl Rahner: Theologian of the Graced Search for Meaning,* The Making of Modern Theology Series (Minneapolis: Fortress Press, 1992), 63.

[10] This "quotation" is cited by Vorgrimler, *Understanding Karl Rahner,* 11, who refers the reader to Rahner's, "Rede des Ignatius von Loyola an einen Jesuiten van

Rahner's point of departure for his theological reflections, it can reasonably be said, lies in his personal experience of God, an "experience of grace from within,"[11] which, for him, forms the most important root of all Christian piety and holiness. This experience, in turn, is related to his understanding of the transcendental orientation of the human person to God which has been described as the unifying principle of Rahner's theology.[12] Such a primal orientation to God leads the human subject into an apparently endless search for meaning, culminating in being drawn towards this holy mystery. While this "experience of grace from within" may not always be made explicitly conscious or thematic, nevertheless it is Rahner's conviction that such "unthematic experience" includes the possibility of a more explicit encounter with God in view of God's prior presence within one's personal existence.[13] Moreover, he does not restrict this

---

heute," *ST* XV: 373-408. Vorgrimler's quotation is, in fact, a brief but accurate paraphrasing of Rahner's reflections on the topic of "Unmittelbare Gotteserfahrung," 374-76. While the quote refers to Ignatius Loyola, we hope to investigate how such sentiments on the experience of God also underpin Rahner's spirituality as well as forming the starting-point for his theological reflection.

[11] Rahner, "Rede des Ignatius von Loyola," 378-80. Rahner's notion of "experience" is discussed in Chapter Three. A concise description can be found in his *Theological Dictionary,* 162 (*Kleines Theologisches Wörterbuch,* 107-108), where experience denotes a form of knowledge arising from the direct reception of an impression from a reality (internal or external) which lies outside our control. It is contrasted with that type of knowledge in which the person is an active agent subjecting the object to its own viewpoints and critical investigation. A considerable degree of certainty or evidence attaches to experience, since that which is experienced irresistibly attests its own presence. Religious experience in the strict sense, for Rahner, is that which constitutes faith, "and insofar as it does so, embraces at once the metaphysical, moral and existential experience of being and existence, and the experience of God's self-attestation (*Selbstbezeugung*) in the occurrence of revelation, in which the fact of a divine self-attestation announces itself to the 'conscience'."

[12] Francis Fiorenza, "Karl Rahner and the Kantian Problematic," Introduction to Karl Rahner, *Spirit in the World* (New York: Herder and Herder, 1968), xix-xlv. See also Anne Carr, *The Theological Method of Karl Rahner* (Missoula, Montana: Scholars Press, 1977), 59-88.

[13] "Für mich ist in meiner Theologie die Gegebenheit einer echten ursprünglichen Erfahrung Gottes und seines Geistes von fundamentaler Bedeutung. Diese geht logisch (nicht notwendig zeitlich) der theologischen Reflexion und Verbalisation voraus und wird von dieser Reflexion nie adäquat eingeholt." *Karl Rahner im Gespräch,* eds. Paul Imhof and Hubert Biallowons, 2 vols. (Munich: Kösel Verlag, 1982, 1983), 2: 257.

encounter with God to a privileged few, but presents it as a possibility for anyone (i.e., as an offer) in the midst of their everyday experiences of life.

b. Ignatian Influences

In an interview[14] towards the end of his life, Karl Rahner explicitly acknowledged the profound significance of the spirituality of Ignatius of Loyola on his life and work as a Jesuit. This influence is, above all, evident in his "Rede des Ignatius von Loyola an einen Jesuiten von heute,"[15] where Rahner has Ignatius of Loyola, founder of the Society of Jesus, speak to Jesuits of today. In this piece, Rahner reveals the quite personal and deeply rooted primal experience of God that is at the heart of his theology — especially his understanding of spirituality. Towards the end of his life he came to see this piece as a kind of a testament of his life and work.[16]

Rahner's interest in Ignatian spirituality can be traced back to his earliest major theological studies on the "spiritual senses" according to Origen, and in the Middle Ages — where he focused on the contribution of Bonaventure.[17] These articles arose out of the context of

---

[14] *Karl Rahner im Gespräch* 2: 51, "Aber die Spiritualität des Ignatius selbst, die wir durch die Praxis des Gebetes und eine religiöse Bildung mitbekamen, ist für mich wohl bedeutsamer gewesen als alle gelehrte Philosophie und Theologie innerhalb und außerhalb des Ordens."

[15] Karl Rahner, Helmuth Nils Loose, and Paul Imhof, *Ignatius von Loyola,* Freiburg: Herder, 1978), 10-38. [ET: *Ignatius of Loyola,* with an Historical Introduction by Paul Imhof, trans. Rosaleen Ockenden (London: Collins, 1979), 11-38]. (The text is also to be found in *ST* XV: 373-408).

[16] "Meine 'Rede des heiligen Ignatius an einen Jesuiten von heute' könnte man als eine Art Testament ansehen. Beim späteren Lesen ist mir das bewußt geworden... . Es (handelt) sich um eine Resümee meiner Theologie überhaupt und dessen, was ich zu leben versucht habe." Karl Rahner, "Ermutigung zum Christsein," *Glaube in winterlicher Zeit: Gespräche mit Karl Rahner aus den letzten Lebensjahren*, eds. Paul Imhof and Hubert Biallowons (Düsseldorf, Patmos, 1986), 128.

[17] Karl Rahner, "The 'Spiritual Senses' according to Origen," and "The Doctrine of the 'Spiritual Senses' in the Middle Ages," *TI* 16: 81-134 (*ST* XII: 111-72). These articles first appeared in French: "Le début d'une doctrine des cinq sens spirituels chez Origène," *Revue d'Ascétique et de Mystique* 13 (1932): 113-45; "La doctrine des 'sens spirituels' au Moyen-Age," *Revue d'Ascétique et de Mystique* 14 (1933): 263-99. See also his "Die geistliche Lehre des Evagrius Ponticus. In ihren Grundzügen dargestellt," *Zeitschrift für Aszese und Mystik* 8 (1933): 21-38.

the *Gebetstheologie* of the Ignatian *Exercises* and need to be understood within this framework.[18] Chronologically, too, the early publications of Rahner (on the doctrine of the "spiritual senses" in Origen, Bonaventure, etc.) are prior to the publications of his major philosophical works.[19] Both Karl Rahner and his brother Hugo Rahner closely followed, as well as contributed to, the new research on the person of Ignatius and on the original sources of Jesuit spirituality, undertaken in the period immediately before the Second World War.[20] During this period, there was a change in the then prevailing "baroque" view of Ignatius, interpreted primarily as an ascetic, towards a growing appreciation of him as one of the pre-eminent mystics of the Church.[21] Among those responsible for this change were Otto Karrer, Erich Przywara, and Albert Steger, all of whom influenced the young Rahner by their writings, and, in the case of the latter two, by their personal contact with him.[22] Part of the reason,

---

[18] What was this "context"? Beginning in 1894, the *Monumenta Historica Societatis Jesu,* 71 vols. (Madrid — Rome, 1894 — 1948), a collection of source material on the founding of the Society of Jesus, helped shed new light on the origin of the Ignatian *Spiritual Exercises.* In turn, new investigations and research on Ignatius and on the spiritual characteristics of the Jesuit Order were undertaken — in which both Rahner brothers were involved. See Karl H. Neufeld, "Unter Brüdern: Zur Frühgeschichte der Theologie K. Rahners aus der Zusammenarbeit mit H. Rahner," *Wagnis Theologie,* ed. Herbert Vorgrimler (Freiburg: Herder, 1979), 341-54.

[19] Karl Rahner, *Geist in Welt: Zur Metaphysik der endlichen Erkenntnis bei Thomas von Aquin* (2nd ed., rev. by Johannes B. Metz, Munich: Kösel Verlag, 1964). [ET: *Spirit in the World,* trans. William Dych (New York: Herder and Herder, 1968)]. This first major philosophical work of Rahner's was originally completed in May, 1936, and the first edition published by Rauch in Innsbruck in 1939.

[20] The major resource on the origins of the Society of Jesus has been referred to above (n. 16). See also Hugo Rahner, *Ignatius von Loyola als Mensch und Theologe* (Freiburg: Herder, 1964). While both brothers displayed a common interest in Ignatius and in the Ignatian *Exercises,* Hugo Rahner, an historian and an outstanding authority on the subject of Ignatius, was led to delve *backwards* into the tradition of the Founder of the Order. Karl Rahner, on the other hand, starting with Ignatius, moved *forwards* in an attempt to articulate how the Ignatian *Exercises* might be significant for contemporary Christian spirituality.

[21] In Rahner's view, the person most responsible for this growing appreciation of Ignatius was Erich Przywara, a fellow Jesuit and long-time friend. For a personal account of his debt to Przywara, see Rahner's "Laudatio auf Erich Przywara," in *Gnade als Freiheit: Kleine theologische Beiträge* (Freiburg: Herder, 1968), 266-73.

[22] For Karrer, see his *Der Heilige Franz von Borja* (Freiburg: Herder, 1921), 249-74. For Przywara, see his *Deus semper major: Theologie der Exerzitien,* 3 vols. (Freiburg: Herder, 1938-39). Steger was Rahner's spiritual director during the latter's

too, why Rahner showed such a keen theological interest in Ignatius is because he felt that the *Exercises* could form a subject of theology and, in a certain sense, be one of its sources.[23]

c. Rahner's Early Spiritual Theology

During his early theological formation in Valkenburg, Holland (1929-33), Rahner concentrated on the study of spiritual theology, the history of spirituality, and patristic mysticism. We have already referred to his collaborative work with Hugo Rahner in this area.[24] But we need to go further back to discover Rahner's very first published text: "Warum uns das Beten nottut."[25] This work was written by Rahner as a twenty year old in 1924, and is a short reflective meditation on the necessity of prayer. It reveals elements of Rahner's spirituality which he was later to develop, e.g., the heart as symbol for (the inner ground of) the human person, the longing of the Christian to understand and to do the will of God, and, finally, the searching for a God of mystery, who, in the last analysis, is beyond all our understanding and concepts.

However, Rahner's spiritual classic is undoubtedly *Worte ins Schweigen,*[26] a collection of meditations on aspects of God who is

early studies at Pullach, near Munich. See Steger's article, "Primat der göttlichen Gnadenführung im geistlichen Leben nach dem hl. Ignatius von Loyola," *Geist und Leben* 21 (1948): 94-108.

[23] "... Dann können auch die Exerzitien einen Gegenstand der Theologie von morgen bilden, in gewissem Sinn für sie eine Quelle sein, nicht so wie Schrift und kirchliches Lehramt, wohl aber in dem Sinn, daß alles, was konkreter und aus den abstrakten Prinzipien der Theologie allein nicht adäquat ableitbarer Vollzug des Christentums ist, der Theologie etwas zu sagen hat, was sie sonst nicht erkennen kann ..." Karl Rahner, "Die Logik der existentiellen Erkenntnis bei Ignatius von Loyola," *Das Dynamische in der Kirche*, Quaestiones Disputatae 5 (Freiburg: Herder, 1958), 76- 77.

[24] For Hugo Rahner's account of this early *Zusammenarbeit*, see his "Eucharisticon Fraternitatis," *Gott in Welt*, vol. 2, eds. J. B. Metz, W. Kern, A. Darlap, H. Vorgrimler (Freiburg: Herder, 1964), 895-99.

[25] Karl Rahner, "Warum uns das Beten nottut," *Leuchtturm* 18 (1924-25): 10-11. The text is also in: Karl Rahner, *Sehnsucht nach dem geheimnisvollen Gott: Profil, Bilder, Texte*, ed. Herbert Vorgrimler (Freiburg: Herder, 1990), 77-80.

[26] Published in Innsbruck in 1938, this book has been one of the most successful of all of Rahner's works. By 1967 it had reached its tenth edition and been translated into eight languages. Our references are taken from the text in Karl Rahner, and Hugo

encountered in silent, prayerful reflection. In this series of ten meditations, Rahner speaks directly to the one who is God of his life, of his Lord Jesus, of his prayer, of his knowledge, of law, of his daily routine, of those who are living, of his brothers and sisters, of his vocation, and, finally, of the God who is to come. This work, his first book publication, also reveals how central is the question of grace for all of Rahner's theology and spirituality — grace as the self-communication *(Selbstmitteilung)* of God to humanity.

While *Worte ins Schweigen* remains one of Rahner's most successful publications, it is also, theologically, one of his most overlooked texts. One possible reason for this is that, at first sight, we are dealing here with prayers and meditations, which seem to have little "theological" significance. However, on another level, they reveal a characteristic of all Rahner's theological thinking, namely, a return to, or better, a searching for, the source, and a return to an original core experience. In *Worte ins Schweigen,* the theme of the reflections is God — not as a concept or an idea, but as (the searching for) the God of our experience. And it is only when this question of experience is taken seriously that the search for God can, in Rahner's view, be undertaken faithfully and correctly.

What experience is at issue here? One approach to this question is to examine the context out of which the prayers arose.[27] These "conversations" of Rahner with God appeared initially, anonymously, in a pastorally-oriented periodical[28] for clergy in 1937 in Vienna. The background theme or framework for the periodical was the spiritual and pastoral renewal of priests in ministry, and it is precisely within this context of ministry ("Seelsorge") that Rahner intended to describe how God can be discovered. Each of the titles of the ten meditations gives an indication of the place of encounter or experience of God, and forms the starting-point from

Rahner, *Worte ins Schweigen: Gebete der Einkehr* (Freiburg: Herder, 1973). [ET: *Encounters with Silence*, trans. James M. Demske (Westminster, Maryland: The Newman Press, 1963)].

[27] See Karl H. Neufeld, "Worte ins Schweigen: Zum erfahrenen Gottesverständnis Karl Rahners," *Zeitschrift für Katholische Theologie* 112 (1990): 427-36.

[28] *Korrespondenz des Priester-Gebetsvereines — Associatio perseverantiae sacerdotalis* 58 (1937). Rahner's meditations appeared during the year in various issues of the periodical.

which the conversation with God, the "word into the silence," begins.

What is also relevant to the more immediate context of the book's appearance is the fact that, in the winter and summer semesters of 1937/38, Rahner had begun to lecture in Innsbruck on the relationship between theology and philosophy. These lectures were subsequently published as *Hörer des Wortes* in 1941.[29] Thus, both *Worte ins Schweigen* and *Hörer des Wortes* belong chronologically together. However, there is also a thematic relationship between the two works. In *Hörer des Wortes,* Rahner is exploring whether the human person is able to hear a word spoken by God, i.e., to hear a possible revelation proceeding from God. The common denominator in both titles is "Wort." Even the words "Hören" and "Schweigen" indicate a certain correspondence — they indicate the importance of a personal orientation on the part of the person towards God in order that a real communication between God and the person may occur.[30] The term "silence" has two sides. On the one hand, it denotes the silence of God, echoing the silence of the dead, and frustrating any attempts at prayer. On the other hand, and more positively, this "silence" represents that "boundless space" in which, alone, one finds the love to make an act of faith. In Rahner's words:

> "Your silence is the framework of my faith, the boundless space where my love finds the strength to believe in Your love ... Your love has hidden itself in silence, so that my love can reveal itself in faith."[31]

What is at issue here, then, is the question of revelation, but not in the sense of a pure "word" revelation as opposed to a revelation in

---

[29] Karl Rahner, *Hörer des Wortes: Zur Grundlegung einer Religionsphilosophie* (Munich: Kösel-Pustet, 1941, 2nd rev. ed., ed. J. B. Metz, Munich: Kösel, 1963). [ET: *Hearers of the Word*, trans. R. Walls (London: Sheed and Ward, 1969)]. Unless otherwise indicated, we will refer to the second edition.

[30] "Im Grunde spiegelt sich in Hören und Schweigen der Unterschied zwischen Mensch und Gott, anders gesagt, die Notwendigkeit einer eigenen Einstellung, damit es zu einer wirklichen Kommunikation kommen kann und kommt." Neufeld, "Worte ins Schweigen: Zum erfahrenen Gottesverständnis Karl Rahners," 432.

[31] Rahner, "Gott der Lebendigen," *Worte ins Schweigen*, 54, "Deine Stille ist der grenzenlose Raum, worin allein meine Liebe die Tat des Glaubens an deine Liebe zu wirken vermag... . Damit sich meine Liebe im Glauben enthülle, hat sich deine Liebe in die Stille deines Schweigens verhüllt." ("God of the Living," *Encounters with Silence*, 56).

deeds. It would be a misunderstanding of Rahner's notion of revelation[32] to limit the term "word" to a fixed proposition. Rather, the term "word," in the context of these two early Rahnerian works, is to be seen as a metaphor for that process of God's self-communication to humanity which, for Rahner, forms the innermost centre of the Christian understanding of existence.

Worte ins Schweigen, is thus an attempt on Rahner's part to highlight and facilitate in his readers that encounter (*Begegnung*) with God, which, in his view, lies at the heart of prayer and spirituality. Such an encounter transcends all our words and concepts of God, and is not the result of our own speculations:

> "Your Word and Your Wisdom is in me, not because I comprehend You with my understanding, but because I have been recognized by You as Your son and friend. Of course, this Word, spoken as it is out of Your own Heart and marvellously spoken into mine, must still be explained to me through the external word that I have accepted in faith, the 'faith through hearing' of which St Paul speaks."[33]

In 1939 Rahner published, what he called, a brief outline on the themes of asceticism and mysticism in the Patristic era — *Aszese und Mystik in der Väterzeit: Ein Abriß.*[34] In fact, this book was a complete reworking of the French original by Marcel Viller[35] who himself supported the publication of the German text. Writing in the Foreword, Rahner admits how the study of asceticism and mysticism had become almost an independent discipline (or in Rahner's terms a *Geisteswissenschaft*). Yet, the spiritual teaching and heritage of the Church, Rahner stressed, could not simply be a matter of an enthusi-

---

[32] For a development of the notion of revelation as the self-communication of God, see *FCF*, 116-26 (*Grundkurs*, 122-32). For the "God who acts," ("Gott als der Handelnde") as one of God's "characteristics" ("Eigenschaften"), along with his dealing with humanity in an historical dialogue, see Rahner's "Theos in the New Testament," *TI* 1: 105-110 (*ST* I: 120-25).

[33] Rahner, "Gott der Erkenntnis," *Worte ins Schweigen,* 35. ("God of my Knowledge," *Encounters with Silence,* 31).

[34] Karl Rahner and Marcel Viller, *Aszese und Mystik in der Väterzeit: Ein Abriß,* 2nd ed. (Freiburg: Herder, 1989).

[35] Marcel Viller, *La Spiritualité des premiers siècles chrétiens* (Paris: Bloud and Gay, 1930). Rahner's reworking of this text resulted in a work almost twice the size of Viller's original.

astic heart and pious devotion. Rather, it involved a critical or scientific reflection; hence, the importance of a thorough research into the *history* of this spiritual heritage. While a number of detailed studies on specific, individual questions concerning the spiritual life of the Christian were available at this time, there was no introductory text or overview of spirituality available in the German-speaking world. Thus, Rahner regarded his book as an introductory text on the history of spirituality for beginners and interested laity.[36]

What of the structure of the work? Rahner begins by tracing the spirituality of the New Testament, and early Christian writers such as Ignatius of Antioch, Clement of Alexandria, and Origen. This discussion treats of the themes of martyrdom and virginity and their importance in the early Church. There then follow chapters on the monastic life in the East, the role of the Cappadocians in the fourth century, the importance of Gregory of Nyssa as the "father of mysticism," the Greek mystics from the fifth until the seventh century, and monastic life in the West. The importance of Augustine and his pupil Gregory the Great is highlighted in later chapters to indicate the development of patristic spirituality. Finally, Rahner discusses specific questions related to prayer and devotions, the pursuit of "perfection" and whether this was possible outside of monasticism, devotion to the cross and to Mary, and the veneration of the saints.

From plan to publication the work took about three years to complete. Together with *Geist in Welt*[37] it forms one of Rahner's most comprehensive early works. Unlike *Geist in Welt*, however, *Aszese*

---

[36] Rahner, *Aszese und Mystik in der Väterzeit*, vi-viii, was aware of the limitations of his study. He refers explicitly to the "Unbestimmtheit des Begriffes der 'spiritualité'," and translates this as "Aszese und Mystik." However, he did not intend to give an exhaustive historical synthesis of what was meant in German by the term "Frömmigkeit" .

[37] Unlike *Aszese und Mystik, Geist in Welt* was reprinted in 1957. According to Karl Heinz Neufeld in his introduction to the second edition of *Aszese und Mystik*, 13*-15*, this factor has contributed significantly to the tendency to interpret Rahner from the perspective of *Geist in Welt* rather than from *Aszese und Mystik*. In effect, this led some commentators on Rahner to neglect the spiritual origins of his theology, and to offer instead a mainly philosophical treatment and critique of his work. See, for example, Peter Eicher, *Die anthropologische Wende: Karl Rahners philosophischer Weg vom Wesen des Menschen zur personalen Existenz* (Freiburg: Freiburger Universitätsverlag, 1970).

und Mystik found only minor recognition from experts. Even later attempts by Rahner to publish a new edition of the work met without success.

What is the relationship between *Aszese und Mystik* and *Geist in Welt* both of which were published in the same year? In *Geist in Welt,* Rahner attempted "to get away from so much that is called neo-Scholasticism and to return to Thomas himself, and, by doing this to move closer to those questions which are being posed to contemporary philosophy."[38] A similar method can be detected in *Aszese und Mystik* where Rahner attempted to move away from the ambiguous term "Spiritualität," and return to those foundations and witnesses on which contemporary Christian spirituality and piety is based. In this way, he hoped to make accessible a historical resource, namely the spiritual doctrine of the Fathers of the Church, whom, he believed, represented a living power — capable of enriching the spiritual lives of contemporary Christians.[39] In hindsight, one can see in *Aszese und Mystik* the presence of many Rahnerian themes which later became decisive for his theology: grace and sin, creation and redemption, knowledge and will, word and sacrament, freedom and commitment, spirit and world, etc.[40] Further, in attempting to situate *Aszese und Mystik,* it is apposite to mention here Rahner's doctoral dissertation *E*

---

[38] Rahner, "Preface to the Second German Edition," *Spirit in the World,* xlvii. (*Geist in Welt,* v). The "questions" referred to above represent "Rahner's attempt to confront the medieval scholastic philosophy of Thomas Aquinas with the problems and questions of modern philosophy, especially as formulated by Immanuel Kant in his critical and transcendental philosophy." See Francis Fiorenza, "Karl Rahner and the Kantian Problematic," Introduction to Karl Rahner, *Spirit in the World,* xix.

[39] "Aber auch abgesehen von diesem historischen Interesse, kann die geistliche Lehre der Väter unser eigenes Leben im Geiste befruchten... . In einer traditionsgebundenen Gemeinschaft wie die Kirche bleiben die Väter immer eine lebendige Macht für die Gegenwart, die lebendigen Quellen, aus denen sie ihre geistigen Kräfte holt, die Lehrmeister, die wir fragen sollen." Rahner, *Aszese und Mystik,* 316.

[40] This, it seems to me, is the primary value in publishing a second edition of *Aszese und Mystik* — it provides an insight into the historical work of the early Rahner. The text itself remains entirely unchanged and reflects the results of the historical research of over sixty years ago, which have, in the meantime, been superseded. Karl Heinz Neufeld, in the "Vorwort zur Neuausgabe," 14*, does not discuss this question in detail, preferring instead to show how *Aszese und Mystik* is an exemplary expression of the type of theological work with which Rahner was engaged in this period (*c.* 1930-40).

Latere Christi of 1936.[41] While this work is primarily a study of
Scripture and tradition in the context of New Testament symbolism,
it also exhibits a deliberate ecclesial focus (as the subtitle suggests),
emphasizing the communal character of Christian spirituality. As was
the case in *Aszese und Mystik, E Latere Christi* also highlights Rahner's early preoccupation with the study of the sources (i.e., Scripture
and the Fathers) of Christian spirituality and theology.

Reference to two further works will conclude this representative
survey of the spiritual publications of the early Rahner. Both were
published in 1949. The first, *Heilige Stunde und Passionsandacht*[42] is
a series of meditations on the passion and death of Jesus, including a
scriptural meditation on the seven last words of Jesus. The second,
Von der Not und dem Segen des Gebetes[43] is a collection of sermons
delivered in Munich in the immediate aftermath of the Second World
War. These homilies express Rahner's attempts to impart hope to his
listeners in the context of their suffering, encouraging them to turn
toward God in their anguish and fears. In fact, Rahner is dealing in
Von der Not und dem Segen des Gebetes with the difficult problem of
petitionary prayer.[44] How was it possible to overcome the weary
scepticism of many with regard to such prayer? For Rahner, this
meant listening attentively and with sympathy to those on whom the
burden of life had pressed most heavily, and who felt that God had
failed them. Thus, when he looked into the history of humanity, it
was not with the detached, dispassionate eye of one blind to the sor-
row and pessimism around him. There was also a remarkable opti-
mism at work, based on his conviction that each human life is caught

---

[41] Karl Rahner, *E Latere Christi: Der Ursprung der Kirche als zweiter Eva aus
der Seite Christi des zweiten Adam. Eine Untersuchung über den typologischen Sinn
von Jo 19, 34.* This unpublished thesis was defended in December, 1936 at the Jesuit
Theological Faculty, Innsbruck.

[42] Like *Worte ins Schweigen*, this work was also published in Innsbruck but under
the pseudonym Anselm Trescher (Trescher was his mother's maiden name). It was
later reprinted under the title *Worte vom Kreuz* (Freiburg: Herder, 1980).

[43] See *Karl Rahner im Gespräch*, 2: 57, where Rahner draws attention to the
importance of this work: "Das (i.e., the difficult problem of *petitionary prayer*) habe
ich vielleicht für mich zum ersten Mal in dem kleinem Buch *Von der Not und dem
Segen des Gebetes* behandelt und da schon theologische Dinge gesagt, die auch nicht
viel anders in jenen Texten gesagt werden, die mehr wissenschaftlich sind."

[44] Rahner, "Das Gebet der Not," *Von der Not und dem Segen des Gebetes*, 76-92.

up into the unspeakable nearness of the divine mystery hidden in it.[45] It is to this description of God as the mystery in human experience that we now turn — a topic with which we will begin our preliminary investigation of the key themes underlying Rahner's spirituality.

2. Key Themes in Rahner's Notion of Spirituality

a. God as Mystery

While there exist a number of key terms or *Stichworte* linking many of Rahner's key ideas, one of the most significant is his preferred description of God as "holy mystery" (*das heilige Geheimnis*).[46] To be human is, in Rahner's thinking, to be exposed to the "mystery" which pervades all of reality. The "restlessness of heart" — a notion traditionally associated with Augustine in his *Confessions* — has as its counterpart in Rahner's theology that *questioning* which Rahner sees at the root of the human search for meaning and fulfilment.[47] Such questioning provides an important context for Rahner's explanation of the "transcendent" nature of the human person:[48] it helps to explain

[45] Vorgrimler, *Karl Rahner Verstehen*, 29. In *Herausforderung des Christen. Meditationen — Reflexionen — Interviews*, (Freiburg: Herder, 1975), 125-27, Rahner indicates the significance of his more spiritual works within his overall theological corpus thus: "Ich betrachte, wenn ich es einmal so sagen darf, meine frommen Sachen, 'Das kleine Kirchenjahr,' die 'Worte des Schweigens,' das Büchlein 'Von der Not und dem Segen des Gebetes,' die Bände von Betrachtungen in den Ignatianischen Exerzitien und vieles Ähnliche, nicht als ein sekundäres Nebenprodukt einer Theologie, die als L'art pour l'art für sich da ist, sondern als mindestens ebenso wichtig wie die eigentlichen theologischen Arbeiten" (p. 126).

[46] See, for example, Rahner's development of this topic in *FCF*, 42-71 (*Grundkurs*, 52-79).

[47] Significant here is the comment of Lehmann: "Dennoch ist dieses theologische Denken von einer unendlichen Leidenschaft des Fragens gezeichnet. 'Hartes, nüchternes, bohrendes — wenn es sein muß — Fragen ist schon ein Akt der Frömmigkeit, die dem geistigen wachen Christen geboten ist' [Karl Rahner, *Ich glaube an Jesus Christus*, Theologische Meditationen 21 (Einsiedeln, 1968), 8]. Alles wird in strenger Konfrontation mit dem Daseins- und Weltverständnis des heutigen Menschen vor dem Wahrheitsgewissen ver-antwortet, elementar erschlossen und zur konkreten Bewährung gebracht." Karl Lehmann, "Karl Rahner: Ein Porträt," *Rechenschaft des Glaubens*, 26*.

[48] In *FCF*, 31-35, Rahner begins his explanation of how the human person is a transcendent being ("der Mensch als Wesen der Transzendenz"): "One can place everything in question. In one's openness to everything and anything, whatever can come

why we experience a certain dissatisfaction with anything finite purporting to answer, in an absolute way, the question of human existence. In Rahner's own terms, it is in their nature as spirit that people
open themselves to the unlimited horizons of the human search for
meaning. In the depths of one's heart, the individual is a capacity, a
question, to which only the Absolute can answer — one is a "hearer,"
waiting for a word from the Absolute.[49]

Without, at this stage, going into a detailed analysis of Rahner's
presentation of transcendental experience, we can say that, for Rahner, God is the mystery in human experience. In other words, God is
the depth dimension in experiences such as solitude, friendship, love,
hope and death. We have mentioned above how finite objects cannot
fill our infinite horizon. Such encounters with limitation reveal our
essential contingency, our dependency on a power greater than ourselves. These experiences of limit are highlighted in such experiences
as loneliness, disappointment, the ingratitude of others, or, in more
tragic circumstances, suffering, sickness, and death.[50] But Rahner
would claim that such experiences can also be graced moments
because they open us to the transcendent. In being thrown back on
our finite selves we also have the opportunity of experiencing the liberating power of submitting to the mystery that lovingly supports and
draws near to us.

How is Rahner's description of the human person as a questioner
with an infinite horizon related to his description of the person as
spirit? The term, "spirit," when applied to the individual, means, for
Rahner, both self-presence and questioning. In other words, self-presence is not an absolute possession of oneself, but a self-presence that

to expression can be at least a question for the person. In the fact that one affirms the
possibility of a merely *finite* horizon of questioning, this possibility is already surpassed, and one shows oneself to be a being with an *infinite* horizon... . The infinite
horizon of human questioning is experienced as an horizon which recedes further and
further the more answers man can discover." (pp. 31-32) (*Grundkurs*, 42-43).

[49] See *Hearers of the Word*, 3-27 (*Hörer des Wortes*, 15-44), where Rahner discusses the possibility of a *Christian* philosophy, which points beyond itself and introduces "the person to the attitude of attentiveness to a revelation which may possibly
proceed from God. It thus becomes a *praeparatio evangelii*, through its understanding
of the human person as *naturaliter christianus*, as one who stands ready to receive a
revelation" (p. 23).

[50] Rahner, "Gotteserfahrung heute," *ST* IX: 161-76 (*TI* 11: 149-165, esp. 155-59).

goes out of itself and is ordered to the world. One both possesses one-self and is in search of oneself at the same time. Moreover, it is in this context of the questioning nature of spirit that Rahner locates the question of God. Reflecting on one's experience as a questioner, one realizes that the range of questions is open-ended:

> "Every goal that one can point to in knowledge and in action is always relativized, is always a provisional step. Every answer is always just the beginning of a new question. One experiences oneself as infinite possi-bility because in practice and in theory one necessarily places every sought-after result in question. One always situates it in a broader hori-zon which looms before one in its vastness."[51]

In short, in knowing the finite, one is already beyond the finite, i.e., one can only recognize a limit as a limit when one sees it over against the unlimited or the infinite. According to Rahner, when one affirms the pos-sibility of a merely finite horizon of questioning, this possibility is already surpassed, and the individual shows him or herself to be a being with an infinite horizon. If this view of Rahner's is correct, then the question of the religious dimension of experience inevitably arises. With-out an infinite horizon, one would be immersed in a world of objects, ceasing to question, thus evading the experience of transcendence.

Unlike the term spirit, the notion of *transcendence* connotes that the human person is dynamic, a process, on the way toward a goal that is nothing less than the infinite itself. Despite the fact that it is immersed in the world, the individual is also aware of itself as tran-scending the world of its immediate experience.[52] However, one's knowledge of the infinite is never something totally on its own. Rather, a person's experience of God or the Infinite (or God) is given with and through human experiences in the world. For Rahner, there-fore, every human experience has a religious dimension.[53]

---

[51] *FCF*, 32 (*Grundkurs*, 42). In this and in many other English translations of Rahner, I have substituted inclusive language.

[52] Of course the person is an *incarnate* spirit, a self-transcendent being *within* his-tory. One can never be a self-present subject except by being-in-the-world. While we cannot develop it here, one of the consequences which Rahner draws from this is that human transcendence within history means that the human person must seek God, pursue the mystery through ritual, rites, dogmas, prayers, etc. On history as the event of transcendence, see *FCF,* 140-42.

[53] This assertion will be developed, particularly in relation to Rahner's spirituality, in the next chapter.

This conviction of Rahner's, that all human beings are essentially oriented to the Infinite, received its philosophical justification in *Geist in Welt* where he attempted to examine all that is implicitly involved in the concrete act of human knowing. In this metaphysics of knowledge, he sought to show that human beings are finite spirits whose cognitional life can only be properly understood by positing an infinite horizon as its condition of possibility.[54] This thesis, in its many differentiations, remained decisive for Rahner's continued development in theology. In an essay on "The Experience of God Today" (1969), he writes:

> "The moment we become aware of ourselves precisely *as* the limited being which in so many ways we are, we have already overstepped these boundaries.... . We have experienced ourselves as beings which constantly reach out beyond themselves towards that which cannot be comprehended or circumscribed, that which precisely as having this radical status must be called infinite, that which is sheer mystery."[55]

A significant consequence of this insight is that the Infinite (or God or Holy Mystery) is never known or grasped by us as an object. God remains concealed and unknown, since He is never the direct object of knowledge, but is the infinite horizon within which every finite object is apprehended.[56]

Our discussion in the previous sections reminds us that these insights of Rahner in fact predate his more explicitly philosophical works and can also be found in some of his early prayers. One such example is the meditation entitled "God of Knowledge" in *Encounters with Silence,* where he reflects on the limitations of knowledge in penetrating to the heart of things, and to the depths of one's being. Instead, the true heart of reality can only be fathomed when knowledge develops into love, which, in turn, transforms a person in their very self:

---

[54] See Rahner's "Introductory Interpretation," *Spirit in the World,* 15-22.

[55] Rahner, "The Experience of God Today, " *TI* 11:155-56 (*ST* IX: 167).

[56] For a reflection on the person's transcendental orientation towards mystery in the context of the knowledge of God, see *FCF,* 51-71 (*Grundkurs,* 61-79). Later (in Chapter Three), we will discuss in greater detail Rahner's interpretation of the experience of transcendence as an ever-present movement toward the absolute mystery he calls God.

Only knowledge gained through experience, the fruit of living and suffering, fills the heart with the wisdom of love, instead of crushing it with the disappointment of boredom and final oblivion. It is not the results of our own speculation, but the golden harvest of what we have lived through, that has power to enrich the heart and nourish the spirit.[57]

This reflection leads him to assert that he "knows" God not primarily through words and concepts, but through experience — the experience of living and suffering. The meditation also reveals the existential root of all theological knowledge for Rahner — a root based in the experience of being totally grasped by the love of God — captured in the same piece by the pithy phrase: "Du hast mich ergriffen, nicht ich habe dich 'begriffen'."[58]

Our reference to the above meditation also shows how Rahner reflects on the notion of transcendence in two dimensions. The human person is a dynamism of both knowledge and love, and Rahner describes the religious dimension of the person under both these aspects. We have described how Rahner has shown that in knowing anything finite, one also at the same time "knows" the infinite — precisely as the "condition of possibility" of knowing the finite. And the significant consequence Rahner draws from this is that God (or the Infinite, or Holy Mystery) can never be known, i.e., grasped as an object:

> "The concept 'God' is not a grasp of God by which a person masters the mystery, but it is letting oneself be grasped by the mystery which is present and yet ever distant."[59]

A similar type of reflection is operative in Rahner's discussion of the dynamism of love. At the heart of human subjectivity is the mystery of human freedom.[60] The capacity for choosing among alterna-

---

[57] Rahner, "God of Knowledge," *Encounters with Silence*, 30.

[58] Rahner, *Worte ins Schweigen,* 34.

[59] Rahner, *FCF*, 54 (*Grundkurs*, 63). We have also seen this paradoxical presence-in-absence of God in the context of the discussion of Rahner's prayers in *Worte ins Schweigen*.

[60] Rahner deals with this complicated notion in more detail in *FCF*, 26-31, 35-41, and 93-106 (*Grundkurs*, 37-42, 46-53, 101-112). See also his article "Freedom," *TI* 6: 183-86 (*ST* 6: 221-25). A helpful analysis of how the nearness of God as Mystery is the guiding motif of Rahner's entire theology is given by John O'Donnell, "The Mystery of Faith in the Theology of Karl Rahner," *The Heythrop Journal* 25 (1984):

tives, points to a fundamental characteristic of human existence. But freedom of choice is not merely our freedom with regard to a finite object or possibility in the world; rather, it is the capacity for the infinite, the power human beings have to assume responsibility for the totality of their existence, i.e., all the discrete acts of choice of a person are really dimensions of the one freedom by which that person actualizes him or herself. Here again, for Rahner, the religious dimension is evident. Firstly, one is free with regard to any finite object because that finite reality exists within the infinite horizon of one's freedom. And, secondly, if one is conscious that one's freedom exists within this infinite horizon, one is compelled to take a stance towards it. In other words, if one lives within the Mystery, and if this Mystery is the condition of possibility of a person's finite freedom, then the question emerges as to the type of free response possible vis à vis this Mystery: one can open oneself and surrender to the Mystery, or one can absolutize some finite object in the world. The latter approach would be a self-contradictory use of human freedom, as no finite reality can satisfy the dynamism of transcendence. In Rahner's view, God is the only term for which transcendence exists. Thus, even in these brief reflections on the relation between freedom and human transcendence, it becomes apparent that human freedom is ultimately a matter of a fundamental option, an option for or against God.

The reflections above serve to show that, because the human person is spirit, he or she is also transcendence or a dynamism of knowledge and will — oriented to nothing less than the infinite. Rahner's thesis, then, is that the human person is oriented to the Mystery, which he calls God, and that this orientation is a constitutive element of one's being.[61]

Yet, assuming Rahner's philosophical anthropology to be correct, it leads only to modest conclusions. While his reflections reveal that the question of God is unavoidable, they do not explain precisely

301-18. For a succinct consideration of significant elements of Rahner's thinking about God, including his idea of God as the holy mystery and his emphasis on God's incomprehensibility, see John P. Galvin, "Before the Holy Mystery: Karl Rahner's Thought on God," *Toronto Journal of Theology* 9 (1993): 229-37.

[61] Rahner, "The Concept of Mystery in Catholic Theology," *TI* 4: 36-76 (*ST* IV: 51-102). For Rahner's analysis of the subject who is oriented to, and confronted by, Mystery, see the "Second Lecture," 48-60.

how God can be the *answer* to the individual's ceaseless questioning. In order to show that God is not just the silent, nameless, transcendent and distant Mystery, Rahner needs to reflect again on the human person as he or she is revealed to him or herself by God's *revelation*, i.e., the person as a subject of grace. We will develop Rahner's thoughts on this topic, and the implications for spirituality, when we come to a more explicit discussion of the experience of grace in the next chapter.

To conclude this section, we will attempt to formulate some tentative implications for spirituality on the basis of Rahner's reflections.[62] Firstly, in Rahner's eyes, to speak about the human is already to speak about the divine. Underlying the myriad ordinary human events and experiences in which people are thrown back on themselves — moments of deep joy or deep pain for example — "is the one primal experience *(das eine Urerlebnis):* that the human person is more than the sum of chemical elements and processes, that human life rests on an incomprehensible mystery, indeed constantly begins to flow in that direction."[63] Secondly, this explains why, for Rahner, prayer cannot be the sole subject-matter for spirituality. God is not only the mystery in our prayer, but also the mystery we experience in the details of our daily lives *(die Tiefendimension des alltäglichen Lebens).*[64] Thirdly, it can be seen from the above that God's presence cannot be limited solely to those experiences that are filled with consolation, but can also be found in experiences of struggle and suffering.

b. *Christian Life: A Mysticism of Everyday Faith*

A consistent thread running throughout Rahner's writing on the spiritual life is a rejection of what he calls an élitist interpretation of Christianity. In his reflections on spirituality and mysticism, he insists that *everyone* is called to the immediacy of God's self-pres-

---

[62] On this, see Annice Callahan, "Traditions of Spiritual Guidance: Karl Rahner's Insights for Spiritual Direction," *The Way* 29 (1989): 341-47.

[63] Vorgrimler, *Understanding Karl Rahner*, 14 (*Karl Rahner Verstehen*, 25).

[64] Karl Rahner, "Thesen zum Thema: Glaube und Gebet," in *Chancen des Glaubens: Fragmente einer modernen Spiritualität* (Freiburg: Herder, 1971), 65-74, 73.

ence, a call which, of course, can be rejected.[65] Underlying this assertion is God's universal salvific will, and radical self-communication
to all. Here we are touching on an essential foundation of Rahner's
understanding of spirituality, i.e., his theology of grace, a topic to
which we shall return later. In the last section, we have seen how he
sees God as the depth dimension in such experiences as solitude,
friendship, etc. For the moment, however, we wish to explore his
understanding of what he calls a mysticism of "everyday life" (*Mystik des Alltags*).[66]

In Rahner's view, every Christian is called to a mysticism of everyday faith, hope and love that differs only in degree, and not in kind,
from the extraordinary experiences of recognized mystics. One of the
key tasks of Christian theology as a whole (and Christian mystical theology in particular) is to render intelligible how there is an experience
of being referred to Mystery even in the simplest acts of faith, hope,
and love which permeate daily life. In other words, Rahner is moving
away here from an understanding of mysticism as representing the
final stage of Christian perfection.[67] Mysticism is thus not limited to
those who are technically called mystics in the Christian tradition.
Instead, when Rahner says that the devout Christian of the future will
be a 'mystic,' he is stressing how a Christian's faith-conviction will be
intimately related to a genuine and wholly personal experience of God:

---

[65] On the obligation of every Christian to strive for sanctity, see Rahner, "Being
Open to God as ever Greater," *TI* 7: 26, where he is reiterating an emphasis of Vatican II's *Lumen Gentium*, chap. 5 "The Call to Holiness." See *Vatican Council II: The
Conciliar and Post Conciliar Documents,* ed. Austin Flannery, O.P., Vatican Collection Series, vol. 1, new rev. ed., (Dublin: Dominican Publications, E. J. Dwyer, 1992),
396-402.

[66] See, for example, Rahner's meditation on this topic in *Worte ins Schweigen,*
"Gott meines Alltags," 46-51, and also *Karl Rahner im Gespräch* 2: 211-13.

[67] It would be incorrect, however, to claim that Rahner denies that there are no
stages of growth in the spiritual life. Quite apart from Ignatius, he was well
acquainted with the classical mystical works of St Teresa of Avila and St John of the
Cross. He regarded such mystics as "almost irreplaceable teachers" (*fast unersetz-
liche Lehrmeister*) in rendering intelligible their experience of God. See "Lehrerin der
Kirche: Theresia von Ávila," *Chancen des Glaubens: Fragmente einer modernen
Spiritualität* (Freiburg: Herder, 1971), 141-44, 143. [ET: "Teresa of Avila: Doctor of
the Church," in *Opportunities for Faith: Elements of a Modern Spirituality,* trans.
Edward Quinn (London: SPCK, 1970), 123-26]. See also his article on "The Church
of the Saints," *TI* 3: 91-104 (*ST* III: 111-26).

"... The Christian of the future will be a mystic or he or she will not exist at all. If by mysticism we mean, not singular parapsychological phenomena, but a genuine experience of God emerging from the heart of our existence, this statement is very true and its truth and importance will become still clearer in the spirituality of the future... Possession of the Spirit is not something of which we are made factually aware merely by pedagogic indoctrination as a reality beyond our existential awareness, but is experienced inwardly ... The solitary Christian makes the experience of God and his liberating grace in silent prayer, in the final decision of conscience, unrewarded by anyone, in the unlimited hope which can no longer cling to any particular calculable assurance, in the radical disappointment of life and in the powerlessness of death."[68]

So, when Rahner speaks of mysticism, he is not referring simply to extraordinary "mystical" phenomena such as visions, raptures, and ecstasies, but rather to a personal, interior experience of, and union with, God's Spirit. His thesis is that mystical experiences (in the sense of mystical illumination and unification) are simply a variation of that experience of the Spirit which is radically offered to every person and to every Christian. Behind this assertion lies an attempt to move beyond the traditional "divisions" or stages in the spiritual life, through which one must pass on the way to Christian perfection. In other words, Rahner believes, it is incorrect to assume that:

---

[68] Rahner, "The Spirituality of the Church of the Future," *TI* 20:149-50 (*ST* XIV: 368-81). The German phrase, "eine Erfahrung machen" would normally be translated in English as "to have an experience." However, both here and elsewhere in *Investigations* it is often translated more literally, in order to convey the active participation of the subject who "has" or "makes" these experiences.

Rahner first expressed these ideas in "Frömmigkeit heute und morgen," *Geist und Leben* 39 (1966): 326-42. See also "Christian Living Formerly and Today," *TI* 7: 3-23, 15 (*ST* VII: 11-31, 22), where he describes how "der Fromme (the devout Christian) der Zukunft wird ein Mystiker sein, einer der Gott erfahren hat, oder er wird nicht mehr sein." In order to avoid misunderstandings, Rahner does not oppose such mysticism to faith in the Holy Spirit, but identifies it with such faith: "recht verstanden kein Gegensatz zum Glauben im Heiligen Pneuma ist, sondern dasselbe." See also Jörg Splett, "Mystisches Christentum? Karl Rahner zur Zukunft des Glaubens," *Theologische Quartalschrift* 174 (1990): 258-71, who emphasizes the practical nature or "worldliness" (*Weltlichkeit*) of Rahner's treatment of mysticism: "Es geht Rahner um eine Mystik der Praxis, einer Praxis der Einheit von Gottes- und Menschenliebe" (p. 269).

"the 'mystic' is the only one who has gone or goes on that path to perfection of which the last stage directly and alone borders on one's perfection ... All this forbids us to regard mysticism and particularly its
more or less technically and explicitly developed form exclusively as
the necessary and final stretch of the way before attaining perfect salvation or all ordinary practice of Christian life merely as the *preparatory*
phase of the way of salvation which leads to perfection only when it
ends up on the higher path of contemplative mysticism. Christianity
rejects such an élitist interpretation of life, which can see the person's
perfection as attained only in the trained mystic."[69]

It is with this problem of the gradual ascent to Christian perfection
that Rahner is concerned even from the beginning of his more scientific writings on the theology of the spiritual life.[70] Traditional divisions or stages in the spiritual life presupposed a stage-by-stage
process of becoming holy and perfect, which was also equated with a
continual increase in sanctifying grace. Rahner rejects such a quanti-
tative, impersonal, conception of grace, leading only to what he calls
a growth in "ontic" sanctity.[71] This rather artificial approach results
in two irreconcilable conclusions: on the one hand, the "ontic"
approach implies that there should be a continual increase of grace in
the course of a long Christian life, i.e., the person should have
become more "perfect" or holy; yet, on the other hand, experience
shows us that, in most instances, this is not the case. Without going
into a detailed solution to this problem, Rahner hints that a solution is
nonetheless to be found in a more personalist, and less entitative, conception of grace. Even if we cannot here go into a detailed presentation of his understanding of grace as God's *self*-communication or
self-giving (traditionally referred to as "uncreated grace"), as distinct

---

[69] Rahner, "Experience of Transcendence from the Standpoint of Christian Dogmatics," *TI* 18: 175 (*ST* XIII: 208).

[70] Rahner, "Reflections on the Problem of the Gradual Ascent to Christian Perfection," *TI* 3: 3-23 (*ST* III: 11-34).

[71] Rahner, "Reflections on the Problem of the Gradual Ascent to Christian Perfection," *TI* 3: 8-13. An example of the use of such divisions or separate divisions
of the spiritual life given by Rahner is Bonaventure's *De triplici via*. On this,
see, *The Works of Bonaventure: Cardinal, Seraphic Doctor, and Saint I: Mystical
Opuscula*, trans. José de Vinck (Patterson N.J.: St Anthony's Guild Press, 1960), 59-
94. Rahner also refers here to Otto Zimmermann, *Lehrbuch der Aszetik* (Freiburg:
Herder, 1929), 67.

from the effects of this divine self-giving (which scholastic theologians called "created grace"), we wish to draw attention to the pertinence of this notion of grace for all of Rahner's theology, including his thinking on mysticism.[72]

Returning once again to Rahner's understanding of the term *mysticism*, we can say that, for him, the term signifies both "an experience, the interior meeting and union of a person with the divine infinity that sustains him or her and all other being," and "the attempt to give a systematic exposition of this experience or reflection upon it (hence a scientific discipline)."[73] A further distinction in his use of the term may also prove helpful here. We can distinguish between mysticism in the strict sense (i.e., the unusual experiences of the saints) and mysticism in a wide sense (i.e., ordinary Christian experience in the person's natural domain). To be sure, Rahner will concede, the extraordinary mystical experiences of the saints are *psychologically* different from everyday experiences of grace. The saints experience in an extraordinarily psychological way what all Christians experience in a more hidden way. In his argument, Rahner is also concerned to locate the precise role of *faith* in such mystical experience. He criticizes descriptions of mystical illumination and unification in which God communicates himself so "immediately," and intervenes so gratuitously, that such experiences are no longer perceived within the framework of faith. There can be no theologically higher experience on earth than that

---

[72] Rahner, "Mystical Experience and Mystical Theology," *TI* 17: 90-99 (*ST* XII: 428-38). This article was originally written as the preface to Carl Albrecht's book, *Das mystische Wort: Erleben und Sprechen in Versunkenheit,* ed. H. A. Fischer-Barnicol (Mainz, 1974), vii-xiv. There, Rahner acknowledges his debt to Carl Albrecht who was not only a mystic, but also a prominent doctor, psychologist, philosopher and scientist.

[73] Rahner, Vorgrimler, "Mysticism," *Theological Dictionary*: 301 (*Kleines Theologisches Wörterbuch*: 289-90). See also Rahner's contribution to the theological interpretation of mysticism, "Mystik," in Josef Höfer and Karl Rahner, eds., *Lexikon für Theologie und Kirche*, 2nd ed., (Freiburg: Herder, 1986) 7: 743-45, where he comments: "Insofern haben die Vertreter der Lehre, daß mystische Erfahrung sich nicht spezifisch vom gewöhnlichen Gnadenleben (als solchem!) unterscheide, theologisch durchaus recht. Jede andere Theorie der christlichen Mystik wäre eigentlich Gnosis oder Theosophie, würde die Mystik überschätzen oder das 'gewöhnliche' christliche Gnadenleben in seiner eigentlichen Tiefe und Radikalität grundsätzlich unterschätzen" (p. 744).

of faith in the Spirit of God,[74] and a genuine mystical experience is only to be understood as a "variety" of this experience of grace in faith.

Rahner equates the essence of mysticism (in the strict sense) with the classical term "infused contemplation," in which God gratuitously makes Himself known to the individual. So, despite his reservations mentioned above, Rahner still derives "a vague empirical concept of Christian mysticism" from the religious experiences of the saints:

> "... All that they experienced of closeness to God, of higher impulses, of visions, inspirations, of the consciousness of being under the special and personal guidance of the Holy Spirit, of ecstasies, etc., all this is comprised in our understanding of the word mysticism, without our having to stop here to ask ... in what more precisely this proper element consists."[75]

These extraordinary mystical experiences of the saints, however, occur in the normal realm of grace and faith. Rahner consistently emphasizes how even the deepest mystical experiences do not abandon the sphere of faith. In other words, for him, no intermediary stage exists between the everyday life of Christian faith, hope, and love, on the one hand, and the beatific vision on the other. From this perspective, he concludes that, theologically speaking, mystical experience is not specifically different from the ordinary life of grace.[76] Such extraordinary mystical experiences (mysticism in the strict sense) are different from ordinary Christian experiences in that they represent extremely intense instances of a basically universal experience of God (made possible by God's universal self-communication), and hence a deepening and radicalising of the "normal" life of faith.

---

[74] *Faith*, according to Rahner, is "nothing other than the positive and unconditional acceptance of one's own existence as meaningful and open to a final fulfilment, which we call God." See "The Certainty of Faith," in *The Practice of Faith*, 32. On Rahner's reasons for attaching greater importance to the existential aspect of faith (while not denying the need for conceptual articulation), see "Thesen zum Thema: Glaube und Gebet," in *Chancen des Glaubens: Fragmente einer modernen Spiritualität*, 65-74.

[75] Rahner, "The Ignatian Mysticism of Joy in the World," *TI* 3: 279-80 (*ST* III: 332).

[76] Rahner, "Mysticism," *Encyclopedia of Theology: The Concise Sacramentum Mundi* (London: Burns and Oates, 1975): 1010-11. See also on this topic Harvey Egan, "Mysticism and Karl Rahner's Theology," *Theology and Discovery*, 139-58.

We have described how the specific way the saints experience God has different and unusual *psychological* manifestations, which are related to the person's *natural* abilities for concentration, meditation, self-emptying and other contemplative techniques. These unusual psychological manifestations represent a "natural, pure experience of transcendence when the mediation of categories either partly or completely ceases."[77] In the strict sense, then, mysticism implies a "purely nonconceptual experience of transcendence without imagery,"[78] or a "transcendent experience through grace which is not categorial."[79] Such an experience occurs, in Rahner's view, whenever a person's graced orientation to God emerges explicitly into awareness occupying the person's attention without the usual mediation of images and concepts.

However, Rahner maintains a "difference in kind" between human transcendentality (orientation to God) as the necessary condition of any act of the mind, even the most ordinary, and the explicit experience of transcendence. Intense and unusually explicit experiences of transcendence involve a "return" to self (i.e., this grace-elevated experience of transcendence enters into explicit conscious focus without the usual mediation of concepts). This difference between the mysticism of the saints and the less explicit form of ordinary Christian life belongs not to the realm of the supernatural, but to the order of psychology or parapsychology. Mystical experience (in the strict sense) then, for Rahner, does not so much represent a "higher" stage of the Christian life in grace, because the basic experience of God is not the privilege of a few, but is given to all.[80] This experience is not confined to the extraordinary lives of the mystics and the saints, but penetrates every aspect of daily life. Rahner's understanding of mysticism is, therefore, not that of a pure interiority divorced from the world.

---

[77] Rahner, "Mysticism," *Encyclopedia of Theology*: 1011. On "non-conceptual" experience of God, see Rahner's "Die ignatianische Logik der existentiellen Erkenntnis," *Das Dynamische in der Kirche*, Quaestiones Disputatae 5 (Freiburg: Herder, 1958), 113-24. [ET: The Logic of Concrete Individual Knowledge in Ignatius Loyola," *The Dynamic Element in the Church*, trans. W. J. O'Hara, Quaestiones Disputatae 12 (London: Burns and Oates, 1964), 84-170, esp. 129-42].

[78] Rahner, *The Dynamic Element in the Church,* 147 (*Das Dynamische in der Kirche*, 128).

[79] Rahner, "Enthusiasm and Grace," *TI* 16: 43 (*ST* XII: 64).

[80] Rahner, "The Experience of God Today," *TI* 11: 153 (*ST* IX: 165).

We have previously referred to the element of the ineffable, of the mysterious, in human existence, and how Rahner conceives of the human person as a being constantly reaching out beyond him or herself. This element of the ineffable is not something abstract, but is present in the concrete experiences of everyday life. Examples of this mysticism of everyday life include:

> "experiences of '*aloneness*,' ... when everything is 'called in question,' ... when the silence resounds more penetratingly than the accustomed din of everyday life ... when one is brought face to face with one's own freedom and *responsibility*, feeling this as a single and total factor embracing the whole of one's life ... when one suddenly makes the experience of *love* and encounter, and suddenly notices that he or she has been accepted with a love which is absolute and unconditional ..."[81]

For Rahner, *the* secular mystical experience is the courageous and total acceptance of life and of oneself even when everything tangible seems to be collapsing.[82] In short,

> "whenever secular life is lived with unreserved honesty and courage; ... whenever there is a lived moderation without any thought of reward; whenever there is a silent life of service to others, there too, can be found the mysticism of daily life."[83]

Such experiences really do point to that which, or better, to Him whom, we call God. And this experience, while it may be unacknowledged, unreflected upon, or even suppressed, nonetheless takes place for most Christians not in meditation proper, but in the humdrum of everyday life. As a core-experience or experience of transcendence (which is also always an experience of grace), it is mediated unthematically in one's everyday life through the discovery of God in all things (*das Gottfinden in allen Dingen*).[84]

---

[81] Rahner, "The Experience of God Today," *TI* 11: 157 (*STIX*: 168-69). See also his "Reflections on the Experience of Grace," *TI* 3: 86-90 (*ST* XII: 45-48).

[82] I am indebted here to the remarks of Egan, "Mysticism and Karl Rahner's Theology," 155-57.

[83] Egan, "Mysticism and Karl Rahner's Theology," 155. Additional examples of "experiences of grace" can be found in Rahner's "Reflections on the Experience of Grace," *TI* 3: 86-90 (*ST* III: 105-109).

[84] "Es gibt die Mystik des Alltags, das Gottfinden in allen Dingen, die nüchterne Trunkenheit des Geistes, von der die Kirchenväter und die alte Liturgie sprechen, die wir nicht ablehnen oder verachten dürfen, weil sie nüchtern ist." Rahner, *Karl Rahner*

It is to Rahner's credit that he has provided a basis for a mysticism of everyday life which moves away from any élitist interpretations of Christianity. He has managed to separate what is essential, namely, the personal core-experience of transcendence, which is possible under a whole variety of circumstances, from what is secondary, namely the unusual phenomena which sometimes accompany mysticism.[85] Finally, he correctly highlights how a genuine Christian mysticism, far from fleeing the world, involves instead an ongoing attempt to discover and accept the presence of Holy Mystery in everyday life.

We are aware that the foregoing reflections capture only one aspect of Rahnerian mysticism. We have not, as yet, treated the question of the role of Ignatius in Rahner's understanding of mysticism. One of the main claims of this look is that Rahner's theology has a very definite spiritual basis (i.e., in the experience of grace)[86] and that Ignatius plays a crucial role in this context. However, we will postpone, at this stage, our discussion of the importance of Ignatius for Rahner's understanding of spirituality; this is a theme to which we will return in the fourth chapter.

c. Prayer as Surrender of the Heart

A frequently recurring characteristic, which we have noted, of Rahner's theology and spirituality is its starting-point in Rahner's own personal experience of God (with its insights as well as its questions). From this concrete starting-point, he attempts to understand

---

im Gespräch 2: 212. See also, *Worte ins Schweigen*, 46-51, and *Everyday Things,* Theological Meditations 5, ed. Hans Küng (London and Melbourne: Sheed and Ward, 1965), 33-41.

[85] Karl Rahner, "Experiencing the Spirit," *The Spirit in the Church* (London: Burns and Oates, 1977), 3-31. This work is a collection of three articles by Rahner (and hence various translators). This first article, which is relevant to our discussion, is translated from *Erfahrung des Geistes: Meditation auf Pfingsten* (Freiburg: Herder, 1977), 9-23.

[86] This assertion has been made repeatedly by outstanding commentators on Rahner, such as Karl Lehmann, "Karl Rahner, Ein Porträt," in *Rechenschaft des Glaubens,* eds. Karl Lehmann and Albert Raffelt (Freiburg: Herder, 1979), 13*- 53*, esp. 36*-40*. See also Herbert Vorgrimler, "Grundzüge der Theologie Karl Rahners," in Karl Rahner, *Sehnsucht nach dem geheimnisvollen Gott,* 11-50, esp. 14-21.

the traditional faith of the Church.[87] He also invites others to discover similar experiences in themselves, or even to consider theologizing from quite different experiences. In either case, there is the stress on a return to one's personal experience, while attempting, at the same time, to avoid an arbitrary subjectivism in matters of faith. Rahner's theology has occasionally been labelled "anthropological," which, in our present context, means that his theology takes as its starting-point the experiences, fears and questions of contemporary man and woman. What does it mean, then, to describe Rahner's experience of God as mystical? Without repeating what we have discussed before or entering into a detailed technical discussion of the term, "mystical," it means, in the context of Rahner's theology (and of the Jesuit-Ignatian tradition whence he comes), that his theology grows out of *prayer*, is accompanied by prayer, and, finally, leads back again to prayer.[88] Prayer, here, refers to "that mysterious procedure by

---

[87] This is of one the basic characteristics ("Grundzüge") of Rahner's theology according to Vorgrimler, in "Grundzüge der Theologie Karl Rahners," *Sehnsucht nach dem geheimnisvollen Gott*, 14-31. A similar point has been made by J. B. Metz, namely, that Rahner's theology is a "mystical biography of religious experience," ("die mystische Biographie der religiösen Erfahrung"), in "Karl Rahner — ein theologisches Leben," *Stimmen der Zeit* 192 (1974): 308.

[88] Vorgrimler, "Grundzüge der Theologie Karl Rahners," 15. See also Karl-Heinz Weger, "'Ich glaube, weil ich bete.' Für Karl Rahner zum 80 Geburtstag," *Geist und Leben* 57 (1984): 48-52. In this context, the opinion of Josef Sudbrack is apposite: "Karl Rahner nun theologisierte niemals ohne seine Subjektivität, sein Betroffensein, sein Engagement. Er dachte mit dem Herzen und hat dieses Mit-dem-Herzen-Denken in brillanter Intelligenz und wissenschaftlicher Redlichkeit denkerisch hinterfragt und systematisch gestaltet. Diese *Einheit von Kopf und Herz* ist Schlüssel zum Geheimnis seines weltweiten Einflusses." *Der Christ von morgen — ein Mystiker?*, eds. Wolfgang Böhme and Josef Sudbrack (Würzburg: Herder, 1989), 103-104 (italics mine). Metz expresses similar sentiments: "Nur theoretische Naivität kann die Theologen von heute glauben machen, sie könnten ihre Sprache — also ihre Rede über Gott — im Rahmen moderner Wissenschafts- und Sprachtheorien begründen... . Wie kaum ein zweiter wußte Karl Rahner, daß alle Rede über Gott nur so weit ein authentisches sprachliches Fundament hat, als sie in einer Rede zu Gott wurzelt, daß also der theoretisch unableitbare Sprachraum der Theologie die Sprache der Gebete ist. Daher die eigentümliche Oszillation bei Rahner zwischen Gebetssprache und Argumentationssprache, zwischen Mystagogie und Theologie, zwischen Spiritualität und theologischer Intellektualität, die ihm eine gewisse Oberflächentheologie gern als Dilettantismus ankreidete." Johann Baptist Metz, "Karl Rahners Ringen um die theologische Ehre des Menschen," *Karl Rahner in Erinnerung*, ed. Albert Raffelt, Freiburger Akademieschriften, 8 (Düsseldorf: Patmos, 1994), 78-79.

which a person lets him or herself go into the ultimate mystery of his or her existence as such, trustingly, explicitly, thematically."[89] We have previously referred to this 'mystery' dimension in human existence in the context of Rahner's discussion of the transcendental nature of the human person.[90] When he comes to a discussion of prayer, however, the basic question foremost in Rahner's mind revolves around the *possibility* of prayer today, given the unique and changed circumstances of contemporary Christians. A second derivative question follows from this, and concerns the *form* prayer must take, if it is to be meaningful. We will confine ourselves, initially, to these two questions in the following reflections on Rahner's treatment of prayer.

Rahner calls prayer a fundamental act of human existence (*Grundakt der menschlichen Existenz*).[91] For him, it is something that can

---

[89] Karl Rahner, *Christians at the Crossroads* (London: Burns and Oates, 1975), 49. The German original of this book *Wagnis des Christen. Geistliche Texte* (Freiburg: Herder, 1974), now over twenty years old, was written in the context of a period of change in the Church, which, as Rahner admits, many found upsetting. His response, in this book, is to focus on the basic content of the faith in theory and practice — the awareness of the essentials (*die Besinnung auf das Wesentliche*), as Rahner describes it in the Foreword. With regard to our present theme, prayer, it will be seen that the questions Rahner raises are still actual and urgent in contemporary discussions on the theology of prayer. See, for example, John H. Wright, *A Theology of Christian Prayer,* 2nd ed. (New York: Pueblo, 1988).

[90] The relationship between prayer and the transcendental nature of the human person can be detected in another, more comprehensive, Rahnerian description of prayer as a religious act, or *Grundakt*. (In this context, he acknowledges his debt to J. B. Metz). See Rahner, "Some Theses on Prayer 'In the Name of the Church'," *TI* 5: 419-38 *(ST* V: 471-93), where he describes the nature of prayer in general (p. 419) as "an act of an intellectually endowed creature by which the creature turns towards God by acknowledging and praising His limitless superiority explicitly or implicitly and by subjecting itself to that superiority (in faith, hope, and charity). Hence prayer is an act by which (a) a person as a whole 'actualizes' him or herself and (b) by which this thus actualized human reality is subjected and, as it were, surrendered to God." This description is a paraphrasing summary of Metz's article, "Akt, religiöser," *LThK* I: 256-59, where the religious act is described as "*das Sicheinlassen des Menschen auf diese Transzendenz seines eigenen Wesens* ... die Annahme des Menschseins in seinem ursprüngl(ichen) Verfügtsein, Angesprochensein u(nd) Aufgerufensein durch das Geheimnis Gottes ... " pp. 256, 258.

[91] Rahner, *Wagnis des Christen*, 64. Examples given by Rahner of other such fundamental acts include love, loyalty, trust, and hope, the reality of which can only be grasped in their actual performance.

only be properly grasped by its *practice*. It belongs to those fundamental realities of human life (like the reality of love, loyalty, trust,
hope, etc.) that cannot be synthetically investigated "from without".
Prayer, then, can only have a meaning if it is viewed as "a fundamental act (*Grundakt*) of human existence embracing that existence
as a whole and bringing it, in a movement of trust and love, to that
mystery whom we call God."[92] As a fundamental reality of human
existence, Rahner sees prayer as something that has already been
given to us in the depths of our existence, as an offer to our freedom
— which we can either accept or brush aside.

Rahner speaks of the *possibility* of prayer today because he is aware
of the major difficulties (theological and otherwise) that make prayer
hard or impossible. One difficulty has to do with the effects of the phe-
nomenal development in, what he calls, the "exact sciences" (e.g.,
empirical psychology, genetics, biochemistry, and similar disciplines),
leading to an explosion in knowledge about the human person. The
temptation, in all of this, is for the human person to understand oneself
in terms of a computer, without acknowledging the remnant, the not-
yet-known, the "more," which not only persists in these exact sciences,
despite their rapid progress, but which is also experienced (accepted or
rejected) in life as the element of mystery in human existence. Prayer,
however, being a "realization" (*Vollzug*) of the human person, can
never be the object of the exact sciences, because it escapes such exact
and lucid treatment. There is so much more about the human person
than that which can be obtained from a purely technological point of
view.[93] This "more" has been admirably described by Rahner in his
exploration of the transcendent nature of the human person. Nevertheless, scepticism and doubt about the possibility of prayer persist, and
these are further evident in such problems as: the apparent absence and
intangibility of God (which, in turn, threatens belief); the difficulty in
understanding God as a 'person' who addresses us, and whom we can
address; and the difficulty of petitionary prayer.[94]

---

[92] Rahner, *Christians at the Crossroads*, 49 (*Wagnis des Christen*, 64).
[93] Rahner, *FCF*, 26-31 (*Grundkurs*, 39-42).
[94] See Rahner, *Christians at the Crossroads*, 52-69: " ... The person today finds
it very difficult to discover anything in his or her prayerful consciousness which he
or she could interpret as an address by God distinct from his own mental processes"

When Rahner claims that prayer is best grasped by its practice, he means that when a person accepts him or herself in the totality of their existence and so experiences him or herself as confronted with the incomprehensible mystery embracing this existence, then such a person is living out what prayer really is and means. Prayer, then, is the event *of the experience of God himself.* In fact, the question of God and the question of prayer are, for him, two facets of the one question. But, prayer can become a problem *even* for those who accept God as the one ground of all, as the all-permeating mystery, because they think that to address this nameless God, this ineffable mystery is to turn God into an "object" of thought or speech, i.e., to turn God into an idol. Rahner is sympathetic to such sentiments, but he suggests that our attempts to address this incomprehensible God are not based on the patterns of inter-human dialogue. Rather, it is *God* who brings about our prayer when we pray — He is both the ground of our speech and the One spoken to.[95] God has so constituted the human person that, as a creature, he or she can "do business" with his or her Ground (*mit seinem Grund 'verhandeln' kann*), while at the same time realizing that what he or she is doing is also God's work.

Rahner's procedure, then, is to start with the reality of prayer: the human person can and does, in fact, pray. Then, from the reality of this worshipping address, he determines the essence of the human person as the one who can say "You" to God:

> "When this ability to say You to God (*dieses Dusagenkönnen*) is no longer self-evident but experienced as the person's highest possibility, given and disclosed by God, when we notice that the word we speak in

(p. 64). Rahner here is reacting to those who object that nothing in fact "happens" in prayer, and who thus deduce that it is superficial — not effecting any change. Klaus Fischer sees in Rahner's approach a "polemische Stoßrichtung" against these objections. See his "'Wo der Mensch an das Geheimnis grenzt': Die mystagogische Struktur der Theologie Karl Rahners," *Zeitschrift für Katholische Theologie* 98 (1976): 162. See also in this context a letter from Rahner to the Dutch Carmelites entitled: "Das Beten ist auch eine Tat," ("Prayer, too, is action"), *Chancen des Glaubens*, 89-90. For a discussion of some of these difficulties, including prayer to the saints and to the dead, see Rahner's contribution in: Karl Rahner and J. B. Metz, *The Courage To Pray* (London: Burns and Oates, 1980), 29-87.

[95] Rahner, *Christians at the Crossroads*, 54 (*Wagnis des Christen*, 72).

such a way that it can really reach him is worked and spoken by him in us, when we experience that God's Spirit must pray in us, … then our address to God has for the first time found its true essence …"[96]

In his guidelines for education for prayer, he suggests that, prior to any theological treatment of prayer,

> "there should be an attempt at an initiation (*eine Mystagogie*), into one's personal experience of an enduring, if mostly anonymous, transcendence of human existence in its wholeness … reaching into that mystery which we call God and whose reality cannot be merely indoctrinated from outside, but is always experienced by us in our present life mysteriously, implicitly, and silently."[97]

Prayer, then is not to be presented as merely a particular exercise inculcated from outside, and performed as a duty, but rather as an explicit realization of that relationship of the whole person to God. Moreover, Rahner wishes to draw attention to the whole array of "experiences leading to prayer" experiences permeating one's whole life (examples of which, we have previously mentioned). When, a person learns to face and accept (and not repress) these experiences with an incomprehensible courage, then they are already on the threshold of true prayer, and one can speak of a genuine initiation (or mystagogy). A person's apparently secular life, on the one hand, and their explicit prayer, on the other, can thus mutually interpenetrate, or, to put it another way, apparently secular experiences can be regarded as an opening onto more formal prayer.

A further difficulty with prayer today, acknowledged by Rahner, concerns the question of *petitionary prayer*.[98] On the one hand, Rahner dismisses that understanding of petitionary prayer which sees it as a mere demand, on our part, that God comply with our wishes.[99] On

---

[96] Rahner, *Christians at the Crossroads*, 55 (*Wagnis des Christen*, 74). Since English does not have the Du/Sie distinction as in German, some of the original sense is lost here in translation.

[97] Rahner, "Thesen zum Thema: Glaube und Gebet," *Chancen des Glaubens: Fragmente einer modernen Spiritualität*, 72. [ET: *Opportunities for Faith: Elements of a Modern Spirituality*, trans. E. Quinn (London: SPCK, 1970), 59].

[98] For an early Rahnerian defence of petitionary prayer, see "Das Gebet der Not," *Von der Not und dem Segen des Gebetes*, 76-92 (*Happiness through Prayer*, 56-68).

[99] Nor is it a question of trying to change God's mind. On the modern theological difficulties in conceiving petitionary prayer, see Karl Rahner and Karl-Heinz Weger,

the other hand, he is wary of too rash a "demythologizing" of petitionary prayer because, throughout the history of religion, people have resorted to such prayer. It is also important in this context, he feels, to make a clear distinction between the essence of prayer and magical conjuration, e.g., expecting miraculous interventions by God rather than taking responsibility for our situation in the world. A further, related problem asks how petitionary prayer is reconcilable with God's omniscience, which does not need us to inform it of our needs, or with God's providence and its eternal designs. Rahner does not attempt to offer detailed solutions to these problems; instead, two points are sufficient, in his view, to make the possibility and meaning of petitionary prayer intelligible:

> "Firstly, prayer of petition is prayer and meaningful before God only if the desire for a determined and even worldly individual good asked for is also at the same time the person's absolute surrender to the sovereign decrees of God's will. One cannot come to God in prayer without giving oneself, one's whole existence, in trustful submission and love, and in acceptance of the incomprehensible God who is beyond our understanding not only in his essence but also in his free relationship to us and must be accepted as such."[100]

These more abstract thoughts are given flesh in Rahner's prayers where the attitude proposed above is expressed in more personal terms:

> "... The prayer that You require of me must be ultimately just a patient waiting for You, a silent standing by until You, who are ever present in the inmost centre of my being, open the gate to me from within. In this way I shall be able to enter into myself, into the hidden sanctuary of my own being."[101]

Thus, petitionary prayer, in Rahner's view, is always understood within the framework of an unconditional surrender of the person to God. In this sense, it is an expression of a desire to deepen one's relationship of trust and dependence on God.

Our Christian Faith: Answers for the Future, trans. Francis McDonagh (London: Burns and Oates, 1981), 51-69. [*Was sollen wir noch glauben?* (Freiburg: Herder, 1979), 69-87]. See also Karl Rahner and J. B. Metz, *The Courage to Pray* (London: Search Press, 1980), 29-87.

[100] Rahner, *Christians at the Crossroads*, 57 (*Wagnis des Christen*, 77).

[101] Rahner, "God of my Prayer," *Encounters with Silence*, 24 ("Gott meiner Gebete," *Worte ins Schweigen*, 30).

Rahner's second point is that the person who steps into God's presence in prayer does so as a person of daily, profane and banal needs and anxieties. In other words, one places oneself before God in prayer as one is, and not merely as a so-called "religious" person desiring God. Hence, one can place oneself before God, while, at the same time, willing something legitimately. *Petitionary* prayer, then, places the needy person at their most concrete before God: the person is mindful not only of who *God* is, but also of who *he himself* (*she herself*) is. When understood in this way, the question of how petitionary prayer is answered is, for Rahner, of secondary importance.

Prayer, therefore, is not some isolated activity cut off from the rest of our lives, but "must be understood as the expression and execution of our existence in its entirety."[102] Behind this statement lies the truth that God is not just something alongside other things, but their ultimate and incomprehensible ground (*Grund*). The implications for our understanding of prayer, and thus of God, are far-reaching:

> "Do we observe that God really is ineffable, incomprehensible, that he can nowhere be pinned down as it were, that he does not occupy a particular place within the co-ordinated system of our concepts and our experiences ... that our prayer is never anything like a human confrontation of wills in which one finally gives way to the other? Do we observe that we possess God, so to speak, only in silent adoration of the ineffable, sacred, incomprehensible mystery?"[103]

In a similar vein, Rahner sees the various guidelines and practical helps to prayer as helps to an *experience of grace* (i.e., a spiritual experience) which is always present to us as an offer. Once more, we are here moving away from a merely entitative understanding of grace:

> "We do not merely go, so to speak, loaded with God's grace from the liturgy back into a godless world. We come from a world filled with God into a sphere in which what is otherwise covered up, what can be suppressed, what is not clear, what is often for that reason not radically accepted, reaches complete self-awareness."[104]

---

[102] Rahner, *Christians at the Crossroads*, 59, ("... als Ausdruck und Vollzug des einen Ganzen unserer Existenz," *Wagnis des Christen*, 80).

[103] Rahner, "Thesen zum Thema: Glaube und Gebet," *Chancen des Glaubens: Fragmente einer modernen Spiritualität*, 78 (*Opportunities for Faith*, 65).

[104] Rahner, "Thesen zum Thema: Glaube und Gebet," *Chancen des Glaubens: Fragmente einer modernen Spiritualität*, 85 (*Opportunities for Faith*, 71).

The truth behind this assertion is that God is everywhere with his grace; there is, thus, no separate sacral space apart from the world, exclusively reserved for the encounter with God.

The title of this section described prayer as surrender of the *heart*. The word "heart" is significant in Rahner's reflections on prayer because, for him, it is a primordial symbol (*Ursymbol*) of the centre of the human person.[105] In the context of prayer, the heart represents the place of our encounter with, and our surrender to, the mystery of God.[106] Prayer opens our hearts to the mystery of the human condition in that the acknowledgement of one's own worthlessness and nothingness is the prerequisite to discovering the presence of God in one's own despair and suffering.[107]

To conclude our section on Rahner's understanding of prayer, we will return to an idea we mentioned at the outset, namely, prayer as a fundamental act *(Grundakt)* of human existence. By "Grundakt," he means that prayer is not simply one human activity alongside numerous others, but that it is an act, an activity or deed ("Das Beten ist auch eine Tat"),[108] whereby the person embraces the whole of human existence. In a further step, Rahner maintains that such fundamental acts are prior to any subsequent reflection on them i.e., these acts belong on a more fundamental level to the human person than the words, language and concepts in which they are expressed. This is a

---

[105] Rahner, "Die Öffnung des Herzens," *Von der Not und dem Segen des Gebetes,* 7-25. See also Rahner's "'Behold this heart!': Preliminaries to a Theology of Devotion to the Sacred Heart," and "Some Theses for a Theology of Devotion to the Sacred Heart," *TI* 3: 321-52 (*ST* III: 379-418).

[106] "In diesem Gebet sagt der Mensch eigentlich nicht mehr etwas Bestimmtes und Begrenztes: eine Bitte an Gott, ein Bekenntnis seiner Schuld, ein rühmendes Bekenntnis von Gottes Eigenschaften. Er sagt sich selbst, *indem er sich Gott übergibt, sich an Ihn weg liebt, so wie der Mensch eben sich nur an Gott verlieren darf.*" Rahner, "Das Gebet der Liebe," *Von der Not und dem Segen des Gebetes,* 46 (italics mine).

[107] Rahner, "Die Öffnung des Herzens," *Von der Not und dem Segen des Gebetes,* 16-19, describes four 'steps' (omitted in the English translation) in the opening of the heart in prayer: "Das erste: er muß standhalten und sich ergeben ... das zweite, das du in deiner Verzweiflung tun sollst: merken, daß Er da ist, wissen, daß Er bei dir ist... und dann kommt das dritte und vierte von selbst. Dann kommt von selbst die Ruhe. Die Stille, die nicht mehr flieht. Das Vertrauen, das nicht mehr fürchtet. Die Sicherheit, die keine Versicherung mehr braucht."

[108] Rahner, "Das Beten ist auch eine Tat," *Wagnis des Christen,* 89-90.

central Rahnerian thesis on prayer: the completion of the act of prayer takes place *prior* to any attempt to express this in words. Thus, he describes prayer not so much as a "speaking", but in terms of "movement" *(Bewegung)*. In other words, he grounds the meaning of prayer not on the conceptual level ("auf der begrifflichen Ebene") but in the essential core *(Wesensmitte)* of the human person.[109] Our discussion of prayer once again reveals Rahner's basic conviction *(Grundüberzeugung)* that:

> "Kein Mensch kann das Ganze seines Lebens, seiner Grundentscheidung voll zu einer ausdrücklichen Aussage bringen. Er lebt immer aus mehr, als er sich selbst und anderen reflex sagen kann."[110]

The distinction above between prayer as a fundamental act of the person, and the second, conceptual level of expressing such an act in words, language, etc., reveals two aspects of prayer, which Rahner describes as "transcendental" *(transzendental)* and "categorial" *(kategorial)* respectively.[111] By "transcendental," he is referring to that a priori constitution of the human person which is always open to that which he calls "mystery." And, it is on the basis of this transcendental nature of the human person (i.e., one's absolute openness to God), that prayer as a dialogue can be intelligible. In prayer, we experience ourselves as the ones spoken to by God, and,

> "God's most original word to us in our free uniqueness is not a word arising momentarily and categorially in addition to or separate from other objects of experience within a wider area of our consciousness, but is we ourselves as integral, total entities and in our reference to the incomprehensible mystery we call God, the word of God which we ourselves are and which as such is spoken to us."[112]

---

[109] Fischer, "Wo der Mensch an das Geheimnis grenzt," 164. For further elucidation of how this "Wesensmitte" is related to the transcendental nature of the human person, see the first part of this section, and also the first part of Chapter Three.

[110] "Ein Brief von P. Karl Rahner," in Klaus Fischer, *Der Mensch als Geheimnis: Die Anthropologie Karl Rahners. Mit einem Brief von Karl Rahner* (Freiburg: Herder, 1974), 404. The quotation is from Rahner's letter to the author.

[111] Rahner, *FCF*, 31-35, 51-68 (*Grundkurs*, 42-46, 61-76). For a good analysis of the relationship between the transcendental nature of the human person and the experience of God, see Rahner, "Religious Feeling Inside and Outside the Church," *TI* 17: 228-42 (*ST* XII: 582-98).

[112] Rahner, "Is Prayer Dialogue with God?" *Christians at the Crossroads*, 66 (*Wagnis des Christen*, 91).

Thus when we (in the Spirit and by grace), experience ourselves as the ones spoken to by God, understand this as our true essence, and freely accept it in prayer, then our prayer is already a dialogue ("Zwiesprache") with God. Alongside this first transcendental aspect of prayer, Rahner refers to a second "categorial"[113] aspect, namely, the concrete, historical content of one's prayer. Influenced by the Ignatian *Exercises,* Rahner has in mind, here, a particular, categorial "object of choice" which may be understood as part of the dialogical relationship between the person and God within the broader framework outlined above.[114]

Later, we shall return to other aspects of Rahner's considerations on prayer, (e.g., charismatic prayer and the experience of the Spirit, the Ignatian dimension, etc.). Our discussion in this chapter is intended rather to serve as an *introduction* to some of the more significant themes in Rahner's spirituality.

d. Love of Neighbour as Love of God

Like prayer, love, according to Rahner, is not easily defined. It refers to that which a person becomes when they realize their unique essence;[115] it is something known only in its completion. If the prin-

---

[113] *Categorial* represents the other side of the transcendental nature of the human person, because one's transcendentality also has a history: "Der Ausdruck 'kategorial' meint also die konkrete, empirische, raum-zeitliche Wirklichkeit des Menschen, die Welt, an die wir normalerweise denken. Zur kategorialen Wirklichkeit gehört dann aber auch die Geschichte des Menschen und der Menscheit, so daß der Ausdruck 'kategorial' nicht nur das meint, was der Mensch in seiner Erfahrungswelt vorfindet, sondern auch das, was er selbst getan hat ..." Karl-Heinz Weger, *Karl Rahner: Eine Einführung in sein theologisches Denken* (Freiburg: Herder, 1978), 21. See also *FCF*, 170-75 (*Grundkurs*, 173-77).

[114] For a description of how a particular, categorial object of choice may be understood as spoken to us by God in the context of the Ignatian *Exercises*, see Rahner, "The Logic of Concrete Individual Knowledge in Ignatius Loyola," *The Dynamic Element in the Church*, 84-170. We shall discuss Rahner's appropriation of Ignatian spirituality in Chapter Four.

[115] "Sie (die Liebe) ist das Ganze des freien Vollzugs der menschlichen Existenz." Karl Rahner, *Wer ist dein Bruder?* (Freiburg: Herder, 1981), 14. In this book Rahner discusses the theme "die christliche Brüderlichkeit" which, in his view, is a synonym for "Nächstenliebe" (p. 19). He discusses, firstly, some *theological considerations* relevant to the theme, then describes how such Christian fellowship faces a completely *new situation* today, and, thirdly, draws some practical *consequences* for Christian living.

cipal Christian commandment is to love God with one's whole heart
(and the heart, as we have seen, represents the innermost centre of the
person), then it follows that this power to love without measure must,
in Rahner's view, reflect the basic structure of the human person.[116]
One can only speak of a "commandment" of love if one remembers
that this "law" does not command some *thing*, but asks of the person
to be him or herself, that is, to be open to "the possibility of love by
receiving God's love in which God does not give something else, but
Himself."[117] God is not presented here as an unmoved, impersonal It,
but as the "living" God, and all Christian activity of the human person is, for Rahner, essentially a response to God's call.[118] In the case
of the human person, this means that one remains dependent on God,
while realizing that God can never be integrated as an element into
one's understanding. This direct reference to God, however, is necessarily mediated through what Rahner terms "inner-worldly communication":

> "The transcendental message needs a categorial object, a support, as it
> were, in order not to lose itself in the void; it needs an inner-worldly
> Thou. The original relation to God is the love of neighbour. If one
> becomes oneself only through the love of God and must achieve this by
> a categorial action then, in the order of grace, the act of neighbourly
> love is the only categorial and original act in which one reaches the
> whole categorially given reality and thus experiences God directly, tran-
> scendentally and through grace."[119]

---

[116] This starting-point for our reflections is evident in both Rahner's spiritual and
in his more "scientific" writings. See, for example, "Das Gebet der Liebe," *Von der
Not und dem Segen des Gebetes*, 42-59, and also "The 'Commandment' of Love in
Relation to the Other Commandments," *TI* 5: 439-59 (*ST* V: 494-517).

[117] Rahner, *The Practice of Faith*, 112 (*Praxis des Glaubens*, 201). Moreover,
Rahner prefers the term "Brüderlichkeit" to "Nächstenliebe," because the former
term can be less easily misunderstood solely in terms of a factual achievement: "weil
dieses Wort weniger als das Wort Nächstenliebe als Forderung einer sachlichen Leistung mißverstanden werden kann." *Wer ist dein Bruder?*, 41. A similar treatment of
the theme, in the context of a discussion of the theology of freedom, can be found in
Karl Rahner, *Gnade als Freiheit: Kleine theologische Beiträge* (Freiburg: Herder,
1968), 42-46. [ET: *Grace in Freedom* (New York: Herder and Herder, 1969), 214-
21].

[118] See, for example, Rahner, "A Spirituality of Calling," *The Practice of Faith*,
184-87 (*Praxis des Glaubens*, 317-20).

[119] Rahner, *The Practice of Faith*, 112 (*Praxis des Glaubens*, 201).

Rahner also wishes to avoid some inevitable misunderstandings that arise in any discussion of love of God and love of neighbour. A first misunderstanding, already alluded to, occurs when the love of God is simply seen as the observance of one particular commandment among others. The love of God cannot be relegated to the status of one particular goal to be achieved alongside a plurality of others in human life.[120] It is not so much the content of an individual commandment, but forms rather the basis and goal of all commandments. Such love only really takes place where God is loved for His own sake, and not as part of human self-assertion and self-fulfilment.[121] So, Rahner is not speaking here of a particular achievement of the person, but describing the love of God in terms of a *surrender* that, for him, is at once both self-evident and incomprehensible.[122]

Neither, in Rahner's view, is the love of neighbour simply to be regarded as a test case for the love of God. The relationship between the love of God and neighbour is much closer — it is one of mutual conditioning:

> "The love of God unreflectedly but really and always intends God in supernatural transcendentality in the love of neighbour as such, and even the explicit love of God is still borne by that opening in trusting love to the whole of reality which takes place in the love of neighbour."[123]

[120] See Rahner, "Liebe," *SM* III: 234-52, esp. 247-52.

[121] For Rahner's accent on the love of God for God's own sake, see his article, "The Inexhaustible Transcendence of God and Our Concern for the Future," *TI* 20: 173-86 (*ST* XIV: 405-21).

[122] "Wenn auf der Kanzel die Liebe zu Gott als die Bedingung des Heiles gepriesen wird, dann ist nicht eine partikuläre Leistung des Menschen gemeint, sondern der eine totale Selbstvollzug des Menschen, der selbstverständlich und unbegreiflich zugleich ist …" Rahner, *Wer ist dein Bruder?,* 15-16. We are not suggesting here that Rahner's understanding of "Brüderlichkeit" ends up in a type of individualistic spirituality devoid of any political responsibility. On the political responsibility of the Christian, see his "Die gesellschaftliche Dimension der Brüderlichkeit," *Wer ist dein Bruder?,* 52-60.

[123] "Reflections on the Unity of the Love of Neighbour and the Love of God," *TI* 6: 247 (*ST* VI: 295). The immediate context for these reflections was a lecture given to Catholic social workers in Cologne in 1965. For a less technical version of this article entitled "The New, Single Precept of Love," see *Everyday Faith,* 104-117 (*Glaube, der die Erde liebt,* 85-95). Helpful secondary literature on this topic includes: Karl Neumann, *Der Praxisbezug der Theologie bei Karl Rahner,* Freiburger Theologische Studien 118 (Freiburg: Herder, 1980), 107-27; Ralf Miggelbrink,

Thirdly, this relationship of mutual conditioning, however, is not to be understood as a type of secular humanism — whereby the love of God is perceived as an old-fashioned word (ultimately dispensable) for the unselfish love of neighbour. Such love of neighbour, instead, for Rahner, already includes the love of God, since it is oriented towards God by its inescapably given transcendental horizon.[124] His conviction is that God is not one object of our love alongside other objects, but is rather the *horizon* of our loving:

> "God is always given as the subjectively and objectively all-bearing *ground (Grund)* of experience, a ground which is beyond this world; he is therefore given indirectly in a kind of boundary experience ("in einer Art Grenzerfahrung") as the origin and destination of an act which is objectively directed towards the world and which, therefore, is a loving communication with (or 'no' to) the Thou in the world. God is primarily and originally given in (or as) the transcendental, unclassified horizon of the knowing and acting intentionality of a person and not as an 'object' represented by an idea within this horizon."[125]

In *Wer ist dein Bruder?*, Rahner does not go into the detail of this argument. He does, however, provide a more explicit treatment in an earlier article (from which the citation above is taken) entitled: "Reflections on the Unity of the Love of Neighbour and the Love of God" (1965). The intention here is similar, i.e., to inquire into charity (i.e., genuine love of neighbour, including acts of charity) and to reflect on its unity with the love of God. After a brief statement of the urgency of this question, and a survey of the declarations of scripture

---

Ekstatische Gottesliebe im tätigen Weltbezug. Der Beitrag Karl Rahners zur zeitgenössischen Gotteslehre, Münsteraner Theologische Abhandlungen (Altenberge: Telos Verlag, 1989), 185-201; and Andrea Tafferner, *Gottes- und Nächstenliebe in der deutschsprachigen Theologie des 20. Jahrhunderts*, Innsbrucker theologische Studien 37 (Innsbruck/Wien: Tyrolia, 1992), 200-229.

[124] God is the one who provides the human person with their ultimate meaning and dignity — by simultaneously residing at their most innermost centre, while infinitely transcending the human person: "Gott ist nicht der Konkurrent des Menschen, sondern der, der den Menschen erst verständlich macht, ihm gerade seine letzte radikale Würde und Bedeutung gibt, indem er gleichzeitig im Menschen zuinnerst ist und ihn unendlich überragt. *Die Ek-sistenz in Gott hinein ist die innerlichste Innerlichkeit des Menschen.*" Rahner, *Wer ist dein Bruder?*, 18 (italics mine).

[125] Rahner, "Reflections on the Unity of the Love of Neighbour and the Love of God," *TI* 6: 245 (*ST* VI: 292-93).

on the topic, Rahner focuses on the teaching from tradition, in particular the thesis of scholastic theology:

> "that the specific Christian love of neighbour is both in potency and in
> act a moment of the infused supernatural theological virtue of *caritas*
> by which we love God in his Spirit for his own sake and in direct com-
> munity with him."[126]

The implication Rahner draws from this is that the love of neighbour
is not merely the preparation or fruit of the love of God, but is *itself*
an act of love of God, that is to say, it is an act within the total believing and hoping surrender (*Übergabe*) of the person to God. In other
words, for Rahner, all inter-human love is also "caritas" (i.e., also
love of God), since it is oriented towards God by its transcendental
horizon — itself given gratuitously by the ever-present grace of
God.[127] Rahner thus speaks of "the anonymous 'Christianity'[128] of
every positively moral activity," and concludes:

> "... wherever a person posits a positively moral act in the full exercise
> of his or her free self-disposal, this act is a positive supernatural salvific
> act in the actual economy of salvation ... This is so because God in
> virtue of his universal salvific will offers everyone his supernaturally
> divinising grace and thus elevates the positively moral act of a person ...

---

[126] Rahner, "Reflections on the Unity of the Love of Neighbour and the Love of
God," *TI* 6: 236 (*ST* VI: 282). Rahner discusses, elsewhere, the relation between love
and the other virtues and concludes: "There is only one 'virtue' which asks the person for him or herself — really him or herself wholly and completely — and this is
the virtue of love and it alone; all other virtues only 'participate' in this nature of the
one love, in so far as they are destined, even though out of their own nature itself, to
be more than just themselves." Rahner, "The 'Commandment' of Love in Relation to
the Other Commandments," *TI* 5: 451 (*ST* V: 508).

[127] The gratuity of God's grace is a theme found even in Rahner's earliest spiritual
reflections. See his "Das Gebet der Liebe," *Von der Not und dem Segen des Gebetes*,
54: "Wer ehrlich Gott lieben will, der liebt Ihn schon, er könnte es ja nicht wollen,
hätte nicht schon Gottes Gnade an das Herz des Menschen gerührt und schon Besitz
genommen von der letzten Liebessehnsucht."

[128] The term "anonymous Christianity" (*anonyme Christlichkeit*) is a highly
controversial one. Some of Rahner's early reflections on the topic include: "The
Christian Among Unbelieving Relations," *TI* 3: 355-72 (*ST* III: 419-39); "Anonymous Christians," *TI* 6: 390-99; and "Atheism and Implicit Christianity," *TI* 9: 145-
64. For an excellent survey of the origins of this theory in Rahner, see Nikolaus
Schwerdtfeger, "Der 'anonyme Christ' in der Theologie Karl Rahners," *Theologie
aus Erfahrung der Gnade: Annäherungen an Karl Rahner*, eds. Mariano Delgado and
Matthias-Lutz Bachmann (Berlin: Morus Verlag, 1994), 72-94.

Wherever there is an absolutely moral commitment of a positive kind in the world and within the present economy of salvation, there takes place also ... an act of divinising grace, and thus *caritas* is exercised in this."[129]

Rahner's intention, moreover, is to show how the love of neighbour has a special, basic, all-embracing position within the whole of morality:

"The act of personal love for another is the all-embracing basic act of a person which gives meaning, direction and measure to everything else. If this is correct, then the essential *a priori* openness to the other human being which must be undertaken freely belongs as such to the *a priori* and most basic constitution of a person and is an essential inner moment of one's (knowing and willing) transcendentality."[130]

And this *a priori* basic constitution is experienced in the daily concrete encounters with one's neighbour. Love of neighbour is, therefore, a manifestation of the individual's wholeness and essence. We have previously referred to Rahner's understanding of the transcendent dimension of the human person. Here, he focuses on how the love of God can only be achieved by a *categorial* action — the transcendental intentionality needs a categorial object — and the act of neighbourly love is this categorial act. Why does such categorial activity represent the fulfilment of the spiritual and transcendental nature of the human person? Because the encounter with the world — and the individual encounters the world primarily as an environment of persons — is the medium of the original, unobjectified experience of God. Rahner's point is that the person's transcendentally original *a priori* experience of his or her reference to God can

---

[129] Rahner, "Reflections on the Unity of the Love of Neighbour and the Love of God," *TI* 6: 239 (*ST* VI: 285-86). Once again, this quote highlights how Rahner's reflections on the unity of love of God and neighbour merge with his understanding of *grace*. Our love of neighbour "as a response to God's love is sustained by God's love itself, i.e. a love made possible by God's self-communication. This means nothing other, however, than that this our love of God has its real ontological basis in God's love for us, i.e. in His communication of Himself in grace." Rahner, "The 'Commandment' of Love in Relation to the Other Commandments," *TI* 5: 456 (*ST* V: 515).

[130] Rahner, "Reflections on the Unity of the Love of Neighbour and the Love of God," *TI* 6: 241 (*ST* VI: 288).

only be achieved in a going-out into the world, which, understood as the world of persons, is primarily the people with whom one lives. In short, our original experience of God is always given in a "worldly" experience.[131] Our turning towards the people we live with allows us, in Rahner's words, to "experience unreflectedly the transcendental conditions of this act (i.e. the transcendental reference to God and the transcendental openness to the human Thou)."[132]

The above considerations indicate that the love of one's neighbour is not simply a commandment to be obeyed, but represents the complete actualization of Christian existence. As the complete self-realization of the person, this love is not something that we can "have," but which can only be experienced in the movement of an unconditional surrender of oneself to the unknown, namely, to God as the ground and mysterious partner of this love. This love, in an interpersonal encounter, implies the actualization of a spiritual existence which:

> "possesses an absolute depth and an element which is taken up into the 'eternal life' between God and the human person. And ultimately this life always transcends this immediate, corporeal encounter in time and space."[133]

Hence, such love is not confined within the boundaries of an immediate, simply corporeal, experience. Only in transcending these boundaries in faith and hope, does such love of neighbour reach fulfilment.

A final aspect of Rahner's reflections will conclude our section. It concerns the place of *Jesus* within the above framework. If, as we have seen, love for another person is the mediation of the love of God (and forms an inseparable unity with it), then this love can be directed to Jesus. For Rahner, such love represents:

> "the absolute instance of a love in which love for another human person and love for God find their most radical unity and mediate each other mutually. Jesus is the most concrete absolute, and therefore it is in love for him that love reaches the most absolute concreteness ..."[134]

---

[131] In crude form, this is the basic conclusion of Rahner's *Spirit in the World*, 406-408 (*Geist in Welt*, 404-407). See also his "Science as a 'Confession'?" *TI* 3: 385-400 (*ST* III: 455-72).

[132] Rahner, "Reflections on the Unity of the Love of Neighbour and the Love of God," *TI* 6: 246 (*ST* VI: 294).

[133] *FCF*, 309-10 (*Grundkurs*, 302).

[134] *FCF*, 310 (*Grundkurs*, 302).

Jesus is, thus, the neighbour par excellence, and Rahner, in fact, affirms the centrality and significance of a personal relationship with him. Such a relationship only occurs when one takes the risk of encounter ("das Wagnis der Begegnung"), and tries to love Jesus in a really personal way.[135] Every such encounter is a call emerging out of one's concrete life to a discipleship — which is nothing other that a participation in the mystery of the life, death, and resurrection of Jesus. It is only when Jesus is accepted and loved in himself, over and above one's knowledge about him (or one's idea of Christ), that a true relationship, the relationship of an absolute self-abandonment can begin.

These considerations form the starting-point of what Rahner refers to as an *existentiell* Christology, i.e., to that process of personal appropriation and actualization of a Christian's personal relationship to Jesus Christ, something which can also be spoken of in abstraction without such a personal realization. Such an appropriation is important because the danger always exists of turning the relationship with Christ into the cult of an abstract Christ-idea. In Rahner's view, however, one can love Jesus in a true, genuine and immediate love (bearing in mind that it is Jesus who seizes the initiative, and through grace — the divine gift of love of God and Jesus — makes this love of him possible for us).[136] It is not possible to adequately treat of

---

[135] We are following here Rahner's reflections on this topic in *Grundkurs*, 301-303. Rahner is drawing attention "to the fact that the Christian life is not merely about satisfying universal norms which are proclaimed by the official church. Rather, in these norms and beyond them it is the always unique call of God which is mediated in a concrete and loving encounter with Jesus in a mysticism of love." *FCF*, 311. Rahner has dealt with the theme of the love of Jesus more particularly in *Was heißt Jesus lieben?* (Freiburg: Herder, 1982), 14-28 (*The Practice of Faith*, 114-20), where he describes how "every trusting, loving relationship to another human being has an uncancellable 'plus' on the resolution-and-decision side of the balance sheet — as over against the reflective side, the side that tallies up the justifiability and reasonableness of such risk and venture ... But always there remains that 'plus' on the side of the freedom to take a risk — on the side of love, precisely — in a truly Christian relationship to Jesus" (p. 115).

[136] See *Was heißt Jesus lieben?* 25-27, where Rahner speaks of "der Mut Jesus um den Hals zu fallen," ("the courage to throw one's arms round Jesus"). At the risk of sounding too pietistic, Rahner is advocating a love of Jesus "that transcends space and time, in virtue of the nature of love in general and by the power of the Holy Spirit of God" (*The Practice of Faith*, 120). This relationship of discipleship has both a

Rahner's transcendental Christology here. Our concern rather is to reiterate his claim that any understanding of the dogma about Christ only arises "subsequent to and because of a historical encounter with Jesus as the Christ."[137] The starting-point for Rahner's Christology is, therefore, the actual faith relationship between a believing Christian and Jesus Christ.

Our considerations thus far have sought to show that no spatial, cultural or temporal distance between Jesus and us need present an insuperable obstacle to loving the concrete, historical person that Jesus is. Further, this relationship of love, we have seen, in no way constricts or diminishes our love of neighbour. Instead, drawing on Mt 25:40, Rahner sees the love of neighbour as the prerequisite of our love for Jesus.[138] Conversely, the love for neighbour can and should grow through a love for Jesus, "for it is only in a loving relationship with Jesus that we conceive the possibilities of love for neighbour that otherwise we should simply not hold to be feasible, but which present themselves nonetheless wherever we take up our neighbour in our love of Jesus because he or she is Jesus' brother or sister."[139] Finally, while this immediate love for Jesus is not present from the beginning of life, it can grow and deepen through patience, prayer, and an ever renewed immersion in Scripture. As a gift of God's Spirit, it cannot be grasped or commandeered, but "we may always know that the very aspiration to such love is already its beginning, and that we have a promise of its fulfilment."[140]

---

mystical and a societal component. In a previous section, we have discussed the mystical component, and in Chapter Five we will dwell on the political component of Rahner's understanding of spirituality.

[137] *FCF*, 203 (*Grundkurs*, 203).

[138] For Rahner, there is an intimate and reciprocal relationship between love and faith. Authentic faith implies an action, an activity, which in this case is the love of neighbour: "der *volle* Glaube an Christus [kann] gar nichts anderes als die Tat, die Ihm getan wird: Diese ist die Tat der Liebe am Nächsten, und umgekehrt... . Wenn wir so den Text [Mt 25: 31-46] lesen, dann sagt er uns: Wenn du an Jesus glauben, also ihm begegnen, deine Tat ihn erreichen lassen willst, dann triffst du ihn im Nächsten, den du wahrhaft liebst *in der Tat unsentimentaler Alltäglichkeit*." Rahner, *Ich glaube an Jesus Christus*, 27, 28. (Italics mine).

[139] *Was heißt Jesus lieben?* 28, "... wo der Nächste vom einem in die Liebe Jesu aufgenommen wird, weil er Jesu Bruder oder Schwester ist."

[140] *Was heißt Jesus lieben?* 28 (*The Practice of Faith*, 120).

The preceding reflections conclude our initial introduction to some of the key themes underlying Rahner's understanding of spirituality. Moreover, it is becoming clear that Rahner's concern is to overcome the division or compartmentalizing of faith and everyday life by developing a "spirituality of the everyday" (eine *Alltagsspiritualität*).[141] We have seen in this section that, for Rahner, God is not an object of love next to other objects, and that, therefore, the love of neighbour is not in conflict or in competition with the love of God: they form one love. We will continue our exploration of how these themes are operative in Rahner's spirituality in Chapter Three — which is a more specific and detailed examination of the *experiential* dimension of his spirituality. Before that, however, we will now focus more explicitly on what Rahner means by the term "spirituality," and how he links this to his understanding of theology. We then conclude by asking to what extent our definition of spirituality in Chapter One coincides with Rahner's understanding and use of this term.

3. Towards a Definition of Spirituality in Rahner

a. The Link between Theology and Spirituality

In the Preface to his *Foundations of Christian Faith*, Rahner states his intention to give an intellectually honest justification of Christian faith, and to do this on, what he calls, a first level of reflection (*erste Reflexionsstufe*).[142] What does this term mean, and how is it related to

---

[141] Elmar Klinger, *Das absolute Geheimnis im Alltag entdecken: Zur spirituellen Theologie Karl Rahners* (Würzburg: Echter Verlag, 1994), 37. Rahner shows how even negative everyday experiences can become prayer: "Wie wird der Alltag selbst zum Gebet? Durch Selbstlosigkeit und Liebe. Ach, wenn wir willige und verständige Schüler wären, wir könnten für den inneren und geistlichen Menschen keinen besseren Lehrmeister haben als den Alltag! Die langen, gleichen Stunden, die Monotonie der Pflicht, die Arbeit, die jedermann selbstverständlich findet, das lange und bittere Mühen, für das niemand dankt, ..." Rahner, "Gebet im Alltag," *Von der Not und dem Segen des Gebetes*, 72.

[142] *FCF*, xi-xii (*Grundkurs*, 6), "... eine Rechtfertigung des christlichen Glaubens in intellektueller Redlichkeit ... eben auf der Ebene, die wir die 'erste Reflexionsstufe' genannt haben." See also Rahner's, *Zur Reform des Theologiestudiums*, Quaestiones Disputatae 41 (Freiburg; Herder, 1969), 64 (n. 49), where he attributes the term

Rahner's writings on spirituality? It was in the immediate aftermath of Vatican II that the term first appeared in Rahner's writings. The context was the urgent task and duty to initiate a reform of theological study in the light of the Council. Rahner's reflections on this topic appeared in 1969 under the title *Zur Reform des Theologiestudiums*.[143] His aim here was to stimulate discussion on the development of a new concept of theological study, based on the directions given in the Council's Decree on the Training of Priests: *Optatam Totius*.[144] This decree envisaged a type of introductory course, of appropriate duration, whereby:

> "the mystery of salvation (should) be presented in such a way that the students may understand the meaning, arrangement and pastoral aim of ecclesiastical studies, and may be helped at the same time to make faith the foundation and inner principle of their entire lives."[145]

Rahner's contribution to this "cursus introductorius in mysterium Christi" is to develop a scientific-theoretical basis for such a "Grundkurs" or "Einführungskurs."[146] He draws attention to the Council's emphasis on the necessary co-ordination of philosophy and theology in order to reveal "to the minds of the students with ever increasing clarity the Mystery of Christ, which affects the whole course of human history, (and which) exercises an unceasing influence on the Church."[147] In the light of this, Rahner saw his task as that of devel-

---

"erste Reflexionsstufe" to Gabriel Marcel, *Geheimnis des Seins* (Wien, 1952), 112-115, and adds with regard to the explanation of the term: "Indem nämlich hier zum einen nicht so sehr nach den 'historischen' Einzelinhalten des Glaubens gefragt wird, sondern eher nach den (transzendentalen) Bedingungen des möglichen Glaubensvollzugs hinsichtlich eines bestimmten Inhalts, muß auf dieser ersten Reflexionsstufe (eine sehr handfeste) theologische Arbeit, und zwar im strengsten Sinne des Wortes geleistet werden."

[143] Karl Rahner, *Zur Reform des Theologiestudiums*, esp. 51-98.

[144] See *Optatam Totius*, esp. nn. 13-18, which concern the revision of ecclesiastical studies. See *Vatican Council II: The Conciliar and Post Conciliar Documents,* ed. Austin Flannery, O.P., new rev. ed., vol. 1, Vatican Collection Series (Dublin: Dominican Publications, E. J. Dwyer, 1992), 717-21.

[145] *Optatam Totius*, n.14.

[146] This contribution later found a more developed and systematic expression in his *Grundkurs des Glaubens*, (1976) which has as its sub-title: *Einführung in den Begriff des Christentums*. For a personal account of the purpose and content of this work along with a frank admission of some of its limitations, see Rahner, "Foundations of Christian Faith," *TI* 19: 3-15 (*ST* XIV: 48-62).

[147] *Optatam Totius*, n. 14.

oping a scientific basis on which to ground the *inner unity* of all the theological disciplines.[148] Previous attempts at building such a unity in the nineteenth century failed, according to Rahner, because they provided only a superficial overview of the content of the distinct theological disciplines.[149] Neither, according to Rahner, should the *Grundkurs* proposed by the Council be restricted to a pious introduction to theology aimed solely at religious edification.

Yet the problem (in the context of our discussion of the proposed introductory course in theology) of the relationship between spirituality and theology persists. Rahner is aware of this. On the one hand, he sees such an introductory course in theology as being especially concerned with a *personal decision to believe*. On the other hand, he situates this introduction within the framework of intellectual reflection, with all the rigorous thinking that such reflection demands of the student. Ultimately, the question that Rahner is grappling with in this introductory course is: "What is a Christian, and why or how can one live this Christian existence today with intellectual honesty?"[150] And it is here that Rahner makes his distinction between a first and a second level of reflection. The *first level of reflection* is an attempt to give an intellectual justification for faith (*eine Glaubensbegründung*), where faith gives an account of itself. This level is distinguished from the *second* (subsequent) level of reflection,

---

[148] Commenting on the relevant sections of *Optatam Totius*, (nn. 14-15), Rahner states: "Jedenfalls aber wird hier vorausgesetzt, daß das ganze Studium unserer Theologen einen *einheitlichen Sinn und Aufbau* hat, daß es nicht Philosophie und Theologie als zwei völlig unverbundene Größen neben- oder hintereinander gibt, sondern das ganze Studium auf *ein Ziel* hin angelegt ist." Rahner, *Zur Reform des Theologiestudiums*, 54. Rahner, elsewhere, (*Herausforderung des Christen. Meditationen — Reflexionen — Interviews*, 128-29) makes a similar reference to the need for a "universalistische Theologie," whose method, at least indirectly, would point towards the unity of theology (without of course undermining the individual theological disciplines). While Rahner concedes that he never explicitly worked out such a method, it is an underlying reason for his pursuit of a transcendental theological anthropology. This anthropology, as we will see in the following chapter, stresses the "reference" (*Verwiesenheit*) of the human person towards the absolute mystery of God.

[149] See Rahner, *Zur Reform des Theologiestudiums*, 56 (and n. 42), where he refers to the development of the "theological encyclopedias" in German universities.

[150] *FCF*, 2 ("Was ist ein Christ, und warum kann man dieses Christsein in einer intellektuellen Redlichkeit heute vollziehen?" *Grundkurs*,14).

"where the pluralistic theological sciences, each in its own area and each with its own specific method, gives an account of themselves in a way which for the whole of the faith is inaccessible to all of us today, and all the more so to beginners in theology."[151]

Rahner offers a number of reasons for the necessity and urgency of such an introductory course in theology on a first level of reflection. Firstly, the theological student of today is no longer supported by a homogeneous religious environment. The practice and presence of Christianity is not something that can simply be taken for granted. Secondly, Rahner points to a crisis in the situation of faith today, and theological students are not immune from the effects of this. In order to overcome such a crisis, a "foundational course" is required, which is aimed at an intellectually honest affirmation of the Christian faith.[152] It must be possible, he argues, to help the beginner in theology with such an affirmation. Rahner does not think the individual theological disciplines can accomplish this by themselves, because they have become too splintered, fragmented, and specialized.[153] The challenge is therefore to reconcile intellectual honesty with Christian faith. At first sight, it seems that intellectual honesty has to do with maintaining a sceptical reserve, devoid of any personal self-commitment, in a position of dispassionate neutrality. However, for Rahner,

---

[151] *FCF*, 9 (Grundkurs, 21).

[152] "Aus diesem Dilemma (und hier liegt die Grundschwierigkeit für das Selbstverständnis heutiger Theologie überhaupt [gibt es sie überhaupt als solche?]) kommt man nur heraus, wenn der Theologe *selber* zurück zur Sache findet und in einem 'Sich-absetzen' (Reflektieren) vom (über den) Gegenstand dem zuwendet, was dieser *in sich* eigentlich *bedeutet*." Rahner, *Zur Reform des Theologiestudiums*, 58 (n. 42).

[153] Christian faith today, Rahner argues, is in a state of "gnoseological concupiscence." By this he means that it has become impossible for a Christian or for a theologian to order his or her knowledge into a more or less well-structured system (as was the case in the 16th and 17th centuries, for example): "Our minds are fed with disparate insights and pieces of information from a great range of sources of knowledge and these do not admit any longer of a positive and complete ordering into a coherent whole." Rahner, "The Foundation of Belief Today," *TI* 16: 6 (*ST* XII: 21). Rahner's response to this situation is to concentrate on the innermost kernel of faith, which involves an "ultimate trust in the complete and all-embracing meaning of human existence ... (and) reaches out finally to what we call God." *TI* 16: 13-14 (*ST* XII: 29-30). This "Christentum von innen heraus" (as opposed to "eine Indoktrination von außen") is a consistent Rahnerian emphasis and is intimately bound up with his understanding of mystagogy. See *Karl Rahner im Gespräch* 2: 69-70, and our own further discussion of this theme in Chapter Four.

intellectual honesty is not at all like this. In fact, any attempt on the part of someone to live without self-commitment, to remain in the dimension of "brute fact," and, in this sense, to remain "neutral" is *itself* a decision:

> "There is no such thing as remaining poised in some dimension which is *prior* to decision. The attempt to remain neutral, therefore, is in practice only the refusal to bring one's powers of speculative thought to bear upon the decisions entailed willy nilly in the fact of living one's life at all. For in this there is one decision at least which we must arrive at: whether life is to be regarded as absurd or as filled with ineffable and mysterious meaning."[154]

Likewise, faith involves the "taking of sides," i.e., a decision, whereby "the ultimate meaning of existence is accepted and embraced as God's word to us."[155] Such faith is courageous when the decision is made even though we may feel weighed down by uncertainty, darkness and danger. While Rahner is not downplaying the intellectual element in faith, he is highlighting, what he calls, the "existential difference" between our lived experience and our theoretical evaluation of such experience:

> "The intellectual life of the human person is always, fundamentally and inevitably designed in such a way that a perceptible existential difference prevails between that which is implied in the very fact of living and that which is the outcome of scientific speculation upon one's life. One cannot shape one's existence solely and exclusively on the basis of factors which one has made one's own by a process of scientific investigation, and which one has 'proved' to oneself in *this particular* manner."[156]

The second reason for such an introductory course follows from the above, and relates to the *pluralism* in contemporary theology and philosophy. Each theological discipline, it seems, is treating an enormous amount of material with its own particular methodology, and fre-

---

[154] Rahner, "Intellectual Honesty and Christian Faith," *TI* 7: 49 (*ST* VII: 56).

[155] Such a decision is prior to any theorizing on our part, i.e., it is not the result of a process of speculative reasoning. "Intellectual Honesty and Christian Faith," *TI* 7: 56-57 (*ST* VII: 62). Rahner also describes faith as a decision of hopeful courage, which is "nothing other than the positive and unconditional acceptance of one's own existence as meaningful and open to a final fulfilment, which we call God." Rahner and Weger, *Our Christian Faith: Answers for the Future*, 25. See also his "Faith as Courage," *TI* 18: 211-25 (*ST* XIII: 252-68).

[156] Rahner, "Intellectual Honesty and Christian Faith," *TI* 7: 53 (*ST* VII: 59-60).

quently without much reference to other theological disciplines. Rahner acknowledges this pluralistic situation, which he characterizes as "interdisciplinary fragmentation."[157] Nonetheless, he admits that such a situation renders a scientific theology very difficult, because theology itself has developed into a vast number of individual sciences.

Rahner's conception of an introductory course in theology on a first level of reflection is not to be seen as unscientific because it "merely" offers the student a *basic* understanding of the Christian faith. His plan is also to offer a *foundation* for such an understanding. It is not necessary to be able to work one's way through the pluralism of the theological disciplines in order to develop an initial intellectual justification of the Christian faith. Therefore, Rahner's does not only focus on the contents, methods and aims of the individual theological disciplines, but primarily on the believing subject him or herself. In other words, he is enquiring into the *a priori* conditions in the believer which enable him or her to both hear a possible revelation from God, and to respond in faith.[158] Traditional fundamental theology failed to do this, because it attempted instead to prove, in a rather formal way, the facticity of divine revelation. Very often, such a theology remained unfruitful for the life of faith of the believer, who did not regard the facticity of revelation as something absolutely clear and certain. Thus, the contemporary demand is for fundamental theology "to try to bridge the gap ... between the grounds of credibility of Christian revelation and the actual decision to believe."[159]

---

[157] *FCF*, 8 (*Grundkurs*, 19). On the question of pluralism in theology, see Rahner, "Pluralism in Theology and the Unity of the Creed," *TI* 11: 3-23 (*ST* IX: 11-33); and "Possible Courses for the Theology of the Future," *TI* 13: 32-60 (*ST* X: 41-69).

[158] The foundational course, according to Rahner, must reflect firstly upon the human person as the universal question which he or she is for him or herself. "This question, which the person *is* and not only *has*, must be regarded as the condition which makes hearing the Christian answer possible *Secondly*, the transcendental and the historical conditions which make revelation possible must be reflected upon in the manner and within the limits which are possible on the first level of reflection, so that the point of mediation between the question and answer, between philosophy and theology will be seen. *Thirdly* and finally, we must reflect upon the fundamental assertion of Christianity as the answer to the question which the human person is, and hence we must do theology." *FCF*, 11 (*Grundkurs*, 22-23).

[159] Rahner, "Reflections on a New Task for Fundamental Theology," *TI* 16: 164 (*ST* XII: 208).

There is, it seems, a *tension* present in Rahner's thought here, a tension which is reflected in both his theological and more spiritual writings. On the one hand, he is attempting an introduction to the idea or concept (*Begriff*) of Christianity on a first level of reflection. This introduction is not to be restricted to a mystagogical initiation into Christianity, which is a concern of Rahner's more spiritual writings.[160] However, on the other hand, a neat distinction between Rahner's spiritual and theological writings is, for the most part, artificial.[161] There is always a tension, he concedes, between our theological concepts and our attempts to relate these concepts back to an original experience. This tension, moreover, indicates Rahner's basic conviction (*Grundüberzeugung*) that theological concepts are, at best, a rather limited expression of what has already been experienced and lived through, more originally, in the depths of one's existence.[162] Further, Rahner never considered his more strictly "theological" writings (e.g., in the *Schriften*) as "scientific" in the strict sense of the term — even these writings were to have an "edifying" purpose ("eine 'erbauliche' Absicht").[163]

---

[160] See, "Thesen zum Thema: Glaube und Gebet," *Chancen des Glaubens*, 65-74. Yet, in Rahner's conception of the basic formation of theology students, such a "spiritual mystagogy" seems unavoidable: "Was die Struktur der Grundausbildung der Theologen angeht, so könnte man ja auf das zurückgreifen, ... daß es einen, wenn auch reflex in gewissem Sinne dilettantischen theologischen Universalismus geben muß, der alle fachtheologische Arbeit trägt und der dem jungen Theologen als Nächstes einmal vermittelt werden muß. Das ist dann natürlich beinahe zwangsläufig auch so etwas wie *eine spirituelle Mystagogie* in einen echten, schon bis zu einem gewissen Grad reflektierten, aber nicht fachwissenschaftlich reflektierten Grundvollzug des eigenen Glaubens." Rahner, "Gnade als Mitte menschlicher Existenz. Ein Gespräch mit und über Karl Rahner aus Anlaß seines 70 Geburtstages," in *Herausforderung des Christen: Meditationen — Reflexionen — Interviews* (Freiburg: Herder, 1975), 144 (italics mine). Such a mystagogy is necessary because: "Heute aber kommen Menschen in die Theologie, die noch suchen, was eigentlich Christentum ist, die vielleicht sogar höchste Bedenken haben, ob man überhaupt beten kann, was es eigentlich heißen soll ein personales Verhältnis zu Jesus haben" (p. 146). The concept of mystagogy is explored in more detail in Chapter Four.

[161] Rahner's comment on the underlying intention of the different essays in volume 16 of *Investigations* indicate his intention "to show how religious experiences of a spiritual or mystical kind can overflow and be transposed into the idiom of theological reflection. In this way the rift, all too common even today, between lived piety and abstract theology may be bridged." *TI* 16: 72, n. 12 (*ST* XII: 100, n. 12).

[162] *FCF*, 17 (*Grundkurs*, 28).

[163] "Brief von P. Karl Rahner," in Fischer, *Der Mensch als Geheimnis*, 402.

What is at issue here is that all theological reflection begins and ends in the holy mystery of God. It involves a being led back into mystery ("Reductio in Mysterium").[164] A theology that does not acknowledge this dimension of mystery, the *reductio in mysterium* (or more precisely, a "reductio in mysterium Dei"[165] of theological propositions, has, in his view, failed in its true mission. It has failed to recognize the analogical nature of such theological propositions, and remained stuck on the conceptual level.[166] It is here that the borders between Rahner's spiritual and more strictly theological writings become rather fluid.[167] For even in his spiritual writings, Rahner is theologizing on a first level of reflection — reflecting, as he describes

[164] This idea is further developed by Rahner in his third lecture on "Reflections on Methodology in Theology," *TI* 11: 101-114 (*ST* IX: 113-26). See also his article "Theologia crucis," *LThK* 10: 61.

[165] On this, see Rahner's "The Concept of Mystery in Catholic Theology," esp. the "Third Lecture," *TI* 4: 60-73 (*ST* IV: 82-99), and "The Hiddenness of God," *TI* 16: 227-43 (*ST* XII: 285-305).

In his description of some of the fundamental characteristics of Rahner's theology, Karl Lehmann gives the "spiritual element" pride of place, seeing in this the living source or ground for the dynamism of Rahner's theology: "An erster Stelle steht das spirituelle Element ... In der Herzmitte dieser Spiritualität lebt eine große Leidenschaft für die Unermeßlichkeit und Unbegreiflichkeit dessen, was wir 'Gott' nennen. Aus diesem stets lebendigen Quellgrund schöpft Rahners Theologie immer wieder ihre ganze Dynamik, zerbricht sie immer wieder die Krusten aller theologischen Begriffe und findet stets wieder zurück in eine sie verjüngende Unerschöpflichkeit des Denkens, der Meditation, der spirituellen und theologischen Rede." Karl Lehmann, "Theologie aus der Leidenschaft des Glauben: Gedanken zum Tod von Karl Rahner," *Stimmen der Zeit* 202 (1984): 294.

[166] On the occasion of his eightieth birthday, Rahner gave a lecture to the Catholic Academy of the archdiocese of Freiburg (11/12 February, 1984) entitled "Erfahrungen eines katholischen Theologen," in which he highlights once more the analogical nature of all theological language ("die Analogheit aller theologischen Aussagen"). *Karl Rahner in Erinnerung*, ed. Albert Raffelt, Freiburger Akademieschriften, 8 (Düsseldorf: Patmos, 1994), 134-148. See also Rahner's, "What is a Dogmatic Statement?" *TI* 5: 42-66 (*ST* V: 54-81).

[167] "Der oben angesprochene Unterschied zwischen den von anderen mir zuerkannten 'wissenschaftlichen' Arbeiten und den 'erbaulichen', 'spirituellen' ist dann sehr relativ, zweitrangig und hat gänzlich fließende Übergänge. Auch in den erbaulichen Schriften suche ich zu denken, weil ich sonst mich und andere nicht wirklich (im biblischen Sinn) heute 'erbauen' kann." "Brief von P. Karl Rahner," *Der Mensch als Geheimnis*, 402. For Rahner's reluctance to have his writings classified as works of theological scholarship, see "Some Clarifying Remarks About My Own Work," *TI* 17: 243-48 (*ST* XII: 599-604). His preference is to describe his writings as "the work of a dilettante" (p. 246).

it, on Christian faith considered as a whole ("das Ganze des Christ-seins").[168] We have already seen in our discussion of prayer, in the previous section, how Rahner understands this not simply as a partic-ular exercise, but as a *Grundakt,* and as an explicitation of the rela-tionship of the whole person to God.

Fundamental acts of human existence like prayer and trust, hope and love are relevant to our discussion here. As examples of a basic realization ("Grundvollzug") of human existence, such acts are *prior* to our reflection on them. These acts belong more fundamentally to the human person than do any thoughts, concepts, words, etc., which we might use to try to understand, or to express what has taken place. In the example of prayer, we find that the distinction between the two levels of reflection reflects this twofold movement in his theology. On the second level of reflection, prayer can be discussed and explained on a more conceptual level with regard to its objective form, i.e., with regard to its contents, aims, structure, etc. The first level of reflection, on the other hand, concerns itself with a consider-ation of the more basic movement (*Grundbewegung*) that constitutes the act of prayer itself, and which has its roots in that act of trust on the part of the person towards the mystery we call God.[169]

It might be added here that the two levels we have been discussing are not to be separated. In fact they are linked:

> "The believer recognizes that the logical and the existential factors in his awareness constitute a unity, and he cannot and will not schizo-phrenically divide them one from another ... The intellectual life of the human person is always, fundamentally and inevitably designed in such a way that a perceptible existential difference prevails between that which is implied in the very fact of living and that which is the outcome of scientific speculation upon one's life."[170]

---

[168] Rahner, "Intellectual Honesty and Christian Faith," *TI* 7: 58-60 (*ST* VII: 59-60).

[169] "Nachdenken über das Gebet auf der ersten Reflexionsstufe aber ist dann gegeben, wenn die Reflexion sich gleichsam nochmals zurückwendet auf die allen objektivierten Gehalt tragende Grundbewegung des Betens selbst und deren Ursprung im Wagnis des Vertrauens und der Hingabe des Beters an jenes Geheimnis, das christlich Gott, ja 'Vater' heißt." Fischer, "Wo der Mensch an das Geheimnis grenzt," *Zeitschrift für Katholische Theologie* 98 (1976): 165.

[170] Rahner, "Intellectual Honesty and Christian Faith," *TI* 7: 53 (*ST* VII: 59-60).

This "existential difference" manifests itself also in the distinction Rahner makes elsewhere between the "concrete lived faith" and "theological reflection."[171] There is the "always more" that is entailed in the decision to believe, to live in a particular way, and such a decision cannot be solely the outcome of rational speculation. Moreover, Rahner considers his more "spiritual" writings as pre-scientific (*vorwissenschaftlich*), and situates them on a first level of reflection. Just as Rahner distinguishes between two levels of reflection (while also highlighting their interconnectedness), he makes a similar distinction (while also noting their fundamental unity) between his spiritual writings on the one hand, and his more strictly theological works on the other. We have seen that Rahner's "spiritual" writings consist primarily in prayers, meditations and homilies, aimed less at scholarly precision than as a stimulus to help people discover and "make" a similar experience themselves. The boundaries between spirituality and theology are blurred in that theology *also* has a "mystagogical" task.[172] All theological reflection, for Rahner, begins and ends in prayer.[173]

Elmar Klinger, a former pupil of Rahner's, has recently offered some perceptive comments on this problem of the relationship between theology and spirituality in Rahner.[174] He finds a point of

[171] "Brief von P. Karl Rahner," *Der Mensch als Geheimnis*, 402.

[172] Theology, in this sense, becomes "instruction in the experience of mystery" ("Einweisung in die Erfahrung des Geheimnisses schlechthin ..."). Referring to the theology of Thomas Aquinas, Rahner reflects " ... that the highest precision and sober objectivity of true theology ultimately serve only one purpose: to force one out of the lucid clarity of one's existence into the mystery of God, where one no longer grasps but is moved, where one no longer reasons but adores, where one does not master but is overpowered. Only where the theology of concepts and comprehension raises itself ("sich selbst aufhebt") and is transformed into the theology of overwhelming incomprehensibility is it really theology. Otherwise it is at bottom merely human chatter, however correct it may be. The 'Adoro te devote, *latens* Deitas, quae sub his figuris vere latitas' must not always be recited lyrically; it must be the central principle of all theological thought and knowledge." *Everyday Faith*, 189-90 (*Glaube, der die Erde liebt*, 152-53).

[173] The experience of God in prayer (as well as in other situations and activities) is one of the basic characteristics linking Rahner's spirituality and theology. See Vorgrimler's comments in Karl Rahner, *Sehnsucht nach dem geheimnisvollen Gott: Profil, Bilder, Texte*, ed. Herbert Vorgrimler (Freiburg: Herder, 1990), 14-24.

[174] Elmar Klinger, *Das absolute Geheimnis im Alltag entdecken: Zur spirituellen Theologie Karl Rahners* (Würzburg: Echter Verlag, 1994), esp. 47-60.

intersection between theology and spirituality in Rahner with the notion of the experience of God.[175] The Rahnerian notion of spirituality, Klinger argues, consists essentially in an experience of God, which is at the core of what it means to be Christian. Theology, then, in a second step:

> "… denkt über diese Erfahrung nach, berichtet von ihr, klärt sie auf und läßt sie zum Gegenstand einer genauen, aber auch weiterführenden Erörterung werden. Sie erwächst selber dem geistlichen Leben und bleibt ihm verpflichtet. Beide kommen nicht ohne einander aus."[176]

Yet, theology is *also* more than this:

> "Die Theologie ist bei Karl Rahner ein Reden von Gott und Gotteserfahrung zugleich. Sie ist die Rede vom Gott des eigenen Lebens aus der Erfahrung dieses Lebens. Sie ist Rede vom Leben selber, dem Ort der Begegnung mit dem absoluten Geheimnis, in dem Gott erfahren wird … Theologie ist Rede von diesem Gott. Sie führt in sein Geheimnis ein und ist die Rede von diesem Geheimnis. Sie geht aus ihm hervor und bleibt von ihm umfangen. Dieses Geheimnis ist die Grenze der Theologie, aber auch ihr innerstes Wesen … Sie ist, mit einem Wort Rahners beschrieben, eine 'reductio in mysterium'."[177]

In effect, Rahner understands theology as the "science of mystery," which ultimately transcends the formulation of mere human words and which calls for an attitude of trembling and silent adoration. Thus, the task of theology (in all the various forms in which it is objectified) is to appeal to the basic experience of grace, that is:

> "to bring all human beings again and again to a fresh recognition of the fact that all this immense sum of distinct statements of the Christian faith basically speaking expresses nothing else than an immense truth, … the truth namely that the absolute mystery that is, that permeates all things, upholds all things, and endures eternally, has bestowed itself as itself in an act of forgiving love upon human beings, and is experienced in faith in that ineffable experience of grace as the ultimate freedom of human beings."[178]

---

[175] See also our discussion of this issue in Chapter One, "Spirituality and Experience."

[176] Klinger, *Das absolute Geheimnis im Alltag entdecken*, 49-50.

[177] Klinger, *Das absolute Geheimnis im Alltag entdecken*, 52.

[178] Rahner, "Reflections on Methodology in Theology," *TI* 11: 105 (*ST* IX: 123).

Theology, in this understanding, has to do not only with the *fides quae* (i.e., the content of one's beliefs), but also with the *fides qua* (i.e., the faith by which), the act itself of believing and trusting. It is in this latter element that, we believe, the overlap between Rahner's theology and spirituality lies.[179] Both his spiritual and more scholarly writings constitute a "mystagogia," namely, an initiation, or leading of people to such an "experience of grace," not to be misunderstood as some form of pious feeling, but rather denoting those:

> "moments and events in which a person's whole existence comes into play, in which a person is brought up against his or her life in its entirety, in which the meaning of that life is weighed in the balance ... At those moments attitudes are formed and decisions are taken which are not wholly or rationally explicable in purely inner-worldly terms, and which are without an ultimate grounding in the solely here and now."[180]

It is not a question here of Rahner confusing theology with kerygma or paranesis, but rather a reminder, on his part, to theology that:

> "it derives from the utterance of the Spirit and has to serve it. For unless this utterance of the Spirit and the theology deriving from it are related to the ultimate experience of the Spirit in human beings' lives, they lose their distinctive subject matter altogether."[181]

This section has examined a number of the connections that exist between Rahner's theology and spirituality. In so doing, we have also attempted to indicate the mystical structure of his theology.[182] Our

---

[179] "Alle subtile Theologie, alles Dogma, alles Kirchenrecht, alle Anpassung und alles Nein der Kirche, alle Institution, alles Amt und alle seine Vollmacht, alle heilige Liturgie und alle mutige Mission haben nur das einzige Ziel: Glaube, Hoffnung und Liebe zu Gott und den Menschen. Alle anderen Pläne und Taten der Kirche würden absurd und pervers, wollten sie sich dieser Aufgabe entziehen und allein sich selbst suchen." Karl Rahner, *Das Konzil — ein neuer Beginn* (Freiburg: Herder, 1966), 24.

[180] Rahner, *Christians at the Crossroads*, 60 (*Wagnis des Christen*, 81-82). See also his "Reflections on the Experience of Grace," *TI* 3: 86-90 (*ST* III: 105-110). We have previously discussed this question in the context of the "Christian Life as a Mysticism of Everyday Faith" in the second part of this chapter.

[181] "Reflections on Methodology in Theology," *TI* 11: 105 (*ST* IX: 123-24). See also Rahner's Foreword to *TI* 16: *Experience of the Spirit: Source of Theology*, vii-xii, where he describes the importance of grounding theology on a living experience of faith.

[182] Rahner's theology can be called mystical for three reasons: "1) It takes seriously the experience, although often hidden or repressed of God's self-communication; 2) it leads persons into their own deepest mystery by awakening, deepening, and

final section will focus, more particularly, on Rahner's use of the term "spirituality," the contexts in which this term arises, and the meaning he attributes to it. In addition, we will recall our provisional definition of the term in the first chapter, and ask whether this definition can (or cannot) also be applied to Rahner's understanding of spirituality .

b. Components of a Definition

Part of our task in Chapter One was to isolate the "core" meaning of the term "spirituality," and, in so doing, we drew on the German theologian Josef Sudbrack, as well as on the development of his thought by the moral theologian, Bernhard Fraling. This core, we saw, involved a number of elements: a "being-grasped" of the whole person (*ein Ergriffenwerden des Subjekts*), a personal encounter with Christ relevant to our contemporary situation *(Begegnung mit Christus; auf unsere heutige Situation hin verdeutlicht),* and a "concretisation" *(Verleiblichung)* in the specific historical context of each person *(Situationsbezogenheit).*[183] It will be our contention in this section that this core meaning is also applicable to Rahner's understanding of spirituality. While Rahner, it seems, was not disposed to provide a neat definition of the term, "spirituality," it is possible to deduce from his writings what he means by it, and what he considers to be the more important elements in Christian spirituality. We have already examined a number of the "themes" which we regard as integral to his understanding of spirituality. We are now in a position to provide a more precise indication of how *the term itself* was employed by Rahner in his spiritual writings.

In Chapter One, we distinguished between different uses of the term "spirituality" in terms of various levels, one of which referred to the *study* of various spiritual doctrines, traditions, and practices,

---

explicating what every person already lives; and 3) it attempts to compress, to simplify, and to concentrate all Christian beliefs by indicating how they evoke the experience of God's loving self-communication to us in the risen Christ." See Harvey D. Egan, *An Anthology of Christian Mysticism* (Collegeville, Minnesota: The Liturgical Press, 1991), 600.

[183] See Chapter One, n. 92.

i.e., spirituality understood in terms of an academic discipline. While Rahner was always reluctant to make a hard and fast division of spirituality and theology into two separate academic disciplines (as we noted in the previous section), it is noteworthy that one of his earliest publications, *Aszese und Mystik,* consisted precisely in a historical study of early Christian asceticism and mysticism. We saw that this work was a re-working of an original book by Marcel Viller, *La spiritualité des premiers siècles chrétiens* (1930). But why did Rahner change the original French title for the German version? One reason is given in the "Introduction," where he speaks of the indefinite and uncertain nature of the term "spirituality" ("Unbestimmtheit des Begriffes der 'spiritualité'").[184] Possibly, he felt that, had he retained the term "spiritualité," he would have been obliged to provide a detailed exposition of how the term was understood and developed in France. Further, he was unsure whether the more recent term "spirituality" was a suitable category which could be applied, without qualification, to the writings of the Church Fathers. And, finally, he was reluctant to use the term "spirituality" in the title, in case he gave the impression that he was providing a complete history of spirituality ("Frömmigkeit") in all its aspects.[185] Hence, he preferred to use, what he considered, the somewhat more restricted terms "Aszese" and "Mystik," even if it could also be argued that these terms themselves are not without a certain ambiguity.

It is especially in such early publications of Rahner that we find the term "Frömmigkeit" (rather than the term "Spiritualität") to designate a piety that was frequently associated with the pursuit of Christian perfection.[186] While the term "Frömmigkeit" can be translated as

---

[184] Rahner, "Vorwort des Bearbeiters," *Aszese und Mystik,* vi.

[185] In *Aszese und Mystik,* 316, Rahner points out that the historical investigation of the spiritual teaching of the early Church Fathers could serve as a basis for enriching the spiritual life of contemporary Christians. No historical epoch, he believed, could itself claim to have the fullest expression of Christian spirituality. Hence, the value of examining how such spirituality was expressed and practised over the centuries.

[186] See, for example, the Index in *ST* II: 387, where there is an entry under "Frömmigkeit," but nothing under "Spiritualität." Under "Frömmigkeit," the reader is also referred to what is considered a related term, namely, "Vollkommenheit" or "perfection," which gives an indication of how the spiritual life was frequently understood at that time.

"piety" or "devotion," it would be inaccurate to restrict the use of this term, in Rahner, solely to his early writings.[187] It is probably more correct to say that Rahner uses the terms "Frömmigkeit" and "Spiritualität" interchangeably, without making a sharp separation between them. We saw in the first chapter that the term "Spiritualität" (unlike "Frömmigkeit") is a relatively recent addition to the German theological vocabulary; thus, this term also makes its entrance correspondingly later in Rahner's own writings. A good example of such an interchangeable use of the two terms is to be found in an article of Rahner's entitled "Christian Living Formerly and Today" ("Frömmigkeit früher und heute")[188] Here "Frömmigkeit" is translated as "Christian living," but it is also equated with "Spiritualität." In other words, "spirituality," too, has to do with Christian living, and is described by Rahner as the "intense realization of the Christian reality in the individual person as individual."[189] Rahner was aware of the individualistic connotations that make up much of traditional piety and devotion. Hence, he later came to regard the terms "piety" and "devotion" as less apt to express this Christian reality.[190] When Rahner uses the term "Frömmigkeit" to designate piety, he means:

> "the personally adopted and freely accepted relatedness of a person to God in faith, hope and love; but a relatedness that is Christian, being mediated through Jesus Christ."[191]

There are a number of underlying tensions that Rahner is grappling with in his discussion of what spirituality involves. One of these is what he calls the church-relatedness of personal piety. In other words, a person's relationship with God is shaped by (though not identical

---

[187] For example, piety (Frömmigkeit) is the theme of Rahner's article, "Religious Feeling Inside and Outside the Church," *TI* 17: 228-42 (*ST* XII: 582-98). See also the later essays: "Devotion to the Sacred Heart Today," *TI* 23: 117-28 (*ST* XVI: 305-20) and "Courage for Devotion to Mary," *TI* 23: 129-39 (*ST* XVI: 321-35).

[188] Rahner, "Christian Living Formerly and Today" *TI* 7: 3-24 (*ST* VII: 11-31).

[189] Rahner, "The Spirituality of the Church of the Future," *TI* 20: 143-53 (" ... als intensiver Selbstvollzug des Christlichen im einzelnen Menschen." *ST* XIV: 368).

[190] Rahner, "The Spirituality of the Church of the Future," *TI* 20: 143-53 (*ST* XIV: 368-81).

[191] Rahner, "Religious Feeling Inside and Outside the Church," *TI* 17: 228-42 (*ST* XII: 582-98).

with) their relationship to the Church. Christian spirituality, for
Rahner, involves *both* these elements: the Church and the individual.
However, the matter is also more complicated than this, because,
while there is a legitimate ecclesial dimension to spirituality, there
also exists spirituality (and piety) outside the Church. To return to the
ecclesial aspect, Rahner concedes that the importance one ascribes to
this dimension depends on one's view of the Church, and the question of its indispensability or otherwise for the salvation of humanity.[192] In his view, Christianity (and this includes Christian spirituality) is essentially ecclesial, in that it is more than an affair of a
person's subjective and pious dispositions. Thus, Christian spirituality can never be the ideological creation of a religious enthusiasm, or
of the religious experience of an individual:

> "Obviously a Christian is a Christian in the innermost depths of his
> divinised essence ... . But the very thing which he is in his innermost
> depths ... this very thing comes from the concrete history of salvation
> to meet him in the concrete as his very own: it comes in the profession
> of faith of Christians, in the cult of Christians, in the community life of
> Christians, in a word, it comes in the church."[193]

In short, Rahner sees no inherent contradiction between spirituality
understood as an absolutely personal experience of grace in the individual, and the fact that this spirituality can (and must) find a concrete
ecclesial expression, both in the sacraments of the Church, as well as
in its devotional life and practices.[194] In fact, Rahner's view is that cer-

---

[192] We cannot go into Rahner's ecclesiology here, but merely draw attention to
what he terms the "new ecclesial aspect" of spirituality, which is a direct consequence of the changed ecclesiology of Vatican II. "We do not see the Church so much
as the *signum elevatum in nationes*, as it was acclaimed at the First Vatican Council.
What we now see is the poor Church of sinners, the tent of the pilgrim people of God,
pitched in the desert and shaken by all the storms of history, the Church laboriously
seeking its way into the future, groping and suffering many internal afflictions, striving over and over again to make sure of its faith." Rahner, "The Spirituality of the
Church of the Future," *TI* 20: 152-53 (*ST* XIV: 380-81).

[193] *FCF*, 389 (*Grundkurs*, 376).

[194] "In piety, both elements, the Church and the individual, are related to each
other. The nature of the human person makes it impossible for either one of them to
be fully eliminated; and yet the mutual relationship of these two factors is not rigid
and unalterable. The Church's part in piety can be subjectively experienced as the sustaining foundation for its understanding, its certainty and its vitality; but this ecclesiastical form can also be experienced as something secondary, as a kind of merely tol-

tain ecclesial expressions of piety are secondary, and do not form the essential core of what makes up Christian spirituality.[195] One must not confuse too readily, he reminds us, particular *church* forms of piety with that "anonymous" piety that exists *outside* of the Church.[196] However, Rahner also maintains a oneness of piety in the Church and outside it. This oneness resides in the primal experience of God which, as we have seen, is an *a priori* transcendental experience of the human person, and is either freely accepted or rejected. Rahner concludes his reflections by insisting that Christian spirituality in the future will concentrate on what is *most essential* to Christian piety.

What does Rahner think is most essential to Christian spirituality? Our reflections in this chapter lead us to conclude that there lies at the heart of Rahner's spirituality a *personal experience of God*. In the next chapter, we will examine this Rahnerian terminology of religious experience in more detail.[197] Moreover, it is this experience of

---

erated appendage of piety in its solitary relationship to God, the certainty and power of which come from within." Rahner, "Religious Feeling Inside and Outside the Church," *TI* 17: 229 (*ST* XII: 583).

[195] Rahner is attempting to keep room in the Church for the specifically "less devout in the Church's sense." Excessive emphasis on specific devotional practices (as a criterion for a person's relationship to God or as an instrument for binding people to the Church) could force such people into the situation of "fringe" Christians. "Religious Feeling Inside and Outside the Church," *TI* 17: 229-30 (*ST* XII: 583).

[196] For Rahner, non-church piety is also efficacious for salvation: "The Christian ought not to see it as a mere human attempt to set up a relationship to God 'from below.' For it is really inwardly sustained by the free grace of God, which is offered everywhere and effects salvation wherever one obeys the absolute command of his conscience, and realizes and objectifies this obedience, at least in some form of devotion, as an explicit relation to God. So the Catholic Christian and theologian can basically recognize that in fact all conscientious, honest piety is saving, is sustained by grace, and in this sense already Christian in the anonymous sense." Rahner, "Religious Feeling Inside and Outside the Church," *TI* 17: 231 (*ST* XII: 585-86). For another discussion of this problem, see Rahner's "Observations on the Problem of the 'Anonymous Christian'," *TI* 14: 280-94 (*ST* X: 531-46).

[197] Some of the (interrelated) terms Rahner uses to describe this experience of God include: "experience of transcendence" (*Transzendenzerfahrung*), "experience of the Holy Spirit" (*Erfahrung des Heiligen Geistes*), "experience of grace" (*Erfahrung der Gnade or Gnadenerfahrung*), "mystical experience" (*mystische Erfahrung and Mystik*), and "experience of enthusiasm" (*enthusiastische Erfahrung or Enthusiasmus*). For a helpful analysis of these terms and the distinctions between them, see James A. Wiseman, O.S.B., "'I have experienced God': Religious Experience in the Theology of Karl Rahner," *American Benedictine Review* 44:1 (March 1993): 22-57.

God which forms the most primal and sustaining ground of all spirituality — both inside and outside the Church. Further, we indicated how Rahner distinguishes between a primal experience of God, and a reflective, verbally objectifying knowledge of God. In other words, he distinguishes (as well as connects) personal spiritual experiences (such as love, joy, fear, etc.) and their verbal objectification in reflective form. And we also saw how this primal experience of God belongs to the transcendental nature of the human person, as the direction towards which this transcendence tends.[198]

Why does Rahner's repeatedly stress that the spirituality of the future needs to be based much more "on a solitary, immediate experience of God and his Spirit in the individual"? One reason, to which we alluded is that, especially in the first world, there is no longer a relatively homogeneous Christian environment which supports or even takes for granted a decision to believe. In the light of such a secularized milieu, the decision of faith can no longer depend upon the support of a Christian environment. Hence, Rahner speaks of the "lonely responsibility" and the "solitary courage" required of the individual in the decision of faith.[199] And such a solitary courage can only exist if it lives out of this wholly personal experience of God and his Spirit. It was in this context that we interpreted Rahner's remark that the Christian of the future will be a mystic or will not exist.

An objection to Rahner's proposal might be made at this point. Is his understanding of the essential core of spirituality not advocating a return to the "spiritual individualism" of the past? He is aware that many Christians of his generation could certainly be accused of this, but in his vision of a spirituality of the future, he also outlines the importance of "fraternal community," even if he is hesitant to pin-

---

[198] "… This goal towards which transcendence tends can only be thought of as the infinite, unlimited reality which remains at root a mystery: that is to say, God." Rahner, "Religious Feeling Inside and Outside the Church," *TI* 17: 233-35, 235 (*ST* XII: 585-87).

[199] Rahner, "The Spirituality of the Church of the Future," *TI* 20: 149 (*ST* XIV: 375). See also Karl Rahner, "Theology and Spirituality of Pastoral Work in the Parish," *TI* 19: 97-98 (*ST* XIV: 160-62), where Rahner speaks of "the courage for a lonely decision contrary to public opinion, the lonely courage analogous to that of the martyrs of the first centuries of Christianity, the courage for the decision of faith that draws its strength from itself and does not need public support."

point what exactly he means by this. It seems he wishes to leave open the possibility of what he calls "a communal experience of the Spirit."[200] He was reluctant to dismiss phenomena (such as baptism in the Spirit, and speaking in tongues, etc.), which he believed could (and did) occur in prayer groups of the Charismatic and Pentecostal movements. His intuition, at any rate, (even if he did not offer any recipes of how this could come about), was that a more fraternal or communally lived spirituality was something that still needed to be developed.

Summing up, we can conclude that Rahner is constantly attempting to make a greater link between spirituality and everyday life. His early historical studies of spirituality taught him how this "spiritual" life was often presented as a type of sublime superstructure placed over (in the sense of above) the normal Christian life. Thus, the "spiritual" people lived in monasteries, convents, or similar institutions, and were considered "professionals" in Christianity. There, they were able to pray, do penance, and strive after holiness and perfection, without having to be "distracted" by everyday, worldly concerns. Today, that situation has changed. The atheistic milieu, and the constant threat of the annihilation of humanity are just two characteristics of modern society, which, he argues, make it impossible and irresponsible for the contemporary Christian to remain untouched by the world in a type of spiritual paradise. Indeed, for Rahner, a person will only be able to come to terms with this world to the extent that one is radically Christian.[201] This, we have seen, means an experience

---

[200] Rahner, "The Spirituality of the Church of the Future," *TI* 20: 151 (*ST* XII: 377). This experience, therefore, is not only a purely solitary occurrence on the part of the individual alone. In the next chapter, we will see how the later Rahner moved away from such a spiritual individualism and made room for the possibility of a common experience of the Spirit. Our contention will be that it is mainly in his later writings that he succeeded in holding together these two aspects of spirituality (the loneliness of faith, on the one hand, and the fraternal fellowship of faith, on the other) in a dialectical unity. In other words, we will try to show that there has been a growing awareness, on Rahner's part, of the communitarian aspects of spirituality.

[201] " ... Insofern rücken Spiritualität und normales christliches Leben heute enger zueinander. Sie durchdringen sich gegenseitig und fordern einander heraus. Heute kann niemand mehr wie in früheren Zeiten in einem Paradies spiritueller Unberührtheit von der Welt leben, und man wird auch mit dieser konkreten Welt, so

of God in the depths of one's being, which he describes as "mystical," but not in an élitist sense.

Rahner has described spirituality as "simply a question of coping with our life's work in a Christian way."[202] Even given the great variety of expressions of Christian life, the root of all spirituality lies in the act of entrusting the plurality of one's life calmly and silently to God. Rahner's concern, moreover, is not to speak of spirituality in an abstract way. Instead, spirituality is primarily Christian life in faith, hope and love:[203]

> "In the last resort spirituality is our absolute transcendence, beyond any categorial reality in us or outside us, into the absolute mystery that we call God; it is ultimately a transcendentality dying, crucified, becoming torn apart with Christ, not as a theory but as what happens in us in our concrete existence when we confront this life with its ultimate dependence on the incomprehensible mystery of God and achieve the acceptance, the endurance, of this life concretely with Christ through all categorial breakdowns, through all death, through all disappointment ... In this sense spirituality is understood as truly Christian life emerging from the innermost centre of our own existence and not merely as a fulfilment of religious conventions prevailing in Christianity and in the Church."[204]

In short, it is our claim that the original definition of spirituality (in Chapter One, and repeated again at the beginning of this section) does not do violence to Rahner's conception of the term. However, the reader may get the impression that it is primarily the first part of the definition of spirituality (i.e., the *Begegnung* mit Christus) that gets prominence in Rahner's writings. The second half of our definition, however, referred to the need for concretisation *(Verleiblichung)* in the specific historical context of each per-

---

meine ich wenigstens, nicht mehr fertig, wenn man nicht eben doch radikal Christ ist." Karl Rahner, "Wissenschaftlichkeit der Theologie und Begegnung mit Gott," *Glaube in winterlicher Zeit*, 77.

[202] " ... das christliche Bestehen seiner Lebensaufgabe." Karl Rahner, "The Spirituality of the Secular Priest," *TI* 19: 103 (*ST* XIV: 166).

[203] It is not without significance that the anthology of Rahner's spiritual writings, *The Practice of Faith* (1983) is divided into three thematic categories of the Christian life, that is, the three theological virtues of faith, hope and love.

[204] Karl Rahner, "The Spirituality of the Priest in the Light of His Office," *TI* 19: 121-22 (*ST* XIV: 187).

son. We have indicated some ways whereby Rahner provides a concrete shape to his understanding of spirituality.[205] Later, we shall return to this aspect of our definition when we explore in greater detail the development which occurred in Rahner's understanding of this term.

[205] We shall not, at this stage, develop the political dimension of spirituality. It would be a misunderstanding, however, to think that Rahner was unaware or uninterested in this aspect: "I do not think that we must or should practise politics in a banal, commonplace sense. But I think that the unity of love of God and love of neighbour, the knowledge that where we stand by the poor, persecuted, underprivileged there is or can be an intimate experience of grace, and that an ultimate transcendentality of the person radicalized by grace into the mystery of God and a self-renunciation in love of neighbour represent the two aspects of the one Christian life, the unity of love of God and love of neighbour — in the last resort, that is what I understand here as the political dimension of spirituality; and that is something quite important." Rahner, "The Spirituality of the Priest in the Light of His Office," *TI* 19: 137 (*ST* XIV: 206).

CHAPTER THREE

THE EXPERIENTIAL DIMENSION OF RAHNER'S NOTION OF SPIRITUALITY

Introduction

The focus of this chapter is on the notion of religious experience in Rahner, and on the significant role which this plays in his understanding of spirituality. We will see that the theme of experience is one of the most elusive and ambiguous concepts in Rahner's thought. He frequently employs the term "experience" without actually defining it. Rahner claims that there are certain basic experiences that happen to everyone, and maintains that God is the depth dimension in every personal experience of love, faithfulness, joy, and so on. He further describes the experience of God as simultaneously an "experience of transcendence." It will be necessary to explore what Rahner means by the designation "transcendental" in this context. We shall show that, in considering God as the infinite horizon or as the term of transcendence, Rahner reveals the core of his transcendental-anthropological method. The conclusion of the first part of our chapter will then argue that Rahner's metaphysical anthropology can provide the foundations for what can be termed a dialectical spirituality.

In the second part of the chapter, we continue our delineation of the central features of Rahner's understanding of religious experience by concentrating on the experience of the Spirit and on the accompanying phenomenon of religious enthusiasm. Crucial to our discussion will be the question Rahner raises about where and how such experiences take place. While he is convinced of the importance of a thematic experience of God for the contemporary Christian, he feels that, for the most part, Christians overlook this possibility of an experience of God in the everyday routine of life. The final section of part two examines the experience of the Spirit from another point of view, namely from that of the theologian Heribert Mühlen. His approach, we believe, complements and even goes beyond that of Rahner's by indicating that the experience of the Spirit is never a purely private process, but also has specific social and communal implications.

The third and final part of the chapter consists in a discussion of Rahner's presentation of the experience of grace. Rahner reinterpreted the traditional view of grace in at least four significant ways. Drawing on both Scripture and on the Fathers, his aim was to develop a more personal understanding of grace as the *self*-communication of God to humanity. His starting-point and conviction is that the Christian believer is called to share God's intimate life. Part of his reinterpretation of grace entailed the introduction of a new term, the "supernatural existential," by virtue of which, he claims, the human person is not neutral with regard to God. Linked to this notion of the supernatural existential is Rahner's emphasis on the universal salvific will of God. Hence, he develops an understanding of grace as present to everyone in the mode of an offer — an offer which can be freely accepted or rejected. Yet, Rahner's proposals are not without their ambiguities, and we will mention a few of these towards the end of our exposition.

In the light of the foregoing reflections, we will conclude the chapter by noting some consequences which ensue for Rahner's understanding of spirituality. This discussion begins by tracing a transition or a movement in Rahner's thought from an anonymous, unthematic experience of God, on the one hand, to the need for a more explicit Christian interpretation of this experience on the other. How Rahner makes this transition, and to what extent he merely ends up with a vague or "anonymous" spirituality, are questions that will occupy us in this and in the final chapter. The question can also be phrased in terms of the "specifically Christian" nature of Rahner's conception of spirituality. Rahner, we contend, is convinced of the need to move from an anonymous experience of grace to a more explicit interpretation and appropriation of this experience in the context of Christian faith. Thus, our concluding remarks will try to elicit (albeit in a fragmentary way) Rahner's specifically Christian interpretation of spirituality. The substance of these remarks will then be taken up again and expanded further in the last chapter of our work.

1. The Rahnerian Notion of Religious Experience

a. Rahner's Concept of Experience — Terminological Clarification

i) Experiential and Conceptual Knowledge

Throughout his writings Rahner frequently uses the term "experience" without defining it. In addition, he uses the term in a variety of interlinked ways, the most common of which include the following expressions: experience of God *(Gotteserfahrung)*, "experience of transcendence" *(Transzendenzerfahrung)*, "experience of the Holy Spirit" *(Erfahrung des Heiligen Geistes),* "experience of grace" *(Erfahrung der Gnade or Gnadenerfahrung)*, "mystical experience" *(mystische Erfahrung and Mystik)*, and "experience of enthusiasm" *(enthusiastische Erfahrung or Enthusiasmus)*. The closest we come to a definition of the term is in his *Theological Dictionary*, where *religious* experience is described as "the inner self-attestation *(innere Selbst-Bezeugung)* of supernatural reality (grace)."[1] Such religious experience is only possible, according to Rahner, "in conjunction with objective, conceptual reflection *(mit einer gegenständlich begrifflichen Reflexion)* of the mind upon itself."[2] In other words, we cannot make a clear-cut distinction between the creative working of God's grace and our conceptual interpretation of it, since God and his activity can never be grasped in isolation, or clearly distinguished from the reflective activity of the created mind.

Experience, then, is a rather elusive and enigmatic concept in Rahner's writings. It refers to a source or to a particular form of our

---

[1] "Religiöse Erfahrung als innere Selbst-Bezeugung der übernatürlichen Wirklichkeit (Gnade) ist dem Menschen bzw. der Menscheit in ihrer Glaubensgeschichte nur zusammen mit einer gegenständlich begrifflichen Reflexion möglich." Karl Rahner and Herbert Vorgrimler, *Kleines Theologisches Wörterbuch*, unter Mitarbeit von Kuno Füssel, Herderbücherei 557 (Freiburg: Herder, 1961, 1976; 13th. ed., 1981): 108 (Rahner, Vorgrimler, "Experience," *Theological Dictionary*: 162).

[2] Rahner, Vorgrimler, "Experience," *Theological Dictionary*: 162. See also Rahner, "The Experience of God Today," *TI* 11: 151-52 (*ST* IX: 163): "Experience as such and subsequent reflection upon this experience, in which its content is conceptually objectified are never absolutely separate one from the other. Experience always involves at least a certain incipient process of reflection. But at the same time the two are never identical. Reflection never totally includes the original experience."

knowledge arising from "the direct reception of an impression from a reality (internal or external) which lies outside our free control."[3] Thus, for Rahner, experience is one of the ways we grasp the objects of knowledge. If experience is a way of knowing, then whatever we discover about experiential knowledge in general, will help illuminate the dynamics of our experience of God. Rahner further maintains that the dynamics of our experience of God are comparable (but not identical) to what happens in typical human experiences such as joy, faithfulness, trust, and love. But our experience of God is also atypical — it cannot simply be grouped together with these other experiences[4] — since God is so radically different from the objects of ordinary experience. Thus, there is an ambiguity operative from the outset in Rahner's notion of experience. Commentators on Rahner[5]

---

[3] Rahner, Vorgrimler, "Experience," *Theological Dictionary*: 162. See also Karl Lehmann, "Experience," *Sacramentum Mundi* 2: 307 (*SM* I: 1117-18), who describes "external" experience as involving corporeal objects perceived directly through the natural senses, whereas "inner" experience includes "that of one's own state of mind and soul (representations, imaginations, etc. in the direct mental processes), and self-consciousness in reflection."

[4] Thus, at the beginning of their discussion of Rahner's understanding of experience, some commentators refer to how he sometimes uses the singular (die Erfahrung), and at other times the plural (die Erfahrungen). We will see that Rahner's intention is to show that the experience of God is not so much given to us in addition to other experiences, but rather lies *hidden within* every human experience. See William J. Hoye, *Gotteserfahrung? Klärung eines Grundbegriffs der heutigen Theologie* (Zurich: Benziger, 1993), 112-114.

[5] As well as Hoye (see above), some of the commentators referred to in this chapter include: Klaus P. Fischer, *Gotteserfahrung: Mystagogie in der Theologie Karl Rahners und in der Theologie der Befreiung* (Mainz: Grünewald, 1986), esp. 43-74; Herbert Vorgrimler, "Gotteserfahrung im Alltag: Der Beitrag Karl Rahners zu Spiritualität und Mystik," *Karl Rahner in Erinnerung*, ed. Albert Raffelt (Düsseldorf: Patmos, 1994), 100-117; Karl Lehmann, "Karl Rahner. Ein Porträt," *Rechenschaft des Glaubens: Karl Rahner Lesebuch,* eds. Karl Lehmann and Albert Raffelt (Freiburg: Herder, 1979), 13-53; Bert van der Heijden, *Karl Rahner: Darstellung und Kritik seiner Grundpositionen,* Sammlung Horizonte 6 (Einsiedeln: Johannes Verlag, 1973), 200-28; Karl-Heinz Weger, *Karl Rahner: Eine Einführung in sein theologisches Denken* (Freiburg: Herder, 1978), 11-98; James J. Bacik, *Apologetics and the Eclipse of Mystery: Mystagogy According to Karl Rahner* (Notre Dame: University of Notre Dame Press, 1980), 20-38; Stephen J. Duffy, *The Graced Horizon: Nature and Grace in Modern Catholic Thought,* Theology and Life Series 37 (Collegeville, Minnesota: The Liturgical Press, 1992), 85-114, 206-34; Donald L. Gelpi, *The Turn To Experience In Contemporary Theology* (New York/Mahwah, N.J.: Paulist Press, 1994), 90-107; J. Norman King. "The Experience of God in the Theology of Karl Rahner,"

usually deal with this difficulty by focusing on a number of distinctions which Rahner himself makes. An example of this distinction is that between the "transcendental" and the "categorial" dimensions of experience. The category "transcendental" points to a dimension of human experience and to a level of consciousness that is deeper, more significant, than the dimension of reflected, articulated, conceptualized experience which is termed "categorial." Why is this? One reason is Rahner's wish to lead his readers beyond or behind the world of doctrines, propositional language, and the like, to their primordial ground in the mystery of God. So, while Rahner is not opposed to the conceptual (i.e., categorial) dimension of experience, his real concern is the transcendental dimension of experience which, he holds, can even constitute an *a priori* way of knowing.

This claim is best clarified by contrasting experiential knowledge with conceptual knowledge.[6] In conceptual knowledge, the person is an active agent, subjecting the object to his or her own viewpoints and methods, to critical investigation, and to discursive thought. In experiential knowledge, on the other hand, the knowing subject is more passive. Experiential knowledge involves a minimal amount of analysis and examination. Rather than trying to grasp its objects and place them into precise categories, experiential knowledge provides

Thought 53 (1978): 174-202; Heribert Mühlen, "Der gegenwärtige Aufbruch der Geisterfahrung und die Unterscheidung der Geister," *Gegenwart des Geistes: Aspekte der Pneumatologie*, ed. Walter Kasper, Quaestiones Disputatae 85 (Freiburg: Herder, 1979), 24-53; George Vass, *The Mystery of Man and the Foundations of a Theological System: Understanding Karl Rahner,* 2 vols. (London: Sheed and Ward, 1985), 2: 59-83; James A. Wiseman, O.S.B, "'I have experienced God': Religious Experience in the Theology of Karl Rahner," *American Benedictine Review* 44 (1993): 22-57; Paul M. Zulehner, *"Denn du kommst unserem Tun mit deiner Gnade zuvor ..." : Zur Theologie der Seelsorge heute. Paul M. Zulehner im Gespräch mit Karl Rahner* (Düsseldorf: Patmos Verlag, 1984), 40-82.

   [6] See, for example, Michael Skelley, *The Liturgy of the World: Karl Rahner's Theology of Worship* (Collegeville, Minnesota: The Liturgical Press, 1991), 65-74. Rahner describes such conceptual knowledge as reflexive, interpretive, thematic, and conscious. See, his "Experience of Self and Experience of God," *TI* 13: 122-24 (*ST* X: 132-34). Karl Lehmann, "Experience," *Sacramentum Mundi* 2: 307-309 (*SM* I: 1118), also refers to this contrast: "Experience is also used to designate the knowledge and sense of reality gained from direct intercourse, in contrast to a 'book knowledge' which remains external" (p. 307).

us with a kind of knowledge that is more immediate and complete than our conceptual grasp of reality.

The differences between experiential knowledge and conceptual knowledge also emerge when we compare the ways we experience and conceptualize ourselves. We gain a conceptual grasp of self through stepping back and actively analyzing ourselves, our likes and dislikes, our strengths and weaknesses, and, more fundamentally, through our attempts to define who we are, and where we fit into the human community. However, we also have another way of knowing ourselves, namely, through basic self-experience, which, to some extent, comes to us whether we seek it or not, and through which we have a much more immediate grasp of ourselves than we are ever able to articulate conceptually. In Rahner's words: "One always experiences more of oneself at the non-thematic and non-reflexive levels in the ultimate and fundamental living of one's life than one knows about oneself by reflecting upon oneself whether scientifically or (mainly in one's private ideas) unscientifically."[7]

Nevertheless, experiential and conceptual knowledge are also related to one another. Within this relationship, experience is logically (though not necessarily chronologically) prior to conceptual knowledge: it is possible to have a conceptual understanding of love before we have had any experience of it. Yet, all our conceptual knowledge of realities such as love, fear, etc., is, ultimately, an attempt to interpret our *experiences* of these realities. It is in this sense that Rahner claims that experience can be considered an *a priori* way of knowing.[8]

With regard to the experience of *ourselves* we can say that we always know more about ourselves than we are able to say. Conceptual knowledge can never totally capture and fully communicate the deepest levels of our experience of self. We can never give our experience of ourselves wholly and completely to another person. In fact,

---

[7] Rahner, "Experience of Self and Experience of God," *TI* 13: 123 (*ST* X: 134).

[8] Rahner is not denying the importance of what he calls "reflexive" or "interpretive" knowledge, but claims that "the struggle for conscious knowledge, objectified and explicitated in conscious terms, constitutes only a modest and secondary part of life." Rahner, "Experience of Self and Experience of God," *TI* 13: 124 (*ST* X: 134-35).

even if we do reflect on our self-experience, our conceptual interpretation can be inaccurate or distorted. The transition from experience to conceptual knowledge can be difficult, but it can also be rewarding. When we make a successful transition from experience to conceptual knowledge, this, in turn, can help us to be more clearly attentive to, and aware of, such basic human experiences as love:

> "It is true that such basic experiences are prior to any conceptual objectification or interpretation of them, and are in principle independent of these processes. But however true this may be, still we cannot regard this process of objectifying reflection as superfluous... The experience itself as such can in itself be accepted more profoundly, more purely, and with greater freedom when we achieve a knowledge of its true nature and its implications at the explicitly conscious level."[9]

Finally, compared to conceptual knowledge, Rahner describes such basic human experiences (of love, faithfulness, trust, etc.) as inescapable *(unausweichlich)*. Moreover, conceptual knowledge requires a greater amount of active participation on our part. Our conceptual grasp of something is related to the amount of time and energy invested in analysis and reflection. Experiential knowledge, on the other hand, is not in our control to the same degree. To sum up, Rahner's claim is that we cannot avoid experiencing *ourselves*, regardless of how inadequate and inaccurate our conceptual interpretations of ourselves may be. While we might not make the transition from experiential to conceptual knowledge (or might make the transition only partially), it does not follow that we do not have such basic experiences, (including, Rahner will say, the experience of God), however we may try to ignore, suppress, or deny them.

ii) Human Experiences and the Experience of God

We concluded our previous sub-section by noting the "inescapability" of basic human experiences. But Rahner goes further. While it is, of course, possible that someone might not have had such basic experiences (of love, etc.,) as those mentioned above, Rahner's contention is that it is impossible for anyone not to have a basic experience of God. Everyone, in his view, has an experience of the absolute

---

[9] Rahner, "The Experience of God Today," *TI* 11: 152 (*ST* IX: 164).

mystery, explicitly or implicitly, whether suppressed or accepted, whether rightly or wrongly interpreted.[10] The reason for this will be developed more fully in the following section. In short, however, the experience of God is utterly inescapable because we experience God whenever we experience our transcendence.[11] Whenever we know or choose anything, we experience the absolute mystery as the term of our transcendence. Leaving aside discussion of Rahner's transcendental method for the moment, our point here is that while the experience of God is different from any other human experience, it is not to be thought of as one particular experience among many other human experiences. On the contrary, the basic experience of God constitutes:

> "the ultimate depths and the radical essence of *every* spiritual and personal experience (of love, faithfulness, hope, and so on), and thereby precisely constitutes also the ultimate unity and totality of experience, in which the person as spiritual possesses him or herself and is made over to him or herself."[12]

---

[10] "... (die) Erfahrung, ... die in jedem Menschen gegeben ist (reflex oder unreflex, verdrängt oder angenommen, richtig oder falsch interpretiert oder wie immer), daß diese Erfahrung *einerseits* ursprünglicher und unausweichlicher ist als ein rationales Kalkül ... daß aber *anderseits* diese Erfahrung sich nicht so (wie die vom Vorhandensein eines sinnlichen physikalischen Erfahrungsdatums oder einer vitalen Empfindung) aufdrängt und unwiderstehlich ist, daß der Übergang von der Erfahrung zu ihrer expliziten, reflexen und interpretierenden Erkenntnis und Aussage unwiderstehlich wäre." Rahner, "Gotteserfahrung heute," (*ST* IX: 162).

[11] We began our discussion of the religious dimension in every human experience in Chapter Two. See also Rahner, "The Experience of God Today," *TI* 11: 153 (*ST* IX: 164-65); "Experience of Self and Experience of God," *TI* 13: 123-24 (*ST* X: 133-34); "Reflections on the Experience of Grace," *TI* 3: 86-87 (*ST* III: 105-106); "Experience of the Spirit and Existential Commitment," *TI* 16: 27-29 (*ST* XII: 45-47); and "Experience of the Holy Spirit," *TI* 18: 195-99 (*ST* XIII: 232-38).

[12] Rahner, "The Experience of God Today," *TI* 11: 154 (*ST* IX: 166). We are indebted here also to Michael Skelley's helpful comments, in *The Liturgy of the World: Karl Rahner's Theology of Worship*, 70-74. Although we have treated of the ambiguity of the term "spiritual" in Chapter One, a similar problem is evident in English translations of Rahner. The reason for the ambiguity is because the term "spiritual" sometimes translates the German *geistig*, as in the reference above, whereas, at other times, it is used to translate the term *geistlich*. It would be less confusing, I think, to confine the adjective "spiritual" to the translation of "geistlich," and use "intellectual" to translate the adjective "geistig". For an example of the former use, see Rahner's discussion of "spiritual experience" in the context of the experience of the Spirit in section two of this chapter.

The ambiguity in Rahner's understanding of experience, which we mentioned at the beginning of the chapter, is again in evidence here. On the *one* hand, Rahner states how the experience of God is more basic and more inescapable than any subsequent process of rational and conceptual reflection. On the *other* hand, this experience does not impose itself upon us in the fashion of a datum of sense experience or an organic sensation that we *automatically* make the transition from the experience itself (which is inescapably present) to a recognition and interpretation of it at the conceptual and reflexive level. We might not even make this transition, or our interpretation of such basic experiences might be erroneous. Rahner's point, however, is that we cannot help experiencing God, however dimly, at some level of our being whenever we experience anything, and he appeals to us to attempt to discover this experience (perhaps previously quite unrecognized or suppressed) within ourselves. This experience of God as the absolute mystery is not therefore confined to the individual "mystic," or to those who interpret their lives in explicitly religious categories. In fact, Rahner even claims that those who expressly deny it, may also implicitly experience God:

> "Wherever there is selfless love, wherever duties are carried out without hope of reward, wherever the incomprehensibility of death is calmly accepted, wherever people are good with no hope of reward, in all these instances the Spirit is experienced, even though a person may not dare give this interpretation to the experience."[13]

We have seen that when Rahner describes how this experience is present to everyone, he is careful to nuance his assertion by noting that it can be suppressed or rejected, or can be rightly or wrongly interpreted. Here, another possible ambiguity in our understanding of the term "experience" emerges, since Rahner links our experience of God with the ordinary, everyday human experiences of life. Concrete experiences of life can provide the locus for our experience of God. The experiences Rahner has in mind here include such basic experi-

---

[13] Karl Rahner, "How is the Holy Spirit Experienced Today?" in *Karl Rahner in Dialogue: Conversations and Interviews, 1965-1982*, eds. Paul Imhof and Hubert Biallowons, trans. & ed. Harvey D. Egan (New York: Crossroad, 1986), 142 (*Karl Rahner im Gespräch* 1: 278-79).

ences as joy, anxiety, faithfulness, love, trust, responsibility, etc.[14] A person *has* such experiences before he or she reflects on them, or attempts to analyze them. The experience of God at issue here:

> "is not some subsequent emotional reaction to doctrinal instruction about the existence and nature of God which we received from without and at the theoretical level. Rather it is prior to any such teaching, underlies it, and has to be there already for it to be made intelligible at all. This experience of God is not the privilege of the individual 'mystic,' but is present in every person even though the process of reflecting upon it varies greatly from one individual to another in terms of force and clarity... We should say, rather, that God is present as the asymptotic goal (*das asymptotische Woraufhin*), hidden in itself, of the experience of a limitless dynamic force inherent in the spirit endowed with knowledge and freedom."[15]

In exploring the question of the experience of God, Rahner assumes, first of all, that such a thing exists, i.e., that God as a reality exists, a reality to which every human person is related. Secondly, the phrase "experience of God" implies, for Rahner, "that there is something more, something different, and something more fundamental than that knowledge of God which can be acquired through the so-called proofs of God's existence."[16] Once again, the basic experience of God is prior to, and more fundamental than, our subsequent attempts at conceptual interpretation and verbalization. While such proofs may be meaningful in their own right, Rahner's claim is that they are more the outcome of an *a posteriori* process of reasoning, or the conceptual objectification of what is called the experience of

---

[14] In Chapter Two, 2, c, "Prayer as Surrender of the Heart," we noted how experiences and events of this kind have an inner nucleus or ultimate point of reference in the one primal experience: that the human person "is more than the sum of chemical elements and processes, that human life rests on an incomprehensible mystery, indeed constantly begins to flow in that direction." Vorgrimler, *Understanding Karl Rahner*, 14 (*Karl Rahner verstehen*, 25).

[15] Rahner, "The Experience of God Today," *TI* 11: 153 (*ST* IX: 164-65). Rahner also emphasizes that this "dynamic force" within the human person can also be experienced as grace-given, in that it includes within itself "the powerful hope of achieving a state of ultimate proximity and immediacy to that goal towards which it is tending." We will treat of the experience of grace in a separate section.

[16] Rahner, "The Experience of God Today," *TI* 11: 149 (*ST* IX: 161). See also Hoye, *Gotteserfahrung? Klärung eines Grundbegriffs der heutigen Theologie*, 112-70, esp. 116-18.

God.[17] Rahner also cautions against a too facile identification of our experience with "God," or with "the absolute mystery," for fear of presupposing beforehand that we know what is meant by these terms.[18]

Throughout his discussion of the experience of God, Rahner warns that such experience must not be conceived as though it were merely *one* particular experience *among* others. Rather, it constitutes "the ultimate depths and the radical essence of *every* spiritual and personal experience (of love, faithfulness, hope, and so on)."[19] Here we touch on the heart of Rahner's understanding of the experience of God. His aim is to draw attention to this experience, and to enable others to discover it within themselves. And this is only possible, he claims, to the extent that one recognizes that it has been present all along in one's life. Further, the discovery of such an experience of God (or absolute mystery) within one's life, as well as the process of transition from an unthematic awareness of the experience to a more explicit recognition of it at the conceptual level, constitute the "mystagogical" task of Christianity. A more detailed discussion of this notion will be provided in the following chapter.

Even in his somewhat abstract treatment of this topic, Rahner is referring to something extremely concrete, which he describes as "the element of the ineffable in the concrete experience of our everyday life."[20] Certain experiences or episodes of a person's life mani-

---

[17] In fact, the task of Rahner's theological programme is aptly described in the *Grundkurs* as: "unsere theologische Begrifflichkeit in ihre ursprüngliche Erfahrung hinein zurückzuverweisen" (p. 28).

[18] Rahner, "Erfahrungen eines katholischen Theologen," *Karl Rahner in Erinnerung*, ed. Albert Raffelt, Freiburger Akademieschriften, 8 (Düsseldorf: Patmos, 1994), 134-148. This personal reflection on the analogical nature of theological statements was Rahner's last public lecture (a month before his death). The lecture, in effect, constitutes a *Rückblick* over his whole theological enterprise.

[19] "Die Gotteserfahrung ist ... die letzte Tiefe und Radikalität *jeder* geistig-personalen Erfahrung (der Liebe, Treue, Hoffnung und so fort) und ist somit gerade die ursprünglich eine Ganzheit der Erfahrung." Rahner, "The Experience of God Today," *TI* 11: 154 (*ST* IX: 166).

[20] Rahner, "The Experience of God Today," *TI* 11: 157 (*ST* IX: 168). Rahner is drawing attention to the depth dimension (or dimension of the ineffable) located in everyday experiences. In Chapter Two, we saw how Rahner based this assertion on his understanding of the transcendental orientation of the human person "to the incomprehensible and ineffable Mystery which constitutes the enabling condition for

fest this dimension of the ineffable more clearly than others. Rahner has in mind experiences where the individual, normally lost amid the myriad of activities and tasks of daily life, is suddenly thrown back upon him or herself, and when everything is "called into question." In such experiences, one is brought face to face with one's *aloneness*, and, at the same time, with one's *freedom* and *responsibility*. This is also the case with regard to the experience of personal *love*, where one notices that "he or she has been accepted with a love which is unconditional even though ... he or she can assign no reason whatever, find no adequate justification, for this unconditional love that reaches out to him or her from the other side."[21] Rahner's aim is to show that this single, basic experience of the human person is an orientation towards mystery that is the ground of each one's personal life.[22]

We saw above that, when Rahner asks where *concretely* in our everyday experiences the experience of God can be found, he provides examples of both a positive and negative kind. He calls these the *via eminentiae* and the *via negationis* respectively. Together, these represent two aspects of one and the same experience of God. For some this experience takes place there where "the greatness and glory, goodness, beauty, and transparency of the individual reality of our experience point with promise to eternal light and eternal life." For others, this experience occurs when the "lights shining over the tiny island of our ordinary life are extinguished and the question

knowledge and freedom," and which in itself "implies a real, albeit a non-thematic experience of God." See, "Experience of Self and Experience of God," *TI* 13: 123 (*ST* X: 134). The metaphysical and philosophical basis for the presupposition that the human person is *a priori* open towards a possible revelation forms the major theme of Rahner's earlier work, *Hearers of the Word*, esp. 3-27, 53-68. [*Hörer des Wortes: Zur Grundlegung einer Religionsphilosophie*, 2nd ed., revised by J. B. Metz (Munich: Kösel, 1963), 17-40, 63-77]. See also *Spirit in the World*, 393-400 (*Geist in Welt*, 392-99), where this question is discussed by Rahner in the context of the possibility of metaphysics.

[21] Rahner, "The Experience of God Today," *TI* 11: 157-58 (*ST* IX: 169).

[22] "This orientation towards mystery is ... the innermost essence of transcendence in cognition and freedom, because it is the condition of the very possibility of cognition and freedom as such. Consequently it is the ground of one's personal life as such; one's ground lies in the abyss of mystery, which accompanies one always throughout life." Rahner, "Mystery," *Sacramentum Mundi* 4: 135 ("Geheimnis," *SM* II: 192).

becomes inescapable, whether the night that surrounds us is the void of absurdity and death that engulfs us."[23] Rahner's preference is for the *via negationis*.[24]

Rahner himself provides some examples of concrete experiences of God, with the purpose of striking a responsive chord in his readers, thus helping to bring to conceptual awareness the mystery which lies hidden in life. In his essay, "Experience of the Holy Spirit" (1977), he gives twelve examples of such everyday experience of God through the *via negationis*. One such example should reveal the letting-go, the experience of risk, and of overwhelming trust that is involved here:

> "Here is someone who cannot get their life's accounts to come out right, who cannot balance the entries in these accounts, consisting of good will, mistakes, sin and disasters, even if they try (impossible as it may seem) to add repentance to these entries. The accounts simply do not add up and they do not know how they can insert God as an individual entry in order to strike a balance between debit and credit. And this person, unable to balance his or her life's accounts, surrenders him or herself to God or, to put it both more and less precisely, to the hope of an incalculable final reconciliation of their existence, marked by the presence of the One whom we call God."[25]

Are such experiences of God in and through our ordinary experiences of life merely a question of an unverifiable mood or feeling, a factor confined to our private, interior lives? Rahner does not think so. He argues, on the contrary, that experiences of the kind we have

---

[23] Rahner, "Experience of the Holy Spirit," *TI* 18: 199 (*ST* XIII: 238).

[24] A possible explanation of Rahner's preference for the *via negationis* can be located in his early works on prayer. For example, *Von der Not und dem Segen des Gebetes* is a collection of homilies, whose immediate background was the suffering experienced as a result of the Second World War. We will see later that the reasons for his preference for the *via negationis* are also related to his suspicion of the more enthusiastic manifestations of the experience of the Spirit. See also, Vorgrimler, "Gotteserfahrung im Alltag: Der Beitrag Karl Rahners zu Spiritualität und Mystik," *Karl Rahner in Erinnerung*, 106-110.

[25] Rahner, "Experience of the Holy Spirit," *TI* 18: 200 (*ST* XIII: 239). The translation has been altered with a view to inclusive language. See also his "Gebet im Alltag," *Von der Not und dem Segen des Gebetes*, 60-75, and "Gott meines Alltags," *Worte ins Schweigen*, 46-51. We discussed some of the (constant) features of this basic experience of letting-go, of trust, etc., in the context of our discussion of prayer in the previous chapter.

discussed above *also* have a public and social significance. For the experience of God is expressed, however unreflectedly, in terms of faithfulness, responsibility, love, and hope, and such experiences, according to Rahner, "do in fact sustain the social level of human living."[26]

Drawing together some of the characteristics of Rahner's presentation of the experience of God thus far, we can say, firstly, that *everyone* has such an experience, however diffuse and unthematic it may be. Secondly, such experience is both *unthematic* and *prior* to any subsequent attempt, on our part, at conceptualization and analysis. Thirdly, this experience of God is, at the same time, an *experience of the self*, especially in those limit situations (examples of which we have provided above), where the individual is thrown back onto him or herself. In the words of Bacik, a perceptive commentator on Rahner:

> "The self-experience of every person inescapably contains a religious dimension whether it is conscious or not, accepted or rejected, rightly or wrongly interpreted. Hence it is available to everyone and not just to a privileged few, or the explicitly religious. It is more fundamental than all rational calculation about it since it is the necessary condition of all knowing."[27]

Fourthly, the experience of God constitutes the radical *essence* of every personal experience (of love, faithfulness, etc.). Hence, Rahner attempts to show how the common features of human experience point in this direction. In other words, God may indeed be "met" in our experience, though it is always as holy mystery that he is encountered.[28]

Fifthly, religious experience involves *gradations* — ranging from ordinary experiences of grace to more mystical experiences. We shall deal more fully with this aspect in our discussion of Rahner's treat-

---

[26] Rahner, "The Experience of God Today," *TI* 11: 160 (*ST* IX: 171). Religion, in this context, according to Rahner, consists "in a conceptual reflection upon, and a social institutionalization of this experience of God." In other words, religion is a social reality which constantly draws life from this experience.

[27] Bacik, *Apologetics and the Eclipse of Mystery*, 36.

[28] See Nicholas Lash, *Easter in Ordinary: Reflections on Human Experience and the Knowledge of God* (London: SCM, 1988), 242-53.

ment of the experience of the Spirit. Sixthly, religious experience is *susceptible of reflection and objectification.* Some people have a greater ability than others to identify and articulate such experience, e.g., the prophet, the mystic, or the poet. Seventhly, the experience of God takes place in concrete, everyday experiences of both a *positive* and *negative* kind. In instances of the former kind, we are more conscious of our union with God as the gracious mystery, and of the peace and integration that comes from living in harmony with this mystery. The most complete manifestation of this is the ecstatic experience of intense union known as mysticism. In instances of the latter kind, we are reminded of our limitation and essential contingency, our dependency upon a power greater than ourselves. It is the painful experience of realizing that we do not control our existence and must find our fulfilment outside of ourselves.

The foregoing list of characteristics of Rahner's notion of religious experience is not meant to be exhaustive.[29] In the following section, we will develop the transcendental dimension of the experience of God. Our presentation to date has aimed to show that religious experience necessarily involves a dynamic interplay of the *transcendental and categorial* realms. In the working out of this dialectical relationship, and in order to highlight the (frequently concealed) depth dimension of human experience, we attach a certain primacy to the transcendental dimension. At the same time, we have and shall continue to stress that we are not undervaluing the concrete historical (categorial) aspects of existence. It has always been Rahner's contention that we realize or achieve ourselves, not in an abstract spiritualized inwardness, but in external interaction with other persons and with our environment.[30]

---

[29] For a similar attempt at gathering together the defining characteristics of the experience of God in Rahner's writings, see Denis Edwards, "Experience of God and Explicit Faith: A Comparison of John of the Cross and Karl Rahner," *The Thomist* 46 (1982): 33-74, esp. 69-70.

[30] "Our life consists for the most part of actions which are performed *ad extra*, of activities in which one is occupied with something other than oneself, actions by which one intervenes, and effects something in the external world of things and fellow human beings. Without these activities one could not fulfil one's life at all. One cannot live in pure inwardness. One cannot make oneself a pure spirit... . Not only would this be impossible, even if one wanted to withdraw oneself into one's interior-

b. Experience of God as Experience of Transcendence

When Rahner reflects on the particular situation of the experience of God *today*, he calls to mind in the first place the "transcendental" character of this experience. What does he mean by this phrase? He approaches the question by comparing how, in earlier times, the average Christian was able to conceive of God as part of the reality of the world. In this way, God was rendered "comprehensible." "He was the 'good God' who acts as ruler of the world, acting to ensure the good moral conduct of its inhabitants and at the same time capable of restoring it to his grace."[31] But today, this kind of God or this primitive idea of God is, according to Rahner, no longer in vogue. On the contrary, our ever increasing understanding of the world leads to the elimination of the divine from it. God, it seems, has become unspeakably remote. This desacralization of the natural world leads him to conclude that, in our day, the initial impetus for the transcendental experience of boundless mystery will not come from the world around us, but from the world within — human existence with its unfathomable depths.[32] Hence the importance of the "transcendental" character of the experience of God today. In Rahner's words: "This experience of God, precisely as it exists *today* is much more clearly and radically than in earlier times, an experience of transcendence."[33] In fact, Rahner is not overly concerned about making a precise distinction between the experience of God and experience of transcendence. For him, the more important issue is to show how the goal or term of transcendence "can only be thought of as the infinite, unlim-

---

ity, but one would soon notice that one's inner experience would become thin and unreal, and that one would not be achieving what one wants, viz. the intensification and deepening of one's 'interior life.' Hence one must have actions *ad extra*, and this is just as much part of one's life — and more precisely, of one's spiritual life — as the inner processes." Rahner, "Some Thoughts On 'A Good Intention.'" *TI* 3:105-106 (*ST* III: 127-28). See also Bacik, *Apologetics and the Eclipse of Mystery*, 22-25.

[31] Rahner, "The Experience of God Today," *TI* 11: 161 (*ST* IX: 172).

[32] Rahner, "Experience of the Holy Spirit," *TI* 18: 196 (*ST* XIII: 233-34). See also his article "Religious Feeling Inside and Outside the Church," *TI* 17: 235-40 (*ST* XII: 590-96). Pertinent here, too, is the discussion of Wiseman, "Religious Experience in the Theology of Karl Rahner," *American Benedictine Review* 44 (1993): 29-38.

[33] Rahner, "The Experience of God Today," *TI* 11: 161 (*ST* IX: 173).

ited reality which remains at root a mystery: that is to say, God."[34] Rahner calls transcendental experience "the subjective, unthematic, necessary and unfailing consciousness of the knowing subject that is co-present in every spiritual act of knowledge, and the subject's openness to the unlimited expanse of all possible reality."[35] He describes it as an *experience* because it is ever-present, albeit unthematic, and a condition of possibility for every concrete experience of any and every object. It is *transcendental* because it belongs to the "necessary and inalienable structures" of the knowing person, "and because it consists precisely in the transcendence (*Überstieg*) beyond any particular group of possible objects or of categories."[36] Further, the term of this transcendental experience, namely God, can only be spoken of indirectly. God, as the term of our experience of transcendence can never be situated within our system of coordinates, can never be objectified in the sense of being understood as one object among other objects, or be adequately defined conceptually.

[34] Rahner, "Religious Feeling Inside and Outside the Church," *TI* 17: 235 (*ST* XII: 590).

[35] Rahner, *FCF*, 20 (*Grundkurs*, 31). We have already reflected on the human person as transcendent being in Chapter Two. Our aim here, however, is not to provide a detailed investigation of the origins of the notion of transcendence in Rahner. Our point is rather to show that transcendental experience refers to a "basic mode of being which is prior to and permeates every objective experience." It is not the "thematically conceptualized 'concept' of transcendence" that is at issue here, but "rather the a priori openness of the subject to being as such, which is present precisely when a person experiences himself as involved in the multiplicity of cares and concerns and fears and hopes of his everyday world. Real transcendence is always in the background, so to speak, in those origins of human life and human knowledge over which we have no control." *FCF*, 34-35 (*Grundkurs*, 45).

[36] Rahner, *FCF*, 20 (*Grundkurs*, 31). See also Herbert Vorgrimler, "Der Begriff der Selbsttranszendenz in der Theologie Karl Rahners," *Wagnis Theologie. Erfahrungen mit der Theologie Karl Rahners,* ed. Herbert Vorgrimler, (Freiburg: Herder, 1979), 242-58.

According to Van der Heijden, "transcendental" means for Rahner either: i) the quality of a particular mode of knowledge or ii) the quality of a particular mode of being that is connected with the transcendental mode of knowing. In the first meaning, "transcendental" refers to the way in which persons know themselves, being, and God. In the second meaning, "transcendental" refers to some of the realities that correspond to our transcendental mode of knowing. Here "transcendental" refers not to our knowing in a non-objective (*ungegenständlich*) fashion, but rather to that which is transobjective (*übergegenständlich*). Van der Heijden, *Karl Rahner: Darstellung und Kritik seiner Grundpositionen,* 101-104.

Rahner is aware of the difficulty of the task involved if Christianity is to help people discover the experience of God within themselves, to accept it, and to give their allegiance to it. This is not an easy task, since, as we have seen, we do not automatically make the transition from the experience itself to a recognition and interpretation of it at the conceptual level. In fact, we will see later that what is at issue here is a choice between acceptance and rejection. It may not be a particularly dramatic choice — rejection usually takes the form of evasion or postponement. Acceptance, on the other hand, involves an act of surrender and trust, something we discussed previously in the context of prayer.

While this implicit experience of God is present, unthematically, according to Rahner, in every exercise of our intellectual faculties, it is particularly manifest in those experiences where we are "thrown back on ourselves" — when we are no longer able to overlook factors in our life which we would rather evade: loneliness, suffering, ingratitude on the part of others, and especially the reality of death. At retreat conferences, Rahner would often urge his hearers to take the time to ponder such realities as a prelude to a possible experience of God:

> "Be still for once. Don't try to think of so many complex and varied things. Give these deeper realities of the spirit a chance now to rise to the surface: silence, fear, the ineffable longing for truth, for love, for fellowship, for God. Face loneliness, fear, imminent death! Allow such ultimate, basic human experiences to come first… . Then in fact something like a primitive awareness of God can emerge."[37]

The experience of God and the experience of transcendence form a unity in diversity, in that God is the term of the movement of transcendence.[38] Instead of the term "God," Rahner frequently prefers to use the term "holy mystery." We have already alluded to his reasons for this. In his own words:

> "Because God is something quite different from any of the individual realities which appear within the realm of our experience or which are inferred from it, and because the knowledge of God has a quite definite

---

[37] Karl Rahner, *Meditations on Priestly Life*, trans. Edward Quinn (London: Sheed and Ward, 1970), 7-8. [*Einübung priesterlicher Existenz* (Freiburg: Herder, 1970), 18-19].

[38] Wiseman, "Religious Experience in the Theology of Karl Rahner," 36.

and unique character and is not just an instance of knowledge in general, it is for these reasons very easy to overlook God. The concept of 'God' is not a grasp of God by which a person masters the mystery, but it is letting oneself be grasped (*ein Sich-ergreifen-Lassen*) by the mystery which is present and yet ever distant."[39]

What lies behind Rahner's interpretation of the experience of transcendence as an ever-present movement toward the absolute mystery he calls "God"? Firstly, running throughout Rahner's argument is a certain pre-understanding, or pre-apprehension (*Vorgriff*) of what is being sought.[40] Secondly, alongside this pre-understanding is Rahner's acknowledgement of some kind of direct experience or personal encounter with this term of transcendence within a context of faith. Even Rahner's remarks on the so-called "proofs" for God's existence bring out this fact. For him, the "proofs" are not to be viewed in contrast to an "experience" of God. Rather, they constitute an objectively conceptualized articulation of this experience.[41] Rahner is theologizing out of a faith experience that had its roots early in his life, and which he later acknowledged without hesitation:

---

[39] Rahner, *FCF*, 54 (*Grundkurs*, 63). We have already referred to Rahner's understanding of experience in terms of knowledge at the beginning of the chapter. In this section of *FCF* (Chapter II: Man in the Presence of Absolute Mystery), Rahner also describes the experience of God as "transcendental" knowledge, which, at the same time, is an a posteriori knowledge from the world: "Our transcendental knowledge or experience has to be called a posteriori insofar as every transcendental experience is mediated by a categorial encounter with concrete reality in our world." *FCF*, 52 (*Grundkurs*, 61).

[40] The notion of "pre-understanding" is not unique to Rahner. For example, the American philosopher John E. Smith has described this pre-understanding as "a certain *pre-experience*." In the context of arguments for God's existence, he comments: "No argument for God can take place without an initial idea of God's nature, and this in turn can be reached only through direct experience or encounter. Unfortunately, the limitation of our understanding becomes most evident at this point, because this encounter can never have the clarity and obviousness of ordinary perception." *Experience and God* (New York: Oxford Univ. Press, 1968), 127.

[41] "A theoretical proof for the existence of God, then, is only intended to mediate a reflexive awareness of the fact that one always and inevitably has to do with God in one's intellectual and spiritual existence, whether one reflects upon it or not, and whether one freely accepts it or not.... . The point of the reflexive proofs for the existence of God is to indicate that all knowledge ... takes place against the background of an affirmation of holy mystery, or of absolute being." *FCF*, 69 (*Grundkurs*, 77).

"Where are we to start when it is a question of stating and showing that one may have the courage of one's belief? … I begin with the fact that I have — quite simply — always been a believer and that I have met with no reason which would force or cause me not to believe any more. I was born a Catholic because I was born and baptized in a believing environment. I trust in God that this faith passed on by tradition has turned into my own personal decision, into a real belief, and that I am a Catholic Christian even in my innermost being. This, in the last analysis, remains God's secret and an unreflected reality deep down within me which I cannot express even to myself."[42]

Our discussion up to now reveals Rahner's basic personal conviction that both he and others could, and did, have an experience of God. While his argument is somewhat circular, his basic question has to do with *intelligibility*, and has two aspects. Firstly, *how* is such an experience of God (which Rahner assumes to be both possible and desirable) most adequately to be conceived and expressed? And, secondly, what is there about the constitution of the (finite) human person that makes experience of the infinite One possible? We have already reflected on Rahner's approach to the second question by pointing to the openness of the human mind and heart to the infinite.[43] In fact, in Rahner's view, both these questions are connected,

---

[42] Rahner, "Thoughts on the Possibility of Belief Today," *TI* 5: 4 (*ST* V: 12). While the text cited above may be considered more a testimony to belief than to an experience, we also refer to Rahner's early prayers as providing the most lucid examples of such a faith experience: "Dank deiner Barmherzigkeit, du unendlicher Gott, daß ich von dir nicht bloß weiß mit Begriffen und Worten, sondern dich erfahren, erlebt und erlitten habe. Denn die erste und letzte Erfahrung meines Lebens bist du… . Du hast mich ergriffen, nicht ich habe dich 'begriffen,' du hast mein Sein von seinen letzten Wurzeln und Ursprüngen her umgestaltet, du hast mich deines Seins und Lebens teilhaftig gemacht, …" Rahner, "Gott der Erkenntnis," *Worte ins Schweigen*, 34-35.
Commenting on the notion of the experience of God in Rahner's theology, William J. Hoye, *Gotteserfahrung?* 113-14, notes: "Die Theologie Rahners ist im vollen Sinne des Wortes eine Erfahrungstheologie. Alle theologische Erkenntnis expliziert die eine Gotteserfahrung." He then cites Rahner: "Theologische Aussagen verbal thematischer Art (und erst so sind sie 'Aussagen') verweisen darum immer trotz ihrer rationalen Struktur, die sie natürlich auch haben (weil sie sonst keine Aussagen wären), auf die ursprüngliche, vorthematische, transzendentale Erfahrung und sind nur unter dieser Bedingung wirklich verstehbar." Rahner, "Zum Verhältnis zwischen Theologie und heutigen Wissenschaften," *ST* X: 107-108.
[43] In mystical writers of the Middle Ages, this capacity was often referred to in terms of a faculty or power called the *Seelenspitze* or *apex affectus* or *apex mentis*.

and we will address this relationship in the subsequent discussion of his transcendental-anthropological method. Moreover, these two questions also provide an indication of the interrelatedness or unity of theology and philosophy in Rahner's writings, in which this circular movement between question and answer is again evident. In other words, the *question* which the human person is, is the condition of possibility of the hearing of the answer which is the Christian revelation:

> "This question, which the person is and not only has, must be regarded as the condition which makes hearing the Christian answer possible.... . The question creates the condition for really hearing, and only the answer brings the question to its reflexive self-presence. This circle is essential and is not supposed to be resolved in the foundational course, but to be reflected upon as such."[44]

The question of the human person as the subject of a pre-apprehension or "Vorgriff," which has no intrinsic limit, was examined by Rahner even in his earlier and more philosophical works, *Geist in Welt* and *Hörer des Wortes*. In *Geist in Welt*, Rahner uses a Thomistic metaphysics of knowledge, explained in terms of transcendental and existential philosophy, to define the human person as "that essence of absolute transcendence towards God insofar as man or woman in his or her understanding and interpretation of the world respectfully 'pre-apprehends' (*vorgreift*) towards God."[45] This thesis remained decisive for Rahner. It recurs again in the *Grundkurs des Glaubens*, where the human person is described as:

> "a transcendent being (*das Wesen der Transzendenz*) insofar as all of one's knowledge and all of one's conscious activity is grounded in a pre-apprehension (*Vorgriff*) of "being" as such, in an unthematic but ever-present knowledge of the infinity of reality."[46]

Rahner himself used such terms in some of his earlier writings. See Rahner, "The Doctrine of the 'Spiritual Senses' in the Middle Ages," *TI* 16:104-34, esp. 122-26 (*ST* XII: 137-72). Later, he came to favour terms more common in modern philosophy, such as "the transcendence of the (human) spirit" or, with Heidegger, "the *Ek-sistenz* of the human person."

[44] Rahner, *FCF*, 11 (*Grundkurs*, 22-23).

[45] See J. B. Metz, Foreword — "An Essay on Karl Rahner," *Spirit in the World*, xvi.

[46] Rahner, *FCF*, 33 (*Grundkurs*, 44).

The theological implication of this thesis is that all our conceptual expressions about God, however necessary they are, "always stem from the unobjectivated experience of transcendence as such: the concept from the pre-conception, the name from the experience of the nameless."[47] In short, when Rahner speaks of God as the infinite horizon or as the term of transcendence, he is declaring our inability to situate God within some well-defined system of coordinates. God, as the Whither of transcendental experience, is indefinable, and cannot be conceived adequately as an individual existent alongside of other existents. "The ultimate measure cannot itself be measured. The limit by which everything is 'defined' cannot itself be defined by a still more ultimate limit."[48]

c. Rahner's Transcendental-Anthropological Method

Our reflections on Rahner's understanding of the experience of transcendence bring us to the heart of what he has called his "transcendental-anthropological method" in theology.[49] We have seen how he takes for his starting-point the individual's ability to *question*.[50] Indeed, his transcendental method has been described as "a particular way of questioning."[51] The fact that the individual raises questions

---

[47] Rahner, "Über den Begriff des Geheimnisses in der katholischen Theologie," *ST* IV: 70 (*TI* 4: 50): "Die begriffliche Aussage über Gott, so notwendig sie ist, lebt immer von der ungegenständlichen Erfahrung der Transzendenz als solcher, der Begriff Gottes also vom Vorgriff, seine Nennung also von der Erfahrung des Namenlosen."

[48] Rahner, *FCF*, 63 (*Grundkurs*, 72). Rahner's intention is to depict the transcendental knowledge of God as an experience of mystery. He accomplishes this by turning to the term ("das Woraufhin") and source ("das Wovonher") of human transcendence. *FCF*, 59 (*Grundkurs*, 68). His primary aim is to draw attention to our unthematic knowledge and experience of God, and to help this (knowledge) become more explicit.

[49] Rahner, "Theology and Anthropology," *TI* 9: 28-45 (*ST* VIII: 43-65).

[50] "The transcendental subject, even in the boundlessness of his own transcendentality, ultimately apprehends himself as a *question*. For he always experiences himself in this transcendentality of his as open, as of himself an empty question, as that which refers beyond and outside of himself to that which he himself is not." Rahner, "Reflections on Methodology in Theology," *TI* 11: 88 (*ST* IX: 99). [Attempts to use inclusive language in the above citation have proved too unwieldy!].

[51] "Die transzendentale Methode ... *ist vielmehr eine bestimmte Weise des Fragens.*" Weger, *Karl Rahner: Eine Einführung in sein theologisches Denken*, 27.

about him or herself, and is thereby opened to the unlimited horizons of such questioning, means that this person "has already transcended him or herself... . In doing this one is affirming oneself as more than the sum of (the) analyzable components of one's reality."[52] It is in this radical questioning (i.e., in the encounter of oneself in a question), and also in the going beyond or transcending every possible empirical and partial answer, that the human person experiences him or herself as a subject oriented towards the totality (*Bezogensein auf das Ganze*)[53] and as "pure openness for absolutely everything, for being as such" (*die reine Geöffnetheit für schlechthin alles*).[54]

Rahner postulates an "a priori" givenness in the human person. By this he means that the particular constitution of the human person is not derived simply from one's interactions with the world of experience.[55] This *a priori* constitution of the human person is not exhausted in the *a posteriori* experiences that we have in our everyday, *categorial* world.[56] Rather, the a priori dimension of the human person precedes that encounter with the world of experience, and not just in a temporal sense (as we saw in the previous section in the context of experiential and conceptual knowledge). However, at the same time, nothing can really be known about the a priori constitution of the human person without the a posteriori experiences that a person has.[57] It is important to bear in mind here that Rahner always sees the human person as constituting a unity.[58] The human person is always

---

[52] Rahner, *FCF*, 29 (*Grundkurs*, 40).

[53] Rahner, *Grundkurs*, 41.

[54] Rahner, *FCF*, 20 (*Grundkurs*, 31).

[55] "To say that one is person and subject, therefore, means first of all that the human person is someone who cannot be derived, who cannot be produced completely from other elements at their disposal. He or she is that being who is responsible for him or herself. When one explains oneself, analyzes oneself, reduces oneself back to the plurality of one's origins, one is affirming oneself as the subject who is doing this, and in so doing one experiences oneself as something necessarily prior to and more original than this plurality." Rahner, *FCF*, 31 (*Grundkurs*, 42).

[56] The contrast between the two terms "kategorial" and "transzendental" was discussed in the previous chapter.

[57] See Rahner, "Reflections on Methodology in Theology," *TI* 11: 89 (*ST* IX: 100) where he mentions "the constant danger of interpreting the *a priori* element as that which alone is important, of being intolerant of the historical element and failing to take it into account."

[58] See, for example, *FCF*, 42-43 (*Grundkurs*, 52-53).

matter and spirit, subject and object, an individual and a member of society, free and unfree, and so on. To sum up, while Rahner sees the person living and acting in the concrete world, or *categorial* reality, as he calls it — a world increasingly characterized by pluralism and constant change — he also sees the "more" of the human person in the "a priori", or, to put it in another way, in the transcendental dimension of the human person.[59] The transcendental method, then, attempts to show that this *a priori* element in the human person exists, and to elaborate and clarify its meaning.

A further characteristic of Rahner's transcendental method is the continual return to foundational human experiences (*Grunderfahrungen*), which, he says, remain always and everywhere the same: "The person of today is never *merely* a person of today. This is indeed something he or she must not be."[60] In other words, for Rahner, the human person is more than "a finite system of individual, distinguishable elements."[61] Further, *Grunderfahrungen* (such as the experience of personal love, facing one's personal responsibility, the approach of death, etc.) are but different expressions "of this single, basic experience of the human person present in a thousand different forms, and in this experience it is borne in upon him or her that his or her existence is open to the inconceivable mystery."[62] In this sense,

---

[59] Commenting on what he calls "die apriorische Verfaßtheit des Menschen," Weger describes this as "a kind of metahistorical dimension" ("eine Art übergeschichtliche Dimension"). However, it is not a question of placing this a priori dimension over or beyond history. Rather, the importance of history resides in the fact "... daß Geschichte Antwort sein kann auf genau jene Fragen, die wir nicht 'erfinden' (und aus diesem Grund auch apriorisch mit der menschlichen Existenz gegeben sind) und denen wir nicht entrinnen." Weger, *Karl Rahner: Eine Einführung*, 27.

[60] Rahner, "The Man of Today and Religion," *TI* 6: 3 (*ST* VI: 13).

[61] Rahner, *FCF*, 29-30 (*Grundkurs*, 40).

[62] Rahner, "The Experience of God Today," *TI* 11: 158 (*ST* IX: 169). In *Spirit in the World*, the human capacity to question is also the starting-point of metaphysics: "Ausgangspunkt ist der fragende Mensch." *Geist in Welt*, 74. Further, such metaphysics "is always concerned with things which we 'always know and always have known'... . (It) is the methodical, reflective, knowledge of that which one has always known." *Hearers of the Word*, 31 (*Hörer des Wortes*, 47). In pursuing this question, the person is made aware of what he or she is in the ground of their being: "der nach dem Sein Fragenmüssende." *Geist in Welt*, 72. Hence, for Rahner, the practice of metaphysics is unavoidable: "Der Mensch fragt notwendig. Diese Notwendigkeit kann aber allein darin gründen, daß dem Menschen Sein überhaupt nur als Fragbarkeit erschlossen ist, daß er selbst ist, indem er nach dem Sein fragt, daß er selbst als Seins-

Rahner insists that there is present in such transcendental experience "an unthematic and anonymous, as it were, knowledge of God." This theme is beautifully captured in the following image:

> "In the ultimate depths of one's being, one knows nothing more surely than that one's knowledge, that is, what is called knowledge in everyday parlance, is only a small island in a vast sea that has not been travelled. It is a floating island, and it might be more familiar to us than the sea, but ultimately it is borne by the sea and only because it is can we be borne by it. Hence the existentiell question for the knower is this: Which does one love more, the small island of one's so-called knowledge or the sea of infinite mystery? ... Only when one turns one's attention to the scope of knowledge and not only to the objects of knowledge, to transcendence and not only to what is understood categorically in time and space within this transcendence, only then is one just on the threshold of becoming a religious person."[63]

In Rahner's view, there will always be a tension between such original human basic experiences *(Grunderfahrungen)*, and our attempts to describe these in concepts and language. Religious language is also characterized by this tension, and, within theology, there will be a tension between original self-experience acquired through what we do, suffer, etc., and our attempts to express such self-experience in conceptual terms. Hence, Rahner saw one of the most significant tasks of theology as the attempt to relate all our theological concepts back to our original experience.[64]

Rahner's transcendental method is best described in terms of its aim. We have mentioned how Rahner posits an *a priori* "givenness" in the individual which is not reducible to particular actions in the categorial world. This becomes clearer in his analysis of the faculty of knowledge and the role of the subject (person) in this process. The

---

frage existiert.... Die Frage nach dem Sein im Ganzen ... ist die einzige Frage, von der er sich nicht abkehren kann, die er fragen muß, wenn er überhaupt sein will." *Geist in Welt*, 71.

[63] Rahner, *FCF*, 22-23 (*Grundkurs*, 33-34).

[64] "We should show again and again that all these theological concepts do not make the reality itself present to the individual from outside of him or her, but they are rather the expression of what has already been experienced and lived through more originally in the depths of existence." *FCF*, 17 (*Grundkurs*, 28). For a discussion of this "dual movement" in Rahner's thought in the context of the relationship between theology and spirituality, see the third section of Chapter Two.

transcendental method is linked with the act of knowledge in that this method, following from the formulation of Kant, seeks to ascertain the conditions of possibility *(Bedingungen der Möglichkeit)* of human knowledge and action. The term "transcendental" itself refers to that necessary and unavoidable metahistorical, a priori disposition of the human person who is oriented beyond all this-worldly, historical and empirical reality. With Rahner, we find the term used in the following associations: "transcendental method" *(transzendentale Methode)*, "transcendental-anthropological enquiry" *(transzendental-anthropologische Fragestellung)*, "transcendental experience *(transzendentale Erfahrung)*, "transcendental subject" *(transzendentales Subjekt)*, and "transcendental reflection" *(transzendentale Reflexion)*.

We began this section by claiming that Rahner's theological starting-point is the questioning subject. But not all questions are equally important. On the one hand, there are those questions which ask for answers of a factual, or empirical kind, e.g., the factual knowledge derived from the natural sciences. On the other hand, there are those *existentiell* questions (examples of which include questions concerning the significance and meaning of human freedom, responsibility, and love), which are qualitatively different, and which cannot be easily evaded.[65]

The anthropological aspect of this method can best be described in terms of the "turn to the subject," credited to Descartes and developed by Kant. (In fact, Rahner's *Geist in Welt* is an attempt to retrieve from Aquinas' theory of cognition an implicit transcendental turn to the subject. Whether Rahner finds this turn to the subject in Aquinas, or reads it into him is an issue beyond the scope of our discussion here).[66] This turn to the subject involves moving away from

---

[65] For a more spiritual, anthropological meditation on the human person considered as a "question," see Rahner, "Was ist der Mensch?" *Wagnis des Christen: Geistliche Texte*, 13-26.

[66] There have been several analyses of Rahner's philosophical foundations, as well as of his dependence on Aquinas. Some of the more significant of these in English include: Thomas Sheehan, *Karl Rahner: The Philosophical Foundations,* with a Preface by Karl Rahner, S.J. (Ohio: University Press, 1987), 173-94; Anne Carr, *The Theological Method of Karl Rahner*, American Academy of Religion Dissertation Series, no. 19 (Missoula, Montana: Scholars Press, 1977), 59-124; and George Vass, *A Theologian in Search of a Philosophy: Understanding Karl Rahner*, vol. 1, (Lon-

a naive understanding of the "nature of knowledge after the model of a tablet on which an object is inscribed, whereby the object comes from outside, as it were, and appears on the tablet."[67] On the contrary, knowledge has a far more complex structure. Kant's concern in *Kritik der reinen Vernunft* was to ascertain the presuppositions or "conditions of possibility" in the knowing subject that enable one to know and make judgements, especially where this knowledge and judgement contains more than what is mediated to the subject in sense perception. Abandoning the prevailing notion of knowledge as a "copy" of objects, Kant sought to show that objects must conform to our knowledge. Such an approach would lead to *a priori* and scientific knowledge, since:

> "... understanding has rules which I must presuppose as being in me prior to objects being given to me, and therefore as a priori. They find expression in a priori concepts to which all objects of experience necessarily conform and with which they must agree."[68]

Kant therefore believed that human knowing involved both the passive perception of objects as well as a "subjective" contribution on the part of the knower. And this subjective element is not the result of knowledge, experiences, or perceptions, but exists already (a priori) in the human person. This is the *a priori* of human knowledge — we can never have knowledge of any object as the "thing in itself," but only in terms of our relations to it, i.e., only as phenomenon.[69] In other

---

don: Sheed and Ward, 1985), 31-45. For Rahner's own assessment of the significance and challenge of Aquinas for contemporary theology, see Rahner's "Einführender Essay," in J. B. Metz, *Christlicher Anthropozentrik. Über die Denkform des Thomas von Aquin* (Munich: Kösel, 1962), 9-20. Also relevant here are Rahner's, "On Recognizing the Importance of Thomas Aquinas," *TI* 13: 3-12 (*ST* X: 11-20); and "Thomas Aquinas: Monk, Theologian, and Mystic," *The Great Church Year*, 309-314.

[67] Rahner, *FCF*, 17 (*Grundkurs*, 28).

[68] Immanuel Kant, *Critique of Pure Reason*, B, xvii, f, cited in Thomas Sheehan, *Karl Rahner: The Philosophical Foundations* (Ohio: Univ. Press, 1987), 24.

[69] Human reason as opposed to divine reason is a finite, receptive reason. It does not constitute the "thing in itself" (the noumenon), but only as an appearance to the human knower. Such an appearance entails what Kant called a receptive, sense intuition on the part of the knower. See Martin Heidegger, *Kant and the Problem of Metaphysics*, trans. James S. Churchill (Bloomington, Ind.: Indiana Univ. Press, 1962), 27-39.

words, whenever one perceives something, one does so with the pre-given "categories" of (pure) human reason, i.e., reason before it acquires its objects — not as chronologically prior, but as the condition for the possibility of any knowledge of objects at all. Thus Kant refers to human reason as that "which contains the principles whereby we know anything absolutely *a priori*."[70] In this context, Kant introduces the term "transcendental:" "I entitle *transcendental* all knowledge which is occupied not so much with objects as with the mode of our knowledge of objects insofar as the mode of knowledge is to be possible *a priori*."[71] Moreover, for Kant, human reason, insofar as it can know *a priori*, can also be *scientific* reason. His point here is that what constitutes reason as scientific is its prior relation to its objects. Herein lies the heart of Kant's Copernican Revolution, and its radical reversal of the prevailing notion of knowledge as a "copy" of objects. In short, knowledge determines rather than copies:

> "Scientific knowledge (or any knowledge for that matter) is never a brute encounter between two "things," the scientist and the datum. Knowledge for a human being requires mediation whereby the data are structured in an intelligible framework 'prior' to the sense encounter (not chronologically, of course), for if the data are to be *known*, they must have some common ground with the intellect, i.e., must conform to some exigency of human knowing."[72]

It would be wrong, however, to assume that Rahner simply takes over Kant's use and understanding of the term "transcendental," without giving it a different nuance of his own. After an intensive private study of the Belgian Jesuit philosopher-theologian Joseph Maréchal's *Le point de départ de la métaphysique*,[73] Rahner devel-

---

[70] Immanuel Kant, *Critique of Pure Reason*, A 11/B 24, cited in Sheehan, *Karl Rahner: The Philosophical Foundations*, 22.

[71] Immanuel Kant, *Critique of Pure Reason*, B 25, cited in Sheehan, *Karl Rahner: The Philosophical Foundations*, 22.

[72] Sheehan, *Karl Rahner: The Philosophical Foundations*, 29.

[73] Joseph Maréchal, *Le point de départ de la métaphysique: Leçons sur la développement historique et théorique du probleme de la connaissance*. 5 vols. (Paris: Descleé de Brouwer; and Brussels: L'Edition Universelle, 1922-26). See especially the final volume: *Le thomisme devant la philosophie critique*, 2nd ed., 1949 (originally published, 1926). Acknowledging Maréchal's influence on his interpretation of Aquinas (particularly in *Geist in Welt*), Rahner says: "I owe my most basic, decisive, philosophical direction, insofar as it comes from someone else, to the

oped an understanding of the transcendental subject which went beyond the a priori conditions for the possibility of knowledge (although he also includes this). Rahner, in addition, gave the term "transcendental" what has been described as a "vertical" orientation (*die vertikale Stoßrichtung*).[74] With this vertical meaning, Rahner recognizes that the term "transcendental" never refers solely to the question of the subjective conditions of the possibility of knowing and acting. Rather, *God* is the pre-supposition, the "condition of possibility" for all human knowledge. In Rahner's view, then, the meaning of the term "transcendental" encompasses the possible (metaphysical) knowledge of God.[75] Moreover, Rahner, in his transcendental method, is concerned to show that the concrete world of experience is not in itself sufficient to account for the human person in his or her totality. Instead, the transcendentality of the human subject is conceived as the openness on our part towards what he calls "Mystery."

Having ascertained what are the "conditions of possibility" which make all our experiences possible, the transcendental method, in a second step, attempts to express in conceptual terms those a priori experiences (of God or of transcendence) which until then had remained unthematic.[76] While we have underscored the a priori ele-

Belgian philosopher and Jesuit, Joseph Maréchal. His philosophy already moved beyond the traditional neo-Scholasticism. I brought that direction from Maréchal to my studies with Heidegger, and it was not superseded by him." Leo O'Donovan, "Living into Mystery: Karl Rahner's Reflections at Seventy-five," *America* 140 (March 10, 1979): 177.

[74] Weger, *Karl Rahner: Eine Einführung*, 30.

[75] "Die Transzendentalität des Menschen meint bei Rahner also immer auch die Offenheit des Menschen auf das, was er 'das Geheimnis' nennt. Die Transzendenz menschlicher Geistigkeit ist das Woher (als Ermöglichungsgrund) und das Woraufhin (Ziel) des gelebten Menschseins selbst, ist, was das Menschsein erst ermöglicht. Es ist weiter das, was auch unabhängig vom Menschen objektiv existiert; das, woran der Mensch teilhat und worauf er verwiesen ist und was er dennoch nie 'hat.' Das 'Wovonher' der menschlichen wie das 'Woraufhin' kann nach Rahner nicht einfach das Leere, das Nichts, das Nicht-Seiende oder nur Projektion des menschlichen Geistes sein, der keine objektive Wirklichkeit entspricht. Die Transzendenz (für Rahner nur ein anderer, 'ursprünglicherer' Name für Gott) ist Wirklichkeit, und transzendentales Subjekt ist der Mensch nur, weil es diese Transzendenz gibt." Weger, *Karl Rahner: Eine Einführung*, 31.

[76] We have discussed in the final section of Chapter Two how Rahner treats of theological statements (which are thematic and verbal in character) by referring

ment of this method, it is also necessary to stress that the transcendental method, in focusing on the knowing subject, does so in the awareness that this subject "apprehends him or herself as inescapably anchored in *history*, and realizes the *a posteriori* nature of his or her experience, something which precisely cannot be reduced to the transcendental dimension."[77]

The anthropological aspect of the method is particularly evident in the starting-point and primary concern of all Rahner's theological considerations.[78] Specifically, this starting-point or context is described by Rahner in terms of the crisis of faith of contemporary Europe. Gone is the previously homogeneously Christian milieu, and this has been replaced by a pluralism of world-views, each vying for attention in the atmosphere of an increasingly secularized world, and against a background of atheism, and technical rationality. It is within such a context that Rahner attempts to provide his intellectual justification for a decision to believe. In Rahner's view, it is only when all the experiences that constitute the self-understanding of the person of today are taken into account, that Christian faith-statements will begin to make sense. Thus Rahner's theological reflections begin with the human person, from below, rather than trying to bring God in "from the outside," in a type of doctrinaire approach.

A number of characteristics of the human person, as interpreted by Rahner, emerge from the foregoing reflections. Let us, by way of a

them back to an original pre-thematic and transcendental experience, and have noted his insistence that it is only on this condition that they are really comprehensible. See Rahner, "On The Relationship between Theology and the Contemporary Sciences," *TI* 13: 97-100 (*ST* X: 107-110). Herein lies the value, even the urgency, of a transcendental enquiry in theology today — if contemporary man and woman are to be genuinely able to assimilate the propositions of faith. On this, see Rahner, "Reflections on Methodology in Theology," *TI* 11: 88 (*ST* IX: 99). For a good "Rückblick" on transcendental theology in the context of Rahnerian research, and on the future possibilities for this method in theology, see Bernd Jochen Hilberath and Bernhard Nitsche, "Transzendentale Theologie? Beobachtungen zur Rahner-Diskussion der letzten Jahre," *Theologische Quartalschrift* (1994) 4: 304-15.

[77] Rahner, "Reflections on Methodology in Theology," *TI* 11: 88 (*ST* IX: 99).
[78] See, for example, Rahner's remarks on the addressee of contemporary theology, *FCF*, 5-8 (*Grundkurs*, 17-20).

summary, bring together some of these characteristics.[79] Then, in the final part of this section, we shall draw out some implications for spirituality that result from Rahner's transcendental-anthropological method.

Rahner has described the human person as "the question to which there is no answer."[80] This is the basic datum of his metaphysical anthropology. Put another way, the person is to be understood as "the essence of an unlimited transcendentality."[81] What is at issue here is both the openness of the human person, as well as one's unfulfilled and limitless transcendentality. This transcendentality has its own historical process of explication, and the transcendental method takes seriously the importance of considering the human person as a historical being. Nevertheless, according to Rahner, the movement of human self-transcendence is constituted by God's *grace*. Clearly, then, Rahner is not attempting to deduce the mystery of the unmerited reality of salvation *a priori* from the mere nature of the person as such.[82] The final statement of Rahner's description of the mode in which the human person is constituted in a state of grace-given transcendentality focuses on the history of this transcendental dimension, that is, on the history of God's self-communication, which he calls saving and revelation history. The history of God's self-communication to the world attains its absolutely highest point, its point of irreversibility, with "the absolute bringer of salvation, Jesus as crucified and risen, the Son of the Father."[83]

---

[79] In the following paragraph our summary is based on Rahner's "five statements," in which he expresses "the mode in which the person is constituted in a state of grace-given transcendentality, and the historical process in which this takes place." Rahner, "Reflections on Methodology in Theology," *TI* 11: 94 (*ST* IX: 106).

[80] Rahner, *Christian at the Crossroads*, 11 (*Wagnis des Christen*, 13).

[81] Rahner, *Christian at the Crossroads*, 14 (*Wagnis des Christen*, 17). See also his "Experience of Self and Experience of God," *TI* 13: 122 (*ST* X: 133), where Rahner describes metaphysical anthropology as an attempt "to understand the whole of reality from one specific point of departure, namely from that finite subject which is nevertheless, open to the infinite."

[82] Apart from Rahner's "Reflections on Methodology in Theology," *TI* 11: 90- 94 (*ST* IX: 102-106), see also his "Theology and Anthropology," *TI* 9: 33-37 (*ST* VIII: 49-54).

[83] Rahner, "Reflections on Methodology in Theology," *TI* 11: 94 (*ST* IX: 106).

d. Implications for Spirituality

It is our contention that Rahner's metaphysical anthropology can provide a basis for what has been called a "dialectical" spirituality.[84] We have seen how Rahner's whole theology flows from his philosophical anthropology. The conclusion of *Hörer des Wortes*, for example, is couched in anthropological terms:

> "What we are engaged in is anthropology insofar as we are concerned with the human person. Insofar as we see the human person as that creature who has to attend in freedom, within one's history, to a possible message from the free God, it is 'theological' anthropology. It is 'fundamental-theological' anthropology insofar as this self-understanding which the person has of him or herself is the presupposition for the fact that he or she is able to hear at all the theology that has actually arisen."[85]

Rahner developed his theological anthropology in terms of a description and analysis of the general formal structures or characteristics of human existence. In our reflections to date we have discussed a number of these characteristics, sometimes called by Rahner "existentials," a variation of a technical term in Martin Heidegger's philosophy.[86] We also find a number of these existentials listed in *Foundations of Christian Faith*, where Rahner provides a theological ordering, describing human beings as persons, transcendent beings, responsible and free, historical, dependent creatures oriented to mystery, beings threatened by sin and guilt, and finally, as the event of God's self-communication.[87] In this, Rahner is not offering a comprehensive theological anthropology, but merely using these characteristics of human existence as a basis for his theological reflections.

---

[84] This claim is made by James J. Bacik, "The Basis for a Dialectical Spirituality," *Being and Truth: Essays in Honour of John Macquarrie,* eds. Alistair Kee and Eugene T. Long (London: SCM Press, 1986), 168-82.

[85] Rahner, *Hörer des Wortes,* 208.

[86] See, for example, Rahner, Vorgrimler, "Existential State," *Theological Dictionary*: 161, where the term refers to the basic disposition of the human person, characterized by 'thrownness' and 'being-in-the-world'. Further, *FCF*, 16, describes the term "Existential," as in Rahner's phrase "supernatural existential," as referring "to an element in the person's ontological constitution precisely as human being, an element which is constitutive of one's existence as person prior to one's exercise of freedom. It is an aspect of concrete human nature precisely as human."

[87] For Rahner's theological anthropology, see *FCF*, Chaps. I-IV, 24-137 (*Grundkurs*, 35-142).

James J. Bacik, in his analysis of Rahner's anthropology as a basis for a contemporary spirituality, organizes Rahner's statements about the fundamental structures of human existence "into pairs of opposites that are dialectically related."[88] One example of such a dialectical pair is Rahner's juxtaposition of the description of the transcendental nature of the human person, and his insistence that such a transcendence also has a history — the categorial dimension. Bacik then groups together those existentials which involve *openness and dynamism*: we are spirit, self-transcendence, individual persons, infinite questioners, and so on, and places them alongside those existentials which reflect some type of *limitation*: we are at the same time contingent, communal, material, finite, historical, sexual, temporal, concupiscent, and subject to death. He (Bacik) then uses the word "spirit" to summarize the first group of characteristics, and "world" to designate the second. In this way, he arrives at Rahner's own characterization of human existence as "spirit in the world." In Rahner's words, we are: "the mid-point suspended between the world and God, between time and eternity, and this boundary line is the point of our definition and our destiny."[89] The two existentials "spirit" and "world" imply each other, and one cannot exist without the other. Both terms have also to be understood in terms of our essential relationship to the absolute mystery. Further, all our encounters with the absolute mystery come precisely in and through finite reality.

Bacik's aim in bringing together seemingly opposite Rahnerian existentials in a type of dialectical tension is to provide a solid and comprehensive basis for working out an approach to the spiritual life for contemporary (Western) society. He sees much of the current spiritual struggle as the attempt to bring apparently opposite and competing tendencies into some kind of integration. Examples of such

[88] Bacik, "Rahner's Anthropology," 175. In the following, we are indebted to Bacik's comments, even if the implications for spirituality which he draws remain at a somewhat abstract and general level. This is surprising, given that Rahner himself has offered far more specific and concrete characteristics of a spirituality of the future. See, for example, his "The Spirituality of the Church of the Future," *TI* 20: 143-53 (*ST* XIV: 368-81).

[89] Rahner, *Spirit in the World*, 407 (*Geist in Welt*, 404).

polarities or tensions include our personal struggles to balance possibility and facticity, rationality and irrationality, responsibility and impotence, anxiety and hope, and the individual and social aspects of our existence. An authentic theological anthropology that refuses to collapse into one or other of the competing poles, focusing instead on the lifelong quest for integration, can serve as a valuable foundation for building a contemporary spirituality. Bacik then argues for a dialectical spirituality rooted both in contemporary experience as well as in a solid anthropology. Such a dialectical spirituality will consist of a number of "ideal characteristics ... expressed in terms of paired opposites in order to reflect our lifelong struggle for integration."[90] A contemporary spirituality will, then, in Bacik's view, include the following characteristics or ideals: i) a *committed-openness*, whereby one is both rooted in one's own religious tradition, but open to the religious standpoints of others in an ongoing search for greater meaning and value; ii) a *reflective-spontaneity*, which fosters a self-evaluation of both our current religious and our other experiences without falling into an excessive self-absorption or narrow introspection; iii) a *hopeful-realism*, which is in touch with the darker and more tragic dimension of existence, while at the same time maintaining a lively hope and confidence in God's final victory over suffering; iv) an *enlightened-simplicity*, which strives for a spiritual maturity based on an adequate theology, i.e., on an adult understanding of our faith, as well as a humble charity based on such insight, combined with an uncomplicated lifestyle, intelligently chosen and worked out, and an utter dependence on God. Such a spirituality will, finally, be v) *prayerfully-prophetic*, combining an interest in prayer with a genuine concern for the needs of the oppressed and disadvantaged.

Even if these characteristics of what Bacik calls a dialectical spirituality are not meant to be exhaustive, they provide a good foundation for any contemporary spirituality, as well as indicating its task. However, it needs to be pointed out that Bacik's categories are not particularly Rahnerian. Rather, Bacik is attempting to employ Rahner's anthropological insights with a view to setting a tone or mapping a direction, as he calls it, for an adequate spirituality that will be

---

[90] Bacik, "Rahner's Anthropology," 179.

closer to the experience of people, and be "a more reliable guide in their quest for meaning, commitment, integration and a richer human life."[91] It would be hard to imagine Rahner disagreeing with Bacik's outline, but it remains rather general. We hope to go beyond Bacik by focusing more specifically on: i) the key themes underlying Rahner's spirituality, an analysis of which we have already begun, and ii) by indicating a *development* in Rahner's thought in the area of spirituality. This development shifted from an early "spiritual individualism" to an increasing awareness of the political dimension of spirituality (partly due to the influence of his former student and friend Johann Baptist Metz). However, our second claim remains to be developed in the course of our work.

Before we return to our investigation of the Rahnerian notion of experience, we will raise some questions and issues arising primarily from the presuppositions in his metaphysical anthropology. Our aim here is not to enter into a detailed criticism of Rahner's philosophical foundations, but rather to indicate some possible *limitations* of his approach and some implications for his understanding of spirituality. The final chapter will offer a more detailed evaluation of this spirituality.

One question raised by Metz and by others concerns Rahner's transcendental-anthropology, which conceives the human person a priori as that being characterized by a transcendence towards God. The problem here is whether such an approach restricts the (necessarily) historically realized salvation of humanity too much "to the question of whether the individual freely accepts or rejects this constitution of his or her being."[92] Metz fears that such an approach runs the risk of restricting the question of salvation to the sphere of the *private* and of not sufficiently preserving the relationship of faith to the world and to history. Another, related, criticism is that Rahner focuses excessively on the questioning and knowing subject.[93] The more polemical of

---

[91] Bacik, "Rahner's Anthropology," 181. An interesting fact in this context is that James Bacik was the principal author of the pastoral letter, *Empowered by the Spirit: Campus Ministry Faces the Future,* issued by the Catholic Bishops of the United States, Nov. 1985.

[92] Metz, "Foreword," *Spirit in the World,* xvii-xviii.

[93] Paul Weß, "Wie kann der Mensch Gott erfahren? Eine Überlegung zur Theologie Karl Rahners," *Zeitschrift für Katholische Theologie* 102 (1980): 343-48.

these criticisms then proceed to accuse Rahner of compromising God's transcendence, and of confusing the object of the Christian faith with the object of philosophical reflection.[94] However, Rahner tirelessly stressed that human transcendentality cannot be understood as that of an absolute subject which experiences and possesses what opens before it as something subject to its power. Rather, our transcendentality is "a relationship which does not establish itself by its own power, but is experienced as established by and at the disposal of another, and which is grounded in the abyss of ineffable mystery."[95]

Rahner's focus on the individual (questioning and knowing) subject, however, does leave him open to the criticism that his anthropology, initially, at any rate, does not adequately explore the *inter-subjective* dimension of human existence.[96] We will not explore this important accusation against Rahner in detail at this stage; a fuller evaluation will come in our final chapter. It is our contention that, while the two dangers or criticisms of Rahner's transcendental-anthropological method mentioned above could lead to serious distortions in

---

[94] An example of such polemic is Paul D. Molnar, "Can We Know God Directly? Rahner's Solution From Experience," *Theological Studies* 46 (1985): 228-61.

[95] Rahner, *FCF*, 42 (*Grundkurs*, 52). See also *FCF*, 67 (*Grundkurs*, 75), where Rahner comments more explicitly: "It would be the greatest misunderstanding, a misunderstanding which would lose all connection with the original experience, if this term (of our unlimited transcendentality) were explained as something in the mind, as an *idea* which human thought established as its own creation. For this term is what opens up and makes possible the process of transcendence. Transcendence is borne by this term, and this term is not its creation."

[96] The philosophical basis for this criticism lies in Rahner's understanding of being. We have discussed his portrayal of the human person as the one who must ask (the metaphysical question) about being ("der nach dem Sein Fragenmüssende"). There is an antecedent knowledge of being in general, so that "one does not somehow first of all have to be brought to being, but the understanding of being which is a person's already must be brought to itself in that person." *Hearers of the Word*, 35 (*Hörer des Wortes*, 52). Being is accessible to a person only as something questionable, i.e., in terms of "questionability" ("Fragbarkeit"). Similarly, being is being-able-to-be-known ("Sein ist Erkanntseinkönnen"). Rahner's presentation of being under the two aspects of "Fragbarkeit" and "Erkennbarkeit" has been criticized for a "Verkürzung des Seins," i.e., for too narrow an understanding of being — effectively identifying it with knowledge: "Sein und Erkennen ist dasselbe." *Geist in Welt*, 82. For a development of this criticism, see Peter Eicher, *Die anthropologische Wende. Karl Rahner's philosophischer Weg vom Wesen des Menschen zur personalen Existenz* (Freiburg/Schweiz: Universitätsverlag, 1970), 330-31, and Hoye, *Gotteserfahrung?* 124-70.

his understanding of spirituality, they do not, in fact, do so. Our main reason for this assertion is that — although Rahner's epistemological presuppositions remained more or less unchanged throughout his career[97] — his theological method of confronting an enormous range of contemporary Christian problems led to a gradual *development* in his reflections both in theology and in spirituality.

2. Experience of the Spirit and Enthusiasm

a. Experience of the Spirit — Terminological Clarification

Another term used by Rahner, which he occasionally identifies with the experience of transcendence, is what he calls "experience of the Holy Spirit."[98] In a rare reference to Scripture, he points out that it does not merely present us with a doctrine of the Spirit, but, at the same time, itself appeals to an experience of the Spirit.[99] Nonetheless,

---

[97] A detailed analysis of Rahner's epistemological presuppositions is beyond the scope of our work. Such an analysis has been offered by Gelpi, *The Turn To Experience In Contemporary Theology*, 90-107. Gelpi's argument hinges on what he calls the fallacies of Kantianism. Kantian logic, he claims, argues by formulating an unproven hypothesis which one then presents as a valid transcendental deduction (p. 95). Kantian logic fails to distinguish clearly between different types of inference, namely, hypothetical, deductive and inductive, but instead regards all inference as deductive. Gelpi then shows how Maréchal and his followers unwittingly took on board this confusion of hypothesis with demonstration. His point is that Maréchal's regrounding of classical metaphysics in a Thomistic theory of knowledge is merely a *hypothesis*, which, in fact, cannot be established *a priori* as universal and necessary. In this context, there arises a further tension between the relatively static, hierarchical universe of classical metaphysics with its fixed and unchanging essences, and Rahner's later endorsement of an evolutionary world-view, particularly in relation to Christology. See *FCF*, 176-203 (*Grundkurs*, 180-202).

[98] "The experience of transcendence permitting God to be present (because of God's salvific will in regard to all human beings, by which one is oriented to God's immediacy) is in fact always experience of the Holy Spirit, whether a person can or cannot interpret explicitly in this way his or her inescapable experience of the unknown God." Rahner, "Experience of the Holy Spirit," *TI* 18: 198 (*ST* XIII: 237). This article also appeared separately in German as *Erfahrung des Geistes: Meditation auf Pfingsten* (Freiburg: Herder, 1977), and in English in Rahner's *The Spirit in the Church* (London: Burns and Oates, 1979), 1-32.

[99] Apart from the testimony of Scripture (he has in mind here Paul's letter to the Galatians and other Pauline and Johannine writings), Rahner also refers to the

while there is testimony to such experience of the Spirit in both
Scripture and in the lives of the mystics and the saints, many Christians fail to discover this experience concretely in their lives. Thus,
Rahner points to the danger that possession of the Spirit comes to be
seen as lying outside one's consciousness and outside everyday piety.
This then leads him to ask when and how such an experience occurs
in us. Rahner's basic thesis here is:

> "that the essential nature of genuine experience of the Spirit does not
> consist in particular objects of experience found in human awareness
> but occurs when one experiences the radical re-ordering of one's tran-
> scendent nature in knowledge and freedom towards the immediate real-
> ity of God through God's self-communication in grace."[100]

The experience at stake here is, according to Rahner, incommensu-
rably different from what we ordinarily describe as "experience"
(especially in a scientific or empirically psychological sense). Experience of the Spirit is not simply one encounter with a particular object
that happens to come upon us from outside. Rather, such an experience begins at the very heart of our existence, at what might be called
its subjective pole. In Rahner's words, the experience of the Spirit has
a transcendental character because it takes place at the innermost
depth of the human person, and constitutes "the singular, original,
primordial experience by the subject of itself, always and everywhere
present behind all representational experiences."[101] The type of experience at issue here, then, is of the individual person as such, who
undergoes a multiplicity of categorial experiences in everyday life. In
other words, "behind all these specific experiences there is a form of
experience which is incommensurable with ordinary everyday
encounters with specific realities,"[102] even though this is generally
overlooked or ignored. A similar danger exists, in Rahner's view,

---

testimony of the saints and the mystics who are "people of the Spirit." Rahner,
"Experience of the Holy Spirit," *TI* 18: 189-95 (*ST* XIII: 226-32). We have discussed
the relation between such "mystical" experience and everyday life in the previous
chapter.

[100] Rahner, "Experience of the Spirit and Existential Commitment," *TI* 16: 27-28
(*ST* XII: 45-46).

[101] Rahner, "Experience of the Holy Spirit," *TI* 18: 191 (*ST* XIII: 228).

[102] Rahner, *The Spirit in the Church*, 5-6 (*Erfahrung des Geistes*, 14).

with the experience of the Spirit: it, too, is liable to be overlooked among the myriad specific experiences of living.

However, like any other experience, the transcendental experience of the Spirit is mediated through categorial objects. The transcendental experience, as we have seen before, must be given objective form, and in this way becomes a definite object of human awareness. Rahner further distinguishes between the experience of transcendence as such, and the objective form in which this is conceived. This distinction also has specific implications for our understanding of where and how we experience the Spirit.[103]

An examination of the context of Rahner's essays on the experience of the Spirit reveals a connection with the charismatic movement which was flourishing (particularly in America, but also in Europe) towards the end of the seventies and early eighties.[104] Rahner was not, however, an uncritical observer of this movement, and once reflected:

> "how naively such people absolutely identify their inspirations, their sense of peace, freedom and being led by the Holy Spirit with the immediate and direct intervention of God... . Such a theology can easily go awry when, for example, its ideas are immediately experienced as the pure gift of God, when in fact they come from somewhere much closer to home."[105]

The examples which Rahner gives of experiences of the Spirit are really the same as those experiences of transcendence, or experiences of grace. These include actions such as forgiving another even when one gains no reward for it, renouncing something without receiving recognition from others or even a feeling of inward satisfaction, or

---

[103] Once again, Rahner begins his discussion of the specific nature of our spiritual experiences by considering the common structure of human knowledge and freedom. "In knowledge and freedom one becomes the very essence of transcendence... One is always simultane-ously concerned with the individually characterized and specifically definable individual object of one's everyday experience, ... *and* at the same time with something beyond all that — even when one takes no notice and does not name or refer to this 'something else' always present outside and beyond the ordinary." Rahner, *The Spirit in the Church,* 12.

[104] Rahner's essay "Experience of the Holy Spirit," was originally a meditation delivered to the Catholic Academy of Bavaria on Pentecost Sunday, 1976. See also Wisemann, "Religious Experience in the Theology of Karl Rahner," 38-41.

[105] Rahner, "Approaches to Theological Thinking," *Karl Rahner in Dialogue,* 33.

making a decision purely in the light of the innermost dictates of one's conscience without being able to make this decision understandable to others.[106] When we act in such ways, *then* God is present with His liberating grace, then we experience the mysticism of everyday life, the sober intoxication of the Spirit of which the Church Fathers and the early liturgy spoke. But what is the difference between the examples of the experience of the Spirit given above, and those found in charismatic circles (e.g., baptism in the Spirit, speaking in tongues), which Rahner is unwilling to interpret absolutely as a special, direct intervention of God? For Rahner, to assume that the experience of the Spirit is limited solely to particular, isolated, special occasions is to adopt a fundamentally mythological understanding of the relationship of God to the world. Instead, even those who do not feel particularly attracted to charismatic groups and practices can still have an experience of the Spirit amidst the routine of ordinary life.[107] We have already noted that the basis for this claim lies in Rahner's analysis of human knowledge and freedom, an analysis which revealed the human person as a being of transcendence oriented to mystery.[108]

Our examination of the context in which Rahner uses the term "experience of the Spirit" leads us to conclude that, for him, the

[106] In the previous section, we noted some examples provided by Rahner, of experiences which, whether one is aware of it or not, are instances of experiences of the Spirit. See "Experience of the Holy Spirit," *TI* 18: 200-203 (*ST* XIII: 239-42).

[107] "In everyday life this transcendental experience of God in the Holy Spirit remains anonymous, implicit, unthematic, like the widely diffusely spread light of a sun which we do not directly see, while we turn only to the individual objects visible in this light of our sense-experience." Rahner, "Experience of the Holy Spirit," *TI* 18: 199 (*ST* XIII: 238). See also, *Karl Rahner im Gespräch* 1: 278, where he describes the experience of the Spirit in similar terms: "Diese Erfahrung (die Erfahrung des Geistes) ist meistens anonym, wird von uns nicht reflektiert, nicht in Worte gefaßt, verbalisiert, wird sogar meistens von uns, die wir zu den einzelnen Gegenständen des Alltags und ihren Aufgaben entfliehen, verdrängt."

[108] In the previous two chapters, we saw that this experience of one's orientation to mystery forms *the* condition for the very possibility of everyday knowing and willing. Rahner concludes: "If we were to use the term 'mysticism' to describe this experience of transcendence in which we always, even in the midst of everyday life, extend beyond ourselves and the specific thing with which we are concerned, we might say that mysticism occurs in the midst of everyday life, but is hidden and undeclared, and that is the condition of the very possibility of even the most ordinary, sober and secular everyday experience." Rahner, *The Spirit in the Church*, 14 (*Erfahrung des Geistes*, 29).

experience of transcendence "is in fact always experience of the Holy
Spirit, whether a person can or cannot interpret explicitly in this way
his or her inescapable experience of the unknown God."[109] Rahner's
examples, which we have adduced earlier, about experiencing the
Spirit in everyday life also indicate how Rahner frequently employs
the expressions "experience of God" and "experience of the Holy
Spirit" synonymously. Nevertheless, he is aware of the criticism that,
in his discussion of the experience of the Spirit, he seems to advocate
a mysticism of everyday life which can be found in most major religions, and which is thus not *specifically* Christian, i.e., not specifically directed to Jesus the crucified and risen Christ.[110] This criticism
is a serious challenge to Rahner's presentation to which we shall not
respond in detail here. However, we shall see in our subsequent discussion of Rahner's reinterpretation of grace that underlying his view
of the experience of the Spirit and the mysticism of everyday life is
his belief in the universal salvific will of God. This belief, in turn,
forms the basis for his claim that God's salvific will also takes effect
in some mysterious way outside the bounds of verbalized and institutionalized Christianity. The importance of the Christ-event within
Rahner's understanding of spirituality will be discussed in the third
part of this chapter. It will be our contention that it is only when Rahner's theology of death and of martyrdom is taken into account that
an accurate picture of his understanding of Christian spirituality can
emerge.[111]

Throughout Rahner's discussion of the experience of the Spirit we
have noted his insistence that such experience needs to be connected
to the ordinary routine of life. Thus, he provides numerous concrete
examples of such experiences, in the hope that the reader may examine his or her own experiences and thereby come to recognize, more
explicitly, the activity of this Spirit within his or her life.

---

[109] Rahner, "Experience of the Holy Spirit," *TI* 18: 198 (*ST* XIII: 239).
[110] Rahner, *The Spirit in the Church*, 24-25 (*Erfahrung des Geistes*, 49-50).
[111] See, for example, Karl Rahner, "On Christian Dying," *TI* 7: 285-93 (*ST* VII:
273-80); and also his *Zur Theologie des Todes*, Quaestiones Disputatae 2 (Freiburg:
Herder, 1958). The consequences for spirituality emerging from Rahner's re-interpretation of grace are treated in section 3, c, of this chapter. The theme of martyrdom
also re-surfaces at the beginning of Chapter Five, (section 1, a.), where Hans Urs von
Balthasar's criticisms of Rahner's understanding of Christianity are discussed.

b. Experience of the Spirit and Existential Decision

Alongside Rahner's concern to link the experience of the Spirit with the ordinary routine of life is his abhorrence of anything that gives the impression of an élitist understanding of spirituality. Perhaps this is the reason for his caution concerning those who wished to set themselves apart from the great mass of so-called ordinary Christians. Rahner preferred to stress how the Spirit could be experienced in a whole variety of situations, above all in the unselfish love of neighbour, and in "the observance of the harsh duty of ordinary life and the resigned acceptance of death."[112] Nevertheless, he would also admit that there is a desire for an experience of the Spirit today, and this is where phenomena such as prayer-groups, group meditation and other spiritual "exercises" come in. They constitute "rehearsals" (*Einübungen*) for admitting and accepting fundamental experiences of the Spirit when and wherever they occur in life. Such "exercises," however, are not the sole place where such explicitations of the experiences of the Spirit occur.

Irrespective of where such an experience of the Spirit occurs, the aim of Rahner's approach is to bring the person to a *decision* or choice which embraces the whole of one's existence, and which will lead to the radical re-ordering of one's transcendental nature towards the immediate reality of God. In other words, the experience of the Spirit is connected to what Rahner calls "existential commitment," examples of which include the choice of a particular career, a specific form of behaviour towards another person, the decision to marry, a particular religious act, and so on.[113] While this existential commit-

---

[112] Rahner, "Experience of the Holy Spirit," *TI* 18: 208 (*ST* XIII: 248). "Experience of the Spirit in the sense meant here as such occurs always and everywhere in the life of someone who has awakened to personal self-possession and to the act of freedom in which one disposes of oneself as a whole. But in most cases in human life this does not come about expressly in meditation, in experiences of absorption, etc., but in the material of normal life: that is, when responsibility, fidelity, love, etc., are realized absolutely." (p. 207). See also Rahner, *Karl Rahner im Gespräch* 1: 277-81.

[113] Rahner's discussion of "existential commitment" in terms of a "choice" which necessitates a "discernment of spirits" is deeply influenced by the *Spiritual Exercises* of St Ignatius Loyola. For a fuller discussion, see Rahner's "The Logic of Concrete Individual Knowledge in Ignatius Loyola," *The Dynamic Element in the Church*, Quaestiones Disputatae 12 (Freiburg: Herder, and London: Burns and Oates, 1964),

ment has both a transcendental and a categorial aspect, it is the categorial aspect of an existential decision that poses some difficulties. The reason for this is that there may be a number of possible categorial objects of choice available to a person, any one of which appears equally legitimate and "good." However, Rahner, on the basis of his understanding of the *Spiritual Exercises*, believes that God can communicate his will to a person.[114] In other words, it is possible, through a real guidance by the Holy Spirit, to choose one particular option from a variety of possible, good alternatives. What is at issue here is a discernment of spirits, or of finding the will of God in daily life, which involves more than a mere rational consideration of general moral principles. In the next chapter we shall return to Rahner's interpretation of the "election" in the *Exercises*, that is to say, to his view that the *Exercises* reflect a unity of spiritual experience and existential decision.

The problem here, then, is how one is to come to an existential decision in the face of a number of worthwhile possibilities. Frequently in the course of daily life, a sincere Christian may experience little difficulty in this area, because he or she has the impression that God "tells" or "inspires" him or her what choice should be made from those available. But it cannot be the case that God always intervenes in a direct way in the form of a "private" revelation. While this possibility is not to be ruled out in principle, it is Rahner's contention that we must move away from such a mythological explanation, and instead see how a specific choice is only possible when there is "a synthesis of the transcendent experience of the Spirit and the encounter with the categorial object of choice freely offered here and now:"[115]

84-156. [*Das Dynamische in der Kirche*, Quaestiones Disputatae 5 (Freiburg: Herder, 1958), 74-148]. We have already noted how some Ignatian themes figure in Rahner's spirituality, e.g., his understanding of Christian life as a mysticism of everyday faith. This discussion will be developed in more detail in the following chapter.

[114] For Rahner's interpretation of the *Exercises* as a practical guide for the recognition of the will of God in order to make a vital decision, i.e., the "Election," see his *The Dynamic Element in the Church*, 89-129 (*Das Dynamische in der Kirche*, 78-100), and "Modern Piety and the Experience of Retreats," *TI* 16: 135-55 (*ST* XII: 173-97).

[115] Rahner, "Experience of the Spirit and Existential Commitment," *TI* 16: 31 (*ST* XII: 49).

"When a Christian is aware of the presence of an ultimate synthesis (not to be produced at will, not open to rational analysis, but simply there as a fact) between the basic experience of the Spirit and the will for a particular individual object of his everyday freedom: then he is acting, not only reasonably and morally, but also charismatically."[116]

Thus, the will of God is also the object of transcendental experience, and this synthesis of the transcendent and the categorial takes place by means of a *choice*, whereby the person is able, in a free and uninhibited way, to fit a particular object of choice (assuming it is morally good) "into the movement of knowledge and freedom which is involved in the transcendent experience of the Spirit."[117] The categorial object of choice, therefore, provides a concrete and practical means of expression for the transcendent experience of the Spirit. Once more the basis for this assertion rests on a tenet of Rahner's (Thomistic) anthropology, namely, that no exercise of freedom, no existential decision is possible without a prior, transcendent grasp of absolute being, or, to put it more theologically, without a reference to God. Experience of the Spirit thus involves, on our part, an acceptance (in the form of an existential decision) of our transcendental nature as this is raised up by grace. Rahner's understanding of the "experience of grace," will be discussed in the third part of the chapter. Before that, however, we will examine the phenomenon of religious enthusiasm, a topic closely related to the experience of the Spirit.

c. Experience of Enthusiasm

Closely associated with the experience of the Spirit are certain phenomena such as speaking in tongues, uttering prophecies, and the experience of radical conversion. Such phenomena, which are evident in various charismatic movements (both Catholic and Protestant), form part of what has been called religious enthusiasm, and offer, in Rahner's view, a real and concrete expression of Christianity.[118] At

---

[116] Rahner, "Experience of the Holy Spirit," *TI* 18: 209 (*ST* XIII: 249).

[117] Rahner, "Experience of the Spirit and Existential Commitment," *TI* 16: 32 (*ST* XII: 50).

[118] We follow here Rahner's reflections on the subject in "Religious Enthusiasm and the Experience of Grace," *TI* 16: 35-51 (*ST* XII: 54-75), and his article "Enthu-

the outset, Rahner stresses that he is interpreting such phenomena not from the point of view of psychology, but from a dogmatic perspective. His concern is to ascertain under what conditions a charismatic phenomenon may be considered an experience of the Spirit. We have previously noted his reservations towards those "100 percent pentecostalists" who too hastily ascribe such phenomena to a direct and special intervention of God. And even if our sense thus far, is that Rahner's preference is not for the extraordinary, but rather for a more "sober" spirituality, it cannot be denied that he had an appreciation for the Charismatic movement as a whole.[119]

Rahner begins his investigation with the question whether the traditional doctrine of the indwelling of the Holy Spirit involves the entry of the Spirit into the realm of human consciousness, or whether this Spirit is only accepted as a reality on the basis of the data of Scripture and the teaching of the Church — what Rahner calls a type of external indoctrination. He cites some schools of post-Reformation

siasmus," in *Praxis des Glaubens: Geistliches Lesebuch*, 124-28. The term, enthusiasm, has historically been regarded with suspicion. The term — derived from the late classical Greek *enthousiasmos* (from *entheazin*, "to be God-possessed") — means to be inspired or even possessed by a god or a divine, superhuman power. In a footnote (p. 35), Rahner notes how, in Protestant circles since Luther, the concept has been associated with emotional excess. For a lengthy historical study of enthusiasm, see Ronald Knox, *Enthusiasm: A Chapter in the History of Religion* (New York: Oxford Univ. Press, 1950). Knox likewise views enthusiasm as a kind of religious eccentricity, linking it with fanaticism and an uncontrolled emotionalism.

[119] In fact, Rahner envisages two "Grundtypen" of spirituality and piety in the future. The first type is a "wintry piety" (eine *winterliche Frömmigkeit*) which, while firmly Christian and sacramental, can identify with the situation of the worried atheist (without itself becoming atheistic). The second type corresponds to the charismatic and enthusiastic movements, whose adherents, at times, claim an almost naive immediacy to God. While Rahner appears rather sceptical here about such Pentecostal movements, he does not deny that such movements could represent a new outpouring of the Holy Spirit in the Church. His fear, however, is that the Church could concern itself overmuch with this second type of spirituality leading to a type of marginalization or ghettoization of Christianity. See, Rahner, "Gnade als Mitte menschlicher Existenz. Ein Gespräch mit und über Karl Rahner aus Anlaß seines 70 Geburtstages," *Herausforderung des Christen: Meditationen — Reflexionen — Interviews* (Freiburg: Herder, 1975), 149-50. In this context, the comment of Metz is petinent: "Er (Rahner) blieb immer ein Universalist, der den von der Kirche verkündeten Gott nie zum Privateigentum seiner Kirche werden ließ. Sein ignatianisches Pathos für den je größeren Gott ließ keine sektierisch anmutende Kirchenfrömmigkeit zu." Johann Baptist Metz, "Fehlt uns Karl Rahner?," *Karl Rahner in Erinnerung*, ed. Albert Raffelt, Freiburger Akademieschriften, 8 (Düsseldorf: Patmos, 1994), 91.

theology (in which the Jesuits were also represented) which understood such an indwelling as a purely ontological reality, lying beyond
conscious awareness. According to this position, the indwelling, or
the illumination, or presence of the Spirit in the person is a reality
that transcends consciousness, even though it is said that the person is
"ontologically" raised up by the grace of God. While Rahner rejects
this position, he notes that it deals neatly with the question of charismatic enthusiasm by classifying this as a purely natural, empirical
phenomenon, which must be judged according to psychological criteria alone.

Rahner's view, on the other hand, attempts to steer a middle course
between two opposing positions. The first position, referred to above,
discounts expressions of religious enthusiasm from the start, regarding such phenomena (e.g., charismatic enthusiasm) as having nothing
to do with Christianity as such, since they are found in various forms
in most religions. In the second position, such expressions are recognized as the unadulterated operation of the Holy Spirit. For Rahner,
despite the variety of expressions of religious enthusiasm, all these
experiences, to the extent that they are genuine, have some generic
sense in common, and "this consists in a transcendent experience
which touches the centre of the religious subject and in which the
subject has an experience of God."[120] However, despite the transcendental experience involved in religious enthusiasm, the *categorial*
element plays a greater role in the objectification of the experience.
In fact, phenomena of religious enthusiasm contain categorial content
of different kinds (which need to be critically evaluated). But this
does not mean that such phenomena cannot enable a person to clearly
experience their own transcendence and inner reference to God. In
short, Rahner describes religious enthusiasm as "mysticism in ordinary dress," ("die Alltagsgestalt der Mystik") or "a sort of mysticism
of the masses."[121] Nevertheless, he warns that, given the various
kinds of categorial content in experiences of religious enthusiasm,
and the fact that they are caused by a variety of factors, the objectifi-

---

[120] Rahner, "Religious Enthusiasm and the Experience of Grace," *TI* 16: 42 (*ST* XII: 62).

[121] Rahner, "Religious Enthusiasm and the Experience of Grace," *TI* 16: 43, 47 (*ST* XII: 64, 69).

cation of the experience of transcendence in religious enthusiasm can easily be distorted. This is why he was suspicious of certain claims made by some charismatics. In sum, Rahner's point is that while expressions of religious enthusiasm *can* be experiences of grace, this is not always the case. Rather than focus solely on the categorial aspect of religious enthusiasm, his approach is to view this phenomenon in its *totality* as an experience of grace:

> "All expressions of religious enthusiasm, whenever they are to some degree genuine and in earnest, are spiritual events in which the grace filled transcendence of the person comes plainly to the fore and in which the subject freely experiences God as both the ultimate goal of this transcendence and the very ground of the experience itself."[122]

Rahner situates religious enthusiasm midway between what he calls mysticism in the strict sense,[123] and the day-to-day awareness of ordinary Christians "who do not encounter with any clarity either the heart of their own subjectivity or God himself in his true self-communication."[124] The spirituality of many Christians is, unfortunately, characterized by the lack of such an authentic experience of God, and they remain stuck at the conceptual level, resting in "the expressions of religion," imprisoned in the objective and categorial reality of everyday existence. In the second part of this chapter, we will see how Rahner's understanding of the experience of religious enthusiasm is intimately connected with his understanding of grace, the essence of which is not captured in propositional formulae, but in the self-communication of God to the transcendent spirit of the person.

---

[122] Rahner, "Religious Enthusiasm and the Experience of Grace," *TI* 16: 45 (*ST* XII: 67).

[123] Rahner has described this as a rare and spasmodic occurrence and as a transcendent experience through grace which is not categorial, that is, a radical experience of faith which destroys the conceptual and the categorial in so far as these claim to be ultimate realities. "Religious Enthusiasm and the Experience of Grace," *TI* 16: 43, 47 (*ST* XII: 64, 69). See also his "Mystical Experience and Mystical Theology," *TI* 17: 90-99 (*ST* XII: 428-38).

[124] Rahner, "Religious Enthusiasm and the Experience of Grace," *TI* 16: 44 (*ST* XII: 65-66). "But the day-to-day awareness of the pious Christian rests on these conceptual and propositional expressions; it is dissolved and remains fixed in them; it confuses, in the words of Scripture, the letter with the spirit, the word about God with the Word of God and with God himself."

Underlying Rahner's analysis, then, is the conviction that genuine experiences of grace do exist, and that they can, in principle, occur in experiences of religious enthusiasm, though they are not limited to these. Further, such experiences (of enthusiasm) must be critically analysed as to their origin and nature, and their possible consequences and distortions.[125] It must be remembered that the categorial content of such experiences of enthusiasm are of human origin, and cannot be interpreted simply as divine inspiration. At the same time, however, a critical analysis of the categorial content of religious enthusiasm does not necessarily undermine the fact that a basic experience of grace and of the Spirit has occurred.[126] In testing the authenticity of the categorial content of such an experience, Rahner also

[125] Rahner has elsewhere examined the question of *criteria* for genuine experiences of religious enthusiasm, particularly in relation to visions and prophecies. See Karl Rahner, *Visions and Prophecies*, Quaestiones Disputatae 10 (Freiburg: Herder/London: Burns and Oates, 1963), 76-106. [*Visionen und Prophezeiungen*, Quaestiones Disputatae 4 (Freiburg: Herder, 1958), 76-107]. The importance of a correct attitude towards visions and prophecies and their relevance to contemporary spirituality is evident from the following quotation from the work cited above: "And if a vision (mystical or prophetic) be recognized in itself as genuine, our reaction to it may still be wrong. One may be deaf, or refractory, to the message. Who can deny that most people do not welcome a call to penance or to a devotion that would be salutary for a given time? But the other extreme is also possible, especially among people of a piety too intuitive and unenlightened. Where private revelations (even genuine ones) are abused to gratify a spiritual sensationalism, those revelations are not correctly understood. If we crave prophecies which are so clear and definite that they take from us the burden of responsible decision and loving abandonment to God's inscrutable Providence, then what we want is sooth-saying and we are no longer capable of interpreting true prophecy aright should such emerge from a real 'apparition'." (p. 84).

[126] Sometimes the question arises in this context about what is from God and what is from humankind. However, Rahner does not regard this question as *so* important, preferring, as we have seen, to show how the "purely human" or everyday domain also comes under God's grace: "Wer sich mit fröhlichem Herzen zum Guten aufgelegt fühlt, wer ein spontan liebevolles Herz dem Nächsten entgegenbringen kann, wenn aus welchen Gründen und mit welchen Mitteln immer der Ausbruch aus einer depressiven Phase in freudige oder wenigstens tapfere Lebenstat gelingt, wer die Worte des Evangeliums wie mit neuen Ohren hören kann, als hätte er sie noch nie gehört, wer in nüchterner Geduld mit sich und seinen Grenzen fertig wird, der darf und muß solches Können und Tun als Gnade Gottes preisen und braucht nicht genau zu unterscheiden, woher es denn komme, weil alles Gute und Helle immer und überall im letzten aus der freien Güte Gottes kommt, die uns geschenkt wird. So kann das Alltäglichste, das zum Heil gereicht, noch als Gnade Gottes verstanden werden, und das außergewöhnlich Charismatische ist immer noch menschlich." Rahner, "Enthusiasmus," *Praxis des Glaubens: Geistliches Lesebuch*, 127.

maintains that the usual rules for the assessment of theological statements should be applied: conformity to the message of the Gospel, to
Scripture, to the faith and mind of the Church, etc.[127] Moreover, any
testing of the authenticity of experiences of religious enthusiasm will
always distinguish "between the real, fundamental experience of
grace in the transcendent being of the person on the one hand and the
categorial content on the other."[128] This categorial content, as we
have seen, can be both the cause and medium of a clearer and more
radical interiorization of the transcendent experience of grace even if
the external manifestations of such experiences appear in retrospect
somewhat dubious. Rahner's main fear about particular experiences
of religious enthusiasm (and he includes under this term prophecies,
private revelations, and visions) is that they could be presented as a
short-cut towards holiness at little cost, changing the way of the
Cross into pure joy; or

> "where the entire spiritual life is reduced to revolving round one reve-
> lation (however genuine in itself), whose content, in comparison with
> the whole wide world of Christian truth by which we should live, is
> bound to be meagre — we can conclude that even genuine revelations
> have certainly been misunderstood and misapplied."[129]

d. Comments and Questions

Having presented Rahner's understanding of the experience of
the Spirit, and the related phenomenon of religious enthusiasm,
we shall now make some initial comments on his position.[130] We

---

[127] We shall not go into the wider (ecclesiological) question here of the relationship of religious enthusiasm to the community and the Church. Rahner has addressed
this problem in his treatment of the charismatic element of the Church and its relationship with the Church's institutional structure. See Rahner, *The Dynamic Element
in the Church*, 42-83 (*Das Dynamische in der Kirche*, 38-73).

[128] Rahner, "Religious Enthusiasm and the Experience of Grace," *TI* 16: 51 (*ST*
XII: 74).

[129] Rahner, *Visions and Prophecies*, 84 (*Visionen und Prophezeiungen*, 83-84). We
will take up later the importance of the Cross for Rahner's spirituality. The topic was a
frequent source of theological and spiritual reflection. See, for example, "The Cross —
The World's Salvation: Meditations on Good Friday," *Opportunities for Faith*, 25-30;
"Self-Realization and Taking Up One's Cross," *TI* 9: 253-57 (*ST* VIII: 322-26).

[130] This section is not meant to provide an extensive evaluation of Rahner's understanding of spirituality. Rather, we make two points which, in our opinion, are important for any understanding of the experience of the Spirit.

follow here some insights of the Paderborn theologian, Heribert Mühlen, who has written extensively on pneumatology, with particular reference to the Charismatic renewal.[131] Mühlen is especially interested in all those "movements" (e.g., Focolare, Cursillo, the Taizé community, the fraternities of Charles de Foucauld, etc.) which, he believes, are good examples of contemporary experiences of the Spirit. Such movements witness to a variety of charisma, or gifts of the Spirit which, whether they be "very remarkable or more simple and widely diffused, ... are fitting and useful for the needs of the Church."[132]

Mühlen's understanding of the experience of the Spirit (*Geisterfahrung*) appears, initially, similar to that of Rahner's. Like Rahner, he points out how the Holy Spirit is beyond all objectivation ("jenseits aller Objektivierung"), and can never simply become an "object" of our experience. Further, he underlines the regulative function of theology to "discern the spirits," to pinpoint distortions and false manifestations of the Spirit. However, Mühlen's presentation also differs from Rahner's understanding in two important respects. Firstly, Mühlen highlights the important role of *conversion* in any experience of the Spirit ("die Umkehrstruktur der Geisterfahrung"), while, under a second aspect, he develops the social or *communal dimension* of this experience.[133] Both these aspects, we believe, provide a challenge to Rahner's conception of the experience of the Spirit, and also take his thought somewhat further. Herein lies the value of introducing Mühlen's reflections at this stage.[134]

---

[131] See Heribert Mühlen, "Der gegenwärtige Aufbruch der Geisterfahrung und die Unterscheidung der Geister," *Gegenwart des Geistes: Aspekte der Pneumatologie*, ed. Walter Kasper, Quaestiones Disputatae 85 (Freiburg: Herder, 1979), 24-53.

[132] Vatican II, Dogmatic Constitution on the Church, *Lumen Gentium*, n. 12.

[133] Mühlen, "Der gegenwärtige Aufbruch der Geisterfahrung und die Unterscheidung der Geister," 30, 41. See also his article, "Soziale Geisterfahrung als Antwort auf eine einseitige Gotteslehre," *Erfahrung und Theologie des Heiligen Geistes*, eds. C. Heitmann and H. Mühlen (Munich: Kösel, 1974), 253-72.

[134] See Klaus P. Fischer, *Gotteserfahrung*, 49, n. 55, who mentions Mühlen's work in passing, but nonetheless regards it as significant: "Der Ansatz Mühlens stellt eine echte Anfrage an Rahners Konzeption der Gotteserfahrung dar und verdient eine ernsthafte Antwort."

For Mühlen, the original form ("Urform") of the experience of the Spirit lies in the gift of prophecy.[135] The prophet does not just speak *as if* God was present in his words. Instead, through the words (and actions) of the prophet, God himself is truly and effectively present (2 Cor 5: 20). This point is at the core of the biblical experience of the Spirit: the human person (in this case, the prophet) cannot pre-empt this experience, cannot strive towards it, but must accept it (and the personal suffering that it frequently entails), and must allow this "event" to happen to him or her. In the New Testament, we see evidence of a *passive* mode of speaking with reference to the reception of the Holy Spirit: the disciples are baptized and filled with the Holy Spirit (Acts 1: 8, 11: 15; 2: 4), and receive him (Acts 2: 38). With regard to the gift of prophecy, Mühlen's contention is that God himself can only be present in the words of the prophet if the latter has experienced a conversion (*Umkehr*) towards an ever deeper dependence on God.[136] Like Rahner, Mühlen stresses that any such process of conversion is itself "co-constituted" ("mitkonstituiert") by God's grace. Accordingly, Rahner's question regarding the apriori conditions that enable the person to be a possible "hearer of the word" (of God's revelation) is reformulated by Mühlen in terms of conversion. In other words, the question is whether the human person, by virtue of their (implicit) transcendental "pre-apprehension" (*Vorgriff*), is oriented towards a possible (explicit) experience of conversion, which itself can be accepted or rejected.

Mühlen explains this experience of conversion by taking the prophet Jeremiah as an example. Part of Jeremiah's experience of the Spirit involves a two-stage process of conversion. His initial

---

[135] In the Old Testament, the Spirit of God comes over Othniel (Judg 3:10), Gideon (Judg 6:34), Jephthah (Judg 11:29), Saul (1 Sam 11:6), David (1 Sam 16:13), etc. The New Testament, for its part, recognized Jesus as the new "prophet," (Lk 24: 19). The Lucan interpretation of the Pentecost event (Acts 2:14-24, following Joel 3:1-5) marks the beginning of the outpouring of the Spirit, and the gift of prophecy throughout the whole Church. See Mühlen, "Der gegenwärtige Aufbruch der Geister-fahrung und die Unterscheidung der Geister," 27-28.

[136] "Wie aber ist solche Interaktion zwischen Menschen so möglich, daß wirklich *Gott selbst* in ihr anwesend wird? Nur durch eine Umkehr zu immer tieferer Abhängigkeit von Gott! Diese aber kann nicht angezielt, gewollt, sondern nur erlei-dend angenommen werden." Mühlen, "Der gegenwärtige Aufbruch der Geister-fahrung und die Unterscheidung der Geister," 30.

reluctance to accept his prophetic vocation (Jer 1: 6) gives way to an experience of joy as a result of the "touch" of God (Jer 1: 6-10). But this initial conversion needs to be deepened when the prophet experiences continued opposition to his message. Mühlen sees in this example the pattern or "Umkehrstruktur" of all charismatic-prophetic experience of the Spirit. Only through a second experience of conversion does the prophet achieve a deeper dependence on God, and an acceptance of personal suffering.[137]

Even Jesus' experience of the Spirit has a similar basic structure. Not that he needed to undergo a process of conversion, but through his baptism in the Spirit, he placed himself on the side of all those who themselves underwent a baptism of repentance. Further, Mühlen shows how Jesus' baptism in the Spirit is linked with his death [on the basis of the opposition to his message (Mk 10:47-40)]. What is paradigmatic here for Mühlen is that Jesus' experience of the Spirit is linked with the power for self-sacrifice ("die Kraft zum Selbstopfer"), which leads to a greater dependence on God through suffering, as we mentioned above.[138]

The experience of the Spirit, in Mühlen's view, then, is not *primarily* an "enthusiastic" phenomenon in the sense of an emotional expression of feeling. Much more is this experience a deepening of one's commitment to God in the form of a radical conversion. Rahner, as we have seen, has a different nuance, linking the experience of the Spirit with existential commitment, i.e., with a *decision* that embraces the whole of one's life. With Mühlen, conversion is itself an ultimate or conclusive ("endgültig") decision for life in the power of the Spirit.[139] (Even the word "decision" ("Entscheidung") implies

---

[137] "Erst wenn er (der Prophet) bereit ist, die eigene menschliche Dynamik an Gott zurückzugeben und sie von der Dynamik Gottes durchkreuzen zu lassen, wird ihm eine *vertiefte* Abhängigkeit von Gott geschenkt... Aus der anfänglichen Umkehr, die noch nicht gereift ist an der Widerständigkeit der Botschaft, entspringt so die zweite, *wahre* Erfahrung dieser ersten Umkehrerfahrung und wird so zu einer *durchgemachten*, tiefer erlittenen Geisterfahrung." Mühlen, "Der gegenwärtige Aufbruch der Geisterfahrung und die Unterscheidung der Geister," 32-33.

[138] For Rahner too, a charism always involves suffering. See his remarks on "the burden of a charism" in *The Dynamic Element in the Church*, 77-82 (*Das Dynamische in der Kirche*, 68-72).

[139] "Umkehr ist in diesem Sinne Entscheidung zum Leben, zum ewigen Leben, zum endgültigen Leben im Geist in der Kraft dieses Geistes... *Umkehr ist nicht ein*

a separation ("Scheidung") that must occur between the old and the new life in the Spirit). Further, the adjective "end-gültig" indicates that the decision is irrevocably oriented towards the end or goal of one's life, a "Lebensentscheidung," in which, according to Mühlen, the proleptic acceptance of one's own death becomes concrete. The experience of conversion is thus associated with suffering and death ("die *Leidensstruktur* der Umkehrerfahrung"). Turning to those Christians who manifest "very remarkable" charisms or "extraordinary gifts" (*Lumen Gentium*, n. 12), the implication is that these gifts represent an "opus arduum," that is, an arduous service for the building up of the Church.[140]

With regard to Rahner, we mentioned that he does not explicitly treat of conversion in his discussion of the experience of the Spirit. However, Rahner does deal with the notion of conversion in the context of his treatment of the history of the sacrament of Penance.[141] We shall not delve into the details of this early piece of Rahnerian *Dogmengeschichte*. His aim there was to shed some light on the traditional Catholic affirmation that the consequences of sin deprived the justified person of "interior personal grace."[142] The result of his

Dauervorgang, sondern ein *einmaliges* Ereignis, das infolge seines proleptischen, vorwegnehmenden Charakters sich in der Lebensgeschichte auszeitigen muß in immer tieferer Rückkehr zu dieser ersten Umkehr (vgl, Offb 2:4f), die ja bereits Umkehr zur Annahme des Todes ... war." Mühlen, "Der gegenwärtige Aufbruch der Geisterfahrung und die Unterscheidung der Geister," 37. For an understanding of the unique, once-off (einmalig) nature of conversion, see Rudolf Schnackenburg, *Christliche Existenz nach dem Neuen Testament: Abhandlungen und Vorträge*, 2 vols. (Munich: Kösel, 1967), 1: 35-61.

[140] Mühlen, "Der gegenwärtige Aufbruch der Geisterfahrung und die Unterscheidung der Geister," 40, is following Thomas Aquinas, *Summa Theologiae* I, Q. 43, A. 6, here. See also the similar interpretation of Francis Sullivan, "Baptism in the Holy Spirit," *Gregorianum* 55 (1974): 49-68. Inspired by Thomas, Sullivan distinguishes between the grace of baptism (gratia gratum faciens) which makes us pleasing to God, and charismatic grace (gratiae gratis datae). Unlike the grace of baptism, which is oriented primarily towards individual salvation, the latter gift(s) of charismatic grace are for *others*, to help them on their way to God.

[141] Rahner's essays on the history of Penance appeared around 1950 and are collected in the eleventh volume of his *Schriften* (=*TI* 15, "Penance in the Early Church"). See also his "Forgotten Truths Concerning the Sacrament of Penance," *TI* 2: 135-74 (*ST* II: 143-83).

[142] Rahner, "Sin as Loss of Grace in Early Church Literature," *TI* 15: 23-53 (*ST* XI: 46-93).

research led him to the conviction that penance (as "conversion to God and aversion to sin")[143] was to be understood not solely as the forgiveness of sins by God, but as reconciliation with the Church ("reconciliatio cum ecclesia").[144] Moreover, for Rahner, conversion is to be seen as both a disposition (*Gesinnung*) and an act — expressed in the opening of oneself as a "hearer of the Word" — a Word that both judges and pardons.[145] It is not a question, as some have said, of Rahner downplaying the role of sin.[146] To a certain extent, it is true, sin is relativized in Rahner's understanding — it is not an "absolute" — God remains "the always greater One," whose universal salvific will cannot be destroyed by the sinful actions of the human person.[147]

The second aspect of Mühlen's presentation focuses on the social or communal aspects of the experience of the Spirit. It cannot be without significance that the recent renewal in "charismatic" experiences of the Spirit has not occurred in private, to isolated individuals, but rather in a more communal manner, in groups, prayer-meetings, etc. Mühlen sees in this "social experience of the Spirit" ("soziale Geisterfahrung") a movement away from the privatized spirituality of previous generations, where any experience of the Spirit was regarded as a highly personal event which had nothing to do with

---

[143] Rahner, "Penance in the Early Church" *TI* 15: 3 (*ST* XI: 21).

[144] This understanding of penance as "reconciliation with the Church" was later to find expression in Vatican II. See, for example, the Dogmatic Constitution *Lumen Gentium*, n. 11. With this emphasis, the excessive privatization that had developed in the understanding of sin and penance receded and the ecclesial dimension came more to the fore.

[145] Karl-Heinz Neufeld, "Umkehr und Buße im Denken Karl Rahners," *Wort und Wahrheit* 30 (1989): 32. This "Akt des Sich-Öffnens" is also evident in some of Rahner's prayers and meditations. See, for example, "Die Öffnung des Herzens," *Von der Not und dem Segen des Gebetes*, 7-25. In reference to the theme of sin and repentance, see "Das Gebet der Schuld," 116-37, and "Gebete der Entscheidung," 138-54 in the same book.

[146] This is one of a number of criticisms directed at Rahner by Hans Urs von Balthasar. See his *Cordula oder der Ernstfall,* Kriterien 2 (Einsiedeln: Johannes Verlag, 1966), 85-97.

[147] "Und das heißt, daß der Sünder letztlich diesen Gott nicht in Frage stellen kann, daß er durch seinen Widerspruch, durch sein Fehlverhalten dennoch nicht den göttlichen Heilswillen und Heilsplan zunichte machen kann, mag er sich selbst noch so sehr davon ausschließen." Neufeld, "Umkehr und Buße im Denken Karl Rahners," 33.

society.[148] "Spirit" ("Pneuma"), however, for Mühlen, refers to the presence of "God with us" (Ex 17:7), and is also described as the "dynamism of God:"

> "Geisterfahrung hat immer etwas mit unserem *dynamischen Verhältnis* durch Christus zum Vater und zu den Mitmenschen zu tun: Der Heilige Geist als die Dynamik Gottes ist die tragende Wirklichkeit in und an diesem unserem Verhältnis. Das Pneuma, die göttliche Dynamik, hat etwas zu tun mit der *dualen* Wirheit zwischen den 'Nächsten,' den Arbeitskollegen, den Ehegatten, den Nachbarn, es hat etwas zu tun mit der *pluralen* Wirheit der Gemeinde, des Volkes, aller Menschen."[149]

We will not pursue Mühlen's investigation any further here. At this stage, we are content to have raised the question of the communal dimension of spirituality, and to have pointed out that the experience of the Spirit cannot be conceived as a purely private process, but also has a communal dimension with specific social consequences.

3. Experience of Grace

a. A Reinterpretation Of Grace

In the third and final part of our chapter, we concentrate on some of the essential features of Rahner's theology of grace which, in turn, have implications for his spirituality. Of course, not all aspects of Rahner's understanding of grace can be presented here. Rather, our aim is, firstly, to highlight how Rahner was responsible for a significant shift in emphasis in modern thinking on grace, and, secondly, how this theology of grace provides the theological foundations for his understanding of spirituality.

---

[148] Following Vatican II (specifically, *Gaudium et Spes*, nn. 4-10, 54), Mühlen speaks of a "new age of human history," beginning in the middle of this century. He then proceeds to draw out the implications of such a changed situation for a contemporary understanding of pneumatology. We can only present here the conclusions of his study in so far as these have consequences for spirituality today. See his article, "Soziale Geisterfahrung als Antwort auf eine einseitige Gotteslehre," *Erfahrung und Theologie des Heiligen Geistes,* 253-72.

[149] Mühlen, "Soziale Geisterfahrung als Antwort auf eine einseitige Gotteslehre," 264-65.

Rahner reinterprets the traditional view of grace in four significant ways.[150] First, since Aquinas, the term *grace* denoted primarily what has been called "created grace," that is, the habit or quality of the human soul infused by God. This sanctifying, created, grace focused on the effects in an individual of God's self-communication. Along-side this, there was the concept of "uncreated grace," which referred to God himself present to, and indwelling in a person. The traditional Scholastic theology of grace, however, gives the priority to created grace, as Rahner explains:

> "However diverse they may be among themselves, it is true of all the scholastic theories that they see God's indwelling and his conjunction with the justified person as based exclusively upon created grace. In virtue of the fact that created grace is imparted to the soul God imparts himself to it and dwells in it. Thus what we call uncreated grace (i.e., God as bestowing himself upon the person) is a function of created grace."[151]

Rahner, on the other hand, reverses the relationship between created and uncreated grace. What is primary in his conception is uncreated grace, or, in more Rahnerian terms, the self-communication of God to human beings. This assertion lies at the heart of his understanding of Christian existence. The human person is:

> "the event of a free, unmerited and forgiving, and absolute self-communication of God... . The term 'self-communication' is really intended to signify that God in his own most proper reality makes himself the innermost constitutive element of the human person."[152]

God's self-communication means, therefore, that what is communicated is really God in his own being, rather than merely knowledge

---

[150] We are indebted here to Roger Haight, "Grace," *NDCS*: 452-64. See also his *The Experience and Language of Grace* (Dublin: Gill and Macmillan, 1979), 119-42. Karl Neumann also offers a good introduction to the theme of grace and experience in Rahner, showing, in particular, how the notions of "Gnadenerfahrung" or "Gotteserfahrung" gain increasing prominence in Rahner's theological and spiritual writings. Karl Neumann, *Der Praxisbezug der Theologie bei Karl Rahner,* Freiburger Theologische Studien 118 (Freiburg: Herder, 1980), 137-200.

[151] Rahner, "Some Implications of the Scholastic Concept of Uncreated Grace," *TI* 1: 324 (*ST* I: 352). For further discussion of this topic along similar lines, see Piet Fransen, *The New Life of Grace,* trans. Georges Dupont (London: Chapman, 1969), 87-106.

[152] Rahner, *FCF*, 116 (*Grundkurs*, 122).

about him. Here Rahner offers a more personal, and more immediately religious, understanding of grace by returning to Scripture and the Fathers.[153] Having examined the primary sources of revelation, his conclusion is that grace is first and foremost a communication of the personal Spirit of God, and that as a *consequence* of this communication there is an inner transformation of the person (what scholastic theology calls created grace). Rahner also refers to the Fathers (especially the Greek Fathers, e.g., St Irenaeus) to support his claim that the created gifts of grace are the consequence of God's self-communication to the human person. Thus, Rahner is moving away from an understanding of grace as a creative effect of God's efficient causality.[154] Created grace, in the scholastic understanding, involved an entitative (*seinshafte*) modification of the person, which formed the basis for a new relationship between God and the individual.[155] The problem for the early Rahner was how to reconcile these two different conceptions of created grace, that is, whether created grace was a *consequence* of God's self-communication, or, whether it formed the *basis* of this communication. On one level, this may appear a rather technical semantic problem, but Rahner's ultimate intention was to recast the traditional understanding of grace using interpersonal categories. His solution was to develop a new concept (the "supernatural existential"), which, he believed, best explained the

---

[153] Rahner, "Some Implications of the Scholastic Concept of Uncreated Grace," *TI* 1: 320-24 (*ST* I: 348-52). See also "Nature and Grace," *TI* 4: 177 (*ST* IV: 223), where Rahner appeals for a more exact concept of "uncreated grace," whereby "... we can also see more clearly how the Catholic theology of grace ... can go beyond the notion of a merely entitative, created state and the *merely* 'ontic' and non-existential element... . Grace is God himself, the communication in which he gives himself to the person as the divinizing favour which he is himself... . Such grace, from the very start, cannot be thought of independently of the personal love of God and its answer in the person. This grace is not thought of as a 'thing'."

[154] With regard to God's self-communication, Rahner speaks of a formal causality as distinct from efficient causality, where the effect is always different from the cause. With formal causality, "... a particular existent, a principle of being is a constitutive element in another subject by the fact that it communicates itself to this subject... . In what we call grace and the immediate vision of God, God is really an intrinsic, constitutive principle of the person as existing in the situation of salvation and fulfilment." *FCF*, 121 (*Grundkurs*, 127).

[155] Rahner, "Some Implications of the Scholastic Concept of Uncreated Grace," *TI* 1: 324 (*ST* I: 352).

relationship between God and the human person. We shall return to this concept in the next section.

The second reversal in Rahner's reinterpretation of grace lies in his response to the implied *extrinsicism* of the traditional understanding of grace. In this view, grace was regarded as a mere superstructure imposed on us by God's decree. God's offer of grace was not regarded as constitutive of the actual condition of human existence. Human nature (i.e., the "addressee" of God's self-communication) was not ordered to grace, but was understood in a sharply circumscribed manner.[156] Further, God's "supernatural" grace comes to this self-enclosed human nature as an external, arbitrary, and merely additional factor. Rahner sees a danger here:

> "... of understanding oneself merely as a nature and of behaving accordingly. And then we will find God's call to us out of this human plane merely a disturbance, which is trying to force something upon us (however elevated this may be in itself) for which one is not made (in this view one is only made and destined for it *after* one has received grace, and then only in a way entirely abstracted from one's experience)."[157]

Instead, Rahner's starting-point is to present the human person as one called to share God's intimate life. A central feature of this claim is that God does not confer on the human person merely created gifts as a token of his love, but communicates *Godself*.[158] The person is thus

---

[156] This "extrinsicism" presupposed that whatever one knew by oneself (independently of Revelation) about oneself belonged to one's "nature." The concept of nature was then contrasted with the superstructure of "supernatural grace" which is imposed upon nature by God's free decree, and which demanded acceptance. See Rahner, "Concerning the Relationship between Nature and Grace," *TI* 1: 298-300 (*ST* I: 324-26).

[157] Rahner, "Concerning the Relationship between Nature and Grace," *TI* 1: 300 (*ST* I: 326). Elsewhere, Rahner outlines the dangers in practice which result from such extrinsicism: "For if it is correct, our known spiritual life must take place within the region of our pure nature, which has two sectors: the 'purely natural' which is totally confined to its own dimensions, apart from an 'elevation' which is outside consciousness, and then a number of acts of knowledge which are (subjectively) composed of purely natural elements and are referred to the supernatural only by their objects (by faith, by a pure intention etc.). If this is true, then it is not surprising — that one should take very little interest in this mysterious superstructure of one's being. After all, one does not find grace where one finds oneself, in the immediate activation of one's spiritual being." Rahner, "Nature and Grace," *TI* 4: 168 (*ST* IV: 213).

[158] Rahner, "Grace," *Sacramentum Mundi* 2: 415 (*SM* II: 451).

enabled to share in the very nature of God. Rahner speaks of a "twofold modality of God's self-communication:"

> "... the modality of the antecedent situation of an offer and a call to one's freedom on the one hand, and on the other hand in the once again twofold modality of the response to this offer of God's self-communication as a permanent existential of the human person, that is, in the modality of an acceptance or in the modality of a rejection of God's self-communication through one's freedom."[159]

In contrast with the extrinsicist approach, God's presence as an offer of salvation is, according to Rahner, part of the very condition of human existence: God's creation (through efficient causality) takes place because God wants to give Godself in love. This grace or divine self-communication has traditionally been understood by Christian theology as God's free gift to the human person. Moreover, if the human person is to accept this offer of grace, there must be an openness on their part to receive it. In other words, the human person must be created in such a way that they *can* receive this Love which is God himself. It (the grace of God's self-communication) can only be received if its very reception is made possible by God: the self-communication as such effects its own acceptance.[160]

However, problems arise, in this context, about how it is possible to conceive of grace as a gift, or, as Rahner says, "unowed" (*ungeschuldet*).[161] Rahner's fear is that if we are said to have a wholly natural disposition to grace, such a disposition could be misunderstood as inevitably attracting grace to itself. This sense of "demanding" grace cannot but conflict with the gratuity of grace. Yet, Rahner holds that human nature *is* ordained to grace. The essence, indeed the paradox, of the human person is that one is both ordained (*hingeordnet*) to personal communion with God in love, and yet one must receive this love as free gift.[162] We will see in our discussion of his supernatural

[159] *FCF*, 118 (*Grundkurs*, 124).

[160] Rahner, "Grace," *Theological Dictionary*: 192-96 (*Kleines Theologisches Wörterbuch*: 156-60).

[161] Rahner, "Concerning the Relationship between Nature and Grace," *TI* 1: 304-17 (*ST* I: 330-45).

[162] The similarly paradoxical nature of human love can serve as a helpful analogy here. See Rahner, "Concerning the Relationship between Nature and Grace," *TI* 1: 305 (*ST* I: 331).

existential that Rahner begins "terminatively," i.e., because God gives humanity a supernatural end (and this end is primary in the divine intention), the human person "*is* by that very fact always inwardly other in structure than they would be if they did not have this end."[163] The extrinsicist approach, on the other hand, claimed that where grace had not laid hold of persons and justified them, their binding ordination to their supernatural finality could only exist in a divine decree that remained wholly external to them. Rahner reverses this by refusing to reduce humanity's existential situation to something purely juridical or moral, grounded in a divine decree. Instead, "what God decrees for human nature must necessarily terminate in an intrinsic, ontological modification of human quiddity."[164] The ordination to a supernatural end constitutes, according to Rahner, a real determination of humanity itself, and is not merely the expression of a divine intention, a decree of God's will. This claim, in turn, will form the decisive argument for Rahner's introduction of his concept of the supernatural existential.

Rahner's third reversal in his reinterpretation of grace lies in his stress on the *universality* of God's salvific will. In contrast to the scholastic position which held that grace is scarce, and that no salvific grace existed outside the Christian sphere, Rahner argued for the universality of grace. The dramatic implications of his view have already been alluded to: no sphere of human life is excluded from the saving presence of God. Rahner's optimistic viewpoint was ratified by the Second Vatican Council in both *Lumen Gentium* and *Gaudium et Spes*.[165] Instead of asking with Augustine how many out of the *massa*

---

[163] Rahner, "Concerning the Relationship between Nature and Grace," *TI* 1: 302-303 (*ST* I: 328). See also the excellent discussion of the nature/grace problematic in Rahner with a particular focus on his supernatural existential in Stephen J. Duffy, *The Graced Horizon: Nature and Grace in Modern Catholic Thought,* Theology and Life Series 37 (Collegeville, Minnesota: The Liturgical Press, 1992), 85-114 and 206-34.

[164] Duffy, *The Graced Horizon,* 94.

[165] For example, *Lumen Gentium*, n. 16, *Vatican Council II*, ed. Flannery, vol. 1, 367, (following 1 Tim 2:4) refers to God's universal salvific will, and continues: "Those who, through no fault of their own, do not know the Gospel of Christ or his Church, but who nevertheless seek God with a sincere heart, and moved by grace, try in their actions to do his will as they know it through the dictates of their conscience — those too may achieve eternal salvation." Similarly, *Gaudium et Spes*, n. 22, *Vatican Council II*, ed. Flannery, vol. 1, 924, speaks of all people of good will in whose hearts grace is active invisibly, and to whom the possibility of becoming partners in the paschal mystery is offered in a way known only to God.

damnata could be saved, Rahner asks whether we may not hope that the majority of humanity will, in fact, be saved.[166] A further consequence of this reinterpretation of grace (also expressed by Vatican II) is the development of a more positive relationship between the Church and the world, where the former barriers between the two give way to a Christian vision of a kingdom of grace beyond the Church.

The fourth reversal or reinterpretation of grace by Rahner is a reaction against the scholastic claim that grace, because it is supernatural, is something totally beyond the region of consciousness. In contrast, Rahner holds that grace can be consciously experienced. He was convinced that both Scripture and genuine theological tradition within the Church point to this different understanding of grace. "Grace, the Holy Spirit, the working of the Spirit of God in the proper sense of divinizing grace ... , all this is something new which in our view ... operates within human consciousness."[167] However, Rahner qualifies this view, since grace is still not experienced directly or unambiguously as grace, in the fashion of the experience of a categorial object. Instead, as we have seen, the essence of grace lies in the self-communication of God to the transcendent spirit of the human person.[168] And it is because of this divine self-communication that the transcendent human spirit is:

> "permanently and necessarily ordered to the direct presence of God, whether this be the object of conscious or thematic reflection or not... . Grace is thus understood as the radical transformation of human transcendence so that God is not merely the final goal of human striving which one may come nearer to but never reach... . Grace is also that which makes it possible for this movement to *reach* God in himself."[169]

---

[166] Rahner, "The Abiding Significance of the Second Vatican Council," *TI* 20: 90-102 (*ST* XIV: 303-318). The pastoral consequences of the change from a "Heilspessimismus" (associated with Augustine) to a "Universaler Heilsoptimismus" is discussed with reference to Rahner's theology of ministry in Paul M. Zulehner, *"Denn du kommst unserem Tun mit deiner Gnade zuvor ..." : Zur Theologie der Seelsorge heute. Paul M. Zulehner im Gespräch mit Karl Rahner* (Düsseldorf: Patmos Verlag, 1984), 40-82.

[167] Rahner, "Religious Enthusiasm and the Experience of Grace," *TI* 16: 38-39 (*ST* XII: 58). See also his article, "Gnadenerfahrung," *LThK* 4: 1001-02.

[168] See, Rahner, "Gnade als Mitte menschlicher Existenz," *Herausforderung des Christen*, 134-37.

[169] Rahner, "Religious Enthusiasm and the Experience of Grace," *TI* 16: 40 (*ST* XII: 60-61).

By linking grace with human transcendence, Rahner intends to show how grace is operative even in cases where an explicit Christian interpretation is absent, or present only in a very obscure manner.[170] Thus, grace is present whenever this self-communication is accepted by someone acting in accordance with the inmost dictates of their conscience. Whenever a person responds in such a way, there occurs the "experience of grace."[171] With this, and with the other theological reversals described above, Rahner broke open the narrow objectivist treatment of grace and showed how grace affects our conscious life, not just our being but our existence.[172] A further conclusion of Rahner's reflections is that this self-communication of God is not imposed upon the human person from without, and merely on the conceptual level, but that this notion really expresses what the human person truly is, and what they themselves experience in the depths of their existence. However, to substantiate this claim it will be necessary to turn to Rahner's description of the offer of the divine self-communication as a "supernatural existential."

b. Rahner's "Supernatural Existential"

In the previous section, we noted Rahner's insistence that grace can be experienced, and that this grace (understood as God's self-communication) is present to all in the mode of an offer — to be

---

[170] A good example of where Rahner identifies the experience of grace with the experience of transcendence, and relates both to the experience of the Spirit, can be seen in the in his essay "Experience of the Holy Spirit" *TI* 18: 198 (*ST* XIII: 237): "... Then, in the actual order of reality, experience of transcendence (which is experience of God) is always also experience of grace, since the radicalness of the experience of transcendence and its dynamism are sustained in the innermost core of our existence by God's self-communication making all this possible, by the self-communication of God as goal and as strength of the movement toward him that we describe as grace, as the Holy Spirit (at least as an offer to our freedom). The experience of transcendence permitting God to be present (because of God's salvific will in regard to all human beings, by which one is oriented to God's immediacy) is in fact always experience of the Holy Spirit, whether a person can or cannot interpret explicitly in this way their inescapable experience of the unknown God, whether or not one has at one's disposal theological expressions such as those we have just been using."

[171] See Rahner's "Reflections on the Experience of Grace," *TI* 3: 86-90 (*ST* III: 105-109).

[172] Rahner, "Nature and Grace," *TI* 4: 178-88 (*ST* IV: 224-36).

freely accepted or rejected. Linked to this claim is God's universal salvific will, i.e., Rahner's belief that all are called to salvation. It is to Rahner's credit that he has expanded this traditional teaching of Scripture and the Church by investigating how it is possible for non-Christians to be saved. Specifically, he searches for some concrete manifestation of this will for all people to be saved, and takes as his point of departure a certain openness on our part to God's self-communication. In what follows, we will expand on what this human openness involves. Previously, our discussion of Rahner's transcendental-anthropological method showed how the human person is an "obediential potency" for a possible revelation of God. Further, we saw how Rahner developed the notion of God as the horizon of our knowing, and the term of our transcendence. Now, however, we see Rahner developing the notion of God communicating himself to humanity. In other words, God is more than the metaphysical condition of the possibility of human knowing and loving. In effect, Rahner's aim to is to present God's self-communication in such a way that the human person can recognize this as the valid expression of, and the key to, their own self-understanding. This is the context for the introduction of the "supernatural existential."

Rahner interprets God's wish to communicate himself as the beginning of His divine plan for humanity. Thus God not only makes a creature He can love, but makes us in such a way that we *can* receive this love which is God himself.[173] Immediately, though, Rahner nuances his position. Firstly, the human person has no claim to this divine self-communication, i.e., the grace of God's self-communication is supernatural.[174] In other words, this grace is "unowed" (*ungeschuldet*), or, more positively, a gratuitous gift of God. Secondly, this grace is permanently present to all in the mode of an offer. It does not exist solely in the thoughts and intentions of God, but is

---

[173] Rahner, "Grace," *Sacramentum Mundi* 2: 415-21 (*SM* II: 450-65). See also "Concerning the Relationship between Nature and Grace," *TI* 1: 310 (*ST* I: 336-37).

[174] "... The grace of God's self-communication is supernatural, in other words one can have no claim to it — quite apart from one's unworthiness as a sinner — nor can *any* creature: it is not entailed by one's inalienable being (one's 'nature'), so that in principle God could deny it to humanity though sin had never been committed." Rahner, "Grace," *Theological Dictionary*: 193-94 (*Kleines Theologisches Wörterbuch*: 157).

an "existential"[175] of each person's concrete existence. By virtue of God's universal salvific will, the human person is pre-determined *a priori* towards their supernatural end in God. Rahner's position is that:

> "the supernatural call made to the person by God's grace is given not simply ontically, but also ontologically. In other words, it is present not only in the order of a person's being, but also in some form in their consciousness, which it determines in some way."[176]

Rahner maintains, then, that there is within the human person a "potency" (*Potenz*), a "congeniality" (*Kongenialität*), or a "disposition" (*Anlage*), enabling us to be able to receive and to accept God's self-communication.[177] This "potency" is "what is inmost and most authentic" in the human person, and God's self-communication represents "that to which one is ordained in the ground of one's being."[178] Throughout his discussion of grace, Rahner is attempting to steer a middle way between that view of the human person as a purely *passive* potency with regard to God's self-communication on the one hand, and, on the other, the view that the person's receptivity to grace is a wholly natural ordination.[179] During the thirties and

---

[175] Rahner, "Supernatural existential," *Sacramentum Mundi* 2: 306 (*SM* I: 1298-99). For our initial reference to the term "existential," see section 1, d, of this chapter.

[176] Karl-Heinz Weger, *Karl Rahner: An Introduction to his Theology* (New York: Seabury Press, 1980), 108. See also Rahner's, "Zum theologischen Begriff der Konkupiszenz," *ST* I: 408: "Die Hinordnung auf das übernatürliche Ziel, die verpflichtend ist für jeden Menschen in der gegenwärtigen Wirklichkeits- und Heilsordnung, kann vielmehr durchaus gedacht werden als ein realontologisches Existential des Menschen, das ihn real und innerlich qualifiziert." The term "übernatürliche Existential," in fact, appeared in an earlier form of Rahner's article (with the same title) in *Zeitschrift für Katholische Theologie* 65 (1941): 61-80.

[177] "... One is only really known in one's 'indefinable' essence when one is understood as *potentia oboedientialis* for the divine life and when this is one's *nature*. One's nature is such that it must look to grace for its *absolute* fulfilment, and hence, as regards itself, it must reckon with a *non-frustrating* absence of an absolute fulfilment." Rahner, "Nature and Grace," *TI* 4: 186 (*ST* IV: 235).

[178] Rahner, "Concerning the Relationship between Nature and Grace," *TI* 1: 311-12 (*ST* I: 338-39).

[179] The issue here is how to explain the capacity of the human person for grace. Aquinas, in his *Summa contra Gentiles* III, speaks of the person's capacity for grace and glory as an inborn desire of the person, a *desiderium naturale*. The problem arose, however, that if this desire is not to be in vain, God must be bound to give the person

forties there was much discussion in theological circles in Europe about this issue, the outcome of which led to a new movement in French theology after the Second World War called the *Nouvelle théologie*.[180] One task which this movement set itself was that of rethinking the problem of the relationship between nature and grace.

Probably the best known theologian of this movement was Henri de Lubac, who, in his major work on the mystery of the supernatural, wanted to revive Aquinas' notion of the *desiderium naturale*.[181] Refusing to conceive human nature in a merely static sense (onto which the supernatural call of God was added), de Lubac argued for a more dynamic understanding of human subjectivity, and held, like Rahner, that the desire for God is a constitutive element of the human subject. However, the official ecclesiastical reaction to de Lubac's position was negative. Even prior to de Lubac's work, Pius XII, in his encyclical *Mystici Corporis* (1943) insisted that God's freedom and the gratuitous character of supernatural grace were not sufficiently guaranteed if the human person of his or her own accord, that is, as a pure creature, was thought to have a right to God's grace. And there was a more specific correction of the views of the *Nouvelle théologie* movement in the encyclical *Humani Generis* (1950).[182]

Rahner, for his part, was not entirely unsympathetic to de Lubac's position. Yet his concern, beginning in *Hearers of the Word*, was to search for the *a priori* conditions of possibility that lie behind this human desire for God. We have already seen in this context how Rahner introduced the notion of *Vorgriff* or "pre-grasp," which referred to the conscious opening up of the horizon within which a

---

the free gift of grace and one could thus lay claim to it. For an account of the origin of Rahner's "supernatural existential," see George Vass, *The Mystery of Man and the Foundations of a Theological System: Understanding Karl Rahner*, 2 vols. (London: Sheed and Ward, 1985), 2: 59-83.

[180] For a helpful survey of this expression and the controversy surrounding it, see Henri Rondet, "Nouvelle Théologie," *Sacramentum Mundi* 4: 234-36 (*SM* III: 816-20).

[181] Henri de Lubac, *Surnaturel: Études historiques* (Paris: Aubier, 1946).

[182] "Others destroy the gratuitous character of the supernatural order by suggesting that it would be impossible for God to create rational beings without ordaining them for the Beatific Vision and calling them to it." *The Teaching of the Catholic Church* (Cork: Mercier Press, 1966), 411 (= DS 3891).

particular object of human knowledge becomes known.[183] In other words, Rahner wished to see being — conceived as an infinite, a priori, non-objectifiable horizon against which limited, finite, particular objects appear — as a participating, constitutive element in all human cognitive and affective activity.[184] The *Vorgriff* is, therefore, directed towards the infinity of being, which Rahner designates as "God." In his metaphysical investigations to define the conditions of a possible Self-manifestation of God in a human word, Rahner concludes that the human person has an "obediential potency" for such a revelation. He revived the notion of obediential potency, a term scorned by de Lubac, giving it a new meaning. No longer was it to be understood as the human person's "non-repugnance" (*Nicht-Widersprüchlichkeit*)[185] to receive God's grace, nor as a merely passive human receptivity. Rather,

> "...obediential potency is a dynamism, in itself not absolute, but conditioned, a dynamism now enhanced by the capacity to strive towards a strictly supernatural goal: the vision of God. For this enhancement he introduced in 1950 the term *supernatural existential*."[186]

Thus, the term "supernatural existential" refers to more than the human person's openness to God. What is at stake here is an enhancement, or, as Rahner has described it, an "ontological modification"[187] and an "existential determination"[188] (*eine existentiale Bestimmung*) of the person. We are dealing here with the crux of the problem of nature and grace. This problem is central to our discussion of Rahner's understanding of the experience of grace. In effect,

---

[183] Rahner, *Hearers of the Word*, 59-60 (*Hörer des Wortes*, 78-79). The *Vorgriff* is clarified by Rahner as "a *capacity* ("Vermögen") of dynamic self-movement of the spirit, given *a priori* with human nature," a movement in which the particular object of knowledge in each act of cognition is grasped not just in its "thisness," but in its limitation and reference to the totality of all possible objects.

[184] Duffy, *The Graced Horizon*, 207-208.

[185] Rahner, "Concerning the Relationship between Nature and Grace," *TI* 1: 314 (*ST* I: 342). "Non-contradiction" is possibly a more accurate translation.

[186] Vass, *The Mystery of Man and the Foundations of a Theological System: Understanding Karl Rahner*, 2: 65. See also Rahner, "The Theological Concept of Concupiscentia," *TI* 1: 374-82 (*ST* I: 377-414).

[187] Rahner, Vorgrimler, "Existential, Supernatural," *Theological Dictionary:* 161 (*Kleines Theologisches Wörterbuch:* 123-24).

[188] Rahner, "Supernatural existential," *Sacramentum Mundi* 2: 306 (*SM* I: 1298).

Rahner is asking about the necessary conditions for the encounter of humanity with God, that is, for a person to be really able to receive the communication of God in Godself. By virtue of this existential, humankind is not neutral with regard to God,

> "... but positively susceptible to willingly accepting as a gratuitous gift a reality not alien to it but striking a resounding chord in its most profound depths.... One is oriented to say 'yes' before doing so."[189]

Moreover, the concept of obediential potency mentioned above:

> "... is no longer presented as a non-resistance of nature to grace, but a positive preapprehension of the God of grace; *pure nature* is no longer an Aristotelian constant of human essence which was once realized in history, but a postulate to affirm the gratuitous unexactedness of God's grace."[190]

Rahner uses the term "nature" as a remainder concept (*Restbegriff*), referring to that "which remains over when the supernatural existential as unowed is extracted."[191] While this may sound like a return to the former compartmentalization (of nature/supernature), Rahner thinks it is necessary to postulate such a term in the human person. Otherwise, the supernatural existential could be conceived as part of the "pure" nature of the human person, and not as a gratuitous gift of God. Nevertheless, Rahner concedes that this term "pure nature" is not one that can be clearly delineated. It can never be found in a "chemically pure" state separated from its supernatural existential. Instead,

> "the strictly *theological* concept of 'nature' therefore does not mean a state of reality, intelligible in itself and experienced by us separately (apart from a grace inaccessible to experience) on top of which, according to revelation, an additional higher reality would be superimposed."[192]

Nonetheless, there is a certain theological ambiguity about Rahner's concept of "pure nature." On the one hand, he wishes to preserve

---

[189] Duffy, *The Graced Horizon*, 99.

[190] Vass, *The Mystery of Man and the Foundations of a Theological System: Understanding Karl Rahner*, 2: 66.

[191] Rahner, "Concerning the Relationship between Nature and Grace," *TI* 1: 314 (*ST* I: 340).

[192] Rahner, "Grace," *Sacramentum Mundi* 2: 417 (*SM* II: 454).

the sovereignty of God, on the other, the autonomy of the individual. We have outlined Rahner's argument that God, on the basis of His universal salvific will, wishes to communicate Himself to humanity, to endow it with grace, and, further, that this grace is the most intimate element of human existence. Yet, in abstracting from this framework a concept of "pure nature" (which he considers more a hypothetical state, or a "remainder concept"), Rahner also leaves himself open to accusations of extrinsicism — in that a person's endowment with grace remains an extrinsic embellishment — the very weakness which his theory of the supernatural existential sought to overcome. By retaining this concept of "pure nature," he leaves open the speculative possibility of some world where pure human nature could have meaning in its own right.[193] Georg Vass, who has highlighted this ambiguity in Rahner's theory, nevertheless offers a guarded defence of Rahner's use of the term "pure nature:"

> "Pure nature with its obediential potency is a requisite for understanding the person on the essential level, its actuation in the supernatural existential is the principle for understanding the person on the level of existence. Roughly speaking the first is the result of an *ontic,* the other of an *ontological* way of thinking."[194]

Rahner is not advocating a return to that primitive view of "pure nature" conceived as a real historical state of humanity to which was added the call of God to a higher "supernatural" destiny. Rather, with

---

[193] A typical example of such an objection to Rahner's theory is that of Hans Urs von Balthasar: "So ist, … die Frage, ob es eine Welt auch ohne diese Gnade hätte geben können, eine müßige Frage." *Karl Barth: Darstellung und Deutung seiner Theologie,* 2nd, ed., (Cologne: Verlag Jakob Hegner, 1962), 312. See also Vass, *The Mystery of Man and the Foundations of a Theological System: Understanding Karl Rahner,* 2: 71-72; and Duffy, *The Graced Horizon,* 220-21, who likewise notes this ambiguity in Rahner, but who maintains that the hypothetical notion of nature is purely a secondary matter for Rahner: "There is no avowal of a real leap from hypothetical nature to actual graced nature; there is simply the contention that an ungraced world is possible, that the actual economy is not the sole possibility, that there is a difference between humanity-as-such and historical humanity." (p. 221).

[194] Vass, *The Mystery of Man and the Foundations of a Theological System: Understanding Karl Rahner,* 2: 72. For the distinction between "ontic" and "ontological," see Weger, *Karl Rahner: An Introduction To His Theology,* 198, n. 29: "'Ontic' means 'in accordance with being', in other words, what *is*; 'ontological', in the sense in which Rahner uses the term, means becoming conscious of what is 'ontic'." (italics mine).

the concept of "pure human nature," he envisages "only an abstract, but valid, presupposition for the human person, not however a world in which it could be realized. Pure nature is not an ontological but merely an ontic principle."[195] In short, the primary function of the theological concept of nature, is, as we mentioned already, a _con- trasting_ concept to highlight the gratuity of grace.

To sum up our discussion of Rahner's concept of the supernatural existential, we can say that, prior to anything that the human person does, he or she is already subject to the universal salvific will of God. Further, this "situation" is not merely an external one, not merely a divine intention, a decree "in God's will," but entails an "objective, ontological modification" of the human person. In this sense, the concept of the supernatural existential discloses our "congeniality" or "disposition" to enter into a relation with a God of love:

> "Thus one must have a real potency ("Potenz") for it (this Love which is Godself)... . This potency is what is inmost and most authentic in one, the centre and root of what one is absolutely. One must have it always ... must ... always remain what one was created as: the burning longing for Godself in the immediacy of God's own threefold life. The capacity for the God of Self-bestowing personal Love is the central and abiding _existential_ of the human person as he or she really is."[196]

---

[195] Vass, *The Mystery of Man and the Foundations of a Theological System: Understanding Karl Rahner,* 2: 73. We agree here with Duffy, *The Graced Horizon,* 106-108, that Rahner's notion of human nature, theologically considered, lacks any refined determination. Rahner's understanding of nature as a *Restbegriff* is his reaction to the traditional, objectivist view where grace was relegated from the world of experience to an objectified spiritual realm beyond human consciousness; it (grace) was perceived as "an unconscious modality of the soul, an ontic state elevating one but discernible only to the eyes of faith." Instead, Rahner's contention is that it is impossible to experience nature at any time as hermetically sealed off from the influence of grace. See, for example his "Reflections on the Experience of Grace," *TI* 3: 86-90 (*ST* III: 105-109).

[196] Rahner, "Concerning the Relationship between Nature and Grace, *TI* 1: 311-12 (*ST* I: 338-39). In an article some years later (1958), Rahner describes how the human person, prior to the subjective appropriation of salvation, is "inwardly determined" (*innerlich bestimmt*) by the supernatural existential: "Prior to any subjective attitude, the human person *is* really different (from what he or she *would* be as mere creature and mere sinner), because redemption has taken place in Christ, because God loves him or her in Christ ... This 'is' which determines the person in not procured by faith and love. One rather 'takes cognizance' of it through faith and love, accepting it of course and ratifying it existentially ... It is not simply a subjective conversion to a

In the light of our reflections on Rahner's understanding of religious experience, we will now examine some consequences which ensue for his understanding of spirituality. We shall attempt to indicate a *link* between transcendental and categorial experience in Rahner's thought. This link is necessary for our claim that Rahner's spirituality is not one of pure interiority — based on a rather vague idea of Christianity — but contains within it a "turn towards the world," where God is encountered in the ordinariness of everyday life.

c. Consequences

i) From an Anonymous to an Explicit Spirituality

Our discussion, thus far, of Rahner's concept of religious experience has shown that there is a distinction between one's ordinary, everyday experiences, and that unique, original, basic experience of oneself as the subject who undergoes all these particular experiences.[197] We have seen that the basis for this claim lies in the transcendental reference of the human person in knowledge and freedom to the mystery of God. In other words, an experience of God is present in *every* human person, by virtue of one's orientation to mystery, or as Rahner sometimes puts it, by virtue of the dynamic structure of the human spirit. Each person possesses a primordial reference to God, the incomprehensible mystery. This does not mean, though, that such an experience of God or of grace is always accepted for what it really is, since the experience of God as such differs from any subsequent conceptual reflection on, or interpretation of, this original experience.

Rahner has thus sought to show a *movement* or transition from an implicit, unthematic experience of God to a more explicit recognition

God who by reason of his metaphysical goodness has to be gracious in any case, if we ourselves are only interested in it... God has done something *to* me *in* Christ before I do anything." Rahner, "Questions of Controversial Theology on Justification," *TI* 4: 200-201 (*ST* IV: 250-51).

[197] Apart from the references provided in section 1, a, i) "Human Experiences and the Experience of God," this distinction also lies at the root of Rahner's claim that it is possible to be an "anonymous Christian." See, for example his "Observations on the Problem of the 'Anonymous Christian'," *TI* 14: 287-94 (*ST* X: 538-46).

of such an experience at the conceptual level. We have already noted
how Rahner gives priority to the unthematic aspect of religious experience. He reacts against the tendency to regard such an experience of
God as deriving from a form of doctrinal instruction "from without."
Yet, it could be asked whether this approach undermines that which
is specifically Christian in spirituality. With the stress on the universal, transcendental character of religious experience, do we not run
the risk of ending up with a merely vague and "anonymous" spirituality? Until now, the impression given has been that this type of universal and anonymous spirituality is Rahner's preference.[198] Yet, this
is not entirely accurate. In the remainder of our work, we hope to
make clear that Rahner also emphasizes the importance of, and the
need for, a specifically Christian spirituality, which he presents as the
making explicit of what is essentially a universally available experience of God.

Rahner's clarification of the experience of God, then, is based on a
twofold conviction: i) that this experience is universal (i.e., God is
that which we encounter in our deepest human experience), and ii)
that the God so encountered is the Father of Jesus Christ whose Spirit
dwells in our hearts.[199] Throughout his writings, Rahner has sought to
stress the importance of a mystagogical initiation into an experience
of God, which occurs when a person "returns to him or herself" in
silent reflection. Such a (spiritual) exercise is an attempt to seek the
unity in the multiplicity of one's activities by returning to the innermost centre ("die innerste Mitte") of one's being.[200] This turning

---

[198] For an attempt to develop an "non-theistic" spirituality that has certain parallels with Rahner's approach, see Leo Apostel, "Een ander geloven. Een nieuwe tran-
scendentie. Over niet-theistische spiritualiteit," *De geur van de roos. Over zingeving
en spiritualiteit*, eds. Ulrich Libbrecht et al. (Leuven: Davidsfonds, 1994), 29-45.
While Apostel shares similar pastoral motives to Rahner in examining how the
"unchurched" and "non-believers" have a spirituality — he even refers to Rahner at
one point (p. 40) —, he differs from the latter in not explicitating an ecclesial dimension to spirituality.

[199] This is the conclusion of J. Norman King, "The Experience of God in the Theology of Karl Rahner," *Thought* 53 (1978): 200-202.

[200] Rahner, "Der Helfer-Geist," *Von der Not und dem Segen des Gebetes*, 37. See
also his "Thoughts on the Theology of Christmas," *TI* 3: 24-34 (*ST* III: 35-46). Rahner's "Konzentration auf die 'Mitte' des Glaubens" is one of the most significant
characteristics of his theological method: "Seine Methode, die als Methode, wie er

inwards *may* then lead to an explicit act of faith. In any event, it is Rahner's belief that such a "spiritual" exercise only finds full expression *exteriorly* — in the routine of everyday life, where the summons of grace makes itself heard:

> "Have we ever kept quiet, even though we wanted to defend ourselves when we had been unfairly treated? Have we ever forgiven someone even though we got no thanks for it and our silent forgiveness was taken for granted? ... Have we ever sacrificed something without receiving any thanks or recognition for it, and even without a feeling of inner satisfaction? Have we ever been absolutely lonely? Have we ever decided on some course of action purely by the innermost judgement of our conscience, deep down where one can no longer tell or explain it to anyone, where one is quite alone and knows that one is taking a decision which no one else can take in one's place and for which one will have to answer for all eternity? ... Have we ever fulfilled a duty when it seemed it could be done only with a consuming sense of really betraying and obliterating oneself, when it could apparently be done only by doing something terribly stupid for which no one would thank us?"[201]

Of course, both a Christian and a non-Christian can have the experiences outlined above. But it is possible, in Rahner's view, to discover in such experiences "a mute pointer in the direction of God, something which in its namelessness and boundlessness gives us a hint that God is more than just another thing, added to those with which we normally have to deal."[202] Rahner further claims that, by silently entering into such experiences, "God allows us to become aware of his presence, if we are quiet and do not take fright and run away from the mysterious being which lives and acts in this

---

selber sagt, sehr vieles Martin Heidegger verdankt, ist die der Konzentration der Vielfalt auf ganz wenige Grundgedanken, ... auf Schlüsselbegriffe oder noch besser auf Schlüsselerlebnisse. *Der* Grundgedanke dieser Theologie oder *das* Schlüsselerlebnis ist, nachlesbar bei Rahner selber, die Erfahrung Gottes." Herbert Vorgrimler, "Gotteserfahrung im Alltag: Der Beitrag Karl Rahners zu Spiritualität und Mystik," *Karl Rahner in Erinnerung*, ed. Albert Raffelt (Düsseldorf: Patmos, 1994), 102. See also Vorgrimler's other article in the same volume, "Versöhnung mit der Kirche," 44-69, esp. 66-69.

[201] Rahner, "Reflections on the Experience of Grace," *TI* 3: 87 (*ST* III: 106-107). See also Karl Rahner, *Sendung und Gnade. Beiträge zur Pastoraltheologie*, 3rd ed. (Innsbruck: Tyrolia Verlag, 1961), 84.

[202] Rahner, "Thoughts on the Theology of Christmas," *TI* 3: 26-27 (*ST* III: 38).

silence."[203] In this way, the experience of mystery (*das Geheimnis*) which is simultaneously incomprehensible *and* self-evident, comes to the fore. This experience of mystery in traditional Christian terms is called the experience of God, but it is not that Rahner is simply imposing a neat concept (God) *onto* all these various experiences in order to render them intelligible. Rather, it is the other way round: it is only from such experiences that what is meant by the term God becomes clear.[204] In other words, those who have experiences similar to those mentioned above have "also already *in fact* experienced the *supernatural*, ... (if even) in a very anonymous and inexpressible manner."[205] The encounter with God, then, takes place not normally in the form of a special divine intervention, but "anonymously" in the everyday routine of life. "Everydayness" ("Alltäglichkeit") is a specific "existential" of human living, and one which, for Rahner, has spiritual significance: it is there in the world of the everyday that one is challenged to discover the "anonymity" or hiddenness of God.[206]

Nevertheless, the examples listed above only represent, in Rahner's eyes, the "lowest step" in the experience of grace.[207] We are dealing here with a graced "root" experience. And just as the fruit is "present" in the root, so too do the different experiences of grace contain the core and source of the Christian message. Such experiences must be "developed," in that they need to be interpreted and reflected on in the light of the Gospel. Herein lies the "strangely ambiguous" (*Zweideutigkeit*) nature of experience.[208] This ambiguity does not remain simply at the theoretical level. The situations

---

[203] Rahner, "Thoughts on the Theology of Christmas," *TI* 3: 27 (*ST* III: 38).

[204] "See also Rahner, "The Concept of Mystery in Catholic Theology," *TI* 4: 48-54 (*ST* IV: 67-75). We are indebted here to some perceptive remarks of Nikolaus Schwerdtfeger, *Gnade und Welt: Zum Grundgefüge von Karl Rahners Theorie der "anonymen Christen,"* Freiburger Theologische Studien 123 (Freiburg: Herder, 1982), 363-80.

[205] Rahner, "Reflections on the Experience of Grace," *TI* 3: 88 (*ST* III: 108).

[206] "Also muß *in* der Welt Gott gesucht und gefunden werden, also muß der Alltag selbst Gottes Tag, die Auskehr in die Welt Einkehr in Gott, muß der Alltag 'Einkehrtag' werden. Es muß der Alltag selbst gebetet werden." Rahner, "Gebet im Alltag," *Von der Not und dem Segen des Gebetes*, 72.

[207] Rahner, "Reflections on the Experience of Grace," *TI* 3: 86 (*ST* III: 105).

[208] Rahner, "Thoughts on the Theology of Christmas," *TI* 3: 27 (*ST* III: 38).

described above also have existential implications. They demand an openness, a renunciation, and a letting go:

> "This infinity, which silently surrounds you — does it repulse you and drive you back into your limited daily life? Does it bid you yourself to go away out of the silence in which it rules? Does it fall upon you with the merciless loneliness of death so as to make you run away from it into the more familiar sectors of your life, until it catches up with you … in death? … Or is it that which waits until you are open *to its very self* as something approaching, coming, the promised beatitude?"[209]

Rahner then develops a specifically Christian interpretation of our experiences. In Christian terms, the kind of renunciation and letting-go that is involved in the experiences referred to above is called the taking up one's *cross*. It is no coincidence that Rahner's examples have to do with self-emptying and renunciation since, for him, every authentic experience of grace is in some way a participation in the death of Jesus.[210] Renunciation (*Entsagung*) occurs when a person "radically submits to God's disposal, [is] seized and overpowered by God … when … one summons up courage (again by God's grace), embracing and surrendering one's whole existence to believe, hope, and love."[211] Yet Rahner concedes that the taking up of one's cross is not confined to Christians alone:

> "The person who, in a hope which no longer seeks to reassure itself, relinquishes oneself in the depths of the mystery of existence, in which death and life can no longer be distinguished because they can only be grasped together, actually believes in the Crucified and Risen one, even if he or she is not aware of it (in conceptual terms)."[212]

This hopeful courage is simply another word for *faith*, which itself has two aspects.[213] There is the "ultimate courage for existence," on

---

[209] Rahner, "Thoughts on the Theology of Christmas," *TI* 3: 27 (*ST* III: 38).

[210] Rahner, "Self-realization and Taking Up One's Cross," *TI* 9: 253-57 (*ST* VIII: 322-26). See also his articles: "Following the Crucified," *TI* 18: 157-70 (*ST* XIII: 188-203); and "Christian Dying," *TI* 18: 252-56 (*ST* XIII: 299-304).

[211] Rahner, "Christian Dying," *TI* 18: 254 (*ST* XIII: 301). See also his "Reflections on the Theology of Renunciation," *TI* 3: 47-57 (*ST* III: 61-72).

[212] Rahner, "Self-realization and Taking Up One's Cross," *TI* 9: 256 (*ST* VIII: 325).

[213] "There can exist an 'anonymous faith' which carries with it an intrinsic dynamism and therefore an obligation to find full realization in explicit faith, but which is nonetheless sufficient for salvation even if a person does not achieve this ful-

the one hand, and "explicitly Christian faith in Jesus, crucified and risen," on the other.[214] In Rahner's view, these two factors do not simply exist alongside each other externally; ultimately, he sees them as one.[215] The peculiarity of Christian faith is that it sees in Jesus the consummation of our hope, a fulfilment also promised by God to us. This forms part of the "content" of explicit Christianity, part of that courageous faith which permits us to hope that our (negative) experiences of futility, darkness and death do not have the last word.

The explicit message of Christianity, therefore, helps us to interpret our experiences correctly. It is not a question of Christianity simply supplying a subsequent, conceptual explanation of our experiences of grace, added, as it were, as a supplementary (but unnecessary) appendix.[216] Rather,

> "the message of faith which comes in the hearing of the word opens the eyes of inner experience so that this experience may have the confidence to understand itself correctly and to accept the sweet comfort of its uncanny mystery as the real meaning of this experience."[217]

Conversely, without reference to our experience, the word of proclamation "from without" remains hollow and empty. In short, Rahner is convinced of the need to move from an anonymous experience of grace to a more explicit interpretation and appropriation of this experience in the context of Christian *faith*:

> "… Human life does of itself present a kind of anonymous Christianity, which explicit Christianity can then interpret, giving a person the courage to accept and not run away from what one experiences and undergoes in one's own life; … This would be putting into practice

---

filment during their lifetime, as long as they are not to blame for this." Rahner, "Anonymous and Explicit Faith," *TI* 16: 54 (*ST* XII: 78).

[214] Rahner, "Faith as Courage," *TI* 18: 223-24 (*ST* XIII: 266-67).

[215] In a variation of an image used earlier, Rahner believes these two forms of courage "differ in fact only more or less as the seed differs from the flower." Hence his conviction that "it is certainly possible for a person to have that innermost faith in courageous hope for the totality of one's existence as oriented to God, to realize it freely in the commonplace routine of one's duty and love and yet inculpably to be unable to produce that courage which is required in principle from the Christian for faith in regard to Christian teaching as a whole." Rahner, "Faith as Courage," *TI* 18: 221-22 (*ST* XIII: 264).

[216] Schwerdtfeger, *Gnade und Welt*, 370.

[217] Rahner, "Thoughts on the Theology of Christmas," *TI* 3: 28 (*ST* III: 39).

what St Paul said of his preaching: 'What therefore you worship (really worship!) without knowing it (as consciously and explicitly interpreted), that I preach to you.' (Acts 17:23)"[218]

The "more" of Christianity, however, is not restricted solely to an increase in knowledge, or to a more reliable foundation for living. Rather, such knowledge must lead to a specific *decision* on the part of the Christian "to abandon oneself all the more decisively to the sovereign will of God's mystery."[219] There is, thus, a definite connection in Rahner's thought between the frequently anonymous experience of grace and the explicit acceptance of the message of faith.[220] In this context, Rahner describes, on the one hand, that "act of hope in one's own resurrection" which takes place in everyone "by transcendental necessity:"

"For every person wants to survive in some final and definitive sense, and experiences this claim in one's acts of freedom and responsibility, whether one is able to make this implication of the exercise of one's freedom thematic or not, and whether one accepts it in faith or rejects it in despair."[221]

Yet, on the other hand, he acknowledges a specifically Christian aspect of hope consisting in:

"... a hopeful knowledge of Jesus' victory in his defeat. And in Christians these two moments, the *letting ourselves fall* (*das Sichfallenlassen*) into God's unfathomability as into our ineffable happiness, and the *confession* (*das Bekenntnis*) of Jesus' victory in his mortal defeat, mutually condition and support each another. And together they form the one Christian hope. Because when people in the experience of their

---

[218] Karl Rahner, *Mission and Grace: Essays in Pastoral Theology*, vol. 1 (London and New York: Sheed and Ward, 1963), 160. [*Sendung und Gnade. Beiträge zur Pastoraltheologie*, 3rd ed. (Innsbruck: Tyrolia Verlag, 1961), 119].

[219] "But the affirmation of an implicit Christianity is also an affirmation that this basic dynamism, like every other potentiality of the human person, cannot be content to remain implicit, but strives after its own explicitness (*Ausdrücklichkeit*) — its 'name'... . The dynamism ... reaches a new degree of articulate recognition (*eine neue, höhere Stufe der Ausdrücklichkeit*) and fulfilment in the explicit confession of faith within the Church." Rahner, "Missions," *Sacramentum Mundi* 4: 80 (*SM* III: 550). See also Rahner, "Faith between Rationality and Emotion," *TI* 16: 60-78 (*ST* XII: 85-107).

[220] Schwerdtfeger, *Gnade und Welt*, 370-371, n. 42.

[221] Rahner, *FCF*, 268 (*Grundkurs*, 264).

own banality and guilt could despair of themselves on the basis of their own resources, they realize in view of Jesus, ... that they should at least not let this life fall desperate into vacuous meaninglessness, but instead must confess him together with his life's destiny as the one living with God forever.... . Then the *experience of God* in the defeat of our hopes as the hope and the confession of the crucified as the conqueror converge in one Christian hope."[222]

These reflections on Christian hope and the cross reveal a link in Rahner's thought between transcendental and categorial experience. The transcendental hope in resurrection is the horizon of understanding (*der Verständnishorizont*) for experiencing the resurrection of Jesus in faith, and "when it is not suppressed, this transcendental hope in resurrection necessarily seeks the historical mediation and confirmation in which it can become explicit."[223]

In short, Rahner's conviction is that everyone experiences God as that mysterious reality behind the gift and summons to silence, courage, self-sacrifice, trust, etc. God is the ground of the definitive meaningfulness of the whole of human life.[224] Nevertheless, even if we are in fundamental agreement with Rahner thus far, we could ask whether the experiences he describes are not those of a rather pious introspection. In other words, is there not here an excessive focus on the subject's "return to oneself"? Does the Christian (whether anonymous or explicit) only experience God by going inwards? If this were the case, we would be back at a rather individualistic understanding of spirituality. In the following section, we intend to show that this

---

[222] Rahner, *Herausforderung des Christen*, 39, [Only portions of this work have been translated into English. The section relevant to our discussion, however, can be found in: Karl Rahner, *The Great Church Year. The Best of Karl Rahner's Homilies, Sermons and Meditations*, ed. Albert Raffelt, trans. Harvey D. Egan (New York: Crossroad, 1993), 166, italics mine]. On the necessity of *both* these elements (*das Sichfallenlassen* and *das Bekenntnis*), see Klinger, *Das absolute Geheimnis im Alltag entdecken*, 27-28, who comments: "Es ist vollkommen abwegig, bei Rahner die verbale Äußerung im Bekenntnis und die unausdrückliche, vorverbale Einstellung, die dieses Bekenntnis übersteigt und auch unaufgebbar trägt, gegeneinander ausspielen zu wollen. Das Bekenntnis geht aus jener Einstellung hervor und bleibt auf sie zurückverwiesen.... . Anonymität und Existentialität, namenlose Dunkelheit und durchdringende Klarheit, ... konkurrieren nicht miteinander, sondern stehen in einem Bedingungsverhältnis."

[223] Rahner, *FCF*, 269 (*Grundkurs*, 264).

[224] King, "The Experience of God in the Theology of Karl Rahner," 200-201.

accusation cannot justifiably be levelled at Rahner. Our defence of Rahner necessitates a brief examination of his idea of a "searching Christology" (eine "suchende Christologie").[225] Our claim will be that it is in this notion of a "seeking" or anonymous Christology that "the significance of explicit Christianity and the reference of anonymous Christianity to Christ coincide, since Rahner tries to demonstrate in them that what is sought in any case is found in Christ."[226]

ii) Rahner's "Three Appeals"

We have previously noted Rahner's insistence on taking seriously Vatican II's teaching on the universal salvific will of God. The issue here is the connection of such a salvific will to the Christ event. With regard to our problematic, the *specific* issue concerns how *both* an anonymous *and* an explicitly Christian spirituality are related to Christ. Although the mode of this relationship will be different in each case, Rahner nevertheless argues "that if a person accepts their existence resolutely, they are really already living out in their existence something like a 'searching Christology' (eine 'suchende Christologie')."[227] He then clarifies this rather general statement and gives

---

[225] On this, see Rahner, *FCF*, 295-98 (*Grundkurs*, 288-91). Christology, Rahner argues, is turning here in a kind of "appeal" to a "global understanding of existence which is already 'Christian' because of antecedent grace." *FCF*, 295 (*Grundkurs*, 288). This claim is related to Rahner's third "reversal" of the traditional interpretation of grace outlined in the previous section.

[226] Weger, *Karl Rahner: An Introduction to His Theology*, 128 (*Karl Rahner: Eine Einführung*, 110). In the context of Rahner's understanding of mysticism (see Chapter Two, Section 2, b), this means "that all mysticism, wherever it exists, has an objective relatedness to Jesus Christ which admittedly is not explicitly grasped in extra-Christian mysticism; ... Christian theology ... can interpret a mysticism of this kind as 'questing Christology', just as Jesus himself rightly understood an act of love of neighbour done without knowledge of him as in fact done to himself." Rahner, "Experience of Transcendence from the Standpoint of Catholic Dogmatics," *TI* 18: 188 (*ST* XIII: 224-25).

[227] Rahner, *FCF*, 295 (*Grundkurs*, 288). Underlying Rahner's discussion are two important assumptions. The first is that all salvation is achieved through Christ, a factor which is significant in any discussion of non-Christian religions and salvation. The second assumption states that all who reach salvation must have a *relationship* to Jesus Christ, who is the "universal cause of salvation." On this, see Rahner, "The One Christ and the Universality of Salvation," *TI* 16: 199-224, esp. 216-24 (*ST* XII: 251-82, esp. 272-82).

it an explicit content through his "three appeals:" the appeal to an absolute love of neighbour, the appeal to readiness for death, and the appeal to hope in the future. By putting these appeals into practice, *both* the anonymous *and* the explicit Christian (in a free and fundamental act) express an "ultimate basic trust in the complete and comprehensive meaning of existence."[228] At the same time, Rahner believes "that this 'searching Christology' encounters what it is searching for precisely in Jesus of Nazareth."[229] Before we deal with the "absolutely particular" significance of belief in Christ, however, we turn to these three appeals and ask how they might constitute an anonymous or searching Christology.

The appeal to an "absolute love of neighbour" has already been discussed in the previous chapter. Without going over ground already covered, the important point in our current discussion is "that through radical and unconditional love of another, a person makes an implicit act of faith and love in Christ."[230] This absolute love is prepared to take risks in directing itself unconditionally to another person.[231]

---

[228] Rahner, Weger, *Our Christian Faith*, 163.

[229] Rahner, *FCF*, 295 (*Grundkurs*, 288). In the context of Rahner's searching Christology, the *difference* between an anonymous and an explicit Christian "is that in the Christology of quest a person does not know that it is in Jesus of Nazareth that what one is seeking is to be found... . This means that the Christological quest possesses a relationship to Jesus, even if one does not know how to call him by his proper name." Rahner, "The One Christ and the Universality of Salvation," *TI* 16: 222 (*ST* XII: 279-80).

[230] Rahner, "The One Christ and the Universality of Salvation," *TI* 16: 222 (*ST* XII: 279-80). See also his collection of meditations, *Ich glaube an Jesus Christus*, Theologische Meditationen 21 (Einsiedeln: Benziger Verlag, 1968), 16-23. This text is also available under the title "Unbedingte Liebe," in *Praxis des Glaubens*, 206-11. Unfortunately, however, the text is not to be found in the English version of this book, *The Practice of Faith*.

A question that arises with regard to Rahner's presentation at this point is that he seems to focus on the intimate rather than on the social dimension of love. It is not accurate, however, to claim that Rahner was unaware of the social and political dimensions of love. See, for example, "A Brief Anthropological Creed," *FCF*, 456-57 (*Grundkurs*, 437-39), where he describes two dimensions of love of neighbour: "an *existentiell* dimension of *intimacy*, and an *historical* and *social* dimension."

[231] "Wenn diese Liebe den Menschen wirklich radikal und ohne Vorbehalt an den Anderen wagt, ... dann ist darin inwendig und vielleicht namenlos — aber wirklich — das erfahren, was mit 'Gott' eigentlich gemeint ist; auch dann ist darin 'Gott' schon erreicht, ..." Rahner, "Unbedingte Liebe," *Praxis des Glaubens*, 208.

Here, too, there is the aspect of renunciation and self-abandonment which surfaced earlier in our interpretation of experiences of grace. Further, this love is subject to disappointment, since our neighbour is finite and unreliable, and cannot in him or herself justify the offer of such absolute love. Thus, a person's experience of trying to love his or her neighbour is an ongoing, often stumbling process, marked by both successes and failures.[232] Yet, when the neighbour is really radically loved without reservations, and not purely as a "means" or as a "proof" of one's love of God, then there is the (perhaps only anonymous and unthematic) consent to God as the _enabling ground_ (als der _tragende Grund_) of that love.[233] Rahner concludes as follows:

> "But a love whose absoluteness is experienced, even though it becomes fully itself not by virtue of itself, but only by virtue of its radical unity with the love of God through Jesus Christ, this love wants more that just a divine guarantee which remains transcendent to it. It wants a unity between the love of God and love of neighbour in which, even though this might be merely unthematic, love of neighbour is love of God and only in this way is completely absolute."[234]

Rahner's contention, then, is that in one's love of neighbour, one is always searching for someone who, as a human being, can be loved with the absoluteness of love for God. This "someone" is to be found in Christ, the "God-Man" ("der Gottmensch"), "whose existence within the single totality of the human race makes possible absolute love of another person."[235]

---

[232] See also Rahner, "Menschliches Scheitern und Weltverhältnis des Christen," _Handbuch der Pastoraltheologie: Praktische Theologie der Kirche in ihrer Gegenwart_, eds. Franz Xaver Arnold, Karl Rahner, Viktor Schurr, and Leonhard M. Weber (Freiburg: Herder, 1966), II/1: 34-38.

[233] "Wir sagen also: Jene Liebe, die den anderen absolut ernst nimmt und sich total anvertraut, erfährt — _wenn_ und _indem_ sie geschieht —, was 'Gott' ist, insofern sie ihn nämlich als Grund und Ermächtigung dieser Liebe erfährt ... Der 'Akt' solcher Liebe des Anderen ist der 'Akt' des Glaubens an Christus." Rahner, "Unbedingte Liebe," _Praxis des Glaubens_, 208, 211.

[234] Rahner, _FCF_, 296 (_Grundkurs_, 289).

[235] Rahner, "The One Christ and the Universality of Salvation," _TI_ 16: 223 (_ST_ XII: 280). Rahner sums up his position as follows: "Der 'Akt,' in dem Christus geglaubt wird, ist gegeben in dem Akt der unbedingten Liebe zum Nächsten, denn in diesem wird Er als Grund dieser Liebe mitbejaht; ein solches radikales Vertrauen

The second appeal is to a readiness for death (*Bereitschaft zum Tode*). Rahner feels that traditional preaching on the death of Jesus tended to concentrate too much on the particular, categorial nature of this event. Such an approach easily gives rise to a theory of satisfaction whereby the death of Jesus is simply regarded as an external and meritorious cause of our redemption.[236] Rahner's approach, on the other hand, is to develop a theology of death in such a way that the event of Jesus' death can be more closely related to the basic structure of human existence.[237] Accordingly, Rahner describes death as "the one act which pervades the whole of life, and in which a person, as a being of freedom, has disposal of him or herself in their entirety."[238] On the one hand, a person is obliged to take a stand towards the phenomenon of death, while, on the other, death reveals one's powerlessness, and must simply be endured. This "permanent dialectic" in the human person cannot be "resolved" by any abstract moral idealism. Instead, Rahner's thesis is that:

> "*the Christian, every Christian at all times, follows Jesus by dying* with him; following Jesus has its ultimate truth and reality and universality in the following of the Crucified."[239]

If Christian spirituality is about the following (*Nachfolge*) of Jesus, then, Rahner argues, there must be something that is unique which forms the content and norm of this discipleship. Traditionally, the history of Christian spirituality has focused on the element of *imitation* of the concrete Jesus through such practices as fasting, poverty, renunciation of power, and so on. Early Christianity also contained

---

liebt nämlich — suchend oder schon explizit findend — im Menschen einen Menschen mit (will sie absolute und *menschliche* Liebe zugleich sein), der die Radikalität solcher Liebe annehmen, tragen und als dem Menschen schlechthin gegenüber legitimieren kann, ohne daß sie ein sich selbst und den Menschen zerstörendes Abenteuer wird." Rahner, *Ich glaube an Jesus Christus*, 25.

[236] For Rahner's criticisms of the satisfaction theory, see his *Zur Theologie des Todes*, Quaestiones Disputatae 2 (Freiburg: Herder, 1958), 54-55. [ET: *On the Theology of Death*, Quaestiones Disputatae (New York: Herder and Herder, 1961), 66-69].

[237] See, Rahner, "Dying with Christ," *On the Theology of Death*, 64-88 (*Zur Theologie des Todes*, 52-72).

[238] Rahner, *FCF*, 297 (*Grundkurs*, 290).

[239] Rahner, "Following the Crucified," *TI* 18: 160 (*ST* XIII: 192).

D. MARMION

numerous examples of those who sought to imitate Jesus by martyr-dom.[240] But problems arose when martyrdom faded as a possibility, and when it became clear that not every Christian could adopt the particular ascetical practices mentioned above. It is in the light of the changing historical forms of the imitative following of Jesus that Rahner asks whether there is a particular, concrete following applica-ble for *all* Christians. The answer to this question lies, according to Rahner, in our participation in his death.

Death is presented here as an event involving the whole person. If the human person is considered as one who does not simply have a body, but *is* body, then death, in a human and Christian sense, is more than the physiological event of a medical exitus. Death is not merely something that happens to a person from outside. Rather, the central mystery of the theology of death has to do with the free act of resigned and self-forsaking surrender (*Selbstweggabe*) by which a person gives himself (or herself) over into the loving incomprehensi-bility of God.[241] In this sense, human death is an existential act which is anticipated throughout life in the "dying in installments" by which we give ourselves over to others and to God in love.[242] This act of self-surrender, Rahner holds, constitutes the "very content" of our relationship to God and reveals the most fundamental nature of

---

[240] While Rahner is aware that imitation and following are not synonymous terms, the former aspect is still important, he believes, since there exists the all too real dan-ger of turning Christian spirituality into a purely internal and private disposition. Such a spirituality can then very easily become a mere exercise in edification. For an excur-sus on martyrdom, see Rahner, *Zur Theologie des Todes*, 73-106.

[241] Rahner, "Following the Crucified," *TI* 18: 164 (*ST* XIII: 196). See also "The Human Question of Meaning In Face of the Absolute Mystery of God," *TI* 18: 99-101 (*ST* XIII: 122-28). In its dialogue with humanism, for example, Christianity "affirms God as the unprescribable absolute future." Such a claim is only the outcome of facing and accepting the mystery of death, something Rahner suspects Western humanism tends to pass over in silence. Rahner, "Christian Humanism," *TI* 9: 197-200 (*ST* VIII: 200-202).

[242] "But these individual decisions are elements of one life's decision only insofar as ... there occurs in them an assent or a refusal to that infinite horizon and objective of freedom which alone makes possible freedom in the proper sense in regard to the subject and its individual objects and in the final understanding is known as God.... This innermost structure of every real decision of freedom insofar as it is an internal factor in human death as an existential act, makes itself clearly felt in what we expe-rience empirically as death." Rahner, "Following the Crucified," *TI* 18: 163-64, 169 (*ST* XIII: 195-96, 203).

love.[243] We also see here some of the features common to Jesus' death and ours:

> "Jesus surrendered himself in his death unconditionally to the absolute mystery that he called his Father, into whose hands he committed his existence, when in the night of his death and God-forsakenness he was deprived of everything that is otherwise regarded as the content of a human existence: life, honour, acceptance, ... In the concreteness of his death it becomes only too clear that everything fell away from him, even the perceptible security of God's love, and in this trackless dark there prevailed silently only the mystery that in itself and in its freedom has no name and to which he nevertheless calmly surrendered himself as to eternal love and not to the hell of futility. In that sense his death is the same as ours, ... "[244]

In death every person has this experience of being deprived of everything, even of oneself; each one alone falls into the dark abyss. Jesus also died such a death. He not only descended into our human life, Rahner reminds us, but also fell into the abyss of our death. The statement that Jesus died as we die can then, he argues, provide an ineffable dignity and consolation for our own death. Further, if we believe what Christian faith says about God assuming our human reality, we believe this also to be true of our death. In other words, human death has been redeemed and emptied of final despair and futility.

However, it is only with reference to the *resurrection* that we really *follow* Jesus' death and that our death is transformed. Rahner stresses the importance of the unity of the death and resurrection of Jesus. The soteriological significance of the fate of Jesus must be situated in both his death and resurrection taken together. For in his resurrection, the death of Jesus "is completed and made effective: the incomprehensible God finally accepted this human reality as redeemed, precisely because the latter was surrendered unsupported and unreservedly into the incomprehensibility of God himself."[245] Rahner stresses that this acceptance by God happens in the first place with Jesus. In this sense, his death is different from ours — his death

---

[243] Rahner, "The Human Question of Meaning In Face of the Absolute Mystery of God," *TI* 18:101 (*ST* XIII: 128).

[244] Rahner, "Following the Crucified," *TI* 18: 165 (*ST* XIII: 197-98). See also Rahner, "Christian Dying," *TI* 18: 252-56 (*ST* XIII: 299-304).

[245] Rahner, "Following the Crucified," *TI* 18: 167 (*ST* XIII: 200).

takes place for us. We appropriate and share in the death of Jesus when we surrender in hope and love to the incomprehensibility of God.[246] As a result of Jesus' death and resurrection, a light is thrown on the ambivalence of our own death. There emerges, in turn, a spirituality of hope as a result of Jesus' resurrection. It is not that Rahner wishes to remove the ambivalence of death. Perplexity, suffering, and death remain permanent existentials of human history, and Christians continue to experience in them the darkness of human existence. Indeed, in seeking to follow the Crucified in Christian life, that is, in the acceptance of everything that is traditionally described as the "cross" (the experiences of frailty, of sickness, of disappointments, etc.), the Christian is continually faced with the question of how to cope with such existentials.[247] Either we become cynical and attempt to cling all the more desperately to what has not yet been taken away from us, or we accept such disappointments with abandoned resignation as events of grace. Only in this second way, Rahner argues, are we taking the cross on ourselves daily, thereby giving concrete expression to the following of the *Crucified* in *life*.

Rahner's third appeal is to hope in the future. Typical of the human person is the ability to plan and to hope, and to project oneself into the unforeseeable. In this sense, a person moves towards their own

---

[246] Rahner is aware that the appropriation of Christ's death also takes place with "social visibility ... in the Church, in the visible signs and rites established by Christ himself. These are the sacraments." Rahner, *On the Theology of Death*, 80-81 (*Zur Theologie des Todes*, 66-67). In Rahner's view, three sacraments in particular (Baptism, Eucharist, and Anointing of the Sick) involve for the Christian a "dying with Christ." This issue will be taken up in the final chapter where the relationship between personal and sacramental piety is discussed. For Rahner's reflections on this topic, see his "Personal and Sacramental Piety," *TI* 2: 109-34 (*ST* II: 115-41), and "Commitment to the Church and Personal Freedom," *Grace and Freedom*, 127-49 (*Gnade als Freiheit*, 91-112).

[247] The importance of contemplating "the death of the Crucified" brings Rahner's reflections to a close: "We must attend to and repeat the words which he uttered, so expressive of the most horrible and the most wonderful aspects of death: 'My God, my God, why hast thou forsaken me?'; 'Father, into thy hands I commend my Spirit'. On each side of him, to the right and to the left — with terrifying symbolism — two others hung in death. Two men, cursing death, because they could not understand it. But who could? Still, one of them looked at Christ. What he saw was enough to make his own death comprehensible to him." Rahner, *On the Theology of Death*, 87 (*Zur Theologie des Todes*, 72). See also, Rahner, "Christian Pessimism," *TI* 22: 155-62 (*ST* XVI: 206-214).

future by overcoming the gap between what they are and what they wish to become. But hope, as a *divine* virtue, is, for Rahner, more than this. It determines our relationship with God.[248] All created, finite realities (including ourselves) stand in a relationship to their creative Ground, God. Anything we experience and think is always mediated by a finite reality. God, in Rahner's transcendental framework, is only given as the Ground — abiding in Himself and mediating Himself via finite realities. In making Godself known, God simultaneously erects a barrier that divides us from God. Yet the claim of the divine virtue of hope is that the human person can dare to reach out over this chasm, this infinite distance, and "grasp for" God.[249] Rahner warns against imagining this hope as a type of analgesic meant to soothe us from the harshness and insecurities of life.[250] On the contrary, for Christians, "it is that which commands them, and at the same time empowers them, to have trust enough constantly to undertake anew an exodus out of the present into the future (even within the dimension of this world)."[251]

In his appeal for hope in the future, Rahner is holding two aspects together in dialectical tension. Firstly, the basic principle of Christian hope, Rahner believes, involves a "self-abandonment" of oneself to God, to a strength that is no longer one's own. But this "heavenly hope" is, secondly, always mediated by something earthly-objective: it is a concrete task in the midst of the banality of everyday life. On

---

[248] Rahner, "Hope," *The Practice of Faith*, 219-25 (*Praxis des Glaubens*, 367-77).

[249] It is not a matter here of the person "possessing" God. Hope, Rahner argues, is not merely a provisional attitude which will be dissolved in the next life — even there God remains as the incomprehensible one. Rahner, nevertheless, still uses the term "possession" of God, but takes this to refer to a "radical transcendence and surrender of self," and "letting of one's self go" ("Sich-selbst Loslassen") out into the incomprehensibility of God. "In the word 'hope' this 'outwards from the self' attitude into God as the absolutely uncontrollable finds expression." Rahner, "On the Theology of Hope," *TI* 10: 250 (*ST* VIII: 568-69).

[250] See Rahner's "Prayer for Hope," *Everyday Faith*, 207-211 (*Glaube, der die Erde liebt*, 169-72).

[251] Rahner, "On the Theology of Hope," *TI* 10: 257 (*ST* VIII: 576). "The Christian must, therefore, impress the form of his or her hope upon the framework of the world he or she lives in. Of course this does not mean ... that certain specific and firm structures of the secular world he or she lives in could ... constitute the enduring objective realization of his or her eschatological hope (in the sense of being established as this once and for all).

the one hand, such a hope does not proclaim any human paradise, while, on the other, it contains a "concrete imperative," which could be called the social dimension of hope. In fact, Rahner speaks of a greater and lesser hope which are linked:

> "In the power of this greater hope one also possesses the lesser hope, namely the courage to transform the 'framework of secular life,' as the Council puts it, and the converse is no less true. In this lesser hope the greater one is made real."[252]

In short, Rahner sees hope as that attitude in which a person dares to commit him or herself to that which is radically beyond all human control. Such an act of radical self-commitment entails an attitude towards the eternal, where this hope finds its ultimate consummation. What Rahner calls "the absolute future of God" is really our own future which also belongs to history in that "history already bears within itself the irrevocable promise of this goal, and ... that, although it is still in progress, history is now already moving in this sense *within* its goal."[253] Thus, hope is not confined to an attitude of one who is weak and who is hungering for a fulfilment that has yet to be achieved, but rather is "the courage to commit oneself in thought and deed to the incomprehensible and the uncontrollable which permeates our existence, and, as the future to which it is open, sustains it."[254]

d. Conclusion: "I believe in Jesus Christ"

In the final chapter of the book *Our Christian Faith*,[255] entitled "I believe in Jesus Christ," Rahner provides an excellent and personal account of what it means for him to be a Christian. In fact, this chap-

---

[252] Rahner, "On the Theology of Hope," *TI* 10: 259 (*ST* VIII: 578). The document of the Council to which Rahner is referring is the Dogmatic Constitution on the Church, *Lumen Gentium*, Chap. 4, n. 35, in Flannery, ed., *Vatican Council II*, vol. 1, 392.

[253] Rahner, *FCF*, 297 (*Grundkurs*, 290-91).

[254] Rahner, "On the Theology of Hope," *TI* 10: 259 (*ST* VIII: 578).

[255] Karl Rahner and Karl-Heinz Weger, *Our Christian Faith: Answers for the Future* (London: Burns and Oates, 1980), 159- 79. [*Was sollen wir noch glauben?* (Freiburg: Herder, 1980), 187-207]. See also Rahner's *Ich glaube an Jesus Christus*, Theologische Meditationen 21 (Einsiedeln: Benziger Verlag, 1968).

ter provides us with a good summary description of Rahner's understanding of spirituality. At the same time, Rahner manages to bring together here, in synthetic form, some of the issues and tensions which have featured in our discussion thus far. Therefore, it offers a suitable focus for bringing our own reflections to a provisional conclusion.

From the outset, Rahner admits that he writes not from a "neutral" point of view, but from a "committed" one, that is, as a Christian who maintains that, in dealing with the ultimate issues of life, a personal Yes or No is demanded. His basic conviction here (and we will shortly discuss the influence of the *Spiritual Exercises* of Ignatius Loyola on Rahner in this regard) is that a person's historical life moves in freedom toward a point of *decision* — in terms of either a final protest or a final acceptance of existence. The hopeful acceptance of existence is interwoven with other specific experiences in life (experiences of meaning, light, joy, love and so on) which make an absolute claim on the person. Further, such a fundamental acceptance of existence (which does not exist only when it is explicitly talked about), entails a movement towards God. Rahner is aware of possible misunderstandings when he designates "God" as the ultimate basis for this hope. We have seen how his response is to develop a notion of God as "incomprehensible mystery," and to view human transcendence in knowledge and freedom as moving towards this mystery. In this sense, we concluded that, for Rahner, the act of accepting existence is "the act of letting oneself sink trustfully into the incomprehensible mystery."[256] Thus Christian spirituality does not primarily provide "explanations" or "instruction" or "final" answers — God is not a determinate number in the equations of people's lives.

In our discussion of Rahner's notion of grace, we saw how he stressed that God is both the initiator and goal of this movement towards Him:

> "Because Christians know that this fundamental trust of theirs … is supported by God himself, they call this most intimate movement of

---

[256] Rahner and Weger, *Our Christian Faith,* 165 (*Was sollen wir noch glauben?* 193).

their existence towards God by the power of God 'grace', and 'the Holy Spirit', and express this single movement towards the immediate presence of God in faith, hope and love."[257]

Moreover, we noted how Rahner does not restrict this intimate movement to Christians alone, but acknowledges that it occurs wherever someone is faithful to the dictates of his or her conscience. Perhaps such a person may not be able to recognize this move for what it really is, or be unable to recognize its "absolutely particular" historical manifestation in Jesus Christ. Nonetheless, Christians hope both for themselves and for others that this movement will find its way through the superficiality and darkness of life to its final "eternal" goal.

In the encounter with Jesus of Nazareth, a "mysterious synthesis" takes place where "primal hope and knowledge of Jesus form a circle which is in the end unbreakable and give each other mutual support and justification."[258] One way in which such a synthesis is achieved, already discussed, is through the love of neighbour, since all love of neighbour is, in Jesus' words, also love of him. This synthesis, Rahner holds, is present in both Christians and non-Christians, but Christians recognize in the person of Jesus "the event of the unique and qualitatively unsurpassable and irreversible approach of God."[259] For the person who hears the Christian message, a new and radical situation of choice has been created, which can lead to the response of explicit faith. We have indicated the significance, for Rahner, of the cross and resurrection in any authentic faith in Jesus.[260] But Rahner

[257] Rahner and Weger, *Our Christian Faith,* 165 (*Was sollen wir noch glauben?* 193).
[258] Rahner and Weger, *Our Christian Faith,* 166 (*Was sollen wir noch glauben?* 194).
[259] Rahner and Weger, *Our Christian Faith,* 167 (*Was sollen wir noch glauben?* 195). Later Rahner adds: "Perhaps it is ordained that many 'find' him more easily by looking for him in anonymous hope without being able to call him by his historical name" (p. 171).
[260] "Jesus is only understood as the Christ, that is, as the definitive and victorious self-communication of mystery to the world, if his cross, his *death*, are accepted as the salvation and surrender of a human person to this mystery, ... All the remaining content of the Christian faith, and especially the social expression of this faith, namely the Church, does indeed consist in categorial data and particular formulations of these data, but it does not form an independent and additional element to this faith which

goes further, and highlights the importance of a *community* of people who believe in Jesus as the one who was crucified and rose from the dead.[261] Christians, through their belief in Christ, cannot be simply religious individualists. Rahner further emphasizes the necessity of a community and social structure if this faith is to be transmitted through the active witness of its members. There are, of course, many other reasons for Rahner's claim that Christianity means Church, which are beyond the scope of our present discussion.[262] For the moment, we are content to have detected a transition in Rahner from a belief in Christ to a stress on the value of the Church, while also bearing in mind that there exists a "permanent tension, which constantly takes different forms and must always be resolved afresh, between Christian freedom and the Christian need for the Church."[263] This is a tension to be endured rather than resolved. One reason for this ongoing tension is the social and historical structure of the Church — in its empirical reality the Church always lags behind its essence. The Church is always the Church of sinners. Yet, the Christian, while maintaining a critical attitude to the Church, can still hope to find in it the liberating spirit of Jesus and his truth.

can only be taught from without; it is rather deduced from the primordial fact of revelation and faith, which is the acceptance of the absolute mystery, first in Jesus and then derivatively in us." The primary realization of faith consists, for Rahner, in the courage to accept one's human existence in unconditional fidelity to one's conscience. The conceptual formulation of this faith in explicitly Christian terms "is in a sense secondary, although not superfluous, in comparison with the primary embodiment of faith ... but this does not mean that the explicit, moral obligation of faith becomes unnecessary." Rahner, "Faith between Rationality and Emotion," *TI* 16: 71-72 (*ST* XII: 97-98).

[261] What we might call the ecclesial dimension of Rahner's spirituality can only be mentioned in passing at this stage. We will return to this aspect in our final chapter.

[262] For an extensive treatment of this topic, see *FCF*, Chap. VII "Christianity as Church," 322-401 (*Grundkurs*, 313-87).

[263] Rahner and Weger, *Our Christian Faith,* 172 (*Was sollen wir noch glauben?* 200).

CHAPTER FOUR

THE IGNATIAN DIMENSION OF
RAHNER'S SPIRITUALITY

Introduction

This chapter, like the preceding ones, is divided into three parts. In the first part, we examine the Ignatian background of Rahner's spirituality. Both Karl and Hugo Rahner spent a considerable part of their early academic life researching Ignatian spirituality. In fact, Hugo Rahner is better known for his historical work in this area over a longer period, whereas Karl Rahner's career developed more in the direction of systematic theology. As part of the Ignatian background to Rahner's spirituality, we will first of all list Rahner's main writings on Ignatian spirituality, and then treat of these in more detail in parts two and three. Since most of Rahner's Ignatian writings revolve around the *Spiritual Exercises*, we will begin with how he understands their nature and function. Then we introduce what he considers to be the more significant elements of Ignatian spirituality. Included here are such themes as: Ignatian mysticism of joy in the world, finding God in all things, and the notion of "indifference." All these themes play a central role in Rahner's appropriation of Ignatian spirituality and particularly his interpretation of the *Exercises*.

The second part of the chapter explores Rahner's interpretation of the *Exercises* in more detail. Central to our discussion is the idea of "choice" or "election" and its significance in the *Exercises*. In other words, we shall see how the dynamic of the *Exercises* involves a "discernment of spirits" facilitating the discovery of God's will for an individual, and culminates in the decision to follow this will. Underlying this dynamic is the Ignatian (and Rahnerian) presupposition that God deals "directly" with the creature. This claim will be investigated in relation to Rahner's interpretation of the Ignatian rules of discernment, and will be seen to be encapsulated in the phrase "consolation without previous cause." How Rahner understands this Ignatian term and the difficulties that emerge from his interpretation are also discussed. The second part of the chapter then concludes with an appraisal of Rahner's Ignatius interpretation. In this context, we shall make specific reference to his retreat conferences based on the *Exercises*.

This chapter also intends to develop Rahner's contention that Ignatius' *Exercises* have something to offer not only to spirituality but also to theology. In teasing out what Rahner means by this, we have already seen how it has to do with the notion of religious or spiritual experience, and with how such spiritual experience constitutes a source for theological reflection. A secondary aim of this chapter, then, is to clarify Rahner's conviction that theology must be built on a living experience of faith. We do this by elucidating how his own theological thinking originates both from a reflection on, and the practice of, the Ignatian *Exercises*, and how such an approach can aptly be characterized as a mystagogical theology. This chapter, therefore, builds on, as well as develops, some themes (e.g., Rahner's concept of grace) which have emerged in our previous three chapters.

The third and final part of the chapter focuses on Rahner's last major article on the contemporary significance of Ignatius. Indeed, this article, where Rahner has Ignatius speak to a Jesuit of today, has come to be regarded as Rahner's spiritual testament. We believe it excellently captures the basic intention behind all Rahner's reflections on spirituality, namely, to lead his readers and hearers into an "experience of mystery." Moreover, Rahner's spiritual testament is further characterized by his retrieval of the patristic notion of "mystagogy." We trace the connection between this idea of mystagogy and Rahner's early studies on the spiritual senses. At issue is the question of an immediate experience of God, an experience, which has to do more with a "felt-knowledge," (a *sentire*, to use an Ignatian term), rather than with an intellectual knowledge. Finally, by way of conclusion, we will gather together some of the key insights from Rahner's appropriation of Ignatian spirituality and outline how these can contribute to a contemporary "mystagogical" Christian spirituality.

1. The Ignatian Background

In a *Festgabe* for Rahner's sixtieth birthday, his brother Hugo refers to their common concern in exploring the contemporary theological and spiritual significance of the writings of Ignatius Loyola.[1] In the case of Karl Rahner, this concern found expression in his foundational essay on the *Spiritual Exercises* of Ignatius, "The Logic of Concrete Individual Knowledge in Ignatius of Loyola."[2] Both brothers also collaborated in the publication of a series of prayers and meditations based on the structure of the *Exercises*, which appeared in 1958 under the title *Gebete der Einkehr*.[3] Karl Rahner himself wrote a number of articles that dealt directly with the spiritual doctrine of Ignatius as well as directing many retreats based on the *Exercises*.[4] Moreover, Rahner's *Theological Investigations* remain a fertile source for his reflections on Ignatian spirituality and on its relationship to theology.[5]

---

[1] Hugo Rahner, "Eucharisticon Fraternitatis," *Gott in Welt* 2: 896.

[2] Karl Rahner, "Die Logik der existentiellen Erkenntnis bei Ignatius von Loyola," *Das Dynamische in der Kirche*, Quaestiones Disputatae 5 (Freiburg: Herder, 1958), 74-148 (*The Dynamic Element in the Church*, 84-170). The essay, however, originally appeared under the more descriptive title: "Die ignatianische Logik der existentiellen Erkenntnis — Über einige theologische Probleme in den Wahlregeln der Exerzitien des heiligen Ignatius," in Friedrich Wulf, ed., *Ignatius von Loyola: seine geistliche Gestalt und sein Vermächtnis (1556-1956)* (Würzburg: Echter-Verlag, 1956), 343-405.

[3] Salzburg: Otto Müller Verlag, 1958. The meditations grew out of a "student-mission" near Freiburg given by both brothers in December 1951. It was published again as *Worte ins Schweigen. Gebete der Einkehr*, Herderbücherei Band 437 (Freiburg: Herder, 1973).

[4] Karl Rahner, *Einübung priesterlicher Existenz* (Freiburg: Herder, 1970), [ET: *Meditations on Priestly Life*, trans. Edward Quinn (London: Sheed and Ward, 1970)]; *Betrachtungen zum ignatianischen Exerzitienbuch* (Munich: Kösel, 1965), [ET: *Spiritual Exercises* (London: Sheed and Ward, 1976, reprint, 1986)]. See also his "Ignatian Spirituality and Devotion to the Heart of Jesus," *Mission and Grace* 3: 176-210 (*Sendung und Gnade*, 510-33); "A Basic Ignatian Concept," *Mission and Grace* 3: 144-75 (*Sendung und Gnade*, 487-509); "Wesensbestimmung und Darbietung der Exerzitien heute," *Wagnis des Christen*, 95-101 (*Christians at the Crossroads*, 70-74); "Im Anspruch Gottes. Bemerkungen zur Logik der existentiellen Erkennt-nis," *Geist und Leben* 59 (1986): 241-47.

[5] See, for example, his "The Ignatian Mysticism of Joy in the World," *TI* 3: 277-98 (*ST* III: 329-48); "Being Open to God as Ever Greater," *TI* 7: 24-45 (*ST* VII: 32-53); "Modern Piety and the Experience of Retreats," *TI* 16: 135-55 (*ST* XII: 173-97);

The majority of Rahner's writings on Ignatian spirituality focus on the *Exercises*.[6] Hence, we will restrict our discussion, for the most part, to Rahner's interpretation of the *Exercises*, and to those Ignatian themes which are central to this interpretation.

a. Rahner and the Exercises: Introduction and Context

Rahner considered the *Exercises* a fundamental document of the post-Reformation Church, and one which had a decisive influence on its history. In his view, the *Exercises* brought something genuinely new into the Church. While, on the one hand, Ignatius was a man of the late Middle Ages and of the "devotio moderna," on the other, he stands at the turning-point towards the age of the rational, the scientific and the technical. This "modern" age could be described in terms of the drive towards control and transformation of the natural world. Moreover, the change entailed a shift from a cosmo-centric worldview to an anthropocentric one.[7] In short, the modern period, in Rahner's view, can be characterized by a

> "turning to the subject, to subjective striving for salvation, to the subjective viewed as a task for the Church, to the attitude of reflection upon one's self, ... to an existential ethic, to a 'choice' in which the subject in some sense exists by his own decision, chooses, transcends, reflects and is ... called by God ... This is, in short, a turning to self-responsibility."[8]

The starting-point is thus the individual subject itself, a subject who is no longer experienced as part of an already given order of reality. We shall see how Rahner portrays Ignatius as also exhibiting a "subjective"

"Reflections on a New Task for Fundamental Theology," *TI* 16: 156-66 (*ST* XII: 198-211); "Christmas in the Light of the Ignatian *Exercises*," *TI* 17: 3-7 (*ST* XII: 329-34). Rahner's final spiritual testament, however, remains: "Rede des Ignatius von Loyola an einen Jesuiten von heute," *Ignatius von Loyola,* 10-38 (*Ignatius of Loyola,* 11-38).

[6] We follow here the translation of the *Exercises* by Louis J. Puhl SJ, *The Spiritual Exercises of St Ignatius. Based on Studies in the Language of the Autograph* (Chicago: Loyola University Press, 1951).

[7] This is the thesis proposed by J. B. Metz, *Christliche Anthropozentrik* (Munich, Kösel, 1962).

[8] Rahner, "Being Open to God as Ever Greater," *TI* 7: 33 (*ST* VII: 40).

approach to salvation. By this Rahner means that, in the *Exercises*, Ignatius aims at "a completely personal relationship" between Jesus Christ, the Lord of the Church, and the retreatant, who, in this way, comes to an experience of his or her calling to serve the kingdom of God and the Church.[9] At the same time, therefore, Rahner stresses that Ignatius was a man of the Church, someone to whom the phrase "sentire cum ecclesia" could most suitably be applied.[10] Nevertheless, Ignatius was primarily concerned with the modern person considered as a personal subject. It should not be overlooked, Rahner reminds us, that the religious path of Ignatius begins with a subjective experience of consolation and desolation.[11] However, Rahner appreciates that, at first sight, it seems somewhat disturbing that Ignatius believed mystical experiences could provide the whole content of faith, including the totality of our understanding of God and of the world.[12]

In order to elucidate the above claim, we need to examine Rahner's understanding of the *Exercises*. Firstly, the *Exercises* are not a series of pious meditations, but represent an attempt, following a certain plan, to enable the retreatant to make a fundamental and free *decision* of life-long importance. Rahner interprets the *Exercises* then, primarily, in terms of a *choice* or an "election," namely, the choice of the means and the concrete way in which Christian faith can become a living reality in us. Secondly, they normally take place in an environment of solitude and prayer, since the dynamic of the *Exercises* assumes a personal encounter with God. The kind of decision at issue here "cannot be deduced from the general principles of the faith or from common human wisdom alone; a decision such as this is received from God and from His grace alone in a kind of existential knowledge gained in

---

[9] Rahner, "Modern Piety and the Experience of Retreats," *TI* 16: 143 (*ST* XII: 182).

[10] See Ignatius' "Rules for Thinking with the Church," *The Spiritual Exercises of St Ignatius*, nn. 352-70.

[11] Rahner, "Modern Piety and the Experience of Retreats," *TI* 16: 140 (*ST* XII: 179). Rahner is referring here to the *Autobiography of St Ignatius Loyola*, nn. 5-8. We follow the translation of the *Autobiography* by Parmananda R. Divarkar in *Ignatius of Loyola: The Spiritual Exercises and Selected Works*, eds. George E. Ganss et al., Classics of Western Spirituality Series (Mahwah, New Jersey: Paulist Press, 1991), 65-111.

[12] *Autobiography of St Ignatius Loyola*, nn. 29 and 30.

prayer."[13] This kind of knowledge emerges from what Rahner terms a logic of existential decision, which Ignatius developed by means of his rules of choice.[14] Rahner subsequently describes this decision as the result of a solitary spiritual process. The assumption operative here lies in Ignatius' intuition that "the Creator can deal directly with the creature, and the creature directly with his Creator and Lord."[15]

Behind the notion of choice, described above, is the attempt to discern the will of God for the retreatant. According to Rahner, Ignatius is only interested that the individual place him or herself before the Lord and ask: "What should I do?" or "What does God want from me now?"[16] The *Exercises* thus presuppose that an existential decision can take place as a result of a personal call of God to the retreatant. Further, Rahner is convinced that if such a logic of existential decision is to remain valid today, "it must be removed from the context of the choice of a vocation in the Church and clearly expressed in terms of its general significance for human existence."[17]

---

[13] Karl Rahner, *Spiritual Exercises* (London: Sheed and Ward, 1967), 8 *(Betrachtungen zum ignatianischen Exerzitienbuch,* 12). Rahner also reminds his readers in the Foreword (p. 8) that the true meaning of the *Exercises* only emerges from their *practice* and not from printed theological meditations. It is not that Ignatius ignores the more rational processes of reflection and decision-making, but he regards these as derivative and secondary, applying when the fundamental choice is either impossible or unsuccessful. *The Spiritual Exercises of St Ignatius,* nn. 175-88.

[14] *The Spiritual Exercises of St Ignatius,* nn. 169-89. See also Rahner, "Modern Piety and the Experience of Retreats," *TI* 16: 144-45 (*ST* XII: 183-84). The "real heart" of the *Spiritual Exercises,* for Rahner, consists in "the existential choice and the achievement of absolute freedom before God (termed indifference), and the experience of the radical immediacy of God in the comfort of the 'first' and the 'second' time of choice.'" (p. 144).

[15] *The Spiritual Exercises of St Ignatius,* n. 15. See also Rahner's "Rede des Ignatius von Loyola an einen Jesuiten von heute," *Ignatius von Loyola,* 12, where he maintains "Gott kann und will mit seinem Geschöpf unmittelbar handeln."

[16] Roland Barthes, *Sade, Fourier, Loyola,* trans. Richard Miller (Berkeley and Los Angeles: Univ. of California Press, 1976), 45, 48, maintains that "this interrogative structure gives the *Exercises* its historical originality; hitherto, ... the preoccupation was more with carrying out God's will; Ignatius wants rather to discover this will (What is it? Where is it? Toward what does it tend?)." The language of interrogation developed by Ignatius is thus aimed "less at the classical question of consultations: *What to do?* than at the dramatic alternative by which finally every practice is prepared and determined: *To do this or to do that?*"

[17] Rahner, "Modern Piety and the Experience of Retreats," *TI* 16: 141, n. 11 (*ST* XII: 180, n. 11).

This choice, this perception and acceptance of God's call effected in a personal, free decision, has two mutually related aspects: a transcendental and a categorial aspect.[18] The transcendental aspect denotes the person's radical decision or conversion to God in faith, hope and love, while the categorial aspect refers to the mediating realization of this decision in the concrete, and implies a particular act, e.g., the choice of a way of life, the love of one's neighbour, the endurance of life's everyday trials, and so on. These two aspects cannot be separated, but neither is their reciprocal relationship a static one; rather, it is a relationship that has a history in the life (i.e., in the historical decision) of an individual. But Rahner fears it is the categorial aspect (that is, what does God want from me now?) that can too easily gain prominence. If this is the case, then the "mystagogical" dimension of the *Exercises* could be undermined. In other words, it can be overlooked that the *Exercises* constitute an initiation or a mystagogy into a basic experience of God.[19] To facilitate such an experience is the main task of the director of the *Exercises*. It is not a question here of a merely theoretical initiation into the essence of Christianity. The *Exercises* are and remain a matter of choice and decision in a concrete life-situation, since the conversion or *metanoia* (sometimes called by Rahner a person's fundamental option) is not just a theoretical occurrence. Rather, the initiation is to an "existentially accepted Christianity in faith, hope and love for God,"[20] and not an abstract indoctrination. This immediate encounter between

---

[18] Rahner, "The *Exercises* today," *Christians at the Crossroads*, 71 (*Wagnis des Christen*, 97).

[19] "Verstehst du schon jetzt, wenn ich sage, die Hauptaufgabe, um die alles andere zentriert ist, müsse für euch Jesuiten das Geben der Exerzitien sein. Damit sind natürlich zunächst und zuletzt nicht kirchenamtlich organisierte Kurse gemeint, die vielen auf einmal gegeben werden, sondern *eine mystagogische Hilfe für andere, die Unmittelbarkeit Gottes nicht zu verdrängen, sondern deutlich zu erfahren und anzunehmen*... . Aber all dieses andere sollte eigentlich von euch als Vorbereitung oder als Folgerung der letzten Aufgabe verstanden werden, die auch in Zukunft eure bleiben sollte: *die Hilfe zur unmittelbaren Erfahrung Gottes,* in der dem Menschen aufgeht, daß das unbegreifliche Geheimnis, das wir Gott nennen, nahe ist, angeredet werden kann ..." Rahner, "Rede des Ignatius von Loyola an einen Jesuiten von heute," *Ignatius von Loyola,* 15. (italics mine). See also Rahner, "Christian Living Formerly and Today," *TI* 7: 11-16 (*ST* VII: 19-24).

[20] Rahner, "The *Exercises* today," *Christians at the Crossroads*, 73 (*Wagnis des Christen*, 99-100).

God and the human person has, Rahner believes, special significance today because:

> "all the societal supports of religion are collapsing and dying out in this secularized and pluralistic society. If, nonetheless, there is to be real Christian spirituality, it cannot be kept alive and healthy by external helps, not even those which the Church offers, even of a sacramental kind, ... but only through an ultimate, immediate encounter of the individual with God."[21]

b. Rahner's Appropriation of Ignatian Mysticism

i) A Tension of Opposites

Before we explore Rahner's interpretation of the *Exercises* in more detail, it may be useful to offer a synthesis of what he considers to be the more significant elements of Ignatian spirituality. In an early essay entitled "The Ignatian Mysticism of Joy in the World,"[22] Rahner presents a picture of Ignatian spirituality as a relentless search for God "in which the paradox of fleeing the world in order to find God *in* the world is reconciled."[23] He begins his reflections by asking what mysticism and Ignatian delight in the world (*Weltfreudigkeit*) can have in common, since mysticism has at times been depicted in terms of opposition to, and even abandonment of, the "world." The question, more precisely, concerns the nature of the mystic's joy in the world, particularly in the case of Ignatius, since not every approving reference to the world is especially Christian or mystical.[24] However, Rahner's discussion in this context (i.e., Ignatian *Welt-*

---

[21] Rahner, "The Immediate Experience of God in the Spiritual Exercises of Saint Ignatius of Loyola: Interview with Wolfgang Feneberg," *Karl Rahner in Dialogue*, 176 (*Karl Rahner im Gespräch* 2: 34).

[22] *TI* 3: 277-93 (*ST* III: 329-48). The article was originally published as "Die igna-tianische Mystik der Weltfreudigkeit," *Zeitschrift für Aszese und Mystik* 12 (1937): 121-37.

[23] Kelly, *Karl Rahner: Theologian of the Graced Search for Meaning*, 80. (italics mine).

[24] Rahner claims that, even on the basis of a vague, empirical concept of mysticism, Ignatius can be considered a mystic. Such an empirical concept of mysticism includes references to the religious experiences of the saints, their experience of closeness to God, of visions, inspirations, and awareness of being under the special and personal guidance of the Holy Spirit. "The Ignatian Mysticism of Joy in the World," *TI* 3: 279-80 (*ST* III: 332).

freudigkeit) is not about mysticism in the strict sense, but about Ignatian spirituality, or in more traditional terms, Ignatian piety (*Frömmigkeit*).[25] In this essay, he outlines two significant characteristics of this spirituality. Firstly, Ignatian spirituality is a spirituality of the *cross*, which both links it with other spiritualities and provides it with a universal character. Secondly, Ignatian spirituality is directed to the God *beyond* the world. These two aspects, Rahner believes, point up the distinctive character of Ignatian spirituality, and provide the foundation for the meaning of its "joy in the world."

Like all forms of Christian spirituality, Ignatian spirituality is a spirituality of the *cross*, which Rahner considers to be its first, fundamental characteristic. Ignatius, in founding his order, continues the line of those Catholic orders which take the vows of poverty, chastity and obedience, and which "take over the attitude of the monk, the *monachos*, of one alone in God far from the world."[26] By "monastic" here, Rahner is not referring to the external arrangement of community living. Rather, the term, monk, refers to the one who has put on the pattern of Christ, who takes upon him or herself the Lord's renunciation, and who attempts to allow that dying with Christ to become a reality throughout the course of his or her life. In this context, Rahner refers to the early Church where Christian perfection and martyrdom were practically synonymous terms.[27] It is this spirit of the early Church which the monk seeks to perpetuate. Ignatius, for his part, also wished to follow Christ in a similar manner, and the summit to

---

[25] Rahner's terminology may appear confusing here. The title of his article ("Die ignatianische Mystik der Weltfreudigkeit") refers to mysticism. But — and we have also seen this in Chapter Two — Rahner's concern here is not so much in isolating "the characteristic of mystic piety" from a "'normal' piety and way of prayer." He concedes that such a distinction exists. Yet, he chooses not to focus on this, but more generally on describing "the character of Ignatian piety (*Frömmigkeit*) from which the fact and the meaning of its acceptance of the world will become understandable." Rahner, "The Ignatian Mysticism of Joy in the World," *TI* 3: 280-81 (*ST* III: 333). We have translated "Frömmigkeit" here as "spirituality;" the reasons for doing so have already been mentioned at the end of Chapter Two.

[26] "Ignatius stands in the line of those who existentially flee into the desert in a violent *fuga saeculi*, even though it may be the God-forsaken stony desert of a city, in order to seek God far from the world." Rahner, "The Ignatian Mysticism of Joy in the World," *TI* 3: 281 (*ST* III: 334).

[27] Rahner, *Aszese und Mystik*, 29-40.

which he leads his followers in the *Exercises* is the "foolishness of the cross."[28]

Such a spirit does not admit of an easy harmony between God and the world. Ignatius' own spiritual theology is characterized by a reverential distance from God and creatures alike. The God of Ignatius was the "God who is always greater," and although Ignatius was favoured with numerous mystical illuminations, he came to respect and preserve a reverent distance from all that is of God.[29] Rahner's second assertion about Ignatian spirituality — that it is directed toward the God who is *beyond the whole world* — can be thus interpreted in terms of an attitude towards everything finite. All things which are not God are grasped as something transparent, something through which God shines forth. When we come to the christological element of the *Exercises*, we shall see that Christ forms the mediator between the "above" of mystical illumination and consolation, and the "below" of a world crying out for redemption. The tension at issue here is pithily captured by Rahner's brother, Hugo: "Only he who has already found God 'above' will also be able to find him 'below'."[30]

Nevertheless, in Rahner's view, the ultimate reason for an Ignatian sacrifice or renunciation of the world (i.e., the abandonment of its goods and values) is the Incarnation, the actual fact that the living, personal God has spoken to humankind through Jesus Christ. No amount of metaphysical searching can lead to the claim that God has revealed Himself in Jesus Christ:

> "Whether God wants to meet us immediately and personally, whether God wants to remain silent, what God will say to us if God does want to speak — all this is an essential mystery for all metaphysics, ..."[31]

---

[28] See for example the "Third Week" of the *Exercises*, nn. 190-209 and Rahner's commentary in *Spiritual Exercises*, 234-43 (*Betrachtungen zum ignatianischen Exerzitienbuch*, 235-44).

[29] Underlying this attitude is Ignatius' *amorosa humilidad* or humility permeated by love (*Spiritual Diary*, nn. 178-182, in Ganss, *Ignatius of Loyola*, 263-64). It is a love inspired by reverence. Ignatius was not only conscious of being directly consoled by God, but aware too that human nature still remained disordered and self-interested.

[30] Hugo Rahner, SJ, *Ignatius the Theologian*, trans. Michael Barry (London: Chapman, 1968, 1990), 9.

[31] Rahner, "The Ignatian Mysticism of Joy in the World," *TI* 3: 284 (*ST* III: 338). See also Rahner, *Hearers of the Word*, 71-82 (*Hörer des Wortes*, 91-104).

In previous chapters, we discussed how Rahner's God is more than the horizon always remaining in the distance. Indeed, Rahner sees the deeper meaning of revelation in Christ as a calling of human beings out of this world into the life of God, whereby they no longer have only the one option of "rounding themselves off" in nature, that is, in that which is essentially a finite or immanent system. Thus, the call of God, while not implying a denigration of the world, nonetheless accords it only a provisional status.[32]

By a somewhat tortuous route — he terms it a theological metaphysics — Rahner concludes his introduction to Ignatian spirituality by stating that we have to do here with a *personal* God who, despite his transcendence, deals with human beings in their concrete historical situation. The latter part of this claim, however, will only be substantiated later, when we come to discuss Rahner's interpretation of the Ignatian *Exercises*. Already though, we note Rahner's attempt to feel his way through this "tension of opposites" which is so characteristic of Ignatian spirituality.[33] The tension at issue in this early essay of Rahner is that of reconciling the personal God of Ignatian spirituality with an image of God as the *Divina Maiestas* beyond the world. Unfortunately, the sparseness of biographical references to Ignatius' life (which would no doubt have shed more light on Ignatius' spiritual experience), means that this early essay remains rather abstract and, at times, ambiguous. Rahner's concern is to show that, for Ignatius, we encounter the absolute God not only in opposition to the world, but also *in* the world. However, despite its occasional abstruseness, the article is significant for its combination of the Ignatian traits of reverence and humble love. This attitude has been

---

[32] "For human beings can only confess existentially ("existentiell bekennen") that God has moved the centre of their human existence out of the world, if they negate their intramundane existence in its immanent signification by a *fuga saeculi*." Rahner, "The Ignatian Mysticism of Joy in the World," *TI* 3: 286-87 (*ST* III: 340).

[33] This is the opinion of such experts on Ignatian spirituality as Hugo Rahner, *Ignatius the Theologian*, 3-31, and Josef de Guibert, *The Jesuits: Their Spiritual Doctrine and Practice. A Historical Study*, trans. William J. Young, ed. George E. Ganss (St. Louis: The Institute of Jesuit Sources, 1972), 70-74. In his concluding synthesis of the personal spiritual experience of Ignatius, de Guibert states that this could be summed up in the two phrases (or tensions): "mystical invasion" and "courageous struggle." For the relevant biographical connections, see especially the first chapter, "The Personal Interior Life of St Ignatius," 21-73.

called by another Ignatian expert, Erich Przywara, the "Ignatian function" within the Catholic world, that is:

> "to be a counter-corrective to all violation of the ultimate distance
> between God and creatures, whether it concerns taking possession of
> God or divinizing creation."[34]

A further characteristic of Ignatian spirituality, which we have seen
in the previous section, and which comes explicitly to the fore in the
Exercises is the search for, or discernment of, God's will.[35] Rahner's
stress is that the retreatant in the *Exercises* encounters this personal
God in the person of Jesus Christ. And, as a result of such an
encounter the retreatant can respond with a readiness for the cross.[36]
Dying to the world, asceticism and renunciation, as an expression
of readiness for the cross, do not, of themselves, guarantee possession
of God. Rather, true asceticism is a gesture of love which reaches out
beyond the world and is an expression of a most fundamental shift in
one's existence.[37] It is above all a free grace of God that enables such
a change in the retreatant, who is thus on the way towards accom-

---

[34] Erich Przywara, *Ignatianisch. Vier Studien zum vierhundertsten Todestag des
Heiligen Ignatius von Loyola* (Frankfurt a. M.: Josef Knecht Verlag, 1956), 115.

[35] This inquiry is a process which necessitates a "discernment of spirits" — the
most important part of the *Exercises* in Rahner's opinion — and which we will treat
later in a separate section. Throughout this process, Rahner maintains, God's *grace* is
at work enabling the retreatant's response to occur; grace, as we saw in the last chapter, "understood as the direct presence of God (*Gottunmittelbarkeit*) to the unique
subject, not as a general principle." Rahner, "Modern Piety and the Experience of
Retreats," *TI* 16: 142 (*ST* XII: 181).

[36] Rahner goes on to conclude (although he does not clearly explain the connection) that, from there "springs that which is in reality Ignatian affirmation of the
world and joy in it." Rahner, "The Ignatian Mysticism of Joy in the World," *TI* 3:
288 (*ST* III: 342).

[37] "Renunciation is a profession ... of a person's shifting the centre of his or her
existence out of the world, since the renunciation of the highest positive values of this
world is either meaningless and perverse within this world or must be regarded as the
believing gesture of that love which reaches out beyond the world and its goods (even
those of a personal nature)." Rahner, "Reflections on the Theology of Renunciation,"
TI 3: 54 (*ST* III: 68-69). In the article we have been following, Rahner remarks: "The
fuga saeculi which belongs essentially to Christian existence appeared to us as the
commitment to God, insofar as God is, as the being beyond the world, the inner centre and goal of our Christian existence; as the existential reaccomplishment of the
shifting centre of our being into the triune God, a shifting already accomplished by
the self-revelation of the God of grace." Rahner, "The Ignatian Mysticism of Joy in
the World," *TI* 3: 288 (*ST* III: 342).

plishing God's will for him or her. The important point for Ignatius
— and Rahner mentions this only indirectly — is that neither prayer,
nor religious experience, nor asceticism exist for their own sake, but
only as *means* to seek, find and accomplish the divine will:

> "The link between prayer, abnegation, and reformation of life, and
> seeking, finding, and executing God's will is a distinctive feature of
> Ignatian spirituality. Ignatius seeks to convert the exercitant into a liv-
> ing and acting incarnation of the divine will."[38]

ii) Ignatian "Indifference"

Our discussion in the previous section leads us to what Rahner calls
the double characteristic of Ignatian "joy in the world," namely, the
maxims of "indifference" and of "finding God in all things." Indifference (*indiferençia*) refers to an attitude of calm readiness for every
command of God, that is to say, a readiness to hear a new call from God
to tasks other than those in which one was previously engaged. In the
Exercises, Rahner maintains, we are dealing with an *active* indifference
and not a resigned passivity. The attitude of indifference does not exist
for its own sake but ultimately for the *choice* of "what is more conducive to the end for which we are created" — God's greater praise and
service.[39] Underlying this view is the idea of God as the always greater
One (*Deus semper major*) which, in turn, calls for "the courage to
regard no way to God as being *the* way, but rather to seek God on all
ways."[40] The challenge and task of indifference, then, is to keep ourselves open for what is greater by becoming open for *the* greater reality,
ultimately, God Himself. In fact, indifference becomes a seeking of
God in *all* things. With such a spirit Ignatius could exhibit a love of the

---

[38] Harvey D. Egan, SJ, "Ignatian Spirituality," *NDCS*: 523. This orientation towards the accomplishment of God's will is sometimes called the "service" dimension
of Ignatian spirituality (in comparison to the "bridal" spirituality of other saints and
mystics, where the divine-human communication is valued above all else). With this
emphasis on the accomplishment of God's will or service, Rahner believes that
Ignatius overcomes any possible misinterpretation of the notion of *fuga mundi*. See
also *The Spiritual Exercises of St Ignatius,* nn. 170-189.

[39] *The Spiritual Exercises of St Ignatius,* n. 23. On the meaning of this "magis" in
the *Exercises*, see Rahner, *Spiritual Exercises*, 23-27 (*Betrachtungen zum ignatianischen Exerzitienbuch*, 27-31).

[40] Rahner, "The Ignatian Mysticism of Joy in the World," *TI* 3: 291 (*ST* III: 345).

cross, but even this love is still ruled by indifference: "the cross, yes, *if* it should please his Divine Majesty to call to such a death in life."[41] In this sense, the *Exercises* are a *means* to enable the retreatant to dispose him or herself to this indifference by underscoring the continual dying in the midst of life that is a necessary part of this task. Indifference is, therefore, the exact opposite to any attitude of unconcern. Rather, it represents the attempt to highlight the relativity of all that is not God.[42] Rahner links this indifference to what he calls the "existentialist" quality of Ignatian spirituality, that is,

> "this attitude of disillusionment, of regarding things as interim and provisional, this faint scepticism, this pressing into service of everything that is not God himself, and along with this the readiness to meet each unique, fresh situation and the fresh summons ever being made in it."[43]

The "existentialist" or existentiell quality, then, lies in a readiness to develop one's own uniqueness not as a wealth to be hoarded but as a service to be shared with and for others. Hence there emerges a relativizing of all particular religious practices, devotions, and methods — God is always greater than what we know of Him. In the light of his discussion, Rahner concludes (and we will return to this point later) that Ignatius was a man of transcendental rather than of categorial spirituality.[44]

---

[41] Rahner, "The Ignatian Mysticism of Joy in the World," *TI* 3: 291 (*ST* III: 345). Elsewhere, Rahner equates indifference with "what Paul calls freedom conferred by the Spirit of God himself — freedom with regard to all the individual powers and forces in our human existence, both in our inner life and in our external situation." Further, this "indifferent" freedom sends us back "into the concrete reality of our life for particular decisions and actions." Rahner, "Christmas in the Light of the Ignatian *Exercises*," *TI* 17: 4, 5 (*ST* XII: 329, 331).

[42] "This indifference, then, is always a mystery. For in this indifference we turn from what we understand to the incomprehensible, from what we are enjoying to what is promised, from the present to the future, from what we can grasp to what we cannot grasp." Rahner, *Meditations on Priestly Life*, 33 (*Einübung priesterlicher Existenz*, 44).

[43] "... mit dem Modewort des Existentialistischen zu bezeichnen." Rahner, *Mission and Grace*, vol. 3: 183, 185 (*Sendung und Gnade*, 515, 516). The English translation, however, seems to overlook the distinction between the two terms "existentiell" and "existential." On this, see Rahner, *FCF*, 16, (Translator's note). On this quality of Ignatian spirituality, see De Guibert, *The Jesuits: Their Spiritual Doctrine and Practice*, 170-72.

[44] Rahner, *Mission and Grace*, vol. 3: 183 (*Sendung und Gnade*, 515).

Rahner even goes so far as to link the notion of indifference with his transcendental analysis of the human person.[45] As we have previously shown, he presents the human person as one who, in the act of knowledge, grasps the finite, individual object while, at the same time, transcending this individual thing, setting it over and against a broader horizon. In this way, the person both dissociates him or herself from, and becomes "indifferent" with regard to, the individual object of knowledge. Thus Rahner concludes that there is a basic "indifference" (*Grundindifferenz*) written into the human person.

Finally, the Ignatian idea of seeking-God-in-all-things forms a synthesis of the "mystical" and "prophetic" dimensions of spirituality. The word "mystical" refers to the aspect of the flight from the world discussed above, while the term "prophetic" pertains to that dimension of spirituality which focuses on work and service in the world. Rahner also notes a dialectic operative here between a flight from, and an acceptance of, the world. This dialectic has found traditional expression in the medieval Christian concepts of *contemplatio* and *actio*. The contribution of Ignatius and his first followers, however, was to combine these different ideas, this tension of opposites, into the formula *in actione contemplativus*:

> "Ignatius seeks only the God of Jesus Christ, the free, personal absolute: *contemplativus*. He knows that he can seek and find God also in the world, if this should please God: *in actione*. And so he is prepared in *indiferençia* to seek God and God alone, always God alone but also God everywhere, also in the world: *in actione contemplativus*."[46]

A danger which Rahner perceives in the notion of indifference is the possibility of Ignatian spirituality becoming rationalistic, and calculating, or cold and sceptical.[47] This can occur through an exaggeration of the relativism of all things other than God in a type of stoic

---

[45] Rahner, *Meditations on Priestly Life*, 30-31 (*Einübung priesterlicher Existenz*, 41-42).

[46] Rahner, "The Ignatian Mysticism of Joy in the World," *TI* 3: 292 (*ST* III: 347).

[47] At times, one could get such an impression. See, for example, Przywara's (*Ignatianisch*, 135) description of the seemingly cool "Sachlichkeit" (factuality) of Ignatian service. In the context of the *Exercises*, the retreatant is expected to become an instrument in God's hands, indifferent to all created things. The election, when it comes, is thus an election of service. See also De Guibert, *The Jesuits: Their Spiritual Doctrine and Practice*, 127.

apathy or lovelessness. Indeed, God can become so transcendent, so nameless and formless, that He ends up merely as an empty word. The "antitoxin" to such tendencies, in Rahner's view, lies in a (properly understood) devotion to the Sacred Heart.[48] In fact, he notes a connection between these two types of spiritualities, in that there was a significant Jesuit influence both at the start, as well as in the development, of Sacred Heart devotion.[49] Such a "spirituality of the heart" can help counteract any form of "loveless" indifference.[50] Why is this?

Rahner believed Sacred Heart devotion to be, despite its limitations, a legitimate expression of the spiritual experience of Christians. It is true that there is often embarrassment today at what appears to have been the rather sentimental and indiscreet character of this devotion. However, Rahner's intention is to highlight the potent symbolism of the heart of Christ and to connect this with some characteristics of Ignatian spirituality.[51] In other words, he moved away from an exclusive focus on the "externals" of such devotion. He describes "heart" as a primordial word, an archetypal symbol that says something about a person's innermost centre, depth and ultimate unity. Moreover, the word "heart" defies definition, pointing beyond itself

---

[48] To treat of Rahner's many writings on Sacred Heart devotion would take us beyond the scope of this section. A representative sample of his writings on this topic include: "'Behold this Heart!': Preliminaries to a Theology of Devotion to the Sacred Heart," *TI* 3: 321-330 (*ST* III: 379-90); "Some Theses for a Theology of Devotion to the Sacred Heart," *TI* 3: 331-52 (*ST* III: 391-415); "Ignatian Spirituality and Devotion to the Heart of Jesus," *Mission and Grace* 3: 176 -210 (*Sendung und Gnade*, 510-33); "Unity — Love — Mystery," *TI* 8: 229-47 (*ST* VII: 491-508); "Devotion to the Sacred Heart Today," *TI* 23:117-28 (*ST* XVI: 305-20).

[49] De Guibert, *The Jesuits: Their Spiritual Doctrine and Practice*, 392-402.

[50] "The death which is indifference can only be life-bearing when it is effected by love and is a dying into love... Indifference must be a readiness of the heart to love." Rahner, *Mission and Grace* 3: 191-92 (*Sendung und Gnade*, 521). The shape and form which such a spirituality of the heart might take is discussed in Annice Callahan, ed., *Spiritualities of the Heart* (New York: Paulist Press, 1990). Also relevant in this context is her doctoral thesis, *Karl Rahner's Spirituality of the Pierced Heart: A Reinterpretation of Devotion to the Sacred Heart* (Lanham MD: University Press of America, 1985), esp. 79-100.

[51] In this context, it is significant that Rahner began his seminal article on "The Theology of the Symbol" by enquiring about the proper object of sacred heart devotion. From there, he was led to clarify the role of symbol in the theology of such devotion. Karl Rahner, "The Theology of The Symbol," *TI* 4: 221-52 (*ST* IV: 275-311).

to the mystery of the always greater God. In the second chapter, we saw how the act of love of neighbour is, at the same time, an act of love of God, i.e., an act within the total believing and hoping surrender of the person to God. This is what Rahner means in the present context by the "indifferent" quality of such love:

> "Not that it does not love the individual, the other. But it takes him or her into that endless movement in which all is loved, all is praised, ... and the name of this 'all' that stands before and behind the sum-total of all individual things and persons loved, is simply God ... Indifference is simply the openness of love to that 'all' which is God ... Hence true indifference is the loving positive relativising of all finite individuals."[52]

True indifference thus opens the person to an all-embracing love and has, what Rahner calls, the character of a heart that has been pierced.[53] This shall become clearer in our discussion of Rahner's interpretation of the *Exercises*. It will become apparent that the challenge for participants in the *Exercises* is to become "women and men of the pierced heart, willing to be in touch with our own hearts and to let our hearts be pierced by suffering and evil in order to reveal the power of God's love in powerlessness and weakness."[54]

This section has intended to serve as a brief introduction to some of the underlying themes, or perhaps more accurately, tensions, inherent in Rahner's appropriation of Ignatian spirituality. Through the Ignatian formula of seeking-God-in-all-things, Rahner hopes to find a higher synthesis — overcoming any tendency to dichotomize spirituality into either flight from the world, or the promotion of any particular system of thought or practice as the *only* possible expression of spirituality. These and other tensions operative in Rahner's appropriation of Ignatian spirituality will emerge again in our discussion of Rahner's interpretation of the Ignatian *Exercises* in the next section.

---

[52] Rahner, *Mission and Grace* 3: 201-202 (*Sendung und Gnade*, 527-28).

[53] "So when we say 'heart of Jesus' we evoke the innermost core of Jesus Christ, ... the heart that was pierced, ... that loves us in the darkness of our hopelessness, that is God's very heart that, without abolishing it, discloses to us God's fundamental mystery." Rahner, "Devotion to the Sacred Heart Today," *TI* 23: 126-27 (*ST* XVI: 318).

[54] Annice Callahan, "Heart of Christ," *NDCS*: 471.

2. Rahner's Ignatius Interpretation

a. The Problem of the "Election" in the Exercises

Although he does not go into the historical background of the debate, Rahner claims that "the nature of the *Exercises* is ultimately determined by the fact that a choice, a vital decision is to be made in them."[55] They are primarily guidelines or instructions towards a discernment of God's will, and culminate in a decision to follow that will. In other words, they are oriented not so much towards edification as towards a particular course of action. Ignatius makes two significant, but unusual, claims in the *Exercises,* and it is these two claims which occupy most of Rahner's attention. The first is that a person can actually seek and find God's specific will for him or herself. The second claim is that God will "communicate Himself to the devout soul" and "deal directly with the creature, and the creature directly with his Creator and Lord."[56] With regard to the first point,

---

[55] Rahner, *The Dynamic Element in the Church,* 89 (*Das Dynamische in der Kirche,* 78-79). The Spanish term "elección" can be translated as "choice" or "selection." However, most of the English literature on Ignatian spirituality retains the traditional term, "election."

The essential aim of the *Exercises* has been much discussed. Broadly speaking, the main writers can be divided into two schools, the "electionists" (e.g., L. de Grandmaison) and the "perfectionists" (e.g., L. Peeters). De Grandmaison maintained that the aim of the *Exercises* is to place a spiritually minded person in a position to discern God's call clearly and to follow it generously, that is, to make a wise election of a state of life in which he or she can serve God best. Léonce de Grandmaison, "Les *Exercices* de S. Ignace dans l'édition des *Monumenta,*" *Recherches de Science Religieuse* XI (1920): 400-408, cited in De Guibert, *The Jesuits: Their Spiritual Doctrine and Practice,* 123. On the other hand, Louis Peeters responded that the end and culminating point of the *Exercises* can only be a union with God which is most intimate and total. Louis Peeters, *Vers l'union divine par les Exercices de S. Ignace,* 2nd ed. (Louvain, 1931), 66 ff., cited in De Guibert, *The Jesuits: Their Spiritual Doctrine and Practice,* 123. De Guibert himself (pp. 122-32) sees these two ends as complementary, not mutually exclusive. The end expressed in Ignatius' printed text of 1548 is to facilitate a good election. But this does not exclude the fact that he also made other uses of the text, for example, by giving the *Exercises* to those (e.g., Xavier, Favre) whose election was already made. Ganss, *Ignatius of Loyola: The Spiritual Exercises and Selected Works,* 390, is also in fundamental agreement with de Guibert.

[56] *The Spiritual Exercises of St Ignatius,* n. 15. In this section, our discussion of these issues is restricted to Rahner's reflections in "The Logic of Concrete Individual Knowledge in Ignatius Loyola," *The Dynamic Element in the Church,* 84-170 (*Das Dynamische in der Kirche,* 74-148).

the question arises as to whether God's will could not be simply deduced by the use of reason within the framework of the general principles of Christian morality. Rahner's point, however, is not to undermine the role of the intellect in any such decision-making process, but to indicate how God may make known some definite will of His over and above what is shown by the use of reason.[57]

According to the Ignatian *Exercises*, the "election" takes place at one of three times.[58] The *first* time is rather rare in that the person is so moved by God that he or she heeds His call without hesitation. In the *second* time, the retreatant reflects on the different movements of desolation and consolation in him or herself, with a view to discerning which movements come from God, and which from the evil spirit.[59] Although Ignatius is convinced that what is at issue here is a real guidance of the Holy Spirit, there is also the danger of illusion or self-deception. The suspicion of a mystical subjectivism is understandable and surfaced even in Ignatius' time. Ignatius' "Rules for the Discernment of Spirits," as well as his insistence on the counsel of a director, both of which are envisaged as integral parts of the *Exercises* were prompted by this concern.[60] It would be wrong to think that the discernment of God's will emerges simply from a type of gut feeling or instinct. Rahner insists that, while rational discursive reflection alone does not *fully* reveal this will, it would be misleading to claim that this process does not involve a "thoroughly intellectual operation of the 'intellect,' ... in which it is capable of apprehending

---

[57] For a meditative reflection on the significance of the election and discernment in the *Exercises*, see Parmananda R. Divarkar SJ, *The Path of Interior Knowledge: Reflections on the Spiritual Exercises of St Ignatius of Loyola*, Study Aids on Jesuit Topics, No. 5 (Rome: Centrum Ignatianum Spiritualitatis (C.I.S), 1982), 87-107.

[58] *The Spiritual Exercises of St Ignatius,* nn. 175-89.

[59] "Consolation" and "desolation" are easily misunderstood terms. The Ignatian term "consolation," for example, always means spiritual consolation, which includes a tendency toward an increase of charity. Such consolation *may* bring with it a concomitant feeling of joy but this is not always the case. Hence, *any* feeling of joy, satisfaction or peace should not be too hastily interpreted as a sign of approval for some choice of action. See Ganss, *Ignatius of Loyola: The Spiritual Exercises and Selected Works*, 425-26.

[60] See, *The Spiritual Exercises of St Ignatius,* nn. 313-36, where Ignatius provides some rules for the "First Week" of the Exercises, and further rules to aid "a more accurate discernment of spirits" more suitable to the "Second Week."

values."[61] However, it is in the *third* time of "election" that the intellect is more predominant. This time is characterized by Ignatius as one of "tranquillity," where the person, not agitated by the various spirits, considers the choice to be made in view of the end for which the person was created, that is, the greater service of God. Yet, even in this third time, the retreatant expects God to guide the decision. In fact, the second and third times of election supplement each other, with Ignatius himself combining them in practice.

Ignatius' belief, then, — and this brings us to his second claim — is that, throughout the three times of election, the Creator is dealing directly with the creature and vice-versa. There is more at work here than the retreatant testing his or her capacities for a particular way of life or course of action solely by rational analysis. On the other hand, we have seen how Rahner also regards rational reflection as an indispensable element in the Ignatian discernment of spirits. The experiences of spiritual consolation and desolation are, after all, experiences with a rational structure and not merely physiological states. Subsequently, we will need to explore in more detail the nature of these spiritual experiences. At this stage, Rahner foregoes a discussion of how the divine will makes itself known in a direct way, except to say that this will can only be apprehended "by a kind of cognition, a making known, which is in some sense directly due to God himself."[62] In fact, theology, he thinks, has traditionally found it difficult to adequately comprehend and deal with the spiritual experience involved in the "election." Thus, the aim of Rahner's reflections is to contribute to a more explicit theology of the *Exercises* by bringing to light the "concrete ontological and gnoseological presuppositions regarding human living that are tacitly made and put into practice by Ignatius."[63]

---

[61] Rahner, *The Dynamic Element in the Church*, 94, n. 9 (*Das Dynamische in der Kirche*, 83, n. 23).

[62] Rahner, *The Dynamic Element in the Church*, 106 (*Das Dynamische in der Kirche*, 93). Rahner further maintains that, while the first mode of "election" involves a type of divine revelation (p. 107), which is extremely rare, this is not the case in the second mode.

[63] Rahner, *The Dynamic Element in the Church*, 109 (*Das Dynamische in der Kirche*, 96). Rahner's thesis is that "Ignatius tacitly presupposes a philosophy of human existence in which a moral decision in its individuality is not merely an instance of general ethical normative principles. There is at least in the domain of

One such presupposition is evident in Ignatius' "Rules for the Discernment of Spirits." We mentioned that these rules serve to facilitate the discovery of God's will for the individual. This complex task necessitates the interpretation of one's own interior experiences or "motions" (*mociones*), which Ignatius depicts as the different movements produced in the soul. Underlying these rules, according to Rahner, is the assumption that there exist divine impulses or movements (that is, whose source is God), and which are perceived by the retreatant as a highly personal influence of God. Now, Rahner is aware of the highly problematical nature of this statement. Firstly, most theologians today have moved away from the image of the God of the gaps who regularly intervenes directly in creation. And, secondly, how many people automatically assume that their different interior impulses are simply to be attributed to either good or bad spirits? Many other factors (e.g., psychological, genetic, social, subconscious, etc.) are acknowledged to be at work.[64] Rahner defends Ignatius, however, by focusing on what he considers to be the core truth of Ignatius' idea of the divine origin of certain spiritual experiences. We have already discussed the basis for this defence in the context of our discussion of grace in the last chapter. There we saw that one of Rahner's reversals of the traditional understanding of grace lay in his claim that grace can be consciously experienced. This conscious experience of grace underpins the recognition of divine impulses (providing a "fundamental evidence and certainty"), and is presupposed by the various rules for the discernment of spirits.[65] In the following section, we will explore in more detail how this fundamental certitude is caused and what form it takes.

b. Discernment of Spirits

Throughout the discussion above on the discernment of God's will (and the decision to follow this will), Rahner maintains that, with the

moral decision an element which is positively individual and unique, ..." (p. 110). For a further development of this thesis, see Rahner, "On the Question of a Formal Existential Ethics," *TI* 2: 217-34 (*ST* II: 227-46).

[64] Schwerdtfeger, *Gnade und Welt*, 305.

[65] Rahner, *The Dynamic Element in the Church*, 130 (*Das Dynamische in der Kirche*, 113).

exception of the first mode of election, the manifestation of this will does not become immediately clear and certain. In fact, he notes a parallel structure between the "ordinary" process of making every-day decisions and Ignatian discernment and decision-making.[66] In the case of important everyday decisions, the individual normally asks him or herself whether the object of choice is appropriate or fitting. It is not simply a question of "thinking it over" in a purely rational analysis of the possible object of choice. Rather, to use more scholastic terms, one inquires whether there exists a "connaturality," or, in Rahner's words, a "congruence" or "synthesis" between oneself and the possible object of choice.[67] If such a congruence exists, it brings with it a sense of inner peace and tranquillity. Moreover, in the *Exercises*, Ignatius mentions the importance of imagining, or putting oneself in, a certain situation in order to make a correct and good choice.[68] We have already seen how the matter can become more complicated when there are a number of possible choices, all of which are morally good, but only one of which expresses the concrete will of God for the individual concerned.[69] Nonetheless, underlying Rahner's Ignatius interpretation is a fundamental *anti-élitism* (a characteristic which has previously surfaced in our discussion of his spirituality), in that *any* person can discover God's will for him or her by following the procedure outlined by Ignatius. In other words, Rahner perceives this method as one accessible to all, and not one restricted to saints or mystics.[70] He then concentrates his discussion

[66] Rahner, *The Dynamic Element in the Church*, 161, n. 43 (*Das Dynamische in der Kirche*, 140, n. 57). See also the helpful comments on this issue by Michael Schneider, *"Unterscheidung der Geister:" Die ignatianischen Exerzitien in der Deutung von E. Przywara, K. Rahner und G. Fessard*, 2nd. ed., Innsbrucker theologische Studien 11 (Innsbruck: Tyrolia, 1987), 79-133, esp. 95-122.

[67] See Rahner, *The Dynamic Element in the Church*, 158-63 (*Das Dynamische in der Kirche*, 138-42).

[68] *The Spiritual Exercises of St Ignatius,* nn. 185-87, 339-41.

[69] However, it is not simply a question of choosing one out of a number of possible courses of action. Ignatius is also concerned that the retreatant's motivation with regard to the object of possible choice should consist in "the desire to be better able to serve God" (n. 155).

[70] Rahner, *The Dynamic Element in the Church*, 119, (italics mine), 127 (*Das Dynamische in der Kirche*, 104, 111). See also Jules Toner, "Discernment in the *Spiritual Exercises*," *A New Introduction to the Spiritual Exercises of St. Ignatius,* ed.

on the second mode of election which he considers the preferred time.[71]

In the *Exercises*, we find two sets of "Rules for the Discernment of Spirits." The first set, which Ignatius claims are more suitable for the first week, contribute to an understanding of the different movements produced in the soul; those spirits that are good are to be admitted, those that are bad are to be rejected. The second set provide "a more accurate discernment of spirits" and are more suited to the second week.[72] It is to these rules for the second week that Rahner turns, since it is only at this time that the choice of a way of life or election takes place.[73] Such a deeply personal decision is not possible at any given moment; thus, the first week of the *Exercises* prepares the retreatant to discover the appropriate way for him or her to follow Christ.[74] Crucial to the second week, however, is a careful attention to the "Rules for Discernment of Spirits," since these rules facilitate that binding choice which truly affects the life of the retreatant. A

John E. Dister (Collegeville, Minnesota: The Liturgical Press, 1993), 66, who maintains that it would be wrong to think that in these rules Ignatius is principally concerned with unusual or sensational spiritual experiences. While the rules do help to deal with such experiences, Ignatius is primarily interested in understanding and responding wisely to the ordinary spiritual or anti-spiritual movements of everyday Christian life.

[71] The first time is regarded as the "the ideal higher limiting case ("der ideale Grenzfall") of the second method," while the third method is the "less perfect mode of the second." Rahner, *The Dynamic Element in the Church*, 106 (*Das Dynamische in der Kirche*, 93).

[72] See *The Spiritual Exercises of St Ignatius*, n. 328. "Spirits," for Ignatius, can mean both the Holy Spirit and created spirits. These latter spirits are themselves divided into good spirits which Ignatius calls angels, and the evil ones, referred to as Satan or demons. The term "discernment," for Ignatius, means to see deeply in order to recognize and separate, i.e., to identify and distinguish the good spirits from the bad.

[73] *The Spiritual Exercises of St Ignatius*, n. 18.

[74] Hence, the purpose of the meditations on the life of Jesus (*The Spiritual Exercises of St Ignatius*, nn. 91-100) "is to discover the imperative in the life of Jesus that applies to me alone, and then to make the choice to carry it out in my life." Rahner concludes his reflections by stating that, "at this point, it is still an open question what the Lord wants me to do, but the fundamental desire for the 'more' of the Foundation, which reveals itself here as readiness for the kenosis of the Lord Jesus Christ, must now be accepted. Anyone who hesitates here should really give up the retreat right now." Rahner, *Spiritual Exercises*, 127, 134 (*Betrachtungen zum ignatianischen Exerzitienbuch*, 129-30, 137).

particular type of "movement" mentioned in this context by Ignatius is described as consolation without a previous cause (*consolación sin causa precedente*).[75]

The phrase "consolation without a previous cause" means for Ignatius "an invasion of God into the soul without any previous use of its own intellectual, volitional, or sense faculties."[76] Further, since it comes from God, it is without error, though careful discernment is necessary to ascertain whether the experience is a genuine case of such consolation. Rahner concedes that in this rule (n. 330) Ignatius has left us a masterpiece of brevity but not of clarity. It is not at all clear what precisely Ignatius meant by the phrase, while Rahner's own interpretation is not without its problems either. In Rahner's view, the term "cause" refers to the "objective ground for consolation which is now consciously present and consoling."[77] But where there is no object present to the senses, or to the understanding, or to the will, which of itself could cause consolation, then the consolation without cause is a consolation *without conceptual object*. Referring to Ignatius' description (n. 330) of the soul being drawn into the love of God, Rahner attempts to explain why "this radical love of God neither states nor presupposes any 'conceptual element' for the experience of consolation."[78] For Rahner, what is at stake here is not the suddenness of the experience but its absence of object. Moreover,

"the absence of object in question is utter receptivity to God ... There is no longer 'any object' but the drawing of the whole person, with the

---

[75] *The Spiritual Exercises of St Ignatius,* n. 330. The full reference is: "God alone can give consolation to the soul without any previous cause. It belongs solely to the Creator to come into a soul, to leave it, to act upon it, to draw it wholly to the love of His Divine Majesty. I said without previous cause, that is, without any preceding perception or knowledge of any subject by which a soul might be led to such a consolation through its own acts of intellect and will."

[76] Ganss, *Ignatius of Loyola: The Spiritual Exercises and Selected Works,* 427.

[77] Rahner, *The Dynamic Element in the Church,* 132 (*Das Dynamische in der Kirche,* 115-16).

[78] Rahner, *The Dynamic Element in the Church,* 134, n. 28 (*Das Dynamische in der Kirche,* 116-17, n. 42). In a passing reference to Bonaventure, Rahner claims that "here on earth there is an experience of the love of God which occurs without the intellect having any share in it." For a more detailed treatment of Bonaventure's contribution, see Rahner, "The Doctrine of the 'Spiritual Senses' in the Middle Ages," *TI* 16: 104-134 (*ST* XII: 137-72).

very ground of his being, into love, beyond any defined circumscrib-
able object, into the infinity of God as God himself ... It is a question
of God and God alone, precisely inasmuch as he is other than any individual object, one might say inasmuch as he is the absolutely transcendent, ..."[79]

In short, when Rahner describes the experience of consolation
without previous cause as "objectless," he is not referring to an
unconscious experience, but to what he calls a "non-conceptual"
experience of God in that the retreatant is drawn up into God's love.[80]
"Without cause" thus refers to God alone, the Creator dealing
directly with the creature, and not to any particular thoughts or concepts, even religious, in which God is known discursively.[81] In contrast to this dynamic, we mentioned other movements that *are* caused
by good or evil spirits. These movements include cognitive acts (e.g.,
thoughts, fantasies, memories), affective acts (e.g., love, desire, hate,
fear, etc.) and affective feelings (e.g., lightheartedness, depression,
gloominess, sweetness, etc.).[82] Ignatius is not so much interested in
all these inner movements of a person's mind and heart as such, but
rather in how they can have an influence on one's Christian life in

[79] Rahner, *The Dynamic Element in the Church*, 135 (*Das Dynamische in der
Kirche*, 117-18).
[80] Thus, we agree with Joseph H. P. Wong, *Logos-Symbol in the Christology of
Karl Rahner*, Biblioteca di Scienze Religiose 61 (Rome: Libreria Ateneo Salesiano,
1984), 55, who claims that "it is not a question of complete absence of object but the
shifting of 'focus' from the particular object to its background, which is pure
dynamism of transcendence." Or, in Rahner's words, "the dynamism itself alone
becomes more and more the essential." Rahner, *The Dynamic Element in the Church*,
145 (*Das Dynamische in der Kirche*, 126).
[81] In the eighth rule (*The Spiritual Exercises of St Ignatius,* n. 336), Ignatius mentions a second period of time (i.e., after the consolation) when the person frequently
forms various resolutions and plans which derive from our reasoning and judgements.
These resolutions may come from the good or evil spirit. Ignatius' point, however, is
that the person "cautiously distinguish the actual time of the consolation from the
period that follows it."
[82] Toner, "Discernment in the *Spiritual Exercises*," *A New Introduction to the
Spiritual Exercises of St. Ignatius,* 65-66. Eugen Drewermann, in an otherwise excessively harsh criticism of Rahner's work, correctly underscores the importance of
incorporating such movements into theological reflection. That Rahner does not discuss such movements leads Drewermann to conclude that Rahner's work is characterized by a "Bewußtseinseinseitigkeit." Eugen Drewermann, *Glauben in Freiheit
oder Tiefenpsychologie und Dogmatik* (Solothurn und Düsseldorf: Walter-Verlag,
1993), vol. 1, *Dogma, Angst und Symbolismus*, 209-226, 224.

acts of faith, hope and charity. Of themselves, these movements do not make someone a better or worse Christian; it all depends on how one understands and responds to them. In the present context, understanding them means to judge what is their source, that is, by what spirit they are prompted.

Returning to the consolation without previous cause, Rahner then explores how such experiences are of divine origin and why they thus possess an intrinsically self-evident and self-sufficient character. His thesis is that this experience of consolation is really an experience of transcendence elevated by grace. Normally, this experience of transcendence is only implicit as the horizon and condition of possibility of any act of the mind. But in the experience of consolation without cause, there is an "*emergence into awareness* (*ein Thematischwerden*) of transcendence and of the term to which it tends, (which) discloses a transcendence qualitatively different from the merely concomitant and implicit form."[83] As we saw in chapters two and three, the human person is not just the subject who reaches out (pre-apprehends) in the act of knowledge towards a limitless horizon, but a subject who is also open and receptive to the infinity of God Himself. Rahner combines this twofold dimension of human transcendence when he describes how the whole of a person's being is poured into a "pure movement of receptivity," ("in diese reine Offenheit der Bewegung")[84] in the experience of consolation. In this experience of transcendence, God is present as the term of the movement. At the same time, Rahner claims that this experience of transcendence or consolation, because it is the condition of possibility of all cognition, is without error and provides the authentic guarantee for us of the term inseparable from it, namely, God. Thus, he concludes that the experience of consolation supplies the ultimate ground of our knowledge of God.[85]

[83] Rahner, *The Dynamic Element in the Church*, 146, n. 34, (italics mine), (*Das Dynamische in der Kirche*, 127, n. 48). "Such a transcendence is the synthesis of the intrinsic transcendent ordination of mind to being in general, and of grace which supervenes to mould this natural unlimited receptivity and make of it a dynamic orientation towards participation in the life of God himself." (pp. 144-45).

[84] Rahner, *The Dynamic Element in the Church*, 149 (*Das Dynamische in der Kirche*, 129-30).

[85] Consolation, then, in Rahner's framework, refers to the "experience of the free transcendence of the whole mind and spirit ... raised by grace to the supernatural ..."

In sum, the consolation without previous cause, for Rahner, is the "thematization" of the human experience of transcendence. He further describes the experience as "wordless," and "without concepts:"[86]

> "On one side there is the pure non-conceptual light of the consolation of the whole human person who is being drawn above and beyond all that can be named into the love of God. On the other there is an instance of being consoled on account of a certain definite limited object."[87]

We are dealing here with an experience which lays open the very centre of a person. Moreover, there is an immediacy about this experience which enables a "perception" or "sense" of God. God, as the source of the consolation, is inwardly "perceived," and not merely inferred as something distinct from the consolation itself. The consolation without previous cause, as part of the "Rules for the Discernment of Spirits," represents, therefore, a type of supernatural first principle and criterion for discovering the will of God in a specific situation:

The Dynamic Element in the Church, 150, and n. 35 (Das Dynamische in der Kirche, 130). This "pure harmony in the depth of one's being" is experienced transcendence, and it is here, Rahner believes, that the real "certitude" of the experience lies. Peace, joy, tranquillity, etc. may be signs of the good spirit, but given the human capacity for self-deception, they cannot in themselves provide this certitude. Rahner nuances his claim even further when he says that the certitude at stake here is "humanly speaking of a limited and ultimately incommunicable kind which cannot be transformed into a deliberate explicit assertion in conceptual terms, (and) cannot really be certitude in the proper sense regarding our own state of grace." For a good exposition and analysis of Rahner's understanding of the election in the Exercises, see Schwerdtfeger, Gnade und Welt, 297-344. He succinctly describes Rahner's understanding of consolation as follows: "Trost ist hier also nicht in einem äußerlich empirischen Sinn als angehängtes Begleitgefühl zur Transzendenzerfahrung verstanden, sondern in einem metaphysischen Sinn als gnadenhaft geschenktes Bei-sich-sein des Menschen im Grunde seines Wesens, insofern dieses von Gott her und auf Gott hin ist." (p. 309).

[86] Rahner, The Dynamic Element in the Church, 153 (Das Dynamische in der Kirche, 133). Rahner refers to Ignatius' letter to Sr. Teresa Rejadell (Ganss, Ignatius of Loyola: The Spiritual Exercises and Selected Works, 337) which he sees as a confirmation of his interpretation of the consolation without previous cause. For a more nuanced interpretation of this letter, and taking into account the varieties of possible translation, see Harvey D. Egan, The Spiritual Exercises and the Ignatian Mystical Horizon, Foreword by Karl Rahner (St. Louis: The Institute of Jesuit Sources, 1976), 46-51.

[87] Rahner, The Dynamic Element in the Church, 137 (Das Dynamische in der Kirche, 119).

"One is deeply drawn affectively towards God as subject without any prior grasp of an attribute through which affectivity might be moved. Very simply this kind of experience occurs when a person finds herself or himself deeply loving God, being drawn totally to God in love, without being aware of how one came to this... It is ... the total movement of affectivity and sensibility towards God without any proportional influence of imaginative or rational intentionality prior to the experience ..."[88]

Further, this experience of consolation is related to a particular characteristic of Ignatian spirituality discussed earlier, namely, the finding of God in all things. In our present context, this characteristic:

"is only the persistent putting into practice of that supernatural concrete logic, of discovering the will of God through the experimental test of consolation. The particular that is met with or that must be chosen, done or undergone, is placed within this pure openness and receptivity of the consciously experienced transcendence towards God, and kept there."[89]

It remains surprising, however, that Rahner, while admitting that this experience can occur on very different levels, does not go into a detailed analysis of these levels. In the next section, we will see that this omission has led to criticism from some commentators. It seems that Rahner is not overly concerned to make precise distinctions between different stages of the experience of consolation without cause. These levels, presumably, would range from the first stage — described as an experience of transcendence of a certain purity and strength — to the higher "mystical" forms of infused contemplation.[90]

Rahner's interpretation has sought to analyze that fundamental certitude which underlies Ignatius' theory for discovering God's will. This will comes as a summons or call to the individual and takes

[88] Michael J. Buckley, "The Structure of the Rules for Discernment," *The Way of Ignatius Loyola: Contemporary Approaches to the Spiritual Exercises*, ed. Philip Sheldrake SJ, (St Louis, Missouri: The Institute of Jesuit Sources/London: SPCK, 1991), 230.

[89] Rahner, *The Dynamic Element in the Church*, 155-56 (*Das Dynamische in der Kirche*, 135).

[90] On this, see Rahner, *The Dynamic Element in the Church*, 144-52 (*Das Dynamische in der Kirche*, 125-32).

definitive, concrete shape in the choice ("election") of a particular course of action. According to Rahner, it is the second "time" which is the normal occasion for making an election. During this time, "much light and understanding are derived through experience of desolation and consolations and discernment of diverse spirits."[91] The discernment of spirits, Rahner argues, is the means of interpreting the *origin* of the experience of desolation and consolation, and, in this way, it permits one to discover God's will.[92] Rahner's aim here is to show how the *Exercises* succeed in *connecting* the election with the experience of consolation. Thus, in the second mode of election, the retreatant attempts to see whether there is a synthesis between the object of election and the fundamental experience of consolation. It is an experimental test to see:

> "whether the two phenomena are in harmony, mutually cohere, whether the will to the object of Election ... leaves intact that pure openness to God in the supernatural experience of transcendence and even supports and augments it or weakens and obscures it."[93]

Testing for this synthesis takes some time, since, unlike the first mode of election, the object of choice is not directly inspired by God. The matter is further complicated, though, in that not all consolation necessarily comes from God, but may also come from created causes — both good and bad. Finally, Rahner considers the period after the

---

[91] *The Spiritual Exercises of St Ignatius,* n. 176.

[92] However, it is also important in interpreting and evaluating experiences of consolation and desolation to note not only their origin, and the accompanying feelings (of joy, anger, guilt, etc.), but also the *direction* in which such experiences are leading. Experiences of desolation are not in themselves destructive, while experiences of consolation can at times be subtly deceptive, something only recognised in hindsight. Further, our interpretation and estimate of the spiritual value of any affective movement also depends upon the *context* in which it occurs. The assumption, of course, in the *Exercises* is that the general direction of the retreatant's life is towards growth in Christian discipleship. On this, see the very helpful comments of David Lonsdale, *Eyes To See, Ears To Hear: An Introduction to Ignatian Spirituality* (London: DLT, 1990), 63-83.

[93] Rahner, *The Dynamic Element in the Church,* 158 (*Das Dynamische in der Kirche,* 138). Schwerdtfeger, *Gnade und Welt,* 320, sums up the retreatant's process of decision thus: "Im Sich-lösen vom einzelnen und im Sich-öffnen für das ursprüngliche Ganze gelangt er dann in die Möglichkeit, sich aus seinem innersten Wesensgrund, und das heißt aus seiner Offenheit für Gott, zu entscheiden."

original consolation as the time for making an election. For only in this subsequent time (and not in the purely divine consolation) is a finite object present as an object of possible choice.[94]

Underlying Rahner's interpretation of the Ignatian Rules of Discernment is the assumption that God communicates through our feelings.[95] In other words, affective states *can* be a guide to the activity of God within us, though one must never lose sight of the fact that these states may well be influenced by psychological forces and factors. Suffice to say that discernment of spirits is not simply a matter of looking into oneself to try to discover natural or supernatural influences. Discernment is more than introspection. It is a matter of noting significant affective "movements" (or what Rahner also calls "motions") in a person's experience and the perceptions, decisions and courses of actions associated with these. By observing such movements it will be possible to discover the leading of God's Spirit as well as the resistances to that leading that might be operating.[96]

c. An Interim Appraisal

i) "Consolation without previous cause"

Since we have not yet considered all of Rahner's writings on Ignatius, we do not claim to offer in this section a complete evaluation of his contribution. Thus far, we have mainly discussed Rahner's essay of 1956, which has had widespread influence on, and provoked

---

[94] The original divine consolation is still present but not in its pure form as the principle of selection. This "second period," or period which follows the actual time of consolation (*The Spiritual Exercises of St Ignatius*, n. 336) is described by Rahner as a "time of testing and trying out how a hypothetically-settled, particular decision would cohere with the fundamental direction of the spirit of which a conscious awareness has been attained." Rahner, *The Dynamic Element in the Church*, 161 (*Das Dynamische in der Kirche*, 140).

[95] I am indebted here to the lucid article of David Lonsdale, "'The Serpent's Tail:' Rules for Discernment," *The Way of Ignatius Loyola: Contemporary Approaches to the Spiritual Exercises*, 165-75.

[96] "Die Lehre von der 'discretio spirituum' ist somit nach dem Zeugnis des Mittelalters kein Stoff der Wissenschaft. Sie ist eher eine 'ars', eine Lehre praktischer Normen und Kriterien als eine 'scientia' oder 'theologia'. Die großen Theologen haben darum von ihr geschwiegen." Leo Bakker, *Freiheit und Erfahrung. Redaktionsgeschichtliche Untersuchungen über die Unterscheidung der Geister bei Ignatius von Loyola* (Würzburg: Echter Verlag, 1970), 299.

a number of critical responses from, Ignatian scholars. One such criticism comes from Jules Toner, who has made an in-depth study of Ignatius' teaching on the discernment of spirits.[97] In an appendix to his work, he turns to Rahner's essay on Ignatian discernment and offers some critical remarks.

At the outset, it is important to bear in mind Rahner's intention in his 1956 essay. This was not meant to be an elaborate study of the Ignatian sources or of the commentators on the *Exercises*. Rather, "the intention has really only been to permit the *Exercises* to put questions to theology."[98] With this caveat, Toner concentrates his attention on the Ignatian discernment of spirits, particularly Rahner's contention that the consolation without previous cause constitutes the principle of spiritual discernment. Toner first asks to what extent the consolation without previous cause can be considered such a principle. Rahner had sought to show that by recognizing a consolation as divine, as coming from God, we are provided with a fundamental certitude in making an election. Granted that such consolation is indeed a privileged way of being moved by the Holy Spirit, providing a particular kind of certainty, the question is whether such consolation and certainty is a pre-requisite for *all* discernment of spirits. It seems Rahner attaches too much weight to the phenomenon of consolation without previous cause. Apart from the two rules (nn. 330 and 336) in which the phrase appears in the *Exercises*, we find no mention of the phrase elsewhere in other works of Ignatius. If such consolation was to be the basic principle of discernment of spirits, then it is surprising that Ignatius did not say so explicitly, or that commentators (e.g., in the directories for the *Exercises*) did not make this point either. Indeed, Toner makes much of the fact that Ignatius (in nn. 331-335 of the *Exercises*) spends the bulk of his time explaining how we can discern what spirit is moving us in consolation *with* previous cause. The evil spirit, which sometimes assumes the appearance of

---

[97] Jules Toner, *A Commentary on St Ignatius' Rules for the Discernment of Spirits* (St Louis: The Institute of Jesuit Sources, 1982), esp. 301-313. See also Toner's second volume on this topic: *Discerning God's Will. Ignatius of Loyola's Teaching on Christian Decision Making* (St Louis: The Institute of Jesuit Sources, 1991), esp. 316-22.

[98] Rahner, *The Dynamic Element in the Church*, 169 (*Das Dynamische in der Kirche*, 147).

the angel of light, can console for purposes that are contrary to the progress of the soul. Thus, Ignatius stresses the importance of observing the whole course of our thoughts: that a course of thoughts disquiets or disturbs the soul is an indication that the thoughts are proceeding from the evil spirit. These rules, then, help us to distinguish whether a good or evil spirit prompts a consolation that could come from either source, whereas neither an evil spirit nor a created good spirit can bring about consolation without previous cause.[99] Toner's point here is that these series of rules indicate that we do not need the phenomenon of consolation without previous cause in order to discern spirits. In other words, the experience of consolation without previous cause is not the *only* way in which such discernment can take place.

The second question put to Rahner concerns the *frequency* of the consolation without previous cause. Toner's position is that we simply do not know how frequently such consolation occurs, since Ignatius himself is not explicit on this matter. Consequently, he dismisses Rahner's reference, in this context, to a letter of Ignatius to a Sister Teresa Rejadell. Rahner believed that this letter contained in effect a commentary on the second and eighth rules for the Discernment of Spirits (nn. 330 and 336).[100] However it must be said *pace* Toner that Rahner adduces this letter not so much as evidence for the frequency of the experience of consolation without cause as for its particular quality: a "wordless" experience without concepts, an experience of immediacy, involving a "perception" or "sense" of God.[101] Yet, since both Ignatius and Rahner see discernment of spirits as an integral and normal part of

---

[99] Toner, *A Commentary on St Ignatius' Rules for the Discernment of Spirits,* 306.

[100] The relevant section is as follows: "It frequently happens that the Lord himself moves our soul and constrains us as it were to this or that action by making our soul wide open. That is to say, he begins to speak within us without any sound of words (*sin ruido alguno de voces*), he draws up the soul wholly to his love and gives us a sense of himself, so that even if he wished, we could not resist. This interior feeling … is filled with deep humility, for, of course, it is God's own Spirit that governs in everything." Rahner, *The Dynamic Element in the Church,* 152 (*Das Dynamische in der Kirche,* 132).

[101] "It is consequently clear too that the 'immediate' derivation of this consolation from God is inwardly 'perceived'… The source itself is perceived, the divine origin of the consolation is not merely inferred, as something distinct from the consolation itself, … there is a non-conceptual mode of knowing, it can only be the non-concep-

the spiritual life of Christians, the question of frequency remains. In Toner's words, "those who think that consolation without preceding cause is rare do not think it necessary for spiritual discernment; whereas those who do see it as the first principle of all discernment think of it as an ordinary experience."[102] Toner places himself in the first group and Rahner in the latter.

This problem can be reformulated in terms of the question: how "ordinary" an experience is the consolation without previous cause? In Toner's, view, only those who have lived a prolonged and intense life of prayer can have such a non-conceptual, immediate experience of God. Rahner, on the other hand, is less exclusive, and suggests that this experience is more common than is often supposed. We have seen that, for Rahner, consolation without previous cause can be described as a basic openness to, and "sense" of, God, and concerns the innermost centre of the human person.[103] The fact that there can be different grades or stages or levels in such an experience (which Rahner, of course, admits) is not his primary concern. Further, this consolation is more than the transcendent horizon which forms the condition of possibility of our acts of cognition. Although transcendence, in Rahner's framework, "designates the immanent, dynamic orientation of mind or spirit above and beyond itself in endless scope towards being in general and, ultimately, to God,"[104] the experience of consolation without previous cause is *qualitatively different* to this. However, since Rahner uses the terminology of transcendence in his discussion of this type of consolation, how can he avoid coming to the conclusion that such consolation is experienced by everyone? It is here that we detect a certain ambiguity in Rahner's presentation. On the one hand, his transcendental theology leads him to depict consolation as the experience of the free transcendence of the whole mind and spirit, elevated by grace, which has emerged *to some degree*

tual awareness of transcendence." Rahner, *The Dynamic Element in the Church*, 154 (*Das Dynamische in der Kirche*, 134).

[102] Toner, *A Commentary on St Ignatius' Rules for the Discernment of Spirits*, 307.

[103] See Josef Sudbrack, "Karl Rahner und die Theologie der Exerzitien," *Gott neu buchstabieren. Zur Person und Theologie Karl Rahners*, ed. Hans-Dieter Mutschler (Würz-burg: Echter Verlag, 1994), 41-50.

[104] Translator's note, in Rahner, *The Dynamic Element in the Church*, 125.

explicitly into conscious focus. But, on the other hand, the consolation at issue here involves a being drawn *wholly* into God's love. In other words, this experience, in Rahner's view, admits of different degrees of intensity, and can occur on very different levels.[105] So, although Rahner foregoes a discussion of the different stages in the experience of consolation, the very existence of such stages or levels underlies his entire presentation. Thus, Harvey Egan, a perceptive commentator on Rahner, can sum up the latter's understanding of the lowest level of the consolation without previous cause as "essentially the becoming thematic or the more explicit experience of the mysticism of everyday life."[106]

However, it would be preferable, we believe, to restrict the notion of consolation without previous cause to those unusual and intense experiences of being overwhelmed by the love of God. While Rahner would not disagree entirely with this description, his confusion of levels of transcendence with degrees of consolation without previous cause gives the impression that such a privileged experience is available to all. Even if we agree with Rahner that, in every conscious act there is at least a vague awareness of God as the "Whither" of transcendental subjectivity, the experience of the consolation without previous cause is more than this. It involves, as we have shown, a communication beyond words:

> "it is not just a conceptual thought of God but an awareness in experience of what alone gives ... such concepts their real meaning."[107]

---

[105] Rahner, *The Dynamic Element in the Church*, 144 (*Das Dynamische in der Kirche*, 125). Egan, *The Spiritual Exercises and the Ignatian Mystical Horizon*, 49 makes a similar point by referring to Ignatius' Rejadell letter mentioned above. There Ignatius describes how "this consolation enlightens some, and to others, He reveals many secrets."

[106] Egan, *The Spiritual Exercises and the Ignatian Mystical Horizon*, 31. Although Toner mentions Egan in his discussion, he regards his position as sufficiently close to Rahner's as to merit the same criticism. Egan (pp. 31-65), following Rahner, interprets the consolation without previous cause with the help of a transcendental theology. Rahner, for his part, endorses Egan's explication of this concept: "This consolation is nothing other than the clear awareness of a person's free, grace-elevated transcendentality which has not been distorted by any categorial object. This graced transcendentality always contains within itself a Christ-directed character." Rahner, "Foreword," to *The Spiritual Exercises and the Ignatian Mystical Horizon*, xv.

[107] Rahner, *The Dynamic Element in the Church*, 149 (*Das Dynamische in der Kirche*, 130).

In short, this consolation has a "disproportionate" quality, it is a pure gift. No spiritual exercise can be devised in order to mediate it, and it can come only from God and immediately from Him. Nevertheless, it is important not to treat the phenomenon of consolation without previous cause in isolation; its proper context is the Rules for the Discernment of Spirits, and is most suited for the second week of the *Exercises*. This context presupposes a retreatant who has shown fervour and generosity in the First Week, and who has the necessary openness to God presupposed by the second time of election. Further, he or she will be able to deal with the "subtle" and "advanced" (n. 9) rules for the discernment of spirits when tempted under the appearance of good.

Perhaps we would be fairer to Rahner if we were to reformulate his basic theological premise in a way that is still in line with Ignatius. This premise is the (thoroughly Ignatian) conviction that the *Exercises* "permit the Creator to deal directly with the creature, and the creature directly with his Creator and Lord" (n. 15). This, in Rahner's view, is the fundamental idea behind every genuine spiritual consolation. Now, within this framework, consolation without previous cause is to be seen as *one* privileged way of being moved by the Spirit. Rather than sharply distinguishing consolation with and without previous cause, it is more constructive to highlight the link between spiritual consolation as such, and Ignatian discernment. The reason Rahner regards consolation without previous cause as the main principle of discernment is because this type of consolation, he believes, gets to the heart of the *Exercises*, namely, an immediate, non-conceptual experience of God.

Yet, it could still be asked wherein lies the difference between consolation with and without previous cause. For Rahner, we have seen the difference has to do with the non-conceptual nature of the latter consolation, its sometimes intense and always disproportionate quality, and, we would add, its utter gratuity. Toner, however, seems to suggest that the consolation itself, in both cases, is the same. Accordingly, Toner concludes that whether the consolation comes from God alone or through some intermediate cause "makes no practical difference."[108] If this is the case, though, why did Ignatius make the

---

[108] Toner, *A Commentary on St Ignatius' Rules for the Discernment of Spirits,* 219.

distinction in the first place? Toner's narrow focus on the term "consolation without previous cause," and the fact that this term occurs nowhere else in Ignatius' writings is enough to convince him of its minor importance. Rahner's approach, on the other hand, attempts to elucidate how a particular form of consolation involves more than our acts of intellect and will, comes immediately from God, and is thus without deception.[109] In the next section, we will explore how such a movement has some form of decision as its intended outcome, traditionally understood in terms of a vocational choice.[110] In other words, religious experience (in the form of prayer, meditations, movements of consolation, etc.) in the *Exercises* does not exist for its own sake, but as a means to seek, find and accomplish God's will.[111]

A further, related, difficulty with Toner's evaluation of Rahner, is his lack of reference to Rahner's transcendental framework of thought. No other Rahnerian works or articles are cited. A greater familiarity with Rahner's notion of transcendental experience (as we have attempted in the previous chapter) might have led him to conclusions less diametrically opposed to those of Rahner. For Rahner's part, it is significant that he never returned to a discussion of consolation without cause in his subsequent writings. Perhaps the ambiguity of the term and the plurality of its possible interpretations became more clear to him.[112] The same is true with regard to the question of the preferred time of election. We have seen that Rahner's preference was for the second time. Yet, this is not the only possible interpretation.

---

[109] While genuine consolation always arises by an interior movement which causes the soul to be inflamed with love of its Creator and Lord (*The Spiritual Exercises of St Ignatius*, n. 316), it is often only *after* a particular experience of God that the retreatant realizes that God was present. This is yet another reason for carefully distinguishing the actual time of consolation from the period which follows it (n. 336).

[110] In the first-time election, for example, there is the profound experience of consolation without previous cause which has as its explicit consequence a particular course of action. But the other times of election show that spiritual consolation is not always experienced in such an intense manner.

[111] Egan, "Ignatian Spirituality," *NDCS*: 523.

[112] I am grateful to Dr Philip Endean SJ, of Heythrop College, London, with whom I discussed the subject matter of this chapter, and who also provided me with some of his writing on Rahner's appropriation of Ignatian spirituality. See his: "The Direct Experience of God and the Standard of Christ: A Critical and Constructive Study of Karl Rahner's Writings on the *Spiritual Exercises* of Ignatius of Loyola" (Dr. Theol. diss., University of Oxford, 1991).

What about the first time of election? And does not the dynamic of this first time bear a close resemblance to the experience of consolation without cause discussed above? We will try to respond to these questions in the next section.

ii) The Preferred Time of Election

We have seen that the *Exercises* do not focus on religious experience for its own sake, but provide a systematic structure to enable a person to discover God's will for them through the practice of the discernment of spirits. At the centre of these *Exercises* lies the Ignatian election. The retreatant, having meditated on the life, death and resurrection of Jesus, is led to choose or "elect" to follow him through a "surrender of self-love and of (one's) own will and interests" (n. 189), and the attainment of an appropriate kind of humility (nn. 164-67).[113] The success of the election, therefore, depends on the quality of the retreatant's spiritual experience over the course of the *Exercises*.

In our exposition of Rahner's interpretation of the three times of election, we quickly passed over the first time, since Rahner considered it rather rare. Instead, his claim is that the normal occasion for making an election is in the second "time." However, some commentators maintain that the first time of election is more significant than is often thought. One such commentator is Leo Bakker, who points out that, at least until 1539, Ignatius expected retreatants to experience the first time of election.[114] Further, Bakker sees in this first time of election a link with the consolation without previous

---

[113] Ignatius (n. 164) speaks of three kinds or modes (*maneras* or "manners") of being humble. They are presented as a consideration which is to pervade the *Exercises* and in particular the days devoted to the election. The first and second kinds of humility are concerned with obedience to God's laws, whereas the third degree moves beyond the law to love and is characterized as an *amorosa humilidad*. See Ganss, *Ignatius of Loyola: The Spiritual Exercises and Selected Works*, 410-411. For a different view of the relationship between the degrees of humility and the election, see William A. M. Peters, *The Spiritual Exercises of St Ignatius: Exposition and Interpretation* (Rome: C. I. S., 1968), 120-29. Peters argues, unconvincingly, that neither the instructions for the reform of one's life nor the third degree of humility belong to the time of preparation before the election.

[114] Bakker, *Freiheit und Erfahrung,* 204-32, 279-90.

cause, and refers to significant experiences from Ignatius' life to support this claim.[115] *The* experience in this regard, according to Bakker, is Ignatius' Cardoner illumination, after which everything appeared to him as in a new light.[116] Although Ignatius does not explicitly say that this experience involved a consolation without previous cause, there seems little doubt that it was not simply an imaginative vision, but a kind of Christian enlightenment, whereby Ignatius received a greater clarity in his understanding.[117] This "illumination" subsequently enabled him to discern true from false consolations. Hence, Bakker and others see in the Cardoner experience the origin (or *Geburtstunde*)[118] for the Rules of Discernment and for the teaching on the election in the *Exercises*.

A related criticism of Rahner's identification of consolation without previous cause as the criterion for the discernment of spirits comes from Peter Knauer.[119] In particular, he objects to Rahner's description of consolation without cause as "objectless" (*ungegenständlich*). Knauer (like Bakker), prefers to identify the *first* time of election with consolation without cause. But, in contrast to Rahner,

---

[115] Bakker, *Freiheit und Erfahrung,* 99-108.

[116] The relevant section from Ignatius' *Autobiography* (n. 30) is as follows: "Once he was going out of devotion to a church situated a little more that a mile from Manresa ... As he went along occupied with his devotions, he sat down for a little while with his face toward the river, which ran down below. While he was seated there, *the eyes of his understanding* began to be opened; not that he saw any vision, but *he understood and learned* many things, both spiritual matters and matters of faith and of scholarship, and this with so great *an enlightenment* that everything seemed new to him. The details that he understood then, though there were many, cannot be stated, but only that he experienced *a great clarity in understanding.* This was such that in the whole course of his life, after completing sixty-two years, even if he gathered up all the various helps he may have had from God and the various things he has known, even adding them all together, he does not think he had got as much as at that one time." Cited from Ganss, *Ignatius of Loyola: The Spiritual Exercises and Selected Works,* 78-79. (italics mine).

[117] See Ignatius' *Autobiography,* nn. 19-36 in Ganss, *Ignatius of Loyola: The Spiritual Exercises and Selected Works,* 76-83, as well as Ganss' own comments, 26-34, 378-79. See also De Guibert, *The Jesuits: Their Spiritual Doctrine and Practice,* 27-33.

[118] Bakker, *Freiheit und Erfahrung,* 105, attributes this phrase to Hugo Rahner, *Ignatius von Loyola und das geschichtliche Werden seiner Frömmigkeit* (Salzburg: Pustet, 1947), 56.

[119] Peter Knauer, "Die Wahl in den Exerzitien von Ignatius von Loyola," *Theologie und Philosophie* 66 (1991): 321-37, esp. 331-34.

he regards this as an "object-related experience of consolation" (*eine gegenstandsbezogene Trosterfahrung*). The two examples he discusses in this context are Ignatius' "meat vision"[120] and his Rejadell letter, the second of which we have already mentioned. These two illustrations from the life and writings of Ignatius exhibit a number of characteristics that apply to both consolation without cause, and to the first time of election. Firstly, they both refer to an activity initiated by God, during which the person is more passive. Secondly, at issue here is an experience which is "without previous cause," in that it is unexpected.[121] Thirdly, a profound certitude is ascertained; there is no doubting the divine origin of the experience; fourthly, it is "object-related," i.e., related to a choice and to a particular course of action.[122] Although it might appear that the above characteristics come close to what one might term a private revelation, this is not the case. Ignatius' Rejadell letter suggests that he did not regard the first

---

[120] Ignatius' "meat vision" is described in his *Autobiography* (n. 27), in Ganss, *Ignatius of Loyola: The Spiritual Exercises and Selected Works*, 79, as follows: "He continued to abstain from eating meat and was so determined about it that *he would not think of changing it* for any reason; but one day, when he got up in the morning, edible meat appeared before him as if he saw it with his ordinary eyes, though *no desire for it had preceded*. At the same time he also had a strong inclination of his will to eat it from then on. Although he remembered his previous intention, *he had no doubt about this,* but rather a conviction that he ought to eat meat. Later when telling this to his confessor, the confessor told him to consider whether this was a temptation; but examining it carefully, *he could never doubt it.*" (italics mine).

[121] The first time of election (n. 175), for example, seems also to come about without previous cause. Ignatius refers to the (unexpected) call of Paul and Matthew, who "without hesitation" respond by following Christ.

[122] Knauer, "Die Wahl in den Exerzitien von Ignatius von Loyola," 333, points out that what is at stake in the Rejadell letter is an experience of God that is related to a particular activity. In this context, then, Knauer speaks of the "Gegenständlichkeit der Tröstung" in contrast to Rahner who described it as a non-conceptual consolation. Bakker, *Freiheit und Erfahrung,* 51-53, is of the same opinion as Knauer. Even a commentator as sympathetic to Rahner as Egan admits that, on this point, Rahner "seems to overlook the importance of conceptual thoughts in Ignatian discernment." Egan, *The Spiritual Exercises and the Ignatian Mystical Horizon*, 49. The key word in this discussion is "sentido" (or "sentir") which, in Ignatius, refers to a type of "knowledge of the heart," a "felt" knowledge or a personal knowledge. "It has nothing to do with any emotional, let alone sensual, impressions; it is a completely intellectual mode of cognition, though it is certainly higher than discursive reasoning ... Ignatius concluded none of his letters without the wish that we may all 'feel' the will of God in order that we may fulfil it perfectly." Hugo Rahner, *Ignatius the Theologian*, 147.

time of election as too unusual. By the same token, Knauer sees in Ignatius' description of the first time of election (n. 175, with the reference to the call of Paul and Matthew) an example of an immediate decision of faith (*unmittelbar Glaubensentscheidungen*).[123] Moreover, the criterion of certitude characteristic of the first time of election is grounded in the fact that here there is a self-communication proceeding directly from God. This is where the parallel with the consolation without previous cause is apparent. For in annotation 330, Ignatius describes how:

> "It belongs solely to the Creator to come into a soul, to leave it, to act upon it, to draw it wholly to the love of His Divine Majesty... without previous cause, that is, without any preceding perception or knowledge of any subject by which a soul might be led to such a consolation through its own act of intellect and will."[124]

However, it would be inaccurate to restrict the decision of faith solely to the first time of election. The preceding comments are simply meant to bring out the significance of this time in the thought of Ignatius, something Rahner does not do in his 1956 article. Indeed, it seems that all three times of election were so much a part of Ignatius' life that he could pass from one to the other with relative ease. The "ideal" election, then, involves an interpenetration of *all* three times. Thus, we agree with Egan in that the three times "are not three distinct ways of finding God's Will, but actually aspects of one core experience and Election in which all three aspects are present in varying degrees of intensity."[125] In the first time, God's immediate, direct action constitutes the core of this experience, while in the second time, this core experience dissipates itself into consolations and desolations. The third time manifests itself as a tranquillity which permits the retreatant to use his or her natural abilities towards a decision unhindered by the agitation of different spirits. We have seen how Ignatius obtained a type of *experiential* certitude in relation to particular decisions, as well as receiving a greater clarity in his understanding. Nevertheless, his *Exercises* also reveal a desire for *reflexive*

---

[123] Knauer, "Die Wahl in den Exerzitien von Ignatius von Loyola," 334.
[124] *The Spiritual Exercises of St Ignatius*, n. 330.
[125] Egan, *The Spiritual Exercises and the Ignatian Mystical Horizon*, 152.

certitude, an example of which is found in annotation 336 (the eighth Rule of the Discernment of Spirits). Here, Ignatius insists on the importance of cautiously distinguishing the actual time of consolation from the period which follows it.[126]

In sum, all three times of election represent an attempt to discover the concrete individual will of God for the retreatant. In the first time of election, the will of God proceeds directly from God (*por ser de sólo Dios nuestro Señor*, n. 336), whereas in the second and third times it is mediated through created reality. Theologically speaking, we see in the interpenetration of the three times of election a harmony of the experience of faith and of the use of reason. Both these aspects — openness in faith and the responsible use of reason — are crucial in discovering God's will.[127] Moreover, Ignatius' life itself offers numerous instances of both divine illumination and a careful searching for the will of God. We saw in the Cardoner experience, for example, how Ignatius became another person with a new understanding. But this is only one side of the coin. This illumination, if we may call it thus, then developed into the need for discernment of spirits. A parallel development noted by Bakker is that the first time of election has to do with a "being chosen" (*Auserwählt-werden*), and, in that sense, is passive, whereas the personal act of choosing denotes a human activity.[128] In fact, there was a

---

[126] See also Ignatius' *Autobiography*, n. 31, in Ganss, *Ignatius of Loyola: The Spiritual Exercises and Selected Works*, 81.

[127] In this context, Hugo Rahner, *Ignatius the Theologian*, 155 states that "all the disciples of Ignatius emphasized the external judgment of the director as a means of controlling inward illumination — Polanco, Miró, Canisius, Nadal and Dávila. Any genuine illumination, any election *sine ratiociniis*, must be able to stand up to examination in the light of *ratio*." Hugo Rahner then concludes that both the second and third times "are closely linked together and act as checks on one another."

[128] Bakker, *Freiheit und Erfahrung*, 280, and 281-85. Bakker notes a transition from the older *Versio prima* (or first translation into scholastic Latin, made most probably by Ignatius himself in Paris by 1534), and the Autograph (Ignatius' own Spanish text left at his death in 1556) in the latter's emphasis on "choosing" rather than on "being chosen." At the same time, however, the first time of election cannot be regarded as a purely passive experience, since a choice does ensue. After Cardoner, for example, Ignatius resolved to go to Jerusalem, to live poorly, to preach to the Muslims, to visit the holy places, etc. Rahner himself similarly describes the election as "the election of being elected" ("die Wahl der Erwähltheit"), i.e., that *we* are elected by God. See his comments on this in the context of the immediacy of the creator to creature in *Meditations on Priestly Life*, 268 (*Einübung priesterlicher Existenz*, 291).

growing insight on the part of Ignatius that the "being chosen" by God also demanded human effort in responding, an effort which, Ignatius believed, some retreatants were either unwilling or unable to make (nn. 18, 169). Hence, from initially favouring the first time of election, he came to emphasize (from 1539-1541) a more gradual calling — corresponding to the second time. We can detect a transition, therefore, in the life of Ignatius from the "pure" mystic, who expected everything directly and exclusively from God, to the man of the Church, and the man who used human "means" in the service of God. Church authorities would, quite rightly, be suspicious of anything that smacked of illuminism, and, although Ignatius always seemed to have had a strong ascetic tendency, his primary concern and wish was to give himself completely to the service of God in the Church. In this context, Ignatius came to a deep appreciation of theological study, and, with regard to the times of election, there emerged a more methodical procedure where human reason came to play an ever greater role.[129]

d. The Christological Dimension of the Ignatian Election

We have looked at some commentators who highlight and develop aspects of the Ignatian election not found in Rahner's treatment of the topic. One such aspect not yet discussed, but mentioned by Bakker and others, is the *christological* dimension of consolation, a dimension to which Rahner devotes very little attention, at least in his 1956 essay.[130] However, in order not to do Rahner a disservice, we need to

---

[129] This is not to contradict our remarks above about the overlapping of the three times of election. It seems Ignatius made his decisions almost always by means of the discernment of different spirits (consolation and desolation) which eventually resulted in him acquiring a certainty about the will of God, and thus arriving at a particular choice. It was not simply a question of rationally working the matter out, of methodically weighing up the pros and cons, though this too played an increasingly greater role. Bakker, *Freiheit und Erfahrung,* 285-90, traces this tendency towards describing the election along more rational lines, that is, by favouring the third time of election as less prone to error. This can be seen, for example, in some of the "Directories" (sets of directives regarding the use and practice of the *Exercises*). One such Directory, which sees the third time of election as "surer and more certain," emerged during the generalate of Claudio Aquaviva (1581-1615).

[130] Referring specifically to Rahner's 1956 essay, Bakker concludes: "Es bleibt allerdings bedauerlich, daß der Trost so wenig christologisch betrachtet wird: ist es nicht so, daß man Transzendenz erst in *Christus* erfahren kann? Dieser Aspekt tritt im

look elsewhere, namely, to his retreat meditations, in order to find the Ignatian process of election depicted in more christological terms. Underlying the necessity and importance of this christological aspect is the presupposition that the experience of God cannot be restricted solely to one's "interiority," as our discussion of Rahner's thesis of a "pure experience of transcendence" might suggest.[131] Rather, since the incarnation, *history* must also be seen as the locus for the encounter with God. Indeed, Rahner himself says as much:

> "We can no longer reach God by leaving the created world or by abandoning time, space, and history; nor can we reach Him through the transcendence of our spirit toward the Absolute. He can only be reached concretely right where we ourselves are — in our flesh and blood. All grace as a participation in the inner life of God is now grace that comes from the Incarnation and therefore grace of Christ."[132]

Furthermore, even a cursory look at the *Exercises* reveals that the decision or election is to be made in the course of a series of meditations on the life of Christ. In his introduction to the consideration of

Artikel nicht hervor, während er in den GÜ zentral ist." *Freiheit und Erfahrung,* 290, n. 54, (italics mine). Avery Dulles makes much the same point in an important article, "Finding God's Will: Rahner's Interpretation of the Ignatian Election," *Woodstock Letters* 114 (1965): 139-52. The christological aspect is relevant to our study particularly in view of our earlier questions regarding the "specifically Christian" aspect of Rahner's understanding of spirituality.

[131] This is Van der Heijden's objection in his discussion of the proper *criterion* for knowing that a person's experience of God was genuine, and thus that the election was carried out correctly. Following Bakker, (see above, note 130), he warns: "Das Kriterium ist nicht mehr bloß und letztlich im inneren Kernerlebnis zu suchen, sondern in Christus." Van der Heijden, *Karl Rahner, Darstellung und Kritik seiner Grundpositionen,* 220. However, the fact that van der Heijden does not include Rahner's retreat conferences in his discussion leads him to the somewhat exaggerated conclusion that the sole criterion for the early Rahner was a pure experience of transcendence. See also Peter Eicher, "Wovon spricht die transzendentale Theologie? Zur gegenwärtigen Auseinandersetzung um das Denken von Karl Rahner," *Theologische Quartalschrift* 156 (1976): 284-95, 291.

[132] Rahner, *Spiritual Exercises,* 80 (*Betrachtungen zum ignatianischen Exerzitienbuch,* 83). For a reflection on Christ as the mediator of all salvation, see Rahner's "The Eternal Significance of the Humanity of Jesus for Our Relationship with God," *TI* 3: 35-46 (*ST* III: 47-60), where he is concerned with overcoming the "unchristian outlook and of solving the *sinful* dilemma into which original sin throws us: God *or* the world... . The Christian attitude, however, would be to honour the world as something willed and loved by God, and to do this in a properly balanced way, ..." (pp. 41-42).

different states of life (n. 135), Ignatius exhorts the retreatant, while *contemplating the life of Jesus,* to "begin to investigate and ask in what kind of life or in what state" God wishes to make use of him of her.[133] By "mysteries" of Jesus' life, Rahner is referring not only to events such as Christ's incarnation, crucifixion and resurrection which have a universal significance for our salvation, but also to "the ordinary, the normal, the commonplace, the boringly repetitive, what all have in common, what is insignificant," or to what he calls the "hidden life" of Jesus.[134] The point here is that the *whole* life of Jesus in all its dimensions possesses redemptive significance, and, in this sense, constitutes a "mystery." Rahner thus reflects on the salvific significance of the hidden life of Jesus, which he presents as forming a unity with all the other, more public, events of his life. In so doing, he intends to underscore the gracedness of *everyday* life. It is not a question, then, of piously meditating on Jesus as an exemplary model of moral behaviour, something, he feels, the meditations on the life of Jesus in the *Exercises* are perhaps overly concerned with.[135]

The reason Rahner portrays the election as *the call of Christ* can be traced to his understanding of the incarnation. God's decision for self-utterance is His basic intention for creation, and also represents a redemptive decision in regard to finite reality. In fact, Rahner presents the fundamental mysteries of Christianity — Trinity, incarnation, grace, and glory — as one comprehensive mystery: that the absolute God goes out as Himself into the non-divine.[136] The

---

[133] For a further collection of theological meditations on this subject as part of Rahner's contribution to a theology of the spiritual life, see his "Mysteries of the Life of Jesus," *TI* 7:121-201 (*ST* VII: 123-96) and his article "Mysterien des Lebens Jesu," *LThK* VII: 721-22. Our claim in this section is that by such contemplation of the mysteries of the life of Jesus, we have a counter-balance to the other main characteristic of Rahner's Ignatian interpretation, namely, that of the Creator dealing directly with the creature.

[134] Rahner, *Meditations on Priestly Life*, 86 (*Einübung priesterlicher Existenz*, 99). See also Rahner, Vorgrimler, "Mysterien des Lebens Jesu," *Kleines Theologisches Wörterbuch*: 287-88.

[135] Rahner, "Mysterien des Lebens Jesu," *LThK* VII: 722.

[136] "This self-communication comes to be in incarnation and grace, ... that is to say, incarnation and divinisation of all reality ... are connected. This one incarnatory-engracing, transfiguring, divinising, self-communication of God to the world, which is created in this decision for his own utterance, reveals precisely what we call the mystery of the Trinity: from this standpoint too the redemptive-historical ('economic')

incarnation, then, in this framework, is not only an event happening in a moment in time, but constitutes also the "inner entelechy" sustaining creation from the very beginning.[137] Creation and incarnation are two moments or phases of the *one* process of God's self-giving and self-expression. God is creator in as much as He willed to be the giver of grace. In other words, the presupposition is that the world was created to receive God's self-communication. In teasing out the meaning of the incarnation, of what it means to say "the Word became flesh," Rahner's accent is on how the *created* reality with its process of becoming is the reality of the Word of God.[138] Moreover, it is incorrect, he claims, to hold that we cannot know any details of the historical Jesus which would be of significance for theology and faith. Otherwise, we simply end up with a contemporary form of fideism, an attempt to emancipate oneself from the burden of history. Instead, Rahner underlines the intrinsic link between faith and history, and, more specifically, asserts that the historical event of Jesus can be seen as the *ground* of faith:

> "Catholic faith and its dogmatics as they have been understood up to now, and also as they will have to be understood in the future, remain indissolubly bound up not only with the historical existence of Jesus of Nazareth, but also with the historical events of a specific kind which took place during his life."[139]

These introductory comments on the meaning of the incarnation serve as a background to Rahner's Ignatian meditations on the theo-

Trinity and the inner, immanent Trinity are intrinsically one." Rahner, *Meditations on Priestly Life*, 74-75 (*Einübung priesterlicher Existenz*, 86-87).

[137] Rahner, *FCF*, 197 (*Grundkurs*, 197). It is beyond our scope here to present a detailed outline of Rahner's Christology. Instead, we confine our discussion to his meditations on the incarnation, and, in particular, on the hidden life of Jesus in the *Exercises* (nn. 101-109, 134, 271). For a synthetic but comprehensive outline of Rahner's Christology, see *FCF*, 176-321 (*Grundkurs*, 180-312); and Karl Rahner, Wilhelm Thüsing, *A New Christology* (New York: Seabury Press, 1980), 3-14. [*Christologie — systematisch und exegetisch: Arbeitsgrundlagen für eine interdisziplinäre Vorlesung*, Quaestiones Disputatae 55 (Freiburg: Herder, 1972), 17-78].

[138] Rahner, *Spiritual Exercises*, 105 (*Betrachtungen zum ignatianischen Exerzitienbuch*, 109). The faith encounter with Jesus as Rahner's christological point of departure is further developed in our final chapter in the context of the Christocentric nature of his spirituality.

[139] Rahner, "Remarks on the Importance of the History of Jesus for Catholic Dogmatics," *TI* 13: 201 (*ST* X: 215).

logical and spiritual significance of the hidden life of Jesus. It is only through meditating on the life of Jesus, he argues, that the retreatant will find the ultimate criterion for making an election.[140] We have seen how the discovery of the right way of following Christ in the *Exercises* is ultimately the result of an individual, personal decision. This "call" to discipleship, however, only takes place when the retreatant is drawn into the concrete historical life of Jesus. A concrete assimilation to Christ takes place which, by the same token, is also a participation in the inner life of God. The "imitation" of Christ at issue here does not, as we have said above, consist in the observance of certain moral maxims, but rather "in a true entering into His life and in Him entering into the inner life of the God that has been given to us."[141] In short, then, the purpose of the meditations on the life of Jesus "is to discover the imperative in the life of Jesus that applies to me alone, and then to make the choice to carry it out in my life."[142]

Although the evangelists give only marginal consideration to the "pre-history" (or hidden life) of the Messiah, — the assumption

---

[140] "The Lord is the ultimate standard; there is none higher than he, since the ultimate standard of necessity is revealed to us just in this actual person. For it is just here that the Logos became man and not simply any man, but this man, so that we cannot really accept a division in the life of Jesus between what is important for us and what can be left aside." Rahner, *Meditations on Priestly Life*, 81 (*Einübung priesterlicher Existenz*, 93).

[141] Rahner, *Spiritual Exercises*, 118 (*Betrachtungen zum ignatianischen Exerzitienbuch*, 121). In fact Rahner goes even further. Given that the Word of God entered the world in a "tangible and public epiphany of grace, and not just as an anonymous historical force," then one can conclude that Christian spirituality "must attain the same level of publicity that He has; it must relate itself explicitly (with the help of Scripture and tradition) to the 'historical' Jesus; it must understand itself as a part of His 'fullness'; in a word, it must be 'ecclesial'!." (p. 117).

[142] Rahner, *Spiritual Exercises*, 127 (*Betrachtungen zum ignatianischen Exerzitienbuch*, 129-30). Later, Rahner adds: "The purpose here in these meditations is to place ourselves in a real, not just abstract, relationship to the event of Jesus' life being considered by means of a salvation-historical and salvation-bringing remembrance. This relationship will bring us the grace necessary to follow Christ... . What takes place in a narrower, sacramental sense in the sacrifice of the Mass, also occurs in a very true sense in the faith-penetrated remembrance of the other events of Jesus' life: And this remembrance is not a mere speculative treatment of Jesus' history — in it, the grace of a definite mystery is revealed and offered to the one praying." Rahner, *Spiritual Exercises*, 162, (*Betrachtungen*, 163).

seems to be that this first part of Jesus' life is not particularly significant for us in that it was so ordinary — Rahner nevertheless discovers a number of characteristics of his hidden life. These christological meditations, we believe, not only complement our previous exposition and discussion of Rahner's Ignatian interpretation, but also offer another insight into his understanding of spirituality.

The first characteristic of this hidden life of Jesus is described by Rahner as *growth*. While not overlooking Jesus' consciousness of a radical and unique closeness to God as part of the hypostatic union, his hidden life "is expressly a life of growth (Lk 2: 40), of change, and thus also a life of surprise, of a life that could not be planned in advance."[143] Linked to this slow growth to maturity is the patient *waiting* for his "hour." This waiting for God, this remaining open (which is not the same as a kind of spiritual fatalism) constitutes, in Rahner's view, a basic structure of Christian living, and thus of spirituality.[144] A third characteristic of Jesus' hidden life (indeed of his whole life) is his *poverty*; not so much as an ascetic practice but as acceptance of the normal, ordinary, average conditions of life at that time. *Work*, too, played a large part in this hidden life; quiet, unobtrusive work and an acceptance of its repetitive and routine nature.[145] The Gospel of Luke (Lk 2: 51) also speaks of the *obedience* of Jesus which belongs to a growing, maturing, human life; an obedience which accorded a certain respect to parental and political authority. Scripture (Lk 3: 21) also attests that Jesus' hidden life is characterized by *prayer*, and this, not only as the consequence of the hypostatic union, but within the framework of traditional and institutionalized Jewish religion, — witnessed, for instance (Lk 2: 41), in his

---

[143] Rahner, *Meditations on Priestly Life*, 88 (*Einübung priesterlicher Existenz*, 101). In this paragraph, we simply present a summary of the seven characteristics of Jesus' hidden life enunciated by Rahner in both *Meditations on Priestly Life*, 86-98 (*Einübung priesterlicher Existenz*, 99-112) and in *Spiritual Exercises*, 121-25; 151-68 (*Betrachtungen zum ignatianischen Exerzitienbuch*, 124-28, 152-69).

[144] On this, see Rahner, "Proving Oneself in Time of Sickness," *TI* 7: 275-84 (*ST* VII: 265-72), and "Intellectual Patience with Ourselves," *TI* 23: 38-49 (*ST* XV: 303-14).

[145] For a theology of everyday things, including work, see Rahner's *Everyday Things*, Theological Meditations 5, ed. Hans Küng (London and Melbourne: Sheed and Ward, 1965).

going up to Jerusalem with his parents for the Passover. Jesus' hidden life can, Rahner believes, be summed up as a *contemplative* life, a life hidden with Christ in God (Col 3: 3), which is the deeper ground of both Jesus' and our ordinary, everyday existence. The seclusion of Jesus' life thus represents a structural principle of our life:

> "It is merely the application and realisation of a living faith that what is most real in our existence cannot be directly grasped and yet is what is most essential to us, for our basic attitude, decisions and way of life... This seclusion — that is, normal, commonplace and often boring life — is the climate in which the hidden supernatural life of the Christian is practised; it is the way in which faith in the hidden God as the centre of our life must be realised."[146]

This average, normal life can be misunderstood in terms of a faint-hearted apathy, but that is not what is meant by the hidden life practised in faith. Rather, the challenge, as we have seen in our second chapter, is to discover in the regular, normal routine of life the Spirit of Christ. Without this Spirit, one's routine, Rahner claims, would indeed degenerate into a kind of institutionalised drudgery. Instead, the point about the meditations on the life of Jesus is to lead the retreatant into a choice for a particular form of discipleship. Such discipleship has a twofold aspect. On the one hand, it is a "following" (*Nachfolge*), not a literal imitation of every aspect of Jesus' life along the lines of a purely external pattern of obedience.[147] On the other hand, Christian discipleship *is* connected to the concrete historical life of Jesus, eliciting a personal decision from the retreatant in his or her always changing historical situation. Rahner's preferred description of Christ in this context is as an "eductive model" (*ein produktives Vorbild*) who forms the retreatant from within through his Spirit.[148] His point is that it is the example of Jesus' life and his Spirit *together* which make him an eductive model of discipleship and obedience.

---

[146] Rahner, *Meditations on Priestly Life*, 96 (*Einübung priesterlicher Existenz*, 110).

[147] For the link between obedience and faith, see Rahner's *Knechte Christi. Meditationen zum Priestertum* (Freiburg: Herder, 1967), 142-75. [ET: *Servants of the Lord*, trans. Richard Strachan (London and New York: Burns & Oates, Herder and Herder, 1968), 127-48].

[148] See Rahner, *Servants of the Lord*, 143 (*Knechte Christi,* 166), and "Following the Crucified," *TI* 18: 162, 165 (*ST* XIII: 194, 197).

Another Ignatian meditation which is of particular importance for the christological aspect of the election is that of the Two Standards.[149] Indeed, Rahner describes it as one of two "decision" meditations (*Wahlbetrachtungen*), the other being that on the "three classes of men" (nn. 149-157). He sees the two standards meditation in conjunction with the temptation of Christ in the desert (n. 274), and finds its general meaning in terms of the call of Christ the king to the retreatant. The problem is once again one of discernment: how can I distinguish a genuine call of Christ from a false impulse? This meditation, Rahner feels, goes some way towards helping the retreatant appreciate the dangers of self-deception and delusion.[150] Despite the simplicity of the image of the two standards — the standard of Satan and the standard of Christ — Rahner sees in it an accurate "existential" that determines human choice. It is not a question of identifying the world with the standard of Satan, and the Church with the standard of Christ. Rather, Ignatius emphasizes the mutual interpenetration of both kingdoms, a dichotomy, which Rahner maintains, goes to the depths of the human person. Such division around us and within us only accentuates the unavoidability of decision, of a real choice. And this inner decision can solely be made in the depths of our existence. The three levels of temptation contained in this meditation, riches, honour, and pride, lead to an absolute self-identification with a particular good, and, ultimately, to an absolute self-assertion against God.[151] In contrast, the call or standard of Christ involves an "existential distancing" from any particular value or good. This active indifference, of not identifying oneself absolutely

---

[149] *The Spiritual Exercises of St Ignatius*, nn. 136-147. We follow Rahner's reflections on this meditation in *Meditations on Priestly Life*, 170-79 (*Einübung priesterlicher Existenz*, 187-97), and in *Spiritual Exercises*, 169-78 (*Betrachtungen zum ignatianischen Exerzitienbuch*, 170-79).

[150] We have previously discussed Ignatius' "Rules for the Discernment of Spirits," where these difficulties are explored in more detail. Moreover, the meditations mentioned above are good examples of what has been described as "a system of virtual or paradigmatic oppositions" (the opposition between the two kings, the two standards, the three classes of men) characteristic of Ignatian language. For an interesting, if at times eccentric, discussion of Ignatian discourse, see Barthes, *Sade, Fourier, Loyola*, 56-75.

[151] Rahner, *Spiritual Exercises*, 175 (*Betrachtungen zum ignatianischen Exerzitienbuch*, 176).

with one particular good, entails a type of *poverty*: "the ability to leave things — a certain abandonment to trust in God ... selfless renunciation, steadfast perseverance ..."[152] Rahner sees such acts of "dying" as highlighting most clearly the christological aspect of the election. They are an imitation of the crucified Christ and *a partici- pation in his death*.[153] Moreover, such a dying is only possible on the basis of the promise of the crucified and risen Christ that this dying is not a falling into an empty nothingness, but a liberation from the illu- sion that any finite good can be given absolute importance.

Rahner's second "decision" meditation on the "three classes of men" (nn. 149-57) brings out in even clearer terms the call of Christ that is at the heart of the election.[154] What counts for Rahner is that the decision is one of personal love for the always greater God, that is, one of unreserved *surrender* (*Hingabe*), to use a more frequent Rahnerian phrase. And, as we have seen, such a decision is not attain- able purely with the aid of rational means, or by appropriating objec- tive moral principles. Rather, it is a question of the person placing him or herself at the disposal of the absolute and personal will of God — something beyond any objective calculation.[155] Such an attitude of

---

[152] Rahner, *Spiritual Exercises*, 176-77 (*Betrachtungen zum ignatianischen Exer- zitienbuch*, 177-78). It is in this existential (and not merely theoretical) transcendence that the always greater God, the *Deus semper major* comes to be known.

[153] "... ein *Partizipation am Sterben Christi* und hat nur von Christus, dem Gekreuzigten und Auferstandenen, her die Verheißung, daß ein solches Sterben möglich ist und nicht im Grunde doch nur ein Fall in eine absolute Leere ist.... . Der Tod dieser Illusion, dieses 'Sterben', das zum Grundakt jeder christlichen Wahl gehört, ist ein Sterben, das in der Gnade Christi mit zusammen geschieht, ob man es reflex weiß oder nicht, ..." Karl Rahner, "Im Anspruch Gottes. Bemerkungen zur Logik der existentiellen Erkenntnis," *Geist und Leben* 59 (1986): 245. (italics mine).

[154] In this meditation it is a question of ridding oneself of all inordinate attach- ments "to be better able to serve God." *The Spiritual Exercises of St Ignatius*, n. 155. For what follows, see Rahner, *Meditations on Priestly Life*, 180-207 and 216-81 (*Einübung priesterlicher Existenz*, 198-227 and 237-304), and *Spiritual Exercises*, 186-202 and 217-85 (*Betrachtungen zum ignatianischen Exerzitienbuch*, 187-203 and 218-303).

[155] Strictly speaking, it could be argued that the two meditations are more about discernment than about choice. In fact, Rahner says of the second that "there is no question here of a concrete decision, but only of the proper religious *attitude* which should precede such a decision. This attitude is the absolutely open surrender of one- self to the sovereign will of God." Rahner, *Spiritual Exercises*, 192 (*Betrachtungen zum ignatianischen Exerzitienbuch*, 193). However, this point does not tell against

detachment, of freely leaving everything to God, is only possible through the grace of Christ's cross. This detachment or active indifference leads to an openness for the greater *service* of God, which Ignatius intends to be the outcome of the election.[156] Throughout the *Exercises*, the retreatant is called towards action, and to ask of God, "What do you want me to do?" This service is the love manifest in deeds, which Ignatius mentions in his contemplation on love (nn. 230-237).

Rahner's retreat conferences, in both *Spiritual Exercises* and *Meditations on Priestly Life*, underscore the significance of the *cross* for spirituality. Moreover, the necessary attitudes mentioned above, and expected of the retreatant, reveal a *dialectical* element in Rahner's appropriation of Ignatian spirituality, namely, to be able to esteem the world, and at the same time, to be able to rise above it in a kind of indifference, in a love for the cross. This realisation of love of the cross is, therefore, in Rahner's view, the innermost existential in the life of the Christian. Properly understood, it challenges a person to find God also in those things that come to him or her as crosses, and raises the question of whether one is prepared for the type of voluntary renunciation or detachment mentioned above, or for what Rahner has described elsewhere as the "new asceticism."[157] Asceticism can

---

Rahner's basic description of the meditations if it is borne in mind that discernment occurs both before, *and after* the election has taken place.

[156] Speaking of such active indifference in the context of the second degree of humility (*The Spiritual Exercises of St Ignatius*, n. 166), Rahner describes it as a love in which "God becomes known in a radical way, existentially, transcendentally, and not merely categorically." Rahner, *Meditations on Priestly Life*, 199 (*Einübung priesterlicher Existenz*, 219).

[157] See Rahner, "Christian Living Formerly and Today," *TI* 7: 19-24 (*ST* VII: 27-31). He sees in this new asceticism of "imposing one's own limits" ("Neue Aszese des selbstgesetzten Maßes") a necessary component of a contemporary spirituality. Traditional Christian ascetic practices were seen as out of the ordinary — life itself was hard enough, and imposed a moderation of its own. Today, with our increasing control over nature and huge progress in science and medicine, a new form of voluntary asceticism is required. Rahner calls this kind of voluntary renunciation an "asceticism in the consumer society" ("Konsumaszese"). It is achieved by "one who is *open to God* ... where *God* is *loved* for his own sake ... (and) consists in sharing in the death of Christ on the Cross, and which is offered to us because today too life still continues mysteriously to be the Passion." (p. 21). For the link between renunciation and love see his "Reflections on the Theology of Renunciation," *TI* 3: 47-57 (*ST* III: 61-72) and our own reflections on Christian hope and the cross in the previous chapter.

thus be described as "a training in readiness for the passion of Christ."[158]

If the cross reveals God's powerlessness in the world, then the resurrection of Christ is its transfiguration and redemption. God's love has ultimately prevailed. Rahner's reminder in this regard, to the priests of his 1961 conference, highlights both his "salvation-optimism" and the graced dynamic operative in the election:

> "... Don't let us preach Christianity as if God had left us our freedom, left the decision to us, had merely offered us in friendliness and benevolence the opportunity to make a right decision and nothing more. This existential, equitable dualism, which we often preach and in our own asceticism mostly observe, is basically false... We must believe in the efficacious grace of God and not merely in sufficient grace."[159]

In short, then, two main points emerge from our discussion of these less philosophical Rahnerian meditations on the *Exercises*. Firstly, these writings place greater stress on the christological basis of his spirituality than do his more speculative works.[160] The retreat conferences or meditations, we believe, thus offer a necessary corrective to his essay in *The Dynamic Element in the Church*. And, secondly, we notice an understanding of grace underlying these meditations which reiterates our presentation of this topic in the previous chapter, that is,

---

[158] Rahner, *Spiritual Exercises*, 243 (*Betrachtungen zum ignatianischen Exerzitienbuch*, 244).

[159] Rahner, *Meditations on Priestly Life*, 246-47 (*Einübung priesterlicher Existenz*, 268-69). See also his *Spiritual Exercises*, 244-50 (*Betrachtungen zum ignatianischen Exerzitienbuch*, 245-51), where he speaks of the importance of considering the whole life of Christ in the retreat — including his resurrection: "Even though we should not forget the *crucified* Lord, still we cannot really understand Him if we do not at the same time believe in Him as the *resurrected* Lord Who, by means of His death, entered into the eternal life of His Father." (p. 245). Yet, the main emphasis in Rahner's conferences, as we have seen, is on the *cross*, and even his references to the "victory" of the resurrection are interpreted from within this framework: "... In spite of everything, we are somehow mysteriously surrounded by something greater, by the victory of Christ... Of course, this victory-confidence ("dieser Siegesmut") of ours is almost identical with the weakness of the cross ("Kreuzesohnmacht"), because the victory was obtained on the cross... We must consider the cross the test of our faith, and at the same time realize that God is stronger in us than is our own fear of the cross." (p. 249).

[160] Rahner himself admits as much. See his "Christian Living Formerly and Today," *TI* 7: 16, n. 12 (*ST* VII: 23, n. 1). For an example of a more speculative treatment of the topic, (other than "The Logic of Concrete Individual Knowledge in Ignatius Loyola"), see Rahner, "Theology and Anthropology," *TI* 9: 28-45 (*ST* VIII: 43-65).

grace conceived as a sharing in the life of God.[161] Since we have discussed this topic already, we will not go into it again here.

Our discussion of Rahner's appropriation of Ignatian spirituality has centred around the difficult process of discerning God's will, the related issues of consolation without previous cause, and the preferred time of election. Further, our analysis revealed certain tensions with which Ignatius, Rahner, and even the retreatant himself or herself have had to grapple. One such tension is that between the role of rational analysis and the place of a Christian enlightenment or "illumination" in the process of making an election. A second tension concerns the question of the passivity or activity of the retreatant. Is it a question of choosing or being chosen? Thirdly (and this applies especially to Rahner's Ignatius interpretation), there is the tension between the transcendental and the categorial aspects of the decision to follow the call of God. In fact, our exposition and discussion of Rahner's position indicate that these two aspects (the transcendental and the categorial) cannot be separated; rather, they mutually complement each other. Moreover, in Rahner's study of the theological problems involved in the Ignatian rules of election, the accent is firmly on the transcendental dimension, whereas, in his Ignatian retreat meditations, the categorial dimension comes to the fore. With regard to a criterion for discovering God's will, it is a question of whether there exists a *synthesis* between the attitude of receptivity and openness to God, on the one hand, and the concrete object of election, on the other.[162] Both the experience of consolation without cause and the meditation on the life of Jesus go hand in hand. Therefore, the fact that consolation without cause (as an "immediate" experience of God) has a wordless and non-conceptual character does not exclude a christological interpretation.[163]

---

[161] "Grace, which is an existential injection of the one graced into the inner life of God, is not just any kind of divinization of the human person ... It is a concrete assimilation to Christ and a participation in His life. Therefore, ontologically and not just morally, it is the *grace of Christ.*" Rahner, *Spiritual Exercises*, 115 (*Betrachtungen zum ignatianischen Exerzitienbuch*, 118).

[162] Rahner, *The Dynamic Element in the Church*, 158-60 (*Das Dynamische in der Kirche*, 138-39). If this is the case, true spiritual joy (i.e., "peace," "tranquillity," "quiet") ensues. *The Spiritual Exercises of St Ignatius*, n. 333.

[163] In his reply to Avery Dulles' article ("Finding God's Will: Rahner's Interpretation of the Ignatian Election," *Woodstock Letters* 114 (1965): 139-52), Rahner responds to Dulles' criticism that his 1956 essay seemed deficient in its failure to

3. Rahner and Ignatian Mystagogy

a. Rahner's Spiritual Testament

In 1977, Rahner wrote his final extended piece on the contemporary importance of Ignatius.[164] Entitled "Ignatius of Loyola Speaks to a Modern Jesuit," it comprises a good synthesis of his previous work on Ignatius.[165] Moreover, it encapsulates the essential core of his notion of spirituality, namely, a direct or immediate encounter with God. We have seen in the previous section how the *Exercises* aim to facilitate such an encounter. Our intention in this section is to return to, and expand on, this theme of the possibility of a non-conceptual experience of God. Right at the outset of the piece in question, Rahner has Ignatius claim: "I had a direct encounter with God. This was the experience I longed to communicate to

accentuate the Christological dimension of the Ignatian election. See Karl Rahner, "Im Anspruch Gottes. Bemerkungen zur Logik der existentiellen Erkenntnis," *Geist und Leben* 59 (1986): 241-47. The article arrived in the USA on 31 January 1969, but was only published posthumously in German. In his response, Rahner acknowledges the central role of the christological dimension in the Ignatian theology of choice: "Diese Dimension gibt es natürlich. Und sie ist bei Ignatius in den Exerzitien durch all die Betrachtungen des Lebens Jesu und auch durch die Betrachtungen der zwei Fahnen usw. sehr deutlich gegeben und praktiziert." (p. 244). Further, he concedes that in his own essay he has not discussed this dimension in any detail. Yet he maintains that this dimension is present in an unthematic way, since all grace is the grace of Christ: "Aber diese Dimension ist da... weil alle Gnade unter den verschiedensten Hinsichten ... Gnade Christi ist und darum auch die Gnade, die als 'Trost' das Wahlgeschäft bestimmt und prägt, immer als Gnade Christi unter all diesen Rücksichten zu denken ist und sonst die ganzen Exerzitien gar nicht verständlich werden." (pp. 244-45). Rahner's final point linking the christological dimension of the election to a participation in the dying of Christ has already been discussed in this section.

[164] Karl Rahner, H. N. Loose, and Paul Imhof, *Ignatius von Loyola* (Freiburg: Herder, 1978), 10-38. The text is also to be found as "Rede des heiligen Ignatius an einen Jesuiten von heute," in *ST* XV: 373-408. [ET: *Ignatius of Loyola,* with an Historical Introduction by Paul Imhof, trans. Rosaleen Ockenden (London: Collins, 1979), 11-38].

[165] "Meine 'Rede des heiligen Ignatius an einen Jesuiten von heute' könnte man als eine Art Testament ansehen. Beim späteren Lesen ist mir das bewußt geworden... Eher handelt es sich um ein Resümee meiner Theologie überhaupt und dessen, was ich zu leben versucht habe." *Glaube in winterlicher Zeit: Gespräche mit Karl Rahner aus den letzten Lebensjahren,* eds. Paul Imhof and Hubert Biallowons (Düsseldorf: Patmos, 1986), 128.

others."[166] Rahner is aware, though, that this claim raises serious theological questions. Firstly, there is the charge of mystical subjectivism, something of which Ignatius himself was accused. Secondly, there is the question of whether Ignatius' claim undermines the importance of the Church and sacraments for spirituality. And thirdly, there is the problem of what it means to say that the experience of God can in some sense be "direct" or "immediate" (*unmittelbar*). We have already explored some aspects of the first and third of these difficulties in previous parts of the chapter. In this section, we investigate the background of the notion of an "immediate" experience of God. This will entail an examination of some of Rahner's early patristic writings — works which form a source for his Ignatian reflections. The underlying assumption running throughout these reflections is that the *Exercises* constitute a *mystagogy*, that is to say, they allow a person to experience a radical immediacy to God.[167] But before we return to this claim, we present an overview of Rahner's article in terms of the *tension of opposites* which we mentioned earlier in our introduction to Ignatian spirituality.

One of these tensions is evident in Rahner's presentation of Ignatius' attitude to the Church. This tension has to do with how a person interprets their attachment or devotion to the Church. For Ignatius, as Rahner sees him, such an attachment, necessary though it is, can never be understood in ultimate terms. In fact, he criticizes some Jesuits for having forgotten this fact in their history.[168] Thus, Ignatius

---

[166] Rahner, *Ignatius of Loyola,* 11 (*Ignatius von Loyola,* 10-11). Rahner's Ignatius continues: "All I say is I knew God, nameless and unfathomable, silent and yet near, bestowing himself upon me in his Trinity, I knew God beyond all concrete imaginings... I encountered God ... God himself: I knew God himself, not simply human words describing him" (pp. 11-12).

[167] " 'Mystagogy' means that the *Exercises* concern themselves not merely and not primarily with an extrinsic indoctrination stemming from dogmatic, moral and ascetical insights, but rather evoke and actualize *the* humanity and *the* Christ-directedness, which through transcendentality and grace (in unity), are always given as an intrinsic, total thrust of the one, whole person into 'loving Mystery.' To be sure, this inner thrust anticipates, corresponds to, and is fulfilled by the history of salvation which encounters a person from the outside." Karl Rahner, "Foreword," to Egan, *The Spiritual Exercises and the Ignatian Mystical Horizon,* xiv. See also Egan's article, "Karl Rahner: Theologian of the *Spiritual Exercises,*" *Thought* 67 (1992): 257-70.

[168] "You have not infrequently defended the Church as if she herself were the ultimate, as if she were not finally, if she is true to her own nature, the phenomenon in

expects his followers to both "sentire cum ecclesia," that is, to think, judge and feel with the Church while, at the same time, remaining aware of its many faults, limitations, and its provisional nature.[169] Consequently, a respectful but critical attitude to the actual official Church can in itself be regarded as "devout."[170] Rahner's point here is that Ignatius' devotion to the Church was geared primarily towards his desire "to help souls." In other words, Rahner claims that Ignatius, in his own life, was able to combine both obedient service to, and critical distance from, the Church. Such a synthesis between profound loyalty to, and critical detachment from, the institutional Church is likewise a hallmark of Rahner's spirituality. Inspired by this Ignatian vision, Rahner can then conceive spirituality in terms of a "mysticism of service," despite the inevitable tensions that will always exist between the ecclesiastical institution and the spirit of the Church.

Rahner is also convinced that Ignatius was able to overcome the tension between the emphasis on the Church as institution and the importance of inner spiritual experience. Ignatius, he believes — despite his conflicts with Church officials — had little difficulty reconciling his personal mystical experiences with his desire to be a man of the Church. Rahner then explores this tension between "religious institution" and "inner experience" a little further.[171] Using

which one silently surrenders oneself to God ..." Rahner, *Ignatius of Loyola,* 14 (*Ignatius von Loyola,* 13).

[169] For Ignatius' "Rules for Thinking with the Church," see *The Spiritual Exercises of St Ignatius,* nn. 352-370. It is beyond our scope to treat Ignatius' concept of Church here in detail, though these rules would be a good starting-point for such a study. *Sentido* has been variously translated as sense, reason, feeling. Here, it refers to a "cognition which is basically intellectual but is savoured so repeatedly that it becomes also deeply emotional and 'satisfies the soul' (n. 2). Thus it becomes a habitual attitude of mind, a frame of reference instinctively used to guide one's life." Ganss, *Ignatius of Loyola: The Spiritual Exercises and Selected Works,* 431. We shall return to this ecclesial characteristic of Rahner's spirituality in our final chapter.

[170] Rahner, *Ignatius of Loyola,* 27 (*Ignatius von Loyola,* 27). "Ecclesial" is possibly a better translation of the word "kirchlich" than "devout." This section of the article is entitled "Kirchlichkeit," which in the English translation is given as "Devotion to the Church."

[171] "Religiöse Institution und Erfahrung von innen" is the title of the relevant section. This section of the article, however, with its stress on the universality of grace, is more a reflection of Rahner's insights than those of Ignatius. Rahner, *Ignatius of Loyola,* 15 (*Ignatius von Loyola,* 14).

metaphorical language, he imagines the human heart as earth or soil which can be either unfruitful or fertile. How does the role of the Church fit into this picture? The traditional view, which Rahner considers incomplete, is to see the Church as setting up "vast and complicated irrigation systems to bring water to the land of a person's heart and to make it fruitful through her word, her sacraments, her institutions and practices."[172] If one is to persist with this image, then it needs to be complemented with the image of water coming not only from without, but also from within. There is *also* a "well" — sited in the centre of the human person, and Rahner's point is that there should be no contradiction between this source and the external "irrigation system." Expressed in more theological terms, this metaphor means that any appeal from outside, in God's name, or any channelling of grace from without, is ultimately only of use if it connects with the grace from within.[173] This is the theological reason behind Rahner's claim that God can be encountered in all things, and not only at special "mystical" moments, even if certain situations (e.g., during the time of the *Exercises*) are particularly favourable for such encounters. Hence, the primary task of Ignatius' disciples is presented in terms of

---

[172] Rahner, *Ignatius of Loyola*, 15 (*Ignatius von Loyola*, 14). Rahner has explored the consequences of this image for the pastoral ministry of the Church with Paul M. Zulehner in: *"Denn du kommst unserem Tun mit deiner Gnade zuvor ..." : Zur Theologie der Seelsorge heute. Paul M. Zulehner im Gespräch mit Karl Rahner* (Düsseldorf: Patmos Verlag, 1984), 7-40, esp. p. 32.

[173] "Immer ist Einführung in den Glauben (besser: in seine weiteren reflexen Etappen) ein Verstehenlassen dessen, was im Grunde des Daseins als Gnade (d.h. als absolute Unmittelbarkeit zu Gott) schon erfahren ist." Rahner, "Glaubenszugang," *SM* II: 415. Yet, in pointing to this experience, and in seeking to draw attention to it, Rahner constantly faced the *dilemma* that: "... we either attempt to touch the spirit, and heart of the individual concerned in the most concrete possible way, and in the particular situation which belongs to him or her personally — and in that case an appeal of this kind gives the impression of expressing something subjective or poetic, a mood which is too vague to be verifiable. And then our appeal is open to the objection that after all it cannot be taken seriously on any realistic view at the 'down-to-earth' level of everyday life. Alternatively the appeal in which we point to this experience is formulated in terms of the greatest possible philosophical exactitude and at the strictly conceptual level. In that case we shall be discussing it in such very abstract terms that they are difficult to understand, and we are faced with the objection that we are indulging in mere subtle word-play, so that in the end the discussion is abandoned from sheer weariness." Rahner, "The Experience of God Today," *TI* 11:154-55 (*ST* IX: 166).

helping others to experience God, and all ministry is to be tested to see if it serves this purpose.

Another way of viewing this tension is in terms of the question about the immediate experience of God mentioned at the outset of this section. On the one hand, Rahner describes the Ignatian experience of God as immediate (*unmittelbar*), while, on the other, he assumes that this experience can be mediated (*vermittelt*) in a variety of ways. For example, the *Exercises*, for all their stress on the transcendental experience of God (and Rahner's emphasis on the significance of the consolation without cause), constitute in themselves a categorial mediation of such an experience. The same is true for other mediations — Jesus, the Church, the sacraments, and so on. We have also seen how underlying the Ignatian election is the assumption that *one* possibility from a variety of legitimate possible options "mediates" God's will for the retreatant. Yet, Rahner's Ignatius is a man of transcendental rather than categorial spirituality: the *Exercises* are *ultimately* concerned with letting the Creator and the creature deal directly with each other:

> "Ignatius presupposes as both possible and actual an experience of God which, however many objectified, verbalized moments or preparations or instrumental helps are included, is not identical with a verbalized, conceptual knowledge of God. In the *Exercises* Ignatius wants to lead one to nothing else besides this experience."[174]

Rahner's spiritual testament also provides other variations of this tension of opposites. There is the stress on the *universal* presence of grace, on the one hand, while, on the other hand, Rahner also underscores the importance and necessity of this presence of God becoming more explicit or thematic. The human person — as essentially receptive and relational — is open to the direct experience of God. We discussed the philosophical basis of this Rahnerian vision of the human person in the second and third chapters. Here, the point at stake is that God is not the object but the sustaining "ground" of our experience, present not just *without* (in the Church's work of religious indoctrination) but also *within* the person. This idea then

---

[174] Rahner, "The Immediate Experience of God in the Spiritual Exercises of Saint Ignatius of Loyola," *Karl Rahner in Dialogue*, 175 (*Karl Rahner im Gespräch* 2: 33).

becomes clearer, as we have mentioned, when seen in terms of its implications for the Church's pastoral ministry: the human person is always one who has *already* met God.[175] Thus, the task of the *Exercises,* and any other apostolic activity, is not to "import" grace into the life of the retreatant. Instead, it will presume the apriori "gracedness" (*die apriorische Begnadetheit*) of the human person, and attempt to bring to awareness the mystery of God who has *always* been present in one's life.[176]

The remainder of Rahner's testament outlines the implications of this mysticism of service in terms of a radical form of discipleship. While he acknowledges the plurality of forms of discipleship, he sees the particular Ignatian contribution in its choice of "the discipleship of the poor and humble Jesus."[177] This is more than a pious formulation. This type of discipleship combines a reluctance to accept positions of ecclesiastical power with a preference for remaining on the fringe of society and the Church.[178] The guiding principle here is that of service without power. Drawing on insights of J. B. Metz, Rahner then focuses on the political and social implications of this form of discipleship. It will have a critical sting and be a dangerous memory of Jesus — challenging the sometimes lethargic immobility of the institutional Church.[179] The new asceticism, which we adverted to

---

[175] Referring to the giving of the *Exercises* today, Rahner claims that "it is more vital today than ever before to have such help towards a direct encounter with God (or should one say: towards an understanding of the fact that the human person has already come to meet God (*daß der Mensch Gott immer schon begegnet ist*)." Rahner, *Ignatius of Loyola,* 16 (*Ignatius von Loyola,* 15). Zulehner, commenting on the pastoral consequences of this insight of Rahner, concludes: "Wir dürfen getrost, bei Getauften *und* Ungetauften annehmen, daß in jedem Menschen Gott schon längst am Werk ist, als seine innerste Sehnsucht nach dem ganzen, dem heilen Leben, nach dem Frieden, nach entgrenzter Freiheit, nach letzter Geborgenheit. Wir können annehmen, *daß nicht nur der Mensch nicht ruht, bis er ruht in Gott, sondern daß auch Gott nicht ruht, bis er ruht im Menschen.*" (*Zur Theologie der Seelsorge heute,* 57).

[176] Rahner, Zulehner, *Zur Theologie der Seelsorge heute,* 52.

[177] Rahner, *Ignatius of Loyola,* 21 (*Ignatius von Loyola,* 20).

[178] For Rahner's insistence on "a will to marginality" as a task of Ignatian spirituality, see his "Ignatius of Loyola," *The Great Church Year,* 329-40 (*Das große Kirchenjahr,* 475-91).

[179] See J. B. Metz, *Zeit der Orden. Zur Mystik und Politik der Nachfolge* (Freiburg: Herder, 1977). [ET: *Followers of Christ. The Religious Life and the Church* (London: Burns and Oates, 1978)].

earlier, is now interpreted along the lines of a social responsibility for justice, and not simply understood as a purely private, self-profiting renunciation. Such options, Rahner maintains, give concrete shape to that "dying with Jesus," to that forgetting of self for God's sake, which is the underlying motif of his understanding of Ignatian spirituality.

Rahner concludes his testament by noting the universality of Ignatian spirituality and its relevance for the "post-modern" era. Despite a certain "religious individualism," he thinks that this emphasis on the individual is pertinent today, where "the individual is threatened with decline and extinction in an organized mass."[180] Indeed, Rahner, for some reason, never showed huge enthusiasm for *communal* expressions of spirituality[181] — hence his warning that the individual must never lose him or herself in community. His preference was more for a solitariness before God and a silence in His immediate presence. In this sense, he understands the mystagogy of the *Exercises* primarily as an individual process rather than as a collective one.[182]

---

[180] Rahner, *Ignatius of Loyola,* 37 (*Ignatius von Loyola,* 37). See also his article: "The Spirituality of the Church of the Future," *TI* 20: 143-53 (*ST* XIV: 368-81), and the final section of our second chapter.

[181] In the previous chapter, we discussed and commented on Rahner's interpretation of experiences of the Spirit and of enthusiasm, (Section 2, c, and d). Rahner thinks communal expressions of spirituality, in liturgy, group prayer services, etc., "can also provide the stimulus for this immediate encounter with God. Yet normally, that immediacy to God, (*jene Unmittelbarkeit zu Gott*) which Ignatius directly intends in his *Exercises*, will only be a subliminal, accompanying symptom in other religious practices and liturgies... I do not wish to say that such (a) common liturgy would not contain anything meaningful or correct or is not indispensable. The liturgy can be the preparation for and the final notes of a mystical experience of God such as usually cannot be accomplished in the liturgy, and which Ignatius sets as a goal in the *Exercises.*" Rahner, "The Immediate Experience of God in the Spiritual Exercises of Saint Ignatius of Loyola," *Karl Rahner in Dialogue,* 180 (*Karl Rahner im Gespräch* 2: 39-40).

[182] However, in the context of the discernment of spirits, Rahner also reflected on the relevance of Ignatius' "deliberatio communitaria" for the Church in the post-modern era. Collective acts of decision could be taken by small ecclesial groups after having engaged in a collective discernment of spirits. Thus, the Church is not merely an objective reality, but an active subject that finds expression in a specific community of believers. Rahner, "Modern Piety and the Experience of Retreats," *TI* 16: 145-55 (*ST* XII: 184-97). On the problems inherent in any attempt at communal discernment of spirits, see William A. Barry SJ, *Allowing the Creator*

We have attempted to discuss Rahner's spiritual testament in terms of a tension of opposites which, we believe, characterizes both Ignatian spirituality and Rahner's appropriation of the same.[183] One such tension not mentioned explicitly by Rahner, however, is also relevant to our discussion of his spirituality. This tension concerns the relationship between the *kataphatic* and *apophatic* traditions of spirituality. From what we have seen thus far in our work, it should be apparent that Rahner's spirituality is more oriented towards the apophatic or negative way. This negative way finds its official ecclesiastical warrant in the declaration of the Fourth Lateran Council (1215) that "between Creator and creature no similitude can be expressed without implying a greater dissimilitude."[184] In the second chapter, we saw how this principle finds expression in Rahner's conception of theology as ultimately a "reduction to mystery." And, in this chapter, we discovered that he interprets the Ignatian consolation without cause as an experience of transcendence devoid of all concepts, images and thoughts. It is important to stress, however, that the apophatic way is more than just a process of negation. The "emptiness" of apophatic spirituality prepares the person for the experience of God's loving self-communication — there is, in other words, a movement from negation to *worship*.[185] The kataphatic or affirmative way, on the other hand, is expressed in the First Vatican Council's (1870) assertion that God "can be known with certainty from the

---

to Deal Directly with the Creature: An Approach to the Spiritual Exercises of Ignatius of Loyola (New York/Mahwah, New Jersey: Paulist Press, 1994), 102-112.

[183] In his lucid "portrait" of Rahner's life and work, Karl Lehmann also refers to "that triad of his tension-filled spirituality (*spannungsgeladenen Spiritualität*) that dominated Rahner's thinking and action to the day he died: (1) the restrained passion of a deep personal piety; (2) the constant struggle with objective forms in the church, theology, and obsolete forms of life; and (3) finding God in all things." Karl Lehmann, "Karl Rahner: A Portrait," *The Content of Faith*, 2-3 (*Rechenschaft des Glaubens*, 14*).

[184] Cited from J. Neuner and J. Dupuis, *The Christian Faith in the Doctrinal Documents of the Catholic Church*, rev. ed. (London: Collins, 1982), n. 320 (=DS 806).

[185] "Because the outstanding apophatic mystics *worshipped* the ineffable, incomprehensible God, they experienced that the negative way is more than transsensual and trans-intellectual negation." Harvey D. Egan, "Negative Way," *NDCS*: 704.

things that were created through the natural light of human reason."[186] Applied to spirituality, the kataphatic way affirms that God
is truly manifest in the world: it "emphasizes the use of images and
words, especially those found in scripture, to transport us into the
mystery of faith."[187] In fact, it would be inaccurate to portray Rahner's spirituality as devoid of all kataphatic elements. Rather, his
appropriation of Ignatian spirituality reveals a synthesis of both the
apophatic and the kataphatic approaches.[188] Rahner is aware that no
spirituality can be purely negative — the human person is, after all,
spirit in the *world,* as his early philosophical work sought to demonstrate.

Although Rahner, as far as we can ascertain, does not use the
apophatic/kataphatic terminology, he does discuss the issues with
which we have been grappling in the course of his reflections on the
significance of private revelations.[189] Such revelations are possible *in
principle* for a Christian, because:

> "God as a free personal being can make himself perceptible to the cre-
> ated spirit, not only through his works but also by his free personal
> word ... in such a way that this communication is bound up with a par-
> ticular place and time, with a concrete word or command, with a finite
> reality or truth, and so that it occurs with, or is connected with, the
> 'apparition' of an object presented to the internal or external senses,
> which object represents and manifests God, his will, or the like."[190]

However, Rahner qualifies his above remarks by situating phenomena such as private revelations and visions within the broader framework of God's self-communication to humanity. In this context, private revelations are an unusual expression of this self-communication

---

[186] Neuner and Dupuis, *The Christian Faith,* n. 113 (=DS 3004).

[187] Wilkie Au SJ, *By Way of the Heart: Towards a Holistic Christian Spirituality*
(New York/Mahwah: Paulist Press, 1989), 96.

[188] Commentators who hold this view include: David Tracy, "Recent Catholic
Spirituality: Unity amid Diversity," *Christian Spirituality: Post-Reformation and
Modern,* eds. Louis Dupré and Don E. Saliers, in collaboration with John Meyendorff,
World Spirituality Series (London: SCM, 1989), 151; Harvey D. Egan, *What Are
They Saying About Mysticism?* (New York/Ramsey: Paulist Press, 1982), 106-107.

[189] We cannot here go into Rahner's interpretation of the theological significance
of such private revelations. For this, see his, *Visions and Prophecies,* 7-30 (*Visionen
und Prophezeiungen,* 13-32).

[190] Rahner, *Visions and Prophecies,* 13-14 (*Visionen und Prophezeiungen,* 18-19).

and, he argues, play a "relative," that is to say, a secondary role. Yet, he also maintains that the history of Christianity would be unthinkable without historical "appearances" ("Erscheinungen") of God in created symbols as documented by Scripture. In spite of his emphasis here on the "sign" character of Christianity, Rahner reveals his apophatic leanings in his warning that:

> "... this basic incarnational structure of the unconfused unity of God and his creatures gives us to understand that we can apprehend God in the sign (or in the form of a vision) only if we do not cling to the sign ... as if it were the ultimate reality, God himself. The sign must be welcomed and passed by, grasped and relinquished."[191]

Returning to Ignatian spirituality, we have seen that the *Exercises* offer one of the clearest examples of the kataphatic mystical tradition. Examples referred to already include the finding of God in all things, and the contemplations on the life of Christ.[192] In the next section, we will see how the retreatant, in the "application of the senses," is also encouraged to use his or her imagination in order to better assimilate the particular Christian mystery that is being contemplated.

b. Mystagogy and the Application of the Senses

Up to now, we have noted Rahner's emphasis on the immediate experience of God in the *Exercises*. Linked to this emphasis is his plea for a new pastoral practice based on the retrieval of the ancient notion of "mystagogy." The term mystagogy refers to that process of initiation which leads a person to an experience of mystery. In other

---

[191] Rahner, *Visions and Prophecies*, 14, n. 12 (*Visionen und Prophezeiungen*, 18, n. 12). Nevertheless, Rahner's emphasizes the *relativity* of private revelations and visions. Otherwise, a distorted spirituality emerges that stresses a "pure spiritual transcendence," or the practice of "pure inwardness," in contrast to that emptying of self (as a participation in Christ's kenosis), and the loving service of one's neighbour.

[192] For an Ignatian-inspired discussion of apophatic and kataphatic approaches to prayer, see Au, *By Way of the Heart,* 85-113. Au rightly advocates a healthy balance between the kataphatic and the apophatic in prayer: "We need to oscillate rhythmically between worship and iconoclasm. Worship consists in meeting the living God in our religious experience; iconoclasm involves destroying all the concepts and images we construct to articulate our religious experience to ourselves and others." (p. 97).

words, it involves an initiation into the sacred.[193] Rahner himself describes Christian mystagogy as:

"the effort to mediate to oneself or, more properly, to another in as clear and as comprehensive way as possible the experience of our pre-given pneumatic existence. Christian mystagogy also refers to the attempt to render comprehensible the fact that a person's 'mystical' experience of the Spirit has been historically and irreversibly confirmed in Jesus Christ."[194]

The term makes an early appearance in Rahner's 1961 retreat conferences on the priesthood. He sees the priest as a "mystagogue of personal piety" (*Mystagoge einer personalen Frömmigkeit*), who will initiate people "into a wholly personal piety."[195] A few years later, in the context of "imperatives for the self-realization of the Church,"

---

[193] Etymologically, mystagogy refers to the action of leading (*agein*, to lead) a person who has been initiated (*mystés*). The term began with the traditional religions of Greece and Rome, and was subsequently taken over by the Christian Fathers in the fourth century (e.g., Bishop Cyril of Jerusalem, whose mystagogic homilies (c. AD 350) are among the earliest of the genre. For a helpful treatment of the origin and development of the term, see Enrico Mazza, *Mystagogy: A Theology of Liturgy in the Patristic Age* (New York: Pueblo, 1989) and David Regan, *Experience the Mystery: Pastoral Possibilities for Christian Mystagogy* (London: Geoffrey Chapman, 1994).

[194] (Translation mine). "Christliche Mystagogie ist *das Bemühen* von jemand, sich oder erst recht einem andern *eine möglichst deutliche und reflex ergriffene Erfahrung seiner vorgegebenen pneumatischen Existenz zu vermitteln*. Christliche Mystagogie ist auch der Versuch, dem konkreten Menschen verständlich zu machen, daß seine mystische Geisterfahrung ihm geschichtlich greifbar und irreversibel durch Jesus Christus zugesagt ist." Rahner, Zulehner, *Zur Theologie der Seelsorge heute*, 51. In this section, we are also in debt to some remarks of Fischer, *Gotteserfahrung*, 27-41. See also his *Der Mensch als Geheimnis*, 41-45, 96-97, 189-93, and the "Brief von P. Karl Rahner," 407-408.

[195] Rahner, *Meditations on Priestly Life*, 149-50 (*Einübung priesterlicher Existenz*, 166). The term is also mentioned by Rahner in his earlier historical discussion of the Greek mystics of the fifth to the seventh centuries. In a letter to me (17 September 1996), Herbert Vorgrimler underlined the significance of mystagogy for Rahner's understanding of ministry: "Wenn man bei ihm (Rahner) nach einer Schwerpunktsetzung sucht, dann liegt sie bei der Mystagogie. Diese ist vielleicht — wie ich aus eigenem Erleben seiner Predigten weiß — durch ein öffentliches Reden möglich. Meist aber wird sie nur im Gespräch überzeugend sein. Der Seelsorger Rahner plädiert primär für Individualseelsorge. Seine Vorbehalte gegen Verkündigung in den Medien, durch 'geistliche Kleidung' usw. waren sehr groß. Immer hat er nach dem Tragfähigen, nach Glaube durch intellektuelle Redlichkeit statt durch Emotionen, gesucht."

Rahner speaks again of the importance of a new mystagogy.[196] Mystagogy, thus, is to be understood as a help towards a direct experience of God (*Hilfe zur unmittelbaren Erfahrung Gottes*), and the Ignatian *Exercises* represent one method of attaining this goal, since they:

> "neither indoctrinate nor introduce some extrinsic value system for digestion. They bring to the fore what is most vital, dynamic and immanent in the depths of every human person."[197]

Indeed, from our study thus far, we could conclude that there is a mystagogical undercurrent running throughout Rahner's theological enterprise, which makes itself felt in *both* his spiritual and theological writings.[198]

Underlying the word mystagogy is the Greek term *mystérion* (Latin *mysterium*). What Rahner has in mind here is an introduction to the "mystery" or secret, hidden in God for long ages and now revealed in Christ (1 Cor 2:1-2). Thus, he places himself alongside Paul in depicting the basic characteristic of mystagogy as an introduction into the mystery of God's love in Christ. Paul equates "the mystery of God" with the crucified Christ, and the primary characteristic of mystagogy or initiation is that it introduces into this mystery of God's love in Christ. Indeed, Paul also identified his "gospel" with "Christ crucified" (1 Cor 1:17, 23-24), and considered himself as a steward dispensing the wealth of this mystery (1 Cor 4:1). This gospel now

---

[196] Rahner explains the urgency of such a mystagogy as follows: "Der Mensch von heute wird auch in der Dimension seiner theoretischen, satzhaften Überzeugungen nur dann ein Glaubender sein, wenn er eine wirklich echte, persönliche religiöse Erfahrung gemacht hat, immer neu macht und darin die Kirche eingeweiht wird. Eine bloße Vermittlung satzhafter, kategorialer Lehrsätze des christlichen Dogmas genügt nicht." Rahner, "Imperative für den Selbstvollzug der Kirche," *HPTh* II/1: 269-70.

[197] Egan, *The Spiritual Exercises and the Ignatian Mystical Horizon*, 31-32.

[198] Our discussion of this claim began in Chapter Two, 3, a, "The Link between Theology and Spirituality." In this chapter it has been substantiated with our exploration of the Ignatian influence on Rahner's thinking. Roman Bleistein makes a similar point in his remarks about the significance of the notion of mystagogy in Rahner's theology: "Die Sache, um die es K. Rahner ging, war schon länger in seinem Denken vorhanden: ein existentieller Ansatz, eine Theologie der letzten Betroffenheit, eine spirituelle Orientierung seiner ganzen Theologie, ..." Roman Bleistein, "Mystagogie in den Glauben. Karl Rahners Anliegen und die Religionspädagogik," *Gottes Weisheit im Mysterium. Vergessene Wege christlicher Spiritualität*, ed. Arno Schilson (Mainz: Grünewald, 1989), 287.

reveals God's plan (Rahner would call this God's universal salvific will), "hidden in him from all eternity (1 Cor 2:7) to bring humanity, Gentiles as well as Jews, to share in the salvific inheritance of Israel, now realized in Christ Jesus."[199]

Similar understandings of mystagogy are to be found in the Patristic Fathers of the fourth century. One example is Maximus the Confessor (d. 662), considered by some as the Father of Byzantine theology. He wrote a *Mystagogia* in an attempt to draw spiritual lessons from liturgical rites such as baptism. Maximus was not primarily concerned with offering a theological commentary on the rites themselves, but with arousing the moral and spiritual sense of his hearers. At the time of his writing, many were leaving the Church in disillusionment, and the aim of his writing and homilies was to recall such Christians to the fervour of their earlier faith. So, even in patristic centuries, mystagogy was practised as a pastoral strategy oriented towards those who had grown indifferent towards the Church, if not towards Christ. In sum, for Maximus, mystagogy consisted:

> "in helping the Christian to gain knowledge (*gnosis*) of the Mystery through contemplating it with the spiritual senses which function as a seeing and hearing which, however, have no visible or audible object. This spiritual sensing can only be accomplished through seeking the Mystery where it is to be found: in creation; in Scripture; in the liturgy, as mediated by symbols. Mystagogy is the means by which this is done."[200]

While a detailed discussion of the early history of mystagogy is beyond our scope, our contention is that this notion runs right through the patristic treatment of Christian initiation. Moreover, the practice of mystagogy is a counterbalance to an exclusively doctrinal catechesis. In contrast to the latter, the mystagogical approach makes use of a whole variety of ways in which we perceive and communicate, including seeing, feeling, and hearing. In the remainder of this section we shall show that Rahner's under-standing of mystagogy is closely linked to his early historical studies of the role of the spiritual senses

---

[199] Joseph Fitzmyer, "Pauline Theology," *NJBC* [82: 33]: 1389.

[200] Regan, *Experience the Mystery,* 21. For a similar view, see Rahner's discussion of Maximus in *Aszese und Mystik,* 240-44, where mystagogy is described as "a mystical explanation of the liturgy" (p. 240).

in Origen, Bonaventure, and in the *Exercises* themselves.[201] Moreover, these studies shed light on the key concept of the immediate
experience of God, an idea crucial to Rahner's Ignatian interpretation,
and evident also in his Spiritual Testament.

The starting-point of Rahner's study of the spiritual senses in Origen and in Bonaventure is that the saints and mystics, in seeking to
express their experience, need to resort to imaginative language. They
are attempting "to express the inexpressible," and they speak of a
spiritual sight, hearing, taste, etc., which they considered to be an
accurate, if incomplete, account of the reality they had experienced.[202]
Rahner regards Origen as the first to have formulated a doctrine of the
spiritual senses. This is a doctrine which uses partly imaginative,
partly literal expressions such as "to touch God" or "to open the eyes
of the heart" (Eph 1:18). Origen's point was that, over and above our
bodily sense faculties, we also have a sense for the divine. According
to Rahner, Origen used Scripture as the main source for his teaching
on the spiritual senses. His exegesis, moreover, is largely allegorical,
and he takes Proverbs 5:2 as a key scriptural text in this context.[203]

---

[201] Karl Rahner, "The 'Spiritual Senses' according to Origen," and "The Doctrine
of the 'Spiritual Senses' in the Middle Ages," *TI* 16: 81-134 (*ST* XII: 111-72). These
articles first appeared in French: "Le début d'une doctrine des cinq sens spirituels
chez Origène," *Revue d'Ascétique et de Mystique* 13 (1932): 113-45; "La doctrine
des 'sens spirituels' au Moyen-Age, en particulier chez saint Bonaventura," *Revue
d'Ascétique et de Mystique* 14 (1933): 263-99. See also his "Der Begriff der ecstasis
bei Bonaventura," *Zeitschrift für Aszese und Mystik* 9 (1934): 1-19. Fischer, *Gotteserfahrung*, 31, also refers to a hand-written script of Frater K. Rahner entitled "Die
Anwendung der Sinne in den Geistlichen Übungen des hl. Ignatius," dated October
1926. However, it is more likely that this essay comes from the pen of his brother,
Hugo. See Roman Siebenrock's review of Fischer's book in *Zeitschrift für Katholische Theologie* 110 (1988): 115-116.

[202] Rahner, "The 'Spiritual Senses' according to Origen," *TI* 16: 81 (*ST* XII:
111). It would be beyond our competence to attempt an evaluation of Rahner's interpretation of Origen. Our aim is to trace a link between "mystagogy," the "prayer of
the senses," and the "direct experience of God," which we maintain are fundamental
components of Rahner's understanding of spirituality. Indeed, these ideas, as Karl-
Heinz Neufeld claims (art. cit., 81, n. 1), point to a line of thought operative, albeit in
a concealed way, throughout his work. Rahner mentions on a number of occasions in
the article (pp. 90, 103) that he is not pretending to offer a comprehensive exposition
of Origen's teaching.

[203] In relation to the doctrine of the spiritual senses, this passage was an important
starting-point for the Fathers of the early Greek Church. The translated Greek Septu-
agint version reads: "My son, hold fast to my wisdom, incline your ear to my words,

Origen also set the pattern for the traditional allegorical interpretation of the Song of Songs. Ever since his interpretation, this has become *the* book for mystics, even if it is now accepted that the Song was not written as an allegory. In fact, Origen believed that, in addition to our five bodily senses, we possess five more spiritual senses. He took unbelief to be a sign of the lack of the spiritual senses, while some Christians may only develop one of their spiritual senses. It is only the "perfect," the "blessed," Origen maintained, who have full control over, and the use of, all their spiritual faculties. These spiritual senses or faculties are developed both through human effort, especially prayer (which leads to a liberation from domination by the physical faculties), and divine grace.

At this point, Rahner returns to a theme which has been a frequent concern of his in his spiritual writings. It is the question of "stages" or "levels" in the spiritual life. Without going into the details of Origen's conception of how these stages of the spiritual life are constituted, Rahner's suspicion is that such a doctrine leads, ineluctably, to two classes of Christian. One class is satisfied with a type of minimal observance of the commandments, while the other achieves perfection in a contemplative life based on a special revelation of the word of God.[204] We have already discussed the fundamental anti-élitism of Rahner's conception of spirituality, its basis in the fundamental equality of all Christians and their *universal* call to holiness as advocated by Vatican II (*Lumen Gentium*, 42). Moreover, we noted how his conception of spirituality led to his advocating an "everyday mysticism." Yet, despite the correctness of Rahner's basic point about the need to move away from a two-tiered system of spirituality, where only some are called to "states of perfection," will there not always be a need for inspiring examples of Christians, traditionally called

that you may keep a good intention: I will give you a sense-perception (*aisthésin*) of my lips". Cited from Hugo Rahner, *Ignatius the Theologian*, 198.

[204] The gnostic overtones associated with this second class of Christians can be traced to an article by Jules Lebreton, "Die Stufen der religiösen Erkenntnis nach Origenes," *Recherches de Science Religieuse* 12 (1922): 265-96, to which Rahner refers at this point in his discussion of Origen's conception of the spiritual life, "The 'Spiritual Senses' according to Origen," *TI* 16: 91, n. 79 (*ST* XII: 123, n. 79). Despite his obvious admiration for Origen, a similar mild criticism is evident in *Aszese und Mystik*, 74.

saints, who live out the decision of faith in a most radical fashion? We have to go elsewhere in Rahner to discover how he deals with this issue. We shall return to it again in our final chapter. Briefly, we can say that Rahner, in later years, came to appreciate the urgent need for a contemporary form of political sanctity. Such a political holiness, developed chiefly by theologians of liberation, arises from an unconditional love for "the least of the brethren" (Mt 25: 40), and, in this, follows the poor and suffering Jesus to the point of death.[205]

Rahner's next major treatment of the spiritual senses is to be found in his article, "The Doctrine of the 'Spiritual Senses' in the Middle Ages," where he focuses on the contribution of Bonaventure.[206] Why is Rahner's essay on Bonaventure relevant in the context of his appropriation of Ignatian mysticism? We have seen how Rahner has interpreted consolation without previous cause in terms of an utter receptivity or openness to God, that is to say, as a non-conceptual experience of God. His concern though, is also to discover the roots of this interpretation of Ignatius in the history of the theory of mystical experience, where "there is an experience of the love of God which occurs without the intellect having a share in it."[207] He considers Bonaventure's mystical theory a significant example in this regard. Like Origen, Bonaventure speaks of three stages of the spiritual life: beginning (purification), development (enlightenment) and perfection. It is in the final stage of perfection that the spiritual senses come into play. The soul, which has lost the delicacy of these inward senses through sin is able to regain them in Christ and through prayer:

> "And once they are attained the soul beholds Christ, hears him, becomes aware of him through his pleasant fragrance, savours him and embraces him. But this can be grasped only by him who receives this

---

[205] On this, see Karl Rahner, "Dimensions of Martyrdom: A Plea for the Broadening of a Classical Concept," *Concilium* 163 (1983): 9-11, and his *Politische Dimensionen des Christentums. Ausgewählte Texte zu Fragen der Zeit*, ed. Herbert Vorgrimler (Munich: Kösel, 1986), passim.

[206] Rahner, "The Doctrine of the 'Spiritual Senses' in the Middle Ages," *TI* 16: 104-134 (*ST* XII: 137-72).

[207] Rahner, *The Dynamic Element in the Church*, 134, n. 28 (*Das Dynamische in der Kirche*, 117, n. 42).

grace of prayer, for this is less a matter of intellectual consideration than of loving experience. Thus at this stage (of prayer) the soul has now won back the interior senses, so that it may behold the supreme beauty, hear the supreme harmony, breathe in the same fragrance, savour the supreme sweetness and touch the supreme delight."[208]

Bonaventure maintained that the five spiritual senses were operations of both the intellect and the will. Spiritual sight and hearing were closely associated with the intellect; taste, smell and touch were related to the will. Although Bonaventure's theory sounds rather forced and artificial to modern ears, Rahner sees in Bonaventure a remarkable attempt to describe the specific character and sublime heights of mystical experience. In Bonaventure's scheme, the closest possible union of a person with God in this life occurs through a direct experience of God called "ecstasy." The notion of ecstasy is not to be equated with the beatific vision; neither is it a type of intellectual knowledge of God. Rather, it is a "feeling God himself," a "sentire Deum *in se*," and, as Rahner says, "it is a question of a mysterious experience, not of intellectual knowledge."[209] In other words, the emphasis is on "sentire," a kind of spiritual touch, rather than on "cognoscere" (knowledge). For Rahner's Bonaventure, this union of the soul with God is realized in what Bonaventure calls the "apex affectus." The "apex affectus" designates the innermost centre of the human person, from which both the intellect and will proceed. As the highest and most interior element in the soul, the "apex affectus" belongs to a deeper level of reality than the

---

[208] Bonaventure, *The Soul's Journey Into God*, ch. 4, n. 3, cited from Hugo Rahner, *Ignatius the Theologian*, 202. [Both Rahner brothers quote from the critical ten volume Quaracchi edition of the works of Bonaventure (1882-1902)]. For Bonaventure, the soul in a state of grace has three modes of operation: through the virtues, the gifts of the Holy Spirit, and the blessings of beatitude. These three modes of operation correspond to the three stages of the spiritual life. Thus, "the perfect person enjoys the sevenfold gifts of the blessings of beatitude and reaches the state of profound peace." Rahner, "The Doctrine of the 'Spiritual Senses' in the Middle Ages," *TI* 16: 111 (*ST* XII: 145).

[209] "Es handelt sich um eine dunkle Erfahrung, nicht um eine Erkenntnis des Intellekts." Rahner, "The Doctrine of the 'Spiritual Senses' in the Middle Ages," *TI* 16: 120 (*ST* XII: 155). It is beyond our scope here to discuss Rahner's treatment of similar issues in, for example, Evagrius Ponticus, or Gregory of Nyssa. On this, see his *Aszese und Mystik*, 97-109, 133-45.

intellect.[210] Further, the "passing over into God in ecstatic contemplation" can only be reached through an "affection," where all intellectual activity is left behind.[211] The understanding of the intellect operative here is "that love is the perfection of knowledge itself."[212] Moreover, since this experience of direct union with God does not involve the intellect, it is an obscure or dark experience; it will only reach its ultimate fulfilment in the beatific vision.[213] Although Rahner

---

[210] "Die ecstasis ist die dunkle, sich im apex affectus allein vollziehende Erfahrung unmittelbarer Liebesvereinigung mit Gott." Rahner, "Der Begriff der ecstasis bei Bonaventura," *Zeitschrift für Aszese und Mystik* 9 (1934): 15. See also, Rahner, "The Doctrine of the 'Spiritual Senses' in the Middle Ages," *TI* 16: 124 (*ST* XII: 160), and Fischer, *Der Mensch als Geheimnis*, 41-43. For a comparison of Rahner and von Balthasar, see Stephen Fields, "Balthasar and Rahner on the Spiritual Senses," *Theological Studies* 57 (1996): 224-41.

[211] Bonaventure, *The Soul's Journey Into God*, ch. 7, n. 3. He continues: "In this passing over, if it is to be perfect, all intellectual activities must be left behind and the height of our affection must be totally transferred and transformed into God" (n. 4). [We have cited here the English translation by Ewert Cousins, based on the Quaracchi edition: Bonaventure, *The Soul's Journey Into God, The Tree of Life, The Life of St Francis,* trans. and ed. Ewert Cousins, Classics of Western Spirituality Series (New York: Paulist Press, 1978), 113].

[212] Rahner, "The Concept of Mystery in Catholic Theology," *TI* 4: 44 (*ST* IV: 61). In this lecture Rahner explores the relationship between mystery and knowledge. He does this by developing the mutual inter-relationship (*perichoresis*) between knowledge and love: "we must understand the act of knowing in such a way that it will explain why knowledge can only exist in a being when and in so far as that one being realizes itself by an act of love... In so far as the reason is more than reason, when it is understood as a potentiality only to be actuated in love, then it must indeed be the faculty which welcomes the greater sight unseen, the faculty of simple rapture, of submissive dedication, of loving ecstasy" (p. 43). Commenting on this, Fischer remarks: "Es handelt sich bei dieser Deutung der Liebe als Vermögen zum Geheimnis um eine der frühsten Grundeinsichten oder Grundintentionen Rahners, die wiederum — in letzter Instanz — von Ignatius angeregt worden sein dürfte." Fischer, *Der Mensch als Geheimnis*, 192. See also Juan Carlos Scannone, "Die Logik des Existentiellen und Geschichtlichen nach Karl Rahner," *Wagnis Theologie*, ed. Vorgrimler, 82-98, esp. 91-92.

[213] Bonaventure's account of the experience of God can be aptly captured, Rahner believes, with the term "contact," whose two distinguishing characteristics are directness and darkness. Rahner, "The Doctrine of the 'Spiritual Senses' in the Middle Ages," *TI* 16: 127 (*ST* XII: 163). Bonaventure's description of loving God as involving an "in caligine sentire Deum" provides the background to the apophatic thread running throughout Rahner's writings on spirituality. Thus, in 1966, he speaks of a mystical approach (or mystagogy) that imparts the correct 'image of God' — that "God is essentially the inconceivable (*der Unbegreifliche*) ... (This) mystical approach ... must teach us in the concrete to maintain a constant

does not go into the matter, we see parallels here between Bonaventure's doctrine and Ignatius' language, where the notion of "sentido," of "felt-knowledge" is also in evidence.[214] Both Bonaventure and Ignatius are dealing here with a direct experience of God based on the distinction between "cognoscere" and "sentire." In our discussion of Ignatian consolation, we noted how this was an "objectless" experience, or a pure experience of transcendence, where a person is deeply drawn affectively towards God.[215] Indeed, Ignatius' earliest disciples did not hesitate to interpret their founder's teaching on the Application of the Senses along the lines of Bonaventure's mystical theory.[216]

What was Ignatius' teaching? In his *Spiritual Exercises* (nn. 121, 133, 227), Ignatius describes a method of meditative prayer which consists in applying the five senses to bear on the subject-matter

closeness to this God; to say 'thou" to him, *to commit ourselves to his silence and darkness,* not to be anxious lest we may lose him by the very fact of calling him by a name ..." Rahner, "Christian Living Formerly and Today," *TI* 7: 15 (*ST* VII: 23), (italics mine). In other words, Rahner believed that a "docta ignorantia" (also a Bonaventurean notion) or a "learned ignorance" is an essential component of spirituality. Rahner, "Zur Spiritualität gehört eine gelehrte Unwissenheit," *Karl Rahner im Gespräch* 2: 206-213. For the theological implications of this intuition, see our reflections on the relation between spirituality and theology in Chapter Two, 3, a.

[214] See Schwerdtfeger, *Gnade und Welt*, 315-21.

[215] Although Rahner, *The Dynamic Element in the Church*, 134-35 (*Das Dynamische in der Kirche*, 117), describes the characteristic of this experience as "its absence of object" ("gegenstandslos"), it might be better to describe it with Fischer as "übergegenständlich," (i.e., "beyond the representational"). "Dunkel ist diese Erfahrung, weil sie gegenstandslos oder besser gesagt übergegenständlich ist... Diese sogenannte reine Transzendenzerfahrung beseitigt nicht den Gegenstand (z.B. einer Betrachtung der Christusgeheimnisse oder auch einer 'Wahl,' einer religiösen Lebensentscheidung), sondern sie läßt diesen ... gleichsam feiner und durchsichtiger werden, transparent auf Gott selbst hin, so daß der menschliche Geist zu sich selbst findet als reine, unbegrenzte Bejahung Gottes." Fischer, *Gotteserfahrung*, 37.

[216] Hugo Rahner, *Ignatius the Theologian*, 204 refers here to the interpretation given to the Application of the Senses by Nadal and Polanco in the Directory of 1599. In the following paragraphs we are indebted to some illuminating remarks of Hugo Rahner on the Application of the Senses (pp. 181-213). [Jéronimo Nadal (1507-1580), from Majorca, joined the Jesuits in Rome in 1545, and played a major role in the consolidation and institutionalization of the Society. Juan de Polanco was appointed as secretary to Ignatius in 1547 and was directly involved in the publication of Ignatius' writings].

of contemplation. The Latin rendering of the original Spanish text is *applicatio sensuum* — hence the term Application of the Senses. Although it is only one part of the Ignatian technique of meditation, it is a most delicate and sensitive form of prayer. In its highest form, the Application of the Senses is the very essence of *sentir* — the feeling for things of God. According to Hugo Rahner, there are two distinct schools of thought concerning Ignatius' teaching in this matter. The first school sees in the Application of the Senses a very simple, almost naive, form of prayer which can be carried out by almost anyone. It is not a discursive method — there is little reasoning or drawing of conclusions — but rather, it is "a more restful manner of absorbing in an affective and more passive way the fruit of the previous contemplations of the day."[217] This method of prayer is less tiring and is thus more suitable to the quiet of the evening. The second school, however, believes the Ignatian Application of the Senses to be a sublime form of prayer which can only be properly carried out by a few. After the meditations of the day, this prayer would take place in the evening because at that time the soul would be more open to divine things. The nerves of the soul would, so to speak, have been laid bare, "so that they are able to react sensitively to the light, the words, the fragrance and the very shape of divine things, in the same way as the nerves of the body, with a spontaneity which does not need to be learnt."[218] While the distinguishing characteristic of the first school is a certain childlike simplicity, and that of the second the beginnings of a mystical technique, we should not see these two interpretations either as mutually exclusive or contradictory.

[217] See Ganss, *Ignatius of Loyola: The Spiritual Exercises and Selected Works*, 403, who also refers to the 1599 Directory (ch. 20, n. 3) in describing this method of mental prayer as "not discursive, but merely rests in the sensible qualities of things, such as the sights, sounds, and the like, and finds in them enjoyment, delight, and spiritual profit."

[218] Hugo Rahner, *Ignatius the Theologian*, 191. When Ignatius in the *Exercises* (nn. 121-125) speaks of applying the five senses to the contemplation of the incarnation, the nativity, etc., he does not provide any theoretical explanation of the spiritual senses. He merely alludes to the five bodily senses assuming that anyone with some experience of prayer would know what he meant.

Initially, the first school of interpretation gained approval. The official Directory of 1599 advocated the suitability of the Application of the Senses for imaginative people, but at the same time it emphasized that this prayer technique leads of itself to a higher form of knowledge. This higher form of knowledge enables the events of salvation to become "present" to the mind. For example, it could take the form of a vivid rendering present of different events and episodes in the life of Jesus, enabling a "writing of Christ's life in the heart."[219] In effect, this method of prayer attempts to put the history of salvation into the present tense. We are now beginning to move away from the simple "imaginative" interpretation towards the view of the second school which considered the Application of the Senses as a form of contemplation. The ultimate end of all prayer for Ignatius was that the soul would feel (*sentido*) the presence of God, thus gaining a "feel" of what God wants of me in my life. In this context, the Application of the Senses can be understood as an attempt to restore this spiritualized sensibility lost to us because of sin, and leading the retreatant deeper into the mystery of union with God.

In sum, it is possible to see in the Ignatian Application of the Senses a sublime form of prayer which echoes Bonaventure's own teaching on the subject. With both Bonaventure and Ignatius, as Rahner interprets them, we are dealing with a "sentire Deum in se," an immediacy of God's presence, which is difficult to translate into teachable maxims other than in images suggested by immediate sense impressions. In Ignatius, this "direct" contact with God finds expression in the notion of consolation; in Bonaventure, in the notion of ecstasy or spiritual touch. Further, with Ignatius we have in the highest form of the Application of the Senses a *synthesis* of the mind and the heart, of reason and imagination.[220] Affectivity and understanding

[219] Hugo Rahner, *Ignatius the Theologian*, 193. For a modern attempt to describe this kataphatic praying with our senses, see Au, *By Way of the Heart*, 103-105. Ignatius himself, in his introductory observations to the *Exercises* (n. 2), underlines the affective foundation of all genuine prayer: "For it is not much knowledge that fills and satisfies the soul, but the intimate understanding and relish of the truth."

[220] Of course, it would be to misunderstand Rahner's interpretation of Ignatius were one to conclude that a person can *only* have a real experience of God when this takes the form of an immediate awareness or strong feeling of God's presence. God is not only to be found in experiences of consolation. We have already discussed in

go hand in hand, and lead to action. In the *Exercises* (n. 1), this consists in the soul ridding itself of all inordinate attachments and, subsequently, in the discovery of God's will. In other words, for Ignatius, no method of prayer exists for its own sake. Rather, the retreatant is to put what he or she has contemplated into action. Thus, the Application of the Senses is more than forming ideas in the mind; it is "open to possible influence from above and provides a point of application for contemplative graces which lead the exercitant deeper into the mystery of union with God."[221] Finally, it is towards such a synthesis of mind and heart — resulting in a decision or choice — that the exercise of the Application of the Senses is oriented.

We have shown how Rahner believes that the Ignatian Application of the Senses can be reconciled with Bonaventure's mystical theory. We have also seen that Rahner's own preferred term in his spiritual testament for the immediate experience of God is not so much ecstasy (Bonaventure), or consolation (Ignatius), but mystagogy. Mystagogy, as the process of initiation into an immediate, personal experience of God, lies at the heart of his interpretation of the *Exercises*. It is not a question simply of intellectual knowledge but more of a "felt-knowledge" (*sentire*).[222] Assuming Rahner's basic interpretation to be correct, we shall now look at some of the consequences for Christian spirituality today. Our broad agreement with Rahner's approach does not imply, though, that his view of the spiritual life (particularly in his early writings) is without its inherent dangers. However, it is in our final chapter that we shall pursue a more detailed evaluation of his conception of spirituality.[223]

Chapter Two the less spectacular "mysticism of everyday life," where a person tries to love God even though no response seems to come from the divine silence, where one seeks to love others even though no echo of gratefulness is heard in return, where one bears the freely accepted burdens of responsibility even when this offers no apparent promise of earthly success. See Rahner, *The Spirit in the Church*, 11-22 (*Erfahrung des Geistes*, 24-45).

[221] Hugo Rahner, *Ignatius the Theologian*, 205.

[222] For a development of a similar idea, that is, reason (*ratio*), and its relationship to love along more theological lines, see Rahner, "The Concept of Mystery in Catholic Theology," *TI* 4: 36-48 (*ST* IV: 51-66).

[223] Nevertheless, we have already indicated some difficulties with Rahner's Ignatian interpretation in this chapter. See our "Interim Appraisal," in Section 2, c.

c. Conclusion: Towards a Mystagogical Spirituality

This chapter has attempted to capture the core experience at the heart of Rahner's interpretation of the *Spiritual Exercises*. Regardless of what words we use to describe this experience (consolation, myst-agogy, etc), the *Exercises* have to do with a *personal encounter with God,* and the *consequences* which ensue from such an encounter. Underlying our approach is the commonly held view that Ignatius himself personally encountered the Lord, and that the *Exercises* are, in effect, the result of his own spiritual experiences.[224] Although we only alluded to some of the more significant spiritual experiences in the life of Ignatius, our study has revealed what Rahner considers to be the most important Ignatian contribution to the Church, namely, that the Christian can experience God directly in some genuine sense.[225] Alongside this insight, is the realization that it belongs to God's very nature to be committed to humanity and its history. While this second point may not be particularly Ignatian, the genius of Ignatius was to show how this reality can be *experienced* in one's prayer life. We can encapsulate these two points as "the *experience* of God acting in our *history.*"[226] Several implications then ensued for our understanding of spirituality, and we will now, by way of a sum-mary, gather these together.

Firstly, we saw how, by reflecting on the alternating experiences of consolation and desolation experienced in prayer during the course of the *Exercises*, a person can come to discern what God is saying to him or her in the particular circumstances of their lives. It is true, of

---

[224] Thus, Bakker, *Freiheit und Erfahrung,* 269 (following Louis Peeters), can claim that the best commentary on the *Exercises* is the life of Ignatius.

[225] In this context, Bakker, *Freiheit und Erfahrung,* 64 asks: "... ob der Nach-druck auf diesem Erfahrungselement, diesem Sich-persönlich-angesprochen wissen, ... nicht vielleicht charakteristisch für ignatianische Spiritualität genannt werden kann." For an attempt to correlate Ignatius' conversion experiences with key points in the dynamics of the *Exercises*, see Walter L. Farrell, "The Background of the *Spiritual Exercises* in the Life of St. Ignatius of Loyola," *A New Introduction to the Spiritual Exercises of St. Ignatius,* 25-39. We are also indebted here to the insightful comments of John E. Dister, "The Core Experience of the *Spiritual Exercises* and Ignatian Spirituality Today," 107-114 in the same volume.

[226] Dister, "The Core Experience of the *Spiritual Exercises* and Ignatian Spirituality Today," 107.

course, that many people arrive almost intuitively, as it were, at an "existential decision" concerning a certain course of action, without any help from Ignatius. But Rahner's contention is that the distinctive Ignatian contribution lay in the development of a careful methodology for coming more clearly to such discernment. We next explored Rahner's interpretation of this methodology in the context of Ignatius' "Rules for the Discernment of Spirits," and of the description of the "Three Times of Election." In fact, Rahner went on to develop an existential ethics which was inspired by Ignatius' teaching on election or choice in the *Exercises*.[227] Underlying this development was the conviction that Ignatius' instructions on the election are not meant exclusively for the time of the *Exercises*. They can guide us not only in making critically important decisions at other times, but also in making ordinary, everyday decisions. For the core of Ignatian spirituality is concerned with striving to achieve a pure heart, a heart suffused with one love for God and neighbour, and so to be able to find God in all things.[228]

Secondly, our study of Rahner's appropriation of Ignatian spirituality convinces us of the importance of a sensitivity to the Holy Spirit in everyday life. The challenge here is to achieve a balance between the excesses of "illumination" (private visions, revelations, and the dangers of what Rahner calls "pure inwardness"[229]), and a concern for history, for concrete service of our neighbour. This rather general principle was given more explicit focus in our discussion of the tensions inherent in coming to an Ignatian-inspired decision. It is a question of combining both openness in faith to the promptings of the Spirit with the responsible use of reason. Indeed, we drew attention to the ever greater role played by human reason in the interpretation of the Ignatian election.[230]

---

[227] Rahner, "On the Question of a Formal Existential Ethics," *TI* 2: 217-34 (*ST* II: 227-46).

[228] Toner, "Discernment in the *Spiritual Exercises*," 71.

[229] Rahner, *Visions and Prophecies*, 14, n. 12 (*Visionen und Prophezeiungen*, 18, n. 12). For our discussion of Rahner's understanding of the "experience of the Spirit" and the associated phenomenon of religious enthusiasm, see section two of Chapter Three.

[230] However, it has been remarked that there is little mention of the Holy Spirit in the *Exercises*. At the time of Ignatius, there was a certain "Spiritphobia," with the

Thirdly, and following on the above, is that although there is a quite *personal* experience of God at the heart of Rahner's conception of spirituality, this is not synonymous with a *private* experience. He has on more than one occasion drawn attention to the deleterious effects for Christianity, of the focus on individual sanctification, for example, the neglect of socio-political issues.[231] This notion of spirituality as at once both personal and relational is, we believe, also Ignatian-inspired. Although some people may have difficulty with the feudal imagery and military language of the *Exercises*, it cannot be denied that Ignatius' aim in writing was to create disciples. In other words, Ignatius was not solely interested in personal conversion but in releasing a man or a woman for action (n. 145). Rahner would, no doubt, agree with Joseph De Guibert's description of Ignatian spirituality as a "spirituality of service" rather than as the solitary preoccupation with one's individual spiritual life.[232] This service of God consists of two factors which are united, namely, a logic of existential knowledge (interpreted by Rahner in the context of the Ignatian guidelines for making an election) and a passionate love for Christ (which, for Rahner, is the aim of the meditations on the life of Jesus). Thus, we are dealing here with a combination, or better, a synthesis of enthusiasm and reason, of heart and understanding.

Fourthly, we saw the prominent role Rahner gives to the notion of indifference or detachment in spirituality. In the *Exercises*, detachment is held out as an ideal enabling us to be both moved by, and respond to, God's Spirit in our lives. Although it can be misunderstood in terms of a resigned passivity or as emotional detachment, this is not what Ignatius meant. Rather, it is the ability to contextualize

Inquisition not particularly receptive to those who claimed to have a direct and personal experience of the Spirit! Whether this was a factor in Ignatius' relative silence on the Holy Spirit or not, it is clear that the role of the Spirit in the *Exercises* is more that of an umpire than that of a messenger. It is the Holy Spirit who gives the power to *discern* between different spirits (1 Cor 12:10; 1 Cor 2:14-16). Tad Dunne, "The Cultural Milieu of the *Spiritual Exercises*," *A New Introduction to the Spiritual Exercises of St. Ignatius,* 19-23.

[231] For example, see his interview, "Following Christ Today," *Karl Rahner in Dialogue*, 181-85 (*Karl Rahner im Gespräch* 2: 41-47).

[232] De Guibert, *The Jesuits: Their Spiritual Doctrine and Practice,* 174-75. See also n. 55.

one's life in the light of a greater purpose.[233] For Rahner, indifference is the freedom conferred by the Spirit of God Himself, an attitude of interior detachment. In effect, it is the acknowledgement that God is the "always greater" One, freeing us to choose "what is more conducive to the end for which we are created" (n. 23), that is, God's greater praise and service.

Fifthly, Rahner's appropriation of Ignatian spirituality encompasses both rational *and* affective elements. Indeed, the retreatant is expected to be *both* active and passive. A genuine spirituality will not neglect the significant role played by affectivity and the emotions in Christian life. This was seen to be one of the strengths of the Ignatian Application of the Senses: it is a prayer method involving not only our mind, but also our imagination, senses and feelings. Despite Rahner's reservations about the contemporary turn to the East in search of new forms of meditation, one reason why these have proved so attractive is their incorporation of the principle that it is with the *whole* body that one prays. In contrast to the old divisions of body-soul, nature-supernature, the Application of the Senses reminds us, too, that it is the *whole* person who encounters God.[234]

Sixthly, and finally, we have noted how seriously Rahner took the Ignatian axiom of the "always greater" God. This gives his spirituality a strong apophatic slant, with a consistent emphasis on the ineffability of the divine mystery. Although Rahner has illustrated how the doctrine of the spiritual senses represents a locus for the experience of God, this experience is, at its most intense, "a purely non-conceptual experience of transcendence without imagery."[235] Every genuine

---

[233] William Thompson, "Renewed Interest in the Discernment of Spirits," *The Ecumenist* 13 (1975): 54-59.

[234] "In diese Dynamik des 'Gott-Schauens' ist der ganze Mensch eingeborgen: Angefangen von der Sinneserfahrung, weitergehend zu Verinnerlichung (Internalisierung) in den 'Sinn' (der Bedeutung für den Menschen) hinein; ... Unterscheidungen wie Leib-Seele-Geist, Natur-Übernatur, Körper-Seele, Aktivität-Passivität sind gegenüber dieser Dynamik nachträgliche Versuche etwas greifbar zu machen, was letztlich nur vollzogen werden kann." Josef Sudbrack, "Die 'Anwendung der Sinne' als Angelpunkt der Exerzitien," *Ignatianisch. Eigenart und Methode der Gesellschaft Jesu*, eds. Michael Sievernich and Günter Switek (Freiburg: Herder, 1990), 112.

[235] "... (eine) rein gegenstandslose Transzendenzerfahrung bildloser Art ..." Rahner, *The Dynamic Element in the Church*, 147 (*Das Dynamische in der Kirche*, 128).

spirituality ultimately results in a dying to all created things in order to surrender totally to loving Mystery. God always remains the *deus absconditus*; the spiritual journey, as Rahner envisages it, thus entails entering into the "darkness" (a "cloud of unknowing"), which arises between God and the contemplative. Only then can there be the realization of the love of God for God's own sake, a love devoid of all concepts, images, and thoughts.[236] We have explained how such love, "beyond" all knowledge, enables the retreatant in the *Exercises* to gain a "sentire" or a "felt-knowledge" of God. But because this negative way of apophatic contemplation is fraught with dangers, Rahner accents the paradigmatic nature of Christ's death and resurrection for Christian living:

> "Cross and resurrection belong together in the authentic witness to Jesus and in genuine and responsible faith in him. The *cross* means the stark demand for a person to surrender him or herself unconditionally before the mystery of his being which one can never bring under one's control, since he or she is finite and burdened with guilt. The *resurrection* means the unconditional hope that in this surrender the blessing, forgiveness and ultimate acceptance of the human person takes place through this mystery."[237]

In short, no spirituality can be purely apophatic, but God's plan is *mediated* through the incarnate Word, and made concrete in the work of the Holy Spirit, and in the Church.[238] Mediation and immediacy are not to be seen as contradictory. For Rahner, there is no

---

[236] On this, see Rahner, "The Inexhaustible Transcendence of God and our Concern for the Future," *TI* 20: 173-86 (*ST* XIV: 405-21), and his "God of My Life," *Encounters with Silence*, 3-10 (*Worte ins Schweigen*, 13-19). See also Egan, *What Are They Saying About Mysticism?*, 105.

[237] Rahner, "The Foundation of Belief," *TI* 16: 17 (*ST* XII: 34). Sudbrack also notes this connection between the experience of transcendence and the death of Christ on the cross in Rahner's thinking: "Doch bei Karl Rahner findet diese — beim ersten Hinblicken — abstrakt-weltlos erscheinende 'Transzendenzerfahrung' des Menschen ihre 'sinnenhafte' Konkretheit im Wesensbezug auf den Tod Jesu Christi. Das 'absolute Geheimnis Gottes', auf das hin die Transzendenzerfahrung des Menschen sich öffnet, ist in der Welt nur da durch das Kreuz." "Die 'Anwendung der Sinne' als Angelpunkt der Exerzitien," *Ignatianisch*, 107.

[238] For a good discussion of both the kataphatic and apophatic dimensions of the Christian mystical tradition, emphasizing that each way contains "moments" of the other, see Harvey D. Egan, "Christian Apophatic and Kataphatic Mysticisms," *Theological Studies* 39 (1978): 399-426.

question of mediations such as Christ, Church, sacraments, etc., disappearing in a person's relationship with God. Rather, such mediation does not

> "remove or obstruct an immediate relationship of (grace-endowed) humanity to God, but makes it possible, guarantees it, and attests it in the historical-categorial dimension of human life. Christian faith denies that radical immediacy to God, who imparts himself to humanity as Godself in God's absolute reality, and creaturely mediation of this self-communication of the absolute are opposed to one another as mutually exclusive alternatives."[239]

We have mentioned how the essence of spirituality, for Rahner, lies in the immediate experience of God. The early Rahner described this in terms of the gradual return to oneself, where the usually only implicit experience of our orientation to God becomes more explicit to our consciousness. Nevertheless, Rahner became increasingly aware of the dangers of conceiving the spiritual life exclusively in terms of an unmediated union with God. Such a view perceives God as a *particular* object of experience, that is, of a very exalted and unusual experience, open to only a few, and made possible by a special intervention of God.[240] As we saw in the last chapter, however, Rahner came to a new understanding of grace as the *universal* presence of God, universally present in human conscious activity, with all the consequences for spirituality that this entails. One such consequence, that frequently surfaced, is the claim that the experience of

---

[239] Rahner, "Experience of Transcendence from the Standpoint of Christian Dogmatics," *TI* 18: 179 (*ST* XIII: 214-15). Hence Rahner sees Church, revelation, sacrament, etc. as "something categorical which points to the transcendental presence of God." He also claims though that if "God is to remain Godself even in being mediated to us, if God is to be present to us in mediated immediacy as the ... ineffable mystery, and if, in this sense, religion is to be possible, then this event must take place on the basis of transcendental experience as such. It must ... allow for an immediacy to God." Rahner, *FCF*, 85 (*Grundkurs*, 92-93). See also his "The Theology of The Symbol," *TI* 4: 244 (*ST* IV: 302).

[240] But in the *Exercises* we are dealing with an immediate communication of God *mediated* through consolations and desolations. Rahner's claim that the consolation without cause provides a criterion for discovering God's will should not, therefore, be seen as a special intervention from above, but as mediated through a process of prudent interpretation codified by Ignatius in his Rules for Discernment. See Juan Luis Segundo, *The Christ of the Ignatian Exercises. Jesus of Nazareth Yesterday and Today,* vol. 4, ed. and trans. John Drury (Maryknoll, NY: 1987), 87.

God (which the later Rahner speaks of in his Spiritual Testament, for example), is not élitist, but applies to all Christians.

In effect, this chapter has explored how Rahner negotiated his way through what has been termed the "tension of opposites" characteristic of Ignatian spirituality. We believe that he has been, in the main, successful. However, this is not to say that there has not been some serious criticism of his position. In our final chapter, we will further examine some of the more serious criticisms of Rahner's understanding of spirituality. Apart from envisaging what form a Rahnerian response to these criticisms might take, we will also look at how some contemporary understandings of spirituality have moved beyond Rahner's position and found expression in a variety of new developments.

CHAPTER FIVE

AN EVALUATION OF RAHNER'S NOTION OF
SPIRITUALITY

Introduction

Our final chapter comprises an evaluation of Rahner's understanding of spirituality. We begin by looking at some of the more fundamental criticisms of Rahner's theology, and seeing how such criticisms, by implication, also apply to his concept of spirituality. Criticism of Rahner came from different quarters; hence, we will offer what we consider to be some of the more representative criticisms of his work. Although Rahner usually chose not to respond *specifically* to critics, we can glean a good picture of what form such responses might have taken from his spiritual and theological writings. Moreover, his many interviews, which have been collected in different volumes, offer further insights into some of the more controversial aspects of his thought.

By way of response to some of the criticisms mentioned in the first part of the chapter, our second section elucidates in greater detail what we maintain is the specifically Christian nature of Rahner's spirituality. Admittedly, some of the issues that will emerge have surfaced in previous chapters. However, the question of the "particularly Christian" nature of Rahner's spirituality, we believe, indicates one of the core problems in our discussion. How we approach this topic shall determine the outcome of our evaluation of Rahner's concept of spirituality. Our claim shall be that Rahner offers a balanced and challenging vision of spirituality, which is of significance and relevance for contemporary Christianity. We establish this by demonstrating that his spirituality is at once Christocentric, ecclesial and sacramental.

Although we have shown ourselves to be in broad agreement with Rahner's basic understanding of spirituality, this does not mean that it is unnecessary to move beyond him. Accordingly, we shall conclude our work by examining two important developments in this regard. The first can be best described as the emergence of a "Liberation Spirituality," which has the continent of Latin-America as its primary context. The second is the development, especially in the Northern hemisphere, of what can be termed a "Feminist Spirituality." By presenting a representative example of each of these advances, we shall show how Rahner's insights have indeed been taken further, and how these developments, in turn, offer exciting and provocative impulses towards the emergence of new forms of contemporary spirituality. Our work closes with a brief Rahnerian retrospective synthesizing some of the main points of our work, and secondly, by outlining the basic contours of a (Rahner-inspired) spirituality of the future.

1. A Synthesis of Various Criticisms

a. Criticism from the Right

In his introduction to Karl Rahner's life and thought, Herbert Vorgrimler concedes that Rahner's theology, like any theology, has its weak points, and is not immune from criticism. He further notes how Rahner's understanding of Christianity was variously attacked for being either too radical, or not radical enough.[1] Thus, Catholic traditionalists complained that Rahner, especially since Vatican Two, had relativised the radical demands of Christianity.[2] In this regard, Rahner's notion of "the anonymous Christian" came in for specific criticism. Yet, underlying this idea of Rahner's is the theological principle of the universality of grace. This principle, moreover, finds expression in the Council's *Pastoral Constitution on the Church in the Modern World, Gaudium et Spes*.[3] Perhaps, too, it was Rahner's

---

[1] Vorgrimler, *Understanding Karl Rahner*, 121-30. We follow here Vorgrimler's basic division of Rahnerian critics, while expanding on some in more detail.

[2] Vorgrimler, *Understanding Karl Rahner*, 122, refers here to an anonymous and polemical attack on Rahner (one of many, it seems) in *Theologisches* 28 (1972): 540, 542.

[3] "All this holds true not for Christians only but also for all people of good will in whose hearts grace is active invisibly. For since Christ died for all, and since all are in fact called to one and the same destiny, which is divine, we must hold that the Holy

influence on some of the key figures of the Council, such as Cardinal König, which gave rise to such resentment and polemic.[4]

A famous example of an adversarial reaction to Rahner's understanding of Christianity is that of Hans Urs von Balthasar in his book *Cordula oder der Ernstfall*.[5] This work seems to mark a significant shift in the relationship between Rahner and von Balthasar. Indeed, Rahner later admitted his puzzlement as to why Balthasar had attacked him so severely.[6] Von Balthasar's book is essentially a reaction to Rahner's anthropologically-oriented theology, which, in his view, tended to reduce Christian living "to a bland and shallow

Spirit offers to all the possibility of being made partners, in a way known to God, in the paschal mystery." *Gaudium et spes*, n. 22, *Vatican Council II*, ed. Flannery, vol. 1, 924. Elsewhere, in the *Dogmatic Constitution on the Church*, it is acknowledged that non-Christians can be moved by grace and achieve salvation through following the dictates of their conscience: "Those who, through no fault of their own, do not know the Gospel of Christ or his Church, but who nevertheless seek God with a sincere heart, and, moved by grace, try in their actions to do his will as they know it through the dictates of their conscience — those too achieve eternal salvation. Nor shall divine providence deny the assistance necessary for salvation to those who, without any fault of theirs, have not yet arrived at an explicit knowledge of God, and who, not without grace, strive to lead a good life." *Lumen Gentium*, n. 16, *Vatican Council II*, ed. Flannery, vol. 1, 367-68.

[4] See, Franz Kardinal König, "Erinnerungen an Karl Rahner als Konzilstheologen," *Karl Rahner in Erinnerung*, 149-64.

[5] Hans Urs von Balthasar, *Cordula oder der Ernstfall*, Kriterien 2 (Einsiedeln: Johannes Verlag, 1966). [ET: *The Moment of Christian Witness*, trans. Richard Beckley (San Francisco: Ignatius Press, 1969)]. A second edition (1967) contained an "Afterword" by von Balthasar as a response to the widespread criticism of his treatment of Rahner in the first edition.

[6] "Warum mein ehemaliger Ordensmitbruder und Freund von Balthasar mich heute so erbittert bekämpft, ist mir ein Rätsel." Letter from Karl Rahner to Horst Georg Pöhlmann, (17th August, 1981) in Horst Georg Pöhlmann, *Gottesdenker. Prägende evangelische und katholische Theologen der Gegenwart. 12 Porträts*, with an Introduction by Milan Machovec (Reinbeck bei Hamburg: Rowohlt Verlag, 1984), 252. It was not always like this. Despite his reservations about Rahner's anthropological method, von Balthasar recognised the theological "courage" of Rahner and spoke of him in 1964 as a "brilliant theologian" (*einen genialen Theologen*). Manfred Lochbrunner, *Analogia Caritatis. Darstellung und Deutung der Theologie Hans Urs von Balthasars*, Freiburger Theologische Studien 120 (Freiburg: Herder, 1981), 123. See also von Balthasar's positive evaluation of the early volumes of Rahner's *Theological Investigations*: "Grösse und Last der Theologie Heute: Einige grundsätzliche Gedanken zu zwei Aufsatzbänden Karl Rahners," *Wort und Wahrheit* 7 (1955): 531-33. For his part, Rahner composed a "Laudatio" for von Balthasar's sixtieth birthday in 1965. Karl Rahner, "Hans Urs von Balthasar — 60. Geburtstag," *Civitas* 20 (1965): 601-605.

humanism."[7] In particular, von Balthasar claimed that Rahner's concept of the anonymous Christian had little to do with the message of the Gospel. This concept, moreover, overlooks what he calls the "Ernstfall" or "decisive moment," which is the cross of Christ:

> "Because one died for all, he has brought us all, including me, to his Cross, so that all, including me, are dead to the law and the world in which this law is valid... Christian belief means the unconditional resolve to surrender one's life for Christ's sake."[8]

Through the cross God's love has been revealed to humanity. The corresponding response, on our side, is a readiness to die for Christ. Thus, von Balthasar lays special emphasis on the value of martyrdom: "Christ himself calls people to martyrdom, and it is this that makes it a special sign of grace."[9] The "Ernstfall," or cross of Christ, becomes the permanent pattern or form of Christian discipleship. This readiness for death by martyrdom is exemplified by Cordula, who, according to legend, initially recoiled from the prospect of martyrdom, but subsequently changed her mind and willingly underwent death.[10]

In *Cordula oder der Ernstfall*, von Balthasar makes three significant, though related, criticisms of Rahner's understanding of Christianity.[11] These are: i) Rahner's unjustifiable identification of God's love for us with our love for neighbour, based in turn on a one-sided

---

[7] Von Balthasar, *The Moment of Christian Witness*, 126 (*Cordula oder der Ernstfall*, 110).

[8] Von Balthasar, *The Moment of Christian Witness*, 24, 27 (*Cordula oder der Ernstfall*, 17, 20).

[9] Von Balthasar, *The Moment of Christian Witness*, 21 (*Cordula oder der Ernstfall*, 15, n.1). It is significant in this context that von Balthasar opens his book with an excerpt from *Lumen Gentium* extolling the value of Christian martyrdom: "The Church therefore considers martyrdom as an exceptional gift and as the highest proof of love... Though few are presented with such an opportunity, nevertheless all must be prepared to confess Christ before humanity, and to follow him along the way of the cross through the persecutions which the Church will never fail to suffer." *Lumen Gentium*, n. 42, cited from *The Moment of Christian Witness, 13* (*Cordula oder der Ernstfall*, 7).

[10] For von Balthasar's reference to "The Legend of the Eleven Thousand Virgins," see *The Moment of Christian Witness*, 133 (*Cordula oder der Ernstfall*, 115).

[11] In this paragraph, we follow von Balthasar's criticisms of Rahner in *The Moment of Christian Witness*, 100-55, esp. 100-113 (*Cordula oder der Ernstfall*, 85-123).

Johannine exegesis; ii) Rahner's lack of an explicit theology of the cross; and iii) the implications of Rahner's notion of the anonymous Christian have not been fully thought through. All three criticisms, we believe, have a direct bearing on spirituality — understood as the concrete living out of one's Christianity in faith, hope and love.

Firstly, Rahner is accused of undermining the absolute priority in Christianity of the love of God for us. Instead, Rahner is said to "identify" love of God with love of neighbour. Von Balthasar's comments are a reaction to an article of Rahner's, that emphasized the *unity* of the love of neighbour and love of God.[12] At the outset of the article, however, it is clear that Rahner's intention is to inquire into the nature of charity by reflecting on its unity with the love of God. In other words, he hoped to demonstrate that neither love of God nor love of neighbour can exist or be practised without reference to each other. Rather than subordinating the love of God to love of neighbour, as von Balthasar suggests, Rahner's aim is to elucidate how the whole truth of the Gospel is hidden and in germ in the love of one's neighbour.[13] Indeed, it is apparent in this article that Rahner is offering

[12] Karl Rahner, "Reflections on the Unity of the Love of Neighbour and the Love of God," *TI* 6: 231-49 (*ST* VI: 277-98). We have previously referred to this article, a talk given by Rahner to social workers in Cologne in 1965 in Chapter Two, 2, d. It seems that one of the reasons for von Balthasar's difficulty with Rahner's thesis is that he (von Balthasar) confuses the terms unity and identity. Although Rahner sometimes used the term "identity," I think his underlying concern was to emphasize a *perichoresis* or mutual conditioning (see below, n. 13) of the two elements: love of neighbour and love of God. As Vorgrimler notes with regard to this thesis of Rahner's: "Einheit bedeutete für ihn *nicht* Identität, aber unverzichtbare Interdependenz, so daß die eine Liebe konkret nicht ohne die andere, nicht unabhängig von der anderen wahrhaft gegeben ist." Herbert Vorgrimler, "Einleitung des Herausgebers," in Karl Rahner, *Politische Dimensionen des Christentums. Ausgewählte Texte zu Fragen der Zeit* (Munich: Kösel, 1986), 10. (Italics mine).
[13] Rahner, "Reflections on the Unity of the Love of Neighbour and the Love of God," *TI* 6: 233 (*ST* VI: 279). Elsewhere, Rahner responded more directly to this criticism of von Balthasar: "Die radikale Liebe zum Nächsten als ursprünglich vollzogene ist vor ihrer Selbstreflexion immer schon ein Ankommen bei Gott und muß es sein. Umgekehrt ist es natürlich auch so. Ich muß den Gott lieben, der mich und den Nächsten liebt. In der Dimension des eigentlichen Vollzugs der Gottes- und Nächstenliebe haben wir von vornherein einmal, so möchte ich sagen, eine Perichorese gegenseitiger Bedingung der beiden Momente." Rahner, "Gnade als Mitte menschlicher Existenz," *Herausforderung des Christen*, 137. See also, Karl Rahner, "Approaches to Theological Thinking," *Karl Rahner in Dialogue*, 124 (*Karl Rahner*

a corrective to at least three distortions which frequently manifest themselves in spirituality. A first distortion is to assume that God can *only* be reached in what he terms a "gnostic-mystic interiority, ... in such a way that he would *thus* be really attainable by love (1 Jn 4:12)."[14] A second distortion consists in any attempt to "compartmentalize" love of God and love of neighbour into two separated spheres of human life. Rahner overcomes this with his conception of love as "a reflected and explicit mode of action and as an unconceptualised transcendental horizon of action."[15] This distinction is based on his notion of a transcendental horizon, which is the "space" within which another human person is encountered, even if such a horizon is usually not explicitly reflected upon or named.[16] Just as the love of neighbour and the love of God can be distinguished but not completely separated, the same holds true for the relation between the transcendental and the categorial dimensions of human love. In other words, Rahner claims that there can be a "transcendental" depth in inter-human love, a love that is at the same time oriented towards God by virtue of one's inescapably given transcendental horizon. Love of neighbour (and we have discussed this in Chapter Two) is the fulfilment of the transcendental nature of the human person, and not simply a "regional" happening in his or her life. Selfless acts of

---

im Gespräch 1: 242). We shall return to Rahner's thesis of the unity of the love of neighbour and the love of God in the third section: "Gathering the Threads."

[14] Rahner, "Reflections on the Unity of the Love of Neighbour and the Love of God," *TI* 6: 235 (*ST* VI: 281). See also his articles: "Liebe," *LThK* VI: 1038-1039, and (more developed) in *SM* III: 234-52.

[15] The heading of this section of Rahner's article is entitled: *Liebe als thematisch-ausdrückliches, kategoriales Tun und als unbegrifflicher, transzendentaler Horizont des Tuns*. Rahner, "Reflections on the Unity of the Love of Neighbour and the Love of God," *TI* 6: 237 (*ST* VI: 284). In every human spiritual act, according to Rahner, one must distinguish between its explicit object (represented in a determined concept and category) on the one hand, and the *a priori* formal object, the transcendental horizon or 'space' within which a determined individual is encountered, on the other.

[16] "In the original and basic act in which God impinges upon a person (and this act precedes all conscious awareness of him) God is always given simply as the ultimate *basis* ("Grund") of experience, that which is beyond the world, upholding it in being and so making the experience possible. In other words God is present here not as a direct object of knowledge or experience but only 'indirectly' as that which is on the horizon of our experience." Rahner, "Why and How Can We Venerate the Saints?," *TI* 8: 17 (*ST* VII: 297).

love, and this points to a third possible distortion in spirituality, are not merely proofs of our love of God but are themselves underpinned and supported by God's divinizing grace. Hence, love of neighbour, according to Rahner, is not simply a stepping-stone on our way to God, but is itself an act of love of God.[17] Since not everyone would view their love of neighbour in such a manner, he is careful to speak in this context only of "the anonymous 'Christianity' of every positively moral activity."[18] Before Rahner's article is dismissed as rather one-sided (and von Balthasar goes even further than this), the original aim of his talk should be kept in mind, namely, Rahner's concern to show how the Christian's relationship to God can be "concentrated" on one's love of neighbour.[19]

In this context, von Balthasar accuses Rahner of a one-sided Johannine exegesis. In his survey of the declarations of Scripture concerning the love of neighbour understood as love of God, Rahner emphasized those Johannine references which claim that when we love our neighbour, God is "in us" (1 Jn 4:12). Von Balthasar, however, claims that Rahner, in his interpretation of John, has left out Christ. Moreover, as we have noted, he detects an over-simplistic identification, on Rahner's part, between love of God and love of neighbour. By contrast, when von Balthasar uses the word "love" he is referring primarily to God's love for us, not our love of God or neighbour. God's love is manifest in Christ, who lays down his life for us (1 Jn 3:16), and who is the expiation for our sins (1 Jn 4:10). Thus, if there

---

[17] This insight of Rahner's is apparent in some of his early spiritual writings, where he describes how an act of love for another person already contains the "image and likeness" of that love, which reaches out toward everything — towards God. Rahner, "Das Gebet der Liebe," *Von der Not und dem Segen des Gebetes*, 48. Thus, even in this early piece, Rahner is aware of the "mysterious more" ("... mit diesem rätselhaften Mehr") that is contained in the genuine love of one person for another.

[18] Rahner, "Reflections on the Unity of the Love of Neighbour and the Love of God," *TI* 6: 238 (*ST* VI: 285).

[19] "... bleibt für uns an diesem Versuch, die Konzentration des ganzen christlichen Gottesverhältnisses auf die Liebe zum Bruder verständlich zu machen ..." Rahner, "Über die Einheit von Nächsten- und Gottesliebe," *ST* VI: 281 (*TI* 6: 235). Of course, Rahner is not saying that *every* act of the love of God is also a formal act of love of neighbour. An explicit relating to God in prayer, for example, has, in his view, a higher dignity, since, in this instance, there is a conscious love of God, which has God as its reflex motive.

is to be an identification between love of God and love of neighbour, it must, von Balthasar argues, be conceived on Christological terms.[20] This leads to von Balthasar's second major criticism of Rahner's work (which we shall take up shortly), namely, its lack of an explicit theology of the cross. For von Balthasar, the only form of love acceptable to God is that which proceeds from the *Ernstfall* (or decisive moment) of the cross. This acknowledgement of the absolute priority of the love of God (a genitive in both a subjective and an objective sense) is *the* primary religious act. One's love of God then "overflows" into one's love of neighbour.

Von Balthasar's third criticism concerns Rahner's controversial notion of the anonymous Christian.[21] This notion, according to von Balthasar, leads inevitably to Christianity becoming dispensable. There is no need, then, for the *Ernstfall*, no need for prophetic witness, no need for martyrdom. If theology goes down this road, von Balthasar argues that it will ultimately become a matter of indifference whether or not one believes in God. However, despite his disagreement with Rahner, von Balthasar does recognize the latter's "legitimate notion that there is a *fides implicita* and a corresponding supernatural love outside the sphere of Christianity and of the Bible, as well as with those who are theoretically atheists."[22] This concession to

[20] "The Christ who lives in me is so deeply within me (and closer to me than I am to myself) because he died for me, because he took me to himself on the Cross and constantly takes me to him again in the Eucharist. How could my relationship with my neighbour be comparable to that — and therefore require the same answering love from me? The bridge to brotherly love in the sense of Christ is the fact that he has done for everyone what he has done for me." Von Balthasar, *The Moment of Christian Witness*, 112-13 (*Cordula oder der Ernstfall,* 96). However, we argued in Chapter Two, 2, d, that Rahner also conceives love of neighbour along Christological lines. In this context, another favourite biblical text of his was Mt 25:31-46, a text which reminds the theologian and the Christian, "so zu denken und so *sein* Dasein zu deuten, daß er die wirklich christliche Dimension aller echten Liebe begreift: seine Liebe zum Nächsten — diese richtig, radikal, d.h. bis in ihre Wurzel verstanden — begegnet real und nicht in einer romantischen, mystischen und mythologischen Identifizierung dem Jesus, den wir als Christus bekennen." Rahner, *Ich glaube an Jesus Christus,* 29.

[21] The primary theological principle underlying the idea of anonymous Christianity (i.e., Rahner's reinterpretation of grace) was discussed in Chapter Three, 3, a, with specific reference to the implications for spirituality.

[22] Von Balthasar, *The Moment of Christian Witness*, 113, n. 42 (*Cordula oder der Ernstfall,* 96, n.1). In an article entitled "Meeting God in Today's World," *Concilium* 6

Rahner (whom he acknowledges to be "inspired by apostolic motives"), is developed in the "Afterword" of *Cordula* with reference to Henri de Lubac's *Paradoxe et Mystère de l'Eglise*.[23] Von Balthasar portrays de Lubac's essay as an attempt to mediate between the positions of Rahner and himself, and therefore as a proposal for reconciliation. De Lubac's proposal rests on a distinction between anonymous Christians and anonymous Christianity. The existence of the former is to be admitted since the grace of Christ operates outside the visible Church, and "in the various milieus of life and culture there are 'anonymous Christians' who in one way or another have received insights originating from the Gospel."[24] However, de Lubac (and von Balthasar agrees with him) does not go any further than this:

> "But it would be a fallacy to conclude from this that there is an 'anonymous Christianity' spread everywhere in humanity, a so-called 'implicit Christianity', which the apostolic preaching would have the sole task of bringing ... to the state of explicitness — as if the revelation brought by Christ had done nothing except bring clearly to light what had already been universally present."[25]

The above comparison of Rahner with von Balthasar clearly highlights serious differences in their conception of how Christianity

---

(1965): 23-39, von Balthasar spoke of recognizing "the free working of the grace of Christ even where there is no explicit Christian belief." (p. 37). Although he saw the need for an alternative to Rahner's theological account of the possibility of salvation of non-Christians, von Balthasar himself did not provide one. See also Eamonn Conway, *The Anonymous Christian — A Relativized Christianity? An Evaluation of Hans Urs von Balthasar's Criticisms of Karl Rahner's Theory of the Anonymous Christian*, European University Studies, vol. 485 (Frankfurt am Main: Peter Lang, 1993), 70, n. 52.

[23] Von Balthasar, *The Moment of Christian Witness*, 148, and 149, n. 7. The reference is to de Lubac's *Paradoxe et Mystère de l'Eglise* (Paris: Aubier, 1967), 120-63.

[24] De Lubac, *Paradoxe et Mystère de l'Eglise,* 150.

[25] De Lubac, *Paradoxe et Mystère de l'Eglise,* 153. Von Balthasar later reiterated this view: "'Anonymous Christians': certainly. There are great human paradigms outside the Church. 'Anonymous Christianity': no, because that implies a relativisation of the objective revelation of God in the biblical event, and would sanction the religious paths of other religions as either ordinary or extraordinary means of salvation. That is biblically not on. But also the expression 'the anonymous Christian' in my opinion remains unfortunate, because being a Christian simply includes confession of a name, the name of Jesus Christ." "Geist und Feuer: Ein Gespräch mit Hans Urs Von Balthasar," *Herder Korrespondenz* 30 (1976): 76. For Rahner's response to De Lubac, see his "Anonymous Christianity and the Missionary Task of the Church," *TI* 12: 162-65 (*ST* IX: 499-502).

should be understood. For the purposes of our study, these differences raise the question about what is the "specifically Christian" in Rahner's understanding of spirituality. Von Balthasar also poses the more fundamental question as to whether Rahner's transcendental method ultimately leads to a relativized Christianity. Further, he asks whether Rahner has subordinated the role of Christ in redemption to the universal salvific will of God. And, finally, does not Rahner's concept of "the anonymous Christian" imply a bland Christianity that is not worth its salt?[26]

The criticism that Rahner's transcendental Christology brackets the historical Christ event and undermines the necessity of an explicit Christianity has already been discussed in the previous two chapters. In both chapters we noted the danger of misjudging Rahner through a selective use of his writings. With regard to his article on the unity of the love of neighbour and love of God, it seems that the difference here between Rahner and von Balthasar (despite the sarcastic tone of some of von Balthasar's comments) is more a question of emphasis. Rahner is primarily concerned that love of God and love of neighbour do not become separated. It is not a question of him substituting an implicit act of love for an explicit confession of Jesus Christ. Rahner never simply equates Christian faith with altruism, which is what von Balthasar's criticisms of him imply. Instead, his point is that a non-Christian, by selflessly loving his or her neighbour, is justified by God's grace and possesses the Holy Spirit. In such persons, Rahner believes, are the seeds of faith, containing their own "inherent dynamism," oriented towards developing into a fully explicit Christian faith as objectified and articulated by the Gospel.[27]

In relation to a theology of the cross, we drew attention to the significance of this in the context of Rahner's appropriation of Ignatian

---

[26] See von Balthasar, *The Moment of Christian Witness*, 127-30 (*Cordula oder der Ernstfall,* 111-113), where he provides a fictitious dialogue between a "Rahnerian" Christian and a well-disposed communist commissar in order to depict the indefensibility and shallowness of Rahner's portrayal of Christianity.

[27] "The seed has no right to seek not to grow into a plant. But the fact that it is not yet developed into a plant is no reason for refusing to give the name which we give to the plant destined to grow from it to the seed as well." Karl Rahner, "Observations on the Problem of the 'Anonymous Christian,' " *TI* 14: 291 (*ST* X: 543).

spirituality in the last chapter. We have also seen how Rahner has worked out a theology of the cross in a variety of articles in *Investigations* and elsewhere.[28] Von Balthasar had suggested that Rahner subordinated the redemption won for us by Christ's death to the eternal saving will of God.[29] But this is not an accurate description of Rahner's position. It is true that Rahner understands the cross as the "cause" of our salvation differently from von Balthasar. However, Rahner is suspicious of any theory of satisfaction that could be misinterpreted as "changing the mind" of an angry God.[30] The idea of Jesus' death as an expiatory sacrifice and as an atonement for the sins of the world must not compromise the Christian's understanding of God as a God of love. Rather, with the death and resurrection of Jesus, Rahner sees God's universal salvific will reaching its historical manifestation as victorious and irreversible. In short, Rahner wishes to move away from an image of a vengeful God demanding retribution for the sins of humanity, which underlies a legalistic theory of satisfaction.[31] The death of Jesus on the cross, he argues, does not so much effect a change in God's relation to humanity as it manifests Jesus' acceptance of God's will:

[28] See, for example, Rahner, "Current Problems in Christology," *TI* 1: 149-97 (*ST* I: 169-222); "Dogmatic Questions on Easter," *TI* 4: 121-33 (*ST* IV: 157-72); "The Scandal of Death," *TI* 7: 140-44 (*ST* VII: 141-44); "Self-Realisation and Taking Up One's Cross," *TI* 9: 253-57 (*ST* VIII: 322-26); "Following the Crucified," *TI* 18: 157-70 (*ST* XIII: 188-203). See also "Theologia crucis," *LThK* 10: 61; *FCF*, 264-85 (*Grundkurs*, 260-79); and with Karl-Heinz Weger, *Our Christian Faith*, 105-23. A representative selection of Rahner's homilies on the theme of the cross and the death of Jesus can be found in *The Great Church Year*, 145-69. For a study of Rahner's soteriology with reference to the role of the cross, see Anselm Grün, *Erlösung durch das Kreuz. Karl Rahners Beitrag zu einem heutigen Erlösungsverständnis,* Münsterschwarz-acher Studien 26 (Münsterschwarzach: Vier-Türme-Verlag, 1975).

[29] Von Balthasar, *The Moment of Christian Witness*, 109 (*Cordula oder der Ernstfall,* 92).

[30] Rahner, *FCF*, 255 (*Grundkurs*, 251).

[31] In this context, Rahner asks whether Western theology could not learn from the East, where, while the significance of the cross was not overlooked, "the redemption was felt to be a real ontological process which began in the incarnation and ends not so much in the forgiveness of sin as in the divinization of the world ..." Rahner, "Dogmatic Questions on Easter," *TI* 4: 126 (*ST* IV: 164). It is beyond our scope here to trace the biblical understanding of the notion of satisfaction and the related notions of atonement, reconciliation, expiation, propitiation, etc. For a helpful discussion of the issues (in relation to Pauline theology), see Joseph Fitzmyer, *To Advance the Gospel: New Testament Studies* (New York: Crossroad, 1981), 162-85.

"... this whole work of redemption, which is supposed to placate God and make him merciful, is the result all along of God's spontaneous desire to save, so that we must (also) clearly say, the saving work of Jesus Christ exists because even before it God was the God who forgives and triumphs over the sins of the world, and not (only) that God is merciful because of the saving work of Christ."[32]

Rahner is grappling here with von Balthasar's question about the meaning of Jesus bearing our sins on the cross. In Rahner's view, God's salvific will is the cause and not ultimately the result of what happened on the cross. While he does not wish to downgrade traditional Christian belief about the saving work of Christ, Rahner's intention is to circumscribe how this work "affects" God. His concern is that the unapproachable sovereignty of God and his will not be obscured. Jesus' death is therefore to be seen as an act of God in the context of his universal salvific will as a whole. It is a universal saving event, not merely the appearance of the Father's salvific will in history, but also the fulfilment of this will.

If Rahner's approach to the death of Jesus is conceived in relation to God's saving will (and partially, too, as a reaction to a distorted theory of satisfaction), then von Balthasar's emphasis is on God reconciling the world to Himself *in* Christ (2 Cor. 5:19).[33] Although von Balthasar laments what he sees as the modern tendency (even among theologians) to diminish the importance of sin, Rahner's claim is that, in the cross and resurrection of Christ, God has the last word over the power of evil in the world.[34] It would be incorrect to say that the death of Jesus merely convinces us of the forgiving and salvific will of God. Rather, Rahner's point is that the redemptive significance of Jesus' death must be seen in union with his life and resurrection.[35] The initiative always lies with God's salvific will, a will that "establishes" the life of Jesus, and which reaches fulfilment in

---

[32] Rahner, Weger, *Our Christian Faith*, 115.

[33] Conway, *The Anonymous Christian*, 131.

[34] We have discussed the notions of death and resurrection in relation to Christian discipleship in Chapter Three, 3, c, ii, "Rahner's Three Appeals." See also our related comments in Chapter Four, 2, d, "The Christological Dimension of the Election."

[35] The relevant section in *Foundations* is entitled: "On the Theology of the Death of Jesus from the Perspective of the Resurrection." Rahner, *FCF*, 282-85 (*Grundkurs*, 276-77).

his death and becomes historically tangible for us in the resurrection.[36]

Von Balthasar's emphasis on the *Ernstfall*, ultimately perceived as a willingness to sacrifice oneself in martyrdom, should not be played off against Rahner's understanding of Christianity. For his part, Rahner has also written on the topic of martyrdom; indeed, towards the end of his life, he pleaded for a broadening of the classical concept of martyrdom.[37] Although the original biblical concept of martyrdom (Gk., *martyr, martyros*) was used in reference to the Apostles (Acts 1:8, 22), Rahner detects the beginnings of a change as early as the second century, where the meaning was extended to all those whose suffering and death bore a striking testimony to their faith in Jesus Christ. Thus, since that period, martyrdom and death are linked: the martyr is a faithful witness through death. In probing the deeper theological meaning of martyrdom, Rahner asks what is the connection between witness to Christ and death. In order to understand martyrdom, death must also be understood. While death is inescapable, martyrdom is voluntary. However, Rahner insists that *every* authentic Christian life must bear some characteristics of martyrdom. Every person is challenged to see death as the act of freedom, not simply as that instant at the end of our lives. There is a "death" we die all through our lives, and Rahner depicts the choice facing the Christian as either viewing death only as the end (in the sense of extinction) or,

---

[36] When Rahner refers to the life and death of Jesus as the "cause" of God's salvific will, he means that "this salvific will establishes itself really and irrevocably in this life and death, in other words, insofar as the life and death of Jesus, or the death which recapitulates and culminates his life, possess a causality of a quasi-sacramental and real-symbolic nature. In this causality what is signified, in this case God's salvific will, posits the sign, in this case the death of Jesus along with his resurrection, and in and through the sign it causes what is signified." Rahner, *FCF*, 284 (*Grundkurs*, 278). For Rahner's understanding of the humanity of Jesus as the self-expression, or the "real symbol" of God, see his "The Theology of the Symbol," *TI* 4: 221-52 (*ST* IV: 275-311). See also Lambert Leijssen, "La contribution de Karl Rahner (1904-1984) au renouvellement de la sacramentaire," *Current Issues in Sacramental Theology*, ed. J. Lamberts (Leuven: Abdij Keizersberg/Faculteit Godgeleerdheid, 1994), 84-102, esp. 96-100.

[37] Karl Rahner, "Dimensions of Martyrdom: A Plea for the Broadening of a Classical Concept," *Concilium* 163 (1983): 9-11. We are indebted here also to his earlier reflections on this topic in *On the Theology of Death*, 89-127 (*Zur Theologie des Todes*, 73-106).

instead, as a "consummation" of his or her life. In the latter instance, death is a falling into the hands of the living God; it entails a surrender of the whole person's uncontrollable and impenetrable existence to the incomprehensible God.[38] When a person freely accepts his or her own finitude and, in this sense, says yes to death, he or she does something, Rahner claims, that could only be achieved by the grace of Christ.[39] What gives the martyr a particular assimilation to Christ, however, is his or her voluntary sharing in Christ's death, thereby offering courageous testimony to the ultimate consequences of Christian discipleship.[40]

Martyrdom, then, traditionally understood, was the free, unresisting acceptance of death for the sake of the faith. Rahner wishes, however, to broaden this traditional understanding. It is apparent that there are many people today who are actively involved in the struggle for justice and peace — both Christians and non-Christians. In some cases, this active struggle for justice ends in death. Rahner's question is whether such people should not also be considered martyrs. Martyrdom, in this view, is not simply the passive endurance of death, but

[38] "Thus death — which can be both the situation of despair and the situation of one's resigning oneself into the hands of the incomprehensible God — becomes also the existentially most radical situation of faith and hope. Dying — at least when it is accomplished in a personal way and by a yes given to the Christian revelation of life — is the most complete and definitive act of hoping faith, and this is the real meaning of Christian death." Rahner, "The Passion and Asceticism," *TI* 3: 75 (*ST* III: 92).

[39] It is significant that one of the earliest appearances of the term "anonymous Christian" appears in this 1957 article of Rahner. His point is that the voluntary and believing acceptance of death can also be practised by those who are "Christian in spirit" ("die anonymen Christen"). Rahner, *On the Theology of Death*, 120 (*Zur Theologie des Todes*, 100). Elsewhere, Rahner speaks of an anonymous Christian *faith* as the acceptance of oneself ("die Annahme seiner selbst"): "Anyone ... who accepts their existence, that is, their humanity — in quiet patience, or better, in faith, hope and love — no matter what they call them, and accepts it *as* the mystery, ... such a one says yes to Christ, even if they do not know that they do... . Anyone who accepts their humanity in full — and how immeasurably hard that is, how doubtful whether we really do it! — has accepted the Son of man, because God has accepted man in them." Rahner, "On the Theology of the Incarnation," *TI* 4: 119 (*ST* IV: 154).

[40] The importance of Rahner's theology of death for his understanding of spirituality is also recognized by Schwerdtfeger: "Sein (Rahner's) ganzes Verständnis vom christlichen Leben ist im Grunde von dort her bestimmt. Christliches Leben ist für ihn grundlegend durch das freiwillige Aufgeben innerweltlicher Werte geprägt, um sich dem Gott der freien Gnade zu öffnen." Schwerdtfeger, "Der 'anonyme Christ' in der Theologie Karl Rahners," *Theologie aus Erfahrung der Gnade*, 80.

also encompasses a more active dimension.[41] In this context, Jesus Christ is the martyr *par excellence* — he not only "passively" endured his death, but his death was the direct consequence of his struggle against the religious and political authorities of his time. His death, therefore, cannot be seen in isolation from his life. If this is the case, we can ask whether those who are not explicitly Christian can also be martyrs. From what we have said above and elsewhere, we believe that Rahner would agree that there can be, what Leonardo Boff describes as "political martyrs," people who "perform virtuous actions in the spirit of Christ."[42] They might not be martyrs of the Christian faith as such, or heroes of the Church, but they are martyrs of the kingdom of God, martyrs to the cause of the Son of God when he was among us. Finally, the Church, too, has its modern martyrs — people like Bishop Romero, for example, who died while fighting for justice in his country. Such people, Rahner insists, highlight the very down-to-earth and practical significance of martyrdom for a contemporary spirituality that is aware of its responsibility for justice and peace in the world.

This section has examined three of von Balthasar's criticisms of Rahner's understanding of Christianity. However, some of the issues have surfaced previously in our discussion of Rahner's spirituality. Our procedure in this (and throughout our work) has been to try to tackle these problems with Rahner rather than against him. In other words, we have sought to draw from within Rahner's own writings

---

[41] However, Rahner is aware of the difficulty of making a sharp distinction between these two types of death, that is, a death for the sake of the faith in active struggle, and a death for the sake of the faith in passive endurance. His point, rather, is that "we should not simply conceive of passively tolerating one's death only in the manner we are used to in the case of the early Christian martyrs brought before a court and sentenced to death. There are quite different ways in which the passive but intentionally accepted toleration of death can occur. Contemporary persecutors of Christians do not give their victims any opportunity to confess their faith in the style of the earliest Christian centuries ... But nevertheless their death in these more anonymous forms of contemporary persecution of Christians can still be foreseen and accepted just as in the case of the old-style martyr. And ... it can be foreseen and accepted as the consequences of an active struggle for justice." Rahner, "Dimensions of Martyrdom," *Concilium* 163 (1983): 10.

[42] Leonardo Boff, "Martyrdom: An Attempt at Systematic Reflection," *Concilium* 163 (1983): 15.

resources to respond to the various criticisms made of him. It is not that we regard Rahner's work as some kind of closed "system" — Rahner never thought of his work in such a way — but we believe that a fair evaluation of Rahner's spirituality cannot be obtained solely on the basis of a limited and arbitrary selection of his works.[43] Rahner acknowledged both the limitations of his thought as well as the need for other thinkers to develop his ideas in new directions.[44] In the next section, we shall see how Rahner's understanding of Christianity has indeed been taken further by one of his former students — Johann Baptist Metz, and how Rahner himself has incorporated some of Metz's insights into his understanding of spirituality.

b. Criticism from the Left

In this section, we briefly present the chief criticisms made by Johann Baptist Metz of Rahner's transcendental approach to theology.[45]

---

[43] This is the perennial danger in any attempt to review Rahner's theology according to J. B. Metz: "... and every review of his (Rahner's) theology seems almost inescapably to be in danger of roughly schematizing it or arbitrarily abridging it." Metz, "Foreword," *Spirit in the World*, xvi. Lehmann voices a similar caveat: "All to easily *one* aspect of his theology considered *without* the other becomes false. Radical immediacy to God, speculative ingenuity, pastoral concerns, sensitivity to the importance of the theological tradition — one would have to be able to say all this and many other things *at the same time* in order to articulate the origin and clarity of his theology." Lehmann, "Karl Rahner: A Portrait," *The Content of Faith*, 11 (*Rechenschaft des Glaubens*, 21*- 22*). See also Lambert Leijssen, "Grace as God's Self-Communication: The Starting-Point and Development in Rahner's Thought," *Louvain Studies* 20 (1995): 73-78.

[44] Rahner, "Gnade als Mitte menschlicher Existenz," *Herausforderung des Christen*, 142.

[45] Metz was a student of Rahner's at Innsbruck in the 1950s and remained a lifelong friend. Apart from editing Rahner's early philosophical works *Geist in Welt* and *Hörer des Wortes*, Metz also commended Rahner's theological work on several occasions. See, for example, his "Laudatio" for Rahner in 1974: "Karl Rahner — ein theologisches Leben. Theologie als mystische Biographie eines Christenmenschen heute," *Stimmen der Zeit* 192 (1974): 305-314; and his two articles: "Karl Rahners Ringen um die theologische Ehre des Menschen," and "Fehlt uns Karl Rahner?" in *Karl Rahner in Erinnerung*, ed. Albert Raffelt, Freiburger Akademieschriften, 8 (Düsseldorf: Patmos, 1994), 70-84, 85-99. For a more critical appraisal of Rahner's theology of transcendence, however, see his *Glaube in Geschichte und Gesellschaft* (Mainz: Grünewald, 1977), 143-48. [ET: *Faith in History and Society: Toward a Practical Fundamental Theology*, trans. David Smith (New York: Crossroad, 1980), 161-68].

Since these criticisms are already well documented, it would seem more constructive, for our purposes, to see how Rahner himself responded to and incorporated Metz's criticisms into his own work.[46] Our contention is that while Rahner's epistemological and philosophical premises remained unchanged during his theological career, he also showed a growing appreciation of the political dimension of Christianity, and that such an awareness, in turn, has implications for his understanding of spirituality.

Metz's political theology is basically a critical corrective to what he sees as the tendency to confine religion to the realm of the private. Political theology is opposed to such "privatization" of religion, to the narrowing down of religion merely to the inner life and to the private sphere.[47] It does not deny, however, the legitimate individual relationship to God. In this sense, political theologians such as Metz would agree that spirituality must always be personal, but never private; it must always be the spirituality of a particular person, while at the same time involved in a variety of social relationships and responsibilities. Not that Metz's political theology is simply advocating a series of human moral imperatives or another form of social ethics. Rather, political theology attempts to formulate the eschatological message in the conditions of present-day society. It claims to be a basic element of critical theological thinking motivated by a new understanding of the relation between theory and practice, and according to which all theology must be "practical," i.e., oriented to action. With regard to Rahner's transcendental theology, Metz argues that it did not give sufficient importance to the societal dimension of the Christian message. The message becomes "privatized" and the practice of faith is reduced to the timeless decision of the person. "The categories most prominent in this theology are the categories of the intimate, the private, the apolitical sphere."[48] Alongside this,

---

[46] See, for example, Rahner, *Politische Dimensionen des Christentums*, 54-77, 170-229.

[47] J. B. Metz, "Political Theology," *Sacramentum Mundi* 5: 34-38 (*SM* III: 1232-1240).

[48] J. B. Metz, *Theology of the World* (New York: Herder and Herder, 1969), 109. [*Zur Theologie der Welt* (Mainz: Grünewald, 1968), 100]. Metz continues: "It is true that these theologians strongly emphasize charity and all that belongs to the field of interpersonal relations; yet, ... they regard charity only as a private virtue with no

Metz notes the transcendental attempt to undermine history. An out and out transcendental theology, he claims, runs the risk of not having to enter the field of history since the human person "is 'always already', whether he or she wants to be or not, 'with God'."[49] Moreover, Metz laments what he perceives as the degeneration of Christianity into a kind of "service-religion" to which one turns in private to be "unburdened" by the exigencies of history.

When it comes to the Church, Metz envisions this as witnessing to and being a bearer of what he calls the "dangerous memory" of Jesus.[50] If the Church lives from the memory of Jesus, the question arises as to what shape such memory takes. The Church, Metz argues, is challenged to remember Jesus as the one who identified himself with those who were being oppressed. To remember Jesus in this way is to give public expression to the dangerous and liberating memory of Jesus. It is a dangerous memory since it forces Christians to call into question all those structures in society which subtly legitimize inequality and suffering. If the dangerous memory of Jesus leads to a liberating praxis, Metz also refers to the "eschatological proviso," or reserve, by which he claims that ultimate liberation is reserved to God alone.[51] Political theology exists within this tension between the eschatological message of the kingdom of God and every particular form of social and political life.[52] Within this framework the

political relevance." The seeds of this criticism are already to be seen in Metz's "Foreword" to Rahner's *Spirit in the World*, xvii-xviii, where he asks whether the transcendental-existential approach to theology conceives salvation in too private a manner, and salvation history too worldlessly.

[49] Metz, *Faith in History and Society,* 160 (*Glaube in Geschichte und Gesellschaft,* 147).

[50] See J. B. Metz, "Prophetic Authority," in *Religion and Political Society*, ed. J. B. Metz, Jürgen Moltmann, et al., trans. David Kelly and Henry Vander Goot (New York: Harper and Row, 1974), 177-209, esp. 203-208.

[51] "The things that lie beyond the range of human freedom and its conflicts — consummation, reconciliation, and peace — are reserved to God and the 'not yet' by virtue of the 'eschatological proviso'." Metz, "Prophetic Authority," *Religion and Political Society*, 205.

[52] Metz's view is that the central promises of the reign of God in the New Testament — freedom, peace, justice, reconciliation — have been made "radically private affairs." Their content has been unduly interiorized, spiritualized and individualized. The society-directed, "public" character of the Gospel then becomes distorted since the Christian considers himself or herself as dispensed from his or her society. Metz, "Political Theology," *Sacramentum Mundi* 5: 36-37 (*SM* III: 1235-37).

Church's task is to call into question any claim by totalitarian systems or ideologies to offer a type of "one-dimensional" emancipation. Given such an eschatological expectation, the Church "is called continually to expect the coming kingdom and so to criticize all efforts at idolatry, whereby particular persons, groups, nations, or empires set themselves up as the lord of history."[53] In short, Metz is promoting a political theology that moves away from the narrow, private and apolitical categories of transcendental theology towards a theology that has a very definite society-directed character.

How did Rahner appropriate these implied criticisms of Metz into his own theological thinking? A couple of years after Rahner's death, Herbert Vorgrimler edited a series of interviews and articles by Rahner covering the political dimension of Christianity.[54] Thus far in our work we have highlighted the spiritual root of Rahner's theology, focusing in particular on his understanding of spirituality gleaned from both his more spiritual writings and retreat conferences as well as from his more "scientific" (*wissenschaftliche*) theological works. Central to our discussion was the recurring theme of the individual's experience of God and the various ways Rahner sought to interpret such spiritual or religious experience. But as Vorgrimler points out (and we have hinted at this before), any investigation of Rahner's spirituality must go beyond this and show that Rahner's thesis of the unity of the love of God and neighbour can be interpreted in terms of the indissoluble unity of the "mystical" and "political" dimensions of Christian spirituality. We have previously explored the mystical dimension of Rahner's spirituality. Now, with Vorgrimler's selection of Rahner's statements on the political dimension of Christianity

---

[53] Matthew L. Lamb, "Political Theology," *The New Dictionary of Theology*, eds. Joseph A. Komonchak, Mary Collins and Dermot A. Lane (Dublin: Gill and Macmillan, Dublin, 1987): 774.

[54] Karl Rahner, *Politische Dimensionen des Christentums: Ausgewählte Texte zu Fragen der Zeit*, ed. Herbert Vorgrimler (Munich: Kösel, 1986). We are also indebted here to the following authors who have made many helpful observations on this aspect of Rahner's theology: Karl Neumann, *Der Praxisbezug der Theologie bei Karl Rahner*, Freiburger Theologische Studien 118 (Freiburg: Herder, 1980); Andrea Tafferner, *Gottes- und Nächstenliebe in der deutschsprachigen Theologie des 20. Jahrhunderts*, Innsbrucker theologische Studien 37 (Innsbruck/Wien: Tyrolia, 1992); Titus F. Guenther, *Rahner and Metz: Transcendental Theology as Political Theology* (Boston: Univ. Press of America, 1994).

— spanning a period of over twenty years — we note how increasingly important this political dimension became for Rahner, though it was never entirely absent.[55] Two points mentioned earlier are worth recalling at this point. Firstly, we have previously indicated how Rahner's definition of the human person as the essence of absolute transcendence towards God, insofar as the human person in his or her understanding "preapprehends" (*vorgreift*) towards God, is not some idealistic abstraction. Rather, this dimension of our personhood is only realized in acts of loving outreach to one's neighbour. Secondly, this neighbourly love is not to be interpreted in a narrow, private sense; it also has a social and a political dimension.[56] Although Rahner's theology of the love of neighbour sometimes gives the impression of being restricted solely to a narrowly interpersonal level (i.e., to one's immediate neighbour), he was convinced that the category of love held out great potential for inter-human solidarity, including with those who are oppressed.[57] In other words, Rahner supported Metz's political theology as thoroughly orthodox,[58] even if he had some reservations about it. Rahner agreed, therefore, that theology must criticize those structures in society that oppress the individual. Moreover, theology must

[55] In his introduction, Vorgrimler emphasizes how: "Rahner war davon überzeugt, daß nur dort, wo Christen die politischen Dimensionen ihres Glaubens begreifen und als praktische Aufgaben wahrnehmen, der Glaube zu jener Tat der Liebe wird, in der nach den Worten Jesu die wahre Anbetung Gottes besteht." He continues: "Es ist wichtig, bei diesen Überlegungen zu Rahnerschen Grundpositionen zu sehen, wie sehr seine Theologie unter dem Einfluß der konstruktiv-kritischen Gespräche mit Johann Baptist Metz sich den Intentionen der Politischen Theologie annäherte." Vorgrimler in Rahner, *Politische Dimensionen des Christentums*, 9, 12.

[56] Rahner, "One Mediator and Many Mediations," *TI* 9: 169-86, esp. 176-77 (*ST* VIII: 226-27).

[57] Regarding the harmony between Rahner's theology and Latin American theology, see Jon Sobrino, "Karl Rahner and Liberation Theology," *Theology Digest* 32 (1985): 257-60; and Sobrino, "Current Problems in Christology in Latin American Theology," *Theology and Discovery*, 189-230. We will return to Sobrino in the third part of the chapter. For Rahner's affirmation of liberation theology, including his last letter before his death to Cardinal Ricketts of Lima in defence of Gustavo Gutiérrez, see his *Politische Dimensionen des Christentums*, 170-88.

[58] Imhof, Biallowons, *Karl Rahner in Dialogue*, 234 (*Karl Rahner im Gespräch* 2: 115-116). For a succinct account of Rahner's academic and pastoral work during the Nazi period and the war, see *Karl Rahner. Bilder eines Lebens*, eds. Paul Imhof and Hubert Biallowons (Freiburg: Herder/Benziger: Zurich: 1985), 32-43.

give rise, in turn, to a socially transformative praxis. However, he further believed that such a theology should also see *God* as a politically
relevant figure.[59] Here we detect Rahner's fear that Christianity might
reduce itself solely to a social liberation movement *(eine gesellschaftliche Emanzipationsbewegung)*. Given his view of the human person
as a being of transcendence, Rahner was never in favour of what he
called a "horizontalist" Christianity, because the individual cannot
simply be reduced to their societal function *(den einzelnen nicht auf
seine gesellschaftliche Funktion reduzieren kann)*. However, Rahner
supported the development of political theology because he saw in it an
attempt to unite the political and mystical components of Christianity.

With the many complex moral issues facing the Christian today,
Rahner's approach is to accent the political and ethical relevance of
conscience.[60] Thus, when discussing the Christian attitude towards
atomic weapons, for example, he insists that the Christian can never
abdicate his or her ultimate responsibility before God or delegate
this responsibility to others.[61] Once again we note Rahner's emphasis
on the *decision of conscience* which always occurs in solitude and
in an immediate responsibility before the inscrutable God. An authentic spirituality, in Rahner's view, then, always involves *both* a mystical *and* a societal component. Both these components form a unity
just as the love of God and love of neighbour constitute a unity. The
solitary mysticism, whereby the creature and the Creator interact
directly, is only possible, however, for a person who loves his or her

---

[59] "Auch Gott ist eine politisch relevante Größe." Rahner, *Politische Dimensionen
des Christentums,* 55. Rahner here alludes to the political and social relevance of the
doctrine of the Trinity, though he does not develop this point. For a discussion of the
practicality of the doctrine of the Trinity and the significance of a Trinitarian faith and
praxis, see Catherine Mowry LaCugna, *God for Us: The Trinity and Christian Life*
(San Francisco: HarperCollins, 1991), 377-411; and John J. O'Donnell, *The Mystery
of the Triune God* (New York/Mahwah: Paulist Press, 1989), 128-44.

[60] Rahner is aware that in morally complex situations the Church can often only
provide certain guidelines or principles which, in turn, can lead to a variety of legitimate possible decisions: "Und innerhalb des moralisch Erlaubten hat die Person das
Recht und die Pflicht, Wahlen zu treffen, die nicht unmittelbar durch Gesetze der
Kirche gelenkt werden. Ein großer Teil des religiösen Lebens eines Christen verläuft
außerhalb des offiziellen juristischen Lebens der Kirche." Rahner, *Politische Dimensionen des Christentums,* 68.

[61] Rahner, "Nuclear Weapons and the Christian," *TI* 23: 16-32 (*ST* XV: 280-97).

neighbour.[62] Hence, love of neighbour is not just a consequence of, but a precondition for, our relationship with God.

So, although Rahner increasingly came to stress the socio-political character of neighbourly love, he is, in fact, attempting to steer a middle course between two possible distortions of Christianity. The first distortion manifests itself in the tendency towards what political theology termed "privatization;" the second lies in the attempt to reduce Christianity to a purely humanitarian commitment.[63] Coming from a slightly different angle, Karl Lehmann has formulated Rahner's approach as the endeavour to resolve the relationship between the transcendental and the categorial-historical dimensions of Christianity. Lehmann regards (correctly, I think) the experience of grace as Rahner's basic theological starting-point. He then makes the following observation which is pertinent to our discussion of Rahner's appropriation of Metz's criticisms of transcendental theology:

> "The transcendental, a priori opening-up of the human person to the triune God, and the God of grace, does not occur in an individualistic and unhistorical introspection... . God's self-communication in grace is certainly a 'transcendental' existential of the human person, but it comes to itself, and to the individual, only as mediated in salvation and revelation history. The transcendental and the historical-categorical moment are not side-by-side, but rather form a unity, and are characterized by their own reciprocal relationship of conditioning each other."[64]

---

[62] Imhof, Biallowons, eds., *Karl Rahner in Dialogue*, 183 (*Karl Rahner im Gespräch* 2: 44). While he does not deny the political dimension of Christianity, this dimension does not occupy pride of place for Rahner: "Es gibt zu wenig Menschen, die daran denken, daß im letzten Verstand nicht Gott für sie, sondern sie für Gott da sind. So im allgemeinen theologischen Geschwätz des Alltags gehöre ich gerade zu den 'anthropozentrischen' Theologen. Das ist *letztlich* ein absoluter Unsinn. Ich möchte ein Theologe sein, der sagt, daß *Gott* das Wichtigste ist, daß wir dazu da sind, in einer uns selbst vergessenden Weise ihn zu lieben, ihn anzubeten, für ihn da zu sein, aus unserem eigenen Daseinsbereich in den Abgrund der Unbegreiflichkeit Gottes zu springen." Rahner, *Karl Rahner im Gespräch* 2: 166.

[63] Karl Rahner, *The Shape of the Church to Come*, trans. Edward Quinn (London: SPCK, 1974), 123-32. [*Strukturwandel der Kirche als Aufgabe und Chance,* 3rd ed., Herderbücherei 446 (Freiburg: Herder, 1973), 131-41]. These distortions also apply, of course, to spirituality as the concrete living out or practical dimension of Christianity.

[64] Lehmann, "Karl Rahner: A Portrait," *The Content of Faith*, 31 (*Rechenschaft des Glaubens*, 39*).

Rahner's interest in political theology, then, can be seen as the natural consequence of his thesis of the unity of the love of God and love of neighbour. However, despite Vorgrimler's collation of different interviews and conversations of Rahner on the political dimension of Christianity, one is left with the impression that many of Rahner's statements now seem a little outdated.[65] Rahner is more at home in critically reflecting on the *Church*, its nature, task, future, etc. Indeed, it is here, in the *ecclesiological* context, that the "political" content of his theology comes most sharply into focus.[66]

Rahner consistently emphasizes that the Church's critical function towards society must always begin with self-criticism. In this, he is in line with Metz's comment that socio-political criticism by the Church must above all be criticism by example.[67] However, the socio-critical function of the Church is only one task among many. Other tasks include:

> "... that the Church believes in the living Lord of all history, and in the blessed end of this history which he has promised; that, contrary to all

[65] Many of the excerpts are over thirty years old. However, Rahner acknowledged in 1983 that, despite their differences of approach, both he and Metz shared a "common basic conviction" about the importance of political theology: "Ich gebe zu, dieser Aspekt [i.e., the political dimension] geht auch über die Grenzen meiner eigenen Theologie hinaus. Die politische Theologie wurde ja nicht von mir, sondern von meinem Schüler Johann Baptist Metz entwickelt. Bei allen Kontroversen in Detailfragen existiert doch zwischen meinem großen Schüler und mir eine gemeinsame Grundüberzeugung: Für die Verkündigung des Evangeliums müssen wir heute die gesellschaftspolitischen Wissenschaften in die Überlegungen der Theologie miteinbeziehen." Rahner, *Politische Dimensionen des Christentums,* 59.

[66] Rahner's *The Shape of the Church to Come,* referred to above, is an excellent example of this. The original title *Strukturwandel der Kirche als Aufgabe und Chance* indicates that Rahner has in mind fundamental structural change in the Church. Similar insights can be found in his "The Function of the Church as a Critic of Society," *TI* 12: 229-49 (*ST* IX: 569-90) and "Transformation in the Church and Secular Society," *TI* 17: 167-180 (*ST* XII: 513-28). See also Guenther, *Rahner and Metz: Transcendental Theology as Political Theology,* 240-65.

[67] Hence, Metz's vision of the Church as the place and institution for socio-political freedom, where "the ecclesial institution, conscious of its own provisional status, does not repress critical freedom but makes it possible, this being the formal contour of the 'servant Church'; how criticism is part of the public life of the Church; how partial identification with the institution is to be positively treasured; how rights and freedom in the Church are not merely constitutional problems but elements of the process of attaining knowledge in the Church's theology;" Metz, "Political Theology," *Sacramentum Mundi* 5: 38 (*SM* III: 1239-40).

the hopelessness which this history continually reiterates, the Church goes on hoping; that it prays for, and feels responsible for, the poor and the oppressed, for people who have not had their fair share of things in this world, and for the dead; that the Church stands in the way when people want to turn history into a mere tale of victors and survivors."[68]

A sociological and political critique of the Church is necessary, according to Rahner because, as a social entity with its own institutions and structures, the Church remains always an *ecclesia semper reformanda*, as the Second Vatican Council declared.[69] The pilgrim Church in history is the "Church of Sinners" whose "concrete forms of social institutionalization" are "open ever anew to criticism."[70] Rahner's ecclesiology thus exhibits a dialectical tension between the divine and human dimensions of the Church. On the one hand, he can claim that the Church represents "the historically real and actual presence of the eschatologically victorious mercy of God," or "the sign of the grace of God definitively triumphant in the world in Christ."[71] On the other hand, there is the need for a critique of the Church, a critique from within, based on the intrinsic tension within the Church between that which it seeks to be and that which it *de facto* is.[72]

The Church, then, exercises its critical function in society by first of all critiquing and reforming its own inner life and structures. If the Church be-comes an exemplar of such structural change, then it, in turn, Rahner believes, can have a greater influence for change on secular society.[73] Rahner's reflections on the Church, especially in *The Shape of the Church to Come*, serve as a continual reminder that Christianity cannot confine the struggle with sin to a wholly private sphere since so much sin has been institutionalized and become

[68] Rahner, "Transformation in the Church and Secular Society," *TI* 17: 171 (*ST* XII: 518).

[69] *Lumen Gentium*, n. 8, *Vatican Council II*, ed. Flannery, vol. 1, 358

[70] Rahner, "The Function of the Church as a Critic of Society," *TI* 12: 231 (*ST* IX: 571). See also his "The Church of Sinners," and "The Sinful Church in the Decrees of Vatican II," *TI* 6: 253-69 and 270-94 (*ST* VI: 301-20 and 321-47).

[71] Karl Rahner, *The Church and the Sacraments* (New York: Herder and Herder, 1963), 14, 18. [*Kirche und Sakramente*, Quaestiones Disputatae 10 (Freiburg: Herder, 1963), 13, 18].

[72] Rahner, "The Function of the Church as a Critic of Society," *TI* 12: 232 (*ST* IX: 572).

taken-for-granted in our world. The Church, he points out, has never interpreted salvation in an individualistic sense as a matter of a person's merely private and interior life.[74] Indeed, if the Church avoids the task of confronting institutionalized sin, it will be regarded as "merely a conservative power, devoted to the defence of things as they are."[75] And, on the other hand, the Church, in order to be outwardly credible, must allow its commitment to justice and freedom to become more effective in its internal life as well.[76]

c. Gathering the Threads

Our discussion of the criticisms of Rahner by both von Balthasar and Metz has provided us with some significant insights into Rahner's understanding of spirituality. Firstly, we believe that the seeds of Rahner's later awareness of the political dimension of spirituality can be traced to his early writings on the unity of the love of neighbour

---

[73] In 1974, Rahner was convinced that "transformations in the Church and the new structures arising out of them could provide a model for secular societies." Rahner, "Transformation in the Church and Secular Society," *TI* 17: 175 (*ST* XII: 521-22). However, in the current ecclesial climate this argument sounds unconvincing. Ten years later, in 1984, Rahner's former utopian view had been replaced by a more pessimistic one. Here, he speaks of the wintry season of the Church ("die 'winterliche' Kirche") and of a European Church on the "defensive." Karl Rahner, *Glaube in winterlicher Zeit*, 232-45. In Chapter Three (p. 147, n. 119), we noted how Rahner refers to a corresponding "winterliche Frömmigkeit" (a wintry piety) which possibly reflects his own style of life and temperament ("wo es im religiösen Leben nicht sehr viel Blüten gibt") as much as it does the contemporary situation of the European Church. *Karl Rahner im Gespräch* 2: 212-13. Rahner envisaged two types of spirituality in the future. The first is the "wintry" or sober spirituality of hope in the midst of a sceptical (and he would include here the "scepticism" of the believer) and an atheistic environment, with which Rahner and his "holy agnosticism" (Metz) could identify. Contrasted with this is the type of spirituality associated with charismatic and enthusiastic movements. Rahner found such expressions of spirituality hard to take as they tended, in his view, to advocate an almost naive immediacy to God and a rather simplistic view of faith. Rahner, *Herausforderung des Christen*, 149.

[74] Rahner, "The Function of the Church as a Critic of Society," *TI* 12: 237 (*ST* IX: 577). In a footnote he adds: "To the extent that political theology is directed against this tendency to restrict salvation to the private sphere it represents a genuine concern for the Church."

[75] Rahner, *The Shape of the Church to Come*, 125 (*Strukturwandel der Kirche*, 133).

[76] Richard P. McBrien, *Catholicism*, 3rd ed. (London: Geoffrey Chapman, 1981, 1994), 693.

and the love of God. This awareness subsequently became more explicit.[77] It is especially evident in Rahner's many conversations and interviews given towards the end of his theological life, where a spirituality emerges which comprises both a *mystical* and a *societal* component. In previous chapters, we explored the mystical component and saw that it had to do with an immediate experience of God mediated, for example, through the Ignatian *Exercises*. Thus far in this chapter, we have examined how spirituality — understood as the practice of Christianity, or discipleship (*Nachfolge*) — also has a societal component.[78] Influenced by his former pupil and friend, J. B. Metz, Rahner came more and more to see how the socio-political backdrop of human life must also be taken into account in any contemporary understanding of spirituality.

If our presentation of Rahner's appropriation of Metz's criticisms indicates a degree of convergence between these two theologians (especially in their emphasis on the mystical and societal component of Christianity), this does not mean that we can gloss over the real differences that exist between their respective theological perspectives. However, our purpose in offering a defence of Rahner's theological approach is to counter a common misunderstanding, namely, that Rahner *exclusively* pursues a transcendental method which then leads to an insensitivity to social problems and to an ineffectiveness in the realm of political and social change.[79] When we discussed the

---

[77] For a discussion of Rahner's later theology, his attempt to find an increasingly temporal and historical conception of God and the people of God, and his developing historical sense of society, see the fine article by Leo O'Donovan, "A Journey Into Time: The Legacy of Karl Rahner's Last Years," *Theological Studies* 46 (1985): 621-46.

[78] "Following Christ Today," *Karl Rahner in Dialogue*, 181-85 (*Karl Rahner im Gespräch* 2: 41-47).

[79] This awareness is evident as far back as Rahner's 1966 address to the conference on "Christian Humanity and Marxist Humanism," where Rahner explicitly states that "theology must always be 'political' theology... The theologian is aware that, according to Christianity, salvation is achieved not only within the explicitly religious sphere but in *all* dimensions of human existence, ... where one loves in an absolutely responsible manner, serves one's neighbour selflessly and willingly accepts the incomprehensible nature and disappointments of one's existence, hoping ultimately to embrace its as yet unrevealed meaningfulness... . In this sense, the whole of the human sphere is religious and the whole of the religious sphere is divine." This lecture reveals Rahner's twin emphasis on God as the absolute future of humankind

significance of themes such as prayer, love, grace, etc., for Rahner's spirituality, we noted how he approached these from both a transcendental and from a historical perspective.[80] Thus, Rahner exhibits a two-fold theological method, or better, a method that incorporates both transcendental and historical reflection. Admittedly, transcendental reflection always runs the risk of failing to take into account the historical dimensions of theological reality.[81] In so emphasizing the self-communication of God to the human person in the transcendental dimension of their being, it can be overlooked that such a self-communication also has a history, "and this is at once the single history of both salvation and revelation."[82] And Rahner, for his part, while consistently arguing for the ever-present interaction of experience and reflection, or for the reciprocal interdependence of transcendental and historical reflection in theology, nonetheless concentrates more on the transcendental moment.[83]

as well as his insistence on "the sober service of 'political' love." Rahner, "Christian Humanism," *TI* 9: 188-189 (*ST* VIII: 240-41). Rahner's awareness of a political dimension to *spirituality* is also in evidence at this time. See his "Christian Living Formerly and Today," *TI* 7: 19 (*ST* VII: 27), where the term "politische Frömmigkeit" is used (though this is unusually translated into English as "the 'political' form of religion").

I am also indebted here to some insightful comments on Rahner's dialectical method by Leo O'Donovan, "Orthopraxis and Theological Method in Karl Rahner," *CTSA Proceedings* 35 (1980): 47-65, and by Mary V. Maher, "Rahner on the Human Experience of God: Idealist Tautology or Christian Theology?," *Philosophy & Theology* 7 (1992): 127-64.

[80] For our discussion of the themes of prayer and love in Rahner's spirituality, see Chapter Two. Rahner's understanding of the "Experience of Grace" is treated in a separate section in Chapter Three. See also his "Reflections on Methodology in Theology," *TI* 11: 84-101 (*ST* IX: 95-113), where Rahner reiterates this twofold method. We concur then with Tafferner's comment that: "Die Verbindung Gottes mit der Menschheit ist bei Rahner immer als eine Verbindung in Geschichte und Transzendenz zu verstehen." Tafferner, *Gottes- und Nächstenliebe in der deutschsprachigen Theologie des 20. Jahrhunderts*, 224.

[81] According to Maher, "Rahner on the Human Experience of God," *Philosophy & Theology* 7 (1992): 148, Metz's critique of Rahner highlights "the need to develop a method for the dialectic (the dialectic *between* the transcendental analysis of human experience oriented toward and by Mystery *and* the attending (dialectically) to the pluralism of social, cultural and historical positions)."

[82] Rahner, *FCF*, 141 (*Grundkurs*, 146).

[83] "... es gibt wenig philosophische, anthropologische und theologische Probleme, die schwerer richtig und ausbalanciert beantwortet werden können als das Verhältnis von Transzendentalität und Geschichte. Insofern bin ich gar nicht verwundert, wenn

By acknowledging and taking on board some of the criticisms of
Metz, however, Rahner opens the way for a more "performative"
understanding of spirituality. The human person is not only a
hearer of the Word but a doer of the word as well. Christian spirituality is not merely an "experiencing" but a "doing," an *activity*,
necessarily involving a "praxis" of solidarity with those who suffer.[84] As we shall see in the final section of our work, it is especially Latin-American theologians who have translated Christianity into a praxis of liberating activity. Commentators who have
examined the relationship between Metz and Rahner agree that,
while the historical moment in Rahner's method could be more
explicitly developed, it would be incorrect to declare his transcendental theology void of any imperatives impelling Christians
towards a spirituality of solidarity. Thus, we agree with Guenther,
who sees in Rahner's thesis of the radical unity of love of neighbour and love of God the foundation for such a spirituality.[85] Yet
Rahner warns that one should not limit oneself merely to a one-
sided social and political engagement. A truly authentic Christian
spirituality will not shy away from the attempt to bring such political engagement into an "inner synthesis" with one's religious life.[86]

---

man mir nachweisen will, daß dieses schwierige Verhältnis in meiner Theologie nicht
umfassend und ursprünglich genug reflektiert wird... . Transzendentalität ist für mich
immer Transzendentalität, die *in* konkreter und letztlich unableitbar Geschichte zu
sich selbst kommt." Rahner, *Herausforderung des Christen*, 130, 136.

   [84] The term "praxis" within liberation theologies is used to accentuate the important distinction (which goes back to Aristotle) between practice (*poiesis*) as a technical skill involved in making something, and practice (*praxis*) as a way of life.
"Whereas the former is a matter of technical skill (*techne*), the latter expresses a basic
way of life... Liberation theologians have followed this direction insofar as when they
affirm that praxis is both the goal and criterion of their theologies, they are affirming
that their goal is not some technocratic organization, some social structure, ... but
rather a way of life. The term *praxis* specifies that the liberation they seek is more
than a mere technocratic or economic development — it is a liberation that has religious, social, political, and personal dimensions." Francis Schüssler Fiorenza,
"Systematic Theology: Tasks and Methods," *Systematic Theology: Roman Catholic
Perspectives*, eds. Francis Schüssler Fiorenza and John P. Galvin (Dublin: Gill and
Macmillan, 1992), 64-65.

   [85] Guenther, *Rahner and Metz: Transcendental Theology as Political Theology*,
271. See also his section: "Rahner's Comments on Political Theology," 292-311.

   [86] Rahner's comments in 1983 once again reveal this inner synthesis of the mystical and societal components of his spirituality: "... ich habe den Eindruck, daß die

This "gathering-in" (*Einbeziehung*) of the concerns of political theology into the broader transcendental framework may take some of the cutting edge off its critical questions (as Lehmann suggests),[87] but Rahner's persistent fear was that Christianity could easily be "reduced" to its purely "horizontal," i.e., political dimensions.

Another concern which Rahner expressed with regard to the modern theology "of the world" is that it can too quickly turn God into a "God-of-the-gaps" (*Lückenbüßer*), that is, a stand-in for the personal happiness and self-fulfilment of the human person.[88] Rahner's claim, on the other hand, is that God does not exist for the human being, but the human being for God — we are only authentically Christian when "with Jesus the crucified One, we let ourselves fall in self-capitulation and without condition into the inscrutable mystery of God."[89] His emphasis is, therefore, on what he terms "the inexhaustible transcendence of God," *(die unverbrauchbare Transzendenz Gottes)*. While "recognizing a mutual dependence between love of God and love of neighbour," Rahner stresses how "the ultimate message of Christianity cuts right across an intramundane humanism, since it involves a *love of God in himself*."[90]

jungen Leute ein sehr starkes soziales und politisches Engagement an den Tag legen. Sie sollten allerdings dieses Engagement in eine *innere Synthese* mit ihrer Religiösität bringen. Es gibt eben doch Gott, es gibt ein personales Verhältnis zu ihm, und es gibt ein personales Gericht Gottes durch den je eigenen Tod hindurch. Alle diese Dinge kann man nicht abschreiben zugunsten eines gesellschaftspolitischen und gesellschaftskritischen Engagements." Rahner, *Glaube in winterlicher Zeit*, 128. (italics mine).

[87] "Die Einbeziehung z.B. von Themen der 'politischen Theologie' in ein größeres Ganzes theologischer Reflexion nimmt jener in gewisser Weise die dezidierte Spitze ihrer Fragestellung (was dann manchmal so gedeutet wird, als würde diese überhaupt nicht 'verstanden'), stellt faktisch aber zugleich eine stille theologische Korrektur dar." Karl Lehmann, "Karl Rahner," *Bilanz der Theologie im 20. Jahrhundert*, eds. Herbert Vorgrimler and Robert Vander Gucht (Freiburg: Herder, 1970), 179.

[88] Rahner, *Glaube in winterlicher Zeit*, 61.

[89] Rahner, *Glaube in winterlicher Zeit*, 61. [ET from Guenther, *Rahner and Metz: Transcendental Theology as Political Theology*, 298, n. 46].

[90] Rahner, "The Inexhaustible Transcendence of God and Our Concern for the Future," *TI* 20: 179 (*ST* XIV: 412-13). (emphasis mine). Rahner's point here is that, in the last analysis, it is not God who exists for us, but we who exist for God. In other words, we cannot *use* God's transcendence for our purposes. See Leo O'Donovan, "A Journey Into Time: The Legacy of Karl Rahner's Last Years," *Theological Studies* 46 (1985): 643, n. 112.

We have previously explored this love of God for God's own sake in the context of the Ignatian *Exercises* and Rahner's interpretation of consolation.[91] However, in this article, "The Inexhaustible Transcendence of God and Our Concern for the Future" (1980), Rahner seems almost to have distanced himself from his previous emphasis on the *unity* of love of neighbour and love of God. Instead, the accent now is on Christianity not becoming stifled in the finite: "God and the world must not be made to coincide simply in a dead sameness."[92] Rahner's point here is that authentic love of God only exists when concern for self is surpassed and relativized by love for God Himself. This transcendence of the human person towards God thus relativizes all individual finite realities (be they particular ideologies, social systems, propaganda, technical developments, etc.), depriving them of their potentially idolatrous

---

[91] See Ralf Miggelbrink, *Ekstatische Gottesliebe im tätigen Weltbezug. Der Beitrag Karl Rahners zur zeitgenössischen Gotteslehre*, Münsteraner Theologische Abhandlungen (Altenberge: Telos Verlag, 1989), 1-42, and 185-201. Miggelbrink grounds Rahner's theory of the unity of the love of neighbour and the love of God in the latter's early work on Ignatius and Bonaventure: "Die ekstatische Liebe konkretisiert sich als Offenheit gegenüber der je größeren Wahrheit und in der Liebe zum Nächsten. Ihr Kern ist eine personalistisch gedachte Gottesbeziehung... . Die Verbindung des Ekstase-Begriffes mit dem Liebesbegriff bei Bonaventura bot Rahner darüberhinaus die Möglichkeit, die tatmystische Dimension der ignatianischen Exerzitien zu integrieren: Bei Ignatius ist der göttliche Trost 'Begleiter' der vollzogenen oder der mit der Festigkeit des Willens vorgestellten innerweltlichen Tat. Hier bereits ist die Überwindung eines rein geistlichen Verständnisses der Gotteserkenntnis 'in ecstatico amore' beschlossen. *Hier hat die These von der Einheit von Gottes- und Nächstenliebe ihren Ursprung.*" (pp. 2, 19-20, emphasis mine). Tafferner, *Gottes- und Nächstenliebe in der deutschsprachigen Theologie des 20. Jahrhunderts*, 201, n. 365, also takes over this thesis of Miggelbrink's: "Rahners theologische Rede über die Liebe zu Gott hat ihren Ursprung in der Überzeugung von der Erfahrbarkeit Gottes in der Überlieferung solcher Gotteserfahrung bei Bonaventura und insbesondere bei Ignatius von Loyola" (p. 224). The distinctive value of her contribution lies in her exposition of a number of lesser known Rahnerian texts where the topic of the unity of the love of neighbour and the love of God is mentioned. See for example, Rahner's discussion of "The Prison Pastorate," ("Gefängnisseelsorge") and "Railway Missions" ("Überlegungen zur Bahnhofsmission") *Mission and Grace* 3: 22-48 and 74-97 (*Sendung und Gnade*, 410-29 and 447-63). Rahner's article "Why and How Can We Venerate the Saints?," *TI* 8: 3-23, esp. 16-21 (*ST* VII: 283-303, esp. 296-300) also contains a section on the unity of the love of neighbour and the love of God pertinent to our discussion.

[92] Rahner, "The Inexhaustible Transcendence of God and Our Concern for the Future," *TI* 20: 180 (*ST* XIV: 414).

character. It is certainly not a question, though, of Rahner bypassing or neglecting the intramundane relevance of the love of God and the consequent requirement of ethical action. Rather, it is yet another example of the ongoing dialectical tension between transcendence and history which lies at the heart of Rahner's twofold theological method. Perhaps we should let Rahner himself have the final word on the relationship between his theology and that of his former pupil:

> "For it has always been clear in my theology that a 'transcendental experience' (of God and of grace) is always mediated through a categorical experience in history, in interpersonal relationships, and in society. If one not only sees and takes seriously these necessary mediations of transcendental experience but also fills it out in a concrete way, then one already practices in an authentic way political theology, or in other words, a practical fundamental theology. On the other hand, such a political theology is, if it truly wishes to concern itself with God, not possible without reflection on those essential characteristics of humankind which a transcendental theology discloses. Therefore, I believe that my theology and that of Metz are not necessarily contradictory."[93]

In this first part of our final chapter, we have sought not only to present some of the chief reservations about Rahner on the part of Von Balthasar and Metz, but also to see how Rahner has responded to and incorporated a number of these criticisms into his theology and spirituality. Central to our presentation has been the claim that Rahner's thesis of the unity of the love of neighbour and the love of God provides the ground for his growing awareness of the political dimension of spirituality. This thesis, in turn, can be traced back to Rahner's early spiritual writings on Bonaventure and on the Ignatian *Exercises*. Combining the core experience at the heart of the *Spiritual Exercises* (a personal encounter with God, as we saw in the previous chapter) with the *Praxisbezogenheit* of Rahner's later writings, we can conclude that Rahner's spirituality has both a mystical and a societal component — even if the latter element was not always brought sharply into focus.

---

[93] Rahner, "Introduction," to Bacik, *Apologetics and the Eclipse of Mystery*, x.

2. The "Specifically Christian" Nature of Rahner's Spirituality

a. The Christocentric Character of Rahner's Spirituality

A key theme running through the first part of this chapter was Rahner's emphasis on the unity of the love of God and neighbour. This theme is a development from our discussions in Chapters Two and Three, where Rahner, following Matthew 25, also asserted a unity between love of Jesus and love of neighbour. For him, every love for one's fellow human being has the character of an absolute commitment to that person. At the same time, such love is a venture, a risk, that hopes not to meet with ultimate disappointment. It is above all in Jesus, Rahner claims, that this hope is confirmed, and whereby we are enabled to commit ourselves in love to our fellow human beings. What is at issue here, and this is all we wish to bring out in this section, is the importance in Rahner's spirituality of a *faith encounter* with Jesus, and how such an encounter forms the point of departure in his Christology. In Chapter Three, we examined three possible approaches to such a relationship when we focused on the consequences for spirituality implied in Rahner's re-interpretation of grace.[94] These three approaches (or three appeals) — love of neighbour, readiness for death, and hope in the absolute future — we argued, "point us on to that relationship with Jesus which alone constitutes the basis for an explicit and genuine Christianity."[95]

---

[94] See Chapter Three, 3, c, ii, "Rahner's Three Appeals." Admittedly, there will be some overlap here with what has been said before. Indeed, the full christocentric basis of Rahner's spirituality only emerges when our discussion of his Christology in Chapters Two, Three and Four (in different contexts) is taken into account. Hence, we will not develop such "christocentric" themes here as Jesus' cross and resurrection, which have been referred to already. However, this second section will develop some of the points — the ecclesial and the sacramental aspects of Rahner's spirituality, for instance, — which have only been hinted at, intermittently, up to now.

[95] Rahner, "The Quest for Approaches Leading to an Understanding of the Mystery of the God-Man Jesus," *TI* 13: 195 (*ST* X: 209). We have previously spoken of a "seeking" Christology in this context in Chapter Three (see above n. 94). Rahner concludes this article (p. 200) with a succinct summary of this Christology: "The questions must be asked how we can love our neighbour unreservedly, committing our own lives in a radical sense on his or her behalf, how such a love is not rendered invalid even by death, and whether we can hope in death to discover not the end but

Anyone who claims to love Jesus, that is, who regards Jesus and his life as making a personal and radical demand on him or her, is not referring to an abstract "ideal" or idea of Jesus. Rather, they are affirming, in effect, that he is living, and has been delivered from death. We saw how Rahner makes this claim in the context of the discussion of the resurrection of Jesus, which constitutes the final and definitive assent of God to us, and forms the basis for our hope that the one and single history of the world as a whole can no longer fail. Alongside this contention is the assumption that it is not possible to say anything of religious or theological significance about Jesus without also describing the essence of *faith* itself (an act whereby Jesus is seen as the Christ).[96] Therefore, *the* point of departure for Rahner's Christology is the faith relationship which a believing Christian actually has to Jesus Christ. Only then does a transcendental Christology reflect upon the conditions of possibility for a reality which we have already encountered.[97] Moreover, a faith in Christ which is not rooted in the actual historical life of Jesus is simply a contemporary form of fideism.[98]

While we agree with Rahner that faith is always more than a dry intellectual assent to propositions, and involves the historical Jesus, one is sometimes left with the impression that his understanding of

the consummation in that absolute future which is called God. And anyone who does ask these questions is seeking thereby, whether he or she recognizes it or not, for Jesus. He or she who really keeps alive this threefold question and does not suppress it will not find it in itself so difficult to discover the answer to these questions in history in the person of Jesus, provided Jesus is preached to them aright... . Traditional christology, which at first sight seems so difficult to understand, ... conveys no other message than that in Jesus God has uttered himself to us victoriously and unsurpassably as the blessed response to that threefold question which is not merely something human beings ask themselves, but which they really are."

[96] Rahner, " 'I Believe in Jesus Christ': Interpreting an Article of Faith," *TI* 9: 165-68 (*ST* VIII: 213-17).

[97] Rahner, *FCF*, 177, 203 (*Grundkurs*, 179, 203). It should be pointed out, however, that Rahner, in the "Introduction" (p. 13) to *Foundations* warns "against taking a *too narrowly Christological approach.*" Thus, he does not begin his foundational course with Jesus since "today Jesus Christ is himself a problem." The German original (*Grundkurs*, 24-25) captures Rahner's intention better here than the English translation: "Man kann also nicht bei Jesus Christus als dem schlechthin letzten Datum anfangen, sondern *muß auf ihn hinführen.*" (italics mine).

[98] Rahner, "Remarks on the Importance of the History of Jesus for Catholic Dogmatics," *TI* 13: 212 (*ST* X: 226). See also Dych, *Karl Rahner*, 50.

faith is in fact *too* fiducial. Faith is repeatedly described as occurring "as a result of an absolute trust," and when "we entrust ourselves to him (Jesus) in a radical way."[99] Clearly, Rahner's view of faith comprises an act of radical self-commitment of the whole human being to Jesus Christ, that is to say, an act of total self-surrender to him. So, while on the one hand, Rahner correctly insists on maintaining an intrinsic connection between faith and history, on the other hand, there is a certain private or individualistic tendency in such a description of faith — despite its value in emphasizing how Christian faith answers our deepest thirst for meaning. In the last section we examined what could be called the social or political dimension of faith, and asked whether this dimension received sufficient prominence in Rahner. The question recurs here in the context of the discussion of faith, whose prophetic and critical function was stressed by Vatican II,[100] a theme which was then further developed by theologians of liberation.

It is significant, for our purposes, to note that, when Rahner treats of the personal relationship of a Christian to Christ in *Foundations*, he does so not in his chapter on Christian life, where one would normally expect such a topic to be discussed, but rather in the chapter on Jesus Christ. Rahner is advocating here what we referred to already as "existentiell Christology."[101] Underlying this approach is the view that "Christianity in its full and explicit form is not merely an abstract theory, ... (but) understands itself as an existentiell process, and this process is precisely what we are calling a personal relationship to Jesus Christ."[102] Christology, then, is not primarily reflection on an idea about Jesus, but a reflection on this lived faith relationship. William Dych, the English translator of *Foundations*, captures this spiritual root and significance of Rahner's existentiell Christology well when he observes:

---

[99] Rahner, " 'I Believe in Jesus Christ': Interpreting an Article of Faith," *TI* 9: 165, 168 (*ST* VIII: 213, 216).

[100] *Gaudium et spes,* nn. 11, 21, 43, *Vatican Council II*, ed. Flannery, vol. 1, 912, 920-22, 943-45.

[101] See the concluding part of our reflections on "Love of Neighbour as Love of God," in Chapter Two, 2, d.

[102] Rahner, *FCF*, 306 (*Grundkurs*, 298).

"For Christian faith is not primarily a theory about Jesus, but a praxis, a way of life. It is the life of discipleship in response to his call to 'follow' him... It is by doing the truth that Jesus did that existentiell Christology acquires its concrete, experiential knowledge of Jesus of Nazareth. One sees here why Rahner accorded such importance to Ignatius Loyola and his *Spiritual Exercises* for his theology. Through the exercise not of the speculative intellect, but of the senses and the imagination, the *Exercises* are designed to put one 'in touch' with the actual Jesus and to give one a 'taste of' and a 'feel for' his life. In this encounter one does not 'grasp' something, but 'is grasped', and the faith which responds and follows is what Rahner calls the point of departure for all Christology."[103]

Without entering into the many special questions which Rahner deals with in his Christology, our focus has been on Rahner's christological *point of departure*, an encounter involving the historical Jesus, and hence an "ascending Christology." It is not that Rahner believes an ascending Christology (proceeding from the human being Jesus) cannot coincide with the classical descending Christology (God becomes a human being). Rather, it is his contention that "this ascending theology shows us how and why an apparently simple relationship of trust in Jesus can contain within itself the whole of classical Christology."[104] In trying to give an account of his or her belief in Jesus Christ, a Christian will reflect first of all on the faith which they already have. In this sense, faith precedes theology. Rahner's christological method, therefore, begins with the soteriological significance of Jesus and his fate for us, and then moves onto a consideration of "Christ in himself."[105] In short, his Christology of ascent is one which takes history seriously. Secondly, it is entirely legitimate to begin such an ascending Christology with statements about the

---

[103] Dych, *Karl Rahner*, 61. Rahner's analysis of the christological dimension of the Ignatian *Exercises* (in the context of the Election) has been discussed in the Chapter Four, 2, d.

[104] Rahner, "Jesus Christ — The Meaning of Life," *TI* 21: 218 (*ST* XV: 215).

[105] "In describing this Christian relationship, in the first instance at least we do not have to distinguish between what Jesus is in the faith of a Christian 'in himself', and what he means 'for us'. For in their unity these two aspects cannot be completely separated from each other. For, on the one hand, we neither could nor would be concerned about Jesus if he had no 'meaning for us', and on the other hand every assertion about his meaning for us implies an assertion about something 'in itself'." Rahner, *FCF*, 204 (*Grundkurs*, 204).

significance of Jesus "for us" (statements which also, of course, express a reality about Jesus "in himself").[106] In fact, Rahner is steering a middle course here: he wants both to retain the classical formulations of Christology, such as Chalcedon, while also striving to obtain new insights from the old formulations, in an attempt to bring Christology into a more positive relationship with current ways of thinking. He does this because he is aware of how traditional Chalcedonian Christology can easily fall under the suspicion of sounding "mythological" (i.e., incredible) to people of today. But far from being embarrassed about the Church's traditional two-thousand-year-old Christology, Rahner's response is to dig deeper into this christological tradition. It is a question of underscoring both the unique permanence of Christian faith while allowing for new formulations of this faith. In our present context, this means that the truth of traditional Christology can be stated in other ways.[107]

What would comprise such a new formulation of faith?[108] With regard to Christology, Rahner believes that there are two aspects or *fundamental insights* in an orthodox Christology. The first lies with Jesus' claim:

---

[106] Rahner, "Christology Today," *TI* 21: 223-24 (*ST* XV: 220-21). Rahner also stresses this unity of Christology and soteriology in his article "Brief Observations on Systematic Christology Today," *TI* 21: 233-34 (*ST* XV: 230-31). Rahner's preference for an ascending Christology can likewise be seen in his 1971 article "The Two Basic Types of Christology," *TI* 13: 213-23 (*ST* X: 227-38). Referring there to the classical descending Christology, he concludes that "in order to achieve intelligibility and to justify its own propositions, [it may] be forced to return to the quite simple experience of Jesus of Nazareth." But, he adds: "Nevertheless it is legitimate, inevitable and sanctioned by the fact that the Church, right from the earliest times down to the present day, has discovered Jesus of Nazareth precisely in these statements of a Chalcedonian christology which seem so abstractly metaphysical, almost irreligious, and strangely inquisitive in character. It has discovered him there afresh again and again." (p. 221).

[107] "... Even loyalty to the faith of Chalcedon permits us and obliges us to inquire beyond these formulations of classical Christology and to search for other more original or at least equally original christological statements which are perhaps closer to Scripture ..." Rahner, "Brief Observations on Systematic Christology Today," *TI* 21: 232 (*ST* XV: 229).

[108] The "Epilogue" of *Foundations,* 448-60 (*Grundkurs,* 430-40) contains three examples of such brief creedal statements oriented towards the essentials of faith. It can be debated, however, whether his three examples actually exhibit the "explicit Christological structure" (p. 453), which he insists they should.

"that there is present with him a new and unsurpassable closeness of God which on its part will prevail victoriously and is inseparable from him. He calls this closeness the coming and the arrival of God's kingdom, which forces a person to decide explicitly whether or not he accepts this God who has come so close."[109]

Jesus, then, through his reality and his word, represents God's universal pledge to humankind, and the unsurpassable access to the immediacy of God in Himself:

"In Jesus (and ultimately only through him) we experience through his life and word that the history of the offer of an unsurpassable and absolute self-communication of God to humankind has entered a phase which can rightly be interpreted as the final phase of the history of human freedom ... In this phase the victory of God's offer of himself to humankind has become irrevocable, as a result of God's action and not merely a posteriori as a result of the actual exercise of human freedom."[110]

Inherent in this claim is that Jesus is the last or "eschatological" prophet — God's final word. This is not because God has arbitrarily ceased to say anything further, but because in offering *Himself* in Jesus, there is nothing to say beyond this.[111] Rahner's second point has been discussed more fully in Chapter Three, and centres on the salvific significance which Jesus' death acquired from the perspective of his resurrection. God's self-offer in Jesus can only be final and victorious if it is *accepted*. It is in Jesus' death and resurrection that such acceptance (of God's offer of Himself to Jesus and in him to humankind) is really actualized and becomes historically present for us.[112]

Our considerations thus far have sought to show what Rahner describes as the abiding significance of Jesus for Christian faith.[113]

---

[109] Rahner, *FCF*, 279 (*Grundkurs*, 274).

[110] Rahner, "Christology Today," *TI* 21: 225 (*ST* XV: 222).

[111] Rahner, *FCF*, 280 (*Grundkurs*, 274). Rahner also maintains that the statement that Jesus is the irreversible pledge of the God who communicates Himself, and not a reality created by Him, is coterminous with the classical statement of Christology concerning the hypostatic union. Rahner, "Christology Today," *TI* 21: 226 (*ST* XV: 222).

[112] "By the resurrection, then, Jesus is vindicated as the absolute saviour." In other words, his claim to have a new and real immediacy of God coming from God Himself has been vindicated with the resurrection. Rahner, *FCF*, 280 (*Grundkurs*, 274).

[113] "But for Christian faith Jesus, his life and the accomplishment of his death, is nothing other than God's definitive invitation to this surrender [by which we allow ourselves to be seized in faith, hope, and love] and the irrevocable promise that this surrender is really accomplished through God's powerful love and not ultimately by

Rahner is convinced that the Church's entire christological teaching can be derived from the fundamental significance of Jesus "for us." This conviction goes hand in hand with the belief that Jesus and his salvific work have made it possible to arrive at an immediacy to the true God. In this respect, Jesus is the unassailable witness — the one who effects that to which he gives witness. We note here, too, a mutual complementarity between the anthropological and christological foci of Rahner's theology.[114] What this means is that, for Rahner, the fundamental or basic statements about Christianity must be related to the intrinsic structure of the human person. By intrinsic structure, Rahner is referring to a finality or dynamism which a person has (at least unthematically, and imparted by God) towards God's self-communication. A transcendental Christology then appeals to a person and asks him or her whether they can freely accept and appropriate such an orientation.[115] The transcendental enquiry at issue here, far from being an abstract, ahistorical process, represents an attempt to *correlate* the historical event of God's saving self-revelation and communication in Christ with the basic structures of human existence and history.[116] Hence, it is the task of an authentic transcendental theology (despite its inherent limitations, as we indicated earlier, and which Rahner acknowledges) to elucidate the connection or correlation, in order to render Christian faith intelligible. Only by showing how the concrete, historical events of salvation history really correspond to the basic structures of the human condition can Christianity claim to affect the human person at the ultimate level of their existence and subjectivity.[117]

the efforts of our own goodwill." Rahner, "Christianity's Absolute Claim," *TI* 21: 180 (*ST* XV: 179-80). See also, Rahner, *Our Christian Faith*, 85-104 (*Was sollen wir noch glauben?*, 105-25).

[114] Rahner, "Theology and Anthropology," *TI* 9: 28 (*ST* VIII: 43).

[115] Rahner, *FCF*, 208-209 (*Grundkurs*, 208-209). "It specifies and vindicates the universal significance of the particular event of Jesus Christ by specifying and vindicating the conditions of its possibility." John C. Robertson, Jr. review of *FCF* in *Religious Studies Review* 5/3 (July 1979), 193.

[116] For a helpful discussion of Catholic methods of correlation in fundamental theology, along with an insistence on the need for some form of transcendental reflection in theology, see David Tracy, "The Uneasy Alliance Reconceived: Catholic Theological Method, Modernity, and Postmodernity," *Theological Studies* 50 (1989): 548-70.

[117] Rahner, "Reflections on Methodology in Theology," *TI* 11: 100 (*ST* IX: 112). See also John R. Sachs, "Transcendental Method in Theology and the Normativity of Human Experience," *Philosophy & Theology* 7 (1992): 213-25.

b. The Ecclesial Aspect of Rahner's Spirituality

In the last section we looked at the significance for Rahner of the personal faith relationship with Christ. We also noted how this "spiritual" foundation forms the starting-point for his christological reflections. But spirituality (or lived Christianity, as Rahner is wont to describe it) also has an essential *ecclesial* aspect. Although the doctrine of the Church cannot be considered the ultimate truth of Christianity — Rahner, as we have seen, also admits the possibility of an "anonymous" Christianity — Rahner does maintain "that church has something to do with the essence of Christianity."[118] The Church represents "the historical continuation of Christ in and through the community of those who believe in him, and who recognize him explicitly as the mediator of salvation in a profession of faith."[119] Rahner bases his claim that Christianity is ecclesial on an anthropology that accents the interrelational nature of humankind. Social intercommunication or interpersonal relationship, in other words, forms an essential part of what constitutes a human being. And if salvation is said to touch the *whole* person in all the dimensions of their life, it would be incorrect to try to limit Christianity to a private kind of interiority. We have already

---

[118] Rahner, *FCF*, 342 (*Grundkurs*, 332). In the following section, we follow some of Rahner's reflections in Chapter VII of *FCF*, "Christianity as Church," 322-401, especially his remarks on the "Fundamentals of the Ecclesial Nature of Christianity," 342-46, and "The Christian in the Life of the Church," 389-401. Other pertinent articles include his "Dogmatic Notes on 'Ecclesiological Piety'," *TI* 5: 336- 65 (*ST* V: 379- 410), and "Religious Feeling Inside and Outside the Church," *TI* 17: 228-42 (*ST* XII: 582-98). Among the secondary literature, two recently published doctoral theses on Rahner's ecclesiology which have been helpful here are Jerry T. Farmer, *Ministry in Community: Rahner's Vision of Ministry,* Louvain Theological and Pastoral Monographs 13 (Louvain: Peeters Press, 1992), and Richard Lennan, *The Ecclesiology of Karl Rahner* (Oxford: Clarendon Press, 1995).

[119] Rahner, *FCF*, 322 (*Grundkurs*, 313). In a very comprehensive early treatment of the fundamental nature of the Church, Rahner offers a similar definition: "Die Kirche ist die gesellschaftlich legitim verfaßte Gemeinschaft, in der durch Glaube und Hoffnung und Liebe die eschatologisch vollendete Offenbarung Gottes (als dessen Selbstmitteilung) in Christus als Wirklichkeit und Wahrheit für die Welt präsent bleibt." Rahner, "Grundlegung der Pastoraltheologie als praktischer Theologie," *HPTh* I/2 (1964): 118. [ET: *Theology of Pastoral Action,* Studies in Pastoral Theology, vol. 1, eds. Karl Rahner and Daniel Morrissey (London/New York: Burns & Oates/Herder and Herder, 1968), 26-27.

discussed the dangers of a purely private understanding of Christianity, in terms of social and political responsibility, in the first part of the chapter. This issue, however, resurfaces in the context of the Church. Spirituality — understood as lived Christianity — involves more than a merely transcendental relation of a person to God; it must take seriously the necessary historical and social mediation of salvation:

> "Either history is itself of salvific significance, or salvation takes place only in a subjective and ultimately transcendental interiority *(Innerlichkeit)*, so that the rest of human life does not really have anything to do with it."[120]

The Church is essential to Christian life and, therefore, to Christian spirituality.

> "It (Church) springs from the very essence of Christianity as the supernatural self-communication of God to humankind which has become manifest in history and has found its final and definitive historical climax in Jesus Christ. Church is a part of Christianity as the very event of salvation. We cannot exclude communal and social intercommunication from a person's essence even when he or she is considered as the religious subject of a relationship with God."[121]

Accordingly, the ecclesial aspect of spirituality is based on the social dimension of the human person. Christian faith comes to an individual from history; it is not the ideological creation of religious enthusiasm or of a particular individual religious experience. Rahner's intention is to show how a genuine Christian spirituality must be both *personal* (affecting a person in the "innermost depths" of his or her existence), while also insisting that such a spirituality is formed by, and finds its fullest expression in, the profession of faith and worship of fellow Christians, in a word, in the *Church*. Rahner is anxious to avoid any false dichotomies here between a personal and ecclesial spirituality:

---

[120] Rahner, *FCF*, 345 *(Grundkurs*, 334). Elsewhere, in relation to the tension between the personal and institutional dimensions of spirituality, he states: "Es gibt zwar kein christliches Frommsein, das sich nicht in einem gewissen Maß notwendig in institutionell verfaßten Formen vollzieht." Rahner, "Die Rücksicht auf die verschiedenen Aspekte der Frömmigkeit," *HPTh* II/1: 76.

[121] Rahner, *FCF*, 334 *(Grundkurs*, 332).

"An absolutely individual Christianity in the most personal experience of grace and ecclesial Christianity are no more radically opposed than are body and soul, than are a person's transcendental essence and their historical constitution, or than are individuality and intercommunication. The two condition each other mutually."[122]

While the ecclesial nature of Christianity was self-evident to him, so, too, were its shortcomings and failures. Indeed, Rahner recognized at an early stage how the sinfulness of the Church could pose a challenge to the believer.[123] Thus, he would encourage Christians to view the Church soberly and honestly, without falsely idealizing it. Indeed, he was more than aware of the many problematic issues — theological, legal, disciplinary — within the Church, and there were hardly any controversial problems affecting the Church's life that escaped his attention and comment. However, these topics are not the focus of our present discussion. Rather, our concern is to tease out what Rahner means by the ecclesial aspect of spirituality, or, more precisely, to come to a greater understanding of the individual's relationship with the Church.

Towards the end of his life, Rahner came to stress what he termed "a new ecclesial aspect" *(eine neue Kirchlichkeit)* to spirituality.[124] It

---

[122] Rahner, *FCF*, 389 (*Grundkurs*, 376). He was to return to this idea many times. See for example his "Courage for an Ecclesial Christianity," *TI* 20: 3-12 (*ST* XIV: 11-22), where he states that "if religion involves what is most real in the human person and the human person in his or her wholeness, then it cannot a priori be merely what is individual and the innermost reality of the individual person alone. Religion must be my own proper and free conviction, must be capable of being experienced at the very heart of existence. But this existence is itself found only in a community and society, being revealed in giving and receiving. Moreover Christianity is a historical religion bound up with the one Jesus Christ. I heard of him only through the Church and not otherwise." (p. 9). For a similar idea, see his "'I Believe in the Church'," *TI* 7: 109-110 (*ST* VII: 112), where he insists that faith "always includes the act of trustful and loving surrender to the faith of the Church, ... Faith does not only mean accepting what 'I' as an individual believe that I have heard. It also means accepting what the Church has heard, giving my assent to the 'confession' of the Church."

[123] Rahner, "The Church of Sinners," *TI* 6: 253-69 (*ST* VI: 301-20). We agree, therefore, with Lennan's assessment that "Rahner attempted to establish a mean between an exaggerated 'ecclesiological piety' and a total lack of appreciation for the Church's role in the economy of salvation." Lennan, *The Ecclesiology of Karl Rahner,* 33.

[124] Rahner, "The Spirituality of the Church of the Future," *TI* 20: 152 (*ST* XIV: 379).

is true that, on a fundamental level, authentic Christian spirituality is clearly ecclesial, since it is rooted in a common faith and always has to be realized sacramentally. But the new ecclesial aspect has to do with a different understanding of, and attitude to, the Church. In the last century of the Pian epoch of the Church, Rahner argues, it was easier for Catholics to identify with the Church "as our natural home, sustaining and sheltering us in our spirituality... The Church supported us, it did not need to be supported by us."[125] Today, this situation has changed, and it is evident in a less triumphalist ecclesiology that acknowledges not only the holiness, but also the sinful nature of the Church.[126] Further, there has been a growing awareness that *all* Christians go to make up the Church. If we only look at the Church from "outside," as it were, then "we have not grasped that we are the church, and basically it is only our own inadequacies that are looking at us from the church."[127] Although Rahner was convinced that attachment to the Church was an absolutely necessary criterion for a fully developed spirituality, he believed that a patient endurance with the present sinful reality of the Church was also required. He was more than aware of how "the Church can be an oppressive burden for the individual's spirituality by doctrinalism, legalism and ritualism."[128]

Two further remarks on Rahner's *Kirchlichkeit* are apposite here in the context of spirituality. One is his stress that spirituality is impossible without a certain *order*. Alongside the truly personal decision that lies at the heart of a "spiritual" life is his claim that there must be a certain system and discipline in the spiritual life.[129] Here the "institutional" spirituality of the Church comes in and makes certain legitimate demands of us in terms of ecclesiastical regulations concerning liturgy, fasting, Sunday Mass, and so on. This leads to our second comment, which concerns the relationship of *Kirchlichkeit* to

[125] Rahner, "The Spirituality of the Church of the Future," *TI* 20: 152 (*ST* XIV: 380).
[126] The impetus for this was, of course, Vatican II. However, Rahner's insights go back even further to the article "The Church of Sinners," *TI* 6: 253-69 (*ST* VI: 301-20) mentioned above, n. 123, which was originally published in 1947.
[127] Rahner, *FCF*, 390 (*Grundkurs*, 377).
[128] Rahner, "The Spirituality of the Church of the Future," *TI* 20: 152 (*ST* XIV: 380).
[129] Rahner, *Grace and Freedom*, 131 (*Gnade als Freiheit*, 95).

the truth (or otherwise) of a person's own opinion. In the area of spirituality, Rahner argues, one must be critical of one's own opinions, "because it is more difficult to be objective about oneself than about others, and so the danger of deceiving oneself is greater than that of being deceived by the opinion of others."[130] Rahner's position is that truth does not emerge from a "solipsistic subjectivity," but only in constant *dialogue* with others and with their truth. This insight also forms the starting-point for his understanding of the ecclesial nature of *theology*.[131] Theology, on a first level of reflection, "presupposes an existentiell relationship to the reality of faith... It is the reflection on a Christianity which is lived and believed existentielly in the Church."[132] Rahner's *Kirchlichkeit,* then, is an offshoot of an anthropology which maintains that a person only discovers him or herself by opening him or herself to others, i.e., our interpretation of self takes place in the risk of such intercommunication. This intercommunication must contain an institutional and social element; otherwise, it remains in the purely private sphere. Truth, then, Rahner continues, has an "institutional" dimension, insofar as this latter "represents that reality through which the other has a true importance for myself."[133] In the case of a theologian, this relationship to the teaching and confession of the official Church is ideally characterized by a constant dialogue in order that the theological thought of the

---

[130] Rahner, *Grace and Freedom,* 170 (*Gnade als Freiheit,* 133).

[131] Speaking of Rahner's *Kirchlichkeit* (or, as he also describes it, "Rahner's konkretes Ja zur Kirche"), Karl Lehmann points out how Rahner never associated himself explicitly with a particular party or faction in the Church: "Er könnte nur diese Position des überall helfenden und vor keinem ängstlich zurücktretenden Für- und Widersprechers einnehmen, weil er um das Ganze der Kirche bemüht bleibt." Karl Lehmann, "Karl Rahner und die Kirche," *Karl Rahner in Erinnerung,* 118-33, 127-28. For Rahner's own thoughts on this, see his "Über das Ja zur konkreten Kirche," *ST* IX: 479-97 (*TI* 12: 142-60). We have already discussed the Ignatian roots of Rahner's *Kirchlichkeit* in the previous chapter (Chapter Four, 3, a, "Rahner's Spiritual Testament"), and which are pithily captured in Ignatius' "Rules for Thinking with the Church," ("sentire cum ecclesia"). See *The Spiritual Exercises of St. Ignatius,* nn. 352-370.

[132] Rahner, "A Theology That We Can Live With," *TI* 21: 101, 103 (*ST* XV: 105, 108).

[133] In other words, the truth of others makes demands on me through its institutional nature. "The truth which must be whole and authentic for myself must also appear as that of others." Rahner, *Grace and Freedom,* 172 (*Gnade als Freiheit,* 134-35).

individual theologian does not become a mere monologue around his or her own ideas. It is not that Rahner was unaware of how conflict-ridden such a dialogue (between theologians and the institutional Church) could be. Neither was he advocating an ecclesiality that shied away from any criticism of the Church.[134] It is rather an acknowledgement that, for a Christian, to profess an ecclesial spiritu-ality is to accept the "cross of institutions," or, more specifically, to endure the, at times, "crucifying antagonism" that exists between the individual and the Church as institution.[135]

From a pastoral point of view, Rahner's ecclesiological reflections were increasingly concerned with those Christians who considered themselves on the margins of the Church. He was concerned that the Church's teaching authority did not seem to be able to cope with such people who, while wanting to be considered Christians, did not feel obliged to follow all of the Church's doctrinal and moral teach-ings.[136] Christians in an age of pluralism, Rahner maintains, are increasingly selecting which of the Church's rules and teachings they will accept and which they will reject. It seems the Church has greater difficulty than in the past in putting its values across. Argu-ments from authority no longer work; today people want to know why and how a particular course of behaviour advocated by the Church is good and of benefit to their lives. Some may see in this an attempt on Rahner's part to sacrifice the demands of the faith. But this is to do him a disservice. We have already seen that being a Christian, in Rahner's eyes, always means going against the tide and carrying the cross. That is not at issue here. What is at stake, how-ever, is the urgent need to separate the essentials of the faith from

---

[134] Dissent (*Diskrepanz*) "from a teaching of the magisterium which does not absolutely engage the Church" is both a right, and sometimes a duty, if the theologian is to continue this intra-ecclesial dialogue. "In such a case he or she must present his view in a way that does justice to the ecclesial importance of his or her opinion, ... and also to his respect for the magisterium's teaching." Rahner, *Grace and Freedom*, 176 (*Gnade als Freiheit*, 139).

[135] Rahner, "Ignatius of Loyola," *The Great Church Year*, 337 (*Das große Kirchenjahr*, 486-87).

[136] On the relationship between the individual believer and the authority of the Church, see Rahner, *Meditations on Freedom and the Spirit*, trans. Rosaleen Ockenden, David Smith, and Cecily Bennett (London: Search Press, 1977), 33-74.

what is secondary.[137] Rahner inquired whether teachers and preachers of the Catholic faith should not ask *themselves*, honestly, which norms, commandments, and regulations they are themselves not fully convinced about, and which ones are crucial to human salvation. This is why Rahner himself concluded his *Grundkurs* with some very brief formulations of, what he considered, the essentials of faith.[138]

The relationship of an individual Christian to the Church is, Rahner admits, a highly complex topic and can take many forms. It can take a position somewhere along the spectrum between "identification" and "distance." Some factors, such as whether or not one is baptized, whether or not one is involved in a visible religious practice, are more easily identifiable. Other factors, such as belief, moral attitude and inner personal commitment also play a role, but are harder to identify. Rahner finds it significant that the Church includes all those who have been baptized in its membership — even if many baptized Christians place little value on such membership. The question he raises in this context is whether a person, who finds it difficult to accept a doctrinal or moral teaching of the Church, can still view themselves as belonging to the ecclesial community as a whole.[139]

---

[137] This is what Herbert Vorgrimler refers to as the "Konzentration" (not "Reduktion") of the contents of faith that is characteristic of Rahner's whole theology. In relation to decisions of conscience, the decisive point is "daß die Verpflichtung aus der innersten Mitte des Menschen und damit aus seiner ureigenen Überzeugung erwächst." With regard to spirituality, the Church is, in a sense, "relativized" but only insofar as it is the personal experience of God that has pride of place, an experience which cannot be confined to the Church, "... wo von der absoluten Erheblichkeit der persönlichen Gotteserfahrung und von der relativen Erheblichkeit der kirchlichen Vermittlung die Rede ist. Der Spiritualität eines Menschen eignet von da her ein befreiter und ein freier Chrarakter." Herbert Vorgrimler, "Gotteserfahrung im Alltag. Der Beitrag Karl Rahners zu Spiritualität und Mystik," *Karl Rahner in Erinnerung*, 109, 111-112.

[138] See Rahner, "Epilogue: Brief Creedal Statements," *FCF*, 448-60 ("Kleiner Epilog: Kurzformeln des Glaubens," *Grundkurs*, 430-40).

[139] For a different nuance, see Rahner, "'I Believe in the Church'," *TI* 7: 110 (*ST* VII: 112-13), where he opines: "However much ... the individual may be sure that 'his' God has bestowed a special revelation upon him, and in a manner exclusive to him alone, he must make sure that in his faith he believes that which all believe... . Always he must submit himself trustfully to the faith of the community of believers, which is always greater and more comprehensive than his own as an individual... . The Church, therefore, is always the measure of our faith, the measure and not that

While this issue raises a host of complicated questions with regard to which teachings of the Church are strictly binding (pertinent here would be the question of the limits of magisterial authority, the hierarchy of truths, etc.), Rahner's position is that conflicts between the doctrinal or moral teaching of the official Church and the individual's subjective conscience can easily arise, and should not be regarded as absolute.[140] The two aspects of the discussion here are, firstly, that the individual Christian should not avoid a really self-critical consideration and examination of his or her conscientious decisions, and, secondly, that such decisions need not *always* and necessarily turn a Christian into a "fringe" Christian. Rahner is aware, though, that these two rather general principles will not, in themselves, remove the inevitability of conflict in the Church. His plea is, rather, for a legitimate "diversity in identification" with the official Church and its official teaching.[141] He further maintains that an individual Christian has more discretion and scope to shape his or her own religious life than is often thought. Indeed, a future ecclesial spirituality, he argues, should focus less on what is "obligatory" in the Church, and more on creatively developing one's spiritual and religious life "claiming Christian freedom boldly without feeling that more is demanded of one officially than one can really honestly and genuinely do."[142]

which is measured." [This article "Ich glaube die Kirche," was originally published in *Wort und Wahrheit* 9 (1954): 329-339]. Incidentally, the English translation of the title of the article could be questioned. The translator has inserted the word "in," and, in so doing, overlooks an earlier distinction made by Rahner in his article "Dogmatic Notes on 'Ecclesiological Piety'," *TI* 5: 336- 65 (*ST* V: 379-410). There, he distinguishes between faith in the Church, and the faith of the Church. What he means is that Christians increasingly experience the Church as an object of their faith but do not believe *in* the Church as the ultimate ground of their faith: "The Church is not the first object of faith; belief in her rests on a faith which does not refer to the Church but to Christ and to God." (p. 352).

[140] In other words, such frustrations, difficulties, and negative experiences with the Church are, according to Rahner, a secondary matter, and should not threaten a person's ultimate attitude towards the Church ("soll sein letztes Verhältnis zur Kirche nicht bedrohen") as the place where one "realizes" salvation ("diese letzte Heilszugehörigkeit zur Kirche ... realisiert"). Rahner, *Glaube in winterlicher Zeit*, 183, 175.

[141] Rahner and Weger, *Our Christian Faith*, 152 (*Was sollen wir noch glauben?*, 180).

[142] Rahner and Weger, *Our Christian Faith*, 157 (*Was sollen wir noch glauben?*, 185). Elsewhere Rahner predicts that "the ecclesial aspect of the spirituality of the future will be less triumphalist than formerly. But attachment to the Church will also

c. The Sacramental Aspect of Rahner's Spirituality

In the previous section we highlighted the ecclesial character of Rahner's spirituality. Following on this, we now claim that this ecclesial dimension is closely connected with what we call the sacramental aspect of his spirituality. Indeed, one of Rahner's abiding theological achievements was to work out a connection between the Church and the sacraments.[143] He accomplished this by presenting the Church as the enduring presence of Christ in the world, and thus as the fundamental sacrament *(Ursakrament)* and the source of all the sacraments.[144] Indeed, he stresses the importance of the sacraments as signs: they are causes of grace precisely because they are signs and symbols of God's presence. The sacraments, it is claimed, are acts fundamentally expressive of the nature of the Church.

Earlier we noted Rahner's description of the Church as "the community, legitimately constituted in a social structure, in which through faith, hope and love God's eschatologically definitive revelation (his self-communication) in Christ remains present for the world as reality and truth."[145] This description has a clear Christological

---

in the future be an absolutely necessary criterion for genuine spirituality: patience with the Church's form of a servant in the future also is an indispensable way into God's freedom, since, by not following this way, we shall eventually get no further than our own arbitrary opinions and the uncertainties of our own life selfishly caught up in itself." Rahner, "The Spirituality of the Church of the Future," *TI* 20: 153 (*ST* XIV: 381).

[143] Karl Rahner, *Kirche und Sakramente,* Quaestiones Disputatae 10 (Freiburg: Herder, 1963). [ET: *The Church and the Sacraments*, trans. W. J. O'Hara, Quaestiones Disputatae 9 (New York: Herder and Herder, 1963)]. An initial sketch of this work appeared as: "Kirche und Sakramente. Zur theologischer Grundlegung einer Kirchen- und Sakramentenfrömmigkeit," *Geist und Leben* 28 (1955): 434-53.

[144] For a discussion of the position of sacramentology within the whole of theology, see Rahner, "Sakramententheologie," *LThK* IX: 240-43. In this article, published in 1964, Rahner's preferred term for the Church was "Ursakrament," variously translated into English as the "fundamental," or "primal," sacrament. Later, however, he came to prefer the term "Grundsakrament," ("basic," or "fundamental" sacrament) for the Church, while reserving the term "Ursakrament," to Christ — the "primordial" sacrament. For a discussion of some of the issues involved, see Farmer, *Ministry in Community,* 113-19, and more comprehensively, Leijssen, "La contribution de Karl Rahner (1904-1984) au renouvellement de la sacramentaire," 84-102, esp. 84-96.

[145] Rahner, *Theology of Pastoral Action,* 26-27. (For the original German, see n. 119).

root. More specifically, Rahner holds that Christ is *the* primordial sacrament *(Ursakrament)*, God's fundamental, original sign: "He (Christ) is the primordial sign because he is what is signified (God's self-communication to humanity); he is the efficacious, manifest sign of this self-communication and its acceptance by humankind, for he is a human person and lives as a human person in time."[146] In developing his ecclesiology, Rahner acknowledges the importance of the visible Church, while, at the same time, wishing to avoid what he called an "ecclesiological Nestorianism," which ignored everything but the visible.[147] The key to achieving this balance was to portray the Church as a sacrament, and central to the notion of sacramentality was Rahner's understanding of the nature of symbol.[148]

For Rahner, the sacraments are neither purely internal and invisible encounters between the grace of God and the human recipient, nor are they merely external signs. Instead, he insisted that, for any authentically Catholic notion of sacramentality, both the "inner" and "outer" aspects of a sacrament are of significance. Accordingly, any definition of sacrament that alludes only to the visible sign *(sacramentum)* and not to what it signifies, that is to say, which fails to regard the sacrament as a symbol of a deeper reality *(res sacramenti)*, is insufficient.[149] When Rahner claims that the sacraments are "causes of grace," he means that "it is a case here of causation by symbols," that

[146] Rahner, *Theology of Pastoral Action,* 45.

[147] Rahner, "Membership of the Church According to the Teaching of Pius XII's Encyclical 'Mystici Corporis Christi'," *TI* 2: 70 (*ST* II: 77).

[148] In the following paragraphs, we outline Rahner's understanding of the sacramentality of the Church and its relation to his notion of symbol. We follow both Rahner's own work on the subject, and also draw on the helpful insights of such commentators as: Michael J. Walsh, *The Heart of Christ in the Writings of Karl Rahner: An Investigation of its Christological Foundation as an Example of the Relationship between Theology and Spirituality*, Analecta Gregoriana 209 (Rome: Università Gregoriana Editrice, 1977), 19-33; James Buckley, "On Being a Symbol: An Appraisal of Karl Rahner," *Theological Studies* 40 (1979): 453-73; C. Annice Callahan, "Karl Rahner's Theology of the Symbol: Basis for his Theology of the Church and the Sacraments," *The Irish Theological Quarterly* 49 (1982): 195-205; Wong, *Logos-Symbol in the Christology of Karl Rahner*, 113-84; Albert Liberatore, "Symbols in Rahner: A Note on Translation," *Louvain Studies* 18 (1993): 145-58; and Lennan, *The Ecclesiology of Karl Rahner,* 18-44.

[149] Rahner, *The Church and the Sacraments*, 34-40 (*Kirche und Sakramente,* 31-37).

is to say, "intrinsically real symbols *(innerem Realsymbol)*."[150] A symbol, for Rahner, is that through which a being expresses itself in a way necessary for its own self-realization.[151] All beings, he contends, are symbolic by their very nature, because they necessarily "express" themselves in order to attain their own nature.[152] It is not a question here of a symbol merely being the image or likeness of something else; rather, a symbol exists in a "differentiated unity" with what is symbolized.[153] Although the symbol and what is symbolized are not the same, they are intrinsically related to each other. Rahner's designation for such a symbolic reality is the term "Realsymbol."

In the second part of his seminal article, "The Theology of the Symbol," Rahner indicates how his ontology of symbol might be applied.[154] Firstly, it can be applied to the theology of the Trinity which constitutes a single entity expressing itself in knowledge and love.[155] The theology of the Logos is, Rahner argues, the supreme

---

[150] Rahner, *The Church and the Sacraments*, 37 (*Kirche und Sakramente,* 34).

[151] Rahner, Vorgrimler, "Symbol," *Theological Dictionary*: 451 (*Kleines Theologisches Wörterbuch*: 398).

[152] This is the basic principle of Rahner's ontology of symbol: "das Seiende ist von sich selbst her notwending symbolisch, weil es sich notwendig 'ausdrückt', um sein eigenes Wesen zu finden." Rahner, "The Theology of the Symbol," *TI* 4: 224 (*ST* IV: 278). In the final section of the essay (pp. 245-52), Rahner examines "The Body as Symbol of the Human," and draws some implications for the meaning of devotion to the heart of Jesus.

[153] Rahner, "The Theology of the Symbol," *TI* 4: 234 (*ST* IV: 289). In *The Church and the Sacraments*, 38 (*Kirche und Sakramente,* 35), Rahner also speaks of distinguishing between "the dependence of the actual manifestation on what is manifesting itself, and the difference between the two." In other words, he is trying to "perceive why the symbol can be really distinct from what is symbolized and yet an intrinsic factor of what is symbolized, essentially related to it."

[154] Rahner, "The Theology of the Symbol," *TI* 4: 235-45 (*ST* IV: 291-303).

[155] Rahner's concept of symbol begins with the fact that "all beings (each of them, in fact) are multiple." See Rahner, "The Theology of the Symbol," *TI* 4: 225-26 (*ST* IV: 279-80). Buckley, "On Being a Symbol: An Appraisal of Karl Rahner," *Theological Studies* 40 (1979): 460, maintains "that there are two notions of multiplicity at work here: (1) there are many entities; (2) each one of these entities is composed of many aspects. All these entities 'agree' or 'represent' (or 'are related to') all other entities 'in some way or another'." We have noted already how they are related in different ways. Sometimes they are related extrinsically, as "merely arbitrary 'signs', 'signals' and 'codes' ('symbolic representations') [*Vertretungssymbole*]." Rahner, "The Theology of the Symbol," *TI* 4: 225 (*ST* IV: 279). On the other hand, when these entities are related symbolically, then they are genuine symbols (*Realsymbole*).

form of the theology of the symbol. In other words, the Logos is the "Word" of the Father, his perfect image and expression, and, in this sense, is the "symbol" of the Father.

Secondly, a theology of symbolic reality applies to Christology, where Rahner explores the statement that the incarnate Word is the absolute symbol of God in the world. It is insufficient to claim that the Logos merely took on a human nature, since this view, Rahner maintains, masks an inadequate theology of symbolic reality. The humanity of Christ is not to be conceived as something in which God dresses up and masquerades. Such a conception would correspond to a merely arbitrary sign or "Vertretungssymbol." Rather, "the humanity (of Christ) is the self-disclosure of the Logos itself, so that when God, expressing God's self, exteriorizes God's self, that very thing appears which we call the humanity of the Logos."[156] The humanity of Jesus is both distinct from and one with the Logos, or, put differently, the humanity of Jesus is "the revelatory symbol in which the Father enunciates himself, in this son, to the world — revelatory, because the symbol renders present what is revealed."[157]

Thirdly, the Church, too, continues the symbolic function of the Logos in the world — it is the symbol of Christ's presence to humanity. Indeed, Rahner's symbolic or sacramental approach to Christology recurs in his ecclesiology. From Christ, the Church has an intrinsically sacramental structure.[158] Two points are important for Rahner in this regard. The first is that although the Church has a juridically determined social structure, this does not make it a merely arbitrary sign *(Vertretungssymbol)*. Rahner does not see any contradiction between the juridical constitution of the Church, and the fact that it is also the symbolic reality *(Realsymbol)* of the presence of Christ in the world.[159] And this is Rahner's second point: the Church is more than a social and juridical entity. It is the symbol of the grace of God, which really contains what it signifies, that is, "it is the primary

---

[156] Rahner, "The Theology of the Symbol," *TI* 4: 239 (*ST* IV: 296).

[157] Rahner, "The Theology of the Symbol," *TI* 4: 239 (*ST* IV: 296).

[158] Rahner, *The Church and the Sacraments*, 18 (*Kirche und Sakramente,* 17). See also his "Introduction," *Meditations on the Sacraments* (New York: Seabury Press, 1974), ix-xvii.

[159] Rahner, "The Theology of the Symbol," *TI* 4: 240 (*ST* IV: 298).

sacrament (*das Ursakrament*) of the grace of God, which does not merely designate but really possesses what was brought definitively into the world by Christ."[160]

The classical place, however, in which a theology of symbol finds expression, Rahner believes, is in the Catholic teaching on the sacraments. It is in the sacraments that the symbolic reality of the Church becomes concrete and actual for the individual Christian believer. Thus, Rahner recalls the description of the sacraments as "sacred signs" of God's grace, effecting what they signify and signifying what they effect. This basic axiom of sacramental theology is based on his notion of "a symbolic reality, which the signified itself brings about in order to be really present itself."[161] In short, the grace of God is the cause of the sacramental "sign" which brings grace about. The sacraments, then, are the visible expression of grace, whereby grace renders itself actively present in space and time.[162]

The sacramental aspect of Rahner's spirituality develops out of the basic insights outlined above. But more still needs to be said. Rahner places the sacramental dimension of spirituality within what he terms the three basic structures of lived spirituality,[163] each of which is presented in terms of the dialectical tension that is so characteristic of Rahner's theological method. They can be depicted as follows: the tension between *the transcendental and categorial* aspects of spirituality; the tension between *the personal and sacramental* aspects of spirituality; and thirdly, the tension between *the institutional and charismatic* aspects of spirituality. We shall outline each of these tensions in turn, since they are interrelated, and then conclude with what we regard as Rahner's most significant contribution towards a sacramental understanding of spirituality.

---

[160] Rahner, "The Theology of the Symbol," *TI* 4: 241 (*ST* IV: 298). See also Eberhard Jüngel and Karl Rahner, *Was ist ein Sakrament? Vorstöße zur Verständigung*, Kleine ökumenische Schriften 6 (Freiburg: Herder, 1971), 65-85. [ET: "What is a Sacrament?," *TI* 14: 135-48].

[161] Rahner, "The Theology of the Symbol," *TI* 4: 242 (*ST* IV: 300).

[162] Callahan, "Karl Rahner's Theology of the Symbol," *The Irish Theological Quarterly* 49 (1982): 197.

[163] "... die drei formalen Grundstrukturen des Frommseins." Rahner, "Die Rücksicht auf die verschiedenen Aspekte der Frömmigkeit," *HPTh* II/1: 64. We follow here Rahner's reflections on pp. 61-79.

We have already discussed the unity, and the mutually influencing relationship, of the transcendental and categorial aspects of spirituality. There is the absolute otherworldliness of God *(Absolute Überweltlichkeit Gottes)*, on the one hand, and, on the other, the fact that God does not remain "jenseitig" — on the other side, but has communicated Himself to humanity in Christ. As far as Christian spirituality is concerned, the challenge is to keep both the categorial and the transcendental aspects together.[164] Rahner's fear, though, is that God has become increasingly "categorialised" *(kategorialisiert)* through a multiplicity of words, rituals, and sacramentals, while the transcendental (or mystagogical) aspect of spirituality has been overlooked.[165]

There is also a certain correspondence between the tension described above, and that which exists between the personal and sacramental aspects of spirituality. A sacramental spirituality, for Rahner, refers to "any activity of the Christian life, which is a sacramental happening, and which receives an historical and ecclesial expression, and thus reveals itself in the dimension of the official Church as an action of God to humankind."[166] At the same time, however, such a sacramental happening also involves the action of the person in the reception and celebration of the sacrament — traditionally called disposition, a disposition which, as Rahner points out, is supported by grace. A sacrament, then, is not only an official-ecclesial salvific act, but also an existentiell salvific act *(existentielles Heilstun)*.[167] The person's free response is itself an event of grace.

---

[164] "Der kategoriale und der transzendentale Aspekt des Frommseins gehören zusammen und bedingen sich gegenseitig, ..." Rahner, "Die Rücksicht auf die verschiedenen Aspekte der Frömmigkeit," *HPTh* II/1: 67.

[165] We have developed this point in relation to Rahner's interpretation of Ignatian mystagogy in the third section of Chapter Three.

[166] Translation mine. The original reads: "Sakramentale Frömmigkeit meint jenen Vollzug des christlichen Lebens, der sakramentales Geschehens ist, im sakramentalen Tun der Kirche eine geschichtliche und kirchliche Ausdrücklichkeit erhält und so in der Dimension der amtlichen Kirche als Tun Gottes am Menschen sich offenbart." Rahner, "Die Rücksicht auf die verschiedenen Aspekte der Frömmigkeit," *HPTh* II/1: 70. See also Rahner's other reflections on the topic: "Personal and Sacramental Piety," *TI* 2: 109-33 (*ST* II: 115-41).

[167] Rahner, *FCF*, 429-30 (*Grundkurs*, 412-13). Rahner is anxious here not to overdo the distinction between the traditional notions of *opus operatum* and *opus operantis*. Both are related. The sacraments are not magic rites; they should not only be received validly but also fruitfully. Hence, his reassertion of the Thomistic stress

Moreover, the dual dynamic of grace — directing the individual towards a sharing of the inner life of God, and towards the transfiguration of the world is again apparent here. In other words, grace has an "incarnational tendency," a social structure, which becomes tangibly historical and reaches its climax in the sacraments.[168] Although grace thus attains a certain "embodiment" *(Leibhaftigkeit)* in the visibleness of the sacraments, there is an inclination, Rahner believes, on the part of many Christians to identify (and so confuse) their personal spirituality with the sacramental life of the Church. It is a distortion, he claims, to restrict God's grace solely to the sacraments. Otherwise, it is only a short step to the equation of personal spirituality with the frequency of reception of sacraments, an unfortunate tendency — more prevalent in the past in Catholic cultures than it is today. In sum, Rahner's comments witness to the shift away from an entitative understanding of grace[169] (whereby an increase in the sacraments implied an increase in grace), to a more mystagogical understanding (as we have seen in previous chapters). Rather than advocating an unrestricted reception of the sacraments, Rahner's concern was to underscore the active role of the person in the sacramental event.[170]

Thirdly, the tension between the institutional and charismatic aspects of the Church also finds an echo in spirituality. Certain manifestations of the work of the Spirit (e.g., various forms of private prayer, private spiritual reading), Rahner believes, should not be "institutionalized," that is to say, should not be simply absorbed into the official hierarchical, liturgical and sacramental structures of the Church. On the other hand, he acknowledges how different charisms associated with the founding of religious orders *have* over time

on the right *disposition*, and his claim that there is always an element of uncertainty about the effect of a sacrament. See his *The Church and the Sacraments*, 24-33 *(Kirche und Sakramente,* 22-30).

[168] Rahner, "Personal and Sacramental Piety," *TI* 2: 119, 125 *(ST* II: 126, 133).

[169] For a discussion of this one-sided understanding of grace in connection with the traditional "Versorgungsseelsorge, see Rahner, Zulehner, *Zur Theologie der Seelsorge heute,* 28-39. Rahner also discussed this question in relation to the Eucharist. See Karl Rahner and Angelus Häussling, *Die vielen Messen und das eine Opfer: Eine Untersuchung über die rechte Norm der Messhäufigkeit,* Quaestiones Disputatae 31 (Freiburg: Herder, 1966).

[170] See Rahner, "Considerations on the Active Role of the Person in the Sacramental Event," *TI* 14: 161-84 *(ST* X: 405-29).

become institutionalized. His concern, though, is to point out the inherent limits of the Church as institution. We have previously mentioned the significance Rahner attributes to the process of coming to personal (*existentiell*) decisions.[171] This is one area where an individual Christian should not expect easy "answers" from those in official positions of authority in the Church. Of course, it will be incumbent on those with such responsibility to exercise their charism of discernment, of testing the Spirits. But the important point, for Rahner, is that the pastoral activity of the Church lead to "Christian maturity."[172] This is the challenge for the "official" ministry of the Church: to respect the charismatic dimension of Christian spirituality by encouraging such phenomena as the discernment of spirits, the personal formation of conscience, and the development of an existential ethics.

Our reflections on the sacramental aspect of Rahner's spirituality have led, in turn, to his stress on the *charismatic* dimension of Christian life.[173] This emphasis was presented as a corrective to the tendency of European Christianity to "rein itself in conservatively, to preserve itself as much as possible, to value caution more than audacious experiments."[174] Indeed, Rahner was aware that the Church as institution was not immune from the temptation to manipulate personal freedom for its own sake.[175] At the same time, however, he consistently presented the Church as the socially constituted presence of

---

[171] "Das konkrete christliche Frommsein, das das ganze Leben des Christen und der Kirche deckt, lebt nicht bloß vom Amt und der Institution, sondern auch von den nicht institutionalisierten Antrieben des Geistes Gottes, von freien Charismen, von Entscheidungen, die nicht eindeutig aus den allgemeinen christlichen Normen abgeleitet werden können, ..." Rahner, "Die Rücksicht auf die verschiedenen Aspekte der Frömmigkeit," *HPTh* II/1: 77.

[172] Rahner, "The Mature Christian," *TI* 21: 115-29 (*ST* XV: 119-32). "Maturity is, first of all, the *courage* and the *resolve* to make decisions and to take responsibility for them even if they cannot be legitimized any longer by universally and universally accepted norms." (p. 119).

[173] We have provided a fuller treatment of this charismatic dimension of Rahner's spirituality in Chapter Three, Section 2, "Experience of the Spirit and Enthusiasm."

[174] Rahner, "The Church Must Have the Courage to Experiment," *Karl Rahner in Dialogue*, 170.

[175] For a discussion of this issue, see Rahner, "Institution and Freedom," *TI* 13: 105-21 (*ST* X: 115-32); and "The Church's Responsibility for the Freedom of the Individual," *TI* 20: 51-64 (*ST* XIV: 248-64).

Christ in history, and therefore as the basic sacrament (*Grundsakrament*) of salvation for humankind. Moreover, his work on the relationship between ecclesiology and sacramentology necessitated a move away from an abstract concept of sacrament unrelated to concrete life-situations. Instead, Rahner's contribution was to show how each sacrament is an "event" (*Ereignis*) of the Church, in which the Church's own being is experienced, celebrated, and realized.[176]

Our aim in this section was not to offer a critical study of Rahner's ontology of the symbol but rather to highlight the sacramental dimension of his spirituality. It would be inaccurate to portray Rahner's spirituality as devoid of any emphasis on the need for sacraments or for liturgy. Nor is it a question of Rahner adopting a narrowly sacramental approach to spirituality, though an isolated reading of *The Church and the Sacraments* might convey such an impression. What has emerged in fact is a vision of Christian spirituality that is *both universal and sacramental*. This conception is directly related to Rahner's understanding of grace, which is offered (transcendentally) to everyone, but which also possesses a sacramental or incarnational character that ultimately refers to the Church.[177]

Finally, although Rahner does not offer many explicit personal reflections on liturgy, he was convinced of the importance of establishing links between worship and the experience of God in daily life. This, in our view, is his most significant contribution towards a sacramental spirituality. In so doing, he has shown sceptical Christians how they can worship with intellectual integrity and honesty. At the same time, he views human history as "the liturgy of the world."[178] In short, all of human life can implicitly be an act of worship. While

---

[176] Leijssen, "La contribution de Karl Rahner (1904-1984) au renouvellement de la sacramentaire," 87, 101.

[177] Rahner, "Faith and Sacrament," *TI* 23: 185 (*ST* XVI: 393). In other words, we have been trying to bring out the sacramental character of all grace, or, in Rahner's words, to "show that *every* divine grace, in which God communicates himself to humanity, has an inner dynamism pushing it to become historically and irreversibly manifest in Jesus Christ, in the Church, and in the sacraments." (p. 188).

[178] "The world and its history are the terrible and sublime liturgy, ... which God celebrates and causes to be celebrated in and through human history in its freedom ..." Rahner, "Considerations on the Active Role of the Person in the Sacramental Event," *TI* 14: 169 (*ST* X: 414). See also Skelley, *The Liturgy of the World*, 92-105.

Rahner never considered the Church's worship as the only liturgy, he nonetheless saw how such ecclesial worship could manifest the holiness of the "secular" dimension of our lives and so be a sign of the fact that this entire world belongs to God.[179]

3. Rahner and Beyond: Towards a New Vision of Spirituality

a. Liberation Spirituality: Jon Sobrino

A number of Rahner's key insights into spirituality have been taken up and developed by theologians of liberation. One of the most interesting "disciples" of Rahner in this regard is the Spanish-born Jesuit, Jon Sobrino. Sobrino received his doctorate in Frankfurt, and has lived and worked in El Salvador since 1957. Sobrino remarks that there are a number of parallels between Rahner and liberation theology, or more specifically, that the basic presuppositions of Rahner's theology are in harmony with Latin American theology.[180] What follows then is a brief presentation of Sobrino's understanding of spirituality, along with some indications of convergence and divergence between his views and those of Rahner. Such an approach, we believe, will provide us with a better picture of the contours of a contemporary spirituality — influenced by Rahner — which incorporates the concrete context of the poor and the victimized, and a commitment to their liberation.

Sobrino's discussion of spirituality emerges from the practice of liberation within the context of Latin America. He is convinced of the urgency of giving the practice of liberation "spirit." Spirit and practice, he maintains, must be brought closer together — hence his

---

[179] "This ecclesial worship is important and significant, not because something happens in it that does not happen elsewhere, but because there is present and explicit in it that which makes the world important, since it is everywhere blessed by grace, by faith, hope and love, and in it there occurred the cross of Christ, which is the culmination of its engraced history and the culmination of the historical explicitness of this history of grace." Rahner, "On the Theology of Worship," *TI* 19: 147 (*ST* XIV: 234).

[180] Jon Sobrino, "Karl Rahner and Liberation Theology," *Theology Digest* 32 (1985): 257-60, 259.

insistence, from the outset, on the importance of "living with spirit."[181] This is how Sobrino understands the traditional phrase "spiritual life." It means "life with a certain spirit, life lived in a particular spirit — specifically, in the case of the Christian spiritual life, life lived in the spirit of Jesus."[182] He also sees spirituality as a basic dimension of theology. The important factor here is the spirit with which theology is done and the spirit communicated by the theology that is done. A purely doctrinal theology no longer suffices; rather, the alternative "theologal" model advocated by Sobrino is that "God is to be contemplated and to be practised."[183] We shall explore in the following paragraphs what he means by this.

The main influence on Sobrino's reflections on liberation spirituality has been Gustavo Gutierrez and, in particular, the latter's book *Beber en su proprio pozo.*[184] Rahner and von Balthasar are likewise commended in having made genuine attempts to forge greater links between spirituality and theology.[185] Finally, Sobrino pays tribute to Metz's idea of a "mysticism and politics of discipleship." In this regard, Sobrino adverts to Metz's emphasis on both contemplation and action. It is an admission that practice is not everything. For

---

[181] We shall follow here Jon Sobrino, *Spirituality of Liberation: Toward Political Holiness,* trans. Robert R. Barr (Maryknoll, New York: Orbis, 1988), 1-102; and a shorter article: "Spirituality and the Following of Jesus," *Systematic Theology: Perspectives From Liberation Theology,* eds. Jon Sobrino and Ignacio Ellacuría, trans. Robert R. Barr (London: SCM Press, 1996), 233-56. We are also indebted to Manuel R. Pajarillo, "Confrontation With The Real: Jon Sobrino's View of Spirituality: Analysis and Study of Its Presuppositions," (STL diss., Katholieke Universiteit Leuven, 1995).

[182] Sobrino, *Spirituality of Liberation,* 2.

[183] Sobrino, "Spirituality and the Following of Jesus," 253. Sobrino is referring here to Gustavo Gutierrez' work: *El Dios de la vida* (Lima: Centro de Estudios y Publicaciones, 1981), 6. "Theologal" (*teologal*) means "related to God," as distinct from "theological" (referring to the study of theology).

[184] Lima: Centro de Estudios y Publicaciones, 1971, 2nd rev. ed., 1983. [ET: *We Drink from Our Own Wells: The Spiritual Journey of a People.* Translated by Matthew J. O'Connell. London: SCM, 1984]. See also Sobrino, *Spirituality of Liberation,* 46-79.

[185] The two texts to which Sobrino refers are: Karl Rahner, "Thomas von Aquin," *Glaube, der die Erde liebt: Christliche Besinnung im Alltag der Welt,* 152 (*Everyday Faith,* 188); and Hans Urs Von Balthasar, "Theology and Sanctity," *Word and Redemption: Essays in Theology,* vol. 2., trans. A. V. Littledale and Alexander Dru (New York: Herder and Herder, 1965), 49-85.

Sobrino, the task of a spirituality of liberation is not simply to achieve an integration of theory and praxis, but to emphasize the importance of the "spirit" in which this is done.

Like Rahner, Sobrino views spirituality as involving the whole person; the spiritual life is not confined to a particular "region" of a person's life. Indeed, he even claims that the term "spiritual life" is tautological, since everyone lives their life with some form of spirit. Spirituality, according to Sobrino, is *the spirit with which we confront the real*, the spirit with which we confront the concrete history in which we live with all its complexity.[186] In order to do this three prerequisites are necessary: i) honesty about the real, ii) fidelity to the real, and iii) a certain "correspondence" by which we permit ourselves to be carried along by the "more" of the real.[187] Sobrino is underscoring the relational and historical nature of spirituality. He thus hopes to overcome the temptation to "leave reality to itself" to the extent that the spiritual life and historical life never meet.

Honesty about the real means the recognition of reality as it is. This involves both the intellectual grasping of the truth of reality and responding to this reality. At the risk of sounding too abstract, Sobrino provides an example, namely, how we recognize the truth about human beings. He feels that humanity, particularly in the First World, is too often spoken of in a rather universalist fashion. For Sobrino, however, to talk of "humankind" or "humanity" is to speak, in the first instance, of the *majority* of humanity, a majority who are the victims of poverty and institutionalized violence. This insight (or noetic moment) is not meant for the benefit of the agent of knowledge but is intended to benefit the reality known by the agent. An honesty with regard to the real will therefore require the practice of love in the form of justice. Inspired by the vision and ministry of Jesus, such honesty recognizes that *homo vivens, gloria Dei*. Indeed, the description of Jesus in the Gospels as being so often moved with compassion constitutes for the disciple the primordial act of spirit.[188]

---

[186] Sobrino, "Spirituality and the Following of Jesus," 236.

[187] See Sobrino, *Spirituality of Liberation,* 13-22.

[188] Commentators have drawn attention to this explicitly christological dimension of liberation spirituality. Roger Haight, referring to both Sobrino and Gutiérrez, describes this spirituality as "the traditional imitation of Christ, but within the context

Drawing on the good Samaritan who was "moved to pity" (Lk 10:33), Sobrino regards this "primordial mercy" as the correct response to the challenge to be honest with reality.[189]

The second prerequisite follows from the first. Honesty about the real must be maintained through the vagaries of history. This will mean faithfully persevering as well as struggling with the sin inherent in reality. Here, too, "we need spirit to maintain our honesty regardless of where it leads."[190] Jesus is presented as the archetype of this steadfast honesty, as one who never wavered in his fidelity to the real. Alongside fidelity and honesty regarding the real is an active hope that seeks to enable concrete reality to become what it is called to be. In other words, history is not sheer negativity and Sobrino, inspired by Paul (Rom 8:18-25), emphasizes how creation lives in the hope of its own liberation. This leads to the third presupposition of spirituality, namely, allowing ourselves to be led by the real. If concrete reality is also steeped in grace, this means that we allow ourselves to be supported and carried along by the "gracedness," by the "more," inherent in reality. This, likewise, is an act of the spirit and is reminiscent of Rahner's own ideas about the universality of grace.

The prerequisite for a specifically *Christian* spirituality, according to Sobrino, lies in an experience of God. Yet he deliberately avoids beginning his discussion of spirituality in terms of a relationship with God. This is not because he considers such a relationship unimportant. Rather, Sobrino is fearful that spirituality might be relegated to the "purely spiritual," and historical reality bypassed. However, the prerequisites mentioned above also correspond to a Christian view of reality. Without an honesty and fidelity to the real we are unable

of one's particular historical and cultural situation." Roger Haight, *An Alternative Vision: An Interpretation of Liberation Theology* (New York, Mahwah: Paulist Press, 1985), 235. For Sobrino's own christological approach to spirituality, see especially his *Christology at the Crossroads. A Latin American View,* trans. John Drury (Maryknoll, New York: Orbis, 1978), 388-95. Sobrino's essay "Current Problems in Christology in Latin American Theology," *Theology and Discovery,* 189-221, also describes the experience of God from the perspective of "the church of the poor." It is noteworthy that the essay appears in a collection to honour Rahner's theological achievement.

[189] "... In Jesus' life one may find a partiality and a solidarity [with the poor] that are historically constitutive." Sobrino, "Current Problems in Christology," 213.

[190] Sobrino, "Spirituality and the Following of Jesus," 239.

either to grasp or respond to God's revelation and communication.
Indeed, the question of spirituality for Sobrino is simply "the question of a correspondence to God's revelation in real history."[191] Presupposed here is the fact that God continues to manifest Himself in history, and that, accordingly, an experience of God is possible.
Therefore, Sobrino believes that his three prerequisites can serve as foundations of a radically anthropological spirituality. These prerequisites, he maintains, permit us to keep on hearing God in history, while also expressing the structure of our response to God's word.

Sobrino realizes that, among those Christians committed to liberation, there are some who regard spirituality with mistrust and suspicion (for reasons mentioned above). However, he is convinced that spirituality is both demanded and fostered by a practice of liberation.
Indeed, a key insight of the early theologians of liberation (e.g., Gustavo Gutiérrez), and one which has been insisted upon from the beginning, is that at the basis of all innovative practice on the part of the Church, there lies, concealed and latent, a typical religious experience. There is demanded, too, "a vital attitude — global and synthetic — calculated to inform our lives in their totality and in every detail."[192] Both this attitude and this experience are historically connected with the practice of liberation. From the perspective of the liberation theologians, then, the "poor" (however we might wish to define this term) constitute the historical locus of an encounter with God. In responding to reality by following the three prerequisites of Sobrino, "we have the experience of God in history."[193]

Spirituality is necessary for the practice of liberation for other reasons too. Groups engaged in liberation practice can become overly competitive and fragmented. Further, these groups, like any other, are prone to the abuse of power and leadership, to dogmatism in their interpretation and analysis of a particular situation, and so on. Only a liberation imbued with spirit, Sobrino argues, can overcome such

---

[191] Sobrino, *Spirituality of Liberation,* 21.
[192] Sobrino, *Spirituality of Liberation,* 24, is citing Gustavo Gutiérrez, *A Theology of Liberation: History, Politics and Salvation,* trans. and ed. Caridad Inda and John Eagleson (London: SCM, 1974), 203. See also Gutiérrez, *We Drink from Our Own Wells,* 33-53.
[193] Sobrino, "Spirituality and the Following of Jesus," 241.

negative elements. In short, the practice of liberation "brings the Christian face to face with ultimate realities, to which the spirit must respond with ultimacy."[194] While this practice is a process involving many steps (e.g., personal conversion, prophetic denunciation), Sobrino insists that what is at issue here is a fundamental *decision* of spirit. The practice of liberation that emerges from such a decision must therefore be founded on what Sobrino has described as, a "theologal" spirituality.

This "theologal" spirituality is far removed from that spiritual mentality that equates "spiritual" with pure interiority as opposed to the encounter with history. Although Sobrino concedes that his is an idealized vision — it is the spiritual mentality "that time and again proposes the ideal, refusing to let us strike a compromise with the factual,"[195] — it is not an idealistic one. The reality in Latin America has been one of persecution and martyrdom, and it is these two traits in particular which form the culminating expression of any spirituality purporting to be honest with this reality.[196] Martyrdom is not to be considered, he maintains, as an isolated, autonomous occurrence, but as the culmination of the process of persecution. Conflict, risk, persecution all form part of that "political holiness" which Sobrino sees exemplified in the life of Archbishop Romero and countless others.[197]

---

[194] Sobrino, *Spirituality of Liberation*, 30.

[195] Sobrino, *Spirituality of Liberation*, 39.

[196] In outlining his vision of a spirituality of persecution, Sobrino has been influenced by the person and writings of Oscar Romero. For Romero's four Pastoral Letters, see his *Voice of the Voiceless*, trans. Michael J. Walsh (Maryknoll, New York: Orbis, 1985), to which Sobrino refers on a number of occasions. Inspired by Romero, Sobrino notes that, in Latin America, there have been numerous examples of the presence of spirit in persecution, i.e., where persecution has been lived with spirit. In the midst of such persecution he sees a "fruitful spirituality" characterized by a spirit of fortitude, impoverishment, creativity, solidarity, and joy. Sobrino, *Spirituality of Liberation*, 96-102. See also his "Bearing with One Another in Faith," *Theology of Christian Solidarity*, eds. Jon Sobrino and Juan Hernández Pico, trans. Philip Berryman (Maryknoll, New York: Orbis, 1985), 1-41.

[197] Sobrino, *Spirituality of Liberation*, 80-86. Sobrino acknowledges that martyrdom was likewise a significant theological theme for Rahner. Sobrino, "Karl Rahner and Liberation Theology," 258. See also Rahner, "Dimensionen des Martyriums. Pläydoyer für die Erweiterung eines klassischen Begriffs," *Concilium* 18 (1983): 174-76, where Rahner makes explicit reference to Romero.

With regard to the relationship between Rahner and Sobrino, there is no doubt that Sobrino has been influenced by Rahner. A number of themes which we have seen in Rahner's discussion of spirituality also appear in Sobrino's writings. For example, both authors exhibit an anti-élitism in their understanding of spirituality and a candid admission of the limitations of praxis. Underlying the anti-élitist approach of Sobrino is "the attitude and the conviction that the Christian does not go to God alone. We are saved as members of a people."[198] More specifically, it means forging a spirituality whose subject is a people rather than an isolated person. In relation to the limitations of praxis and the dangers of an out and out horizontalist understanding of Christianity, it is probably fair to say that Rahner, in his emphasis on the transcendent dimension of the human person, highlights these concerns more than does Sobrino. However, Sobrino is aware of the tendency to idealize the poor, and to make their struggle the sole focus of theological reflection.[199]

Another parallel between Rahner and Sobrino lies in the latter's use of the term "mystagogy" — an introduction to the mystery of God. Sobrino's intention is to elucidate how the practice of liberation and the struggle for human rights, introduces a person to the reality of God.[200] In other words, he is attempting to clarify his assertion that

---

[198] Sobrino, *Spirituality of Liberation,* 100. Sobrino is following the insights of Gutiérrez, *We Drink from Our Own Wells,* 72-89, where Gutiérrez describes spirituality in terms of "the journey of an entire people and not of isolated individuals" (p. 72). The underlying biblical motif here is the exodus of the Jewish people (Ex 6:2-8). Thus, spirituality is not a purely inward journey but a collective adventure. It is not a question of eliminating the personal dimension but of developing a more all-embracing perspective (p. 88) which excludes no area of human life — personal or communal — from the exigencies of discipleship. While Sobrino, *Spirituality of Liberation,* 59, 75, does use the terms "elitism" and "elitist," he is in fact reacting against an individualistic understanding of spirituality. However, it has been asked whether his claim that the church of the poor has a privileged hermeneutical position in contrast to other groups' experiences of God is itself somewhat élitist by ascribing a privileged status to one particular group, namely the poor. See Fernando Segovia, "A Response to Fr Sobrino," *Theology and Discovery,* 222-27.

[199] Sobrino, *Spirituality of Liberation,* 112. Sobrino acknowledges that "liberated from one form of their own poverty, the poor can become 'little oppressors'." That said, however, one sometimes gets the impression that Sobrino himself is not free from such an idealizing tendency.

[200] For a different approach to mystagogy, a "*mystagogia* into the mystery of sin" in the context of God's forgiveness (and where Sobrino acknowledges his debt to

the experience of God is "historicized" in the struggle for human rights and for the life of the poor. There is an element of the "sacred" involved in this struggle which "implies salvation for the one who will respond to it and be introduced into it."[201] Like Rahner, Sobrino frequently refers to Matthew 25 in order to underpin the claim that our reaction to the presence of God in "the least of these brothers (and sisters)" is fundamental and decisive.[202] In short, the defence of the life of the poor constitutes a mystagogy or initiation into the very mystery of God.[203]

On a personal level this struggle involves a "de-centration" of self, i.e., a transfer of one's ultimate concern from oneself to the life of those who are on the fringe. This notion of "de-centration" is not unlike Rahner's understanding of the interpersonal nature of the human person as "ec-static," "stepping away from oneself," that is to say, oriented towards the love of neighbour.[204] Far from promoting an individualistic, ahistorical conception of spirituality, both authors (albeit with different approaches) refuse to confine the "spiritual" to a particular "region" of life. Instead, they both understand spirituality in a holistic and relational way. This is especially evident in their common emphasis

Rahner), see Jon Sobrino, *The Principle of Mercy: Taking the Crucified People from the Cross* (Maryknoll, New York: Orbis, 1994), 88-91.

[201] Sobrino, *Spirituality of Liberation,* 105.

[202] Sobrino, "Current Problems in Christology," 214-16.

[203] Like Rahner, Sobrino claims that theology also has a mystagogical task, or, in his terminology, it must be "theologal." "Theology must see to it that its doctrine on God, and its doctrine on whatsoever theological content, genuinely facilitate the experience of God. A theologal theology must be a mystagogy — an introduction into the reality of God as God is: transcendent mystery, utterly resistant to manipulation, and yet our Father, near at hand, good, and saving." Sobrino, *Spirituality of Liberation,* 72. This last sentence could very easily have been written by Rahner. But Sobrino goes further: God must not simply be a reality for theology, but a reality in *action*. "There can be no encounter with the God of Jesus without an encounter with the poor and the crucified of this world." Sobrino, "Spirituality and the Following of Jesus," 256.

[204] See Rahner, "Liebe," *SM* III: 239-40. We discussed Rahner's understanding of *love* as the complete actualization of the human person in Chapter Two, 2, d. The Bonaventurean roots of the notion of "ecstasis" were treated in the previous chapter. In short, Rahner uses the term "ecstasis" to describe either: i) God's love for humanity, or ii) our love of God. For an example of the former, see his "The Position of Christology in the Church Between Exegesis and Dogmatics," *TI* 11: 200 (*ST* IX: 213); and for the latter, "The Question of the Future," *TI* 12: 189 (*ST* 9: 526).

on the unity between love of God and love of neighbour. To be sure, Rahner is not a liberation theologian and Sobrino does not consider him as one. There *are* divergences in their respective approaches to spirituality, but these have primarily to do with the vastly different *contexts* in which each theologian lived/lives and worked/works. For Sobrino's part, his is a context of oppression. Not only is the context different, but Sobrino makes this context the starting point for all his theological reflection. Indeed, the notion of spirituality operative among European theologians, such as Rahner, is often criticized as apolitical and individualistic.[205] We have shown, however, that the later Rahner incorporated a number of these criticisms into his own reflections. In general, Rahner *was* a supporter of the theology of liberation as indicated, for example, by his last letter to the archbishop of Lima in support of the work of Gustavo Gutiérrez.[206]

There are at least three "formal characteristics" which Sobrino sees in Rahner's theology that bring it into harmony with the fundamental concerns of liberation theology. We also detect a parallel between these characteristics of Rahner's theology and Sobrino's own three presuppositions for a genuine spirituality. Further, these three characteristics inform the understanding and practice of spirituality because they are crucial in coming to an understanding of spirituality in terms of a discipleship of the poor. The first characteristic of Rahner's theology noted by Sobrino is an *openness to the new*. Rahner was not threatened by the positive renewal process of Vatican II, for example. In fact, in his own writings and teaching, he actively set about implementing and inculcating the key insights of the Council. In the same way, he was open to the "newness" of the theology of liberation. Secondly, Rahner's theology can be regarded as both *intellectually honest and pastorally inspired*. Both his pastoral and spiritual publications, argues Sobrino, are a clear indication that his dogmatic writings were decisively connected with the realities of history and the Church. Thirdly, Rahner's *readiness to serve* the Church and to see his theology as such a service reveals an attitude of com-

[205] On this, see our discussion of Metz's criticisms of Rahner in the first part of this chapter.
[206] Rahner, *Politische Dimensionen des Christentums,* 187-88, and "Salvation and Liberation," *Karl Rahner In Dialogue,* 342-45. See also n. 57.

passion and mercy, an attitude which Sobrino claims is implicit throughout Rahner's theology. This last attitude is apparent in Rahner's writings on the tension between "charism" and "institution." We have referred to this before, but it is pertinent here in that Sobrino also notes a similar tension within the Latin American Church.[207] This tension, in turn, gives rise to the presence of *conflict* within the Church. In order to deal with this, Sobrino proposes a spirituality of conflict which does not gloss over this reality, but honestly recognizes it and attempts to resolve it.[208] A spirituality of conflict requires an honest dialogue and an openness to the argumentation of others. Ultimately, Sobrino concludes, it forces us back to the question of our love of neighbour, our love for the Church, and a recognition of the limitation and sin not only of our neighbour, but also of ourselves.[209]

Our brief comparison of Sobrino with Rahner as regards the former's understanding of spirituality demonstrates not only the influence of Rahner on Sobrino, but also the way in which Sobrino has taken Rahner's thought further. Sobrino achieves this by clarifying how a truly Christian spirituality "must enable us to confront our current history as Jesus confronted his."[210] Moreover, Sobrino's understanding of spirituality alerts us to the whole variety of factors that underlie our image and experience of God, factors which include our culture, social class, family background, race, gender, personality, etc. It leads him to be suspicious of any spirituality that is apolitical or which eschews involvement in social issues.[211] In contrast to Rahner, the context of oppression in which Sobrino works gives a greater sense of historical urgency and concreteness to his reflections. At the same time, Sobrino concurs with Rahner's attempts to safeguard God's transcendence. There can be no attempt to identify the reign of God with any particular social order:

---

[207] Sobrino, *Spirituality of Liberation,* 43, and 141-49.

[208] For Rahner's discussion of conflict in the context of discipleship, see his "Ignatius of Loyola Speaks to a Modern Jesuit," *Ignatius of Loyola,* 23-29 (*Ignatius von Loyola,* 23-29). Sobrino also reflects on the role of conflict in discipleship in the context of the Ignatian *Exercises* in "The Christ of the Ignatian *Exercises,*" *Christology at the Crossroads,* 396-424, esp. 404-412.

[209] Sobrino, *Spirituality of Liberation,* 148-49.

[210] Sobrino, *Spirituality of Liberation,* 176.

[211] Sobrino, "Spirituality and the Following of Jesus," 245.

"... The affirmation that the God of the Kingdom 'is near' breaks through that fundamental symmetry of distance and nearness, it does not abolish the dialectic of the presence and the hiddenness of God — a dialectic which has been summarized in the well-known expression, 'already, but not yet'. Indeed, the need to preserve that dialectic represents one of the fundamental experiences of the mystery of God as mystery, since the 'not yet' of God is perceived as always surpassing his 'already'."[212]

We see in Sobrino's understanding of spirituality, then, both a supplement and a challenge to Rahner's presentation. It should not be a question of universalizing one particular approach to the detriment of the other. To do so would be to betray the basic conviction of both theologians that theological pluralism is a gift rather than a threat to the Church. Although liberation spirituality could be seen, on one level, as a reaction to a rather one-sided view of the Christian life, it, too, has had to struggle with the tensions or polarities that govern Christian living.[213] We mentioned above the tension between the "already" and the "not yet" in connection with the experience of the reign of God. While Rahner's emphasis was more consistently on the "always greater" God, the God of "incomprehensible mystery" who always transcends our particular experience, this emphasis is certainly not absent from Sobrino.[214] For Sobrino, however, the "otherness" or transcendence of God is mediated through the otherness of the poor. Jesus' partiality for the poor and the outcast leads, then, to a spirituality that is grounded in the same identification with the powerless and dispossessed of society.[215]

b. Feminist Spirituality: Anne Carr

Feminist spirituality, like Latin American spirituality, begins with the concrete experience of a particular group, namely, women. In

---

[212] Sobrino, "Current Problems in Christology," 205.

[213] For a succinct summary of some of the tensions that have surfaced in our discussion thus far, see Haight, *An Alternative Vision,* 236-39.

[214] "From its very beginnings liberation theology has preserved the dimension of the mystery of God as mystery, even if it has done so in the context of an examination of the spirituality of liberation rather than in the context of a systematic study of God." Sobrino, "Current Problems in Christology," 190, n. 5. Sobrino refers also in this context to Gutiérrez, *A Theology of Liberation,* 189-208.

[215] See Roberto S. Goizueta, "Liberation Theology, Influence On Spirituality," *NDCS*: 599.

previous chapters, we have described Christian spirituality in terms of our personal appropriation and response to the salvation offered by God in Jesus Christ, a response that occurs through the working of the Holy Spirit. A Christian *feminist* spirituality understands itself as the style of response of those who have appropriated the central elements of feminist criticism of what is termed the "patriarchal" tradition.[216] Feminist spirituality is "the spirituality of those who have experienced feminist consciousness raising and so have critical questions about inherited patterns and assumptions about gender differences and the implications of these for social and ecclesial roles and behaviour."[217] This spirituality does not confine itself to the experience of prayer, but is aimed at shaping behaviour and attitudes, and leads to a commitment to achieving an alternative vision in the sociopolitical order (i.e., in the family, society, and in the Church). In this sense, feminist spirituality can be described as holistic. It encompasses all one's relationships: to God, self, others, society, nature, etc. While this may not sound particularly feminist, a *specifically* feminist spirituality refers to:

> "that mode of relating to God, and everyone and everything in relation to God, held by anyone, female or male, who is deeply aware of the historical and cultural restriction of women and their related gender roles to a narrowly defined 'place' within the wider human 'world'.[218]

---

[216] "Patriarchy" means literally "the rule of the fathers." Anne Carr observes: "As the dominant political, social, and familial structure in Western Christian history, patriarchy has served to stabilize a Christian church and social order that is both hierarchical and androcentric." Anne E. Carr, *Transforming Grace: Christian Tradition and Women's Experience* (San Francisco: Harper and Row, 1988, 1990), 135. Carr adds (p. 146), however, that "Christianity was not itself originally patriarchal. Patriarchy is far older and more widespread than Christianity, and it is found in many other religions." For an alternative description of patriarchy "understood as divinely derived because it reflects the natural order and thus is the order of creation," see "Dialogue on Women in the Church: Interim Report," *Origins* 11 (25 June 1984): 90. The dialogues were between representatives of the Women's Ordination Conference and of the National Conference of Catholic Bishops of the U.S. On the gradual development of patriarchy in society, see Gerda Lerner, *The Creation of Patriarchy* (New York: Oxford University Press, 1986); regarding patriarchy in the Church, see Elisabeth Schüssler Fiorenza, *In Memory of Her: A Feminist Theological Reconstruction of Christian Origins* (New York: Crossroad, 1983).

[217] Carr, *Transforming Grace,* 206.

[218] Carr, *Transforming Grace,* 207.

A feminist spirituality, then, draws attention to many women's experience of historical exclusion and oppression both in the Church and in society.[219] This spirituality is not a purely critical response, however. The feminist spiritual vision is also characterized by the watchwords: equality, relatedness, and inclusiveness, as opposed to élitism, individualism, and discrimination. Many Catholic feminists experience an intense existential anger as a result of their alienation or exclusion from many aspects of the life of the Church. At the same time, "a Christian feminist spirituality calls everyone to wider visions of human mutuality, reciprocity, and interdependence before God who seeks the unity and community of all."[220]

In this section, we focus on the work of Anne E. Carr for a number of reasons. Firstly, her book, *Transforming Grace,* represents a well-balanced introduction to feminist questions, including spirituality.[221] Secondly, she is very much acquainted with, and indebted to, Rahner's theology.[222] Both in her theological anthropology and methodology, she relies on insights from Rahner (among others), while, at the same time, developing his thought further in the direction of a Catholic feminist spirituality. Thirdly, she has succeeded in situating the particular feminist theological contribution within the much larger theological tradition. And, fourthly, Carr's focus is primarily on the experience of those *Roman Catholic* women who feel excluded from what they see as the non-participative structures in the Church. Carr, then, belongs to that group of mainstream feminist theologians, who, while they share a "feminist consciousness," have remained within the Church.[223] Rather than moving on to different forms of

---

[219] See Sandra M. Schneiders, "The Effects of Women's Experience on Their Spirituality," *Women's Spirituality: Resources for Christian Development,* ed. Joann Wolski Conn (New York/Mahwah: Paulist Press, 1986), 31-48.

[220] Carr, *Transforming Grace,* 208.

[221] For a variety of different reviews of this work, including a response from the author, see the "Review Symposium," *Horizons* 15 (1988): 365-78.

[222] We have already referred in Chapter Two (n. 12) to her doctoral dissertation, *The Theological Method of Karl Rahner* (Missoula, Montana: Scholars Press, 1977).

[223] Some other leading Catholic feminist theologians include: Sandra Schneiders, to whom we referred in our opening chapter. See her illuminating article "Feminist Spirituality," *NDCS*: 395-406. Elizabeth Johnson is involved in a feminist revisionist criticism of traditional discourse about God, Christ, and Mary and the saints. See her *She Who Is: The Mystery of God in Feminist Theological Discourse* (New York:

post-Christian feminist spirituality, they have chosen to direct their considerable theological and other energies towards a reform of the institution from within.

It is only in the final chapter of her work that Carr explicitly treats of feminist spirituality. However, previous chapters explore the real *theological* concerns of feminist theologians.[224] These concerns, in turn, have a direct impact on the feminist understanding of spirituality and are, therefore, relevant to our discussion. Carr notes a number of characteristics of this spirituality. Firstly, feminist spirituality advocates an appropriate personal *autonomy* and self-transcendence of both men and women. This is a recognition that the goals of human and personal development go beyond mere conformity to rules. In other words, *freedom* is important in contemporary Christian feminist spirituality. The term "liberation" is used to capture the political dimension of this freedom. Concretely, liberation means liberation *from* patriarchy, which to date remains more a hope than a lived reality.[225] On the other side, the virtues associated with *relatedness* are encouraged. One such virtue is that of solidarity, giving rise to a spirituality which is global in outlook, i.e., inclusive rather than élitist. This latter point is important given the danger of the women's movement becoming a luxury for the educated and the affluent. Also interesting is Carr's hint that a strictly feminist spirituality (with its emphasis on women's support groups, storytelling, consciousness-raising, etc.,) might only be a temporary stage on the way to a fuller human and Christian spirituality.[226]

Crossroad, 1993); and "Saints and Mary," *Systematic Theology: Roman Catholic Perspectives*, 469-501. In the area of trinitarian theology, see Catherine Mowry LaCugna, *God for Us: The Trinity and the Christian Life* (San Fransisco: Harper Collins, 1991).

[224] See Carr, *Transforming Grace,* especially Chaps. 7, 8, and 9.

[225] For a similar list of characteristics (inclusivity, connectedness, embodiment, and liberation) of feminist spirituality, see Sally B. Purvis, "Christian Feminist Spirituality," *Christian Spirituality: Post-Reformation and Modern*, 500-519.

[226] Carr, *Transforming Grace,* 210. In other words, "a 'separatist' position cannot be a final one for Christians: the ultimate goal is an inclusive mutuality: 'all one in Jesus Christ'." (p. 129). It should be pointed out, though, that there have been attempts made to provide a spirituality that is specifically oriented to male spiritual needs (see below, n. 228). This can be seen partly as a reaction to feminist spirituality, or, at least to the perception that mainline spirituality is female. It seems that, for

With its emphasis on *inclusiveness*, feminist spirituality cannot be considered to be simply the prerogative of women. Carr believes that men who have identified with the struggle of women can also share such a spirituality. Nevertheless, the temptation to universalize the experience of women remains. Any attempt to absolutize a particular set of women's experiences, however, overlooks the fact that the majority of Catholic women would probably not consider themselves feminist.[227] A self-critical Christian feminism, something Carr also accents, can thus be a corrective to the anti-male rhetoric that crops up in the literature from time to time, even among mainstream feminists.[228]

Carr is more at home in reinterpreting traditional formulations of the doctrine of God in the light of women's experience. There is no doubt that many feminist women find the metaphors "Father" and "Son" troubling. Yet, on the other hand, the Father-Son analogy is both well attested to in Scripture (e.g., in John's Gospel) and in tradition. Drawing on Rahner, Carr insists that:

> "no image or symbol is an adequate 'picture' of God... All human knowledge of God is analogical, and as the tradition maintains, analogies are more unlike than like in their comparison of aspects of human reality or of creation to God."[229]

the moment, men and women are journeying apart: men are too fearful of matriarchy, women too abused by patriarchy.

[227] See Schneiders, "Feminist Spirituality," *NDCS*: 401. As Purvis, "Christian Feminist Spirituality," 504, notes: "As white women speak of their experience as 'women's experience', women of colour and women from minority cultures ... see themselves disappearing just as women in general disappear when male experience defines 'humanity'."

[228] For example, what is one to make of the following generalized statement of Schneiders, "As men have raped women for their own pleasure and utility, so have they raped the environment for the same purposes." Schneiders, "Feminist Spirituality," *NDCS*: 400. And how are men expected to react to such a declaration? One interesting reaction to what he perceives as the anti-masculinity or reverse chauvinism within some quarters of the Christian feminist movement is that of Patrick M. Arnold, "In Search of the Hero: Masculine Spirituality and Liberal Christianity," *America* 161 (1989): 206-210. While his point that "theologians, teachers pastors ... [should] wake up to ... explicitly male spiritual needs" (p. 210) is well taken, his reluctance to name some of the feminist theologians to whom he is referring detracts from the force of his argument.

[229] Carr, *Transforming Grace,* 140-41, where she cites Rahner: "The true radicalism in the doctrine of God can only be the continual destruction of an idol, an idol in the place of God, the idol of a theory about God." Rahner, "Observations on the Doc-

This principle that every statement we make about God must be negated is what Rahner calls "the sober humility of the true relationship with God."[230] Theological feminism, too, plays its part in a critique of the propensity "to literalize metaphors for God and to forget the dissimilarity in every analogy."[231] While Carr admits that many women find exclusively male symbolism for God alienating, she does not go so far as to claim that calling God "Father" is *always* patriarchal. She notes that symbols are deeply ambiguous. Moreover, it is doubtful whether calling God "Mother" adequately counterbalances the undoubted over-masculinization of the God-image in traditional theological discourse.[232]

Underlying Carr's contemporary reformulation of the doctrine of God is the Rahnerian notion of the incomprehensibility and hiddenness of God. Following Rahner, Carr acknowledges the danger of "objectifying" God, of rendering the reality of God as one object beside other objects of human knowledge. "'Incomprehensible mystery' reminds Christians always that they do not really grasp the one to whom the symbols point, the God who is dimly known as the mystery, source, fountainhead, and matrix of being that surrounds

trine of God in Catholic Dogmatics," *TI* 9: 127 (*ST* VIII: 165). It is significant in this context that in Rahner's last public lecture before his death, he lists a number of his "experiences" or convictions as a Catholic theologian. The "first experience" he mentions is the analogical nature of all theological statements (*die Analogheit aller theologischen Aussagen*), something which, he thinks, theology has largely forgotten about. Karl Rahner, "Erfahrungen eines katholischen Theologen," *Karl Rahner in Erinnerung,* 134-48.

[230] Rahner, "Observations on the Doctrine of God in Catholic Dogmatics," *TI* 9: 128 (*ST* VIII: 166). Rahner continues: "The unique character of our relationship with God and his existence for us is shown by the fact that when we have renounced a knowledge of God which *conquers* him by means of affirmation or negation, God does not disappear, but precisely at that point commits himself to us."

[231] Catherine Mowry LaCugna, "The Trinitarian Mystery of God," *Systematic Theology: Roman Catholic Perspectives,* 181.

[232] We cannot go into the complicated issue of God's Fatherhood here. The difficulties involved are well captured by LaCugna: "Feminine imagery for God in the Bible or in some mystical writers does not establish that God has 'feminine aspects' any more than masculine imagery establishes that God has 'masculine aspects'. In addition, this type of interpretation tends to incorporate sex-stereotypes (women are compassionate, men are strong) and to suggest that God is primarily masculine but with a feminine side." LaCugna, "The Trinitarian Mystery of God," *Systematic Theology: Roman Catholic Perspectives,* 183.

humankind in inexhaustible light."[233] This image of a God who is "more" resonates with women who, despite their negative experiences, remain faithful to the One whom the Church proclaims.

In attempting to re-conceptualize the symbol or doctrine of God, Carr employs a dialectical interpretative strategy. She is engaged in a critical correlation of the contemporary experience of women, on the one hand, with Scripture and tradition on the other.[234] Unlike some of the more radical, post-Christian feminists, she is convinced that Christianity contains the resources to affirm and empower contemporary women. This conviction then leads her to a new understanding of God in dynamic and relational terms. Drawing on Sallie McFague, Carr suggests that the image of *friendship* "shows us the love of God as desiring and giving humankind the equality of friendship."[235] The revisioning of God in more relational terms entails a distancing from descriptions of God as male, king, all-powerful, etc. These latter images, Carr argues, have proved alienating for women, supported dominating modes of Church structure, and have adversely affected relations between women and men.[236] Further, the reinterpretation of God in relational terms has implications for the understanding of God's *power*. For feminist theologians, this problematic notion is recast in relational terms as empowerment of the other. The emphasis shifts from "power over" in the sense of controlling another to achieve one's own ends to "power with others," or mutual

---

[233] Carr, *Transforming Grace,* 156.

[234] Carr, *Transforming Grace,* 166-67. Although she does not go into it in detail, Carr at one point (p. 161) mentions the notion of a "hermeneutics of generosity *and* suspicion." This phrase aptly captures the two moments of Carr's dialectical method, namely that of retrieval and critique which are apparent throughout the book. See William M. Thompson's comments on this in the "Review Symposium," *Horizons* 15 (1988): 370, and Carr's response (p. 376), where she maintains that *Transforming Grace* was perhaps too conciliatory and not suspicious enough!

[235] Carr, *Transforming Grace,* 150. See also Sallie McFague, *Metaphorical Theology* (Philadelphia: Fortress Press, 1982).

[236] See Schneiders, "The Effects of Women's Experience on Their Spirituality," 39, who refers to the "masculinizing" of religious experience and its negative impact on women's spiritual formation: "The predominance of the intellectual over the affective approach to the knowledge of God, of method over intuition in prayer, of Christian warfare over friendship as the model of the spiritual life, of asceticism over mysticism, of submission to authority over personal initiative in the apostolate have all expressed the concerns of men and the experiences of men."

empowerment. In a relational and incarnational framework, God's power is in humans through whom God's liberating action occurs. This idea of the self-limitation, or the gentle power, of God also heightens awareness of human freedom and responsibility. It underscores the dialectical relationship between dependence on God and personal autonomy and responsibility in history.[237] In fact, the relationship between personal spiritual growth and transformation, and a politics of social justice is probably the most important characteristic of feminist spirituality.[238] For example, many people are first exposed to feminism via the issue of inclusive language. Then, in attempting to develop liturgies that include women, they become more starkly aware of the alienating and dominative aspects of the more traditional liturgical practice.

Although we cannot pursue the matter in detail, Carr also continues her feminist hermeneutical retrieval in other areas of theology, including Christology, salvation, Mary, and the Church. In relation to Christology she raises a fundamental question for feminist theologians: can a male saviour help women? She describes how many women, despite their awareness of how the maleness of Jesus has been used to justify the exclusion of women from full sacramental participation in the Church, continue to pray to Christ, and with Christ to God. An important task of a feminist Christology, therefore, is to show that Jesus is not a symbol of patriarchal male supremacy, but rather a powerful symbol of its subversion.[239] Mary, too, can become a powerful female symbol for the religious lives of women. Traditionally, Mary embodied the feminine dimension — the mercy, tenderness, and compassion — of the biblical God. But, Carr argues,

---

[237] Carr, *Transforming Grace,* 152. This dialectical interdependence between power and freedom has also been explored by Rahner: "The Theology of Power," *TI* 4: 391-409 (*ST* IV: 485-508).

[238] Schneiders, "Feminist Spirituality," *NDCS*: 400. This insight is succinctly captured in the feminist rallying cry: "The personal is the political."

[239] Carr, *Transforming Grace,* 160. See also Sandra Schneiders, *Women and the Word* (New York: Paulist Press, 1986), 50-71. Another important contribution to this discussion is Elizabeth A. Johnson's "Jesus, the Wisdom of God: A Biblical Basis for Non-Androcentric Christology," *Ephemerides Theologicae Lovanienses* 61 (1985): 261-94, where she explores the tradition of personified Wisdom or *Sophia* in early Christian reflection on the salvific significance of Jesus.

she can also be seen as a "role model of resistance," one who speaks on behalf of the oppressed, and as "the poor one in whom God does great things."[240] And, finally, the self-understanding of the Church must be subject to a theological critique based on an historical awareness of pluralism. Drawing on the work of Elisabeth Schüssler Fiorenza, Carr refers to the "lost" history of women in the early Christian communities. The egalitarian and inclusive character of these communities led to the emergence of a "discipleship of equals" and of women as "paradigms of true discipleship."[241]

We seem to have come a long way from Rahner. Our goal has not been to present a comprehensive account of feminist spirituality in all its aspects, but rather an introduction to some of the issues involved. We also indicated some common areas of concern between Rahner and Carr. Though it would be anachronistic to call Rahner a feminist, it cannot be said that he was altogether oblivious to the significance of the issue of women in the Church.[242] Some of his earlier reflections on this topic, it has to be said, are rather ambiguous and limited.[243] One such example is his collection of essays in *Sendung und Gnade,* where there is a major section entitled "People in the

---

[240] Carr, *Transforming Grace,* 193. Carr concludes: "Mary ... as a central Christian symbol ... signifies autonomy *and* relationship, strength *and* tenderness, struggle *and* victory, God's power *and* human agency — not in competition but cooperation."

[241] See Fiorenza, *In Memory of Her: A Feminist Theological Reconstruction of Christian Origins,* 315-33; and, more recently, her *Discipleship of Equals: A Critical Feminist Ekklesia-logy of Liberation* (New York: Crossroad, 1993).

[242] In this context, it is noteworthy that Rahner maintained a close friendship for over 22 years with the German Catholic writer Luise Rinser. This relationship was reflected in their correspondence — letters, postcards, and telegrams, of which Rahner sent no fewer than 1,800. The letters cover intimate and personal concerns, and include discussion of such matters as priestly celibacy, the relationship between priests and women, growth in the spiritual life, etc. While Rahner was unwilling for his letters to be made public, Rinser's letters have been published. Luise Rinser, *Gratwanderung. Briefe der Freundschaft an Karl Rahner 1962-1984,* ed. Bogdan Snela (Munich: Kösel, 1994). For a good overview of reactions to *Gratwanderung* (literally, 'a walk on the edge'), see Roland Hill, "A walk on the edge," *The Tablet* 249 (9 September 1995): 1136-1137.

[243] For a critical appraisal of the *Frauenbild* in Rahner's theology, see Herlinde Pissarek-Hudelist, " *'Die Frau ist der Frau aufgegeben'.* Die Entwicklung des Frauenbildes bei Karl Rahner," *Wie Theologen Frauen sehen — von der Macht der Bilder,* eds. Renate Jost and Ursula Kubera (Freiburg: Herder, 1993), 159-92.

Church."[244] However, these essays, which were variously published between 1943 and 1958, are primarily concerned with *male* roles in the Church: the bishop, parish priest, deacon, the academic, the theologian, etc. In the essay, "Men in the Church" (1956), Rahner even called for the return of a more masculine Christianity in the Church![245] This was because he feared Christianity had gone "feminine:" women were more devout than men in practice. One way Rahner proposed to redress the balance was to stress the transcendental aspect of spirituality which, he thought, would appeal more to men than the categorial side.[246] If this essay betrays the traditional stereotyping of women, a more enlightened piece appeared in 1964, during the time of Vatican II, entitled "Die Frau in der neuen Situation der Kirche."[247] While Rahner is aware of the unity of the Church, the emphasis here was on the "new situation" of pluralism, of multiplicity and diversity within the Church. The Church could no longer be equated with the culture of the West, but had become a world Church. With regard to the situation of women in the Church, Rahner insisted that authorities in the Church should move beyond paying mere lip service to the equal status of women. A new kind of relationship, he felt, was needed between clergy and women, one which went beyond the "patriarchal attitudes" of the past.[248] He speaks of "the Church of women themselves," whose task it is to devise the concrete model or pattern of life for women today.[249]

[244] Rahner, *Sendung und Gnade*, 235-391 (*Mission and Grace*, vol. 2).

[245] Rahner, *Sendung und Gnade*, 291 (*Mission and Grace* 2: 81).

[246] As regards the "transcendental" side: "It is possible to be unemotional about religion out of reverence; to be reserved out of adoring faith. It is possible to be mistrustful of one's religious feelings not because one is 'tepid' but because one knows that God is as inexpressibly above all our feelings as he is above our thoughts." Rahner, *Sendung und Gnade*, 297-98 (*Mission and Grace* 2: 90).

[247] Rahner, "The Position of Woman in the New Situation in which the Church Finds Herself," *TI* 8: 75-93 (*ST* VII: 351-67).

[248] Rahner, "The Position of Woman in the New Situation in which the Church Finds Herself," *TI* 8: 85 (*ST* VII: 360).

[249] Rahner, "The Position of Woman in the New Situation in which the Church Finds Herself," *TI* 8: 88 (*ST* VII: 362). Carr, *Transforming Grace,* 200, also quotes this article with approval. Rahner concludes his article by referring to the place of a "spirituality of women" (*Frömmigkeit der Frau*), though what precisely such a spirituality comprises is not developed. That, in his view, was a matter for woman herself to decide: "Die Frau ist der Frau aufgegeben." (p. 367).

Drawing on the insights of Vatican II, Rahner also provided stimuli for a new understanding of Mariology and Marian devotion.[250] Starting with the basic principle that Christian dogma has a history, Rahner applied this to the changing image of Mary in the Church. He was concerned to purify Mariology from pious exaggerations and speculations.[251] In his view, "mariological statements refer to a particular individual, an historical and finite human being, who has a definite (albeit unique) place in humankind as a whole and in its history."[252] Just as in Christology there has developed a "Christology from below," something similar could happen in Mariology. Rahner held that such a Mariology "from below," when developed with the more classical Mariology, would make it easier for contemporary believers to identify with Mary as a real person and a model of discipleship.[253]

Our brief survey of some of Rahner's more significant writings on women in the Church reveals that he was aware of the need for a spirituality that would incorporate the specific experiences of contemporary women. If some of his ideas sound very general and abstract, this is partly because he did not see it as his task to develop the details of such a spirituality. However, in the first part of this section, we described how Anne Carr, building on many of Rahner's insights, described this feminist spirituality in more concrete terms. The particular value of Carr's contribution, we believe, lies in her method of dialectical retrieval: like Rahner, she

---

[250] See his "Mary and the Christian Image of Woman," *TI* 19: 211-17 (*ST* XIII: 353-60); and "Courage for Devotion to Mary," *TI* 23: 129-39 (*ST* XVI: 321-35).

[251] "It is not always a sign of neurotic sensitivity when married women suspect in many an image of the Virgin Mother a quiet kind of discrimination. Do we not often have to do with a myth about Mary rather than with faith in Mary?" Rahner, "Courage for Devotion to Mary," *TI* 23: 138 (*ST* XVI: 333).

[252] Rahner, "Mary and the Christian Image of Woman," *TI* 19: 213 (*ST* XIII: 356). He continues: "It is only the Church as a whole that gives reality to Mary, ... which she does not have when considered independently." (p. 214).

[253] "Mary must be seen also as the woman of the people, as poor, as a learner, who lives in the light of the historical, social and religious situation of her time and her people. She is to be seen, not as a heavenly being, but as a human person, as active and suffering for herself and others, as learning in the midst of many uncertainties, as accepting her function in salvation history in faith, hope, and love, and by this very fact, as model and mother of believers." Rahner, "Mary and the Christian Image of Woman," *TI* 19: 215 (*ST* XIII: 358).

attempts to receive, reformulate and reappropriate some of the major Christian symbols from within the context of faith. This struggle to integrate women's personal experience of suffering and discrimination with an ongoing effort to change institutional structures is one of the main characteristics and tasks of feminist spirituality today.[254]

4. Retrospect and Prospect

Shortly before his death, Rahner offered a brief retrospective on his life's work as a theologian.[255] Entitled "Experiences of a Catholic Theologian," Rahner focused on four central "experiences" which, by the end of his life, could be considered key theological convictions governing his method of theological reflection. By outlining these four "experiences" (which, in fact, are also theological statements), we highlight an important conclusion of our work, namely, the spiritual root, or more specifically, the Ignatian inspiration underlying Rahner's theological method. Our contention has been that there is no sharp division between spirituality and theology within Rahner's work. Despite his prodigious literary output, his central theological concern has always been with the notion of the *experience of God*.[256] And it is this personal experience of God "from within" as opposed

---

[254] We have deliberately avoided a discussion of the complicated and controversial question of women and ministry in the Church. That the ordination of women to the priesthood is a focal symbol for feminist theology is beyond dispute. For Carr's examination of some of the presuppositions entailed in the ordination question, see *Transforming Grace*, 43-59. Rahner, commenting on the Declaration of the Congregation for the Doctrine of the Faith on the "Question of the Admission of Women to the Ministerial Priesthood" (15 October 1976), concluded with a plea for the discussion to continue. Rahner, "Women and the Priesthood," *TI* 20: 35-47 (*ST* XIV: 208-23).

[255] Rahner, "Erfahrungen eines katholischen Theologen," *Karl Rahner in Erinnerung*, 134-48. This final public lecture was held in the Catholic Academy of the archdiocese of Freiburg in February 1984. To the best of my knowledge this lecture has not been translated into English.

[256] Hence our exploration of this issue in previous chapters of our work, especially in Chapter Three, where we made a theological investigation of the Rahnerian notion of spiritual experience. We sought to clarify the meaning of this term in Rahner as well as asking such questions as: *Who* experiences God? *How* is this process to be understood theologically? and *What* does it look like in practice?

to "from without" (in the form of an external indoctrination) that constitutes the basis of any genuine Christian spirituality.[257] The *first* experience discussed by Rahner has surfaced before in our work and concerns the analogical nature of all theological statements. The reason Rahner asserts this seemingly obvious axiom is that he believes it to have been largely ignored in theology. We saw in Chapter Four how this mode of speaking about God received its official expression at the Fourth Lateran Council (1215). We have also mentioned how the negative or apophatic way of speaking about God is favoured by Rahner who consistently emphasizes the incomprehensibility *(Unbegreiflichkeit)* of God.[258] In Chapter Two we explored Rahner's depiction of God as "Mystery," and the consequences ensuing from this description in terms of his theological method. The numerous examples of experiences of mystery provided by Rahner lead to a theology of mystery, or more exactly, a theology before *the* Mystery.[259] Underlying this move is a new concept of mystery. Mystery is no longer depicted negatively in terms of truths that are provisionally incomprehensible but more positively:

---

[257] We have already noted how this "Gotteserfahrung" finds expression in love of neighbour *(Nächstenliebe)* involving a *Lebenspraxis* that has both a social and a mystical component. Thus it is erroneous to suggest that Rahner's notion of spirituality has a passive or quietistic flavour to it.

[258] "... Ich möchte nur die Erfahrung bezeugen, daß der Theologe erst dort wirklich einer ist, wo er nicht beruhigt meint, klar und durchsichtig zu reden, sondern die analoge Schwebe zwischen Ja und Nein über dem Abgrund der Unbegreiflichkeit Gottes erschreckt und selig zugleich erfährt und bezeugt. Und ich möchte nur bekennen, daß ich als einzelner armer Theologe bei all meiner Theologie zu wenig an diese Analogheit aller meiner Aussagen denke. Wir halten uns zu sehr in der *Rede* über die Sache auf und vergessen bei all dieser Rede im Grunde die beredete Sache selber." Rahner, "Erfahrungen eines katholischen Theologen," *Karl Rahner in Erinnerung*, 137-38.

[259] One such example relevant to our discussion can be found in Rahner's "Experiences of the Holy Spirit," *TI* 18: 201-202, 203 (*ST* XIII: 241, 242), where we find the description of "someone who sees that his or her clearest ideas and the most intellectual operations of his or her thought are disintegrating, that in the breakdown of all systems the unity of consciousness and what is known consists only in the pain of not being able to cope with the immense variety of questions and yet of not being allowed and not being able to cling to what is clearly known from individual experience and from learning." Rahner concludes: "Where a person entrusts all their knowledge and all their questions to the silent and all-sheltering mystery which is loved more than all our individual perceptions ... *then* God is present with his liberating grace."

"What if we must take the mystery not as the provisional but as the primordial and permanent ...? What if there be an 'unknowing', ... which ... is not a pure negation, not simply an empty absence, but a positive characteristic of a relationship between one subject and another? What if it be essential and constitutive of true knowledge, of its growth, self-awareness and lucidity, to include precisely the unknown, to know itself orientated from the start to the incomprehensible and inexpressible, to recognize more and more that only in this way can it truly be itself and not be halted at a regrettable limit?"[260]

We shall not enter again into Rahner's exploration of the human person as the subject who is confronted by mystery, and as a being of unlimited transcendence, whose primordial and original knowledge of God is given in the experience of transcendence. Our interest here is to recall the point that Rahner's radical reinterpretation of the traditional notion of mystery had methodological consequences for his theology. One consequence was his stress on the incomprehensibility of God; another lies in what he calls a necessary "creaturely modesty" in all theological discourse. Further, we noted Rahner's conviction that all methodological endeavour in theology should try to bridge the gap between the credibility of the Christian message and the *decision* of faith.[261] Rahner's theological reflection is characterized, therefore, by what has been described as an "existentielle Betroffenheit

---

[260] Rahner, "The Theology of Mystery," *TI* 4: 41 (*ST* IV: 57). In this first lecture Rahner eschews the traditional understanding of mystery — regarded as a merely provisional deficiency in knowledge. Instead, he attempts to harmonize the notions of knowledge and mystery by claiming that "the supreme act of knowledge is not the abolition or diminution of the mystery but its final assertion and total immediacy... It (the concept of mystery) is no longer the limitation of a knowledge which should by right be perspicuous... We must understand the act of knowing in such a way that it will explain why knowledge can only exist in a being when and in so far as that one being realizes itself by an act of love." (pp. 41-43). The idea of reason as a potentiality only to be actuated in love has its roots in Rahner's early study of Bonaventure's notion of ecstasy, as we saw in Chapter Four.

[261] This is one of the main tasks facing fundamental theology today according to Rahner. See his "Reflections on a New Task for Fundamental Theology," *TI* 16: 156-66 (*ST* XII: 198-211), where there is explicit mention of the Ignatian undertones of such a theology of decision.

und Ergriffenheit,"[262] the roots of which lie in his experience of the Ignatian *Exercises*.

Rahner's *second* experience brings us to what he considered the centre *(die Mitte)* of the Christian message: the *self*-communication of God. We noted his reluctance in *Foundations* to begin with a too narrowly Christological approach. It is not a question of starting with Jesus Christ but of go-ing further back than this in order to justify why and in what sense one may "risk one's life in faith in this con-crete Jesus of Nazareth as the crucified and risen God-Man."[263] God's self-communication to the human race is various-ly described as a "process," an "event," and a "movement," which reaches its climax in Jesus Christ. We saw how Rahner demonstrated how the mystery of Christ affects the whole history of the human race and how it is possible for someone who has not heard the explicit preach-ing of Christianity to accept the offer of God's self-communication. Indeed, Rahner sees in this concern for the salvation of one's non-Christian neighbour a sublime form of *Nächstenliebe*, whereby Chris-tian hope is not restricted to the individual Christian alone but includes everyone, and where God's grace is not confined solely to sacraments but is universally present. Rahner acknowledged that God's self-communication to humankind has a certain priority in his theology over the confession of the sinfulness of humanity.[264] It is not that he is denying that the experience of grace can coincide with the

[262] Bernd Jochen Hilberath, *Karl Rahner: Gottgeheimnis Mensch* (Mainz: Grüne-wald, 1995), 227. See also Böhme, and Sudbrack, eds., *Der Christ von morgen — ein Mystiker?*, 100-105. Our analysis of Rahner's interpretation of the *Exercises* under-scored the "always more" in such a decision, that is to say, the conviction that God's will, which requires an absolute commitment, arises primarily from an experience of grace. Summarizing Ignatius' position, Rahner says: "An absolute decision to embrace the will of God founded upon rational consideration of the object is left by Ignatius to the third time of choice, but in his view this takes second place to the two others since it applies to cases where no decision has been possible at the first and second time of choice." Rahner, "Reflections on a New Task for Fundamental The-ology," *TI* 16: 162 (*ST* XII: 206).

[263] Rahner, *FCF*, 13 (*Grundkurs*, 24).

[264] "... Man (darf) ruhig die Selbstmitteilung Gottes an die Kreatur als zentraleres Thema denn Sünde und Sündenvergebung empfinden... Es dürfe der Glaube an die Selbstmitteilung Gottes in freier Gnade etwas dem Bekenntnis zur Sündigkeit des Menschen vorgeordnet werden." Rahner, "Erfahrungen eines katholischen Theolo-gen," *Karl Rahner in Erinnerung*, 141.

experience of forgiveness. Rather, it is a question of emphasis, or, more precisely, a question of a shift in emphasis *(Akzentverschiebungen)*. We investigated this shift in terms of Rahner's reinterpretation of grace in Chapter Three. Rahner conceded that his theology might be criticized as eclectic in that he has a variety of philosophical and theological sources. However, he considered a certain one-sidedness unavoidable in any theological method since no theologian could be expected to treat every aspect of Christian faith to the same degree. Formulated more positively, this attempt to focus on the core of the Christian faith which undergirds Rahner's theological method does not issue in a reduction of the essentials of faith, but in "a concentration of the plurality into very few basic thoughts" or key terms *(Schlüsselbegriffe)*, of which the most basic is the experience of the self-communication of God.[265] Like Aquinas, Rahner "always thinks on the basis of the whole and in relation to the whole."[266] Once more, we note Rahner's attempt to get to the depths of what theology entails and to clarify the ultimate aim of all theological endeavour.[267]

Rahner's *third* retrospective experience is that, as a member of a religious order (the Society of Jesus), his theology has some affinity

---

[265] Although we have referred to it earlier, we consider this insight of Herbert Vorgimler's to be pivotal to both the structure of our thesis and to the conclusions we have been drawing: "Seine (Rahners) Methode, ... ist die der Konzentration der Vielfalt auf ganz wenige Grundgedanken, wie er sagt, auf Schlüsselbegriffe oder noch besser auf Schlüsselerlebnisse. *Der* Grundgedanke dieser Theologie oder *das* Schlüsselerlebnis ist, nachlesbar bei Rahner selber, die Erfahrung Gottes." Vorgrimler, "Gotteserfahrung im Alltag: Der Beitrag Karl Rahners zu Spiritualität und Mystik," *Karl Rahner in Erinnerung*, 102.

[266] Rahner, *Everyday Faith*, 188 *(Glaube, der die Erde liebt,* 151).

[267] See Karl-Heinz Weger, "'Ich glaube, weil ich bete.' Für Karl Rahner zum 80. Geburtstag," *Geist und Leben* 57 (1984): 49, where Weger cites a talk of Rahner's on Bavarian Radio (precise references not given) concerning the task of theology: "(Die) Theologie darf heute keine esoterische Geheimwissenschaft sein, die sich mit sublimen Fragen beschäftigt, die nur Fachwissenschaftler interessieren... Die Theologie muß als Wissenschaft der Verkündigung des Evangeliums und den Menschen von heute dienen." In fact, Rahner refused to consider himself a scholar: "I only attempt to clarify those individual questions that modern readers are interested in understanding better. I would say that I have always done theology with a view to kerygma, preaching, pastoral care... In short, I am not a scholar and don't intend to be one." *Karl Rahner In Dialogue*, 256 *(Karl Rahner im Gespräch* 2: 150).

with the spirituality of this order. At least, that was Rahner's hope — that he would be able to incorporate some of what he calls the "existentialism of Ignatius" into his own way of theologizing. In Chapter Four we offered a critical appraisal of Rahner's theological investigation of the spiritual experience at the heart of the Ignatian *Exercises*.[268] We described how he was deeply influenced by certain key Ignatian themes: the centrality of a direct experience of God, the emphasis on the always greater God, and the development of a mysticism of everyday life. Like Ignatius, Rahner was not afraid to limit himself to a few basic spiritual principles, while, at the same time, allowing for a plurality in contemporary forms of discipleship.[269] As a well-known commentator on Rahner puts it: "His own thinking was influenced continually by his desire to work out the theological implications of the spiritual stimulus in the Ignatian *Exercises*."[270]

A *fourth* and final experience enunciated by Rahner — although it lies latent in the previously mentioned experiences — is what he calls the "incongruence" of theology with the other sciences. Rahner acknowledged the theological significance of the various natural sciences and of artistic expressions such as music and poetry. If the theologian is not to preoccupy him or herself with a purely abstract concept of God, then he or she will see that these other sciences and arts not only reveal the hand of God, but also raise countless questions that challenge contemporary theology. Surprisingly, Rahner summarizes his own experience with regard to these other sciences as basically one of ignorance. He is referring in particular to the relation of theology with the natural sciences whose findings, on one level

[268] Of course, Ignatius was not the sole influence on Rahner the theologian. Rahner acknowledged a variety of sources of inspiration, e.g., Maréchal's reinterpretation of Thomistic philosophy. In this sense, Rahner did not consider himself a "systematic" theologian. He preferred to characterize his work as eclectic, as that of a dilettante, and marked by openness and dialogue towards the multiplicity of other anthropological sciences. Rahner, "Erfahrungen eines katholischen Theologen," *Karl Rahner in Erinnerung*, 143-44. See also Neufeld, *Die Brüder Rahner*, 344, 359.

[269] Philip Endean, "Die ignatianische Prägung der Theologie Karl Rahners: Ein Versuch der Präzisierung," Private Paper, London, 1989, 7-8.

[270] See Harvey D. Egan, "Karl Rahner: Theologian of the *Spiritual Exercises*," *Thought* 67 (1992): 258, 261. In Chapter Four we saw how Rahner's experiences with the *Exercises* form the basis for this claim that theology should exercise a mystagogical function by initiating people into their foundational experience of God.

at least, seem to undermine much of what theology takes for granted, for example, the divine origin of the world. In the light of such an explosion in scientific knowledge Rahner became more and more aware of the "emptiness" and "abstractness" of his theological concepts. On the other hand, however, Rahner was one of the first theologians to enter into dialogue with experts from other secular disciplines, including Marxists, atheists, and natural scientists.[271] Moreover, his theological career evinces a move away from the narrow confines of Thomism where the natural sciences had their place to his later attempt to situate Christology within an evolutionary view of the world.

This experience of "not-knowing" *(des Nichtwissens)*, of not being able to provide any clear answers to many of the problems and questions thrown up by natural sciences led Rahner, as we have noted, to plea for a greater modesty in theological discourse: "A theology that wishes to answer all questions clearly and thoroughly is guaranteed to miss its proper 'object'."[272] This experience of helplessness *(Ratlosigkeit)* brings us back to the central tenet of Rahner's theology, namely, to the God of incomprehensible mystery, who cannot be explained with rationalistic clarity. In sum, Rahner's lifelong testimony to the mystery of God as integral to the Christian tradition is considered by some commentators to be the greatest achievement of this "unsystematic" theologian.[273]

Rahner then concludes his retrospective by returning to a familiar emphasis on God as the absolute future, a future which can only be

[271] See Hans-Dieter Mutschler, ed., *Gott neu buchstabieren. Zur Person und Theologie Karl Rahners* (Würzburg: Echter, 1994), 97-119.

[272] "Why Doing Theology Is So Difficult," *Karl Rahner In Dialogue,* 216 (*Karl Rahner im Gespräch* 2: 89).

[273] "The absence of system in Rahner's theological program finds its final explanation in the nature of this mystery." DiNoia, "Karl Rahner," *The Modern Theologians,* 202. DiNoia refers in this context to the conclusion of an interview given by Rahner on the occasion of his 75th birthday: "The true system of thought really is the knowledge that humanity is finally directed precisely not toward what it can control in knowledge but toward the absolute mystery as such; that mystery is ... the blessed goal of knowledge which comes to itself when it is with the incomprehensible one... In other words, then, the system is the system of what cannot be systematized." See "Living into Mystery: Karl Rahner's Reflections at Seventy-five. A Conversation with Leo O'Donovan," *America* 140 (March 10, 1979): 180.

reached through the medium of death. Death and eternal life constitute radical *caesurae*, which he can only describe in the paradoxical language of emptiness and fulfilment, darkness and light, question and answer.[274]

Rahner's retrospective provides us with an opportunity to review some of the themes that we have been grappling with in the course of our work. One such theme that arose right at the outset was the separation between religious experience and intellectual reflection, broadly described in terms of a separation between spirituality and theology. We have indicated how Rahner has managed to incorporate reflection on a whole variety of spiritual experiences into his theological project. In so doing, he has made a significant contribution towards overcoming the mutual marginalization between religious or spiritual experience and the theological academy.[275] He has taken seriously the dictum *lex orandi, lex credendi* (the law of prayer establishes the law of belief), and shown that the specific way Christians pray, meditate and contemplate constitutes an important element for theological reflection.[276] In other words, Rahner's assumption has always been that theological reflection must be built on a living experience of faith. For all his emphasis on the ineffable God, Rahner did not stop at pure negation but used this as a springboard into the search for unity with the transcendent.[277]

---

[274] Rahner, "Erfahrungen eines katholischen Theologen," *Karl Rahner in Erinnerung*, 147-48. We shall not repeat here what we have described elsewhere as Rahner's realistic pessimism where perplexity, suffering, and death are seen as permanent existentials of human history. In the reference above the emphasis is on the silent, faithful, and hopeful acceptance of death in the knowledge that our perplexity is redeemed. See also Rahner, "Christian Pessimism," *TI* 22: 155-62 (*ST* XVI: 206-214), and "Living into Mystery: Karl Rahner's Reflections at Seventy-five," *America* 140 (March 10, 1979): 178-79.

[275] In the Foreword of volume sixteen of *Investigations*, entitled "Experience of the Spirit: Source of Theology," vii-xii, Rahner identifies and develops a theme that "is of crucial importance for [my] whole theological activity." (viii).

[276] For an application of this principle to liturgical theology and the sacraments, with particular reference to Rahner, as one who "sought to overcome any dualism in Christian life and worship that would separate the sacred from the secular," see Kevin W. Irwin, "Sacramental Theology: A Methodological Proposal," *The Thomist* 54 (1990): 311-42.

[277] For a good introduction to the various tensions at work in the Christian apophatic tradition, see Deirdre Carabine, *The Unknown God. Negative Theology in the Platonic Tradition: Plato to Eriugena*, Louvain Theological & Pastoral Monographs 19 (Louvain: Peeters Press/ W. B. Eerdmans, 1995).

But spirituality is not just about experience; it also entails a concrete lived *practice*. We discussed a common criticism of Rahner's transcendental method in this regard, namely, that his method is insensitive to social problems and ineffectual in the area of social change. Against this, we emphasized how Rahner increasingly sought to complement his transcendental approach with an incorporation of a more historical perspective — testified, for example, in his choice of theological topics.[278] If we agree that Rahner considered the transcendental method to be only one part of theology,[279] albeit a necessary one, we also concur with his view that Christians today no longer accept theological propositions of faith which have no apparent connection with their own understanding of themselves. Thus Rahner could agree with the characterization of his theology as a "transcendental anthropology," as long as this description did not give the impression that he had bracketed the complicated question of the relation between transcendence and history.[280] Theology has to speak about the human person "who is a potential hearer of the word by nature, but all the more so by grace and the historical event of divine revelation."[281] Moreover, the "anthropological turn" in Rahner, as we noted in this and in the previous chapter, is ultimately related to his Christology: "Christology is the end and beginning of anthropology;"[282] the Incarnation is the necessary and permanent beginning of the divinization of the world as a whole.[283]

---

[278] Referring to the extraordinary fruitfulness of Rahner's transcendental method, Lehmann comments: "Es war verblüffend, wie leistungsfähig seine transzendentale Methode philosophisch und vor allem theologisch war." Karl Lehmann, "Philosophisches Denken im Werk Karl Rahners," *Karl Rahner in Erinnerung*, 26.

[279] In other words, we are not presenting Rahner's transcendental approach as the last word; rather, the procedure followed has been to see him as a helpful guide (*ein hilfreicher Wegweiser*) whose insights into spirituality and theological method represent one attempt to explicate how God's self-communication in grace affects the whole person and the whole of life. See Bernd Jochen Hilberath and Bernhard Nitsche, "Transzendentale Theologie? Beobachtungen zur Rahner-Diskussion der letzten Jahre," *Theologische Quartalschrift* (1994) 4: 304-15, 311.

[280] Rahner, "Gnade als Mitte menschlicher Existenz," *Herausforderung des Christen*, 129-30.

[281] "Theological Thinking and Religious Experience," *Karl Rahner In Dialogue*, 326.

[282] Rahner, "On the Theology of the Incarnation," *TI* 4: 117 (*ST* IV: 151).

[283] Rahner, *FCF*, 181 (*Grundkurs*, 183).

We have seen how Rahner's "anthropological turn" or "turn to the subject" placed a high priority on spiritual experience, as witnessed in his discussion of the Ignatian *Exercises*, and, increasingly, on history and, in particular, on the ambiguities of history. Further, we traced a development from a (somewhat caricatured) image of the isolated, self-sufficient, rational subject of Rahner's early philosophical works to a recognition that human beings are essentially interdependent, in short, to a more *relational* anthropology. In the first section of this chapter, we have sought to gain some critical distance from Rahner by offering two examples of how such a relational anthropology finds expression in both liberation and feminist theologians. These theologians (we examined Jon Sobrino and Anne Carr) provide a necessary critique of the self-sufficient subject of modern anthropology[284] and take the axiom "to be is to be in relation" to more radical conclusions than Rahner did. We recalled how liberation theology, for example, has rediscovered that human beings are not only interpersonal but exist of necessity in relationship to social and institutional structures.[285] In other words, there has been a retrieval of the social and communal nature of the individual. It is not that Rahner is completely unaware of this retrieval but, as far as his understanding of spirituality is concerned, it finds only limited expression. We indicated this shortcoming in our discussion of the "experience of the Spirit" in Chapter Three. Rahner's accent is primarily on a personal experience of God. Initially, he showed little appreciation for the possibility of communal experiences of the Spirit; the examples he adduced focused almost exclusively on the solitary individual before God.[286]

However, as this study has endeavoured to illustrate, Rahner's spiritual theology is dynamic and flexible enough to cope with both the

---

[284] For a good overview of the critiques of modern anthropology along with some suggested openings for an alternative anthropology, see Dermot Lane, "Anthropology and Eschatology," *The Irish Theological Quarterly* 61 (1995): 14-31.

[285] Janet K. Ruffing, "Anthropology, Theological," *NDCS*: 49.

[286] Is the reason for this because Rahner's generation were "spiritual individualists" (Rahner's description) and that the Ignatian *Exercises* tend to have an excessively individualist focus? For a discussion of some of these issues, with special reference to von Balthasar and Rahner, see Gerard O'Hanlon, "The Jesuits and Modern Theology — Rahner, von Balthasar and Liberation Theology," *The Irish Theological Quarterly* 58 (1992): 25-45.

permutations of history and the shifting priorities thrown up by our historical contexts. By way of conclusion, then, we shall attempt to briefly synthesize some of the essential elements of a Rahner-inspired spirituality of the future. In a short article entitled "The Spirituality of the Church of the Future" (1977),[287] Rahner has brought together five points which he regards as essential to this discussion. These points, which we have already explored, offer a good summary of Rahner's conception of spirituality. His first point is that, for a Catholic, any future spirituality must preserve an element of *continuity* with the spirituality of the history of the Church. Consequently, such a spirituality will never degenerate into mere humanism. It will always be a spirituality of adoration of the incomprehensible God, find historical expression in discipleship of Jesus, and be lived in the Church. This ecclesial spirituality will also have an explicit political dimension, acknowledging its this-worldly responsibility. In short, it will be a spirituality of hope, awaiting an absolute future and not placing its hope in an earthly utopia. The challenge, then, as Rahner sees it, is for spirituality to learn both positively and negatively from the Church's past: to be lovingly immersed in the Church's spiritual heritage, while also remaining open for new Pentecostal beginnings emerging "from below" under the influence of the Spirit.

A second point is that spirituality should concentrate on what is *most essential* and decisive for Christian faith. Rahner is not disparaging various types of liturgical and other devotions, but he thinks that spirituality in the future will concentrate on the "ultimate data" of revelation, namely, that God is, and that we can communicate with Him, and that, as ineffable mystery, God is at the heart of our existence. This focus on what is most essential to Christian spirituality leads to Rahner's third point, namely, that *it is the experience of God which is the real basic phenomenon of spirituality.*[288] This claim lies at the heart of our work and encapsulates the essence of Rahner's understanding of spirituality. All our analyses of Rahner, e.g., of how

---

[287] Rahner, "The Spirituality of the Church of the Future" *TI* 20: 143-53 (*ST* XIV: 368-81).

[288] This is the assumption behind the oft-quoted phrase of Rahner's that the Christian of the future will be a mystic or he or she will not exist at all.

he has integrated spirituality and theology, the mystagogical structure of his theology, the Ignatian dimension, and so on, rest on this basic premise. Despite the various and often justified criticisms levelled against Rahner's understanding of spirituality, we believe his basic claim above to be correct, even if we have diverged from him on certain points.

This immediate and personal experience of God involves a decision of faith, the responsibility for which lies with the individual alone. The previous external, i.e., societal, supports for living Christian faith are diminishing, and Christians find themselves more and more living in a milieu that is at best secular, or at worst atheistic. Thus Rahner speaks of the solitary courage and the lonely responsibility of the individual in their decision to believe. Rahner's fourth remark is a corrective to the individualistic overtones of his third point. Here he leaves room for the possibility of a *communal experience of the Spirit*. He gradually came to see the value and importance of "fraternal community" in any future spirituality, and also referred to the communal discernment of spirits in this context.[289] His final point is described as the *new ecclesial aspect* of spirituality. We have discussed how, for Rahner, an ecclesial spirituality is rooted in a common faith and is sacramentally realized. At the same time, this spirituality will exhibit a patience with those negative aspects of Church life which can be a burden for a person's spirituality.

The two guiding questions at the outset of our work (Chapters One and Two) were: i) what is spirituality? and ii) what is Rahner's understanding of spirituality? These questions were posed in the awareness of a division or split currently existing between spirituality and theology. We have found Rahner to be a helpful guide in attempting to harmonize what have effectively become two separate disciplines. Not only does he manage to bring out the necessary interrelationship that should exist between spirituality and theology, but he has managed to rethink the notion of theology as a science of mystery. According to Rahner, theology goes beyond perception, and leads to a decision or response to the mystery of God in Christ. Put

---

[289] Rahner, "Modern Piety and the Experience of Retreats," *TI* 16: 145-55 (*ST* XII: 184-97).

differently, the tension that we have been analyzing has to do with the role of spiritual or religious *experience* in theology (Chapter Three). Our assumption has been that the cleavage between the "intellectual" and the "affective," if we may put it like this, has been detrimental to both spirituality and to theology. In contrast, we have underscored how both these disciplines can serve each other. Spirituality reminds theology of its mystagogical task, while theology provides spirituality with a necessary foundation and with criteria for judging between authentic and distorted spiritualities.[290] We have analyzed various attempts to effect a closer co-operation between these two disciplines — the many difficulties inherent in this effort notwithstanding. Without going over the same ground again, two difficulties remain. A first problem, frequently cited by Rahner, is the explosion of knowledge of all kinds, including theological knowledge, the effect of which is an ever growing specialization. Theologians are themselves becoming increasingly segregated within their own specialities, a factor that can undermine interdisciplinary co-operation within the academy. A second problem lies in the temptation to offer a too broad, and ultimately amorphous, definition of spirituality, devoid of any Christian specificity. This difficulty is not that easy to overcome. The Christian theologian of spirituality has to walk a tightrope between not excluding anything from the purview of spirituality, on the one hand, and a willingness to interpret the variety of spiritual experience according to specifically Christian and theological criteria, on the other.[291] That Rahner rose to this challenge is beyond dispute; to what extent he succeeded is for the reader to judge.

---

[290] Of course, the issue is more complicated than this, as our discussion in the third part of Chapter One, "Theology and Spirituality" has shown.

[291] Otherwise, we can end up with a vague description of spirituality along the lines of "an experience of the numinous." Such definitions are of little help, since not every experience of the numinous can be considered a genuinely spiritual experience. The importance of the theological foundation of any spirituality as well as the need for criteria for interpreting spiritual experience once again becomes apparent. See D. A. Carson, "When is Spirituality Spiritual? Reflections on Some Problems of Definition," *Journal of the Evangelical Theological Society* 37 (1994): 381-94. For a discussion of different strategies to overcome the mutual marginalization between religious experience and the theological academy, see Philip Endean, "Spirituality and the University," *The Way Supplement* 84 (1995): 87-99.

INDEX OF NAMES AND SUBJECTS

Analogy, and theology, 358

Anonymous Christianity, 178, 282-284, 289

Anthropology, theological, Rahner's, 55-61, 130-140, 173-175, 365-366; and spirituality, 140-145

Application of the Senses, 270-273, 277-278

Asceticism, 51-54, 210-211, 249, 257-258

Au, W., 260-261, 272

Bacik, J., 112, 122, 140-143

Bakker, L., 228, 235-237, 239-241, 274

Balthasar, H. Urs von, 18-19, 25-26, 162, 176, 283-296, 337

Barry, W. A., 258-259

Barthes, R., 204, 247

Bechtle, R., 1

Bekker, J. C., 7

Benjamin, H. S., 5

Bernard, C. A., 20-21, 30, 37, 39

Bleistein, R., 263

Boff, L., 295

Bonaventure, 30, 46-47, 64, 267-268, 272-273

Bornkamm, G., 7, 9

Bouyer, L., 5, 21, 24-25

Brown, R., 8

Buckley, J., 328-329

Buckley, M. J., 226

Callahan, A., 61, 214-215, 328

Carabine, D., 364

Carr, A., 45, 134, 346-357

Categorial, 79, 84, 131-132, 154-155, 251, 286, 331

Chenu, M. D., 36

Christology, and anthropology, 365; and the "election," 240-249; *existentiell*, 86-87, 194-197, 312-318; searching, 186-194

Church, critical function in society, 303-305; institutional and charismatic aspects of, 324, 331, 333-334

Clarke, T. A., 34

Congar, Y., 5, 7

Consolation, without previous cause, 222-226, 228-234, 251; and the "election," 227

Conn, J. W., 2

Conway, E., 289, 292

Cousins, E., 1, 3, 22, 33, 37, 269

Cross, 207-208, 249-250, 278, 284, 290-293

Daniélou, J., 25

Death, 149, 182, 189-192, 292-295

Decision, to believe, 90-93, 359; and the *Exercises* ("election"), 203-

205, 216-219; and existential commitment, 150-152, 160, 184, 187, 195, 199, 204-205, 341

De Guibert, J., 1, 17, 209, 212-216, 236, 276

De Lubac, H., 173, 289

Descartes, R., 134

Deus semper major, 248

Devotio moderna, 31

DiNoia, J. A., 363

Discernment, of spirits, 150, n. 113, 210, n. 35; and the *Exercises*, 151, 199, 219-222, 227-228, 258, 275

Discipleship, 187-190, 194-197, 246, 306, 337

Dister, J. E., 221, 274

Divarkar, P, R., 203, 217

Downey, M., 1

Drewermann, E., 223

Duffy, S. J., 112, 168, 174-177

Dulles, A., 241, 251-252

Dunne, T., 276

Dupuy, M., 24, 31, 33

Dych, W. V., 313, 315

Edwards, D., 123

Egan, H. J., 38, 43, 66, 68, 100, 185, 211, 225, 232, 234, 237-238, 253, 259-260, 263, 278, 362

Eicher, P., 52, 144, 241

Endean, P., 37, 234, 362, 369

Evdokimov, P., 30

Experience, of enthusiasm, 152-155; of God, 42-46, 58, 73, 104, n. 197, 115-124, 179-182, 357, 367; of grace, *see Grace*; of mystery, 59, 127; of the Spirit, 106, 145-150; terminological clarification, 111-115; of transcendence, 55-57 124-128, 148-149, 224; transcendental, 125, 137; transcendental and categorial, 78, 123, 154; unthematic, 122, 148

Faith, 66, 91-92, 182-184, 313-314, 325; and hope, 184-185, 193

Farmer, J. T., 319, 327

Farrell, W. L., 274

Fiorenza, E. S., 347, 354

Fiorenza, F. S., 45, 53, 308

Fischer, K., 73, 78, 94-96, 112, 158, 262, 270

Fitzmyer, J., 5, 6-8, 264, 291

Fraling, B., 10, 15, 20, 27, 100

Fransen, P., 164

Freedom, 59-60, 349

Galvin, J. P., 60

Ganss, G. E., 203, 217, 222, 235-237, 271

Garrigou- Lagrange, R., 17, 22
Gelpi, D. L., 112, 145
Grace, created and uncreated, 164-165; experience of, 68-69, 76, 98, 155-157, 169-170; as God's self-communication, 49, 64, 139, 360-361; and nature, 166-167, 170, 174-177; reinterpretation of, 163-170; and spirituality, 178-182, 333; universality of, 168-169, 256-257, 279
Groote, G., 32
Grün, A., 291
Guenther, T. F., 299, 308
Gutierrez, G., 2, 36, 337
Haight, R., 164, 338-339, 346
Harrington, D. J., 8
Heart, as symbol, 77, 214-215
Heidegger, M., 140
Heijden, B. van der, 112, 125, 241
Hilberath, B. J., 138, 360, 365
History, 274; and spirituality, 10-18, 107, 306
Hoye, W. J., 112, 118, 128, 144
Ignatius of Loyola, influence on Rahner, 46-48, 199-280, 201-202, 212-213, 362-363
Indifference, 211-214, 276-277
Irwin, K. W., 364
Jesus Christ, contemplating the life of, 242-246
John of the Cross, 62, 123
Johnson, E. A., 348-349
Kant, I., 134-136
Kelly, G., 44
Kempis, Thomas à., 32
King, J. N., 112, 179, 185
Klinger, E., 88, 97-98, 185
Knauer, P., 236-239
Knowledge, existential, 203-204; experiential contrasted with conceptual, 113-115; and mystery, 269; transcendental, 136-139
Knox. R., 153
König, F. Cardinal, 283
LaCugna, C. M., 301, 349, 351
Laguë, M., 36
Lamb, M. L., 299
Lane, D., 366
Lash, N., 122
Lateran Council IV, 358
Latourelle, R., 22
Lebreton, J., 266
Leclercq, J., 1, 4, 9-19, 29-31
Lee-Pollard, D., 2
Lehmann, K., 1, 42, 44, 55, 69, 95, 112-113, 259, 296, 302, 309, 323, 365

Leijssen, L., 293, 296, 327, 335
Lennan, R., 319, 321, 328
Lex orandi, lex credendi, 364
Liberatore, A., 328
Lochbrunner, M., 283
Lonsdale, D., 227-228
Louth, A., 40
Love, of neighbour and of God as a unity, 79 -85, 108, n. 205, 187-88, 285-287; political dimension of, 300
Lubac, H. de, 173
Maher, M. V., 307
Maréchal, J., 136-137, 145
Martyrdom, 267, 284, 293-295, 341
Mary, and feminist spirituality, 353
McBrien, R. P., 38, 305
McFague, S., 352
McGinn, B., 3
Megyer, E., 3, 29, 31
Method, Rahner's theological, 129-140, 290, 306-307, 311, 331, 361, 365-367
Metz, J. B., 42-43, 47, 70-71, 74-75, 129, 135, 143-144, 153, 202, 257, 296-300, 337
Meyendorff, J., 3
Migglebrink, R., 81-82, 310
Molnar, P., 144
Moltmann, J., 2, 30
Mühlen, H., 113, 158-163
Mutschler, H-D., 363
Mystagogy, 74, 99, 179, 262-265, 273, 342-343; and the Application of the Senses, 261-270; and the Exercises, 205, 252-256, 258; and spirituality, 274-275; and theology, 97, 99, 200, 362
Mystery, God as, 358-359, 363
Mysticism, 43, n. 5, 62, 65-69; and asceticism, see Asceticism; and the Spiritual Exercises, 206; of everyday life, 61-63, 68, 88, 117-118, 149, 154, 181, 266; of service, 213, 254, 257
Neufeld, K. H., 42, 47, 49-50, 52-53, 162, 265, 362
Neumann, K., 81, 164, 299
Nitsche, B., 138
Nouvelle Théologie, 173
O'Donovan, L., 137, 306, 307, 309, 363
O'Donnell, J., 59, 301
O'Hanlon, G., 366
Origen, 46, n. 17, 265-267
Paul, and spirituality, 4-9
Peeters, L., 216
Peters, W. A. M., 235

Pissarek-Hudelist, H., 354
Pourrat, P., 16, 21
Praxis, 308
Prayer, 69-74, 77-79; petitionary, 74-76; and prayers, 48-52, 54-55, 121, n. 24
Principe, W., 2, 14, 16, 18-19, 35-37
Przywara, E., 47, 210
Puhl, L. J., 202
Purvis, S. B., 349-350
Raffelt, A., 44, 70, 119
Rahner, H., 47-48, 201, 208-209, 237, 239, 270-273
Realsymbol, 329-330
Regan D., 262, 264
Revelation, private, 260-261
Rinser, L., 354
Sachs, J. R., 318
Sacred Heart Devotion, 214-215
Saudreau, A., 17
Scannone, J. C., 269
Schneider, M., 220
Schneiders, S., 1, 3, 4, 21-22, 24, 26, 28, 34-39, 348, 350,
Schweizer, E., 4, 7, 8
Schwerdtfeger, N., 83, 181, 183-184, 219, 225, 227, 270, 294
Segundo, J, L., 279
Sentire, 200, 268, 270, 273, 278
Sheehan, T., 134
Sheldrake, P., 3
Siebenrock, R., 265
Skelley, M., 113, 116, 335
Sobrino, J., 2, 300, 336-346
Solignac, A., 4, 10-11, 15, 19-21, 23, 26, 29, 31
Spirit, 275-276; experience of, *see Experience*
Spirituality, apophatic, 259, 277-278; introduction to, 1-4; communal expressions of, 106, 152-153, 158, 258, 368; definition of, 18-19, 26-28, 100-108; as christocentric, 196, 312-319; and Church, 103-104, 197, 254, 319-327, 368; and death, 189-192, 248, 364; and experience, 33-34; feminist, 282, 346-357; and the future, 63, 106 153, n. 119, 192-194; kataphatic traditions of, 259-261; and liberation, 282, 336-346; political dimension, 81, 305, 308, 311; and practice, 365; sacramental aspect of, 327-334; and spiritual theology, 19-24; and spiritualities, 24-26; terminological

development of, 9-18; and theology, 29-33, 88-93; transcendental aspect, 251, 256, 331, 355; and worship, 259, 335-336, 364, n. 276
Spiritual Exercises, 47, 195, 202-206; and the "election," 235-240
Spiritual senses, 46, 265-274
Splett, J., 63
Sudbrack, J., 10, 16, 20, 25-27, 70, 100, 231, 277-278
Supernatural Existential, 140, 168, 172-175
Tafferner, A., 82, 299, 307, 310
Tanquerey, A., 17, 22-23
Teresa of Avila, 62
Tetlow, J. A., 1
Theology, introduction to, 88-93; mystical dimension of, 99-100; and spirituality, 94-100; and other sciences, 362-363; political, 297-299; and pluralism, 92-93; transcendental, 302, 306-307, 318, 331, 365
Thomas Aquinas, 42-43, 134-135
Thompson, W. M., 352
Thüsing, W., 243
Tinsley, L.,10, 15
Toner, J., 220, 223, 229-234, 275
Tracy, D., 260, 318
Transcendence, 57-60
Vandenbroucke, F., 22, 25, 30, 33
Vass, G., 113, 134, 173-177
Vatican II, 62, 158, 163, 169, 314; and Church, 304; and ecclesiastical studies, 89-90; and God's universal salvific will, 168, 282-283; and Mary, 356; and penance, 162; and spiritual theology, 23
Via Negationis, 121
Viller, M., 1, 17, 44, 51, 101
Vorgrimler, H., 42, 47, 55, 69-79, 97, 111-112, 118, 121, 125, 140, 180, 262, 282, 285, 300, 303, 325, 361
Walsh, M. J., 328
Weger, K. H., 70, 74, 79, 112, 130, 132, 137, 172, 176, 186-187, 194-197, 326, 361
Weismayer, J., 25
Wiseman, J. A., 104, 113, 124, 126, 147
Wong, J. H. P., 223, 328
Wulf, F., 201
Zizioulas, J. D., 6
Zulehner, P. M., 113, 169, 255, 257, 262, 333